D1429052

India's struggle for independence was arguably the most momentous of the twentieth century, and central to it was the generation of powerful nationalist forces. In a series of detailed studies Anthony Low shows how the ambiguity of the British position conditioned the distinctive character of this struggle: how the British determination to hold fast to their Indian empire (unlike the Americans in the Philippines) prior to 1942 was nonetheless complemented by a reluctance to resist their nationalist opponents in the unyielding ways of the French in Vietnam and the Dutch in Indonesia. Much that Gandhi did, Professor Low concludes, would have been unnecessary in the Philippines and impossible in Indonesia and Vietnam, but astutely fitted the peculiar conditions of the nationalist struggle against the British in India. Published on the fiftieth anniversary of Indian independence, *Britain and Indian nationalism* makes a major contribution to the historiography of modern India, to Britain's relations with its empire, and to the history of decolonisation in the twentieth century.

Britain and Indian nationalism

Britain and Indian nationalism

The imprint of ambiguity 1929–1942

D.A. LOW

Emeritus Smuts Professor of the History of the British Commonwealth in the University of Cambridge and University Fellow, The Australian National University

 CAMBRIDGE
UNIVERSITY PRESS

8223 312393

PUBLISHED BY THE PRESS SYNDICATE OF THE UNIVERSITY OF CAMBRIDGE
The Pitt Building, Trumpington Street, Cambridge CB2 1RP, United Kingdom

CAMBRIDGE UNIVERSITY PRESS
The Edinburgh Building, Cambridge, CB2 2RU, United Kingdom
40 West 20th Street, New York, NY 10011-4211, USA
10 Stamford Road, Oakleigh, Melbourne 3166, Australia

First published 1997

Printed in the United Kingdom at the University Press, Cambridge

Typeset in 10/12 Monotype Plantin   [SE]

A catalogue record for this book is available from the British Library

Library of Congress Cataloguing in Publication data

Low, D.A. (Donald Anthony), 1927–
    Britain and Indian Nationalism: The imprint of ambiguity 1929–1942 /
D.A. Low.
       p.   cm.
    ISBN 0 521 55017 3 (hb)
       1. Nationalism–India–History.   2. India–History–British
occupation, 1765–1947.   3. India–Politics and
government–1919–1947.
    DS480.45.L68   1997
    954.03′59—dc21   96-49356   CIP

ISBN 0 521 55017 3 hardback

954.03
RSDOLD

To
The Four Regiments of Sepoys

I have one ambition. I'm going to set these people free.
Frank Murphy, Governor-General of the Philippines Islands [May 1933]

We have ruled here for 300 years with the whip and the club and we shall still be doing it in another 300 years.
de Jonge, Governor-General of the Netherlands Indies, 1931–6

A government worthy of the name could not support a measure that would give over power in one bloc into the hands of a crowd that is incapable of using it rationally and which, from the very first attempt, would break the instrument that it was given, just as a clumsy child breaks a toy.
Albert Sarraut, twice Governor-General of Indochina [1923]

I don't believe that . . . it is impossible to present the problem in such a form as would make the shop window look respectable from an Indian point of view . . . while keeping your hand pretty firmly on the things that matter.   Lord Irwin, Viceroy and Governor-General of India, 1926–31

Contents

Maps

Preface

The unravelling of the former, seemingly impregnable, colonial empires must be accounted one of the principal sagas of the twentieth century. Aside from some residual episodes the generation of powerful indigenous nationalist forces was almost invariably central to this. Their growth has frequently been described. A good deal of attention has been given too to the courses adopted by the imperial powers. The heart of the whole story lay, however, in the multiplicity of interactive struggles between the one and the other. In many instances these have not had the close attention which they warrant.

The character which these struggles displayed varied greatly. On the one hand they amounted to little more than robust and determined elite negotiation. On the other they could relapse into bloody and implacable colonial war. In each instance the form which the conflict took, so it is argued here, principally derived from a notably close and symbiotic relationship between the nationalist thrust involved and the particular imperial posture which it then confronted.

This book is designed to cast a sharper beam of light on arguably the most momentous of all these struggles, in India against the British. In general its characteristics fell somewhere near the middle of the range of alternatives which can be traced. Since in a way that has not been widely appreciated it was contemporaneous with three other nationalist-imperialist struggles elsewhere in Asia which displayed some very different characteristics, not only does its consideration in this wider context pose a number of comparative questions, but to an altogether new degree serves to highlight its distinctive nature. Since, moreover, it broadly coincided with several other fundamentally similar struggles against the British that nature can be depicted rather more precisely.

Three particular features warrant emphasis. As the struggle in India was principally characterised neither by elite negotiation nor by violent conflict, much turned on a spectrum of major propaganda battles between its principals for the moral primacy. Periodically these could be fought out on a very public stage. They could be keenly followed, therefore, not merely in India and Britain, but even further afield as well. Their conduct called for great political skill, and an adroit and taxing care for detail. It is this range of considerations which has largely determined the form that this book takes.

In the making of several chapters in it I have been greatly assisted by other people. I am particularly indebted to Robert Tombs, Christopher Andrew, Anthony Reid, David Marr, Milton Osborne, John Legge, Jamie Mackie, Al McCoy, Freddie Madden, David Fieldhouse, John Charmley, Merle Ricklefs and Ray Ileto for most helpful advice upon a variety of matters in Chapter 1. Wang Gungwu provided the original impetus to Chapter 2. Gyan Pandey, Peter Reeves and Gyanesh Kudaisya have all been especially generous with their time and assistance over Chapter 3, which they have each been good enough to read. Keith Mitchell, Head of the Cartography Unit in the Research School of Pacific and Asian Studies at the Australian National University, used his singular expertise to draw the maps based upon the Survey of India's *Lucknow Guide Map*, 2nd (revised) 1933 edition, based on a survey in 1929–31, generously lent to me by Peter Reeves. Ralph Bultjens read Chapter 5 with a wonderfully sharp eye. Gyanesh Kudaisya very kindly lent me his extensive collection of photostats of the Haig Papers, on which I have drawn so fully in Chapter 7. He and Vinita Damodaran were good enough to let me see their M.Phil. theses from Jawaharlal Nehru University which each dealt in part with many of the same issues; while at a crucial stage Carl Bridge made some most helpful comments on Chapter 8.

I am very indebted too to the organisers of and participants in seminars at which I have sought to outline the arguments in this book, in Melbourne, Sydney, Canberra, Brisbane, Austin (Texas), Oxford, London, Cambridge, Norwich and Hull, and to a great many conversations over the years with many friends in Delhi.

My greatest debts are, yet again, to Belle for all of her support.

I am also immensely indebted to those who over so many years have smoothed the paths into the uniquely important archives in Delhi. In the National Archives of India I think of S. Roy and R.C. Gupta, and especially of the very particular kindnesses of V.C. Joshi and Dhan Keswani. In the incomparable Nehru Memorial Museum and Library I owe so much to the constant help and encouragement of B.R. Nanda and Ravinder Kumar and their staffs both in the archives and in the library. While in Cambridge I have been greatly assisted in a variety of ways by Lionel Carter, Gordon Johnson, Janet Hall and Richard Fisher, in London by Richard Bingle, in Oxford by Judith Brown, and in Canberra by Jan Bretherton and Norma Chin. I very sincerely thank them all.

Over the years it has been my special privilege to have supervised for their theses in three different universities a quite remarkable succession of graduate students. Many years ago a colleague in another field dubbed us 'the Sepoys'. The 1st (Canberra) Regiment comprised Peter Reeves, John Broomfield, Ravinder Kumar, Hugh Owen, Piet van den Dungen, and W.H. (Bill) Hale. The 2nd (Sussex) Regiment was composed of Christine Furedy, David Arnold, Jim Manor, David Hardiman, Bonaventure Swai, Robin Jeffrey, Humaira Momen, Richard Butler, Anne Thompson and included Phares Mutibwa, Anne Sutton and Margaret Kiloh. The 3rd (Canberra) Regiment was made up of Brij Lal, Imran Ali, Stephen Henningham, Andrew Major and Dipesh Chakrabarty; while the 4th (Cambridge) Regiment included Richard Aldrich, Michael Coleman, Vinita Damodaran, David Lowe, Tan Tai Yong, Gyanesh Kudaisya, Medha Malik Kudaisya, Emmanuel Pondi, John Deverall, Derek da Cunha, Matthew Neuhaus, James Burns, Swarna Aiyar and Philip Charrier. In very deep gratitude this book is dedicated to them for all they have given me. I am enormously grateful to the Australian National University, the University of Sussex, and the University of Cambridge who made all this possible, and much else besides.

An earlier version of Chapter 2 appeared as Chapter 7 in Wang Gungwu, ed., *Self and Biography. Essays on the Individual and Society in Asia*, Sydney 1975. I thank the Australian Academy of the Humanities for permission to rework it here. Parts of Chapter 6 appeared in a different context in Chapter 7 in R. Sisson and S. Wolpert, eds., *Congress and Indian Nationalism. The Pre-Independence Phase*, Berkeley 1988 and I am grateful to the Regents of the University of California for the opportunity to draw upon it here. Likewise I am indebted to the editors of the *Journal of Imperial and Commonwealth History* for the use I have made in Chapter 8 of my article in its Volume 12, no. 2, of 1984. I am grateful too to Deryck Schreuder who published a precis of my argument as Chapter 6 in *"Imperialisms". Explorations in European Expansion and Empire* which he edited for the History Department at the University of Sydney in 1991, and to Mushirul Hasan and Narayani Gupta who included it as Chapter 16 in *India's Colonial Encounter. Essays in Memory of Eric Stokes* which they edited for Manohar, Delhi, in 1993.

The references in the opening pages of Chapter 1 and the footnotes, particularly in that chapter, indicate the sources which have been used, while the primary material that has been drawn upon, and its whereabouts, is indicated in the List of Abbreviations below.

Anthony Low

Abbreviations

AICC	All India Congress Committee, and their archives, NMML.
AP	Andrews Papers, Visha Bharati, Santiniketan.
Assam	Government of Assam.
B&O	Government of Bihar and Orissa.
BDEEP	*British Documents on the End of Empire Project*, Series A, B, C, London 1992– .
Bombay	Government of Bombay.
CID	Criminal Investigation Department.
Comm.	Commissioner.
CP	Government of the Central Provinces.
CS	Chief Secretary.
CWC	Congress Working Committee.
CWMG	*The Collected Works of Mahatma Gandhi*, 90 vols., Ahmedabad 1958–84.
DCC	District Congress Committee.
Dep.	Deputy.
enc.	enclosure in . . .
FR	Fortnightly Reports of the GoI or provincial governments.
G	Governor.
GoI	Government of India.
Govt	Government.
HD	Home Department of the GoI.
HgP	Haig Papers, IOL.
HP	Hailey Papers, IOL.
H.Pol.	HD Police files, NAI.
H.Poll.	HD Political files, NAI.
H.Reforms	HD Reforms Branch files, NAI.
IAR	*Indian Annual Register.*
IOL	Oriental and India Office Collections, The British Library, London.

IP	Irwin (Halifax) Papers, IOL.
JNP	Jawaharlal Nehru Papers, NMML.
JP	Jayakar Papers, NAI.
KW	'Keep With', i.e. papers retained with others.
LGs	Local Governments (i.e. Presidency and Provincial Governments).
LP	Linlithgow Papers, IOL.
MN–JNC	Motilal Nehru–Jawaharlal Nehru Correspondence, NMML.
MNP	Motilal Nehru Papers, NMML.
Mss. Eur.	Manuscripts, European, IOL.
NAI	National Archives of India, Delhi.
nd	no date.
NLI	National Library of India, Calcutta.
NMML	Nehru Memorial Museum and Library, Delhi.
NWFP	Government of the North West Frontier Province.
PCC	Provincial Congress Committee.
PSV	Private Secretary to the Viceroy of India.
RPCSD	V. Choudhary, *Dr Rajendra Prasad: Correspondence and Select Documents*, 4 vols., Delhi 1984– .
RPP	Rajendra Prasad Papers, NAI.
SmP	Smuts Papers, South African Archives.
SoS	Secretary of State for India.
SP	Sapru Papers, NLI.
StP	Sastri Papers, NAI.
Supt	Superintendent.
SWJN	S. Gopal, ed., *Selected Works of Jawaharlal Nehru*, Vols. I– , Delhi 1972– .
tel.	telegram.
TF	P.N. Chopra, *Towards Freedom*, Vol. I, *Experiment with Provincial Autonomy. 1 January–31 December 1937*, New Delhi 1985.
ThP	Thakurdas Papers, NMML.
TOP	Nicholas Mansergh, *Constitutional Relations between Britain and India. The Transfer of Power 1942–47*, Vol. I, *The Cripps Mission, January–April 1942*, London 1972.
TwP	Templewood (Hoare) Papers, IOL.
UP	Government of the United Provinces.
V	Viceroy of India.
WP	Willingdon Papers, IOL.

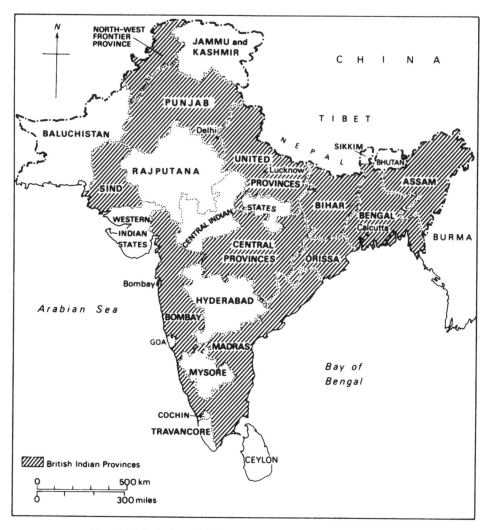

Map 1 India before 1947

1   Introduction: contemporary encounters

Damn the Americans. Why don't they tyrannize us more?
> Manuel Quezon, President of the Philippines Senate

The Gandhis and the De Valeras would have long since entered heaven
had they been born in one of the French colonies.
> Ho Chi-minh, *L'Humanité*, 25 May 1922

There is no more slippery customer than the British Government. The
British Government are past masters in the art of political chicanery and
fraud, and we are babes at their game. We can never in future listen to
any declaration unless action follows.   Jawaharlal Nehru, January 1931

On 8 November 1927 Lord Birkenhead, Britain's Secretary of State for
India, announced the appointment of a statutory commission under the
chairmanship of the Liberal politician, Sir John Simon, to review the
Indian constitution. No Indian was appointed to it. The Indian nationalist elite of all colours was outraged, and over the next two years there built
up in India the potential for another major countrywide agitation of the
kind that Gandhi had led in the early 1920s. In October 1929, in an
attempt to preempt this, the Viceroy, Lord Irwin, formally declared that
in the British view 'the natural issue of India's constitutional progress . . .
is the attainment of Dominion Status', and announced the calling of a
Round Table Conference in London on constitutional reform. This,
however, served to assuage very few, and in March 1930 Gandhi
launched the Indian National Congress upon a major Civil Disobedience
campaign. That was vigorously repressed, and twelve months later, following an agreement between Gandhi and Irwin, it was formally called
off. Yet early in 1932 Civil Disobedience was renewed. This time it was
even more resolutely repressed; and as a consequence by the mid 1930s
Congress gradually moved towards participating once again in the
constitutional politics on which the British set great store.

To its delight Congress then won substantial electoral victories, first at
the elections for the central legislature in 1934, and then more particularly
in the provincial elections in 1937. Following upon these latter, despite

1

some initial hesitation, Congress came eventually to form 'responsible' governments, in accord with the provisions of the new Government of India Act of 1935, in seven of the eleven provinces of India. But two years later, on the outbreak of the Second World War, in protest against the determination of the British to deny Indian political leaders anything but a merely advisory role in the mobilising of Indian support for the war effort, these Congress ministries resigned, and over the ensuing year a further nationalist agitation began to mount. In August 1940 Gandhi declared that this should take the form of a succession of individual acts of civil disobedience rather than a mass movement since eight years before the British had shown how quickly they could defeat that.

Sixteen months later this campaign was overtaken by very much larger events, when late in 1941 the Japanese launched their assault upon the western empires in South and Southeast Asia. At this critical juncture the British Government sent Sir Stafford Cripps to Delhi to try to effect a settlement with the Congress leaders. But since the Cripps Offer fell short of their immediate demands, it was summarily rejected. As it happened the Japanese were then checked at the gates of India. But not before the Congress had launched its great 'Quit India' movement of August 1942, the largest uprising the British had ever had to face in India since 1857. Whilst this was repressed, sometimes brutally, the tide had now turned, for by the terms of the Cripps Offer the British had promised that once the Second World War was over they would grant India the independence it had sought for so long, and in 1947 amid a great deal of turmoil proceeded to do so.

That is the conventional story of India's political history from the late 1920s to the mid 1940s, such as will be found in every standard account.[1]

Over recent decades the story has been filled out in a number of different directions. There have for a start been a number of important accounts of the British side. These have included studies of the Irwin Viceroyalty, of the Round Table Conferences, and of Linlithgow's Viceroyalty,[2] together with a particularly valuable account of the economic side of Britain's involvement in India in the years before independence.[3] Upon the central

---

[1] The most recent include S. Wolpert, *A New History of India*, New York 1977; S. Sarkar, *Modern India 1885–1947*, Delhi 1983; J.M. Brown, *Modern India. The Origins of an Asian Democracy*, 2nd edn, Oxford 1994; B. Chandra *et al.*, *India's Struggle for Independence 1857–1947*, Delhi 1988. See also J.M. Brown, *Gandhi's Rise to Power. Indian Politics 1915–1922*, Cambridge 1972, and *Gandhi and Civil Disobedience: The Mahatma in Indian Politics*, Cambridge 1977.

[2] S. Gopal, *The Viceroyalty of Lord Irwin 1926–1931*, Oxford 1957; R.J. Moore, *The Crisis of Indian Unity 1917–1940*, Oxford 1974; G. Rizvi, *Linlithgow and India*, London 1978.

[3] B.R. Tomlinson, *The Political Economy of the Raj, 1914–1947: The Economics of Decolonisation in India*, London 1979.

political issues it is now well understood that alongside Winston Churchill's robust opposition in the early 1930s to Indian constitutional reform, his opponents, Stanley Baldwin, Lord Irwin, and Sir Samuel Hoare, proceeded on the principle that if constitutional reform could be carried through skilfully, British control at the centre could actually be strengthened, even whilst control over India's provincial governments was relinquished to popularly elected ministries.[4]

We now know a good deal more too about the Congress – the quarters from which it secured support, the processes by which this was generated, the forms that it took. For some while the role of 'those who had been to school and college' has been well understood.[5] More work needs to be done on the important contribution of India's merchant communities.[6] A major clarification, moreover, came from tracing the long succession of adherences to Congress of the more well-to-do peasant communities from around the end of the First World War in Bihar, Gujarat, west Bengal, and parts of the United Provinces, then quite dramatically at the end of the 1920s from the Frontier Province, and thereafter from Madras and Maharashtra in the early 1930s, and the Princely States by the 1940s.[7] There have been studies too of the part played by India's embryonic capitalists,[8] and the role of the Indian Princes.[9]

---

[4] C.R. Bridge, *Holding India to the Empire. The British Conservative Party & the 1935 Constitution*, Delhi 1986.

[5] A. Seal, *The Emergence of Indian Nationalism*, Cambridge 1968; S.R. Mehrotra, *The Emergence of the Indian National Congress*, Delhi 1971; S.R. Mehrotra, *A History of the Indian National Congress*, vol. I, *1885–1918*, Delhi 1995; B. Chandra, *Rise and Growth of Economic Nationalism in India. Economic Policies of Indian National Leadership 1881–1915*, Delhi 1966.

[6] C.A. Bayly, *The Local Roots of Indian Politics: Allahabad 1880–1920*, Oxford 1975; A.D.D. Gordon, *Businessmen and Politics: Rising Nationalism and a Modernising Economy in Bombay 1918–1933*, Delhi 1978; D.A. Low, *Eclipse of Empire*, Cambridge 1991, ch. 4.

[7] D.A. Low, ed., *Congress and the Raj: Facets of the Indian Struggle 1917–1947*, London 1977; D. Hardiman, *Peasant Nationalists of Gujarat: Kheda District 1917–1934*, Delhi 1981; G. Pandey, *The Ascendancy of the Congress in Uttar Pradesh 1926–34: A Study in Imperfect Mobilization*, Delhi 1978; S. Henningham, *Peasant Movements in Colonial India: North Bihar 1917–1942*, Canberra 1982; D.A. Arnold, *Congress in Tamilnad: Nationalist Politics in South India 1919–37*, Delhi 1977; S. Rittenberg, *Ethnicity, Nationalism, and the Pakhtuns*, Durham, N.C. 1988; J. Manor, *Political Change in an Indian State: Mysore 1917–55*, Delhi 1977.

[8] B. Chandra, *Nationalism and Colonialism in Modern India*, Delhi 1979, pp. 144–203; R. Ray, *Industrialization in India: Growth and Conflict in the Private Corporate Sector 1914–1947*, Delhi 1979; C. Markovits, *Indian Business and Nationalist Politics 1931–39*, Cambridge 1985; M.M. Kudaisya, 'The Public Career of G.D. Birla 1911–47', Cambridge PhD thesis, 1992.

[9] B.R. Ramusack, *The Princes of India in the Twilight of Empire*, Columbus, Ohio 1978; R. Jeffrey, ed., *People, Princes and Paramount Power: Society and Politics in the Indian Princely States*, Delhi 1978; S.R. Ashton, *British Policy towards the Indian States 1905–1939*, London 1982; I.F. Copland, *Unwanted Allies. The Princes of India in the Endgame of Empire*, Cambridge 1997.

A great deal of important detail has been unearthed too on the extent to which Indian involvement in the new institutions the British fashioned was characterised by local interests, by factionalism and self-seeking. The 'Cambridge School' of the 1970s aroused a good deal of ire in India for drawing attention to this; ideology and the strong personal commitment that satyagraha entailed were much too easily brushed aside.[10] Yet it would be foolish to suggest that all the political infighting that plagued India after independence sprang hydra-headed just as the British left.

At the same time some important new work has been done on the major theme of Muslim alienation from the Congress and the eventual creation of Pakistan.[11] More than one case has been made here that cuts across the earlier accounts.[12] More has now been retailed, moreover, about the areas that became Pakistan.[13] Curiously it is only now that detailed work is being done on the horrendous partition massacres, from which a very variegated picture is beginning to emerge.[14]

During the 1980s India's modern historiography was greatly enlivened by the 'Subaltern' school, which took its name from Gramsci's somewhat confusing term for the non-elite. Under Ranajit Guha's energetic direction this underlined not only the key importance of the structural contradictions which imperial rule necessarily involved, but the subordinate role imposed on very many disadvantaged communities within Indian society itself; and in a succession of volumes it produced abundant evidence of the extent to which the often different concerns of subordinate communities were both exploited and repressed by the more elitist activists in the

[10] J. Gallagher, G. Johnson, and A. Seal, *Locality, Province and Nation. Essays on Indian Politics 1870–1940*, Cambridge 1973; G. Johnson, *Provincial Politics and Indian Nationalism. Bombay and the Indian National Congress 1880–1915*, Cambridge 1973; F. Robinson, *Separatism among Indian Muslims: The Politics of the United Provinces Muslims 1860–1920*, Cambridge 1974; D.A. Washbrook, *The Emergence of Provincial Politics: Madras Presidency 1870–1920*, Cambridge 1976; C.J. Baker, *The Politics of South India 1920–1937*, Cambridge 1976. For the contrary view see Chandra, *India's Struggle for Independence*, and B. Chandra, *Indian National Movement: The Long Term Dynamics*, Delhi 1988.

[11] Especially Robinson, *Separatism among Indian Muslims*; D. Page, *Prelude to Pakistan. The Indian Muslims and the Imperial System of Control*, Delhi 1982; M. Hasan, *Nationalism and Communal Politics in India 1885–1930*, D. Gilmartin, *Empire and Islam. Punjab and the Making of Pakistan*, Berkeley 1988; R.J. Moore, *Escape from Empire. The Attlee Government and the Indian Problem*, Oxford 1982.

[12] A. Jalal, *The Sole Spokesman. Jinnah, the Muslim League and the demand for Pakistan*, Cambridge 1985; J. Chatterji, *Bengal Divided. Hindu Communalism and Partition, 1932–1947*, Cambridge 1994.

[13] Rittenberg, *Ethnicity, Nationalism, and the Pakhtuns*; S. Ansari, *Sufi Saints and State Power. The Pirs of Sind, 1843–1947*, Cambridge 1992; Tai Yong Tan, 'The Military and the State in Colonial Punjab, 1900–1939', Cambridge PhD thesis 1992.

[14] S. Das, *Communal Riots in Bengal 1905–1947*, Delhi 1991, ch. 6; V. Damodaran, *Broken Promises: Popular Protest, Indian Nationalism and the Congress Party in Bihar 1935–1946*, Delhi 1992, ch. 6.

Congress, both in the urban and more particularly in many of the rural areas of India.[15]

As studies of modern Indian nationalism prior to independence develop further so such matters as the rituals of politics,[16] the creation of communities,[17] the supports for the colonial state,[18] the effects of the world's slump,[19] the visions of independence,[20] the huge plethora of India's discrete arenas and their complex relation to its polity,[21] along with the erosion of imperial authority, have come to engage attention; while the middle decades of the twentieth century are now being studied not just in terms of Independence and Partition (which, quite understandably, have so far preoccupied attention) but in relation to both the immense disruptions and the significant continuities that occurred,[22] and the ways that these spilled across into the post-independence history of the countries of South Asia.[23]

In the 1980s there were at the same time two rather disconcerting tendencies. Chiefly perhaps because in 1985 the Indian National Congress celebrated the centenary of its founding a great deal of attention was devoted to the history of the Indian nationalist movement.[24] That provided a great many welcome new insights. It rarely focussed, however, upon the actualities of the interactive conflict with the British Raj, and there were some disturbing signs of a reversion to uncritical paeans, even on occasion to outmoded hagiography. The more worrying development came from the British side. For as the British documents came increasingly to be studied so the unwary allowed themselves to be trapped into supposing that the processes of decolonisation turned principally on

[15] R. Guha, ed., *Subaltern Studies*, vols. I–VI, Delhi 1982–89.

[16] D.E. Haynes, *Rhetoric and Ritual in Colonial India. The Shaping of a Public Culture in Surat City, 1852–1928*, Berkeley 1991.

[17] S.B. Freitag, *Collective Action and Community: Public Arenas and the Emergence of Communalism in North India*, Berkeley 1989.

[18] G. Kudaisya, 'State Power and the Erosion of Colonial Authority in Uttar Pradesh, India 1930–42', Cambridge PhD thesis 1992.

[19] D. Rothermund, *India in the Great Depression 1929–1939*, Delhi 1992.

[20] For one example see M.M. Kudaisya, 'G.D. Birla'.

[21] G. Johnson, *The New Cambridge History of India* (forthcoming volume).

[22] E.g. Das, *Communal Riots in Bengal 1905–1947*, chs. 5 and 6; Damodaran, *Broken Promises*, chs. 3–6; D.A. Low, ed., *Freedom, Trauma and Continuities: Northern India in the 1940s*, Delhi 1997.

[23] E.g. D.A. Low, ed., *The Political Inheritance of Pakistan*, London 1991.

[24] B.N. Pande, general editor, *A Centenary History of the Indian National Congress*, 3 vols., Delhi 1985; P.R. Brass and F. Robinson, eds., *Indian National Congress and Indian Society, 1885–1985*, Delhi 1987; R. Sissons and S. Wolpert, eds., *Congress and Indian Nationalism. The Pre-Independence Phase*, Berkeley 1988; M. Shepperson and C. Simmons, eds., *The Indian National Congress and the Political Economy of India 1885–1985*, Aldershot 1988; D.A. Low, ed., *The Indian National Congress. Centenary Hindsights*, Delhi 1988; J.L. Hill, ed., *Congress and Indian Nationalism*, London 1991.

imperialists' decisions; occasionally they even permitted themselves to marginalise the Indian national movement to little more than a distant irritant.[25] There need be no doubt that the decisions of the imperial power were of major importance to the processes of decolonisation. They often had, moreover, a sequence to them that warrants the illumination they have received. Yet it is quite erroneous to suggest that all this somehow unfolded within an imperialist vacuum; worse still, that imperial rulers were the olympian masters of their empire's fate.

These tendencies can be fairly readily corrected by calling in aid a larger perspective drawn from the protracted tale of multiple decolonisations across the world in the middle decades of the twentieth century. For that clearly shows that whatever the particular triggers – intellectual breakthroughs, rising ambitions, state crises, or a complex of these and other factors – the growth and development of a vigorous nationalism was all but essential to any sustained progress towards the ending of imperial rule. That seems to have been as true for Egypt as for Zaire, for Vietnam as for Indonesia, for India as for Zimbabwe (and for many others too). Where by contrast nationalism developed relatively slowly – in the Princely States in India, or in Malaya as compared with Indonesia, or in tropical Africa as compared with monsoon Asia – the onset of decolonisation took a good deal longer to occur.

At the same time too narrowly focussed a concentration upon the development of the nationalist movement in any one place can seriously distract from any fully rounded understanding of the course that a particular conflict took, and it is precisely at this point that it seems vital to allow a major place for the policies of the corresponding imperial power. For whilst the generation of nationalist impulses seems to have been of critical importance for any movement towards nationalist independence, not only does the character of the encounter which then ensued appear to have been principally determined by the nature of the particular imperial reactions which these encountered, but the manner in which nationalists responded to these seems to have been principally conditioned by those reactions too.

So soon as one links these together it is, for example, far from surprising that whilst the processes of decolonisation in West Africa in both the French and British territories after mid-century were generally peaceful, those in Britain's East and Central African colonies were marked by violent revolt and major disturbances; whilst those in Algeria, Rhodesia,

---

[25] This at all events is how I read M. Beloff, *Dream of Commonwealth 1921–42*, London 1989. See also Bridge, *Holding India to the Empire*, and R.F. Holland, *European Decolonization 1918–1981*, London 1985.

and the Portuguese colonies were scarred by guerilla war. For these marked differences mirrored very precisely: the readiness of the British and then of the French to grant independence to all-black West African governments without too much resistance; the long-running opposition of the British to proceeding similarly where there were white settler minorities; and the absolute determination of the French in Algeria, the whites in Rhodesia, and the Portuguese throughout their African colonies to maintain their hold at whatever cost.[26]

In considering the Indian case it now takes a peculiarly blinkered view to underplay the major role played by India's surging nationalism in determining the course of the Indo–British conflict. An immense amount of data has been trawled upon this subject and countless studies have been produced to put the question beyond dispute. Nevertheless despite the many contributions which have been made to it in recent years it remains a striking feature of the historiography of modern India that the distinctive (and in contemporary comparative terms decidedly eccentric) character of the Indo–British conflict is all too often substantially ignored. The conflict is treated as its own paradigm. The course which events took is largely taken for granted. There is little or no recognition of the key contingent variables on which so many of them turned; while the idiosyncratic quality of the actual cut and thrust of the interactive conflict in India is rarely given prominence. As a consequence crucial features of the encounter can be seriously underplayed, important nuances missed, and one is left with the supreme irony that the very particular singularities of this quite extraordinary encounter are often overlooked altogether.

The problem here stems characteristically from the propensity of almost all the available accounts of India's political history for the years before independence (not least by the present author) to confine themselves almost entirely to data which relate to India only. There is, of course, a great deal of this and there no doubt remain many caches to be trawled. Nevertheless this whole approach is now seriously limiting understanding. One is all too frequently confronted by a one-country myopia. The wider setting is hardly noticed. Next to no attention is paid to comparative material and comparative issues. And so much of the essence of this major story is as a consequence too often lost to sight.

As it happens, standing close by is one especially helpful way out of this whole tangle. For if we will only lift our eyes and consider a whole series of events elsewhere in Asia which were simultaneously occurring nearby, a

---

[26] I have sought to explore these various points in D.A. Low, *Eclipse of Empire*, Cambridge 1991, esp. chs.1, 3, 5, and 9.

shaft of new light can very soon be cast upon the nature, quality, and character of the course, conduct, and denouement of the Indo–British conflict in a way that is now overdue. Very occasionally, as we shall see, it is worth taking a brief look at what was happening in China away to the northeast where the governing Kuomintang was by the early 1930s in mounting armed conflict with the southern Communist forces under the redoubtable Mao Zedong. It is principally, however, to Southeast Asia that we need to look. For there running parallel to the Indo–British struggle during the first half of the twentieth century there ran three other, major, nationalist–imperialist encounters, each of a broadly similar kind to the Indo–British conflict, each of which nevertheless followed a quite distinctive course to that pursued in India.

Whilst, of course, we must allow for the very important respects in which these countries differed from each other, and *a fortiori* with India, in their size, their previous history, their economies, the developments to which they had lately been subjected, and so on, the pertinent distinctions in the present case all the same remain. In pursuing them it seems critically important (as in the African instances cited above) to pay close attention to the particular circumstances and policies of the imperial power by whom they were confronted in relation to the crucial impact these characteristically made upon their corresponding anti-imperialist thrusts, since in the end there seems little doubt that the principal clues to a great deal else that follows lie here.

The principal facts can be briefly stated. Besides the confrontation between the two World Wars between India's nationalists and the British, there ran upon the one hand the relatively non-confrontational encounter between the Filipino nationalists and the Americans, and on the other not only the eventually unrelieved conflict between the Indonesian nationalists and the Dutch, but the sometimes quite horrendous contest between the Vietnamese nationalists and the French. So soon as these are brought to view not only does any lingering notion that there was something prototypical about the Indo–British story have to be very soon discarded. By exposing the comparisons which these other stories provide it becomes possible both to embark on a much closer scrutiny of the singularities of the Indo–British conflict and to particularise its specific character and quality in a very much sharper form. A brief outline of each of these other encounters must serve to determine the distinctions to be drawn.

Back at the turn of the century during the course of the Spanish–American War of 1898, the United States had sent troops to wrest the

Philippines' islands from the Spanish.[27] There they soon confronted the new, indigenous Philippines Republic, which the Filipino landowning elite had first established amid the earlier Philippines' revolution against the Spanish in 1896–7, following their supersession of the non-elite Katipunan movement in its leadership. Though the Americans refused to recognise the new Republic and between 1898 and 1902 conducted a bloody conquest of the Philippines, they soon established a close alliance with leading figures in the Filipino elite, who, fearful of popular insurgency against them, soon threw in their lot with the new rulers. Thereafter non-elite movements and non-elite nationalism was often vigorously suppressed.[28]

The Americans nonetheless pursued a policy of what they called 'benevolent assimiliation'. By 1913 70 per cent of government posts were held by western-educated Filipinos; by the late 1920s nearly all of them. During the course of the first decade of American rule, municipal, provincial, and legislative assembly elections were all held, and as early as 1907 a Nacionalistas party under the Philippines' longest-running elite nationalist leaders, Osmena and Quezon, secured 72 per cent of the seats in the American-created legislature, with Osmena becoming its Speaker. From the very beginning there were, moreover, Filipino members of the American colonial executive; while by 1925 the only American in the American Governor-General's Cabinet was the Secretary of Public Instruction.

At the outset there had been a good deal of American opposition to the annexation of the Philippines, and many Americans remained opposed to any involvement in a directly imperial role. Formal empire was never central to the American self-image. In many respects it deeply offended against it. Nor was it important for their economy. The number of Americans employed in the government of the Philippines was never at all large. They were generally well content to allow the Filipino elite a much larger role in the governance of the islands than was ever enjoyed by corresponding colonial elites elsewhere. Even, moreover, before the outbreak of the First World War the Democratic Party in the United States had begun to support independence for the Philippines. In 1916 they secured the passage through the Congress of the Jones Act which promised the Philippines its independence 'as soon as stable government can be established'. In the years that followed a succession of Philippines'

[27] There is a summary of the whole story in H.W. Brands, *Bound to Empire. The United States and the Philippines 1890–1990*, New York 1992, Parts I and II.
[28] It is difficult to think of a better study of 'subaltern' activity in Asia and its repression than R. Ileto, *Pasyon and Revolution: Popular Movements in the Philippines, 1840–1910*, Quezon City 1979.

Independence missions thereupon visited Washington so as to secure this. During the 1920s they ran into a number of difficulties with the American Republican Administrations – which by contrast with right-wing regimes elsewhere did not deny the Philippines' right to independence, but simply avowed that it was not as yet ready for it. Since, however, there were clear economic advantages for the Filipino elite in the American connection, and important political ones as well – non-elite movements continued to be suppressed – they were cautious about mobilising mass support against the Americans even whilst regularly proclaiming their nationalist commitments.

With the onset of the depression in the early 1930s and the return of the Democrats to power following the election of Franklin Roosevelt as President in 1932, two further Philippines' Independence missions finally secured a breakthrough. Not least under pressure from the American farming organisations and the American Federation of Labor (which objected to the harm being done to their members' interests by too much Philippines' competition), the passage was eventually attained of two Philippines' independence acts, first the Hare–Hawes–Cutting Act of 1933 which was then amended at Filipino instance and replaced by the Tydings–Macduffie Act of 1934.[29] In this process care was taken to ensure that power would be transferred to a right-wing landed regime,[30] which would remain tied to the United States by fiscal, trade and defence connections, but this was what the Filipino elite wanted too, and thereupon the Philippines finally secured full internal self-government in 1935 with a promise of full independence ten years later.[31]

[29] On the whole story see also U. Mahajani, *Philippine Nationalism. External Challenge and Filipino Response 1565–1946*, St Lucia 1971; S. Karnow, *In Our Image. America's Empire in the Philippines*, London 1990, chs. 4–9; T.A. Agoncillo, *Malolos: The Crisis of the Republic*, Quezon City 1960; R.E. Welch, *Response to Imperialism. The United States and the Philippines American War, 1899–1902*, Chapel Hill 1979; S.C. Miller, *"Benevolent Assimilation": The American Conquest of the Philippines 1899–1903*, New Haven 1982; P.W. Stanley, *A Nation in the Making: The Philippines and the United States, 1899–1921*, Cambridge, Mass. 1974; Stanley, ed., *Reappraising an Empire: New Perspectives on Philippine–American History*, Cambridge, Mass. 1984; D.R. Sturtevant, *Popular Uprisings in the Philippines, 1849–1940*, Ithaca 1976; G. May, *Social Engineering in the Philippines: The Aims, Execution and Impact of American Colonial Policy*, Westport 1980; N.G. Owen, ed., *Compadre Colonialism, Studies on the Philippines under American Rule*, Ann Arbor 1971; B.R. Churchill, *The Philippine Missions to the United States*, Manila 1983; T.W. Friend, *Between Two Empires: The Ordeal of the Philippines, 1929–1946*, New Haven 1965; J.W. Howard, *Mr Justice Murphy*, Princeton 1968, chs. 4 and 5; S. Fine, *Frank Murphy: The New Deal Years*, Chicago 1979, chs. 1–5.
[30] The last Republican Governor-General remarked that its leaders were seeking: 'The Philippines for the Filipino politicians, a small group in the islands who already exercised despotically what powers they have', N. Roosevelt, *The Philippines: a Treasure and a Problem*, New York 1926, pp. 46–7.
[31] It was actually attained in 1946 following upon the end of the Second World War.

All this stood in marked contrast to what was happening in the Netherlands East Indies close by.[32] There the Dutch East Indies Company had first established its trading stations in what is now the Indonesian archipelago back in the seventeenth century. Following upon the supersession of the Company by direct governmental rule at the beginning of the nineteenth century, the Dutch came to secure extensive control over Java by 1830, and in the final years of the nineteenth and into the first decades of the twentieth century completed their conquest of the Indonesian archipelago. Considerable numbers of Dutch people thereupon made their homes in the Netherlands Indies. Relative to the overall population there were soon eight times as many of them as there were of their British counterparts in India; while the ratio of European officials to the local population became nearly fifteen times that in India. There were, moreover, almost as many high-ranking Dutch civil service positions in the Indies as in the Netherlands itself.

The first shoots of what was to develop, however, into Indonesia's nationalist movement appeared in the founding of Budi Utomo ('the beautiful endeavour') in 1908. During the course of the First World War this was extensively overtaken by Sarekat Islam, a much larger movement of Indonesia's majority Muslim community, which by 1919 claimed to have two million followers. But because of Communist infiltration, it then began to fall apart, and in 1926–7 there was a spate of Communist-led revolts in Java and Sumatra which the Dutch resolutely repressed. Thereafter the leadership of the Indonesian nationalist movement fell into the hands of secular nationalists, amongst whom the leading figures were Mohammed Hatta, who headed Perhimpunan Indonesia, the organisation of Indonesian students studying in Holland, and the consummate orator and locally educated engineer, Sukarno, who not only succeeded in establishing in 1927 what soon became the Partai Nasional Indonesia, but during 1928 managed to unite a number of other Indonesian movements under an umbrella organisation, the PPPKI.

Back in 1918 the Dutch had begun to establish a Volksraad (People's Council) in the Netherlands Indies – though upon extremely restricted lines. They were not, however, prepared to tolerate Sukarno's increasingly vociferous activities for very long, and in 1929 arrested him, and, following his trial in 1930, sentenced him to four years' imprisonment. As a parting gesture the somewhat liberal-minded Dutch Governor-General, de Graeff, decided to release him in 1931. But upon his release Sukarno found the unity of the Indonesian national movement in considerable

---

[32] The most useful introduction is M.C. Ricklefs, *A History of Modern Indonesia*, London 1981, especially pts II–IV.

disarray. The position worsened when Hatta returned to Indonesia in August 1932, since there soon developed a sharp difference of opinion between them over precisely what anti-colonial policy it would now be best to pursue. Hatta inclined to the view that a class-based cadre-led party would be essential to moving the Dutch, whilst Sukarno instinctively favoured a less structured mass-based multi-class nationalist movement. Before long Hatta gained control of PNI Baru (the new PNI, originally Sukarno's own creation), while Sukarno moved into the leadership of its rival, Partindo. Both then made considerable progress in winning support, particularly in the towns. So much so indeed that de Graeff's much more conservative successor, de Jonge, finally decided in August 1933 to arrest Sukarno and his associates, and then early in 1934 Hatta and his, and to exile them to some distant islands for life. 'If the political independence of the Netherlands-Indies is preached', de Jonge proclaimed in October 1933, '. . . then His Excellency will indeed silence these expressions of the National Movement'.[33] Thereafter the only Indonesian political parties which were allowed to operate at all openly were those prepared to collaborate with the Dutch; and even they received short shrift when in the Soetardjo Petition of 1936 they sought to secure discussions with the Dutch on some modest constitutional reforms. They were not even accorded the benefit of a reply till over two years had passed.[34]

Throughout these years the Dutch remained implacably committed to maintaining their empire in the Indies. It was almost all they had left of their three centuries of overseas endeavour. They remained wedded, moreover, to 'Ruste en Orde' (tranquillity and order) and from the 1930s onwards to 'Rijkseenheid' (imperial unity) as well. Apart from a brief flowering of the more liberal *De Stuw* group in 1930–3 (backed by the Oriental Faculty at Leiden University), most Dutch residents in the Indies were thoroughly conservative, represented from 1929 onwards in the Vaderlandsche Club (and buttressed by the new Indology Faculty at Utrecht University). Major Dutch commercial companies were heavily involved in Indies affairs. Directors of Royal Dutch Shell were both Colonial Ministers and Governor-Generals in a way that was scarcely conceivable elsewhere. From the mid-nineteenth century onwards there was, moreover, a strong belief amongst the Dutch that possession of the Indies was absolutely vital to the economic health of their homeland (perched as it was uncertainly upon the edge of the North Sea). Income remitted to the Netherlands from Indonesia represented an 8 per cent

---

[33] It was only with the Japanese conquest of the Netherlands East Indies in 1942 that they were eventually released.

[34] S. Abeyasekere, 'The Soetardjo Petition', *Indonesia*, 15, 1973, pp. 81–108.

addition to its domestic product, and comprised most of its foreign earnings. The Indies (so the clichés ran) were the 'cork' on which the Netherlands floated; the horse pulling its economy along; *Indies Gone, Prosperity Done* (as a 1914 pamphlet title put it). Should the Indies be lost, not only would the Netherlands be reduced to penury was it believed, but 'to the ranks of a country such as Denmark'. Amid a plethora of political parties in the Netherlands itself there was in any event little faith by the 1930s in the democratic process so that its introduction in the Indies was altogether inconceivable, especially since, so one Dutch Colonial Minister argued, Indonesia's nationalists were no more than a 'superficial layer of the population, as thin as the silver skin of a grain of rice'. All of which was reinforced by what the Dutch saw as their firm commitment from the beginning of the twentieth century onwards to their 'Ethical Policy'. That in their view provided a complete justification for their continued rule in the Indies. Dismembering 'the Realm' would therefore constitute not only rank treachery to their tiny homeland, but a grave dereliction of their self-imposed duty.[35]

The French in the 1930s were even more determined to hold fast to their empire.[36] Back in the late 1850s they had embarked on the conquest of the states of Indochina, and eventually completed this in the 1890s. They had already lost two empires – one in the Americas and India; a second, upon the defeat of Napoleon, in Europe. They were in no mind to lose the third. Since the days of their pre-Revolutionary monarchy, the

---

[35] See also J. Ingleson, *Perhimpunan Indonesia and the Indonesian Nationalist Movement*, Clayton 1975; Ingleson, *The Road to Exile. The Indonesian Nationalist Movement, 1927–1934*, Singapore 1979; B. Dahm, *Sukarno and the Struggle for Indonesian Independence*, Ithaca 1969; J.D. Legge, *Sukarno. A Political Biography*, London 1972; M. Rose, *Indonesia Free. A Political Biography of Mohammed Hatta*, Ithaca 1987; R. van Neil, *The Emergence of the Modern Indonesian Elite*, The Hague 1960; R. McVey, *The Rise of Indonesian Communism*, Ithaca 1963; D. Noer, *The Modernist Muslim Movement in Indonesia, 1900–1945*, Singapore 1973; S. Abeyasakere, *One Hand Clapping: Indonesian Nationalists and the Dutch, 1939–1941*, Clayton 1976.

[36] Convenient introductions are W.J. Duiker, *The Rise of Nationalism in Vietnam, 1900–1941*, Ithaca 1976, and Duiker, *The Communist Road to Power in Vietnam*, Boulder 1981. See further J. Buttinger, *The Smaller Dragon: A Political History of Vietnam*, New York 1958; Buttinger, *Vietnam. A Dragon Embattled*, New York 1967, vol. I, chs. I–VI; R. Giradet, *L'Idée Coloniale en France, 1871–1962*, Paris 1972; D.B. Marshall, *The French Colonial Myth and Constitution-Making in the Fourth Republic*, New Haven 1973, ch. 2; P.S. Sorum, *Intellectuals and Decolonisation in France*, Chapel Hill 1977; M.J. Murray, *The Economic Development of Capitalism in Indochina (1870–1940)*, Berkeley 1980; S.M. Persell, *The French Colonial Lobby 1889–1938*, Stanford 1983; J-M. Mayeur and M. Reberioux, *The Third Republic from its Origins to the Great War 1871–1914*, Cambridge 1984, pp. 272–8; J. Marseille, *Empire Colonial et Capitalisme Français: Histoire d'un Divorce*, Paris 1984; A. Plessis, *The Rise and Fall of the Second Empire 1852–1871*, Cambridge 1985, pp. 42–50; B. Brotel, 'Imperialist Domination in Vietnam and Cambodia: a Long-Term View', in W.J. Mommsen and J. Osterhammel, *Imperialism and After. Continuities and Discontinuities*, London 1986, pp. 172–6.

administration of France itself had been characterised by centralised control. This had been replicated in the role of the Intendants in its first empire in Canada, and was then reinforced both by the Jacobins and by the Napoleonic state at home. All that in turn came to be underpinned by an ideology of the French state as a rational, corporate institution possessing rights as well as duties *vis-à-vis* its subjects.[37]

This whole approach came to be given full expression in the very centralised and highly autocratic system of direct rule first established in Indochina by Governor-General Doumer (1897–1902). As a consequence there came to be three times as many French officials in Indochina as there were British officials in India (where the population was ten times as large), while all the way down close to the very bottom the colonial administration was staffed by French officials. Ideologically France's colonial regime remained deeply committed both to France's *mission civilatrice* and to its doctrine of *la mise en valeur* (development). During the interwar years that seems to have entailed an extension of the process by which through various economic and social developments during the preceding half century or so, steps were taken to draw the populations of France's provinces into the culture of its metropolis.[38] Whilst France's earlier commitment to the 'assimilation' of its colonial peoples into the French state now tended to be reduced to 'association', one of the principal aims of French policy in Vietnam was always to build up a Vietnamese elite that would be at once French in its loyalties even while encouraging their commitment to Confucian values.

By the opening decades of the twentieth century a Vietnamese nationalist movement had nevertheless begun to raise its head. For many years this was symbolised by Phan Boi Chou, a remarkable man who in 1905 formed the Association for the Modernisation of Vietnam. Eventually in 1925 the French kidnapped him, and after sentencing him to hard labour for life confined him to his house instead. From the outset the French made it abundantly clear that they would not in any way countenance nationalist ambitions in Vietnam, and throughout their rule banned every political party with nationalist aspirations which was launched there.

That situation was underscored during the interwar years in two important respects. As France's position *vis-à-vis* Germany's declined, so empire came to be seen as of critical importance in securing France's proper standing in the world. That was reinforced by the major monopo-

---

[37] E.g. H.S. Jones, *The French State in Question. Public Law and Political Argument in the Third Republic*, Cambridge 1993.   [38] E. Weber, *Peasants into Frenchmen*, London 1977.

listic interests many Frenchmen enjoyed in Indochina in mining, rubber, and the export of rice; by the preeminent role they held in the tea, coffee, timber, and textile industries; and by the immense profits procured by the French-based Banque d'Indochine. Whilst some rather more liberally minded French Governor-Generals were occasionally appointed to Indochina, they made little impact on the local scene.

Following upon the creation of an ineffectual Vietnamese Constitutionalist Party in the early 1920s, an elite secular nationalist party, the VNQDD (Viet Nam Quoc Dan Dang), eventually came to be formed in 1927. In the oppressive conditions then prevailing this soon committed itself to political violence, and in February 1930 precipitated a mutiny at several places in the French colonial army. The French reacted to this with great ferocity by launching their so-called 'White Terror'. Eighty VNQDD leaders were swiftly executed. Hundreds were sent to a penal colony.

To the dismay of the French these events were then immediately over-taken by a whole series of peasant revolts in Indochina during 1930–1, particularly in Nghe An and Ha Tinh provinces and in the Mekong delta, where the newly formed Indochinese Communist Party was soon playing a leading role. Thereupon the 'White Terror' was immeasurably extended. Thousands of Vietnamese peasants were killed. Upwards of 700 people were executed without trial in 1930 alone. Hundreds were sent to the guillotine;[39] while tens of thousands were incarcerated in either mainland prisons or an island penal colony. Although there were several outraged protests, and although the French Colonial Minister went to Vietnam to review future policy there, it was not until the advent of the left-of-centre Popular Front government in France in 1936 that there was any significant let-up in this repression, and even that soon gave way to still more repression in 1939–40, particularly of the Vietnamese Communists and their allies.

Underlying all of this lay the widespread view of a great many Frenchmen that the universalist superiority of their own culture and civilisation made any serious nationalist opposition to their colonial rule essentially malign. For the French Right that called for police surveil-lance, stern repression, and a ready use of penal colonies. For the Left it necessitated not independence but a far greater concern for the colonies' development. France's fundamental attitude towards its empire through-out these years was most clearly expressed at the Brazzaville Conference which de Gaulle called in 1944 which roundly declared that:

[39] Buttinger, *Dragon Embattled*, I, p. 219.

The aims of France's civilizing mission preclude any thought of autonomy or any possibility of development outside the French empire. Self-government must be rejected – even in the more distant future.[40]

One must, no doubt, be cautious about presenting too rigid a classification of these varying imperialist positions during this interwar period along these lines. We have noted, for example, that the Republican regime in the United States was a good deal less sympathetic to Philippines' aspirations for independence than the Roosevelt Administration that followed it. During the late 1920s and the early 1930s there was a somewhat more liberal-minded Governor-General in de Graeff in the Netherlands East Indies; while similar appointments were made on occasion in Vietnam as well (and there was even that brief hiatus in French repression in Vietnam in the Popular Front years). Yet the principal distinctions stand. Whereas by the mid 1930s the Americans had clearly determined to relinquish formal control over their Asian colony (so long as they kept a number of important links with it), both the Dutch and the French were absolutely determined to stay. They were adamant that this would be vital to maintaining their proper status in the world. They were completely convinced of the abundant moral justifications in their colonial subjects' own interests for doing so; and they displayed few qualms about the iron-handed measures they took to check the nationalist forces arrayed against them.

These clear-cut distinctions can, moreover, be quite pithily epitomised. On his appointment as Governor-General of the Philippine Islands by President Roosevelt in 1932 the later Supreme Court Judge, Frank Murphy, declared: 'I have one ambition. I'm going to set these people free.'[41] By contrast, at around the same time, Governor-General de Jonge

---

[40] E.J. Hammer, *The Struggle for Indo-China 1940–1955*, Stanford 1966; R. Betts, *France and Decolonisation 1900–1960*, London 1991; A. Short, *The Origins of the Vietnam War*, London 1989, pp. 27–33; W.G. Langlois, *André Malraux. The Indochina Adventure*, London 1966; D.G. Marr, *Vietnamese Anticolonialism 1885–1925*, Berkeley 1971; Marr, *Vietnamese Tradition on Trial 1920–1945*, Berkeley 1981; A.B. Woodside, *Community and Revolution in Modern Vietnam*, Boston 1976; J.T. Macallister, *Vietnam. The Origins of Revolution*, New York 1970, chs. I–III; M. Osborne, 'Continuity and Motivation in the Vietnamese Revolution: New Light from the 1930s', *Pacific Affairs*, Spring 1974, pp. 37–55; D. Hemery, *Révolutionnaires Vietnamiens et Pouvoir Coloniale en Indo-Chine*, Paris 1975; R.F. Turner, *Vietnamese Communism: Its Origins and Development*, Stanford 1975; J.C. Scott, *The Moral Economy of the Peasant: Rebellion and Subsistence in Southeast Asia*, New Haven 1976, pp. 114–19; D. Pike, *History of Vietnamese Communism, 1925–1976*, Stanford 1978; P. Morlat, *La Répression Coloniale au Vietnam (1908–40)*, Paris 1990; Huyn Kim Khanh, *Vietnamese Communism 1925–1945*, Ithaca 1982; P. Bernard and H. Dubief, *The Decline of the Third Republic 1914–1938*, Cambridge 1985, pp. 193–7; C.M. Andrew, 'France: Adjustment to Change', in H. Bull and A. Watson, eds., *The Expansion of International Society*, Oxford 1984, pp. 435–44; J. Jackson, *The Popular Front in France: Defending Democracy, 1934–38*, Cambridge 1988, pp. 154–9.   [41] Fine, *Murphy*, p. 38.

in the Netherlands Indies announced that 'we have ruled here for 300 years with whip and club and we shall still be doing it in another 300 years'.[42] While following upon the issuing of orders to French Foreign Legionnaires in Vietnam in 1931 to kill nine out of ten prisoners whom they took in armed encounters with rebellious peasants,[43] a scion of a notable French colonial family, Pierre Lyautey, pronounced in a widely quoted book that 'French expansion is an enduring and permanent phenomenon'.[44]

A preliminary glance at the corresponding British position quickly reveals that it possessed a very different character both from the American position on the one hand and from both the Dutch position and the French position on the other.

By contrast with the Americans the British during these interwar years were always quite determined to do everything they could to hold on to their empire. Not only was its possession an essential buttress to their self-image. It was of critical importance, as they saw it, to securing their strategic and economic interests in the world at large. A vast amount of their present position, and an immense legacy from their heroic past, was tied, moreover, to their Indian empire in particular. They had no intention of relinquishing it, and with considerable assiduity and often steely resolve gave their minds to maintaining it. Before 1942 no British government ever contemplated any early move towards India's independence. Prior to 1938 no British political party ever fully committed itself to this – in the way that the Democratic Party in the United States had done two decades earlier for the Philippines. Paradoxically this hardline position was never more precisely displayed than in the response of the principal Conservative Party leaders to Winston Churchill's thunderous denunciations of the reforms they were introducing in India in the early 1930s as presaging the end both of the British Empire and of Britain's leading place in the world. On their side they persistently countered that far from endangering Britain's dominion over India, constitutional reforms were the one way to 'hold India to the empire', which they were as anxious to ensure as he was.[45] In so many respects the British position was thus the polar opposite of the American.

---

[42] Quoted, S. Sjahrir, *Out of Exile*, New York 1949, p. 212.

[43] Quoted Osborne, 'Continuity and Motivation in the Vietnamese Revolution', p. 47.

[44] P. Lyautey, *L'Empire Colonial Français*, Paris 1931, p. vii. Cf. the statement from the Department of Public Affairs in the French colonial ministry of 30 Jan. 1931: 'France will not abandon Indochina . . . Indochina is necessary for France as much from a political point of view as from an economic point of view', quoted Hemery, *Révolutionnaires Vietnamiens*, footnote p. 32.   [45] Bridge, *Holding India to the Empire*, passim.

Yet at the same time it was very different from the Dutch and from the French as well. Whilst totally excluding any early move towards full independence for India, the British never ruled out, as both of those countries did, the prospect of self-government altogether. By declaring indeed in 1929 that India could at some time have Dominion Status, the British conceded that one day India could have as much self-government as Canada and all the other Dominions in the empire. Whilst, moreover, being quite prepared to suppress nationalist agitations and imprison those who participated in them (for a while at least); whilst being very ready to use troops to halt internecine violence,[46] and against those who employed force against them;[47] whilst, moreover, never hesitating to treat political killings as murder,[48] unlike the Dutch the British never banished India's nationalist leaders for life, let alone like the French put hundreds of them to death.[49] By comparison with the Dutch they remained staunch in their support for the principles of parliamentary government (and were much less prone to argue their inappropriateness for India than before), while by contrast with the French they never believed that the superiority of their own culture and civilisation justified the suppression of those who challenged their authority.

If, however, there were clear distinctions between the British position upon the one hand and the American position on the other, and between the British position and both the Dutch and the French upon a third, where did the British really stand?

If we are to come to grips at all closely with this question it seems quite essential once again to take a wider view. For if we confine ourselves to the Indo–British conflict we not only deprive ourselves of substantial parts of the available evidence, but run the risk of suggesting that the phenomena with which we are concerned were confined to India only. That was far from being the case. If we are, however, to fathom at all fully what was involved here it is imperative that we should reach out once again, and this time into the very much larger context within the very much wider British empire in which the Indo–British conflict came to be fought out. For so soon as we do that we not only bring into view a great

---

[46] They were very often used in India to suppress communal disturbances.

[47] This was to be especially the case in Palestine, Kenya, Malaya, and Aden. It should be added that the British had few qualms later on in using *force majeure* against Communists or 'crypto-Communists', particularly in Malaya and British Guiana (Guyana).

[48] In India those whose death sentences were commuted, or who were convicted of complicity, were often sent to the penal colony in the Andaman islands.

[49] The British had exiled for life some who had been involved in the early rebellions against imperial rule, and they later deported, for example, the Kabaka of Buganda in 1953, and Archbishop Makarios in 1957, but before very long both were allowed to return to their countries.

many more manifestations of the otherwise seemingly idiosyncratic practices of the British in India, but we can begin to identify far more closely than before the characteristic stock-in-trade of the British as they came to face the many anti-imperialist thrusts they confronted in these years.

To this end it is important to recall that throughout the interwar period the British Empire remained the world's most portentous imperial power. Along with India, four white Dominions – Canada, Australia, New Zealand, South Africa – constituted its principal supports. It included as well a number of other Asian colonies, Burma, Ceylon, and Malaya more particularly. It encompassed a plethora of island colonies both in the West Indies and in the Southwest Pacific. There were four British colonial territories in West Africa (including the very large Nigeria); ten more in east, central, and southern Africa (Kenya and Southern Rhodesia especially amongst them), and the 'Anglo-Egyptian' Sudan. Spread across the globe there were a number of strategically placed (usually island) territories: Gibraltar, Malta, Cyprus, Aden, Singapore, Hong Kong; while beyond these stood a penumbra of formally independent countries that constituted Britain's 'informal empire': including Egypt, the Persian Gulf Sheikhdoms, and Thailand.[50] Following the peace settlement in 1919 several parts of both the former Ottoman and German empires in the Middle East, Africa, and elsewhere were made British 'mandates', with the consequence that in the 1920s the British empire reached its largest dimensions ever.[51]

For the most part it was not ruled by systems of direct administration such as both the Dutch and the French employed in their empires, but, in accord with a very longstanding English and British tradition, by means of compacts with leading local figures who were granted the right to exercise local control over local affairs so long as they accepted the overall authority of the British.[52] Since such people frequently found this to be the surest way of sustaining their own authority within their own local bailiwicks (and in many instances their security against external threats as well), these arrangements generally proved to be mutually quite acceptable. Thus it was that elected white elites in British settler colonies; Princes and large landowners in India; landed western-educated professional men in

---

[50] Here and elsewhere reference may be made to the general histories, e.g. Bernard Porter, *The Lion's Share. A Short History of British Imperialism, 1850–1993*, 2nd edn, London 1985; T.O. Lloyd, *The British Empire 1558–1983*, Oxford 1983, chs. 7–11; and R. Hyam, *Britain's Imperial Century 1815–1914*, 2nd edn, London 1993.

[51] J. Gallagher, *The Decline, Revival and Fall of the British Empire*, Cambridge 1982.

[52] On all this see F. Madden with D. Fieldhouse, *"The Empire of the Bretagnes", 1175–1688*, and subsequent volumes of their *Select Documents on the Constitutional History of the British Empire and Commonwealth*, Westport 1985– .

Ceylon;[53] Malay Sultans, Fijian High Chiefs, Nigerian Emirs, Ugandan rulers, and a multiplicity of others,[54] all enjoyed considerable political authority within their own local areas, and very effectively underpinned the wider British empire without the British ever having to import a large British bureaucracy.

At the core of this whole structure stood the United Kingdom of Great Britain and Northern Ireland – whose Royal and Merchant Navies bestrode the seas; whose Imperial General Staff masterminded its imperial military strategy; whose capital constituted the world's principal commercial centre; and whose currency dominated the world's financial systems. Here, besides the War Office, the Air Ministry and the Admiralty, there stood four great offices of state – the India Office, the Colonial Office, after 1925 the Dominions Office, and, in respect of such places as the Sudan and Egypt, the Foreign Office (along with, in certain instances, the Bank of England too).[55] Together they held the reins of imperial power. Scattered around the globe Governors and Governor-Generals, along with a miscellany of Residents, Consul-Generals, High Commissioners, Ministers, Financial Advisers, etc. (where these at the periphery were the more appropriate titles) were their centrally selected appointees, as were the supervising cadres in the 'dependent' territories – of the Indian Civil and Political Services, the Colonial Administrative Service, the Malayan Civil Service, and the Sudan Political Service. All in all it composed a most formidable edifice.

That, however, did not make it immune to serious challenge. During the interwar years it found itself facing indeed a whole series of fateful, and some even thought mortal, threats to its hold.[56] In at least half a dozen places there were major thrusts towards full independence in the British empire in these years. Since the British confronted these in much the same manner that they faced the Indian challenge, it proves to be par-

[53] E.g. M. Roberts, *Collective Identities, Nationalism and Revolution in Modern Sri Lanka*, Colombo 1979; Roberts, *Caste Conflict and Elite Formation: The Rise of a Karava Elite in Sri Lanka*, Cambridge 1982; J. Manor, *The Expedient Utopian: Bandaranaike and Ceylon*, Cambridge 1989.

[54] For some general comments on this see D.A. Low, *Lion Rampant*, London 1973, ch. 3 'Empire and Traditional Authority', and e.g. J.M. Gullick, *Residents and Rulers. Influence and Power in the Malay States 1870–1920*, Kuala Lumpur 1991; T.J. Macnaught, *The Fijian Colonial Experience*, Canberra 1982; A.H.M. Kirk-Greene, *The Principles of Native Administration in Nigeria*, London 1965.

[55] For a remarkable account of this contingency see R.J. Aldrich, *The Key to the South. Britain, the United States, and Thailand during the Approach of the Pacific War, 1929–1942*, Oxford 1993.

[56] See e.g. P. Williamson, *National Crisis and National Government. British Politics, the Economy and Empire, 1926–1932*, Cambridge 1992; J. Barnes and D. Nicholson, eds., *The Empire at Bay. The Leo Amery Diaries 1929–1945*, London 1988; J. Charmley, *Lord Lloyd and the Decline of the British Empire*, London 1987, passim.

ticularly valuable to consider the three other leading cases very briefly, namely Egypt, the white Dominions, and Ireland.

Back in 1882, after eighty years of a modernising independence, 'informal' British control had first been extended over Egypt. On the outbreak of war between Britain and Egypt's superordinate power, Turkey, in 1914 a full-scale British Protectorate was proclaimed over Egypt. That, however, soon generated a mounting Egyptian nationalist assault against it. So as to halt this, Curzon, Britain's Foreign Secretary, despatched in 1919 Field Marshal Allenby, the conqueror of the Turks in Palestine in 1918, to be British High Commissioner in Egypt. Allenby soon decided, however, that the way in which to deal with the situation would be by reaching an accommodation with the Egyptian leaders; and via a mission headed by Lord Milner (once the high priest of British imperialism) he eventually persuaded the British government to terminate the British Protectorate over Egypt in 1922.

Since, however, the Egyptians refused to accede to the accompanying British demand that they should sign a treaty under which, among other things, British troops could remain posted in the Suez Canal zone, a British army of occupation continued to be stationed throughout Egypt, and ironically it was then Allenby who forced an Egyptian Prime Minister to resign following the murder of the British army commander in 1924 by parading a regiment of British cavalry before his house. His successor Lord Lloyd (a former Governor of Bombay) took a similarly high imperial line, so much so that in 1929 the new Labour government, with the full support of the Foreign Office and the silent acquiescence of the main Conservative leaders, eventually forced him to resign for doing so too unremittingly. The crisis with the Egyptian leaders nonetheless continued, and it was not until they had become unsettled by Italy's aggression in Abyssinia that they eventually signed the Anglo–Egyptian Treaty of 1936.[57]

Parallel to this there had been a much more extensive development within the British empire at its core. During the course of the middle and later nineteenth century most of the British 'white' colonies had secured full control over their own internal affairs by means of the introduction of 'Responsible Government'. Along with the making of the federations of

---

[57] The confrontation, of course, rumbled on till it reached its fateful denouement at Suez in 1956. On the earlier story see J. Darwin, *Britain, Egypt and the Middle East. Imperial Policy in the Aftermath of War 1918–1922*, London 1981; Lord Lloyd, *Egypt since Cromer*, 2 vols., London 1933–4; A.P. Wavell, *Allenby in Egypt*, London 1943; Charmley, *Lord Lloyd*, chs. 16–22; J. Marlowe, *Anglo–Egyptian Relations 1800–1953*, London 1954.

Canada in 1867, Australia in 1901, and South Africa in 1910, each of them, together with the fourth Dominion, New Zealand, then began to develop its own distinctive nationalism. Over a number of years, in order that this should not pull the empire apart, there was a succession of moves to create an 'Imperial Federation' or some other form of 'closer union'. Since that inevitably would have locked the Dominions into a new system of control from London they all regularly rejected them. During the course of the First World War their Prime Ministers were nonetheless corralled, first in 1917 and again in 1918, into an Imperial War Cabinet in London, and thereafter made members of the 'British Empire Delegation' to the Paris Peace Conference. All of which, however, they very skilfully turned to their own advantage, and in 1919 succeeded in securing international recognition for each of their countries individually as founding members of the new international body, the League of Nations.

There then followed in 1922, however, a bruising incident when in connection with the so-called Chanak crisis the British Cabinet sought to drag the white Dominions into a further conflict with the Turks. Canada in particular reacted against this very strongly; and there then ensued a sustained campaign by Ireland, South Africa, and Canada in particular to throw off all remaining imperial checks on their autonomy. And with that the otherwise portentous British empire faced a major crisis.

It was soon substantially ameliorated, however, with the aid of an ingeniously worded formula, first crafted in the Balfour Report of 1926 and later embodied in the Statute of Westminster of 1931, by which the Dominions – along with Britain – were all now to be recognised as 'autonomous communities, equal in status, in no way subordinate one to another', who nevertheless were still bound together in what was henceforth to be called 'the British Commonwealth of Nations' by their 'common allegiance to the [British] Crown'. That outcome was then reinforced by a new system of 'imperial preference' that was principally fashioned at the Imperial Economic Conference in Ottawa in 1932, and despite the bitter exchanges which occurred on that and other occasions, the old imperial connection seemed, for a while at least, to remain intact.[58]

These arrangements entirely failed, however, to assuage the Irish. In the course of the late nineteenth and early twentieth centuries they had

---

[58] N. Mansergh, *The Commonwealth Experience*, 2nd edn, 2 vols., London 1982, passim; P.G. Wigley, *Canada and the Transition to Commonwealth. British–Canadian Relations 1917–1926*, Cambridge 1977; R.F. Holland, *Britain and the Commonwealth Alliance 1918–1939*, London 1981; K.C. Wheare, *The Statute of Westminster and Dominion Status*, Oxford 1938.

long demanded 'Home Rule'. For three decades Britain's Conservative Party which was in office for much of that time not only opposed this vehemently, but nailed its opposition to its masthead by renaming itself the Conservative and Unionist Party. Thereafter it was not until the advent of a Liberal government in 1906 (together with the passage of the Parliament Act of 1911 that curbed the obstructive capacity of the Conservative-dominated House of Lords) that an Irish Home Rule Act eventually became law in 1914. Unfortunately, however, its implementation was immediately suspended following the outbreak of the First World War, and eighteen months later Irish impatience finally snapped.

In 1916 the Easter Rising took place in Dublin. Not only did the British vigorously suppress this. They summmarily executed fifteen of its leaders. And with that there was no turning back. The newly formed Irish Dail (parliament) thereupon took steps in 1919–21 to create an independent Irish Republic. The British attempted to suppress this, more especially by using their paramilitary 'Black and Tans'. Yet so unacceptable did the indiscriminate killings this entailed become to large swathes of British elite opinion that a new settlement with Ireland soon became unavoidable. Late in 1921 an Anglo–Irish Treaty was accordingly signed by which Ireland was granted not the 'Home Rule' which had been talked about for so long, but – in accord with the then still developing formula – 'Dominion Status'; and despite the appalling trauma of the Irish civil war that followed a majority of the Irish electorate initially accepted this.[59]

But in 1932, within months of the passage of the Statute of Westminster of 1931, the principal Irish nationalist leader, de Valera, and the Fianna Fail party he created in the late 1920s, not only won control of the Irish government, but promptly set about removing all the remaining signs of Ireland's subordination to British supremacy. Once again the British tried to suppress Ireland's aspirations, with the consequence that a bitter trade-sanctions war soon broke out between them. Undaunted, however, de Valera not only set about abolishing such emblematic bonds as the Irish oath to the British crown, but in December 1936 seized the opportunity of the sudden abdication of King Edward VIII to proclaim 'Eire' a republic, select a non-executive President as its head of state (instead of the previous Governor-General), and limit the role of the

[59] On the Irish story see R.F. Foster, *Modern Ireland 1600–1972*, London 1988, Part 4; J.J. Lee, *Ireland 1912–1985*, Cambridge 1989; D.W. Harkness, *The Restless Dominion: The Irish Free State and the British Commonwealth of Nations 1921–31*, London 1969; C. Townshend, *The British Campaign in Ireland 1919–1921*, Oxford 1975; P. Canning, *British Policy towards Ireland 1921–1941*, Oxford 1985; N. Mansergh, *The Unresolved Question. The Anglo–Irish Settlement and its Undoing 1912–1972*, New Haven 1991.

British king in Irish affairs to nothing more than the right to sign letters of appointment of Irish ambassadors overseas.[60]

Over the year that followed the British finally conceded defeat, and in April 1938 an Anglo–Irish Agreement was eventually signed that not only settled a series of long-running disputes between them, but even went so far as to transfer to Irish hands the southern Irish ports (which the British had hitherto held on to because of their critical strategic importance to them).[61] What was then particularly notable was that none of the Dominion governments, nor the British government either, ever suggested that Ireland's implied rejection in all of this of its 'common allegiance to the Crown' – the crucial bond that was meant to be binding the new British Commonwealth together – constituted a compelling reason for expelling Ireland from it.[62]

The significance of these contemporaneous encounters for our present story is not only that they constituted the very much broader context within which the Indo–British conflict came to be fought out and that they serve to explain the origins of many of the expedients the British employed in India – 'Responsible Government', 'Federation', 'Dominion Status', 'the signing of a Treaty . . . between Her Majesty's Government and the constitution-making body' (as the Cripps' Offer put it in 1942) – but that they quite vividly reveal the persistent characteristics of the British responses at this time to a whole series of major challenges to their imperial hold.

There were two striking dimensions to these. In each instance the British invariably took quite deliberate steps to sustain their overall authority. In Egypt Curzon appointed Allenby to curb Egypt's nationalists. His successor Lord Lloyd bore down upon them all but unrelentingly. British troops continued to be stationed throughout Egypt till an Anglo–Egyptian Treaty had been signed. Successive attempts were made meanwhile to bring the Dominions into what would inevitably have been a British-controlled 'closer union'. When these came to naught moves were then made to bring their leaders into a British-dominated Imperial

---

[60] Especially helpful on this whole story is D. McMahon, *Republicans and Imperialists. Anglo-Irish Relations in the 1930s*, New Haven 1984.

[61] Not only did this enable Ireland to remain neutral during the soon impending Second World War. It deprived the British of a vital strategic asset when they came to fight the future fateful battle of the Atlantic.

[62] De Valera remained equivocal about Ireland's precise relation to the British Commonwealth throughout his term in office which lasted until 1948, hoping against hope that if he refrained from breaking the final link a chance might remain of bringing Ulster back into a united Ireland. His successors snapped this in 1949: D.W. Dean, 'Final Exit? Britain, Eire, the Commonwealth and the Repeal of the External Relations Act, 1945-1949', *Journal of Imperial and Commonwealth History*, 20, 3, Sept. 1992, pp. 391–418 sets out the details.

Cabinet. When that proved difficult to sustain in peacetime, deliberate steps were taken to lock them into the new 'British Commonwealth of Nations' through their 'common allegiance to the [British] Crown', and to tie them into a British imperial trading bloc as well. Over several earlier decades Irish demands for Home Rule were quite persistently rejected. Armed force was then used not only against the moves to create an independent Irish republic in 1916, but in 1919–21 too; while trade sanctions were later employed in the mid 1930s in a strenuous attempt to compel the Irish to maintain their commitments to the British.

Yet in every one of these cases the British also bent. They abandoned the British Protectorate over Egypt in 1922. They forced Lloyd to resign in 1929 for being too overassertive towards Egypt's politicians. They acquiesced in the Dominions' demands for full control of their external (and not just their internal) affairs, and reached the point where they conceded that they should not only be 'autonomous', but 'equal in status, in no way subordinate' to Britain itself. By signing the Anglo–Irish Agreement in 1921 they abandoned their attempts to suppress Irish nationalism by force; and in the later 1930s relinquished their attempts to coerce the Irish government by sanctions. They even went so far as to acquiesce in Ireland's repudiation of its 'common allegiance to the Crown', in spite of the disturbing precedent that this palpably entailed for the still very new 'British Commonwealth of Nations'.[63]

Underneath all of this there ran a protracted consideration in a good many intellectual and political circles in Britain during the 1920s and 1930s over how precisely to reconcile the conflicting demands of *imperium* and *libertas*.[64] Empire and all it involved was still of crucial importance to very many British people as a principal support for their preeminent position in the world. A whole series of imperial celebrations – such as the Empire Exhibition at Wembley in 1924 (which attracted 17 million visitors), King George V's Silver Jubilee in 1935, and King George VI's Coronation in 1937 – dramatised the tight hold it held upon the public imagination, while the entrenching of 'imperial preference' in the depths of the economic depression fed the very strong sense that the empire still had some highly practical advantages to it. As late as the 1930s there was next to no thought in Britain of 'giving up' the empire.

And yet from their bitter experience earlier in America, which was now

---

[63] It is not always realised that this provided a precedent for the decision in 1949 to accept India as a Republic within the Commonwealth. Later, in the cases of South Africa in 1961 and Fiji in 1987, countries were in effect forced to leave when they broke a later requirement of membership – non-racialism.

[64] This was the theme of W.K. Hancock's magisterial *Survey of British Commonwealth Affairs*, vol. I, *Problems of Nationality 1918–1936*, Oxford 1937.

being replicated in Egypt, Ireland, and even in certain respects the white Dominions, the British had also learnt of the dire consequences that could flow from resisting nationalist demands too unreservedly – and by contrast from their more general experience in a number of other respects of the white Dominions (and above all, in the persons of Botha and Smuts, of South Africa) of the advantages that might accrue from assuaging these.[65] There was at the same time a long-established British tradition of opposition to arbitrary rule – stemming from the English Revolution of the 1640s, the 'Glorious Revolution' of 1688, Burke's denunciations against tyranny in the late eighteenth century, and so on – that ran at odds with the inherent nature of an empire. There was frequently great antipathy too to the wanton use of force – by no means only at Delhi in 1858, or at Amritsar in 1919[66] – as exemplified in the anti-slavery and aborigines protection movements through much of the nineteenth century, and more particularly in the denunciations of Governor Eyre in Jamaica in 1869, of the 'methods of barbarism' employed in South Africa in 1901–2, and most recently of the Black and Tans in Ireland. There had long been much enthusiastic British support for independence movements in other people's empires – in the Spanish and Portuguese empires in Latin America; in the Austro-Hungarian empire in Italy and central Europe; and in the Ottoman empire in Greece, Bulgaria, and most recently in the Near East. It was unlikely that in the end such predilections could long be foregone in the British empire too.

And so the British oscillated. As they came to face the various challenges to their imperial hold during the interwar period they regularly displayed a deeply laid double-think. In any one case it was rarely at all clear how they would in the end reconcile their conflicting instincts. Whilst all the time desperately trying to hold fast to their empire, they found it extremely difficult in the end to bring themselves to do this without regard to its human cost or their own international reputation. Their position during the 1920s and 1930s was characterised by a deeply laid ambiguity. They found it exceedingly difficult to reconcile their intense imperial instincts with the liberal political values they held so dear.

[65] Cf. Francis Bacon: 'Neither doth it follow that because these fames are a sign of troubles, that the suppressing of them with too much severity should be a remedy of troubles. For the despising of them many times checks them best; and the going about to stop them doth make a wonder long lived', 'Of Seditions and Troubles', *The Essayes, or Counsells, Civill and Morall*, XV, 1625.

[66] Consider only the endless succession of 'small wars' and 'punitive expeditions' that punctuated its creation, e.g. J.M. Lonsdale, 'The Politics of Conquest: The British in Western Kenya 1894–1906', *Historical Journal*, 20, 4, 1977, pp. 841–70; or H. Reynolds, *The Other Side of the Frontier*, Townsville 1981.

The implications of all of this for the Indian story can now be drawn out. At the very time when the Indian National Congress started during the years immediately following the First World War to challenge British rule in India as never before, it is important to bear in mind that there were several other major threats to British supremacy too. Taken together these clearly raised the stakes in India. For if India was now to go the way the United States had gone before – and Ireland seemed bent on going too – just at a time when the new bonds that had been established with the recently restless older Dominions stood upon a highly ambiguous formula, whose rejection the Irish case showed by 1938 could not effectively be resisted, and when, moreover, there was still a sharp conflict with Egypt, the prospects for the previously portentous British empire, even in its rejigged form as the 'British Commonwealth of Nations', began to look dire indeed. From the late eighteenth century onwards India had been of major importance to the global standing of the British. Its army remained of vital importance to their military power in the world. Its markets and foreign exchange were of major consequence for crucial parts of their economy. If their dominion there was now to be undermined, let alone to collapse altogether, that would be an immense blow not only to the British position in the world, but to their *amour propre* as well. Not surprisingly, therefore, immense efforts were made throughout the 1930s by the British to push the genie of India's nationalist demands for complete independence back into its bottle once again.

Considering, however, the way in which they were conducting the other imperial struggles in which they were engaged elsewhere, and the liberal traditions to which they were the heirs, there was a real question whether the British would be prepared in the last resort to suppress India's nationalist movement with quite the relentless determination the Dutch were displaying in the Netherlands Indies, let alone the draconian force employed by the French in Vietnam. They were much more likely to equivocate, prevaricate, and play an ambidexterous hand.

It needs all the same to be remembered that throughout these years the British Raj in India remained a most forbidding edifice. Where Mughal and earlier Indian Emperors had stood before there now ruled the imperious British Viceroy, powerfully supported by a remarkably well-articulated administrative regime, in firm control of India's fiscal system, and backed by a substantial army. Beneath this imposing superstructure there stood, as characteristically elsewhere in the British empire, a countless array of local men holding local control over local arenas in firm alliance with their British overlords. The pivotal role was played here not as is generally suggested by the provinces of 'British India', but by the Indian Princely States, 560 of them or so all told, large and small, scattered around a third of the country.[67] Following upon some earlier toing and froing, their rulers had been promised in 1909 a loosening in British oversight over their internal affairs in return for their reinvigorated loyalty.[68] During the 1920s they tried to push this advantage further, and in the early 1930s numbers of them joined with some liberal politicians from British India in trying to create an All-India Federation in which they would play a major role. Although both of these moves failed, throughout these years every British Viceroy and many an Indian Prince sought assiduously to cultivate each other (Viceregal tiger shoots with an Indian Prince figuring largely in their diaries);[69] and there is a tell-tale indication of what was involved here in the decision by the British quite deliberately to construct *three* council halls in the 'Council House' they tardily built in their new capital of New Delhi in the 1920s:[70] one for a 'lower house', one for an 'upper house', and one – on an equal scale – for the 'Chamber of Princes'. Until well into the late 1930s the Princes overwhelmingly maintained autocratic control over their States against any challenge from the Congress, whilst as late as the Second World War they ordinarily remained staunch in their allegiance to the British, even at the time of Congress's 'Quit India' movement in 1942.[71] Till very late in the day, that is, the Indian Princely states constituted a much more substantial part of Britain's Indian Empire than is ordinarily suggested.[72]

They did not, moreover, stand alone. For to a much greater degree than is customarily acknowledged the basic principles of their association with the British governed the relations between the British and the *pirs* in Sind,[73] the 'great Khans' in the Frontier Province,[74] the Taluqdars of Oudh (in the classic case of 'the natural leaders of the people' being linked with the 'Oudh Policy' of the 'Oudh men' of the British administration),[75] the military/landed elites in the Punjab (in similar

---

[67] M.H. Fisher, *Indirect Rule in India. Residents and the Residency System 1764–1857*, Delhi 1991.

[68] I. Copland, *The British Raj and the Indian Princes. Paramountcy in Western India 1857–1930*, Bombay 1982.

[69] E.g. Earl of Halifax, *Fulness of Days*, London 1957, pp. 139–42.

[70] Now Parliament House, see R.G. Irving, *Indian Summer: Lutyens, Baker and Imperial Delhi*, Delhi 1981.   [71] Low, *Congress and the Raj*, chs. 13 (Manor), 14 (Jeffrey).

[72] Ashton, *British Policy towards the Indian States*; Ramusack, *Princes of India*; Jeffrey, *People, Princes and Paramount Power*; Copland, *Unwanted Allies*.

[73] R.A. Huttenback, *British Relations with Sind 1799–1843*, Berkeley 1962; Ansari, *Sufi Saints and State Power*.

[74] E.g. O. Caroe, *The Pathans 550 B.C.–A.D.1947*, London 1958, Part IV; Rittenberg, *Ethnicity, Nationalism and the Pakhtuns*, chs. 1–3, 6.

[75] T.R. Metcalf, *Land, Landlords and the British Raj. Northern India in the Nineteenth Century*, Berkeley 1979; P.D. Reeves, *Landlords and Government in Uttar Pradesh*, Bombay 1991.

association with the 'Punjab School' of British administrators),[76] and many a powerful zamindar as well.[77] Where in the provinces of 'British' India the British did apply more 'direct' rule they were careful, moreover, to draw into their administrative structure India's traditional 'service' communities in exactly the same way that many of these indigenous rulers did.[78]

Following upon the traumatic shock of the revolt of 1857 the British took a number of steps, moreover, to buttress their position further. They reorganised the army; built new cantonments and new strategic railway lines; rebuilt some key cities so as to make them easier to control; established police forces with a principal responsibility for maintaining imperial authority; maintained detailed anti-riot plans so as not to be caught out unprepared; allocated around a third of the Army in India, and twenty-eight and more of its British battalions, for internal security purposes,[79] and endlessly nurtured the military labour market of the Punjab as the ultimate bulwark of their Raj.[80] They took steps, moreover, by means of an endless stream of rent restriction, tenant security, and moneylender limitation acts to limit the discontents of the better-off peasantry.[81] They developed techniques to check the social upheavals which accompanied famines.[82] They became increasingly adept at defusing disruptive popular agitations.[83] And in the earlier part of the twentieth century they displayed considerable skill in manipulating the politics of the new legislatures to their own advantage.[84] Whilst their colonial state was always a good deal 'thinner' on the ground than those of both the

[76] This found extremely strong expression, of course, in the non-, even anti-Congress Punjab Unionist Party of the 1920s to 1940s. See generally P. van den Dungen, *The Punjab Tradition*, London 1972; Imran Ali, *The Punjab under Imperialism, 1885–1947*, Princeton 1988; I. Talbot, *Punjab and the Raj 1849–1947*, Delhi 1988; Low, *Political Inheritance of Pakistan*, chs. 1–5, 11.

[77] See the striking accounts in A.A. Yang, *The Limited Raj. Agrarian Relations in Colonial India, Saran District, 1793–1920*, Berkeley 1989, and S. Henningham, *A Great Estate and its Landlords in Colonial India. Darbhanga 1860–1942*, Delhi 1990.

[78] E.g. B. Stein, *Thomas Munro. The Origins of the Colonial State and his Vision of Empire*, Delhi 1989, esp. ch. 7; and C.A. Bayly, *Rulers, Townsmen and Bazaars. North Indian Society in the Age of British Expansion, 1770–1870*, Cambridge 1983, passim.

[79] E.g. V.T. Oldenburg, *The Making of Colonial Lucknow 1856–1877*, Princeton 1984; D. Arnold, *Police Power and Colonial Rule. Madras 1859–1947*, Delhi 1986; Kudaisya, 'State Power . . . in Uttar Pradesh', passim; P. Mason, *A Matter of Honour*, London 1974, esp. Part IV; H. Poll.79/30.   [80] Ali, *Punjab under Imperialism*; Tan, 'Colonial Punjab'.

[81] D. Rothermund, *Government, Landlord and Peasant in India. Agrarian Relations under British Rule 1865–1935*, Wiesbaden 1978.

[82] B.M. Bhatia, *Famines in India 1860–1945*, London 1963.

[83] For some striking examples from the Punjab and the United Provinces see Ali, *Punjab under Imperialism*, pp. 66–72; Reeves, *Landlords and Governments*, chs. 3 and 4; J.W. Cell, *Hailey. A Study in British Imperialism*, Cambridge 1992, chs. 8–14.

[84] E.g. J.H. Broomfield, *Elite Conflict in a Plural Society: Twentieth Century Bengal*, Berkeley 1968, ch. VII; Washbrook, *Emergence of Provincial Politics*, chs. 6–7.

Dutch and the French,[85] their hold upon their Indian empire till at least the mid 1930s was in no way any less. This was most strikingly demonstrated in their success in withstanding Gandhi's Non-Cooperation movement of 1920–2 and his Civil Disobedience movements in the early 1930s; in their ability to maintain each of the new provincial 'dyarchy' regimes they had constituted under the Government of India Act of 1920 despite the hostility of Congress towards them; and in their success in doing all this without having to increase their coercive forces at all substantially.[86]

All of which is particularly worth recalling since it serves to emphasise the immense obstacles that the Indian National Congress faced in its momentous battle with the British. For the British were a far more formidable foe than either Congress's conventional panegyrists or its gratuitous detractors readily allow. Most Princely States,[87] and even a good many zamindars' estates, were generally closed territory to it. Almost invariably the Indian 'services', civilian as well as military, remained entirely loyal to their British masters. After 1857 a successful armed revolt never looked like a practical possibility (as was clearly shown in the rapidity with which the British suppressed the 'Quit India' movement of 1942, precisely the kind of revolt they had been preparing to resist ever since 1857). Though there were two or three traditions of opposition to imperial rule upon which the Congress could draw,[88] and whilst there were several crises in the colonial state which it could exploit, in the end these rarely gave it the decisive leverage that it needed.[89]

As a result Congress had to confine itself very largely to the interstices in Britain's Indian imperial body politic: principally the towns and cities of 'British' India;[90] or where there were no governing elites;[91] or where these were stumbling badly.[92] Painfully it had to work out its objectives and then determine the most appropriate ways in which to move forward.[93] As a great many ordinary people were understandably very reluctant to chance their futures in what for many years seemed a hapless

---

[85] See the suggestive Table 1.1 in R. Jeffrey, *Asia – The Winning of Independence*, London 1981, p. 5 that shows that in the 1930s the proportion of Europeans to total population was 1:3,650 in India, 1:475 in Vietnam and 1:200 in Indonesia.

[86] Kudaisya, 'State Control . . . in Uttar Pradesh'; Arnold, *Police Power*, pp. 101, 124–7.

[87] For a striking recognition of this as late as 1937 see Prasad to Nehru, 24 Dec. 1937, RPP 1/37/1.

[88] E.g. T. Raychaudhuri, *Europe Reconsidered*, Delhi 1988, ch. 3; R.I. Cashman, *The Myth of the Lokamanya. Tilak and Mass Politics in Maharashtra*, Berkeley 1975.

[89] Cell, *Hailey*, chs. 8–14; Reeves, *Landlords and Government*, chs. 3 and 4; Pandey, *Ascendancy of the Congress*, chs. 6 and 7; Damodaran, *Broken Promises*, ch. 2.

[90] E.g. Bayly, *Local Roots*; R. Ray, *Urban Roots of Indian Nationalism*, Delhi 1979.

[91] E.g. Hardiman, *Peasant Nationalists of Gujarat*.

[92] E.g. Pandey, *Ascendancy of the Congress*.

[93] E.g. Chandra, *Rise and Growth of Economic Nationalism*; J.V. Bondurant, *Conquest of Violence*, Princeton 1958.

cause, Congress had then to proceed first by cobbling together an amorphous miscellany of disaffected elements that showed themselves ready to support its cause, and then by putting together an extensive portfolio of propaganda methods by which to whittle out far wider popular support than was otherwise forthcoming. For most dedicated nationalists it was all a most heart-rendingly chequered and elongated process, which called for great personal fortitude in withstanding severe batterings by the police, numbing periods of imprisonment, and a good deal of political seduction too.

All the same as in Egypt, in the white Dominions, and in Ireland, India's nationalist movement nevertheless found that it was possible whilst building upon an increasingly deep-laid nationalist ideology to gnaw away at the vitals of Britain's imperial rule without being halted altogether, since by contrast with both the Dutch and the French the British were greatly inhibited from using the ultimate sanctions of lifelong banishment and mass killings against them.

As they squared up to meet their nationalist opponents the British not only did so with a mind well apprised of the other imperial conflicts in which they were involved. They endlessly replicated the ambivalences and oscillations they were displaying elsewhere. Within India they regularly drew lines in the sand and generally exhibited considerable ability in standing fast upon them. Yet they knew very well that in maintaining their dominion in a country as complex as India excessive aggravation could well make their task a good deal more onerous than it need be, whilst judicious assuagement might well save them a great deal of trouble. They accordingly periodically made significant concessions in the hope of reducing the number of their activist opponents and even perhaps splitting the opposition towards them altogether. As, however, it was rare for these concessions to be entirely wholehearted they could just as easily be adversely exploited as compliantly received. They often had therefore to be counterweighted by some much more rigid measures.[94] As a consequence the British frequently found themselves trapped in the coils of their own ambivalence.

That ambivalence was extensively displayed too in the oscillations in the realms of their high policy towards India, particularly in the context of their wider imperial concerns. By the end of the First World War the Government of India had become transfixed upon Indian 'sedition'[95] and

[94] There are several examples of all this in the chapters which follow, perhaps ch. 4 especially.

[95] *Sedition Committee 1918, Report*, Calcutta 1918. There is an extensive story to be told about the hard imperialist line taken by Sir Reginald Craddock during his period as Home Member 1912–17 of the Government of India, see e.g. Broomfield, *Elite Conflict in a Plural Society. Twentieth Century Bengal*, pp. 73–7, 80–1.

proceeded to promulgate the ill-fated 'Rowlatt Bills' against 'revolution-ary crime', against which they always vigorously proceeded. Over exactly the same period, however, following the Montagu Declaration of August 1917 which declared that the goal of British policy was 'the gradual development of self-governing institutions' in India, the Secretary of State joined with the Viceroy to introduce the Montagu–Chelmsford reforms of 1919. During the early 1920s there was keen anxiety in British governing circles as to whether they could thereafter hold the line against Gandhi's Khilafat and Non-Cooperation movements, just at the time when they found themselves having to make sudden concessions both in Egypt and in Ireland (and to some degree to the old Dominions too). Almost by chance, however, this was done,[96] and thereafter during the mid 1920s they generally stood their ground as well.

However, in the face of the next great wave of Indian agitation between 1928 and 1931, they first bent and sought to apply the newly evolving formula of Dominion Status, which appeared to be satisfying Canada, South Africa, and even, to begin with, Ireland, in the hope that it might satisfy India too. But in the event neither the Irwin Declaration of 1929, nor the first Indian Round Table Conference of 1930, nor the Gandhi–Irwin Pact of 1931 succeeded in checking Congress's commit-ment to Gandhi's Civil Disobedience, and that created a deep crisis for the British over precisely what they should do next. Upon the one side leading figures like Winston Churchill and Lord Lloyd, who were vehe-mently opposed to any concessions, were reported to be in

a fearful state of mind about India and cannot conceive of any other point of view as due to anything but cowardice and time serving.

Whilst others took their cue from Irwin who avowed that:

the day is past . . . when Winston's possessive instinct can be applied to Empires . . . That conception of imperialism is finished, and those who try to revive it are as those who would fly a balloon that won't hold gas.[97]

As it happened, amidst the maelstrom of British politics at the time it was these latter views at the hands of the Conservative Party leader, Stanley Baldwin, who was profoundly anxious not to have 'another Ireland in India',[98] which prevailed.

It was all, however, a very close call. Had Baldwin early in 1930 lost the

[96] D.A. Low, 'The Government of India and the First Non-Co-operation Movement 1920–1922', in R. Kumar, ed., *Essays on Gandhian Politics*, Oxford 1971, ch. X; A. Rumbold, *Watershed in India 1914–1922*, London 1979.
[97] Quoted, Charmley, *Lord Lloyd*, pp. 177, 172.
[98] K. Middlemas and J. Barnes, *Baldwin*, London 1969, chs. 20, 22, 26. And see quotation from Crozier papers, H.M. Hyde, *Baldwin*, London 1973, pp. 352–3.

leadership of the Conservative Party as at one stage seemed very probable, or had the Conservatives continued in opposition – or *per contra*
formed a government on their own – in the course of the major British
political crisis of August 1931, things could all have been very different.
Churchill's influence could very easily have become very much more
potent than it did.[99] Even as it was no sooner had Sir Samuel Hoare been
installed as the new National Government's Secretary of State for India in
August 1931 than he told Irwin's successor as Viceroy, Lord Willingdon,
in no uncertain terms, that:

My own view . . . is that the great body of opinion in this country is dead against
anything in the nature of a surrender on the lines of the Irish Treaty.[100]

As it happened Willingdon was very well versed in the wider imperial
crisis to which Hoare here referred. For after having served first as
Governor of Bombay and then of Madras, back in 1926 he had been hurriedly despatched to serve as Governor-General of Canada following a
bitter clash between his predecessor, Lord Byng, and the intensely
nationalist Prime Minister of Canada, Mackenzie King, in order to
rebuild crucial imperial fences there.[101] He accordingly promptly told
Hoare he could

confidently rely on my supporting your view that we should never do anything out
here in the nature of surrendering on the lines of the Irish Treaty . . .[102]

And thereafter he gave stern effect to that assurance in his government's
suppression of Gandhi's second Civil Disobedience movement early in
1932.

Oscillation all the same continued. For within a very short while it was
Hoare and the Cabinet who were urging restraint upon Willingdon in his
campaign against Civil Disobedience at precisely the time that the
'diehard' wing of the Conservative Party under Lloyd and Churchill escalated their denunciations at the imperial backslidings they saw all around
them. Still smarting at his curt removal from the High Commissionership
in Egypt, Lloyd, for example, now cumulatively denounced:

the policy of the Imperial Conference of 1926, as recently embodied in the
Statute of Westminster, [which] has weakened to the point of absolute renuncia-
tion the Constitutional framework of the Empire, [and] that post war policy, as
evidenced in our repeated and hardly foiled attempts to abandon great duties in
Egypt, [and] in the feeble and loosely worded Declaration of Dominion Status for

[99] I owe these suggestions to Dr John Charmley; see also Williamson, *National Crisis*,
passim.   [100] Hoare to Willingdon, 2 Sept. 1931, TwP 1.
[101] R. Graham, *The King–Byng Affair*, Toronto 1967.
[102] Willingdon to Hoare, 15 Sept. 1931, TwP 5.

India [that] has needlessly destroyed our own authority and prestige in the East.[103]

At the same time when with de Valera's victory in the Irish election of 1932 the Irish situation took a new turn and threw the very idea of Dominion Status as the principal solution to Britain's imperial difficulties into serious doubt, it was the Cabinet which proceeded to downplay the thought of eventually granting Dominion Status to India, so much so indeed that the term figured nowhere in the ensuing Government of India Act of 1935. At one stage they even toyed with going ahead with Responsible Government in the provinces of British India on their own.[104] In the end in the Government of India Act of 1935 they did provide for an All-India Federation with 'responsibility-at-the-centre'. But they so hemmed this in with such a formidable array of imperial 'safeguards', and with a legislature so constituted with Indian Princely nominations and Muslim seats as to ensure that Congress should never win a majority there, that they totally failed to assuage Indian opinion in the way which had originally been intended.

That failure soon became all too obvious in the great success of the Congress in the provincial elections of 1937. Characteristically that precipitated two very different responses from the British side. Upon the one hand the new Viceroy, Lord Linlithgow, strove to clamp the new constraining structure of the Government of India Act of 1935 firmly upon India; he successfully enticed the Congress to accept office at the provincial level, and thereafter sought to do everything he could to bring the highly restrictive All-India Federation into operation – unsuccessfully as it happened – while holding fast to his own overall authority and to the Act's 'imperial safeguards'. Before long, however, at a meeting between several British opposition Labour Party leaders and Jawaharlal Nehru at Sir Stafford Cripps's house at Filkins on 24 June 1938, several leading British opposition Labour Party members finally acknowledged that if and when they came to power they would forthwith institute a full transfer of power in India. It is significant that they talked of a treaty to encompass Britain's residual interests there.[105] For this meeting took place within weeks of the signing of the Anglo–Irish Agreement in April 1938, which is one more sign of the close correspondence there could be between events in two quite separate quarters.

Ambivalence, however, continued. It was to be most graphically displayed in 1942, once again in conjunction with very much wider affairs.

[103] *The Graphic*, Apr. 1932, quoted Charmley, *Lord Lloyd*, p. 181.
[104] Moore, *Crisis of Indian Unity*, ch. 6.
[105] R.J. Moore, *Churchill, Cripps, and India 1939–1945*, Oxford 1979, p. 4.

On 7 December 1941 the Japanese attacked the American fleet in Pearl Harbor and launched themselves on their conquest of all of Southeast Asia. On 27 December 1941 (in a telling statement presaging the further break up of the British Empire) John Curtin, the Australian Prime Minister, declared that in this dire situation 'Australia looks to America, free of any pangs as to our traditional links or kinship with the United Kingdom',[106] and thereafter in March 1942, following upon the fall of Singapore on 15 February 1942, the British coalition government, pressured by those same Labour members, precipitously announced that India could have full independence as soon as the Second World War was over. When, however, in August 1942 Congress launched its 'Quit India' campaign to force the British to leave India there and then, they strongly supported the Government of India in suppressing this to the full.

It needs to be emphasised that this pervasive dualism in the British stance towards India, as in other places too, was at once longstanding and deliberate. In 1886, for example, within months of the foundation of the Indian National Congress the year before, Kimberley, the Liberal Secretary of State, wrote to Dufferin, the Viceroy in India, saying:

I have no faith in a repressive policy. Apart from all other objections, sentimental or practical, the English democracy will never allow such a policy to be firmly and continuously pursued . . . We must go forward; to stand still and simply resist is not in our power, even if we were convinced it would be the safest course. The conclusion, therefore, at which I arrive is that *some* concessions to this native movement will have to be made, but I would use the utmost caution in making them, not going an inch beyond the necessity of the case, and, above all, carefully avoiding anything that might tend to fan the flame.[107]

While in the following year Arthur Balfour, the Conservative Chief Secretary for Ireland, avowed that:

It is on the twofold aspect of my policy that I rely for success. Hitherto English Governments . . . have either been all for repression or all for reform. I am for both: repression as stern as Cromwell; reform as thorough as Mr. Parnell or anyone else can desire.[108]

'We stated clearly', Willingdon later recalled, 'that our policy was of a dual nature'; along with insisting upon 'the due observance of the laws' their purpose was always, he said, 'to push forward the new Reform scheme' as well.[109] 'Preventive action is only one part and that, I hope, an

---

[106] *Melbourne Herald*, 27 Dec. 1941.
[107] Kimberley to Dufferin, 22 Apr. 1886, Dufferin Papers, quoted Mehrotra, *Indian National Congress*, I, p. 136.
[108] B. Alderson, *Arthur James Balfour*, London 1903, p. 71.
[109] Note by Willingdon, undated, WP, 2nd Ser., 20.

ephemeral part [of our policy]', Haig, the Home Member of the Government of India, declared in 1932. 'Constitutional advance is the other and more important side.'[110] 'Firmness with what can loosely be described as progress', 'Rab' Butler, sometime Under-Secretary for India, called it.[111]

This ambidexterousness was at the same time unblushingly disingenuous. Even the 'saintly' Lord Irwin could remark in private that 'what is required is some facade that will leave the essential mechanism of power in our hands'.[112] While Sir Samuel Hoare unhesitatingly advised his colleagues that:

It is possible to give a semblance of responsible government and yet retain in our hands the realities and verities of British control.[113]

Cast in those terms British policy was at once dissembling and duplicitous. That, however, does not quite catch its total flavour. For upon occasion, as we shall see, 'progress', 'advance', and 'reform' were indeed made; and in any case it was entirely delusory of the British to think that they could somehow go on maintaining an even balance between 'progress' and 'firmness'. For if real 'progress' was to be made, 'firmness' in the end would have to be abandoned – as they were to discover.

That did not, however, happen till the mid 1940s, and in the meantime British policy towards India remained deeply dualist, disingenuous, and delusory. That meant, both for its enforcers, and for those who were subjected to it, that its application upon any one occasion was rarely at all clear. It was deeply and perennially ambiguous.

One can see this most vividly exemplified in two important but rather different instances. When Irwin was authorised as Viceroy to make his declaration in 1929 promising that India would have 'Dominion Status', in the very same breath this was qualified by the statement that this could only be 'the natural issue of India's constitutional development' – which by clear implication meant it was not to be entertained for a long while yet – and that it would have to be 'within the British Empire' – which meant that complete independence, if that was what India wished, was ruled out altogether. It was exemplified too in the manner in which from 1932 onwards the British regularly curbed Civil Disobedience: not by trials, banishments, or wanton killings, but by indeterminate (that is, one to two years') imprisonment without trial. 'Civil martial law', a British official

[110] Haig to Mieville, 13 Apr. 1932, copy in HP 1.
[111] Butler to Brabourne, 21 May 1937, IOL, Brabourne Papers 21. See also Williamson, *National Crisis*, pp. 83–91, 487–92.
[112] Irwin to Ormsby Gore, 10 Jan. 1929 (and to Dawson 6 May 1929), HP 18.
[113] 'Conservative Policy at the Round Table Conference', 12 Dec. 1930, TwP 52, 9.

neatly called it,[114] thereby giving classic expression to the ambiguity that lay at the heart of the British stance between the American position on the one hand and the Dutch and the French on the other.

Such dualism immersed in ambiguity was clearly recognised upon the Congress side as well.

The Government policy which was enunciated by Lord Irwin towards the end of 1929 [Rajendra Prasad declared as President of Congress in October 1934] . . . has always had a double aspect . . . It has been claimed that this . . . on the one hand aims at advancing constitutional reforms, and on the other seeks to suppress what the Government considers to be subversive and revolutionary movements . . . To Indians it seems that the second policy has not only been much more in evi dence and . . . [has been] responsible for . . . the enactment of laws which have taken away the ordinary rights of citizens but effectively prevented perfectly constitutional agitation also. The reforms side of the policy has succeeded only in feeding credulous people on hopes of something which may not come.[115]

What then needs to be brought right to the forefront of the argument is the preeminent fact that in the course of these interwar years it was the basic postulates of these four western colonial powers that in their quite distinctive ways critically conditioned the most salient anti-colonial strategies that their principal nationalist opponents mounted against them. As in the earlier examples we quoted from Africa the very different stances of the corresponding imperial powers crucially determined the principal corresponding nationalist assaults that were later developed there. This phenomenon applied in both Southeast and South Asia too. In the Philippines the Filipino nationalist elite never sought to organise a major popular agitation against their American overlords, since, given the generally accommodating position of the Americans, sustained lobbying in Washington generally sufficed to secure their ends. As there was never any prospect that any such approach would prove in any way feasible in Indonesia, some Indonesian nationalist leaders concluded that only massive multi-class pressure would move the Dutch, whilst others believed that this could only be done by putting a firmly cadre-led class party together first. When neither proved possible to effect a younger generation of Indonesian nationalists seized a later opportunity at the end of the Second World War to mount a hastily armed insurrection that was then bolstered by the creation of a national army.[116] Meanwhile in Vietnam neither the nationalists nor the communists had any faith that

[114] D.A. Low, "'Civil Martial Law": the Government of India and the Civil Disobedience Movement, 1930–34', Low, *Congress and the Raj*, ch. 6.
[115] Rajendra Prasad's Presidential Address, Bombay Congress, 26 Oct. 1934, *RPCSD*, 1, pp. 236–7.   [116] A.J.S. Reid, *Indonesian National Revolution 1945–50*, Hawthorn 1974.

anything short of an armed uprising would ultimately move the French. As a result both the Vietnamese secular nationalists and the Vietnamese communists committed themselves in the early 1930s to armed insurrection upon a scale that was nowhere replicated elsewhere in the western empires at this time, and in due course amid the turmoil and aftermath of the Second World War a grassroots' nationalist front sprang up that came to be backed by carefully trained Communist cadres and an ultimately indomitable guerilla army.[117]

In their differing ways these, however, were the relatively straightforward cases. Precisely because the British were so inherently ambidexterous, it was in India that a far more complex situation arose. In India there was for a long while a running conflict between those who believed that because of Britain's utter determination to hold on to its empire only uncompromising resistance that bordered upon, where indeed it did not actually cross over into, violence would ever succeed in moving them,[118] and those who believed that given Britain's commitment to doctrines of parliamentary government, skilful negotiation with them was far more likely to bring about effective political advance than would ever be achieved either by anomic violence or by activist extremism.[119] There were, however, large elements of wishful thinking in both these ways of thinking. While each quite accurately reflected one of the poles in the British position neither encompassed its overall duality.

It was precisely in this respect that Gandhi made his quite momentous contribution in India.[120] Since it was a vital part of his extraordinary political genius that he not only overrode this fruitless difference, but seized hold, not of one of the poles in the British position, but of their very co-existence. Whilst vehemently denouncing any resort to violence he never conceded that negotiations on their own would ever succeed in moving the British. Only completely self-sacrificing, non-violent agitations would, he believed, serve to force their hand and make them grant India the *swaraj* it demanded in accord with their self-avowed liberal values. It is now indeed possible to see that it was above all Gandhi's masterly grasp of the critical requirements of the Indian national movement in its momentous battle with India's profoundly ambiguous British rulers that gave him the towering position he came to hold in the Indian national move-

---

[117] D.G. Marr, *Vietnam 1945. The Quest for Power*, Berkeley 1995, chs.3, 6–8.

[118] This was particularly in Bengal, see, A. Tripathi, *The Extremist Challenge*, Bombay 1967; T. Sarkar, *Bengal 1928–1934. The Politics of Protest*, Delhi 1987.

[119] E.g. D.A. Low, 'Sir Tej Bahadur Sapru and the First Round Table Conference', in D.A. Low, ed., *Soundings in Modern South Asian History*, London 1968, ch. 10.

[120] The latest biography is J.M. Brown, *Gandhi. Prisoner of Hope*, New Haven 1989; see also B. Parekh, *Gandhi's Political Philosophy*, London 1989; D. Dalton, *Mahatma Gandhi. Nonviolent Power in Action*, New York 1993.

ment. In the Philippines it is more than probable that he would have been marginalised[121] as having very little to offer elite negotiation in Washington. In Indonesia it is well-nigh certain that he would have been exiled to some distant island for life: while in Vietnam (or so Ho Chi Minh believed from a very early date) there is every likelihood that he would have been done to death. By contrast in India his satyagraha doctrine proved to be quintessentially functional to the ambivalence of the British, having the critically important merit of facing very directly the equivocation inherent in it.[122] Once its appositeness for the Indo–British struggle came to be fully grasped by the serried ranks of the Indian nationalist movement, it soon became eagerly adopted as the preeminent weapon in its armoury, and he its undisputed leader.

Thus it was – to put it pithily – that the double-think at the core of Britain's imperial posture towards India during the interwar years crucially determined the most substantial nationalist response that was launched against it, and so moulded the main forms of the interwar Indo–British conflict which in nature differed so substantially from those in the rest of western-dominated Asia at that time. To a much greater degree than is generally appreciated British ambiguity conditioned both the overall pattern of events and very many particulars in the story, and gave it those quite distinctive characteristics that served to shape its striking singularity.

Now those are bold claims. The rest of this book is therefore devoted to exploring these issues further, not by way of yet another extended account, but through exploring a number of particular episodes in considerable detail. Three related questions variously raised their heads: whether the British were in any way prepared to respond positively to the clamant Indian demand for independence; where lay the limits to British resilience in withstanding nationalist opposition; how far were they prepared to go in assuaging India's principal nationalist leader. Each episode quivered on the ambiguous equilibrium that attended one or more of these issues. The second chapter thus explores the way in which ambiguity on the British side fuelled a major debate amongst India's principal political leaders about how precisely they should respond to a deftly composed British initiative. The third chapter offers a case study of the

---

[121] As his closest disciple, Vinoba Bhave, was to be in the very different political circumstances after India's independence.

[122] Since he comes at the issues from a very different angle it is, it may be suggested, striking how close Professor Bipan Chandra's conclusions, that in its final decades British rule in India was 'semi-hegemonic' and that Gandhi's strategy was a response to this, stands to those which have been reached here, see e.g. Chandra, *Indian National Movement: The Long-term Dynamics*, Delhi 1988.

manner in which British ambiguity conditioned the nature of a series of violent clashes with defiant nationalist supporters in a major Indian city. The fourth traces the corrosive effects of British ambiguity on a protracted attempt by both Gandhi and the British Government of India to sustain a political rapprochement between them; while the fifth describes the fetters which their ambiguity placed upon them as they tried to silence Gandhi altogether. In the sixth we note how British ambiguity unexpectedly provided the Congress with an opportunity to register its widespread support in terms the British acknowledged as fully legitimate. The seventh traces the roles it successively played in the late 1930s in relation to Congress's acceptance of provincial office. While in the eighth the suggestion is made that it was precisely because the British needed to maintain both parts of their persistent ambiguity that they were finally propelled into acceding to India's claim to independence in 1942 within a specified and (everyone hoped) not too distant future. None of this, to repeat, is to suggest that nationalist initiatives were not of preeminent importance. They initiated the encounter, and their aggregated responses finally won the day.

2 Vortex debate: the *purna swaraj* decision 1929

> What is required is some facade which will leave the essential mechanism of power in our hands.   Lord Irwin, Viceroy of India, 30 July 1929

On 31 December 1929, at Mahatma Gandhi's instance, and under Jawaharlal Nehru's presidency, after two years of constant discussion and often heated debate, the Indian National Congress at its Lahore session took two of the most momentous decisions in its history. It confirmed that henceforward its objective would not be Dominion Status within the British Commonwealth, but *purna swaraj*, complete independence. It also authorised the All India Congress Committee, 'whenever it deems fit, to launch upon a programme of civil disobedience' under Mahatma Gandhi's leadership so as to bring British rule in India to an end.[1] Thereupon there ensued between 1930 and 1934, with an interval during 1931, the most widespread and prolonged confrontation between the forces of Indian nationalism and the British Raj that ever occurred.

On the day after the great decisions had been taken, Jawaharlal Nehru, in his capacity as President of the Indian National Congress, received the following letter from one of his most respected predecessors, Pandit Madan Mohan Malaviya. This ran:

As I do not agree with the resolution passed by the Congress yesterday relating to its policy and programme, I think it is due to the Congress and myself that I should not continue to be a member of its Working Committee. I therefore respectfully tender my resignation of the Committee.[2]

There were soon a few further resignations, including that of another ex-President, Dr M.A. Ansari,[3] and from such previously active

---

[1] For a brief and remarkably accurate summary of the whole affair from the British point of view, see GoI to SoS, tel., 9 Jan. 1930, H.Poll.98/30.

[2] Malaviya to Jawaharlal, 1 Jan. 1930, AICC G115/1929. Note: references in this chapter to Motilal and Jawaharlal are to the Nehrus father and son, respectively.

[3] Ansari to Sec. Delhi PCC, 6 Jan. 1930, Ansari to Gandhi, 10 Feb. 1930, NMML Ansari Papers. For Ansari's moving correspondence over this see Ansari to Gandhi, 13 Feb. 1930, Gandhi to Ansari, 16 Feb. 1930, Motilal to Ansari, 17 Feb. 1930, Ansari to Sherwani, 6 Jan. 1930, AICC G115/1929, and M. Hasan, ed., *Muslims and the Congress.*

Congressmen as Aney, Kelkar, Bhagwan Das, and Khaliquzzaman.[4] The record shows, however, that if the outcome of the intense debate within the ranks of the Congress leadership over the previous two months had eventuated differently, it would not have been these men who would have resigned their membership of the Congress. It would have been Jawaharlal Nehru who would have resigned its Presidency.

The outlines of the story are well known. At the Madras session in 1927, Congress, already embittered by Britain's appointment of the all-white Simon Commission to determine India's future over India's head, had declared 'the goal of the Indian people to be complete independence'.[5] There was then established, under the auspices of an All-Parties Conference, a committee to draft a National Constitution for India. Under Motilal Nehru's chairmanship, its two most prominent participants were Jawaharlal, his son,[6] and their fellow Kashmiri member of the Allahabad Bar, Sir Tej Bahadur Sapru. The Nehru Committee's recommendations aroused sharp opposition from many prominent Muslim leaders. They also ran foul of many of the younger members of Congress. The younger Nehru had looked to the committee to endorse the commitment to complete independence. The Nehru Committee, however, came out for Dominion Status.[7] As a consequence at the ensuing Calcutta session of Congress in December 1928 there was very considerable argument. Gandhi, who had lately not played a large part in the Congress's affairs, was urged by Motilal Nehru to attend the session, and there supported the Nehru Report; but under persistent pressure from the younger men, led by Jawaharlal Nehru and Subhas Bose from Bengal, he eventually agreed that if by the end of the following year the British had not granted India Dominion Status, Congress should there and then switch its objective to *purna swaraj*, and forthwith launch a mass civil disobedience campaign.[8] By 1929 'Dominions', according to the Balfour Report of 1926, were conceived to be, as we have seen, 'autonomous communities . . . equal in status, in no way subordinate one to another in any aspect of their domestic or external affairs'. From the outset, moreover, Canada, Australia, New Zealand, South Africa, and

Select Correspondence of Dr. M.A. Ansari 1912–1935, Delhi 1979, pp. 94–104. See more generally M. Hasan, *A Nationalist Conscience. M.A. Ansari, the Congress and the Raj*, Delhi 1987, ch. 9.

[4] Jawaharlal to Kelkar, etc. 26 Mar. 1930, AICC G(iii)/1930. For further details see AICC G125(ii), G130/1930.

[5] N.N. Mitra, *Indian Quarterly Register, Oct.–Dec. 1927*, Calcutta 1928, pp. 353–419.

[6] He was not formally a member of the committee, but was much involved in its work.

[7] *Report of the Committee appointed by the Conference to Determine the Principles of the Constitution of India*, Allahabad 1928; *Proceedings of the All-Parties Convention, 22 December–1 January 1930*, Allahabad 1929.   [8] *CWMG* 38, passim.

Ireland – the five existing white Dominions – had been full members in their own right of the League of Nations. Yet, in the terms set out in the Balfour Report, they were at the same time still 'within the British Empire'; 'united by a common allegiance to the [British] Crown', and 'members of the British Commonwealth of Nations'.[9] Congress's more radical supporters would have none of the latter. They sought nothing less than a complete break with Britain, and full independence for India on its own.

In the aftermath of the Calcutta Congress Gandhi expressed himself deeply worried by the disarray into which the Congress movement had fallen since he was last closely involved in its affairs in the early 1920s. In propelling Jawaharlal Nehru into his then role of Congress's General Secretary, he accordingly urged upon him the prime necessity of turning the Congress into a more 'living thing'.[10] For his own part he spent a good deal of the rest of the year harping on the need to develop khadi (home-spun) and the boycott of foreign cloth as a principal means of bringing home to the greatest and humblest in the land their connection with Congress's ultimate purpose. At the same time he was acutely aware that if there was to be a countrywide satyagraha in 1930, as the Calcutta resolution seemed to threaten, then none of the necessary arrangements had even been considered.[11]

Congress's agitational unpreparedness was soon starkly revealed when in May 1929 the Viceroy, Lord Irwin, unexpectedly extended the life of the central and several of the provincial legislatures, and Motilal Nehru called upon the Congress members to boycott them.[12] For immediately there were vehement and successful protests against this from such prominent Congressmen as B.C. Roy, J.M. Sen Gupta, and Subhas Bose in Bengal, S.K. Sinha in Bihar, G.B. Pant in UP, Satyamurti in Madras, and Vithalbhai Patel, Jamnadas Mehta, and K.F. Nariman in Bombay.[13] In July 1929 the Tamilnad Congress Committee went so far indeed as to

[9] K.C. Wheare, *The Statute of Westminster and Dominion Status*, Oxford 1938.
[10] Gandhi to Jawaharlal, 12 Jan., 1 Feb., 10 May, 5 June 1929, JNP G1. On Gandhi in 1929 see J.M. Brown, *Gandhi and Civil Disobedience. The Mahatma in Indian Politics 1928–1934*, Cambridge 1977, pp. 42–55.
[11] *CWMG* 39–41, passim. Cf. GoI letter, 24 June 1929, H.Poll.179/29.
[12] Circular letter by Motilal, 1 June 1929, AICC G40/1929.
[13] 'Indian National Congress' file C, MNP, contains material on this matter, including communications from B.C. Roy, 15, 24 June 1929, J.M. Sen Gupta, 23 June, Subhas Bose, 25 July, S.K. Sinha, 27 June, G.B. Pant 5, 19 June, Satyamurti, 24 June, Jamnadas Mehta, 13 June, K.F. Nariman, 22 June. Motilal replied to Roy, and Mehta, 20 June. For Patel's view see Patel to Motilal, 20 July 1929, 'Indian National Congress' file P6. For the climbdown see Motilal to Rivett Carnac, 30 July 1929, 'Indian National Congress' file R9, and *CWMG* 41, pp. 228–9. Note: references in this chapter to Patel are to Vithalbhai Patel; those to his brother Vallabhbhai Patel are so specified.

propose that some of their number should even accept provincial min-
isterships[14] – a move which Congressmen had always hitherto sharply disdained. The whole situation from the Congress point of view during these
same months was made still more difficult when the protracted negotiations between all-India Hindu and all-India Muslim leaders, in which
Motilal Nehru had played such a major role over the preceding year or so
following the Nehru Report, finally collapsed.[15] There was at the same
time a great deal of confusion within the Congress leadership over
whether Gandhi or Jawaharlal Nehru or Vallabhbhai Patel (the hero of the
Bardoli satyagraha of 1928) should become the next President – a confusion which was only resolved in September 1929 when Gandhi insisted
that Jawaharlal should be made President-elect in circumstances which
Jawaharlal himself felt to be personally humiliating.[16] Moreover, for all of
Gandhi's and Motilal's constant reminders that a major conflict with the
British was very much in the offing, even Gandhi himself remained com-
pletely uncertain throughout 1929 about exactly how it should be con-
ducted.[17] There were a great many signs, that is, during 1929 that
Congress was in no shape at all to launch a major campaign against the
British such as the Calcutta Congress had portended.

Ever since the previous autumn Lord Irwin, the Viceroy, had, however,
been giving his mind to the whole political and constitutional situation in
India, and in the new year Motilal Nehru was soon being made aware that
the Viceroy was in no way impervious to the Congress demands. By
March 1929 Motilal Nehru himself, and more particularly his fellow
Kashmiri, Sir Tej Bahadur Sapru, were being actively consulted on the
Viceroy's behalf by the Chief Justice of their Allahabad High Court, Sir
Grimwood Mears.[18] Sapru in response expressed himself as well content
with Mears' suggestion that the British should call a Round Table
Conference at which the case for Dominion Status for India could be
put,[19] and when he visited Delhi in April he pressed this case upon the
Viceroy personally.[20] In the discussions which occurred Motilal Nehru
had from the outset gone rather further. He wished (so Mears reported to
Irwin on 26 March) that any conference 'should be preceded by a plain
acceptance of the principle of Dominion Status';[21] and in July 1929 in an

---

[14] 'Indian National Congress' file C, MNP.
[15] E.g. Motilal to Gandhi, 14 Aug. 1929, MNP G1; Jayakar to Gandhi, 19 Aug. 1923, JP
407.   [16] SWJN 4, pp. 155 ff.
[17] For Motilal's determination see Motilal to Iswar Saran, 1 Aug. 1929, MNP 13; to Jal
Naoroji, 5 Aug. 1929, ibid. N2; to B.C. Roy, 10 Oct. 1929, MNP R10.
[18] R.J. Moore, The Crisis of Indian Unity 1917–1940, Oxford 1974, ch. 2. See especially Irwin
to Peel, 24 Jan., 4 Apr. 1929, IP 5; V to SoS, tel., 1 Apr. 1929, IP 10.
[19] Mears to Irwin, 26 Mar. 1929, IP 23.   [20] Irwin to Peel, 4 Apr. 1929, IP 5.
[21] Mears to Irwin, 26 Mar. 1929, IP 23; Moore, Crisis, p. 54.

anxious letter to *The Leader* of Allahabad Motilal proceeded to call publicly for a Round Table Conference 'to discuss the constitution of India
with a Committee of the [British] Cabinet on the basis of Dominion
Status before it was too late'.[22]

By then, Irwin, who had been subjected to similar pressure from,
among others, Vithalbhai Patel, the President of the central Legislative
Assembly,[23] had gone on leave to London,[24] and in the ensuing four
months there occurred there protracted, and in the end acrimonious
negotiations between the leaders of the three British political parties, on
the issue of what the British should do next. By the following November
these jagged divisions were to lead to a series of angry debates in both
Houses of the British Parliament which, since these were immediately
reported in the Indian press, gravely aggravated the exceedingly delicate
political situation which had by then developed there.[25] Irwin, however,
was eventually authorised by the new Labour Government to issue the
landmark Irwin declaration, we have earlier noted, of 31 October 1929 in
which 'in view of the doubts which have been expressed [he] was author-
ized on behalf of His Majesty's Government to state clearly that in their
judgment . . . the natural issue of India's constitutional progress . . . is the
attainment of Dominion Status'. He was authorised as well to indicate the
Government's intention to invite 'representatives of different parties and
interests' in India to a Round Table Conference in London to formulate
new constitutional proposals for India in full discussion with British political leaders.[26]

The critical issue over the next eight weeks, until the Congress meeting
in Lahore in Christmas week 1929, was accordingly how India's nationalist
leadership would ultimately respond to this new British declaration. Would
they agree in principle to settle for Dominion Status as their ultimate
objective, and attend a Round Table Conference in London? Or would
they spurn Irwin's declaration, endorse *purna swaraj* as their principal
objective, and launch their long-heralded civil disobedience movement?

In view of the uncertainties in the Congress ranks the effect of Irwin's
declaration on the Congress was truly disconcerting.[27] The newspapers
gave full vent to the issues.[28] Congress Provincial Committees discussed

[22] 1 July 1929, MNP L2.
[23] Irwin's Note, 11 Jan. 1929, IP 5; Irwin to Birkenhead, 18 Jan. 1929, IP 4; Irwin to Peel, 24
Jan., 28 Feb. 1929, IP 5.
[24] Sapru wished him 'every success in your high mission', Sapru to Irwin, 23 June 1929, SP
15.
[25] Moore, *Crisis*, ch. 2; Irwin's 'Narrative of Events . . .', 4 Nov. 1929, Cabinet Paper
307(29), Secret, IP 5.   [26] *The Gazette of India, Extraordinary*, 31 October 1929.
[27] Irwin to Benn, 31 Oct. 1929, IP 5, reporting a conversation with Vithalbhai Patel.
[28] For summaries see FRs for Nov.–Dec. 1929, H.Poll.17/29.

them vigorously. There were various intermediate circles of prominent individuals who shared actively in the mounting debate.[29] But at its centre, so the evidence makes plain, were four men, Gandhi and the three Kashmiri Pandit lawyers from Allahabad, Motilal Nehru, Jawaharlal Nehru, and Sir Tej Bahadur Sapru.

In 1929 Gandhi was aged sixty. It was just ten years since he had launched his first countrywide agitations in India, which, true to his non-violent principles, he had twice called off when they erupted into violence. During the mid 1920s he had not played a major role in Congress's political affairs, but by 1929 he was back in his former position as the undisputed leader of the Indian national movement.[30] In 1929 Motilal Nehru was aged sixty-eight, President of the Congress for the year, and the disillusioned leader of the Congress forces in the central Legislative Assembly.[31] Jawaharlal Nehru was forty, the idol of the younger generation and of his father.[32] Sapru was fifty-three, a one-time Congressman who eight years previously had been Law Member of the Viceroy's Council, and who now counted as India's foremost constitutional lawyer.[33] It was the complex interaction between these four men that dominated the ensuing argument. The eventual outcome was by no means the foregone conclusion which existing accounts suggest.

Shortly before the Irwin declaration was issued, Sir Grimwood Mears had on 25 October 1929, at Irwin's instance, seen both Sapru and Motilal separately in Allahabad to tell them of what stood in the wind.

Sapru's attitude [Mears wrote to Irwin that evening] was most encouraging. Motilal's quite encouraging enough. Your Excellency may take it as a matter of certainty that Mr Gandhi (if health permits), Motilal and Sapru will most readily go to London. Sapru is my authority as regards Mr Gandhi and is quite sure about it.[34]

Having, whilst on the Viceroy's Council in 1921, come within an ace of securing a Round Table Conference with the British, and having in the intervening years worked for the goal of Dominion Status for India as being a perfectly satisfactory resolution (as for the white Dominions) of

[29] E.g. JP 451(b); ThP 41; G.I. Patel, *Vithalbhai Patel*, Bombay 1951, ch. 40.
[30] J.M. Brown, *Gandhi. Prisoner of Hope*, New Haven 1989.
[31] R. Kumar and D.N. Panigrahi, eds., *Selected Works of Motilal Nehru*, vols. I– , Delhi 1972– .
[32] S. Gopal, *Jawaharlal Nehru. A Biography*, 3 vols., London 1975–84 (see especially here vol. I, ch. 9) ; S. Gopal, *SWJN*, vols. I– , Delhi 1972– .
[33] M. Kumar, *Sir Tej Bahadur Sapru. A Political Biography*, Gwalior 1981.
[34] Mears to Irwin, 25 Oct. 1929, IP 23. Irwin was much encouraged by this report, Irwin to Benn, tel., 29 Oct. 1929, IP 10, and 31 Oct. 1929, IP 5. See also Mears to Sapru, 5 Sept. 1929, SP 37.

India's aspirations, Sapru was naturally delighted with all the Irwin declaration promised. While warning the Viceroy that he 'anticipated some trouble from the Congress',[35] he told him, when he saw him in Delhi on 30 October, how pleased he personally was with the declaration, and reiterated his enthusiasm in a follow-up letter written later on that day.[36]

As became his official position as the current President of Congress, Motilal was more guarded. But there can be little doubt that when he first saw the text of the Irwin declaration, he was by no means unsatisfied with it. Like Sapru in 1921, Motilal had made an abortive attempt in 1924 to secure a Round Table Conference with the British.[37] Now at last one was being offered; and if there were some ambiguities in the text of Irwin's declaration, these were much on a par with the ambiguities in Motilal's own statements earlier in the year.[38]

I am grateful to Your Excellency [Motilal accordingly wrote to Irwin on 30 October] for your letter of the 26th October giving the purport of the statement you are going to make shortly. The matter is of great importance and I feel I will not be justified in expressing any opinion without consulting my colleagues. To this end I am calling an early meeting of the Working Committee of the Indian National Congress and shall meanwhile informally discuss the matter with leading Congressmen and other prominent nationalists. Thanking you for your courtesy.[39]

On the evening of 31 October 1929, the day the declaration was published, several Bombay politicians, including Jinnah, Jayakar, and Setalvad (who like Sapru and Motilal had been informed by Irwin of its text in advance), issued a statement expressing their enthusiastic support for it.[40] The Nehrus, however, in their capacities as President and General Secretary of Congress successfully urged upon most other such people to hold their tongues until there had been a considered discussion first in private in Delhi.[41]

---

[35] Sapru to Sastri, 10 Nov. 1930, SP 101.

[36] Sapru to Polak, 28 Nov. 1929, SP P77; Sapru to Irwin, 30 Oct. 1929, IP 23, 454; Mears to Irwin, 30 Oct. 1929, IP 454a; Sapru to Sastri, 10 Nov. 1929, SP P101. For Sapru's press statement see *Times of India*, 1 Nov. 1929.   [37] See MNP B12, D3, S23, W2.

[38] Mears to Irwin, 26 Mar. 1929, IP 23, 289a; 1 July 1929, MNP L2.

[39] Motilal to Irwin, 30 Oct. 1929, IP 23, 451; V's letter forwarding secret copy of declaration, 26 Oct. 1929, AICC G113/1929. For Motilal's pleasure with the declaration at this point in time, see Mears to Irwin, 30 Oct. 1929, IP 23, 454a.

[40] Setalvad to Irwin, 28 Oct. 1929, IP 23, 443. They issued a further statement on 5 November, *Times of India*, 6 Nov. 1929. On the Indians who were given advance information about the declaration, see Irwin to Benn, tel., 29 Oct. 1929, IP 10; Jayakar Diary 29–31 Oct. 1929.

[41] Motilal to Jinnah, nd, Motilal's tels. to Thakurdas, Jayakar, Sarojini Naidu, J.M. Sen Gupta, B.C. Roy, S.C. Bose, A.K. Azad, Birla, Sardul Singh, Mangal Singh, Gopichand, Dunichand, Alam, Kadir Kasuri, Ansari, Aney, Kitchlew, Imam, Rajendra Prasad, Jinnah, Gandhi, Malaviya, 28–29 Oct. 1929, AICC G113/1929. Jawaharlal to editors of national newspapers, 29 Oct. 1929, and to all members of the CWC, 29 Oct. 1929, *SWJN* 4, pp. 163–4.

Gandhi at this time was touring in the United Provinces.[42] When it came to be rumoured that the Viceroy would shortly be making an important constitutional announcement, he had mechanically reiterated the existing Congress position that 'if Dominion Status was not granted within this year, he would be for complete independence from the next year'.[43] When, however, Vithalbhai Patel brought him[44] the text of the declaration, and explained something of its genesis, Gandhi was so impressed by all the personal efforts which the Viceroy had made to be conciliatory that he readily agreed to attend the meeting of political leaders in New Delhi which the Nehrus were calling for 1 November.

From the outset the Mahatma was nevertheless very much in two minds about how to respond to the Irwin declaration. He was never, as it happened, very much interested in constitutional formulae. But on reaching Delhi he consulted his old Madrasi friend, Srinivasa Sastri, and was soon taking a somewhat different line than in his orthodox press statement of a few days previously. Gandhi, so Sastri was soon recording,

assured me that he does not wish the next Constitution to embody full Dominion Status straight away. He knows it to be impossible. Limitations regarding the Army etc. and the Indian States must be there. Only (1) they must be removable automatically on a specified date or on the happening of some event, (2) they must be introduced with our full consent.[45]

Gandhi, however, was at the same time very much concerned about the need for an amnesty for some political prisoners who had been arrested earlier in the year, and when Sastri pointed out that there could be difficulties in making satisfaction on such matters 'conditions precedent' to Congress attendance at a Round Table Conference, 'Gandhi only said "he didn't mind a bit" and looked forward to an early victory' over the British such as Sapru had nearly secured for him back in 1921.[46]

Thereafter, as arranged, a meeting of prominent political 'leaders' was held in New Delhi at the home of Vithalbhai Patel, the President of the Legislative Assembly, at 2 pm on 1 November 1929.[47] Despite a remark-

[42] CWMG 42, pp. 69–72.   [43] CWMG 42, p. 64.
[44] K.C. Roy to Irwin, 29 Oct. 1929, IP 23, 449.
[45] Sastri to Vaman Rao, 7 Nov. 1929, StP 525.
[46] Ibid. Cf: 'from what I saw of Gandhi at the Leaders' Conference at Delhi I have an impression that he has fully realised his blunder of having once rejected the offer of a Round Table Conference of Lord Reading', NLI, Moonje Diary, 12 Nov. 1929. Gandhi's friend Polak wrote of the lost opportunity in 1921, Polak to Sapru, 8 Nov. 1929, SP 33. On this whole episode see CWMG 21, 22, and D.A. Low, 'The Government of India and the First Non-Cooperation Movement, 1920–22', Journal of Asian Studies, 25, 2, Feb. 1966, pp. 241–59 (reprinted as ch. X in R. Kumar, ed., Essays in Gandhian Politics. The Rowlatt Satyagraha of 1919, Oxford 1971).
[47] See Ansari to Sapru, 31 Oct. 1929, SP A131.

ably favourable press for the Irwin declaration,[48] differences of outlook were soon apparent, and the meeting thereupon adjourned until the following day to allow Gandhi, Sapru, and Jawaharlal each to draw up for consideration a draft statement in response to the Irwin declaration.[49]

The eight manuscript pages of Jawaharlal's proposals survive in his archives, as does his scored and annotated copy of the critical passages in the Irwin declaration. Shortly before he first saw the Viceroy's statement, he had told a correspondent that it was 'highly unlikely to be satisfactory',[50] and so soon as it lay before him his eye quickly fastened on those key phrases in it such as 'natural issue' (marginal note: 'Emphasis on stages'), and words like 'ultimately' and 'ultimate purpose'.[51] In the draft which he then penned for the leaders' statement he began by recalling the Calcutta decisions of the Congress ten months previously, and, whilst acknowledging the conciliatory tone of Irwin's declaration, very soon made the point that 'there is no assurance in it that our demands will be acceded to in the near future'. He then pressed the point by noting that by 1929 all parties in the country 'have based their minimum demand on dominion status', and he thereupon roundly asserted that:

It is on the basis of this minimum demand alone that any fruitful conference can take place between the representatives of India and the representatives of the British Govt. There can be no common ground if even dominion status is considered a distant objective to be arrived at by successive steps.

On subsequent pages he gave expression to the strength of feeling in many Congress circles about the political prosecutions and imprisonments which had lately been occurring, and eventually climaxed his draft with a sharp demand for 'an immediate change in the present methods of administering the country'. All in all it was a reasoned but passionate call for the summary rejection of the Irwin declaration.[52]

Sapru on the other hand put forward a no less carefully reasoned but unequivocal acceptance of the Irwin declaration; while Gandhi for his part largely concentrated on the need for a series of 'conditions precedent' to Indian attendance at a Round Table Conference.

When the leaders met again at Vithalbhai's house at 2 pm on 2 November, Gandhi pressed his view that it was necessary to secure some sort of assurance, public or private, from the Government that the

[48] Irwin to Benn, 2 Nov. 1929, IP 10; FR mid Nov. 1929, H.Poll.17/29. For one example of the declaration's enthusiastic reception see Ramabhadrier to Jawaharlal, 1 Nov. 1929, AICC G113/1929.   [49] C.P. Ramaswamy Aiyar to Sapru, 9 Nov. 1929, SP A116.

[50] Jawaharlal Nehru to R.S. Ruiker, 29 Oct. 1929, AICC 12/1929.

[51] AICC G113/1929.

[52] Jawaharlal Nehru's draft, nd, ibid. It is printed in *SWJN* 4, pp. 175 ff., but seems rather misplaced there.

constitution to be discussed at the Round Table Conference would be based on Dominion Status, as well as a commitment that they would cast their own influence in that direction too.[53] Sapru's own personal desires ran along similar lines, but he argued strongly against any use of the term 'conditions precedent', and eventually Gandhi agreed to give way to him.[54] Thereafter an agreed public statement was drafted and signed. That evening *The Times of India*'s correspondent recorded that the statement which was then issued was Gandhi's 'via media between Sir T Sapru's [draft] and Mr J's, having more in common with the former'.[55]

For Jawaharlal the Delhi manifesto of 2 November 1929, as the leaders' statement came to be called, was a clear setback. 'We hope', it said, in contradistinction to his approach, 'to be able to tender our cooperation to His Majesty's Government in their effort to evolve a scheme of Dominion Constitution suitable for India's needs'. At the same time, however, it 'deemed it necessary that certain acts should be done . . . so as to inspire trust' (it mentioned, among other things, 'a general amnesty' and 'a more liberal spirit in the government of the country'); and it also expressed the hope that it would be the Viceroy's view that the projected 'Conference is to meet not to discuss when Dominion Status is to be established, but to frame a Dominion Constitution' for India.[56]

In this and other respects the manifesto was not therefore an altogether unambiguous response to the Viceroy's initiative, and Sapru, who was in touch with Irwin once again, found himself having to defend his signature of it both to the Viceroy[57] and to some of his more cautious fellow non-Congressmen.[58] But he did so without compunction as being required by the need to keep the Congress leaders from going their own way immediately. As it stood, the manifesto was evidently acceptable to Gandhi; and there can be little doubt that at this point in time Motilal Nehru was well content with it as well, since in his capacity as President of Congress he despatched telegrams all over India in the next day or so directly soliciting

[53] T.H. Horne to Irwin, 4 Nov. 1929, IP 23.
[54] Sapru to Sastri, 10 Nov. 1929, SP S101; Sapru to Mitter, 11 Nov. 1929, SP M119; Sapru to Sethna, 12 Nov. 1929, SP S142; Sapru to Munshi, 15 Nov. 1929, SP M171; Sapru to Polak, 28 Nov. 1929, SP P77; Sastri to Vaman Rao, 7 Nov. 1929, StP 525.
[55] Despatch dated Delhi, 2 Nov., *Times of India*, 4 Nov. 1929. Sapru himself said: 'Part of the Manifesto was taken from my draft, and the rest from Mr Gandhi's', Sapru to Munshi, 15 Nov. 1929, SP M171. See also Sapru to Polak, 28 Nov. 1929, SP P77; Birla to Thakurdas, 3 Nov. 1929, ThP 91.   [56] For its text see *CWMG* 42, p. 80.
[57] Sastri to Sapru, 7 Nov. 1929, SP S100; Sapru to Sastri 10 Nov. 1929, SP S9; Sapru to Irwin, 11 Nov. 1929, SP 19; Sapru to Mitter, 11 Nov. 1929, SP M119. On Irwin's own attitude see Irwin to Benn, tel., 2 Nov. 1929, IP 10, and 6 Nov. 1929, SP 5.
[58] S. Aiyar to Sapru, 6, 16 Nov. 1929, SP A157, A159; Sapru to Sastri, 10 Nov. 1929, SP 57; Sapru to Besant, 11 Nov. 1929, SP B80; Sapru to S. Aiyar, 12 Nov. 1929, SP A158; Sapru to Sethna, 12 Nov. 1929, SP S142; Sapru to Dalvi, 12 Nov. 1929, SP 15; Sapru to Munshi, 15 Nov. 1929, SP M171.

support for it.[59] From the many press statements,[60] and the many telegrams which survive in Motilal's own papers,[61] the number of prominent adherents to the manifesto seems soon to have grown to nearly seventy.[62]

Motilal meanwhile had one great anxiety: his son; and this not only gave him a sleepless night on the train down to Lucknow. It impelled him to seek reassurance there from his old friends Khaliquzzaman and Mohanlal Saxena. Motilal, it must be remembered, was deeply attached to his only son, and he was acutely aware that quite suddenly Jawaharlal was embroiled in a great personal crisis.[63] For when the time came on 2 November for the leaders to sign the manifesto, so one diary account tells us,

All signed it except Jawaharlal and Subhas Chandra Bose. Jawaharlal was hesitating but when Mahatmaji told him that though one is entitled to have his own views he can not remain a member of the Working Committee and also President of the Congress if he is singled out from his other colleagues over an important matter like this, face of Jawaharlal changed immediately and his tone indicated pliability but still he wd not sign. Mahatmaji then impressed on him the teaching of the Great Lokamanya by saying that Tilak used to preach that if you have secured 4 annas, keep it and deriving strength from it press on and fight on for securing the whole Rupee of 16 annas.[64]

While another account tells us that:

When Jawaharlal was signing he was in tears & Gandhi said 'Jawahar think well. If you put your signature honour the responsibility.'[65]

And in a subsequent letter Motilal told his son that at this moment:

[I] pointed out to Gandhiji the difference between a decision arrived by the Cabinet meeting as such and that of a mixed gathering like the one we had in Delhi . . . After that I went to the bath room and returning soon after found that you had signed at Gandhiji's insistence. There was then nothing to be said.[66]

But there was; and three days later Motilal wrote from Lucknow to his son: 'your action in the matter has been simply splendid and brings out clearly the distinction between the genuine and the spurious article'.[67] For immediately after Jawaharlal had signed the manifesto there was an ominous contretemps. As Motilal put it: 'that signature gave the opportunity of their lives to two sets of individuals. Those who are consumed by

[59] Motilal to Jawaharlal, 5 Nov. [1929], MN–JNC.
[60] e.g. *Times of India*, early Nov. 1929, passim.
[61] These are scattered through the individual correspondence files in MNP.
[62] *Times of India*, 18 Nov. 1929.   [63] Motilal to Jawaharlal, 7 Nov. [1929], MN–JNC.
[64] Moonje Diary, 2 Nov. 1929.
[65] Mears to Benn, 1 Dec. 1929, IOL L/PO/14, based, it would seem, on reports from Sapru etc.   [66] Motilal to Jawaharlal, 7 Nov. [1929], MN–JNC.
[67] Motilal to Jawaharlal, 5 Nov. [1929], MN–JNC.

personal jealousy and those who do not like your election to the Congress chair.'[68] And before the day was out, Subhas Bose, Jawaharlal's great Bengali rival for the plaudits of the younger and more radical supporters of the Congress, had indeed not only ostentatiously refused to sign the manifesto; he had published a condemnation of it,[69] and written a courteous but nevertheless pointed letter to Motilal resigning his membership of the Congress Working Committee. Bose, like Jawaharlal himself until this moment, was altogether opposed to the idea of Dominion Status, and was wholly committed to *purna swaraj*, and his letter to Motilal pierced to the heart of the situation (it is particularly revealing of the attitude that day of Gandhi):

I feel it is my duty [Bose wrote] to express my views publicly to explain the attitude of the Independence School. After hearing Mahatmaji's remarks at the Conference this afternoon I feel I should not do so while I am a member of the Working Committee.[70]

Three days later, on returning to Calcutta, Bose wrote bitingly to his mother: 'Jawaharlal has now given up independence at the instance of the Mahatma.'[71]

Jawaharlal would not have quarrelled with that judgment. For within hours (so he was soon telling Gandhi) something 'snapped inside me', and (he went on) 'the fever in my brain has not left me'.[72] Before leaving Delhi for his home in Allahabad he wrote to Gandhi an anguished letter. This does not seem to have survived, lost no doubt somewhere on Gandhi's renewed tour in the UP. But Gandhi's reply survives – and it is vintage Gandhi too.

I have just got your letter [he wrote to Jawaharlal on 4 November]. How shall I console you? Hearing others describe your state I said to myself, 'Have I been guilty of putting undue pressure on you?' I have always believed you to be above undue pressure. I have always honoured your resistances. It has always been

[68] Motilal to Jawaharlal, 7 Nov. [1929], MN–JNC.

[69] N.N. Mitra, *The Indian Quarterly Register*, July–Dec. 1929, Calcutta 1930, pp. 50–1. See more generally L.A. Gordon, *Brothers against the Raj. A Biography of Indian Nationalists, Sarat and Subhas Chandra Bose*, New York 1990, ch. 6.

[70] Bose to President, Indian National Congress, 2 Nov. 1929, AICC G115/1929. Jawaharlal acknowledged this letter on behalf of his father, Jawaharlal to Bose, 7 Nov. 1929, AICC G115/1929.

[71] Bose to his mother, 5 Nov. 1929, S.C. Bose, *Correspondence 1924–1932*, Calcutta 1967. Cf. 'You should not undervalue the gain that we have been able to carry with us extremists like Jawahar Lal Nehru and others', Birla to Thakurdas, 9 Nov. 1929, ThP 91. For a milder approach by Satish Chandra Bose see Bose to Jawaharlal, 4 Nov. 1929, AICC G113/1929. Jawaharlal's position was vigorously challenged by Srinivasa Iyengar, with whom he had only recently clashed, see their letters of 20, 23, 27 Aug., 3 Sept. 1929, AICC G40/1929, and 8, 11, 12, 15 Nov. 1929, AICC G113/1929, and 20 Nov. 1929, AICC, G115/1929. See also Shiva Rao to Sapru, 16 Nov. 1929, SP R74.

[72] Jawaharlal to Gandhi, 4 Nov. 1929, J. Nehru, *A Bunch of Old Letters*, Bombay 1960, p. 76.

honourable. Acting under that belief I pressed my suit. Let this incident be a lesson. Resist me always when my suggestion does not appeal to you head and heart. But why are you dejected? I hope there is no fear of public opinion in you. If you have done nothing wrong, why dejection? The ideal of independence is not in conflict with greater freedom.[73]

That last sentence was a fantastic one. The distinctions between complete independence and Dominion Status were, as it happened, of no great importance to the Mahatma. But, following the debates of the last two years, they were of fundamental importance to Bose, the younger Nehru and their like.

But before Jawaharlal could expostulate in reply, back in Allahabad he wrote to Gandhi once again, and this time much more deliberately. He recalled that in addition to being General Secretary and President-elect of Congress, he was President of the Indian Trade Congress, Secretary of the Independence for India League, and intimately connected with the Youth movement. 'What shall I do with allegiance to these and other movements I am connected with?' he cried. He now felt he had to say that the Delhi manifesto was 'a wholly unsatisfactory reply' to the Irwin declaration. 'I am afraid', he told Gandhi, 'we differ fundamentally on that issue'. The Mahatma, he felt sure, would soon 'agree to any modifications of the conditions which the British Government might suggest. In any event it is quite clear to me that my position in the Congress will daily become more and more difficult.' All the same he was anxious to be as little disruptive as he could, and to this end he made two alternative suggestions. Either, he said, it could be announced that Gandhi himself had now agreed to preside at the next Congress, and accordingly he, Jawaharlal, could excuse himself. Or, if it was too late for that, he would resign the Presidency 'immediately after Congress is over', but would, in the meanwhile, 'act as the Chairman, and the Congress can decide what it likes regardless of me'. Whatever happened he had determined to resign the General Secretaryship of the Congress forthwith, and was sending his letter of resignation, together with a copy of this second letter to Gandhi, to the President, his father, in Lucknow.[74]

When Motilal received his son's letter with its enclosures, the great personal crisis which had haunted him ever since he had left Delhi immediately erupted.

I have been dreading [Motilal wrote to Jawaharlal on 7 November] the action you propose to take from the moment you came back from Ansari's house just before I left Delhi. The distress of your mind was quite apparent from your looks but I felt that that was not the time to discuss the matter ... Your letter with enclosures

---

[73] Gandhi to Jawaharlal, 4 Nov. 1929, *CWMG* 42, p. 26.
[74] Jawaharlal to Gandhi, 4 Nov. 1929, *Bunch of Old Letters*, pp. 76–8, also *SWJN* 4, pp. 166–8.

came just as I was going to Court and I could only glance through a part of it as I had to resume my opening speech ten minutes later. I have never made a feebler opening of a case in my life.[75]

Motilal was so distraught that he clutched at straws. He turned for comfort to Saxena and Khaliquzzaman, and also Dr Ansari, who had just come down from Delhi. He made a feeble defence to Jawaharlal of his recent statement that Jawaharlal's signature on the manifesto had been 'simply splendid'. All those telegrams he had sent, he now stated, were designed to secure 'the consensus of opinion of practically all schools of Indian politicians on the propriety and reasonableness of the conditions imposed' – when he knew very well that the phrase 'conditions precedent' had been deliberately omitted.

As you say [Motilal went on] it is almost certain that the Govt. will not accept the 'conditions' however mildly put in the statement. This will be demonstrated during the Parliamentary debates of this week. The Working Committee will meet later and have all the material before it. I do not see how it can come to any conclusion other than there has been a definite 'rejection' of the demand and there is nothing for it but to recommend to the Congress to inaugurate a campaign for civil disobedience with complete independence as the goal . . . It is only a matter of a few days. My advice to you is to sit tight till the Working Committee meeting at which I expect the action taken will fully accord with your own views. In any case you can take no definite action till the Committee meets. All I plead for is that you will not anticipate that action in whatever you say or do.[76]

To help Motilal in his confusion, Ansari wrote to Jawaharlal as well, and in so doing contravened his own favourable response to the Irwin declaration. 'I believe myself', Ansari wrote, 'that there is a greater chance of the Congress coming over to your view, than your having to resign from the presidentship owing to your views being opposed to those prevalent in the Congress'.[77] And as, later in the day, news of the acrimonious debates in London reached Lucknow, Motilal dashed off a second letter to his son.

Congrats [he wrote]. It is just what we anticipated. There is no question of resignations now. The dust bin is the only safe place for the Delhi statement.[78]

But it was not to be quite so straightforward.

When Gandhi had received Jawaharlal's second letter on 6 November, his reaction was less agitated than Motilal's, but if anything even more concerned. The position for Gandhi can be readily imagined. His devotion to and admiration for Jawaharlal were second to none. He had turned to him earlier in this same year to revivify the Congress organization, and, if

[75] Motilal to Jawaharlal, 7 Nov. [1929], MN–JNC.   [76] Ibid.
[77] Ansari to Jawaharlal, 7 Nov. 1929, JNP Ansari file.
[78] Motilal to Jawaharlal, 7 Nov. 1929, MN–JNC.

success had been limited, the fault had not been Jawaharlal's. Whichever path was now taken there would almost certainly be a crisis for the Congress by the end of the year or soon after. It was inconceivable that at this stage Jawaharlal should be separated from him. It was now two years since Gandhi had thought of him as a possible President of Congress.[79] In the end, in 1929, despite the pressure upon Gandhi himself to become the next President of Congress (as well as the availability of such as Vallabhbhai Patel) Gandhi had insisted that Jawaharlal should 'wear the crown', and had even declared that if this happened Jawaharlal would be his *alter ego*.[80] The central consideration here was that in this way the looming generation gap in the Congress leadership would be bridged, and its younger elements could thereby be held from sliding over into the violence Gandhi so dreaded.[81] All these plans were now in danger of grave disruption. What was more, Jawaharlal's response was this time quite unprecedented. Back in 1928 when Gandhi had felt that Jawaharlal's speeches after his return from Europe were far too radical, he had rebuked him sharply, and threatened to break off their political relationship. In 1928 Jawaharlal had meekly submitted to the Mahatma's bidding.[82] Then at Calcutta in December 1928 there had been another confrontation. Although in the end Gandhi made some significant concessions, he had once more pulled the younger man back into line.[83] But this time the situation was altogether different. For the first time Jawaharlal had evidently determined to stand his ground, and Gandhi could obviously not, therefore, respond to Jawaharlal's second letter in the half-bantering tone in which he had responded to the first. Jawaharlal's suggestions, moreover, as to how the crisis might be limited made very little sense. If Gandhi took over the Presidency of Congress, the reasons would soon become publicly apparent. If, alternatively, Jawaharlal went to Lahore and simply acted as a neutral chairman, the disarray within Congress would know no bounds. Accordingly, on this second occasion Gandhi responded to Jawaharlal with immense care and consideration. From Muttra on 6 November, he sent him a telegram.

Deeply appreciate [this ran] moral difficulty your second letter but there should be no hurry arriving at decision. Resignation must not be pressed. If still agitated meet me wherever you like.[84]

And when, two days later – such was the perturbation in Gandhi's entourage – Pyaralel, Gandhi's secretary, sent on to Jawaharlal a telegram which

[79] Motilal to Jawaharlal, 11 Aug. 1927, MN–JNC.   [80] *CWMG* 41, pp. 303 ff.
[81] E.g. 'Youth on Trial', *Young India*, 3 Oct. 1929, *CWMG* 41, pp. 499–500.
[82] Gandhi to Jawaharlal, 4, 11, 17, 26 Jan. 1927, JNP Gandhi file.
[83] *CWMG* 38, pp. 307–17.
[84] Gandhi to Jawaharlal, tel., 6 Nov. 1929, *CWMG* 42, p. 101.

had been received from Gandhi's old friend Horace Alexander in England, he was careful to add: 'I hope you have received Bapu's long wire.'[85] And so soon, moreover, as Gandhi could find a spare moment amid his busy UP tour, he wrote to Jawaharlal once again.

I have your letter [the Mahatma began]. You must have got my wire. You must not resign now. I have not time to argue my point. All I know it will effect the national cause. There is no hurry and no principle at stake. About the crown; no one else can wear it. It never was to be a crown of roses. Let it be all thorns now . . . let us reserve the whole of this for calm & detached discussion when we meet.[86]

Seen in this sequence the detailed evidence indicates that between 6 and 8 November 1929, Gandhi in one crucial respect shifted his position towards the Irwin declaration. His reason for this can be illustrated by comparing the two last sentences of his two replies to Jawaharlal's successive letters. He ended the first with the quip: 'If you can, do wire that the blues are over.'[87] He concluded the second with a prayer: 'Meanwhile may God give you peace.'[88] The shift was soon public too. Back on 3 November, immediately after the Delhi meetings, Gandhi had responded to a newspaper enquiry by emphasising that he was 'dying to give and secure true heart co-operation' with the British.[89] But on 8 November, after getting Jawaharlal's second letter, he responded to another newspaper enquiry very differently: 'Unless', he said, 'there is a full response to what must be frankly considered to be the conditions enumerated in the leaders' manifesto there can be no peace'.[90]

The overall change was soon picked up by Sapru.

Pandit Moti Lal Nehru came to me last night [Sapru wrote from his home in Allahabad on 11 November to Srinivasa Sastri] and I went to him this morning. I discussed the thing with him again at great length and pointed out to him the inadvisability of such a course and its repercussions in the country. I said the enemies of Indian progress would very much like that the chances of the conference coming about in London and being attended by the Congress-men should be spoiled and they (the enemies) would welcome a decision by the Congress to withhold themselves from the Conference. He said to me in reply that what they intended to say at the meeting of 16th November was that they would go to the Round Table Conference only if their conditions were fulfilled. I begged of him to postpone such a decision and then suggested to him that he might see the Viceroy. He agreed to go if summoned. I further pointed out to him that by taking the threatened action he would make the task of those of us who were willing to work

---

[85] Pyaralal to Jawaharlal, 8 Nov. 1929, AICC G113/1929.
[86] Gandhi to Jawaharlal, 8 Nov. 1929, *CWMG* 42, p. 116.
[87] Gandhi to Jawaharlal, 4 Nov. 1929, *CWMG* 42, p. 96.
[88] Gandhi to Jawaharlal, 8 Nov. 1929, *CWMG* 42, p. 116.
[89] Gandhi to *Daily Express*, London, 3 Nov. 1929, *CWMG* 42, p. 87.
[90] Gandhi to Editor, *Kaisar-i-Hind*, 8 Nov. 1929, *CWMG* 42, p. 123.

for the fulfilment of what I call expectations and they call conditions extremely difficult. I thought when I left him that he was to some extent impressed by my earnest pleading . . . I am most anxious that if we can avoid a split and take the Congress people with us to the Conference we should do so. It is only when this becomes patently impossible that I shall go my own way and they theirs . . .'[91]

The struggle was now on. Sastri realised that the whole situation was now very uncertain. After reading some of Gandhi's articles at this time in *Young India*[92] and *Navajivan*,[93] he told a friend: 'Gandhi is making it hard for us by rushing into print with his interpretation.'[94] The Viceroy was soon seized of the situation as well. On 13 November he wrote to the Secretary of State in London:

Jawaharlal thinks he has sold his soul by signing the leaders' manifesto, and . . . is being consoled by the elder men on the lines of their saying that inasmuch as Government will not fulfil their conditions . . . his path is again quite clear to carry Congress with him in a policy of rejection and of renewed advocacy of civil disobedience.[95]

Two days before, the United Provinces Provincial Congress Committee, with Jawaharlal present, but not in the chair, had indeed passed a resolution denouncing the Irwin declaration root and branch.[96]

There were nevertheless other forces with which Gandhi had to contend. He was strongly pressed by G.D. Birla, one of his principal business supporters, to go to London.[97] A number of Bombay men, Moonje, Jayakar, Kelkar, Jinnah, Munshi, along with both Vithalbhai and Vallabhbhai Patel, held a variety of meetings there at which they expressed their keen concern lest (as the latter put it) 'Mahatma Gandhi surrounded as he is at present by the Nehrus, father and son and also committed to the Calcutta Congress Resolution may be prevailed upon to repudiate the Delhi Manifesto.' Although Moonje believed that Gandhi 'fully realised his blunder of having once rejected the offer of a Round Table Conference of Lord Reading' in 1921, and would 'do his best to see, in his own peculiar way that this offer of a Round Table Conference is not rejected', others were not so sanguine. It was, therefore, agreed that the Patels should urge on Gandhi that the door should not be closed immediately on all future negotiations with the British. They

---

[91] Sapru to Sastri, 10 Nov. 1929, SP S101; see also Sapru to Patel, 11 Nov. 1929, SP P12, and Sapru to Mitter, 11 Nov. 1929, SP M119.

[92] 'Is it true?', *Young India*, 7 Nov. 1929, *CWMG* 42, p. 112.

[93] 'Conditions for Cooperation', *Navajivan*, 10 Nov. 1929, *CWMG* 42, pp. 122–3.

[94] Sastri to Vaman Rao, 13 Nov. 1929, StP 528. See also Mitter to Sapru, 14 Nov. 1929, SP M120.   [95] Irwin to Benn, 13 Nov. 1929, IP 5.

[96] Report from Allahabad, 11 Nov, *Times of India*, 13 Nov. 1929.

[97] E.g. Birla to Gandhi, 11 Nov. 1929, G.D. Birla, *In the Shadow of the Mahatma*, Bombay 1968, pp. 40–1.

suggested too that if there was a further announcement from the British on the composition of a Round Table Conference and a general amnesty, that could be 'evidence of a change of heart'. They even canvassed the idea of extracting from the British a further statement that they intended the proposed Conference 'to frame a scheme for Dominion Status'. Whilst they recognised that this would be very difficult, Vallabhbhai Patel nonetheless wrote to Gandhi on 11 November (in cautious terms, since he had no desire to be left out upon a limb), that 'this needs to be discussed with you since there could be no two opinions that under the present circumstances no government would make any such announcements'.[98] By now, moreover, Gandhi had received cables from Fenner Brockway, Horace Alexander, and other supporters in England, along with representations from his two principal British friends in India, Stokes and Charlie Andrews, all of whom urged the great importance of making a positive response to Irwin's declaration.[99]

However, in an article in *Young India* on 14 November, Gandhi stated flatly: 'It is highly likely that the Labour Government has never meant all the implications mentioned by me', and in a speech in Allahabad on 17 November he went a step further: 'What India was to get', he declared, 'would not come from London but would come from the Indians themselves from their own strength', and accordingly people should 'organize themselves for the work to attain Swaraj'.[100] As Sastri was aware, Gandhi was all along wondering whether the developing situation did not present him with 'a great opportunity for his mighty weapon'[101] of satyagraha, and 'seemed rather carried away by the idea that the Congress ultimatum fixing the 31 December had won its object, and that promise of further result lay along similar lines and not along a different procedure which might give us unripe fruit'.[102]

Nevertheless the Mahatma had still not finally decided between his various options. By now the Nehrus had arranged that a meeting of the Congress Working Committee should be held in Allahabad on 16–18 November to discuss the issues fully,[103] and when Gandhi was asked if in

[98] Vallabhbhai Patel to Gandhi, 11 Nov. 1929, *CWMG* 42, p. 517, and tel., 11 Nov, and Gandhi to Vallabhbhai Patel, tel., 13 Nov. 1929, *CWMG* 42, p. 142; Patel to Sapru, 13 Nov. 1929, *Vithalbhai Patel*, p. 1062. For Patel's caution at this moment see Moonje Diary, 12 Nov. 1929.

[99] 'My Position', *Young India*, 14 Nov. 1929, *CWMG* 42, p. 150. Brockway to Jawaharlal, and Gandhi, 1 Nov. 1929, Horace Alexander to Jawaharlal, 4 Nov. 1929, AICC G113/1929; Gandhi to Brockway, 14 Nov. 1929, *CWMG* 42, p. 161.

[100] Ibid., pp. 179–80.

[101] Sastri to Sivaswamy Aiyar, 2 Dec. 1929, T.N. Jagadishan, ed., *Letters of the Right Honourable V.S. Srinivasa Sastri*, Bombay 1963, pp. 183–5.

[102] Sastri to Vaman Rao, 7 Nov. 1929, StP 525.   [103] Agenda papers etc., AICC 17/1929.

association with this there could be a further meeting of the signatories of the Delhi manifesto, he readily agreed to this.[104] Thereafter it was in the course of those three-day meetings that Gandhi himself, and all the issues which were now involved, came to a very fine point. Nine members attended the Working Committee meeting, including Subhas Bose from Bengal, whom Jawaharlal had ultimately persuaded to attend,[105] and thereafter forty people attended the further special meeting of the signatories to the Delhi manifesto on 18 November.[106]

On 16 November Sapru had a long talk in Allahabad with Gandhi, Motilal Nehru and Madan Mohan Malaviya, a former President of Congress. Whilst Malaviya warmly supported him, Sapru came away with real misgivings. But on the following day at Anand Bhavan, Motilal's house in Allahabad, he had a further meeting, and this time found the discussion 'eminently reasonable'.[107] On the eighteenth, the signatories of the Delhi manifesto were due to meet at Anand Bhavan at 5.30 pm, and Sapru had an hour's talk with Gandhi immediately beforehand.[108]

There can be no doubt that by this time the Mahatma's mind was dominated by thoughts of Jawaharlal and the young men. (He will no doubt have had by now the heart to heart talk with Jawaharlal which he had foreshadowed in his 8 November letter.) Gandhi, so Sapru later recorded of the last-minute conversation he now had with him,

felt that the situation was such that the country expected that something should be done by the Government which would enable him to put the advanced section of his following consisting mostly of young men in a reasonable and hopeful frame of mind.[109]

In particular he mentioned an amnesty for political prisoners.[110] But once again Sapru resisted every suggestion of 'conditions precedent', and once

[104] Patel to Sapru, 8, 13 Nov. 1929, SP P11, P13; Motilal to Sapru, 13 Nov. 1929, SP N39; Motilal to Jayakar, tel., 14 Nov. 1929, JP 451(b); Sapru to Irwin, 15 Nov. 1929, SP I11; Natesan to Motilal [14 Nov. 1929], NMML Natesan Papers.

[105] Bose to Jawaharlal, 11 Nov. 1929, Jawaharlal to Bose, 14 Nov. 1929, AICC G115/1929.

[106] See the list in AICC G113/1929.

[107] Sapru to Irwin, 25 Nov. 1929, SP I13; Sapru to Thakurdas, tel., 16 Nov. 1929, ThP 91; see also Sapru to Irwin, 15 Nov. 1929, SP I11. For Malaviya's support for the Irwin declaration from the outset see Irwin to Benn, 18 June 1929, IP 10; Malaviya to Irwin, 30 Oct. 1929, IP 23; Moonje Diary, 2 Nov. 1929; Malaviya to Sapru, 25 Nov. 1929, SP 5. For some of the prevailing conflicts see Shiva Rao to Sapru, 15 Nov. 1929, IP R73, and Sethna to Sapru, 15 Nov. 1929, SP S143.

[108] Hailey to Irwin, 20 Nov. 1929, IP 23.

[109] Sapru to Irwin, 25 Nov. 1929, SP I13 and IP 23.

[110] The GoI was in no mood to have responded to this demand, PSV to HD, tel., 1 Dec. 1929, Petrie's Note, 4 Dec. 1929, H.Poll.299/29.

again Gandhi eventually gave in, so that in the end Sapru 'succeeded in persuading him that the proper attitude was to give the Government an opportunity of showing it is in earnest over its recent declaration'.[111] And with that the two men went to the Leaders' meeting.

At this Jawaharlal spoke vehemently against both the Irwin declaration and the Delhi manifesto,[112] and was strongly supported by Jamnadas Mehta, Subhas Bose, J.M. Sen Gupta, and several others of those present. Motilal argued (as he had in his second letter to Jawaharlal on 7 November) that the hostility which had been shown towards the Irwin declaration, and all that it involved, in the recent debates in the British Parliament, provided ample warrant for its complete rejection. But the majority of those present stood with Sapru, who now read a cable which had just been received from London from Henry Polak, Gandhi's old friend from his South African days, which argued that it would be an egregious error if the Congress were to respond negatively to the Labour Government's offer; and when Gandhi then referred to his earlier discussion with Sapru the meeting adjourned till later in the evening.[113]

A supremely critical moment had now arrived. For if, at this point in time, Gandhi were to break with the majority of the 'leaders', he would plainly have put himself gravely in the wrong. For like them he had signed the Delhi manifesto. He had, moreover, readily agreed that they should meet with the Working Committee in Allahabad. What was more, he had allowed himself earlier in the evening to accept Sapru's suggestion that the Government should be given more time to make some further response. But at the same time it would have been no less disastrous for him if, by anything he did or said at this stage, he were to alienate the young men. So it is to that evening's interval that we may therefore attribute two remarkable notes dated 18 November which survive in the Nehru archives. The first was Gandhi's draft resolution for the Congress Working Committee which was to meet later that evening, before the resumed meeting of the leaders, and this ran as follows:

---

[111] Hailey to Irwin, 20 Nov. 1929, Sapru to Irwin, 25 Nov. 1929, IP 23.
[112] On the 'distance' between Jawaharlal and Sapru see Jawaharlal to S. Sadanand, 5 Aug. 1929, AICC G40/1929; on the relatively good relations between Motilal and Sapru see Sapru to Motilal, 29 Aug. 1929, MNP Meerut conspiracy case file.
[113] Kunzru to Sapru, 14, 22 Nov. 1929, SP 33, P75; *Times of India*, 18 Nov. 1929; Hailey to Irwin, 20 Nov. 1929, IP 23; FR late Nov. 1929, H.Poll.17/29. Jayakar had shrewdly argued that 'the difficulty with Pandit Motilal is that he is in both camps, and I am not sure that his views of the Viceroy's announcement will not be coloured very largely by his conception of what view the Congress is likely to take', Jayakar to Kelkar, 29 Oct. 1929, JP 451(b). See also Polak to Sapru, 8 Nov. 1929, SP P73; Chintamini to Jawaharlal, 20 Nov. 1929, AICC G113/1929; and Employees Association draft resolution for AITUC at Nagpur, 28 Nov. 1929, AICC 12/1929.

Having considered the Viceregal pronouncement of 1st instant and the manifesto bearing the signatures of Congress members and members belonging to the other political parties in the country, the events that have happened thereafter both in India and England and the advice tendered by friends and well-wishers, the Working Committee approved the action taken by Congressmen and defer further consideration pending the holding of the forthcoming session of the National Congress.[114]

That, on the face of it, gave Sapru all he wanted.

But there was then the second note, and this was addressed to Jawaharlal personally.

Here is my draft [it ran]. I want you to consider it carefully and take your full share in the discussion tonight. I do not want you to suppress yourself in any way whatever except where you feel that self-suppression is better than self-expression on particular occasions. After all we must each serve according to our lights, not borrowed.[115]

With these Janus-like notes, Gandhi brilliantly secured his dangerously exposed position.

During the evening's discussions the last part of Gandhi's draft resolution was changed to say that 'the Working Committee confirms the action taken by Congressmen at Delhi, it being clearly understood that this confirmation is constitutionally limited to the date of the holding of the forthcoming session of the Congress'. It would seem, therefore, that Jawaharlal had taken the Mahatma at his word and suggested an amendment.[116] The draft of the new conclusion survives in the Congress archives with 'Passed M.N.' in Motilal's bold handwriting in the margin.[117] Thereafter the resolution reached the press some time after midnight; and a 'Leaders' resolution confirming the Delhi manifesto in essentially complementary terms was issued at 1.15 am.[118]

Equally important, two marginal scribbles in the Congress papers show that at Allahabad both Subhas Bose and Jawaharlal withdrew their letters of resignation from their Congress offices.[119] What was more, within the next few days Jawaharlal was assuring outside critics on his own side[120] that the situation was not all it might seem.

The position created here [at Allahabad, he wrote to one correspondent on 23 November] was such that some of us thought it better from the point of view of a

---

[114] Gandhi to Jawaharlal, 18 Nov. 1929, *CWMG* 42, p. 181.
[115] Ibid. See the original in JNP Gandhi file.   [116] See the drafts in AICC G113/1929.
[117] Ibid.   [118] *Times of India*, 19 Nov. 1929; Sapru to Polak, 28 Nov. 1929, SP P77.
[119] 'Resignation withdrawn in response to Wg C's resolution 19.XI', note in Jawaharlal's hand on Bose to President, Indian National Congress, 2 Nov. 1929, AICC G115/1929. See also Caveeshar to Jawaharlal, 8 Nov. 1929, AICC G113/1929.
[120] On these see e.g. *SWJN* 4, pp. 169–70.

campaign for full independence at the Lahore Congress to give some rope to those here who wanted to adopt a compromising policy. They laid down a number of conditions and as it is certain that none of these conditions is going to be fulfilled, the Congress will meet in Lahore much stronger for effective action. Anyhow the next few weeks will show whether some of us have made a great mistake or not. I myself have been exceedingly troubled and anxious. On the whole, however, I feel that in spite of what people, ignorant of the conditions here may say we have prepared the ground better for the struggle next year.[121]

Sapru, on his side, was being warmly congratulated for his success at Allahabad, for to outward appearances so it seemed.[122] But he had no illusions himself on this score,[123] and after seeing the Governor of the United Provinces, Sir Malcolm Hailey, he wrote shortly afterwards to the Viceroy saying that it was now absolutely vital that he should see Gandhi.[124]

During the next few weeks there was as a consequence a flurry of telegrams since the Viceroy was away on tour. An individual invitation from him to Motilal was still outstanding.[125] There was an unsuccessful attempt by Sarojini Naidu to arrange a meeting between the Viceroy and Gandhi in Bombay.[126] And it was then suggested that, when they did meet, Sapru, Jinnah, and Vithalbhai Patel should be present as well.[127] Despite his initial hesitations, Gandhi was eventually persuaded by Jinnah and the Patel brothers at a meeting on 1 December that 'if there was an interview with the Viceroy, we would be free to discuss all the terms of the Manifesto'.[128] Motilal, however, now wired to Gandhi that

[121] Jawaharlal to R. Bridgman, 23 Nov. 1929: for this and similar letters see *SWJN*, pp. 170 ff.

[122] Patel to Sapru, 19 Nov. 1929, SP P15; Mitter to Sapru, 20 Nov. 1929, SP M121; Irwin to Sapru, 21 Nov. 1929, ibid. I12; R. Iyengar to Sapru, 23 Nov. 1929, SP A42; C.P. Ramaswamy Aiyar to Sapru, 17 Dec. 1929, SP A118; Bajpai to Sapru, 26 Nov. 1929, SP 5; Mears to Benn, 1 Dec. 1929, IOL L/PO/14.

[123] Sapru to Thakurdas, 24 Nov. 1929, ThP 91; Sapru to R. Iyengar, 28 Nov. 1929, SP A43; Sapru to Mitter, 6 Dec. 1929, SP M123; Sapru to Basu, 17 Dec. 1929, SP 5. For the GoI's appreciation see HD to PSV, tel., 24 Nov. 1929, H.Poll.98/30; Irwin to Benn, 26 Nov. 1929, IP 10; Irwin to Halifax, 3 Dec. 1929, IP 27.

[124] Sapru to Irwin, 25 Nov. 1929, SP I13; Sapru to Thakurdas, 24 Nov. 1929, ThP 91; Sapru to Patel, 24 Nov. 1929, SP P16. Hailey had dinner at Sapru's home on 21 Nov., Sinha to Sapru, 14 Nov. 1929, SP S365 etc.

[125] Sapru to Irwin, 11 Nov. 1929, SP I9; Sapru to Mitter, 11 Nov. 1929, SP M119; Irwin to Sapru, 12 Nov. 1929, SP I10; Irwin to Benn, 15 Nov. 1929 IP 11; Sapru to Irwin, 15 Nov. 1929, IP 23.

[126] Gandhi to Sarojini Naidu, and to Motilal, tels., 14 Nov. 1929, *CWMG* 42, pp. 162–3, and footnotes Motilal to Patel, tel., 15 Dec. 1929, MNP P16.

[127] Patel to Motilal, 2 Dec. 1929, MNP P16; Jinnah to Irwin, 3 Dec. 1929, IP 23; Jinnah to Sapru, 3 Dec. 1929, SP 31; Sapru to Jinnah, 5 Dec. 1929, SP J39; Sapru to Patel, 5 Dec. 1929, SP P18; Irwin to Sapru, 3 Dec. 1929, SP I14; Sapru to Mitter, 6, 12 Dec. 1929, SP M123/124; Sapru to Irwin, 13 Dec. 1929, SP I15; Sapru to Jinnah, 13 Dec. 1929, SP J40; Jinnah to Sapru, 14 Dec. 1929, SP J41; Sapru to Patel, 17 Dec. 1929, SP P19.

[128] Gandhi to Motilal, 30 Nov. 1929, *CWMG* 42, p. 224; Patel to Sapru, 2 Dec. 1929, SP

the 'presence of non-Congressmen with entirely different views will not help'.[129] Whereupon Gandhi suggested that Motilal should go on his own.[130] But Motilal quickly replied: 'Think your presence interview indispensable.'[131] Shortly afterwards the Viceroy, because of the charged atmosphere in Britain following the angry debates in Parliament on his declaration, became very perturbed about his own position following a report in the press that he had invited Gandhi and the others to see him.[132] In the end, however, everyone agreed that an official statement should simply state that it had been suggested to the Viceroy that he should invite five leaders to call upon him, and arrangements for such a meeting were made for 23 December when he was due to be back in Delhi.[133]

Throughout these weeks Sapru was insistent that the Government must make some additional gesture to enable Gandhi 'to hold the extreme wing in the Congress'.[134] On 9 December, Motilal told Vithalbhai Patel, however, that he did not believe the Government would make any concessions. 'At present', he affirmed, 'all roads lead to Lahore'.[135] By December, moreover, Motilal and Sapru were openly at odds with each other, as, from Sapru's point of view, Motilal was 'continuously . . . reviving the talk of "conditions"',[136] although, as we have seen, 'conditions precedent' had always hitherto been rejected. In addition the Congress newspapers were now markedly hardening against the Irwin declaration,[137] and in UP, Bombay, Bihar, Madras, and Bengal,

P17; Patel to Irwin, 2 Dec. 1929, *Vithalbhai Patel*, pp. 1067–8; Jinnah to Sapru, 3 Dec. 1929, SP 31; Thakurdas to Sapru, 6 Dec. 1929, ThP 91.
[129] Motilal to Gandhi, tel., 5 Dec. 1929, MNP G1; Motilal to Jawaharlal, 5 Dec. 1929, MN-JNC; Sapru to Jinnah, 5 Dec. 1929, SP 31; Motilal to Patel, 9 Dec. 1929, *Vithalbhai Patel*, pp. 1070–1. Gandhi had met Motilal for an hour at Rae Bareli on 21 Nov., *CWMG* 42, pp. 198–9.
[130] Gandhi to Motilal, tel., 6 Dec. 1929, *CWMG* 42, p. 244; Patel to Gandhi, Gandhi to Patel, tels., 9 Dec. 1929, *CWMG* 42, p. 253; Jinnah to Irwin, 14 Dec. 1929, IP 23; Jinnah to Sapru, 14 Dec. 1929, SP 31; Patel to Jinnah, 10 Dec. 1929, to Irwin, 11 Dec, to Patel, 12 Dec, *Vithalbhai Patel*, pp. 1071–3.
[131] Motilal to Gandhi, tel., 7 Dec. 1929, MNP G1; Sapru to Jinnah, 13 Dec. 1929, SP 31.
[132] Irwin to Sapru, 3 Dec. 1929, SP I14; Irwin to Benn, 12 Dec. 1929, IP 5; Sapru to Irwin, 13 Dec. 1929, SP I15; Irwin to Patel, 14 Dec. 1929, *Vithalbhai Patel*, pp. 1073–4; Shiva Rao to Sapru, 16 Dec. 1929, SP R74; Patel to Irwin, tels., 17, 18 Dec. 1929, G UP to V, tels., 18, 19 Dec. 1929, Sapru to Irwin, 19 Dec. 1929, Hailey to Irwin, 19 Dec. 1929, IP 23; Sapru to Jinnah, 19 Dec. 1929, SP J42; Sapru to Motilal, 19 Dec. 1929, SP N40; Sapru to Ramaswamy Aiyar, 20 Dec. 1929, SP A119; V to Sapru, nd, SP I20; Sapru to Motilal, nd, ibid. N41; G UP to G Punjab, nd, MNP G12.
[133] Sapru, Gandhi, and Jinnah to PSV, tels., 20 Dec. 1929, IP 23. For several letters at this point see *Vithalbhai Patel*, pp. 1074–82.
[134] Hailey to Irwin, 20 Nov., 4 Dec. 1929, IP 23; Sapru to Irwin, 25 Nov. 1929, SP I13.
[135] Motilal to Patel, 9 Dec. 1929, *Vithalbhai Patel*, pp. 1070–1.
[136] Hailey to Irwin, 19 Dec. 1929, IP 23; Sapru to Patel, 17 Dec. 1929, SP P19.
[137] FR mid Dec. 1929, H.Poll.17/29.

the Provincial Congress Committees had all come out against Irwin, with only Assam and the Punjab in his favour.[138]

Nevertheless the central issue still remained undetermined. In a heated debate at Monghyr, for example, the Bihar Provincial Congress Committee only had a majority of 36 for *purna swaraj* out of a total vote of 242.[139] There were leading Congressmen, moreover, who still held to the Delhi manifesto. Rangaswami Iyengar, the Editor of *The Hindu*, and a good friend of Motilal's, reverted, for example, at this moment to the idea of Dominion Status 'with safeguards'.[140] Whilst Malaviya was looking forward to an immediate amnesty for political prisoners, and, astonishingly, to a State Opening of a Dominion Parliament for India in February 1931.[141]

The upshot, however, still lay with Gandhi, and to judge from the amendments which were set down at Lahore the options before him were still quite numerous.[142] For example, the Congress leaders, before reaching any decision, might have explored things further with the Government,[143] which, despite the upheaval of the angry debates in London in November, had just seen, in December, a much more liberal motion by Fenner Brockway accepted without a division in the House of Commons.[144] Congress might, on the other hand, have declared for independence – but still gone to the Conference. Or a final decision about its future policy could have been postponed until after the Conference had been held – which in turn might only have been attended by those who believed in its efficacy. At Lahore Malaviya even advanced the forlorn hope that Congress should reconvene the All-Parties Conference which in 1928 had sponsored the Nehru Committee.[145]

More to the point, it is important to remember that within six months Gandhi from behind his prison walls at Yeravda was at Motilal's instance to enter into negotiations through intermediaries (Sapru and Jayakar) with the Viceroy, and that, while those talks failed, just eight months later he made his momentous Pact with Irwin which never even mentioned anything like a grant of independence but under which he undertook to

[138] Ibid., and FR end Dec. 1929, ibid.; *Times of India*, 13, 18 Nov. 1929.
[139] FR mid Dec. 1929, H.Poll.17/29.
[140] R. Iyengar to Motilal, 13 Dec. 1929, MNP I4(iii).
[141] Mears to Irwin, 11 Dec. 1929, IP 23.
[142] AICC 32/1929. See also Sir P. Pattani to Gandhi, tel., 22 Nov. 1929, AICC G113/1929.
[143] The Home Department of the GoI was not, it is true, in any mood to bargain, HD to PSV, tel., 3 Dec. 1929, H.Poll.299/29.
[144] A convenient summary is *Indian Quarterly Register*, July–Dec. 1929, pp. 455–60. Brockway to Benn, 21 Nov. 1929, HD to PSV, 30 Nov. 1929, H.Poll.299/29; Brockway to Editor, *Servant*, 27 Nov. 1929, StP 534; Malaviya to PSV, 20 Dec. 1929, IP 23; Sapru to Ramaswamy Aiyar, 20 Dec. 1929, SP A119.
[145] Malaviya's draft amendment, AICC 32/1929.

attend a Round Table Conference in London after all.[146] He was, moreover, to show himself grossly frustrated first later in 1931, and then
throughout 1933, when the Government from their side would not talk to
him.[147] At heart he was essentially a conference goer if ever there was one.
The chief, open, question in the Mahatma's mind in November and
December 1929, as his successive press articles readily demonstrate, was
accordingly whether the 'peace conference' which he always saw as the
climax to his agitations should be entered into now when it was offered, or
only when the satyagraha campaign which was otherwise due in 1930 –
but about whose vitality he was still very dubious – had occurred.[148] He
certainly wanted more than Irwin had set forth on 31 October.[149] So in
the end the significant sequence seems to have lain in Gandhi's successive
responses to Sapru's successive suggestions that more might be secured
from the Government – by going to the Conference; by inviting
Government to make a voluntary addition to their concessions; and then
by tackling the Viceroy direct. For over the weeks Gandhi was clearly
raising his bid, because, given his situation as he saw it, he had no alternative, since none of Sapru's earlier suggestions was likely to satisfy
Jawaharlal and the young men, and, at this particular juncture in the
unfolding nationalist saga, Gandhi became increasingly determined that,
even though he would not allow the young men to precipitate him into
premature action, if in the very last analysis anyone was to be overthrown,
it would have to be the old men, not the young ones.

On 3 December 1929, Sherwood Eddy, an American missionary, who
had seen Irwin, and then for three days Gandhi, wrote to the Viceroy to
say that the situation was 'far more serious than I had realised'. The four
points of the Delhi manifesto had now become firm conditions, and
Gandhi 'had little hope that an agreement could be reached'. Gandhi's
only remaining suggestion was that the British Prime Minister, Ramsay
Macdonald, should commit the Labour Government to staking its political life on effectively granting Dominion Status to India at the Round
Table Conference, but should say so in confidence to a few Indian leaders

---

[146] S. Gopal, *The Viceroyalty of Lord Irwin 1926–1931*, Oxford 1957, ch. VI.
[147] See ch. 5 below.
[148] E.g. 'Honest Differences', *Young India*, 21 Nov. 1929, *CWMG* 42, pp. 192–5; 'Some
Posers', *Navajivan*, 21 Nov. 1929, 'My Notes', *Navajivan*, 24 Nov. 1929, 'Some
Significant Questions', *Navajivan*, 8 Nov. 1929, *Navajivan*, pp. 202–5, 208–9, 428–51.
[149] E.g. Gandhi to Andrews, 19 Nov. 1929, *CWMG* 42, pp. 86–7. There is nothing to
suggest that the GoI was in any mind to make any further concessions, see HD to PSV,
tel., 3 Dec. 1929, V to SoS, 6 Dec. 1929, SoS to V, 9 Dec. 1929, HD to G UP, tel., 13
Dec. 1929, and to PSV, 15 Dec. 1929, H.Poll.299/29.

only.[150] No British Prime Minister could, of course, have done any such thing.

On 10 December, that shrewdest of Indian observers, Srinivasa Sastri, wrote to a friend:

Is Jawaharlal going to swallow Gandhi? No doubt in my mind that Gandhi will be feeling perfectly happy in that event. Sapru must prepare himself to eat the bitterest pill of his life.[151]

And a week later, J.M. Sen Gupta wrote a letter to Motilal Nehru from Calcutta which went straight to the heart of the matter as it stood by that time:

The biggest of all questions today to my mind [Sen Gupta wrote] is how to preserve the unity and solidarity of the Congress in the face of conflicting ideas, opinions and programmes. If the Congress splits up, everything goes. What might remain would not even be a shadow of the present Congress which commands the confidence of the country and the respect, if not fear, of its opponents. It cannot be gainsaid that a conflict between Youth and Age has begun in the Congress and that younger men are chafing at the restraints imposed upon them by the elders and are anxious to shake off the spirit of caution which has guided the activities of Congress . . . In order that the older leaders may be in a position to continue to guide and assist the younger men it is absolutely necessary to give effect to the Calcutta Congress resolutions at Lahore.[152]

That by early December 1929 had become very precisely Gandhi's view. By this time, moreover, Jawaharlal had spoken out vigorously against a settlement with the British in his presidential address to the Nagpur meeting of the Indian Trade Union Congress[153] (which had then proceeded to split). By early December, moreover, his presidential address for the Lahore meeting of the Indian National Congress had been written. It had been seen, amended and then approved by Motilal, and probably by Gandhi, whilst its purport was being very carefully kept secret from Sapru.[154]

There was still, however, the meeting to be held with the Viceroy.

Since 23 December, the day the party of five – Gandhi, Motilal, Sapru, Vithalbhai Patel, and Jinnah – was due to meet the Viceroy, was one of

---

[150] Sherwood Eddy to Irwin, 3 Dec. 1929, IP 23; Irwin to Benn, 12 Dec. 1929, IP5; Irwin to Benn, 12 Dec. 1929, tel., IP 10; Sapru to Natesan, 15 Dec. 1929, SP N18.

[151] Sastri to S. Aiyar, 10 Dec. 1929, *Letters of V.S.S. Sastri*, pp. 185–6.

[152] Sen Gupta to Motilal, 18 Dec. 1929, MNP S10(ii).

[153] For his presidential speech see *SWJN* 4, pp. 49–55. See also *Indian Quarterly Register*, July–Dec. 1929, pp. 424–9. For Sapru's anxiety as a consequence see Sapru to Jinnah, 5 Dec. 1929, SP 31; Sapru to Patel, 5 Dec. 1929, *Vithalbhai Patel*, pp. 1069–70.

[154] Sapru to Irwin, 13 Dec. 1929, SP 31; Hailey to Irwin, 19 Dec. 1929, IP 23; Sapru to Haksar, 15 Dec. 1929, SP H26.

Gandhi's days of silence, there was no discussion with the Mahatma beforehand. Nevertheless (so Sapru later recorded)

right up to half past three both Jinnah and I were talking to Pandit Motilal Nehru and we felt everything was going right. The only questions we discussed were those relating to political prisoners, the date of the Round Table Conference and the personnel. We were all agreed about them.[155]

Shown into the Viceroy's room at 4.30 pm the visitors began by expressing their very real sense of shock at the attempt that morning to blow up the Viceroy as his train had entered Delhi; but as they then turned to the business in hand it was immediately clear that Gandhi and Nehru were bent on a break.

'Mr Gandhi', Sapru wrote, 'took Jinnah, Patel and me by storm and held out an ultimatum to the Viceroy'.[156] At one point (so the Private Secretary to the Viceroy's extensive minutes recorded) 'a discussion then followed between Sir T.B. Sapru, Mr Jinnah and Mr Patel on the one side and Mr Gandhi and Pandit Motilal Nehru on the other'. At another – when Irwin referred to Hindu–Muslim differences – 'Mr Gandhi then said that . . . while India was disunited . . . and while there were these vast differences of opinion among his friends, there was no use in going to London unless they knew that the Viceroy and the British Government were with them'.[157]

I can't help feeling [the Viceroy bluntly told the Secretary of State shortly afterwards] that the main idea operating in their minds is that Indian differences are too deep seated either to be concealed or surmounted at any conference, and that participation therefore in a conference would leave them with their platform so badly riddled as to be incapable of reconstruction.[158]

Before long the talks broke down and that evening the official communique was descriptive but brief. It ended with the curt sentence: 'Conversation then concluded.'[159] The breach was now out in the open.

On the following morning Sapru wrote to the Viceroy giving vent to his bitter disappointment.[160] He then left for the annual meeting of the

---

[155] Sapru to Chhatari, 6 Jan. 1930, SP 1.   [156] Sapru to Ali Imam, 5 Jan. 1930, SP 2.

[157] Minutes by PSV, 23 Dec. 1929, MNP, V's Conference file, and SP P93–103. See also PSV to Sapru, 27 Dec. 1929, SP I19; Sapru to Cunningham, 4 Jan. 1929, SP I23.

[158] Irwin to Benn, 26 Dec. 1929, IP 5. See also Irwin to Halifax, 24 Dec. 1929, IP 27; V to SoS, tel., 24 Dec. 1929, IP 10; Sapru to Chhatari, 6 Jan. 1930, SP 1. Sapru told Ali Imam, 5 Jan. 1930, SP 2, that Gandhi had said: 'I cannot go to England. I am weak. That there were differences and divisions and enormous difficulties in the way.'

[159] *Indian Quarterly Register*, July–Dec. 1929, p. 52.

[160] Sapru to Irwin, 24 Dec. 1929, SP I17; Irwin to Sapru, 25 Dec. 1929, SP I18; Thakurdas to Sapru, 27 Dec. 1929, ThP 91; Sapru to Chhatari, 6 Jan. 1930, SP 1; Sapru to Ali Imam, 5 Jan. 1930, SP 2.

Liberal Party in Madras, where he made it plain that he at least would travel to London to attend the Round Table Conference.[161] The others meanwhile left for Lahore where soon afterwards Jawaharlal was riding into the Congress camp in Lahore on a white horse, and as the new year broke was dancing on the banks of the Ravi following the passage of the Congress Resolution confirming *purna swaraj* as its principal objective, and a civil disobedience campaign as its early intention.[162] Motilal was in Lahore too, plainly very embarrassed by the course he had recently taken, but by now riveted to 'the clarion call of the country'.[163] Gandhi was there as well, now exceedingly worried by the signs that violence might be taking control of his movement, and, while greatly relieved that he still held the initiative, remained quite undecided, as he had all the year long, about when and how the civil disobedience campaign, now due in the following months, should be launched.[164] In the event it was not until the third week of February 1930 that he hit upon the brilliant expedient of breaking the Salt Laws,[165] and only then that he set loose the great civil disobedience movement which, with an interval in 1931, lasted until 1933–4 – but never broke the hold of the British over India.[166]

There are two preliminary comments to be made here. A number of Jawaharlal's biographers imply, where they do not state, that in a crisis he always deferred to Gandhi.[167] The events of November–December 1929 lend some colour to this view. But such commentators overlook the fact that any such relationship was never one-sided; and the seeming corollary was not true – that Gandhi invariably forced Jawaharlal to defer to him. On the contrary, at this critical juncture at least, it was Gandhi who

[161] D.A. Low, 'Sir Tej Bahadur Sapru and the First Round Table Conference', in Low, ed., *Soundings in South Asian History*, London 1968, pp. 294–329.
[162] For his speeches at Lahore see *SWJN* 4, pp. 183–97.
[163] R. Iyengar to Motilal, 15 Mar. 1930, MNP I4(iv); Motilal to Ansari, 17 Feb. 1930, ibid. Ansari file. Cf. 'Rangaswami Iyengar . . . told me in confidence that not only he, but Ansari, Abul Kalam Azad, Sarojini Naidu, in fact all Pandit Motilal's intimate friends are feeling that he has let them down', Shiva Rao to Sapru, 9 Jan. 1930, SP 54.
[164] E.g. 'Interview to the Press', *Young India*, 30 Jan. 1930, 'The Cult of the Bomb', *Young India*, 2 Jan. 1930, *CWMG* 42, pp. 360–4. 'The fact is that we have still not arrived at definite and final conclusions about the precise method of the actual start', Motilal to B.C. Roy, 25 Feb. 1930, MNP R10.
[165] See more particularly D. Dalton, *Mahatma Gandhi. Nonviolent Power in Action*, New York 1993, ch. 4.
[166] Brown, *Gandhi and Civil Disobedience*, passim; D.A. Low, '"Civil Martial Law": The Government of India and the Civil Disobedience Movements, 1930–34', in Low, ed., *Congress and the Raj. Facets of the Indian Struggle 1917–1947*, London 1977, pp. 165–98.
[167] See e.g. M. Brecher, *Nehru. A Political Biography*, London 1959, index references under 'his relations with Mahatma Gandhi'.

deferred to Nehru. From this point onwards Jawaharlal therefore knew that whenever he was firmly convinced that his own judgment was correct, this could happen, and that made the relations between the two men much more subtle than is sometimes suggested.

At the same time there is a clear example here of Gandhi's quite extraordinary political skills. At a moment of crisis many another anti-imperialist movement has split. In the early 1930s Indonesia's nationalists became divided between Sukarno's Partindo and Hatta's PNI (Baru).[168] In 1947 Kwame Nkrumah broke with the United Gold Coast Convention and formed his own Convention People's Party.[169] In 1960 Kenya's nationalists divided into the Kenyan African National Union and the Kenyan African Democratic Union,[170] and so on. Back in 1907 the Indian National Congress had indeed split (for a decade at all events),[171] and then in 1918 saw the breakaway of the Moderates/Liberals.[172] But no such rift occurred during the three decades in which the Congress stood under Gandhi's leadership, and the events of late 1929 make it plain that this was not simply good fortune. It was palpably good management as well. Aside from the resignations of several individuals acting on their own and the open split in the former All-Parties Conference, Gandhi, to his own immense relief and the chagrin of the British, led an all but united, but potentially very divided, Indian National Congress across an ominous, yawning, generation gap. Had he misjudged or spurned his Jawaharlal it could so easily have been otherwise.

In the present context there are three more substantial points to be made. Looked at closely the Irwin declaration was a very carefully crafted announcement which, quite typically of the British – who were anxious both to hold on to their empire and to exemplify their own strongly held political principles – was deeply ambiguous too. Whilst it made some enticing promises about India's constitutional future and held out the unprecedented offer of a full-scale conference in London between 'representative' Indian politicians and British ministers, it quite deliberately ruled out any commitment, not just to the more radical Indian demands for full independence, but even to the more moderate desire of many Indian political leaders for early Dominion Status. As one of Jawaharlal's correspondents appositely remarked:

[168] Ingleson, *Road to Exile*, ch. 3.
[169] *The Autobiography of Kwame Nkrumah*, London 1957, chs. 6 and 7.
[170] G. Bennett and C. Rosberg, *The Kenyatta Election 1960–61*, London 1961.
[171] G. Johnson, *Provincial Politics and Indian Nationalism. Bombay and the Indian National Congress, 1880–1915*, Cambridge 1973, ch. 4.
[172] S.R. Mehrotra, *A History of the Indian National Congress*, vol. I, *1885–1918*, Delhi 1995, ch. 6.

I very much feel that the whole affair is very much sob stuff, for everything about it is indefinite & hollow . . . It is just the diplomatic ruse to draw away the peoples' mind from political agitation & also from the rousing idea of Independence.[173]

The initial response of a great many of India's political leaders was nevertheless remarkably positive. They soon became inextricably entwined, however, in an ardent debate about whether they should accept the offer of constitutional discussions in London along the lines Irwin had promised, or not. Sapru, Sastri, Malaviya, Jinnah, Jayakar, Vallabhbhai Patel, Vithalbhai Patel, Aney, Ansari, Birla, Moonje, Munshi, Kelkar, Rangaswami Iyengar, Khaliquzzaman – a significant array of political figures at the time if ever there was one – along with Indian nationalism's principal British supporters, Stokes, Charlie Andrews, Horace Alexander, Henry Polak, Fenner Brockway, and Colonel Wedgwood, all argued strongly that despite the all too evident weaknesses of the declaration the opportunities it opened up should be seized upon and exploited. On the other side Subhas Bose, Jawaharlal Nehru, Jamnadas Mehta, J.M. Sen Gupta and a great many others insisted, however, that its quite palpable shortcomings would fatally hamstring any attempt to secure India's principal nationalist demands in the foreseeable future.

There was no such debate in the Philippines. By this time there was never any doubt in the minds of its nationalist leaders as to whether they should travel to Washington to discuss Philippines' constitutional matters with their American counterparts whenever an opportune moment occurred. And for a very good reason too, which can best be illustrated by comparing the proceedings of the three Round Table Conferences on India that were held in London over the next few years with the series of negotiations that took place at essentially the same time between Philippines' delegations and American government and Congress leaders in Washington. Whilst in London some essentially limited changes in India's constitutional position were open for discussion, anything that smacked of independence, even of early Dominion Status, was still beyond the pale. In Washington in contrast early political independence for the Philippines was soon the principal item upon the agenda.[174]

Nor were there any such debates in these years in Vietnam or in Indonesia. Even the most modest of constitutional changes was in both cases quite out of the question. The thought, moreover, that the French might at this stage invite Vietnamese nationalist leaders to hold high-level discussions with them in Paris, or that the Dutch might offer to conduct

[173] Divekar to Jawaharlal, 11 Nov. 1929, AICC G40(i)/1929 I.
[174] Friend, *Between Two Empires*, Parts 2 and 3; Churchill, *Philippine Independence Missions*, chs. XI and XII.

constitutional negotiations with Indonesia's nationalist leaders in The Hague, was, quite simply, inconceivable.[175] In the Philippines, that is, there was no need for any such debate. In Vietnam and Indonesia there was never any occasion in these years for one. It was only in India that any such debate took place since only there did the ambiguity in the position of its imperial overlords raise such an issue for decision. These multiple differences reflected respectively the more accommodating stance of the United States towards independence for the Philippines; the adamant opposition to any such idea of the French in Vietnam and of the Dutch in Indonesia; and the patent ambiguity towards Indian independence in these years of the British.

It was this ambiguity that characteristically spawned the singular sequence of events which engulfed so many of India's principal political leaders in the last two months of 1929. Without that ambiguity the great debate into which they found themselves ineluctably drawn would never have occurred at all. It turned upon the question of which of the two voices in Britain's duality – its accommodating or its resistant one – should be heeded most. Neither was at all clear cut, so quite contrary conclusions were both arguably tenable. During the years that followed British ambiguity continued to pervade the momentous encounter between Indian nationalism and British imperialism to mark it out as the distinctive anti-colonial struggle that it was.

---

[175] Ingleson, *Road to Exile*, ch. 7; McAlister, *Vietnam*, chs. 4–7. These only occurred later in the very different circumstances following the end of the Second World War.

3   Holds barred: anatomy of a satyagraha, Lucknow, May 1930

I often picture to myself what would happen if we introduced the Mussolini system of government . . . We should, I presume, arrest everybody who made an anti-Government speech, close down all the Press, who supported the agitation, deport, intern, etc., etc., until no doubt at the end of a month or two we should probably succeed in creating a wilderness and calling it peace. Not, though, I think till we had had a good deal of shooting and that sort of thing . . . it would seem to me that the only result we should have achieved would have been to make our main problem of keeping India within the Empire a hundred times more difficult.   Irwin to Lord Mildmay, 23 January 1930

Out of four prisoners we had to kill three; out of ten we had to kill nine and only keep one for interrogation. These were our unwritten orders.
      Le Gallic, Legionnaire, 4th Bn, French Foreign Legion, Vietnam, 1931

On 12 March 1930 Gandhi set out from his Sabarmati Ashram at Ahmedabad on his march to Dandi on the Gujarat coast to start the Salt Satyagraha that was to launch the Civil Disobedience movement upon which Congress had decided at its Lahore Congress in the previous December.[1] Until shortly before it had still not been at all clear how Civil Disobedience was actually to be offered. On 26 January 1930 'Independence Day' had been celebrated in many parts of India. Everyone had then waited for Gandhi to determine both the form and the starting date of the struggle that was due. His tactics had now been revealed. He called on every Indian to manufacture salt. Since under India's British law salt manufacture was a government monopoly, that entailed a clear defiance of their edicts. As a commodity of importance not least to the poorest in the land, its illegal manufacture provided a striking symbol of the demand of Indians to be freed from British over-lordship. In a large numbers of places there accordingly ensued a whole series of confrontations between Congress supporters and the British.

Amongst the many clashes which occurred several became notorious.

---

[1] Dalton, *Mahatma Gandhi*, ch. 4.

On 21 April a group of Bengali terrorists stormed the Chittagong police armoury, and fought a pitched battle the next day on a nearby hill. Two days later widespread popular violence erupted in Peshawar in the North West Frontier Province, and imperial authority collapsed there for much of the next fortnight. Twelve days later martial law was declared in Sholapur in Maharashtra on 16 May when the situation passed out of British control for a while there as well. Thereafter, however, the most famous of these episodes occurred at Dharasna in western India from 21 May onwards when 3,000 Congress volunteers advanced upon the Government's salt works to offer Gandhian-style non-violent satyagraha, to be met by police with their metal-tipped staves (lathis) who beat them quite remorselessly. Three hundred serious casualties were counted, and the whole affair was widely reported in the world's press.[2]

As some of these episodes illustrated, civil disobedience periodically entailed violent clashes. Yet the commitment to Gandhi's satyagraha doctrine amongst very many of his followers was at once quite remarkable and very widespread. Not all of them sustained their initial enthusiasm for the illegal manufacture of salt, but overwhelmingly they did keep to non-violent civil disobedience and sought peaceful means to demonstrate their defiance of the British.

Satyagraha was so distinct a method by which to confront imperial rulers, and so closely associated with India's struggle, that the manner in which it was actually offered needs to be quite precisely discerned if the characteristic nature of the struggle is to be properly perceived. It is quite impractical of course to detail each of the hundreds of episodes which took place. What is offered here is a close look at just one sequence of the very many satyagraha confrontations that occurred to give some indication of what they could involve.

It happens that some quite detailed accounts are available of a series of episodes that culminated in two days of substantial confrontation in the city of Lucknow in northern India on 24–25 May 1930. This was by no means as large an affair as the others we have mentioned; nor as occurred over many more days in a place like Bombay.[3] It was, however, a much larger affair than generally occurred elsewhere and may, therefore, pass as a middle-of-the-range example of what a Gandhi-inspired Congress satyagraha actually entailed. It happens, moreover, that back in December 1928 Lucknow had seen a much more widely noticed affair, about which we have more extensive information, which helps to

[2] Brown, *Gandhi and Civil Disobedience*, ch. 3 provides a useful summary.
[3] J. Masselos, 'Audiences, Actors and Congress Dramas: Crowd Events in Bombay City in 1930', in J. Masselos, ed., *Struggling and Ruling. The Indian National Congress 1885–1985*, Delhi 1987, pp. 71–86.

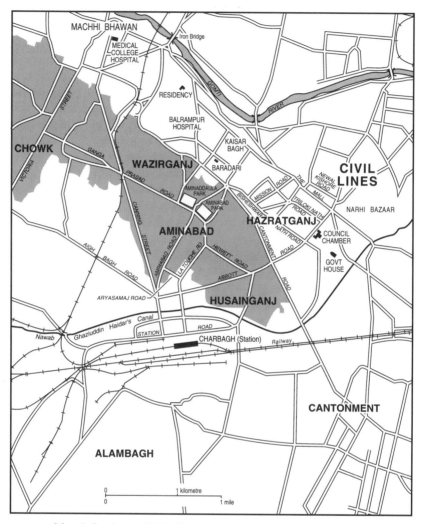

Map 2 Lucknow 1928–30

underscore the issues that arose in May 1930. Differing though they did
in some highly relevant respects, as we shall see, both took place in the
same general area of Lucknow city. The first raised issues that climaxed in
the second. Both turned, moreover, on the physical configurations of the
city, so it first becomes necessary to see how these were disposed.

Lucknow has its origins back in the far distant past. It lies to the southwest of some bends in the River Gomti, 300 miles east-southeast of Delhi.

Its original node was a small hillock, Lakshman Tila, which formed the core of the later Machhi Bhawan, the fort that commanded the ground between the original bazaar area, the Chowk, and the river. Even in the sixteenth century Lucknow seems to have flourished. Akbar greatly admired it, and not only made it the seat of the Governor of his Subah of Oudh, but took a considerable interest in its physical extension to the south. Already it was both a Hindu and a Muslim city, and Brahmins, Kayasths, Sheikhs, and Saiyids in particular made their homes there. Between 1747 and 1754, Oudh's Governor, Saadat Khan, rebuilt the Machhi Bhawan, and later, between 1775 and 1797, major extensions – including the great Imambara in the fort, a palace to the west, and several new neighbourhoods, notably Wazirganj to the east of the Chowk – were built by Asaf-ud-daula, who transferred the capital of his Nawabi of Oudh there from Fyzabad in 1775.

Over the next forty-five years Lucknow became a thriving commercial centre as skilled traditional craftsmen and traders were attracted to it as the administrative and commercial centre of the largest Indian state in north central India that was not under direct British control. And so the city grew once again.

For our present purposes the most important new extensions came as late as the mid-1840s when the then Nawab, Amjad Ali Shah, not only built the iron bridge over the Gomti adjacent to the fort, but developed Hazratganj, 'the market of His Highness', towards the river bend to the east of the main city; whilst his minister, Amin-ud-Daula, built the new Aminabad bazaar between that and Wazirganj and the Chowk to the west. Thereafter the great palace of the Kaisarbagh, with the audience hall, the Baradari, at its centre, came to be built by Nawab Wajid Ali Shah in those *fin-de-siècle* years before Oudh was finally annexed by the British in 1856.[4]

During the Mutiny and Revolt of 1857–8 which followed, Lucknow, with Delhi, became one of the two main storm centres. The saga of the beleaguered British garrison in the Residency in Lucknow became engraved in the annals of British rule in India. The consequences for Lucknow quite precisely set the scene for the story we have to tell. For major steps were taken thereafter to make certain that no British enclave there should ever suffer the same fate again.[5] Within half a mile of the Machhi Bhawan the old city was razed to the ground. Two wide roads

---

[4] H.R. Nevill, *Lucknow. Gazeteer,* Allahabad 1904, pp. 137–53; Abdul Halim Sharar, *Lucknow: The Last Phase of an Oriental Culture,* London 1975, pp. 60–3, 205–22; R. Llewellyn-Jones, ed., 'Lucknow before 1856', in K. Ballhatchet and J. Harrison, *The City in South Asia. Pre-Modern and Modern,* London 1980, ch. 5.

[5] On this whole fascinating story see V.T. Oldenburg, *The Making of Colonial Lucknow 1856–1977,* Princeton 1984.

were then driven through the Chowk – Victoria Street and Canning Street (named after Britain's Queen and the Governor-General) – so as to give quick access to its core. Thereafter police posts were built upon these that would be easy to reinforce from outside the main city, and from where the Chowk and the main Indian city could be more readily controlled. Lying between the fort and the Nawab's Kaisarbagh, the former much battered British Residency was left standing as a perpetual, deserted memorial to the eventual triumph of the British. The Kaisarbagh itself was handed over as a meeting place to the Taluqdars, the 'Barons', of Oudh, who whilst by no means always 'loyal', had at least in the last stages of the revolt transferred their allegiance to the British and thereby secured their hold upon their previously appropriated lands.

Thereafter the British established their main presence to the south and east of the core of the Indian city upon both sides of the Nawab Ghaziuddin Haidar canal which runs eastwards here to the Gomti. To its north they took over a good deal of Hazratganj, adjacent to the relatively recently built Aminabad bazaar. To the south, for their new and much more formidable military garrison, they built a large military Cantonment. And in between, parallel to and immediately to the south of the canal, they built their escape route, the railway line. This first reached Lucknow in 1862. The main railway station which was built here at Charbagh was deliberately constructed as a fort through which beleaguered British families could – should there be a next time – escape with their lives. Lucknow, that is, was quite deliberately reshaped in the aftermath of 1857 so as to preclude any recurrence of the events of that year. Thereafter for its Indian citizens it bore all the marks of an age-old Indian city that had been forced to bend its knee to its alien rulers.

Over the following decades Lucknow did not become the administrative headquarters of the (eventually named) United Provinces of Agra and Oudh which the British formed in 1877, but the Lieutenant-Governor took over a refurbished suburban Nawabi residence, and immediately to its north the British built for the provincial Legislative Council a Council House that served as well as a Secretariat. This stood on the broad Abbott Road that linked the southern ends of both Victoria and Canning Streets, and two through roads to Charbagh, with, at a right angle at its east end, the main shopping and business street, The Mall (which was often indeed simply called 'Hazratganj'). Here was the heart of Lucknow's much vaunted British Civil Lines, where one could find a number of British banks and business houses and several British missionary societies too, along with the city's administrative headquarters, the City Magistrate's court, the Post Office, and a number of 'English' hotels. Beyond the Kaisarbagh to the north, upon either side of the Residency, stood the main European Club, the Chief Court, and four or five hospitals. Here and to the east were the bungalows of the British civil community built so as to make middle-class life in the tropics as tolerable as possible.[6] All told these occupied the whole of the area between the river and the crowded bazaar areas of Aminabad, Wazirganj, and Chowk.

In the second half of the nineteenth and the first decades of the twentieth century Lucknow's economic status went through a double shuffle. On the one hand following not only the passing of the Nawabi, but the advent of the railway (which destroyed much of its river traffic), it lost much of its old commercial and artisanal primacy. But at the same time new road and rail connections soon gave it back some of the commercial and trading position it had enjoyed in the past, while the advent of new industry not only brought new employment but some prosperity too. A paper mill was opened in 1879. Iron and steel foundries began to be built, and flour, biscuit, printing and ice factories as well. The railway workshops, and the accompanying subcontractors, were particularly important. Furthermore, there was soon a great increase in the number of Indian clerks and officials, as well as the first new professional men – teachers, doctors, lawyers, journalists, many of whom were initially Bengalis. All this attracted a growing number of retail traders – cloth merchants, butchers, market gardeners, moneylenders, and so on; and the coolie labourers who toiled for them.

For our present purposes the changes that resulted from all of these developments had several important consequences. They shifted the city's centre of gravity from the Machhi Bhawan and the Chowk to several of the new areas towards the southeast. Traditional handicraft industries continued to be plied in the older parts, and in the Chowk the old established, and generally still very wealthy, Rastogi bankers and businessmen continued to live. But by 1921 the largest assemblage of city markets was to be found in Aminabad, and the main concentrations of the city's population were now to be found there and in the newer surrounding areas.[7] All this had a significant demographic and communal aspect. Whilst by the 1920s Muslims still comprised 50 per cent of the population of Chowk, in Aminabad and its environs they comprised only something between 29 per cent and 37 per cent.[8]

---

[6] A.D. King, *Colonial Urban Development. Culture, Social Power and Environment*, London 1976, ch. 6 (1), is especially helpful on this; also King, 'Colonialism and the Development of the Modern Asian City: Some Theoretical Considerations', in Ballhatchet and Harrison, *City in South Asia*, ch. 1.

[7] D.A. Thomas, 'Lucknow and Kanpur. Stagnation and Development under the Raj, 1880–1920', *South Asia*, New Ser., 5, 2, Dec. 1982, pp. 68–80. See also his University of Sydney M.A. thesis 1975, 'Lucknow and Kanpur, 1880–1920. Studies in Indian Urban History'.

[8] A.C. Turner, *Census of India 1931*, vol. XVIII, *United Provinces of Agra and Oudh*, Part I, *Report*, Allahabad 1933, Subsidiary Table V, Housing Statistics (Tenement Census) – (i) Lucknow Municipality, pp. 156–71.

The Lucknow Municipal Board had been considerably caught up in these developments. Created in 1862 and chaired at first *ex officio* by the city's Deputy Commissioner, it was composed after 1904 of twenty-four elected and eight nominated members, a number later increased to thirty-six. For twenty-seven years its leading figure was Ganga Prasad Verma, member of a prosperous Khattri family who owned and ran the local Urdu newspaper, *The Hindustani*. By the interwar period Muslim and Hindu chairmen alternated with each other. After 1919 the Board was closely associated with the Town Improvement Trust Committee, and was responsible for much of the new building (principally for the benefit of the city's wealthier Indian families) down La Touche and Hewett Roads and in the Civil Lines over to the east towards the Gomti.[9] That last extension had the very important consequence for our present purposes of turning the very much older Narhi bazaar into a distinctive enclave completely surrounded by the Civil Lines.

All this had a further consequence too. For whereas in the minds of the British the Civil Lines and Hazratganj were deemed to be essentially their parts of the city – refashioned as it had been in the aftermath of 1857 – not only did Indians own shops and businesses there (from which they served both the British and more well-to-do Indians), but large numbers of Indians lived there as well. The true dimensions of the situation were revealed in the 1931 census returns. These showed that whereas Hazratganj had 5,151 'Others' – and thus by implication more Europeans than anywhere else in the city – it also had 46,114 Hindus and 25,337 Muslims.[10] Whether or not it was thus a British quarter, or much more properly an Indian one, went, as we shall see, to the heart of the episodes we shall be recounting.

When the Indian National Congress was first launched in 1885, small meetings in its support, particularly among the Bengalis, began to be held in Lucknow. Before the decade was out there were many more. Over the turn of the century Ganga Prasad Verma, Lucknow's leading Municipal Commissioner, was also its principal Congress figure. In 1916 Lucknow saw meetings of the Indian National Congress and the All-India Muslim League which eventuated in the Lucknow Pact between them, and in 1921 it became the seat of UP's legislature.

[9] P. Geddes, *Town Planning in Lucknow. A Report for the Municipal Committee*, Lucknow 1916. For *inter alia* some details about the Municipality see S. Ganju, 'The Muslims of Lucknow – 1919–1939', in Ballhatchet and Harrison, *City in South Asia*, ch. 11.

[10] *District Gazetteer of the United Provinces of Agra and Oudh. Supplementary Notes and Statistics up to 1931–2. Lucknow District*, Allahabad 1934, Table II Population by Thanas 1931; R. Mukherjee and B. Singh, *Social Profiles of a Metropolis: Social and Economic Structure of Lucknow*, Lucknow 1956.

There followed at the end of the First World War the first of Gandhi's great satyagraha campaigns against the British. In the course of these Congress became strongly committed to Gandhi's doctrine of non-violence, to non-cooperation and ultimately to civil disobedience, and with that to a readiness to face not only physical repression but imprisonment. These first encounters between the British and the now Gandhi-led Congress were particularly marked by two searing occurrences: the massacre at the hands of British-led troops of a crowd of peaceful demonstrators in the Jallianwallah Bagh in Amritsar in April 1919, and the killing of policemen by a crowd of protesting demonstrators in a police post at Chauri Chaura in UP in February 1922.[11] The first led in part to the formulation of a British Government decision not to employ troops or overwhelming force against nationalist demonstrators if this could possibly be avoided; the second to Gandhi calling off the Non-Cooperation movement of 1920–2 when it erupted in onslaughts he could not support.[12] But at the same time the latter provided a warning to Indian police in British service of what they could expect when faced by a crowd that was greatly aroused. Both cast their shadows across events in Lucknow in May 1930 as we shall see.

The mid-1920s were then doldrum years for the Indian national movement. But a change came in 1927 when the British Government established the Commission under Sir John Simon to report on India's constitutional future to which no Indians were appointed. Congress's riposte to this was double barrelled. With the support of various other political bodies it established its own Nehru Committee to draft a future Indian constitution for itself, and it promoted both a boycott of the Commission and demonstrations against it when it visited India.[13] One of the most famous of the ensuing episodes occurred in Lucknow on 30 December 1928. The background can be recounted in some detail.[14]

It was proceeded by a series of meetings, processions and confrontations in the city which were designed (as the younger Nehru put it) 'both as propaganda and as rehearsals for the actual show'. These all took place (as did the later episodes in May 1930) in the Aminabad/Hazratganj areas of the city (to which we have referred). They did not touch the Chowk,

---

[11] Shahid Amin, *Event, Metaphor, Memory. Chauri Chaura 1922–1992*, Delhi 1995 contains an arresting account of this whole saga.

[12] Low, 'The Government of India and the First Non-Co-operation Movement, 1920–2'.

[13] E.g. B. Stoddart, 'The Unwanted Commission: National Agitation and Local Politics in Madras City, 1928', *South Asia*, 5, Dec. 1975, pp. 48–65.

[14] The following account is based on the extensive note by G.W. Gwynne, 5 Dec. 1928, in CS UP to Sec. HD, GoI, 11 Dec. 1928, and idem to idem (along with further enclosures), 20 Dec. 1928, H. Poll.130/29, together with *SWJN* 3, pp. 106–22, and J. Nehru, *An Autobiography*, London 1936, ch. XXV.

nor the area around Machhi Bhawan. Lucknow's Congress politics were now centred in Aminabad. Here were two open spaces, both named after its nineteenth-century builder. In one, Aminabad Park, the Congress held its meetings. By the side of the other, Aminuddaula Park, Congress had its office. Immediately to the east stood Hazratganj, the core of the Civil Lines, the special preserve, as the British saw it, of the ruling race. Whilst there was never any initial intention on either side to provoke a conflict – and much effort went into preventing it – nevertheless the ground was clearly laid for a clash between all that was new in Lucknow's urban growth over the past half century or so, and the British vision of the special privileges which were theirs here as of right.

The critical events in 1928 began on 17 November when C.W. Gwynne, the British Deputy Commissioner in charge of Lucknow, received information that the city's Boycott committee (in which Congress predominated but in which other parties shared) was proposing to take out a 'black flag' procession to protest against the impending visit to the city of the Simon Commission.[15] Gwynne made no objection to such a procession so long as a police licence for it had been secured. The committee's chairman, Lucknow's leading Congressman, Mohanlal Saxena (who had been amongst those who had captured the Municipality for the Congress back in 1923), was at this point quite prepared to ask for this, and the city's Superintendent of Police duly issued a licence for the route he had proposed. On 18 November news, however, was received that the veteran Punjabi Congressman, Lajpat Rai, had died after being struck by the police during an earlier anti-Simon demonstration in Lahore. The procession was accordingly cancelled and a condolence meeting was held in Aminabad Park instead.

Over the following days the boycott leaders evidently planned their next moves with considerable care. Their main concern seems to have been to generate support for their cause by leading recruiting processions through key areas of the city. Printed leaflets were at all events issued announcing new procession routes for 23, 24 and 27 November. No permission was sought for these from the British authorities, and when Gwynne saw copies of the leaflets, he refused to grant permission for the routes proposed. However, he readily granted permits for the processions of 23 and 24 November for the route agreed upon for the cancelled pro-

---

[15] Gwynne had been involved in the Hindu–Muslim conflicts in Lucknow which had included a major communal riot back in September 1924 in which two people were killed and 163 injured, see D. Page, *Prelude to Partition*, Delhi 1982, pp. 78–80. There was no recrudescence of these in the course of the events addressed here, though the care (see below) which the Congress leaders seem to have taken to avoid leading their recruiting processions through the strongly Muslim-populated Chowk suggests they were being cautious here.

cession on the eighteenth, and then added: 'as regards the procession on the 27th, I suggest you devise any route which does not come into the Civil Lines as no procession can be allowed there'. For the time being Saxena and his committee were ready to settle for this, and on 23 and 24 November they took their processions through the southern streets of Aminabad as had been agreed.

We may note here very particularly exactly where they went. Starting at Aminuddaula Park they moved along Aminabad Road in the direction of the railway station. Before reaching there they turned left into Arya Samaj Road and then moved up La Touche Road to the Kaisarbagh crossing on their way back to the Congress office on the edge of Aminuddaula Park. Since they thus confined themselves entirely to Aminabad, and did not at any point touch on the Civil Lines, these first two processions were allowed to proceed by Lucknow's British rulers without any interference.

On the next evening, of Sunday 25 November, a large public meeting was held in Aminuddaula Park.[16] This was addressed by Jawaharlal Nehru. He himself had already organised a highly successful hartal (closing of shops) against the Simon Commission in his own city of Allahabad earlier in the year, and he was evidently concerned that the Lucknow campaign was not being pressed as vigorously as it might have been. He now issued a rousing appeal to Lucknow's university students to 'take full part in the boycott demonstrations', and in commenting upon Lajpat Rai's death proceeded to ask: 'Is the honour of your country nought that it can be kicked in the dust by policemen clad in the livery of our alien rulers?' Gwynne understandably believed that he was stirring the pot. It was to be a day or two more, however, before it spilled over.

On the following day, 26 November, the British authorities were informed that the boycotters would that evening be taking out a further procession along a new route through the smaller Husainganj bazaar area immediately to the south of Aminabad. Evidently this was designed to expand the boycotters' support beyond that secured by the Aminabad processions. But Gwynne was happy to agree to it.

There is not the slightest official objection [he told the Boycott committee] to your procession and demonstration in an orderly manner on this or any other occasion provided your Committee follows the rules and regulations on the subject of processions in force for some years in Lucknow for all communities in the interest of law and order.

[16] More information might have been provided here and in the pages that follow about 'faces in the crowd', had this been readily forthcoming, but in relation to the issues with which this (already lengthy) chapter is concerned it was precisely their emblematic anonymity that counted.

To which Saxena replied:

My committee is glad to learn that this is the official attitude in regard to our demonstrations. So far as we are concerned, we desire perfectly orderly and disciplined demonstrations and I have no doubts that we shall succeed in this if no unnecessary restrictions are placed.

On 26 November the boycotters accordingly began a march near one of the bridges across the Haidar canal, which then went via Abbott Road into and through Husainganj bazaar before proceeding again along Abbott Road as far as Triloki Nath Road on its way back to the Congress office via the Kaisarbagh crossing, and Aminabad Road. This was clearly a sizeable procession.

Gwynne now realised he had made a mistake. The procession had passed 'through a portion of the city which is technically within the Civil Lines'. By going up Abbott Road before turning left into Triloki Nath Road it had passed in front of the Council House. Gwynne excused his oversight to his superiors by saying that his

intention all along was to prevent a demonstration in front of the Council Chamber or at Hazratganj . . . The time proposed was the evening during which time the shops do their best business and business would thus be materially hampered.

But he was clearly troubled by the decision he had made:

it was this particular portion of the Civil Lines which I had in mind [he went on] and which in my opinion should be kept free from this form of demonstration. A good deal depends on whether we are right in refusing permission to go through this particular quarter. My reasons are: (1) processions are not allowed in this quarter, (2) I was unwilling to give a precedent on which the Swarajists could base a demand at a later date to take a procession right up to the Council Chamber, and I am convinced that the more we give way the more they would demand; (3) this is the European business quarter. It has absolutely no interest in these demonstrations.

His discomfiture clearly led him to stiffen his attitude, and the studied politenesses of a day or two previously began to evaporate.

On 27 November the Boycott committee announced that it would not take out the procession they had originally planned for that day. Instead, so they now told the Superintendent of Police, they would take out a further procession on 28 November, and once again in a new direction. Since they had already woven their way through Aminabad, and then through Husainganj, it was hardly surprising that they should now have planned that their next recruiting procession should go northeastwards to Narhi, the small bazaar area ensconced within the Civil Lines. To get there it would be necessary to go through a part at least of Hazratganj. In seeking the necessary police permission for this, Saxena, however, affirmed that after setting out from the Congress office they would go via Bisheshwar Nath Road to the Lal Bagh, but would then go straight across The Mall, and proceed by the back road, Newal Kishore Road, to Narhi, and then return later along Abbott Road as far as the Husainganj crossing, before turning right into Hewett Road and then back to the Congress office via Sri Ram Road.

But Gwynne, perceiving therefrom that this new procession would intrude much more substantially upon the hallowed precincts of Hazratganj than before, and fearful that it would be even larger than the earlier ones, quickly made it plain he would have nothing of it.

I am sorry [he had his Police Superintendent tell Saxena] but the route proposed by you cannot be sanctioned as no procession can be allowed to go down or across Hazratganj.

And so as to prevent any repetition of his lapse of 26 November, he then specifically added:

As regards Abbott Road there is no objection to your including in your route the part which your procession of the 26th passed, but it cannot come nearer Hazratganj than the Burlington Hotel crossing.

That meant that whatever may have happened on 26 November, no further procession was to be allowed in the Civil Lines past the Council Chamber – and as we shall see he here precisely paved the way for the later major clash in Lucknow in 1930.

His response to Saxena immediately raised the tension, for Saxena felt he had done everything he could to meet British sensibilities.

I myself [he protested] had arranged the route in such a way that there may be very little interference with the traffic on the Mall. I therefore fail to see the reason why you should have thought fit to disallow the procession down or across Hazratganj . . . I assure you that I shall try to take the procession across the Mall as quickly as possible.

But Gwynne was adamant. He interpreted Saxena's letter as 'in effect a challenge to our authority', and as the time when the procession would start was now coming close he sent a police force to Aminabad under his City Magistrate – an Indian officer named Ainuddin – to bring it to a halt. Ainuddin had a discussion with Saxena and two of his associates near the Congress office, and gave them written instructions to say that they were not to lead out the procession as they had proposed. Saxena riposted by saying that the Police Act only required that a licence for a procession should be sought, not that one should actually be issued, and the procession then began to move forward.

But its way was barred by mounted police. Stones began to fly, and before very long the police began to belabour the crowd with their lathis. A considerable fracas then ensued in which Saxena and a number of others were badly hurt. Soon Gwynne arrived, expostulated to Saxena, and because the curbs the police successfully imposed on the procession now brought it to a halt it eventually reverted to being a meeting in Aminabad Park.

The following day, 29 November, was clearly going to be a very difficult one. In accordance with an AICC instruction Lucknow's Congress-dominated Municipal Board had declared that all schools and offices should be closed in protest against the Simon Commission and in memory of Lajpat Rai. In the course of the morning Jawaharlal Nehru, who overnight had heard of the clash on the previous evening, arrived by train from Allahabad, whither he had returned after the meeting on the previous Sunday. Along with several leading Congressmen including G.B. Pant, Khaliquzzaman and H.N. Misra, he went immediately to a small meeting which had been called that day in Narhi. At its conclusion he and several others made arrangements to go to the Lajpat Rai Day meeting that was to be held that evening in Aminuddaula Park. Since it would not be easy to organise an orderly procession at short notice, they decided to go there in small parties of a dozen or so, and – as Nehru himself put it – 'in order to avoid any blocking of traffic or any conflict with the police' go along Newal Kishore Road and then directly across The Mall and 'not to go through Hazratganj, which is the main European shopping quarter'. Saxena's earlier caution about not obtruding upon Hazratganj was here being firmly repeated. But when an Assistant Superintendent of Police, who was present in Narhi, learnt of these plans, he sought to forbid them, and he and Nehru had a curt exchange. In view of all that Nehru had heard previously of the clash with the police on the evening before he was in no mood to parley, and soon he and Pant led out the first parties from Narhi.

The next thing they knew they were being ridden down in Newal Kishore Road by mounted police wielding batons. For Nehru and a number of others who were present this was their first experience of being personally assaulted in this way, and the memory of it – and in Pant's case the injuries – lived with them for ever afterwards.

The small parties halted and sat down in the road. Gwynne then arrived, and there was a protracted argument. He had, he said (in flat contradiction to all he had said earlier), no objection to the parties proceeding as they had originally intended; but they had to secure formal permission for this before doing so. Nehru later recorded:

We told him after police behaviour on two occasions we were not prepared to ask for any formal permission. Thereupon he suggested that he would be satisfied by an oral request, but that too we were not prepared to make. Ultimately he even said he was prepared to treat our conversation as an oral request if we were also prepared to treat it as such. We were unable, however, to agree to this.

A large crowd began to gather, and Gwynne was soon in two minds as to what to do next. Eventually after an hour or so, Pant (according to Gwynne, though there may be some elision here) remarked that 'they would not proceed without permission, and wanted to go'. Gwynne seized upon this as sufficiently meeting his purpose (it was, as Nehru remarked, 'entirely a matter of prestige on either side'), and thereupon gave permission for the procession to proceed. The onlookers were instructed to go by the side roads to Aminabad. But three of the parties from Narhi (contrary, so Gwynne averred, to an explicit agreement) then marched right along The Mall all the way to the Kaisarbagh, 'preceded', as Nehru recorded, 'by the mounted police as a kind of guard of honour in a kind of triumphal march'. They stopped for some while outside Gwynne's own house shouting hostile slogans, and then joined up with a highly excited meeting in Aminuddaula Park.

Gwynne was later to explain to his superiors that he had in the end decided to let the procession proceed because he

did not wish to have a fracas in this quarter of the town, in the European trading centre, at the busy time of the evening and I thought it advisable to get the crowds away. I also wished to help the demonstrators to reach their destination as they wished to participate in a public meeting.

The truth, however, was that whilst Nehru and his associates had suffered a good deal of physical hurt in Newal Kishore Road, they had thereafter, by their refusal to fall in with Gwynne's requirements, and by their triumphal march along The Mall, twisted the lion's tail a great deal more severely than Gwynne or his Superintendent of Police found easy to bear.

The next morning the Simon Commission was due to arrive at the railway station at 8 am. Nehru was probably well warranted in suggesting that after the humiliation Gwynne and his police officers had suffered in Hazratganj the day before, they were now 'nettled', and liable to take any opportunity to reassert their preeminence.

Gwynne, however, had firmly committed himself in the preceding days – in full accord with the UP Government's policy – to allowing a demonstration against the Simon Commission to take place on its arrival in Lucknow. Back on 25 November Saxena had asked him what restrictions if any do you propose to impose on the day the Commission arrives here. I may tell you that we are willing to observe any reasonable orders to regulate traffic so long as we are allowed to hold a black flag demonstration somewhere near the route, or the station within a reasonable distance.

At Gwynne's instance the Superintendent of Police had replied suggesting that the demonstrators should go from the Congress office down La Touche Road direct to the railway station,

where I will allot you a place on the route on the vacant land in front of the station where the members of your procession can congregate and demonstrate.

There had been further exchanges on 27 and 28 November about the exact time of the Commission's arrival, and on 29 November Gwynne had gone so far as to ask Saxena

if you will kindly let me know where you wish to demonstrate near the station . . . so that I can if possible allot ground for the purpose.

That evening Saxena informed him that the Congress procession would go via La Touche Road and form up on the open space behind 'Mr A.P. Sen's bungalow facing Station Road'. Here they would be able to demonstrate against the Commission as it passed in its cars on the way to the Civil Lines.

But Gwynne now had other ideas. Because he had already allotted land in that area to 'the depressed classes' and to the Muslims, the Congress demonstrators would have to confine themselves, so he declared, to an area to the right of the mouth of La Touche Road – opposite where the Commission would enter their cars, but not along their route, and actually about 200 yards distant from them. Not surprisingly Saxena found this quite unacceptable, and not surprisingly too – particularly in view of the emotions which had been aroused on both sides by the events of 28 and 29 November – there was a major clash at the Charbagh on 30 November.

The police were on duty at the railway station at 5.30 am. During the night Nehru and others had tried to persuade the leaders of the 'depressed class' to agree to a reallocation of territory between them. But they were evidently baulked by an intervention by Gwynne. They tried again with Gwynne himself at about 7 am the next morning. There was, they said, plenty of more suitable land still available. But Gwynne (so later Nehru recorded) answered 'gruffly . . . that he was not prepared to argue and that his orders must be carried out'. By now the Congress processionists numbering a thousand or so, who had left the Congress office at about 6 am and had marched down through Aminabad, were standing to the left of the mouth of La Touche Road where their leaders had led

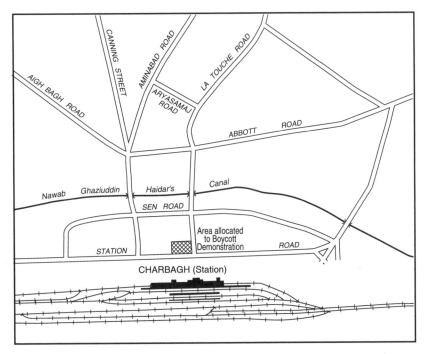

Map 3 Simon Commission demonstration, Lucknow, 30 November
1928

them, rather than in the patch to the right which Gwynne had allocated to
them. Soon the accompanying crowd, eventually of some tens of thousands (Congress's recruiting efforts had evidently been remarkably
successful), was spilling into the area well beyond this. All this made a
mockery of the arrangements that Gwynne had made; and that broke the
dam. Gwynne and his police officers were not merely infuriated. They
were increasingly worried lest by the time the Simon Commission arrived
the situation should have passed out of their control. So, from the east end
of the long open space between the railway and the city, they launched the
full force of their foot and mounted police against the Congress demonstrators and the attending crowd, so as to clear the roadways and much of
the adjacent ground.

There followed the famous fracas outside the railway station at
Lucknow in the hour before the Commission reached the city, in which
Nehru and a great many others suffered severe and long-remembered
beatings. British prestige no doubt was upheld. The Simon Commission
passed on its way to the Civil Lines without personal mishap. But the

Congress purpose was greatly served as well. There were not only processions and meetings throughout the day in Aminabad, and a large mass meeting that evening, but the episode was widely reported both in India and abroad. As Nehru told the press a few days later:

I have not the slightest grievance against the government and officials in Lucknow . . . they had completely played into the hands of the boycotters. They had brought the issues before the people . . . that British rule in India means the policeman's baton.

There had earlier been similar occurrences in several other places (as, for example, in Lahore where Lajpat Rai had been so severely beaten). In UP there was a further demonstration against Simon and his colleagues in Agra on 28 November, and a much more substantial one in Kanpur on 3 December.

On 5 December the Commission were back in Lucknow for a garden party given in their honour in the Kaisarbagh by those arch-supporters of the British Raj in the province, the Taluqdars of Oudh. Gwynne was greatly concerned as to what might occur this time. His chief anxiety was that Congress would send a procession of women to the Kaisarbagh, which he would find it impossible to stop without a major fracas. But this did not eventuate. Instead protest meetings were held outside the Congress office in Aminabad, and at Narhi, and to Gwynne's annoyance the elaborate police precautions he had taken to cordon off the Kaisarbagh, whilst generally successful in letting the garden party gather peacefully, not only angered the influential Maharajah of Mahmudabad whose house stood nearby, and who felt himself to have been inconvenienced. They failed to anticipate both a rowdy Congress demonstration from a nearby house as the party got under way, and the flying of a kite bearing the boycotters' slogan 'Simon Go Back' whilst it was in train. With the Commission's departure from Lucknow, this trail of events, however, came to an end.

They bore half a dozen characteristics which require noting. In the early stages of the build-up to the events on 30 November there was a series of processions and meetings which were principally designed to recruit participants for the final demonstration at the railway station. The processions did not go into the old Chowk area at all; evidently that was not thought to be a good recruiting ground for Congress's activities. Several processions went instead through the main part of the relatively new neighbourhood of Aminabad, and one went to Husainganj. Efforts were then made to enlist supporters in Narhi – with results which markedly heightened the tempo of events.

Throughout these early stages remarkably civil exchanges took place between Lucknow's British officials and the Boycott committee. Whilst the committee was not overly meticulous in the approaches it made for the necessary licences to hold processions, it made little objection to having to do this. The British for their part pressed the point that permission was required, but so long as the routes proposed were confined to the Indian bazaar areas of the city, they gave this fairly freely. None of the episodes was designed on the Congress side at this stage as a deliberate confrontation. The most that was planned for the climax was a noisy demonstration against the Simon Commission when it made its visit to the city.

It is thus most striking that the precipitant of the conflicts which did occur concerned Congress's threatened and then actual intrusions upon the forbidden territory of Hazratganj and the Civil Lines, the hitherto quarantined preserve of Lucknow's imperial masters. It was Gwynne's refusal to contemplate even so minor, and, if one was to march to Narhi from Aminabad, unavoidable an intrusion upon the Civil Lines that precipitated the fracas on 28 November. It was the corresponding action of his Assistant Superintendent of Police which precipitated the assault upon Nehru and his party in Newal Kishore Road the next day. Gwynne justified his refusal to countenance the proposed intrusions upon Hazratganj by reference to the annoyance these would cause to those who lived and worked there (and one can easily imagine the social pressure he will have been under from his own countrymen in Lucknow on this score). But the symbolism of what was involved here is highly revealing. It may be that memories of the Mutiny, and of the steps taken to reconstruct Lucknow in its aftermath, were not part of Gwynne's conscious calculus. But reshaped as the city had been as a consequence of 1857, the Congress threat was not just to a few businessmen and shoppers. It involved *au fond* – as was indeed very widely recognised – a highly symbolic challenge to the essential prestige on which British rule in India was always so dependent.

It is in this connection then especially striking that in 1928 both Saxena and to a marked extent even Jawaharlal Nehru himself deliberately tried to limit the boycotters' intrusions upon the British preserve. Even on 29 November (the day before the station clash), despite the police assault on the evening before, Nehru and his fellows at the Narhi meeting still strove to obviate any direct challenge to British sensitivities about Hazratganj by not organising too salient a procession through it, and by as far as possible using the back streets such as Newal Kishore Road on their way over to Aminabad. On both occasions the processions started out – so they were not completely cowed. But the caution Congress leaders twice displayed provides eloquent testimony to the degree to which the rules which the British laid down still prevailed.

The irony then was that because Gwynne was worried that unless he let the Narhi groups proceed there could be a full-scale riot in Hazratganj just at the peak of its European shopping hour, the Congress had a quite unplanned triumph, when their Narhi parties marched through Hazratganj itself, escorted by the police who less than two hours before had been riding them down. That was so evidently a major blow to British prestige that the scene was then set, not only for a new unwillingness on both sides to be accommodating, but for the Congress's refusal to obey British instructions the next morning, and for the onslaughts of the police at the railway station which then ensued.

It transpires, that is, that the basic precipitant of the famous episode outside Lucknow's railway station in November 1928 was not so much the visit to the city by the Simon Commission, but the highly charged issue of intrusions by the Congress upon the sanctity of the British Civil Lines there.

At the same time one can begin to glean in these 1928 episodes a remarkably clear picture of the kinds of pressures under which India's nationalists laboured as they mounted their campaigns against their British overlords. Congress's dedicated core in Lucknow city now had the resources to organise a city office and a modicum of party workers to manage its affairs and plan its activities. They seemed well seized, more-over, of the precise methods by which they could drum up local support (and, by not venturing into Chowk, of knowing where this might well not be forthcoming). But in Lucknow's British administration they faced a classic British posture. Subject to the strict limits which the British care-fully laid down, Congress was permitted to recruit support for and hold demonstrations against them. But woe betide it if it in any way trans-gressed these, even unavoidably, particularly if a prime symbol of British superordination was in any way trenched upon. If it happened, moreover, that the imperial rulers were then momentarily bettered, the chances were high that they would take an early opportunity to turn the tables on them.

It is at the same time no less remarkable that when, over three succes-sive days, police onslaughts were launched against them both the Congress members and its multitude of supporters remained overwhelm-ingly staunch in their adherence to the doctrines of non-violence which Gandhi had taught them. As Gandhi himself wired to Nehru following the Charbagh affair: 'It was all nobly done'.[17] Clearly the police used considerable violence, both when riding them down, and, more generally, by beating them about the head and body with that fearsome weapon, the

---

[17] See facsimile of Gandhi to Nehru, 3 Dec. 1928, Nehru, *Bunch of Old Letters*, facing p. 56.

metal-tipped bamboo stave, the lathi. But Congressmen used next to no violence against them in reply.

Three other things are notable as well. These assaults were not launched against a noisy procession or a rowdy demonstration; the British conceded the legitimacy of both such proceedings. Whilst, of course, many were hurt, no one was killed. Above all, whilst the large Lucknow cantonment stood just a mile away from where the clashes took place, its resources were never called upon by the British, even to recover the situation created by the march up The Mall. If Gandhi's lessons had thus been quite astonishingly well learned on the Congress side, the lessons of Jallianwallah Bagh had been evidently well absorbed on the British side as well.

One can at the same time see in these 1928 episodes the acute pressures under which the thin red line of British officials found themselves labouring. For all their efforts to play by the book, and to be as reasonably accommodating as possible, nationalist activities did not simply raise questions for them of public order in a busy city. Ultimately they were directed against the very presence of British rule in India itself. As a consequence it was always necessary for British officialdom to be on the *qui vive*, and there were eventually inescapable limits to the transgressing of its orders which it could possibly allow.

But when and where, in their shoes, did one draw the line? At the outset – as the Government of India was soon inclined to think? When the edge of Hazratganj had been crossed – Gwynne at first let this happen, but soon felt it necessary to justify himself for doing so? So soon as Congress sought to lead a procession across the *via sacra* of The Mall? But since processions were allowed down The Mall on other occasions – religious ones for example – could one really be quite so absolute about this? Since in the end the issue was that crucial one, the maintenance of British prestige, no such occasion could be treated at all lightly. Yet it was necessary to take care lest one's decisions suddenly turned a mere episode into a major riot – especially at the wrong time and in the wrong place. There were moments therefore when British officers swallowed their pride, whatever they may have been moved to do afterwards. And if they had to use force, because of past experience, they knew that it was vital to put from their minds, except in quite dire circumstances, the possibility of calling in troops, however close these might be to hand.

In confronting these questions British officials were generally of the calibre, and enjoyed the self-confidence, to take them in their stride. But it would be quite unwarranted to imply that episodes of this kind did not place very considerable pressures upon them. On four successive occasions Gwynne clearly fretted, if he did not indeed become rattled: after letting the 26 November procession move past the Council Chamber; in Newal Kishore Road on 29 November; outside the railway station on 30 November; and on 5 December, the day of the Taluqdars' garden party. Of his own final comments two were probably characteristic of the general British position at the time:

Should we have held the agitation in check [he asked] if we had yielded at every turn to the Congress' demands? I feel sure that had we done so . . . a far more difficult situation would have arisen . . . to control.

And on his refusal to allow the demonstrators to go closer to the railway station on 30 November, he averred:

I had nothing but the word of Mr Jahawir Nehru and Mr Mohan Lal Saxena that their followers would remain quietly behind the police cordon . . . I do not say such promises are deliberately broken, but merely that men of this stamp have no control over . . . their followers . . . when they have aroused feelings of excitement.

Sixteen months later there occurred the further series of episodes in Lucknow city that are the principal interest of this chapter.[18] These have not been nearly so widely noticed as these earlier ones in 1928. Prominent national figures were not involved, and for all their potency by 1930 they did not much stand out amidst the onrush of so many other episodes at that time. The clashes which occurred in Lucknow in May 1930 were, however, much more substantial than those in 1928, and reached their climax not with two unsought for spectaculars, a noisy demonstration and a mounted police charge, but with a carefully structured confrontation, that was deliberately provoked upon both sides. This led to well over one hundred people needing medical attention, the despatch of British troops to the heart of Aminabad to maintain the British position there (in a way that had never even been thought of in 1928), an assault by a city crowd on a police post in the depths of Aminabad (in a way that Gandhi would never have sanctioned), its check by police firing, followed by something of a police rampage, during which four people were killed and a good deal of looting took place. These events led both to an enquiry by a committee of prominent local citizens and to an official British enquiry

---

[18] The account which follows is based on 'Mr. L.S. White's report on the incidents which occurred in Lucknow on May 25 and 26, 1930', 16 June 1930, and his Note, 5 June 1930, in CS UP to Sec.HD, GoI, 10 July 1930; Ma to Hoyle, 21 Apr. 1930; Kidwai to Munro (two letters), 14 May 1930; Munro to Kidwai, 14 May 1930; Kidwai to Irwin, 15 May, 5 June 1930; Munro's press communiques, 26, 27 May 1930, in UP to HD, 2 tels., 27 May 1930, H. Poll.249/30, together with contemporary reports in *The Pioneer*, 18 May–17 July 1930, and in *The Leader*, 17 May–1 June, 15–18 June 1930, along with press coverage of the evidence to Mr White's enquiry, *The Leader*, 7–15 June 1930.

that publicly recorded evidence over several days. On almost every count these events were a good deal more serious than those we have outlined above. At the same time the striking fact is that they occurred in precisely the same general area of the city; erupted on the same question of the special position for the British of Lucknow's Civil Lines and all which that implied; and in many ways simply involved an escalation of the conflict we have already described.

By the middle of April 1930 Congress's Civil Disobedience movement was beginning to make its mark in UP. In twenty-seven of its forty-eight Districts government officials had been given special powers of search under the Salt Act. The number listed was increasing daily, and the provincial government remarked that this was a 'good indication' of the extent to which breaches had occurred or were expected. Seventy people, moreover, had already been prosecuted, and as a consequence there were hartals and demonstrations in several of the UP's more important towns.[19] Chief amongst those imprisoned was Jawaharlal Nehru.

The escalation of political activity in Lucknow had begun on 20 January 1930 when Nehru had addressed a meeting of 500–600 people in Aminuddaula Park, which was followed by the celebrations of Independence Day on 26 January. Already Congress leaders were calling for 'volunteers', and by early April they had established a Satyagraha camp, where to judge from later events 200 or so volunteers were soon being very effectively trained in the Gandhian practice of non-violent satyagraha. February seems to have been a relatively quiet month, but on 12 March a meeting chaired by Mohanlal Saxena brought together a crowd of around 3,000 people to celebrate the start of Gandhi's Dandi march. Thereafter several smaller meetings were held and a number of processions went through the city, all of them to recruit support for the Congress movement.

It seems as if the first illegal making of salt did not occur in Lucknow until 13 April, but in conjunction with a complete hartal on that day upwards of 6,000 people watched a number of Congress supporters making salt, which promptly led to the arrest and imprisonment of seven of their most prominent leaders, Mohanlal Saxena and C.B. Gupta principally amongst them. Over the next week or so a further five or six large meetings of 6,000–7,000 people were held (particularly in connection with the arrest of Jawaharlal Nehru). Soon, however, interest in illegal saltmaking appears to have waned, and by late April the whole emphasis in the Lucknow campaign had switched to the boycott of foreign cloth.

---

[19] For a vivid description of an episode in Agra see Barlow (an ICS Sub Divisional officer) to his parents, 27 Apr. 1930, Cambridge South Asian Archives, Barlow Papers.

Whilst this almost certainly irritated a goodly number of Muslim cloth merchants, a number of significant Lucknow Muslims now threw their support behind the campaign, and during the first two weeks of May an all but continuous series of meetings of between 1,000 and 5,000 people was held in the Aminabad area (particularly to protest at Gandhi's arrest on 5 May), together with further processions through the adjacent city. But so successful was the picketing of foreign cloth – there was an almost complete hartal over five days and all the stocks seem to have been sealed – that the campaign soon began again to lose its bite, and its leaders had then to decide what to do next.[20]

In the course of these early weeks Munro (who was now British Deputy Commissioner in Lucknow) seems to have gone out of his way, like Gwynne before him, to emphasise that Congress was entirely free to hold meetings and lead processions 'inside the city proper'. Following the events of November 1928 the implications of such a statement were palpable, and when for a second time the remaining Congress in the city found itself having to give its campaign a further boost, they eventually seized upon them. On 12 May 1930 they announced that as a further step in their civil disobedience campaign they would on 14 May lead a Congress procession along Hazratganj.

This was to raise the stakes significantly higher than had been done before. Back in 1928 the Congress leaders had taken very deliberate steps to avoid marching straight down Hazratganj, and had been careful to respect the sensitivities of the British on this matter. The conflicts which did then erupt did so, moreover, almost inadvertently. If, for example, Narhi bazaar (where the boycotters had wanted to go, as they had previously been to Husainganj) had not been quite so ensconced within the Civil Lines, there is no reason to believe that the clashes of 28 and 29 November 1928 would necessarily have occurred; and as a consequence it is at least arguable that the Charbagh affray on the following day would not have been as severe as it was. (It is unlikely, for instance, that Jawaharlal Nehru would have been there; it was only the clash with the police on the evening of 28 November – over the proposed procession to Narhi – that brought him hurriedly to Lucknow the following morning.)

But with the onset of Congress's countrywide Civil Disobedience movement in 1930 all such reservations were cast aside. No longer were India's committed nationalists prepared to limit themselves to the boycotting of British dignitaries and noisy demonstrations aimed against them. Under Gandhi's leadership they were now committed to full-scale,

---

[20] These details have been culled from *UP Police Abstracts of Intelligence*, CID Office, Lucknow, Jan.–May 1930. I am very grateful to Dr G. Kudaisya for securing these for me.

non-violent, confrontations with their British rulers, and that entirely changed the nature of the encounters which ensued. Recognition of the fact that a quite new position was in the offing was vividly exemplified when early on the morning of 14 May 1930 Munro mounted a police party brandishing their lathis in order to send a clear signal that if the Congress leaders did proceed to take a procession down Hazratganj it would very promptly be halted.

At this point there was an illuminating correspondence between Munro and Mushir Husain Kidwai, a member of the Indian Legislative Assembly and a prominent Lucknow citizen.[21] On 14 May Kidwai wrote to Munro to reproach him for his apparent intention

to stop the proposed procession [going down Hazratganj] even by violence if need be . . . It is obvious that no Indian whether a Congressman or not can attach any special sanctity to a place where a few Europeans happen to have their shops or a few others pass . . . to their residences or clubs and every citizen has a right to know why the executive authorities in the town feel inclined to make individual distinction between Indian quarters and so called European quarters in the matter of peaceful procession of Indians. Surely the European community enjoying the hospitality of the Indians in Lucknow has not been given any reason to get enraged against the Indian community to the extent of feeling provoked by the mere sight of a peaceful Indian demonstration over public thoroughfare which passes between some of their shops.

Munro, however, was quite unmoved.

No procession [he replied] has in the past ever been permitted to pass up Hazratganj in any circumstances . . . Apart from all other considerations Hazratganj is a busy throughfare over which much motor and other vehicular traffic passes. The Congress party has been allowed to conduct its processions freely inside the city proper. It can have no good reason for wishing to come into Civil Lines where its adherents do not reside and where the presence of a procession will cause disturbance and annoyance to other peaceful citizens . . . I suggest that you use your influence to persuade the Congress leaders to abstain from this unnecessary and provocative step.

To which Kidwai riposted by return that he resented

such racial discriminations . . . The Hazratganj road is wider than the city roads and therefore it should be easier to regulate the procession there in such a way that it does not hinder the traffic . . . such processions as the Corpus Christi processions which obstruct the road just as much are allowed even in Hazratganj.

Whereupon he wrote to the Viceroy to protest to him as well.

Before the issue reached a crisis Munro, in what were now classic

---

[21] For some details of his career see Riaz-ur-Rahman Kidwai, *Biographical Sketch of Kidwais of Avadh*, Aligarh 1987, pp. 122–9.

British terms, nonetheless sought to reach a reasonable compromise with the Congress leaders under which 'the procession should be allowed to proceed to the end of Hazratganj and after being diverted through side streets should proceed on its intended route after striking Hazratganj further down'. That was close to the compromise Nehru and Pant had worked out when they had set out down Newal Kishore Road from Narhi on 29 November 1928, and in other circumstances the Congress Committee might well have accepted it. But now that a full-scale Civil Disobedience movement had been launched, such compromises were very difficult for them to swallow, and they soon brusquely rejected Munro's proposal. To which he replied by formally issuing an order under the Police Act which blandly stated that in view of the fact that no procession had ever been allowed to pass through Hazratganj hitherto, Congress 'were at liberty to take the procession anywhere except Hazratganj'.

The Lucknow Congress was not, however, to be diverted, and on the afternoon of 14 May they led out 'a big procession' headed by Mrs Mitra (who had played a prominent part in the events of 1928) and Messrs Pestonji and Khanna (who were the 'Directors' of the Civil Disobedience movement in the city). Upon leaving the Congress office on Aminabad Park, this went down Hewett Road, then turned left up Abbott Road, and there found its way barred by a large body of police at the Hazratganj corner – i.e. at the entrance to The Mall. For four hours the two sides stood and faced each other. As the evening wore on the main body of processionists started to melt away. But a small group remained resolutely behind, sitting on the ground, confronted by a magistrate and a small body of police, who at 4 am the next morning eventually arrested them, removed them from Hazratganj, and then set them free. They were, however, quickly replaced by a further group of protesters under a Muslim lawyer, Ashfaq Hussain, and during the following morning (15 May) these were periodically superseded by others. There were at the same time reliefs upon the police side as well. Later it was conceded on the British side that in the end this Congress demonstration 'was partially successful', for around 2 pm on the 15th the remaining processionists were eventually allowed to pass through Hazratganj without being stopped. Throughout Munro evidently attempted to play the position coolly, and he was pleased when the local press acknowledged that he had done so.

Here was the eye of the storm. For during the following week the city's Congress leaders had to decide precisely what they should do next, while Munro, a much cooler character than Gwynne, seems to have worked out some of his own future moves as well. On Sunday 18 May a much larger Congress meeting than ever before was held in Aminabad, purportedly attended by 10,000 people. This was addressed by the long-established

Congress figure, Pandit Madan Mohan Malaviya, who stressed the need for a boycott of British goods and for communal harmony. In the course of the meeting salt was again illegally manufactured and this time was sold. However by this stage, in view of what was happening elsewhere across the country, all this was rather tame, and Lucknow's Congress leaders were now in danger of laying themselves open to the charge that they were not prepared to steel themselves for a major clash with the British.

The ideal prescription for a full-scale satyagraha confrontation was as always to conjoin a notorious public grievance with a quite particular place so as to create a controlled but spectacular public episode which would provoke the ugly face of British imperialism and thus evoke extensive publicity and very considerable public sympathy. Elsewhere, at Dandi or Dharasna, the symbolism of the place and the occasion for such a dramatic encounter between Indian nationalism and British imperialism had proved highly potent. Gandhi had quite brilliantly seized on the symbolic issue of salt to launch his countrywide campaign, and at those two places that had served his purpose very successfully. But as the absence of any British response to the further manufacture of salt in Lucknow on 18 May served to confirm, saltmaking seemed unlikely to provoke any significant clash in Lucknow, while the boycott of foreign cloth, though evidently holding up, now seemed very unlikely to create a major confrontation. All of which (as Kidwai explained to the Viceroy following the events of 14 May) threw the Congress leadership back on to the now well-established *cause célèbre* of Hazratganj as the only potent means of precipitating a major confrontation with the British.

Lucknow [he wrote] had no salt factory to be raided. In Lucknow the Congress volunteers had no field of operations against the government so as to win the general sympathy of the masses and the people. Now the government has supplied it in the sacrosanct grounds of Hazratganj.

Some of Kidwai's protestations on this score in his letters to Munro on 14 May were undoubtedly specious in sliding over the direct challenge to the authority of the British which a Congress march down Hazratganj would entail, but some of Munro's responses to him were scarcely less tendentious too. As Kidwai wrote in protest to the Viceroy about the events of 14 May:

even ten Congress volunteers were not allowed to pass through the Hazratganj Road even at a time when there was no traffic at all, all the shops had been closed and hardly any resident was visible . . . [It is] this Shibboleth of prestige with a racial superiority complex which is causing all the trouble . . . It was fortunate that the Congress volunteers succeeded in keeping the mob under perfect control . . . but I wonder how long both sides will be able to bear the strain.

In the prevailing circumstances that was by now by no means an alarm-
ist statement. By late May 1930 a major clash between the Congress and
the British in Lucknow very evidently stood in the offing, and, as Kidwai
noted, when the Congress leaders contemplated their position, they now
found they had really very little option but to attempt once again to
provoke a major clash over the otherwise quite banal issue of whether or
not they should be allowed to take a political procession, not through the
crowded streets of the extensive bazaar area of the city which they had
always been free to do, but along its main, broad shopping street in its
most prosperous new area, the Hazratganj.

Back on 14–15 May they had successfully demonstrated that they no
longer respected British susceptibilities on this score. They had shown
too that they could sit it out with the police for many an hour on end.
They had then been able to organise a series of reliefs when their leaders
were arrested; and they had finally achieved their purpose of marching up
Hazratganj when the opportunity for this eventually opened up. If one
had wanted to encapsulate the gross effrontery that imperial rule in
Lucknow necessarily implied, it would in any event have been difficult to
have improved upon the British administration's persistent determination to prevent a group of politically minded citizens from marching
through Hazratganj when they were perfectly free to do so anywhere else
in their own city. As Kidwai continued to protest to the Viceroy, in their
fixation upon the intensely symbolic importance of preventing the
Congress in Lucknow from taking a satyagraha procession along
Hazratganj Road, 'the authorities themselves have supplied the satyagrahis with a centre for their operations which they did not have before'.

In view of history and circumstance Munro, however, had in the end no
option but to treat the longstanding injunction against political processions through Hazratganj as sooner or later a *casus belli*. Lucknow's Civil
Lines, for all their Indian population, had now stood for nearly seventy
years, not merely as the European sanctuary upon the edge of a major
Indian city, but as the very embodiment of British prestige in one of the
two major cities in which Indians had once challenged British dominion
in India much more forcefully than anywhere else. For all its Indian
inhabitants, the British had long since designated Hazratganj, moreover,
as their space, and if the aura of imperial domination was to be maintained in Lucknow, it was in no way possible to allow Congress to
encroach upon it with impunity. If, after their ultimately successful
attempts on 14–15 May, the Congress in the city was now to break the
British prohibition against political processions in Hazratganj once again,
there was no way that Munro could ultimately treat that as anything but a
quite deliberate attempt to inflict a major propagandist blow against the

primacy of the British in the city as part of Congress's now impassioned campaign to bring British rule in India to an end. In the final analysis no British official could convincingly ignore such a challenge, and Munro was not the man to do so.

The upshot, as Kidwai had already warned the Viceroy, was that the situation in Lucknow now threatened to spill over into the kind of violence which had occurred at Sholapur and Chittagong. That in the event proved to be somewhat of an exaggeration. For as so often in the conflict between the British and the Indian National Congress, the two sides continued to strive hard to hold major violence at bay: the Congress by offering their studied non-violent satyagraha and by disowning the violence of the attending crowd when in fact violence did occur; the British by making only the most minimal calls, when the clashes actually took place, on the available military support from their large Cantonment just a mile or so away. Kidwai's apprehensions, however, were not altogether mistaken. Serious violence did now occur in Lucknow, and upon at least one occasion Munro quite seriously miscalculated its potentiality.

During the week following the events of 14–15 May Lucknow's Congress leaders rustled up a good deal more local support than before, and on Thursday 22 May 1930 eventually decided to set out once again to lead a procession through Hazratganj in direct defiance of a further order from Munro that they were not to do so.

Munro had evidently decided that he would now face them down very directly. The procession was accordingly first formally forbidden at the outset, and then 'when it reached one end of the street [The Mall] it was opposed by a small force of police', and was formally forbidden once again. However, five minutes later it was allowed to proceed. It then did so in a perfectly orderly manner, keeping carefully to the left-hand side of the road so that the ordinary traffic would not be interrupted, while Congress's stewards ensured that the attending crowd blocked neither the road nor the footpaths.

Munro had clearly been taken by surprise. 'The Congressmen on that day', so his Superintendent of Police later explained, 'were much greater in numbers and it was not considered judicious to stop them'. Munro somewhat recovered his position by nevertheless noting that he had successfully tested (as the later British enquiry put it) 'whether the leaders were prepared to proceed in spite of a prohibition, if the police was not adequate to prevent them'. And then, so as to demonstrate that his orders were not to be treated with impunity, on the following evening he arrested thirteen of the Congress leaders. Eleven of them (including

Pestonji and Khanna, the 'directors' of civil disobedience in the city) were then sentenced on 24 May to six months' imprisonment, while the President and Secretary of the Town Congress Committee were let off with a fine. That, however, could only stir the pot further, and with nineteen of the city's principal Congress leaders now in jail, it remained to be seen what the others would do next.

There is some suggestion that at this stage Munro made one further attempt to prevent a final escalation by letting it be known that in spite of all that had already occurred, he would be prepared to allow Congress processions to pass through Hazratganj so long as a licence for these had been sought. But the remaining Congress leadership in the city were not to be so easily diverted from their course, and on 25 May in protest against the imprisonment of their leaders they firmly decided that they would take out a further procession of a still more formidable kind before the day was out.

Once again they planned to take a major procession from the Congress headquarters in Aminabad via Hewett Road till it met Abbott Road. There it would turn left and move up Abbott Road past the Council Chamber, where it would turn left again at the Hazratganj crossing, and then seek to go all the way up the Mall itself, whence it would ultimately return to its starting point. In view of the arrests that had been made two days previously the procession was to be led by Mrs Mitra (the 'only member of the war council so far spared') and a party of ladies. Congress's core supporters were now plainly determined to suffer the full consequences of their actions in offering non-violent satyagraha, and the crucial moment for that had now arrived.

On the British side it was now clearly felt that 'there was ample evidence on that day that the masses in the city were likely to be out of control as they were in an excited state'. Accordingly Munro determined that he would this time halt the procession and use such force as would be necessary to disperse it. As it happened 25 May 1930 was a Sunday. His argument therefore that a Congress procession would interfere with the business and shopping activities of those who worked in and used Hazratganj accordingly looked even thinner on that day than it had before; but it was not of course his major concern. That related to the extraordinary importance attached to the inviolability of Hazratganj as a principal symbol of British imperial prestige in the city. Sunday indeed had its advantages for Munro, for if a major clash did occur, it would interfere a great deal less with Hazratganj's ordinary business than a clash upon a weekday.

In view of the steady escalation of events over the preceding few days, he had, moreover, ample opportunity to concoct his plans. He was now clearly determined that he would not once again leave himself in the posi-

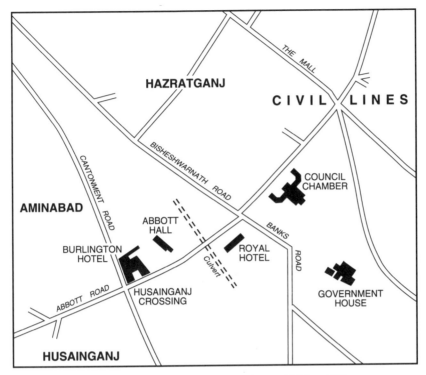

Map 4 Satyagraha confrontation, Lucknow, 25 May 1930

tion of having to let the procession proceed for lack of sufficient police to stop it (as he had on 22 May). He was now in a strong position, what was more, to rebut any suggestion that the Congress processionists would in the end accept his injunctions, for it had now been well established that they would quite certainly not do so.

The point he selected as the place at which he would bring the procession to a halt was in Abbott Road, near where it met Banks Road, opposite the south end of the Royal Hotel compound, close by the Seventh Day Adventists' Mission, and just short of the UP Council building. This was all but precisely the place which Gwynne had defined in November 1928 as constituting the *ne plus ultra* of the Civil Lines and Hazratganj. Here, beyond the Royal Hotel compound a surface drain passed under Abbott Road through a culvert.[22] On either side of the road at this point a narrow lane followed the line of the drain. To the left was an open space on which a new house was being built. Beyond, the ground sloped

[22] As, one may remark, it still did long afterwards, as an inquisitive visitor to Lucknow could readily discern.

upwards past a row of compounds to the Husainganj crossing where the Cantonment road crossed Abbott Road adjacent to the Husainganj bazaar area. From there it was possible for a considerable number of onlookers to view the scene, and that was to add to its fateful consequences. Upon the right-hand side of the road, just beyond the drain, was a building known as Abbott Hall – whose gate had been shut, but from whose grounds it was possible for a number of well-to-do people to watch the events which ensued.

At this chosen point 'a cordon of civil police armed with batons and lathis' together with 'a number of armed police who were carrying batons but no lances' stood ready to block the road where it passed over the culvert and drain; while 'a considerable reserve of police numbering about one hundred and fifty armed for the most part with batons or lathis, was drawn up inside the compound of the Royal Hotel'. Behind the police cordon the streets leading out of Hazratganj towards Abbott Road were sealed off, so that the police could not be attacked from the rear. But the lanes along the drain were not blocked, and in the event provided important getaways for those fleeing from the clash that soon occurred.

Munro and his Superintendent of Police, Chapman, then stationed themselves with the reserve police in the grounds of the Royal Hotel. There they were joined by the Brigade Commander, Colonel Jones, and his chief staff officer, the Brigade Major, Major Benson, who had come from the Cantonment a mile away across the railway line. In the early 1930s the Lucknow Cantonment was the Headquarters of the 6th (Lucknow) Infantry Brigade. This usually included a regiment of British and a regiment of Indian cavalry, two battalions of British and two of Indian infantry, two field batteries of Royal Artillery, and a number of ancillary troops as well.[23] None of these had been called to the scene. As, however, there was now concern that 'the spirit of lawlessness' was spreading, the Brigade Commander and his Brigade Major were there to see how things developed so that should it after all be decided that troops should be called out, they could give their orders very speedily.

Before the procession started on its way a notice under the Police Act to prohibit its movement into the Civil Lines was served on Mrs Mitra. It was, of course, ignored. At about 5.30 pm the procession accordingly moved forward, carrying national flags 'and singing the usual national songs'. It numbered about 200 Congress volunteers, with 30 to 40 women at its head, with Mrs Mitra in the van. They walked in pairs and kept carefully to the left-hand side of the road. They were soon accompanied by a considerable crowd of onlookers, 'who had come to see the

---

[23] *District Gazetteer of U.P., 1931–32,* p. 4.

show', and who spilled across the road, while a further number of people collected near the police cordon, not least in the adjacent open space to the left, to wait upon events. It was later estimated that the attending crowd must well have numbered several thousands.

At about 6.30 pm the procession reached the police cordon stretched across Abbott Road and halted. The City Magistrate, Muhammad Bashir Siddique, then went forward, declared it to be an unlawful assembly, and in a loud voice informed Mrs Mitra that if the procession did not disperse within two minutes it would be dispersed by force. That constituted a major step forward in Lucknow's May 1930 confrontation. Munro had never gone so far before. Nor had he informed the Congress organisers as he did earlier in the evening that this would now be his intention.

A few minutes later, when there was no response, Munro gave the fateful order that the procession should be dispersed. The police moved in to arrest Mrs Mitra, who was taken away in a police van, while the other ladies were hustled into a lorry that was driven away as well. Then after another five to ten minutes a whistle was blown. Mounted police thereupon moved forward down both sides of the road to separate the processionists from the watching crowd – and were not altogether sparing in the use of their batons. They then attempted to remove the processionists – but failed. For the leaders now ordered them to sit or lie down, so that the horses of the police would shy away from them. Three sections of foot police, six men under an NCO each, were then sent forward to pick up the recumbent processionists and carry them off. So far everything had been quite clinically done. The crowd, whilst shouting slogans and obviously sympathetic to the procession, had so far shown no overt hostility to the police, nor any violence either.

But the furies were then let loose. One can imagine the scene. Evidently some of the processionists now resisted the attempt of the police to snatch their flags and carry them off. The police were then given orders by Munro to disperse the 'unlawful assembly' using their lathis, and proceeded to do so without restraint. Twenty minutes of brutal, and in the end quite indiscriminate, police flaying then ensued. Soon the onlookers, who had received no warning that they too were part of this 'unlawful assembly', were being attacked as well. To begin with the crowd fell back, but then surged forward again, whereupon police reserves were called up from the Royal Hotel grounds. Before very long the greater part of the available police force then embarked on assaulting all and sundry in the road, and in the adjacent open space as well. The gate into the Abbott Hall grounds was now opened in order that some of the injured could be carried there for succour. But they were immediately followed by some of the fleeing crowd, with the police in hot pursuit. Some of the better-to-do who had come there to watch events now found themselves being assaulted by the police as well. The vehemence with which the police proceeded is indicated by the subsequently well-testified evidence that amongst those standing in the Abbott Hall compound a 'Mr Kitchlu sustained fourteen bruises or abrasions and three scalp wounds', a 'Mrs Bakhshi received six contusions and a black eye', a 'Mrs Mushran six contusions or abrasions and her son five bruises and a wound on the forehead'.

In the end the Congress volunteers and the watching crowd found themselves forced to withdraw – towards the Husainganj crossing, and down the two side lanes which ran along the open drain to the right and left of the original police cordon. There are no reports of any arrests being made. But on this occasion that was not the purpose. Those who chose to defy the British were to be taught a very much shorter, sharper, and swifter lesson. There were Congress reports that 8 to 10 people had been killed and that 219 cases of injuries were registered that night. On the following day Munro issued, however, an angry press communique in which he suggested that only two people had suffered fractures, '8 or 10 were more or less severely injured, while about 50 of the others received trifling injuries'. But the later British official enquiry did find, not only that considerable numbers were carried off to doctor's surgeries (one doctor saw as many as fifty patients), and to both the Balrampur Hospital a mile away up the river and King George's Hospital a further mile beyond that, but that over one hundred people could be identified as having required medical attention, of whom nineteen 'could be considered serious' (some of them in an unconscious or semi-conscious state), nine having fractures (of the arm, knee-cap, or hand), 'the remainder persons admitted to hospital suffering from the result of a severe beating', of whom several bore evidence of 'a pretty severe beating' or had 'contusions on various parts of the body'. Miraculously there were no deaths, whilst most of those detained in hospital were soon discharged. But the carnage, the pain, the physical damage, and the shock to a peaceful if deliberately defiant procession, and to its large accompaniment of curious and supportive onlookers, can be very easily imagined – the more so when one notes the British enquiry's statement that there was no evidence of any of the police receiving injuries that were anything more than trifling. The evidence is therefore clear that both the processionists, and on this occasion the attending crowd, held to Gandhi's insistence upon non-violence very firmly.

The police assaults, however, immediately created widespread anger in the city. Pandit Ras Behari Tewari, the city's member of the Legislative Council, sent his resignation to the Viceroy the following day, while

Kidwai (Munro's correspondent of ten days before) immediately sent a further protest to the Viceroy. *'Unnecessary violence has been used'*, he inveighed, *'and "brutalities"* . . . *have been perpetrated by the Government's agents'*. Neither the crowd nor the volunteers had shown the least violence.

What was the 'unlawful object' [he disingenuously asked] with which the procession was taken out . . . Instead of committing any lawlessness the processionists only wanted to assert the rights of the people of Lucknow to use one of their own main roads against the high handed action of an irresponsible, autocratic and conceited executive. Any impartial observer could not but see that if there was any lawlessness it was on the side of the executive.

There was nothing contrived, however, about his thunder against those of his

countrymen, who for the sake of a few rupees, had behaved like savages against an unresisting and orderly crowd of their fellow countrymen at the orders of a foreigner . . . The gratuitous attacks of the mercenaries of a foreign government and the brutality of the bureaucracy effectually roused feelings of hostility in the hearts of all the inhabitants of the City and not only in the hearts of those devoted to Congress principles [and] all shades of opinion had become united in looking with abhorrence at the atrocity committed.

More piercingly he asked why the watching crowd was 'not warned beforehand that they would be doing an unlawful act'.

There was particular resentment at the treatment of the ladies. Whisked away from Abbott Road they had been taken by police lorry to the Alambagh police station, two miles out of the city on the western side. There they had been detained for a couple of hours until 9 o'clock at night, when they were

let go in the darkness of the night to find their way through the dangerous and deserted area which lies between it and the city and to be at the mercy of scoundrels and hooligans.

When the Superintendent of Police came to be taxed about this, he mumbled some excuse about not having been able to make the necessary arrangements before they were released. But his action had been palpably deliberate, and the resulting anger was clearly palpable as well. On reaching Aminabad the ladies 'were carried in procession by a huge but orderly crowd with scenes of wild enthusiasm', before being personally escorted back to their homes.

That night there were other consequences as well. As the later official British report put it, there could be 'no doubt that the immediate result of the dispersal of the procession and the crowd on the evening of the 25th May led to a very considerable amount of bitterness'. There was dismay enough that the procession had been dispersed by force. There was outrage that the attending crowd, of all classes, should have been so wantonly attacked as well. Around 9 pm there was a large meeting in Aminuddaula Park (which was evidently orderly). Elsewhere the constable on point duty at the Husainganj crossing had to be rescued. A large crowd gathered outside the Aminabad Police Outpost. Another collected in front of the City Magistrate's office, and stayed there till after midnight, while a third even threatened the police station in the Chowk. Elsewhere an off-duty Head Constable was set upon, and upon the following day several police constables on traffic duty had to be withdrawn.

During the afternoon of 26 May the British administration then learned that notwithstanding the events of the previous day – indeed no doubt because of them – Congress had firmly decided to take out yet another procession that evening in further defiance of the British.

At this point the British clearly decided to raise the odds once again. They now determined to stop the procession before it could ever start. Accordingly they moved onto Congress's own ground within Aminabad itself (which they had always hitherto left it free to occupy as it chose). They sent 200 police to clear the roads, remove the crowds from Aminuddaula Park, and confine as many as possible within the railings of Aminabad Park near by. They then brought in from the Cantonment one squadron of British cavalry from the 3rd Hussars and one company of British infantry from the East Yorkshire Regiment, along with some machine guns – some 200 troops all told – under a Captain Gawan, and around 5 pm posted them immediately in the front of the Congress Office in Aminuddaula Park. An hour later the Police Superintendent ordered, moreover, that the Congress flag which flew there should be pulled down. As a consequence the Congress leaders seem to have decided that the major procession planned for that evening should not now be led out lest some altogether more portentous clash than the one on the day before should now occur.

Yet whilst the backs of the British were turned a batch of eleven Congress supporters carrying a Congress flag set out from the Hewett Road/Abbott Road corner and managed to march through Hazratganj before returning in triumph to the Congress office. Munro and his senior, the Commissioner for Lucknow, when they heard of this, correctly concluded that in view of all the prevailing circumstances it was unlikely that any further Congress procession would be taken out that night. But then in a fateful move, thinking that the organised Congress were the only opponents with whom they needed to concern themselves in the city, made a major, and highly revealing, error. Believing that the situation was settling down, between 7 and 7.30 pm they made a number of new dispositions. Contrary to the views of the Police Superintendent (who was far better informed than they were since his plainclothes agents were milling around in the city's crowd), they sent the troops back to their barracks in the Cantonment; withdrew the mounted police; and then sent the remainder of the police – roughly 200 all told – to spend the night in the Aminabad Outpost nearby in Sri Ram Road. Whereupon they took themselves off to their bungalows in the Civil Lines.

Within half an hour, however, there ensued the major climax to these convulsive days. Upon the previous evening the Aminabad Outpost had already attracted the attention of the Aminabad crowd. During the early evening of the following day, Monday 26 May, the formidable presence of British troops established in Aminuddaula Park effectively smothered their pent-up fury. But with the withdrawal of the British troops, of the mounted police, and of the British officials, the clamps were off. The anger which the police attacks upon the attending crowd had generated on the 25th, stoked as it will have been by the obtrusive demonstration of imperial forces within Aminabad itself on the 26th, eventually spilled over as it was now getting dark. When it did so the foot police in the Aminabad Outpost – numerous as they were – found themselves appallingly exposed. For the Outpost did not stand, as Lucknow's post-Mutiny re-designers had clearly insisted that police stations should all stand, on a broad swathe through the city like Victoria Street or Canning Street, along which it could have been fairly readily protected and relieved. On the contrary it stood on the edge of a narrow street, overshadowed on all sides by much taller buildings, in the depths of the Indian city, within a stone's throw both of the Congress headquarters off Aminuddaula Park and of Aminabad Park where the city's principal political gatherings were always held.

Who exactly started the ensuing fracas it would never have been easy to say, for such situations are highly symbiotic. Whilst it seems that some of the 20,000 or so who had been out and about in Aminabad earlier in the evening – the largest gathering so far seen in these events – now went away home, a sizeable, angry, city crowd remained behind and followed the withdrawing police around the corner from Aminabad Road into Sri Ram Road, shouting abuse as it went, before proceeding to assault them and the Outpost.

The Aminabad Outpost's main building consisted of a long tiled structure standing back from the road, surrounded on three sides by much taller houses. Over to one side stood the house of the Head Constable, with a kitchen behind it. Towards the front of the open courtyard which

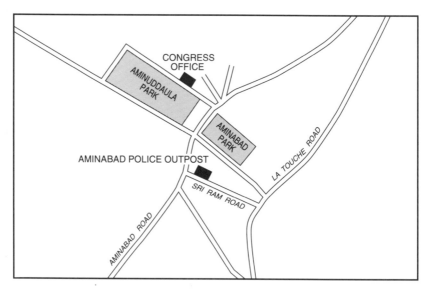

Map 5 Attack on Aminabad police outpost, Lucknow, 26 May 1930

lined the street there was 'a well with a wide masonry plinth about three feet high' (still there for a visitor to see several decades later). The only cover in front of the main building was this plinth, and several police were soon crouching down behind it. One of them was hit on the nose by a brick. The Deputy Superintendent in charge thereupon ordered the crowd to disperse. More bricks were then thrown, whereupon he ordered his Reserve Inspector and some fifty to sixty policemen to make a baton charge. Still more bricks flew. So he doubled the number of police for a further charge. Both were driven back. But the crowd did not disperse and soon almost all the police drew back for safety into the Outpost's main building.

In a situation like this it is quite impossible to keep track of every detail. What is clear is that the situation now rapidly deteriorated. Whilst it was subsequently to be claimed that under the charges of the police the crowds fell back, the police in the Outpost were now not only becoming very frightened but very determined too. So far the main crowd had come from the Aminabad Road end of Sri Ram Road. But a second crowd now advanced from the other end, and began to throw bricks as well. So the Deputy Superintendent went out again, and this time gave a warning that if they did not disperse, the police would open fire upon them. Someone at this point set light to an ice vendor's stall at the corner of the com-

pound. There was clearly here a major threat to the Outpost itself. The
crowd indeed was soon shouting: 'Set fire to the police chowki.' The
Deputy Superintendent then thought he heard two shots being fired at
him from one of the houses immediately opposite, where a number of
people had climbed on the roofs, and were busily throwing stones as well.
Whether visions of Chauri Chaura now crossed his mind and that of any
of his police constables it is not possible to say. But that they had now
become deeply apprehensive that a similar fate could overtake them is not
to be gainsaid. Whilst none of the police had been seriously hurt in the
Abbott Road melee on the previous day, when the police casualties at the
Aminabad Outpost on 26 May were counted the medical evidence
recorded that thirty-four of them had been injured by bricks or broken
bottles and suchlike, or about one in six all told.

So, urged on by his Reserve Inspector, the Deputy Superintendent
decided to open fire. Four rounds of buckshot were directed over the
heads of the people standing on the houses immediately opposite, who
quickly scurried away. 'Then the armed guard of fourteen men fired a
volley of one round each into the crowd towards the Aminabad Road.
The crowd fell back, but soon advanced again still throwing stones, and
a second volley was fired.' The crowd did now retreat to the T-junction
of Sri Ram Road and Aminabad Road, some going to the right, others
to the left, and the police followed after, half of them facing right, half
facing left. As the crowd remained aggressive, further volleys were fired
in both directions. To the right the crowd did then begin to melt away,
but on the left it simply stood its ground further back. By then the
crowd from the other end of Sri Ram Road was advancing again, and
four armed constables and a number of others were sent after them.
Four more shots were fired, whereupon the crowd eventually did disperse.

Already the Deputy Superintendent had telephoned both the
Wasirganj police station to ask for reinforcements of arms and ammuni-
tion, and the City Magistrate to tell him of what was now afoot. When the
firing eventually ceased he telephoned again, this time to his
Superintendent, whom he managed to track down at the Deputy
Commissioner's bungalow. The time was 8.10 pm. It was just about an
hour since the British troops had been withdrawn.

But the night was not over yet. Some of the police now embarked on a
rampage. There were indiscriminate lathi charges in a number of places.
Random shots were fired, and four people were subsequently found dead,
at least two of whom were found well away from the vicinity of the
Outpost. There was looting as well – of a cloth shop, a watch shop, some
fruit stalls, a pan shop and a sharbat shop. Not all of this was necessarily

committed by the police. Others would almost certainly have taken advantage of the prevailing circumstances. But a Head Constable was apprehended driving away with a carriage loaded with rolls of cloth, and soon after 8 pm a retired Deputy Conservator of Forests in Kashmir who was driving at the north end of the road between Aminuddaula and Aminabad Parks found himself accosted by some mounted police who started to beat both him and his driver, till his wife told them that her brother was a Lucknow Police Inspector, when they quickly made off. Meanwhile a fire had been started down Aminabad Road towards the railway station, and the fire service had to be called out. When the night's events came to be tabulated a count showed that the police had fired forty-six rounds of buckshot and four of ball, with seven unaccounted for. There was once again uncertainty about the total number of casualties, but aside from the four dead, and those who went to their city practitioners, the Medical College and Balrampur hospitals treated between them a dozen with gunshot wounds, and upwards of a further twenty suffering from 'contusions'; and there were reports of as many as sixty casualties all told.

Order, however, was very soon restored. The troops, who had only just returned to their barracks, were hurriedly called out once again, and were back in the city by around 9.30 pm. They and the police thereupon picketed its most sensitive points. There was some apprehension lest further episodes might occur, and indeed the Outpost in Husainganj was reinforced when a crowd threatened to attack it. A curfew was then imposed, and prohibitions were issued not only against assemblies or processions of more than five persons, but against the carrying of any weapons of offence.

All this seems to have effectively halted the escalation. The troops took over the two Aminabad parks. A good many arrests were made of those violating the curfew, and over the next two or three days a number of those wearing Gandhi caps were arrested, till Munro halted this. For the next two or three days most of the shops in the area were closed, but on the evidence of the provincial police reports there were no further outbreaks in Lucknow during the weeks which then followed.

The confrontation which the Lucknow Congress finally mounted on Sunday 25 May admirably succeeded in placing the British and their henchmen in a very bad light. Its members had gone out with great courage in the clear expectation that they would have to suffer brutal assaults from the police for their cause. Whilst there was no repetition of Jallianwallah Bagh, a great many of them had been very badly hurt, and the outrage of the city's public against the British administration was correspondingly sharp. In a private letter of 26 May to his (non-Congress) fellow Liberal, Sir Sita Ram, the very distinguished, longserving UP politician, Hriday Nath Kunzru (who had been staying in Lucknow), put it all pithily:

It was intended yesterday to take out a procession through the Hazratganj. Its passage was blocked near the Royal Hotel and the volunteers were mercilessly belaboured. Even women were beaten. Your blood will boil when you read an account of it.[24]

Shortly afterwards M.H. Kidwai vented his anger in yet another letter to the Viceroy.

The first point which I, a Muslim [he expostulated] . . . want to bring to the notice of a Christian Viceroy is that if the executive authorities had not attached such an inviolable, fanatical, sanctity, on racial grounds, to a broad and uncongested (perhaps the broadest and most uncongested) thoroughfare of Lucknow where a few European shop keepers happened to have their shops thinly interspersed among 'mainly' Indian shops (further more Indians than natives of Europe reside on this road), and had treated it as they treated other roads in the city which are far more narrow and congested no trouble would have arisen and no tragic results would have ensued . . . The only reason for treating the Hazratganj as sacrosanct and a forbidden land while the processionists were at liberty to take the procession anywhere except through Hazratganj was that it was a 'European quarter' in the eyes of the authorities. But this reason besides being as outrageous to Muslim sentiment as it should have been to Christian should not have been taken into consideration because this sort of racial Superiority Complex had already caused the greatest possible misunderstanding between the rulers and the ruled in India . . . When the people saw with their own eyes their helpless kith and kin mercilessly belaboured by lathis and heavy bludgeons even though they were meekly lying down on the road receiving blows without the least retaliation (more Christ-like than the Christian District Magistrate), when they found that even respectable Indian ladies were assaulted insulted and ill treated no wonder that every shade of opinion in Lucknow, including the Muslims and the moderates, was roused to indignation.

These were clearly only two of the many expressions of anger that Sunday's melee generated in Lucknow and elsewhere. On the following Tuesday, 27 May, 3,000 people attended a 'Lucknow Day' protest meeting in Allahabad, and about 600 in Kanpur. On Wednesday 28 May a similar meeting was held in Agra, while on 29 May a further protest meeting was held in Allahabad, and a 'Lucknow Day' procession was taken out in Banda. Amongst half a dozen meetings elsewhere, a meeting two days later at Etawah focussed on the Lucknow affair as well. It was

[24] Kunzru to Sita Ram, 26 May 1930, NMML, Sita Ram Papers 29(77).

then rather lost to sight amidst the torrent of other episodes. In this same week, for example, in UP alone, 34 Congress-sponsored meetings were reported by the police at which 1,000 and more people were present. In the following week there were 25 more of that size and all but 200 others – along with a miscellany of picketings, boycotts, salt makings, and the court proceedings which ensued.[25]

What was not, however, lost was the impact of the affair in Lucknow itself. On 26 May Munro issued a press statement about the Sunday affair, and on 27 May about the Monday shooting. At the same time the Oudh Bar Council announced the appointment of a committee of enquiry under Mr St George Jackson, MLC, into the events of 25–26 May, while on 28 May a 'meeting of about twenty-five gentlemen of the city representing all shades of opinion' appointed a committee of inquiry under the chairmanship of S.M. Habibullah, a Legislative Councillor, and a retired Magistrate and Collector, which three days later issued a statement on behalf of 'a very large number of citizens who have always stood for law and order and who have no sympathy for the law breaking programme', which denounced the 'policy of intimidation by means of deliberate and merciless assaults' designed, so it declared, 'to demoralise the citizens of Lucknow by causing serious injuries and by the use of unnecessary force'.

There were now calls for a public enquiry too. In responding to these the Governor of UP, Sir Malcolm Hailey, told the Viceroy that:

My instincts are all against condemning district officers for what they do under provocation; but of course the forcible breaking up of a peaceful procession at Lucknow did actually offend the general principles we had laid down; and writing to you I may say that I think they made a mistake. It may be very satisfactory at times to apply forcible methods to an obstinate lot of 'satyagrahis', but the ulti-mate gain does not always compensate one for the trouble which this causes ... there is no doubt that large numbers of otherwise fairly loyal people in Lucknow have been turned against us by the incident of the 25th May and on the whole it has formed somewhat of an asset to Congress.[26]

Though he remained 'quite clear that the complaints of police excesses and so on have very little real foundation', as 'local Muslims were all joining in the complaints', he decided on 1 June, 'for the necessity of keeping the Muslims straight', to appoint a British Sessions Judge, Leslie White, to conduct a formal enquiry.[27] Two days later White began his hearings and until 14 June continued with the examination of 104 wit-nesses, whose evidence was extensively reported in the UP press. His

[25] *UP Police Abstracts of Intelligence*, 7, 14 June 1930.
[26] Hailey to Irwin, 9 June 1930, HP 18B.
[27] Hailey to de Montmorency, 5 June 1930, H 18B.

eventual report was laid before the UP Legislative Council on 12 July where it was excoriated by the Indian members for the egregious white-wash they believed it to be.

Over the events of 25–26 May there hung a major irony. On the one side they showed just how successful the post-Mutiny replanners of Lucknow had been in accomplishing their principal purpose. Thanks to the building of a large military Cantonment in close proximity to the city, with easy access to its heart, a violent popular uprising had been speedily halted, within indeed little more than an hour. At the same time had the post-Mutiny planners been specifically ordered to provide Britain's more adept Indian opponents with a pristine case on which to mount a major satyagraha success against them, they could scarcely have improved upon their restructuring of Hazratganj, 'His Highness' market', as the sacred heart of the wider precinct of the new British Civil Lines. For this pro-vided the city Congress with a quite superb opportunity for inflicting a major moral defeat upon the British for their racist stance. Like other far-seeing strategists the British in Lucknow in May 1930 very successfully refought the previous war, only to suffer signal defeat in the new.

It is important at the same time to note that the affrays of 25–26 May 1930 did not simply involve Congress's non-violent satyagraha on the Sunday. They included as well the attack on the Aminabad Outpost on the following evening. There were, that is, at least two nationalist forces in Lucknow (aside, that is, from that represented by such people as Kunzru, Kidwai, Habibullah, and their like). There was first the Congress, and then the city crowd,[28] and their *modus operandi* differed very greatly.

Be it noted by your Excellency [Kidwai emphasised to the Viceroy in a letter of 5 June], that the Congress volunteers and officials were not involved in the alleged riot [on 26 May] but that it was one between the police and the *citizens* of Lucknow. The widespread nature of the indignation caused by the police can well be gauged by this.

The clear evidence is indeed that on the evening of 26 May when the troops were withdrawn, not only had Congressmen 'implored the people who followed the police to go away and many obeyed', but that the crowd which assaulted the Police Outpost consisted 'mostly of low classes'. The Lucknow Congress quite correctly insisted that it was in no way responsi-ble for the attack upon the Police Outpost, and that it remained adamant in its opposition to violence of any kind.

Yet its actions had come closer to the wind than its leaders readily

---

[28] This is a striking, and hitherto unnoticed, example of the point the 'Subaltern School' of modern Indian historians have been making, see R. Guha, ed., *Subaltern Studies*, vols. 1– , Delhi 1982– .

allowed. Both in 1928 and 1930 they had begun their campaigns by taking recruiting processions through the newer bazaar areas of the city, not so much with a view to enlisting more enrolled members in their ranks, but so as to secure a much larger penumbra of sympathetic supporters who would give it popular support as their local campaign reached its climax. There were, however, several significant difficulties with this. First, however successful Congress's stewards might ordinarily be in marshalling attending crowds (as, for example, on the occasion of the procession through Hazratganj on 22 May), events both at the railway station in 1928, and in Abbott Road in 1930, showed that once matters had become explosive there was little they could do to ensure that order should prevail. The city crowd acknowledged no absolute commitment to Gandhi's doctrines of non-violence, and evidently saw no reason why it should submit unforgivingly to the beatings of the police – those greatly hated mercenaries of the alien state. As soon as a promising opportunity offered to take physical reprisals against them they were quick to seize it. In Lucknow in May 1930 the British authorities twice played into their hands; first in Abbott Road on 25 May when they let the police abandon their initial discrimination between satyagrahis and onlookers so soon as the men amongst the former resisted arrest; and then by their haughty disdaining of the crowd's fury when they culpably left the Aminabad Outpost utterly at its mercy on the following evening. The launching of a non-violent campaign against the British in no way precluded, that is, the possibility that violence might be resorted to by others.

At the same time these episodes showed that quite apart from its moral content Congress's now ingrained caution against violence had a very real point to it. As the evening events of 26 May demonstrated the British possessed all the means they needed to throttle any resort to actual violence in the city. Popular violence, so the Congress correctly discerned, was not an effective way to move the British.

It is at the same time striking that in the aftermath of the attack on the Police Outpost both the British and the Congress showed every sign of feeling that their actions on 24–25 May had generated a great deal more trouble for themselves than either of them would have wished. Congress had found its initiative in the nationalist campaign wrested from its grasp by the violence of the city crowd; whilst the British (as Hailey clearly recognised) had suffered a considerable propaganda defeat. As a result in an effort to recover their hold of the nationalist movement in the city Congress cut down its campaign of civil disobedience to a symbolic minimum; while the British deliberately moderated their response to it as well.

Early in June 1930 the Congress leadership which was still at large in

Lucknow started to send out batches of half a dozen volunteers each day in defiance of a month-long British prohibition against political processions of any kind. These were sometimes selectively composed: on one day sons of Oudh Taluqdars; on another Brahmins; on a third Muslims. They were all soon arrested and sentenced to six months' imprisonment – but with no further consequences. Congress meanwhile resumed its picketing of foreign cloth shops, and in mid June there was a face-to-face standoff between a number of Congressmen and the police at each of the entrances to Aminuddaula Park over attempts by the Congress to rehoist its flag there.[29] Congress now sent flag bearers, moreover, through various parts of the city not least to Narhi and Chowk. They made no attempt, however, to mount any more large-scale satyagraha marches of the kind they had taken out in May. The British for their part showed every sign of trying to play these later events very coolly too. They arrested none of the flag bearers. Before the end of June they withdrew the troops they had posted in the Aminabad Parks (which allowed the Congress to run up its flag there once again), and they then lifted the general prohibition they had imposed against processions. Congress did make one further, though very limited, attempt to march down Hazratganj, this time from both ends. The small groups at the head of each of these processions were soon arrested (and sentenced to six months' imprisonment), but thereupon the remaining Congress leaders ordered the rest to disperse, and the British were careful not to interfere.

Throughout these weeks the city crowd fell quiescent too. It looks as if it had been cowed by the police shootings, and by the parading of troops; while the relative moderation of both the Congress and the British provided it with no further realistic opportunity to express its still no doubt unassuaged deeper feelings. As a consequence Congress and the British regained control of the nationalist conflict in the city, and the city crowd appears to have left them to it.

This Lucknow story provides one indication out of a great many of the extent to which so many ordinary members of Congress had by the early 1930s come to adopt Gandhi's non-violent satyagraha procedures as their principal means for bringing nationalist pressure upon the British. It is to be emphasised that this was chiefly because Gandhian non-violent satyagraha met so precisely the quite peculiar circumstances of the Indian conflict with the British. By the early 1930s the British no longer ruled out the Indian demand for independence altogether. They were anxious indeed to hold discussions with India's principal nationalist leaders about introducing some constitutional reforms at the margin. They remained

[29] Some additional details are from *UP Police Abstracts of Intelligence*, June 1930.

adamant, however, that they would not relinquish freely their control over the central citadels of British power in India, and it was quite plain that they would not be budged from this position by verbal pressure only.

But they did not seem likely to buckle before violence either. As the episodes in 1930 at Chittagong, Sholapur, and Peshawar all showed, despite any initial setback the British were fully capable of suppressing any armed insurrection that was raised against them. Ever since the Great Revolt of 1857 they had meticulously laid plans against any such event recurring;[30] their Indian army remained overwhelmingly 'loyal' to them;[31] while their police generally made short shrift of the small, violently minded groups which sought to conspire against them.

If neither talk nor violence then seemed at all likely to shift them, some other way of giving effective expression to the vehemence of India's nationalist feelings needed to be found. What was so striking about Gandhi's doctrine of non-violent satyagraha was just how extraordinarily functional it was to the distinctive features of the British stance towards India. While it disdained talk – till at any rate there seemed a real chance the British would make some genuine concessions – it also eschewed violence. At the same time it quite specifically involved a great deal more than simply the creation of a major political movement. Satyagraha had its cutting edge as well. Whilst vigorously non-violent, carefully marshalled, avowedly peaceful and thus morally laudable, it was both physically defiant and formidably antagonistic too, and it was very specifically designed to force the British to resort to some reprehensible action that would rend their moral authority.

The actual operations of a satyagraha confrontation warrant, however, further notice. At the outset, so the Lucknow story indicates, it involved the enlistment of numbers of active Congress members in its ranks who were trained in the patience, orderliness and courageous resolution which Gandhi's doctrine called for. Next, a much wider following of local sympathetic supporters was recruited well beyond the Congress's regular membership. A clear distinction had then to be drawn between protest processions, meetings, and demonstrations whose legitimacy the British ordinarily accepted, and deliberately mounted satyagraha confrontations which they were certain to resist. In mounting the latter it was of special advantage if some striking issue of peculiar local applicability could be latched upon in order to specify and highlight the iniquities of British imperialist domination. Dedicated Congress members had then to

---

[30] Kudaisya, 'State Power and the Erosion of Colonial Authority in Uttar Pradesh', ch. 5.

[31] E.g. Tai Yong Tan, 'Maintaining the Military Districts: Civil-Military Integration and District Soldiers' Boards in the Punjab, 1919–1939', *Modern Asian Studies*, 28, 4, 1994, pp. 833–74.

proceed with completely self-sacrificing determination up to and beyond the point where severe police beatings were not only to be openly courted but willingly sustained as well. If as a consequence an attendant crowd took to violence, major Congress confrontations had, however, to be quickly called off, and more insidious procedures, which would often entail prison sentences, had to be adopted in their place, since so far as Congress was concerned the frontiers of violence were not to be crossed, as that would very directly play into the hands of the British.

In confronting these ingeniously constructed assaults the British had to display all the skills they could muster to ensure that they did not lose the upper hand, either by overreacting or by underreacting. They accordingly looked for every expedient they could find to prevent a serious climax supervening, since they were well aware that in any such theatrically constructed encounter any Congress success could so easily do immense damage to their self-assumed moral primacy on which they always set great store. On many a peripheral issue they were therefore quite prepared to bend. They were careful, moreover, to ensure that as far as possible it was Congress which escalated any encounter that occurred; and when one did so they were at pains to remove the women protestors first before embarking on harsher measures against the men. Yet in the end they never hesitated to enforce their own orders, not least in defence of a racist privilege, as they were quite clear that upon their readiness to do this depended their ability to maintain their imperial hold in India. They were accordingly always prepared to use the force they believed to be necessary to ensure this was maintained. Yet in the aftermath of the Jallianwallah Bagh massacre of 1919 they remained neurotically inhibited from using military force against their nationalist opponents if this could possibly be avoided, and as the Lucknow story very particularly specifies, even where there was a large military cantonment just a mile or so away, they were ordinarily extremely careful when a climax came to use no more than their lathi-armed police to disperse a nationalist demonstration (despite the brutality these could inflict, especially when riding horses) rather than call up the firepower of their soldiery. When they did send for troops they were very careful too, when no counter-violence had been launched against them, to call out no more than a symbolic minimum so as to effect no more than a demonstration, and soon returned them to their barracks as soon as it seemed safe to do so. If violence was then levelled against them they felt under no compunction about recalling troops to the city and maintaining military patrols there for several weeks on end. Yet neither then nor later did they resort to any punitive shootings or to any random arrests either.

An essential feature of the great proportion of the clashes which occurred at this time in the nationalist–imperialist encounter in India was thus that certain holds were barred. Congressmen not only totally eschewed violence. They did everything they could to prevent the city crowd from resorting to it too. While for their part the British substantially modulated their response to the Congress challenge, even when they were prepared to use harsh, coercive force when that seemed to them unavoidable.

All of which stood upon the inherent ambiguity on each side. We saw in the previous chapter how the ambiguity of the British in its declaratory mode generated a sharp debate within the Indian nationalist leadership in the weeks preceding the Lahore Congress in 1929. Here we have explored one example of how British ambiguity in its operational mode directly conditioned the manner in which local representatives of the two sides battled with each other in direct, physical confrontation in the open streets and parks of a major Indian city. The knife edge upon which British ambiguity stood was neatly symbolised in Hailey's private criticism of Munro's actions on 25 May and his appointment of an official enquiry into them, that were quite precisely conjoined with his refusal to upbraid Munro directly and his summary rejection of all nationalist criticisms raised against them. Congress reciprocated. It never sought to mount a major insurrection. It concentrated instead on defying the British and at considerable personal cost discrediting the posture that they took.

Contemporaneously the quite distinctive character of these proceedings can be quite summarily indicated by noting that nothing at all like them occurred in the Philippines at this time since against the much more accommodating Americans anything at all comparable was quite unnecessary there. At the same time they had no counterparts in Indonesia or in Vietnam either. All the signs were that in both places there would have been very much harsher retribution if anything similar had been attempted. These satyagraha confrontations epitomised the singular nature of the Indo-British conflict.

As it was despite the efforts of the British to play these issues cautiously the honours in these Indian clashes went increasingly to the Congress side. As a consequence both the British in India, and those involved with Indian affairs in Britain too, were made to feel that Gandhi's increasingly well-honed satyagraha weapons would continue to be employed against them until the purposes they were designed to secure were attained. They became the principal instruments in the armoury of the Indian freedom movement – not bludgeons that could be easily turned against their wielders, but the deftest of scalpels which sliver by sliver would ultimately pare the imperialist stance to its bone.

4   Peace with conflict: the Gandhi–Emerson talks, March–August 1931

I rather like the look of things in India. The late Lord Salisbury said, quoting an American, there were two ways of governing men – 'bamboozle or bamboo'. You seem to be trying both at once.
Winston Churchill to Sinclair, Liberal Chief Whip, 30 December 1931

One common feature of the final period of imperial rule in many a colonial territory, at all events in the British Empire, was the coming together, and then close conjunction, between the principal nationalist leaders and the last colonial rulers. Perhaps the most notable example occurred in India in 1947 as between Jawaharlal Nehru and Mountbatten. But there were many later cases too: between Senanayake and Soulbury in Ceylon; Nkrumah and Arden-Clarke in Ghana; Tunku Abdul Rahman and MacGillivray in Malaya; Abubaker and Robertson in Nigeria; Nyerere and Turnbull in Tanganyika; Kenyatta and Macdonald in Kenya; even briefly between Mugabe and Soames in Zimbabwe. There were earlier examples too in most of India's Provinces in 1937–9 (as we shall see in chapter 7). The reason for this propensity is not hard to find. For while the incoming nationalist leaders were understandably anxious to secure a firm grasp on the levers of political power, the outgoing rulers were anxious to depart in as orderly and as dignified a manner as possible. Both had a major interest in effecting a smooth transfer of power.

During the early part of 1931 somewhat similar impulses were at work between Gandhi and the Government of India. In an extraordinary way they entered for a while into a closer association with each other than ever before or after. Whilst the British strove to enlist Gandhi's cooperation and that of the Congress in the furtherance of constitutional reforms and in restraining Congress's more activist supporters, Gandhi sought to use the unusual opportunity this gave him to secure for the Indian National Congress an equal partnership with the British in the exercise of overall political power in India. So as to secure their objectives the British were ready to enter into a quite exceptional compact with him. Precisely, however, because, for all the goodwill they were ready to display, they had by this time neither decided to transfer any real power over India, nor been forced to do so, the classic end-of-empire accord never at this time came to fruition here, and, to the contrary, before many months had passed, the close accord they had established with Gandhi lay in ruins. Many of the details of this story have been recounted elsewhere. What is generally missed are both its central determinants, and its cruel denouement. Once again the particular events of a constricted period were critically conditioned by Britain's persistent ambiguity.

In putting this story in context we need briefly first to retrace our steps. By the 1920s, as we have seen, whilst still holding firmly to their dominion over India, the British were committed before the decade was out to review the Indian constitution. So as to forestall the likelihood that this would be conducted under the auspices of a new, more accommodating Labour government, Birkenhead, the Conservative Secretary of State for India, brought forward in 1927 the appointment of a Statutory Commission to put together advice upon this. The egregious decision, at the instance of the new Viceroy, Lord Irwin, and his advisers, to appoint no Indians to this not only led (as we have variously seen in the previous two chapters) to a dramatic closing of the ranks between the followers of the Indian National Congress and the politicians and 'public men' of a 'liberal/moderate' kind who had been separated from it for a decade past. It also precipitated the series of angry boycotts of the Statutory Commission that not only threatened the orderly consideration of constitutional reform in India, but challenged Britain's imperial authority there as well.[1]

In theory it would perhaps have been possible for the British to have responded to these eventualities either by deciding to shelve the idea of further constitutional reform altogether, or by going the extra mile and granting the reaggregated forces of Indian nationalism all that they were seeking. But for reasons that need no reiteration at this stage they were in no mind to do either. Their instinct was rather to wean their nationalist opponents away from their oppositional stance, and channel their energies into more consensual courses. 'By some means or other', Irwin was to state, 'contact had to be regained and confidence in British purpose restored'.[2]

Thus it was that in October 1929 Irwin issued the declaration on behalf of the British Government which promised that in due course India could have 'Dominion Status', and thereupon invited India's political leaders to a Round Table Conference on constitutional reform in London. That, as we have seen, precipitated a major debate within the ranks of India's

---

[1] S.Gopal, *The Viceroyalty of Lord Irwin 1926–1931*, Oxford 1957, chs. I–III.
[2] Earl of Halifax, *Fulness of Days*, London 1957, p. 117.

nationalists that eventuated in a renewed breach between the
'liberal/moderates' who decided they would accept the invitation to go to
London, and the very much more substantial Indian National Congress
which in December 1929 emphatically rejected the British offers.
Thereafter in March 1930 Gandhi unloosed the hosts of Indian nationalism in a sustained, and in the main remarkably non-violent, attack on
British rule in India. Characteristically Irwin initially preferred to treat all
of this calmly; but when it proved to be a great deal more formidable than
his government had expected, he did not hesitate to repress it vehemently,
by arresting thousands of Congress activists, Gandhi in due course
amongst them.[3]

Yet that could only be a holding operation. For as the British had long
since learned repression gave them very uncertain ground on which to
stand. Moreover, they still sought to entice the Congress leaders to the
Round Table Conference. As a consequence between July and September
1930 (when there were some signs that the Congress leaders might be
prepared to compromise) Irwin in the so-called Yeravda negotiations
authorised two leading 'moderates', Sir Tej Bahadur Sapru and M.R.
Jayakar, to seek some compromise agreement with the Congress leaders.
After protracted negotiations that, however, proved to be unattainable.
One side sought too much, the other conceded much too little.[4]

To most people's surprise the Round Table Conference which thereupon took place in London between British ministers and politicians and
a selection of Indian figures, but without participation by the Congress,
did nevertheless by February 1931 produce some very much more
promising results than had ever been expected. Representatives of the
Indian Princes agreed with Indian 'moderate' leaders that an all-India
Federation of India's provinces and princely states could be formed; and
despite the clefts which had been opened up amongst Britain's political
parties by Irwin's 'Dominion Status' declaration, the British Labour
government, with the concurrence of the other parties, not only agreed to
grant full 'responsible government' to British India's provinces, but – so
long as there were several important restraining 'safeguards' in the new
constitution – to grant 'responsibility at the centre' to a government
enjoying the support of a carefully crafted federal legislature.[5]

As has been well recounted elsewhere,[6] in view of this unexpected turn
of events Irwin seized the opportunity that there might just be here, not
only to bring civil disobedience to an end and cease employing so much
repression to maintain British authority over India, but of persuading the

---

[3] Gopal, *Irwin*, ch. V. [4] Brown, *Gandhi and Civil Disobedience*, pp. 153–68.
[5] The text is conveniently printed in *CWMG* 45, App. I.
[6] Gopal, *Irwin*, ch. VI; Brown, *Gandhi and Civil Disobedience*, pp. 171–91.

Congress to settle for the reforms that lay on offer rather than pursuing the chimera of immediate independence.[7] To this end on 25 January 1931 he released Gandhi and the principal Congress leaders unconditionally. There was no immediate response from the Congress side, but eventually, through the good offices of several 'moderate' go-betweens back from London, Sapru and Jayakar not least among them, Gandhi met Irwin in the Viceroy's House in New Delhi on 25 February 1931.

By this time Gandhi was ready for a settlement. Sapru and Jayakar persuaded him that whilst the conclusions of the Round Table Conference held out no hope of *purna swaraj*, they might well contain their own evolutionary potential which could conceivably bring India to within sight of their goal.[8] As a satyagrahi Gandhi was always committed to making a settlement if an acceptable solution stood on offer.[9] More particularly he was now under immense pressure from his staunchest supporters – India's merchant communities – to abandon the civil disobedience campaign lest grave damage be done to their businesses by its associated trade boycott.[10] In this atmosphere the main lines of a settlement were soon agreed. Under it civil disobedience would be called off; imperial repression would cease; and Congress would undertake to attend a second Round Table Conference in London later in the year.

There were, however, a number of attendant difficulties. Gandhi demanded a full enquiry into recent repressive actions by the police. He pleaded for the life of Bhagat Singh, the murderer of a prominent British police officer, who was due to be executed. He argued for the restoration of lands confiscated from satyagrahis in Gujarat, and for the reinstatement there of those who had resigned their offices in his cause; and despite the ending of Civil Disobedience he insisted that lawful picketing must be permitted to continue, and the collection of salt by the poor as well. Irwin refused to meet him on the police, or on Bhagat Singh, but he was prepared to concede (in a way that soon caused major difficulties) that where in Gujarat confiscated land had not been finally sold, and where vacated posts had not been permanently filled, these might be recovered; and that under strict conditions non-oppressive picketing, and salt production for local use, could be allowed.

As a consequence over the course of several meetings the two men developed a close personal rapport with each other, and this was soon

---

[7] Irwin to his father, 10, 30 Mar. 1931, IP 27.

[8] 'To proud Gujarat', *Navajivan*, 15 Mar. 1931, *CWMG* 45, p. 296. See also Low, 'Sir Tej Bahadur Sapru and the First Round Table Conference', pp. 318–20.

[9] E.g., Speech at Karachi Congress, 30 Mar. 1931, *CWMG* 45, p. 364.

[10] S. Sarkar, 'The Logic of Gandhian Nationalism: Civil Disobedience and the Gandhi–Irwin Pact (1930–31)', *Indian Historical Review*, 3, 1, 1976, pp. 114–46.

extended to Herbert Emerson, the Secretary of the Home Department of the Government of India, whom Irwin called in to help with the details. When Irwin first suggested this, Gandhi declared: 'Oh, please let him in. I have heard so much about him, what a hard man he is, so unkind to the poor people.' Thereupon, so Irwin told his father:

I accordingly fetched the luckless Emerson in, who happens to be an admirable type of Indian Civilian, perfectly straightforward, with plenty of character, and, within five or ten minutes, he and Gandhi understood each other perfectly and evidently liked each other very much. The result was that I was tremendously helped in what had hitherto been a single-handed contest.[11]

The Gandhi–Irwin Pact of 5 March 1931 that emerged from these discussions was on the British side a characteristically dual-faced pronouncement.[12] Whilst it put an end to repression, and provided for the immediate release of satyagraha prisoners who had not been involved in violence, and while it formally allowed that Congress could make any case it wished in London, it nevertheless contained no commitment to early Dominion Status, let alone *purna swaraj*, whilst Irwin quite specifically emphasised to Gandhi the extreme foolishness of striving for any more extensive reforms than the Labour Government already had on offer, and warned him that should there be any renewal of civil disobedience it would immediately be suppressed. The Pact succeeded, however, in binding the Congress into undertaking to be represented at the next Round Table Conference and into assuming a degree of responsibility for the restoration of orderly government in India. In classic British manner, by a measured assuagement, Irwin had seemingly fashioned a working concordat with the prime nationalist leader, as a principal means of sustaining British imperial rule in India, and blunting the edge of nationalist opposition to it.

It is upon the aftermath of the Pact that we shall focus here. Upon the Indian side it had from the outset some very strenuous critics. Had Jawaharlal Nehru not been thrown off balance by the recent death of his father Motilal, his considered opposition to it might well have been as strong as it had been against going to London in 1929.[13] As it was Vallabhbhai Patel, the principal Gujarat Congress leader, was always vehemently hostile to it.[14] It gave him none of the assurances which he believed were crucial to his personal position there.[15] Yet Gandhi himself was very

---

[11] Irwin to his father, 10 Mar. 1931, IP 27. See for a slightly differently phrased account Halifax, *Fulness of Days*, p.148.

[12] The text is conveniently printed in *CWMG* 45, App. VI.

[13] Gopal, *Jawaharlal Nehru*, I, pp. 149–51.

[14] E.g. Bombay to HD, 25 Mar. 1931, H.Poll.33/1/31; Bajpai to Sapru, 21 Apr. 1931, SP 5, B14.   [15] *SWJN* 4, pp. 470–82 passim.

well satisfied. Not only had he dramatically elicited from the Viceroy British recognition of the Congress as the principal force with which significant political negotiations in India had to be conducted (rather than with elected legislators, 'moderate' intermediaries, or their like). Without damaging the support of his merchant supporters for the nationalist movement he had met their demand for an end to Civil Disobedience. He had procured the mass release of a great many satyagraha prisoners. He had restored the cooperation with India's 'moderate' leaders – so that all the significant forces of Indian nationalism were now reaggregated once again. He had, moreover, secured a commanding position from which to insist upon the Government's full and generous implementation of the Pact; and he clearly sensed that it had given him an unprecedented opportunity to secure for the Congress a hold over government administration in India of a kind which he had hardly dreamt of before.

Yet in a manner that seems to have been very largely missed the pervasive dualities in the Pact, exemplifying as they did the fundamental ambiguities in the overall British position, immediately created a quite extraordinary situation in India that soon did fatal damage to all that its principal negotiators had had in mind. Given the mutual accommodation which had been achieved, it might have been expected that the Pact would have led to a moderating of populist rhetoric, and the abandonment of ostentatious agitation, whilst each side buckled to the task of constitutional reform to which it was now committed. Certainly Irwin had anticipated that 'the creation of . . . peaceful conditions [and] . . . civil quiet . . . [would secure] for those grave issues calm and dispassionate examination'.[16] But that proved to be a complete miscalculation.

In the immediate aftermath of the Pact the government arranged for the prompt jail delivery of the great majority of the satyagraha prisoners, and very soon rescinded its special coercive powers too.[17] But to its intense dismay every such conciliatory action promptly proved to be totally counterproductive. For far from Irwin's initiatives being extolled as the gestures of goodwill they purported to be – or the Pact being excoriated for its complete failure to meet Congress's insistent demand for *purna swaraj*; or anyone acknowledging that over the turn of the year the steam had largely gone out of the civil disobedience movement – it was instantly hailed across the length and breadth of India as a palpable sign of British enfeeblement and a remarkable triumph for the Congress.[18]

---

[16] V's Statement, 26 Jan. 1931, *CWMG* 45, p. 427.

[17] HD to LGs, tel., 5 Mar. 1931, H.Poll.5/45/31.

[18] E.g. Comm. Lucknow to CS UP, 13 Mar., Emerson's Note, 16 Mar., Jagdish Prasad (CS UP) to Emerson, 25 Mar., Mudie to Harper, 30 Mar., and (a view from the base of the

That conclusion was not in fact all that surprising. Back in 1919 and again in 1922 when nationalist agitation had been called off, it had been brought to a halt by Gandhi himself. When ten years later it was twice resumed, it largely petered out of itself in 1941, and was very largely defeated in 1942. In sharp contrast in March 1931 it was rescinded, not principally at the instance of Gandhi, nor because it had been effectively trounced, but because in their anxiety to limit the damage which flowed from the repressive measures they had taken over the past year and entice Congress into negotiations on constitutional reform, the British had allowed Gandhi to effect a quite extraordinary personal compact with them. That in the eyes of a great many Indians represented nothing less than a comprehensive climb-down from the high peak of imperialist defiance which the British had been displaying over the previous year. Why should Irwin have negotiated with Gandhi (so popular perception had it) and agreed to the precipitate repeal of repressive measures and the summary release of most satyagraha prisoners, if the British had not suddenly become aware, as they had not acknowledged before, that they were no longer able to maintain their previous dominion over India.[19] Amid the baffling melange that was British ambiguity its more conciliatory stance, that is, was extensively interpreted in the aftermath of the Pact not as a genuine attempt to set aside conflict and embark upon negotiations, but as an unmistakable augury that in India British imperialism was beginning to crack.

Within days of the promulgation of the Pact there thereupon followed a mass popular outburst which found expression in a whole series of tumultuous demonstrations, meetings and processions in innumerable towns and villages up and down the country that welcomed home the suddenly released satyagraha prisoners as so many heroes in the nation's cause.[20] The intense euphoria which propelled this drew strength from

government's structure) Kemp (Superintendent of Police, Muttra) 'Report on Political Situation', 31 Mar. 1931, H.Poll.33/11/31; B & O report, 21 Mar. 1931, Hallett to Emerson, 14 Apr. 1931, H.Poll.33/5/31; Punjab to all Comms. etc., 25 Apr. 1931, H.Poll.33/7/31; Jagdish Prasad to Emerson and enc., 16 July 1931, H.Poll.33/24/31; Williams to Emerson, 29 July 1931, H.Poll.33/30/31.

[19] E.g. Montmorency (G Punjab) to Irwin, 11 Mar. 1931, H.Poll.33/2/31; Comm. Jhansi to CS UP, 15 Mar. 1931, H.Poll.33/3/31; Kemp, 'Political Situation' (note 18 above); Speeches by Lakhsmi Chand, 13 Mar. and Mrs Uma Nehru, 15 Mar. 1931, H.Poll.33/24/31.

[20] E.g. Daily police report, Surat, 9 Mar. 1931, in Collins to Emerson, 17 Mar. 1931, H.Poll.33/3/31; Boyd (Lahore) to Emerson, 11 Mar. 1931, H.Poll.33/2/31; Dep. Comm., Rae Bareli to Comm. Lucknow, 13 Mar. 1931, H.Poll.33/11/31; District Officer, Jhansi to Comm. Jhansi, and enc., 14 Mar. 1931, H.Poll.33/3/31; B & O report, 21 Mar. 1931, H.Poll.33/5/31; Hailey to Willingdon, 21 Apr. 1930, HP 20.

the fact that it was still only a year since the Civil Disobedience movement had first been launched; that despite the setbacks it had suffered, and the reservations which existed, popular commitment to it was still running high; and that its agitational propensity remained unabated.

Amidst the accompanying tumult there was at the same time a much more calculating agenda on the part of many Congress leaders. Whereas to Irwin and the British Government the principal merits of the Gandhi–Irwin Pact had been the decisions of the Congress to call off Civil Disobedience, suspend the campaign for immediate *purna swaraj*, and commit itself to being represented at the second Round Table Conference, to a great many Congressmen the Pact presented a quite different face. To them it never constituted anything more than a truce whilst the further talks to which they were committed with the British ran their course. They had no illusion that upon the central issue of *purna swaraj*, on which the great Civil Disobedience campaign had been fought, they had made no progress whatsoever. They had indeed been cajoled into calling it off. They had even been trapped into discussing the much more limited reforms the British had on offer. They had no confidence, moreover, that the forthcoming second Round Table Conference would secure their principal objectives. The probability was therefore that civil disobedience would shortly have to be renewed. It was accordingly vital, so they saw it, that during the currency of the Pact they should take every opportunity to boost popular support for their cause, develop the Congress organisation, enlarge its capabilities, and enhance the momentum of their movement in every way they could.[21]

It was necessary, however, to move cautiously. Although they joined with their fellow countrymen in the excitement that followed upon the announcement of the Pact, they had no desire to provide the British with any excuse for abrogating it – other than at a moment of Congress's own choosing. They had no wish to undermine the plenipotentiary position Gandhi seemed to have secured with the British. And they had no intention of returning to jail whilst the new opportunities the Pact provided for promoting their cause still remained unexhausted. Ordinarily they were careful therefore to obey its *ipsissima verba*.[22]

That was a particularly astute move since the characteristic ambiguities

---

[21] E.g. Gandhi's speech in Bombay, 17 Mar. 1931, *CWMG* 45, pp. 305–7; Nehru to PCCs, 9 Apr. 1931, and several other letters, and Williamson's (Director, Intelligence Bureau) Note, 21 Apr. 1931, H.Poll.33/1/31; Williamson's Note on Emerson's 11 Apr. letter, 28 Apr. 1931, Reid to Emerson, 11 May 1931, Assam to HD, 12 May 1931, Montmorency to Emerson, 13 May 1931, H.Poll.33/7/31. Nehru's speeches Mar. and June 1931, *SWJN* 4, pp. 487–99, 5, pp. 1–7 passim.

[22] E.g. Notice by Sitla Sahai, 8 Mar. 1931, H.Poll.33/11/31; Cotton to Emerson, 26 Apr. 1931, H.Poll.33/30/31.

of the Pact gave them a number of unprecedented opportunities to advance their cause which they could scarcely have fashioned for themselves. Whilst they were prevented from employing by its terms their well-honed stock-in-trade of satyagraha confrontations,[23] by the same token the government was precluded from resorting to the wholesale imprisonment of nationalist activists which they had so extensively employed during the past year. That meant that upon their release Congressmen were generally quite free within the ordinary law to campaign in any other way that they chose. That, as it happened, suited them very well. During the course of the previous year their satyagraha confrontations and their no rent and no revenue campaigns had often entailed considerable personal costs for themselves (frequently indeed many months in jail). There were, however, a good many other, no doubt less heroic, but by no means less potent means by which to launch an assault upon British authority in India. Many of them necessitated considerable popular support. But in the aftermath of the Gandhi–Irwin Pact that was ordinarily forthcoming. Not only were they now free to denounce the government in more unrestrained terms than ever before, and organise all manner of popular nationalist demonstrations against them. Before very long they found themselves able to fasten upon a whole plethora of disputes concerning the Pact's detailed implementation, and in their cause to challenge many a district officer's orders with impunity.[24] Whilst, moreover, the Pact specifically proscribed no rent and no revenue campaigns, because of the severe impact of the 1930s world slump,[25] peasant agitations in several rural areas became all but impossible to hold back. Many soon assumed an anti-government as well as an anti-landlord character, which also suited the Congress very well.[26] For they could now stand forth as champions of the victims of agrarian distress as rarely before or after. Whilst, therefore, they remained careful to hold to the specificities of the Pact, they were now quick to exploit its conciliatory features in every way they could.

This position was officially promulgated within days of the Pact's conclusion by Jawaharlal Nehru as General Secretary of the Congress in a letter of instruction to Congress's provincial leaders.

It is vitally necessary [he wrote to them on 10 March] that you should take immediate steps to consolidate the position gained by the Congress during the last year and to strengthen it still further. The immediate action to be taken is to

---

[23] Mahmud to PCCs, tel., 5 Mar. 1931, *CWMG* 45, pp. 256–7.
[24] All this is fully canvassed below.
[25] E.g. Allahabad CID report, 1 Apr. 1931, Emerson's Notes 3,4 Apr. 1931, Notes by Fazli Husein, 22 June 1931, and Emerson, 1 July 1931, on cuttings from *Hamdard*, 21 June 1931, Emerson to Gandhi, 24 June 1931, H.Poll.33/11/31; Bell to Emerson, 11 Apr. 1931, H.Poll.33/3/31.   [26] H.Poll.33/11/31, 33/24/31 passim.

send out our Workers, those who have been discharged from jails and others to the villages to explain exactly what has been done in Delhi, further to see that there is no harassment or oppression of any kind in the rural areas. If such cases of harassment occur either on the part of police officials or the agents of landlords, our workers should immediately come to the help of the persons harassed and by negotiation try to get their difficulties removed. In case they find difficulty in doing so they should refer the matter to you ... If we now establish firmly definite centres of work and activity in rural areas we shall strengthen our organisation and prepare the people for any contingency that may arise. I need not tell you that the provisional settlement at Delhi means a truce only and no final peace. That peace can only come when we have gained our objective in its entirety.[27]

As a result the celebrations that had accompanied the release of so many Congressmen soon developed into the great Congress 'stir' of mid-1931. Over the course of several months an immense number of rallies, meetings, and marches were mounted,[28] newspaper articles vaunted the nationalist cause high, whilst endless speeches lifted the anti-imperialist rhetoric by many decibels.[29] In particular there was now extensive picketing of foreign cloth and liquor shops.[30] Every opportunity was then seized upon to turn the tables on the government. Every lapse upon the ruler's part was soon transformed into an occasion for great furore. Every opening was exploited to turn the harsh economic conditions arising from the slump into some angry cause to lead against the British. While countless formally correct invocations by the Congress to hard-pressed peasants to pay their rent and revenue became almost invariably qualified by admonitions to pay only what they could afford.[31]

Moreover, Congress provincial leaders soon set about garnishing their provincial campaigns with some special emphases that were locally especially pertinent. In the Punjab loud cries were uttered against the death sentence on Bhagat Singh.[32] In NWFP Abdul Ghaffar Khan seized the

---

[27] Nehru to Secretaries, PCCs, 10 Mar. 1931, *SWJN* 4, pp. 488–90, H.Poll.33/2/31, 33/11/31, 33/24/31.

[28] E.g. several telegrams from LGs in late Mar. 1931, H.Poll.33/1/31, and Apr. 1931, H.Poll.33/2/31 passim.

[29] E.g. H.Poll.33/2/31 passim (e.g. report of speech by S.C. Bose in the Jallianwallah Bagh, Amritsar, 8 Apr. 1931, and Jagdish Prasad to Emerson, 21 Apr. 1931).

[30] E.g. 'My Notes', *Navajivan*, 15 Mar. 1931, *CWMG* 45, pp. 291–3; H.Poll.33/30/31 passim; Police report, Ferozepur, 9 Apr. 1931, H.Poll.33/2/31; Hallett to Emerson and encs, 4 Apr. 1931, Emerson to Gandhi (re B & O), 9 Apr. 1931, H.Poll.33/5/31; Chetti to Patel, 13 May 1931, AICC 17/1931; Jagdish Prasad to Emerson, 2 July, enc. Mudie to Mehta, 1 July, Mudie to Nehru, 30 June and Nehru to Mudie, 1 July 1931, H.Poll.33/24/31; Maxwell to Gandhi, 18 July 1931, H.Poll.33/4/31; H.Poll.33/5/31, 33/27/31 passim.

[31] E.g. Dep. Comm., Sultanpur to Jagdish Prasad, 20 July 1931, H.Poll.33/23/31; Jagdish Prasad to Emerson and encs., 16 July 1931, H.Poll.33/24/31; H.Poll.33/11/31 passim.

[32] H.Poll.33/2/31 passim; Report on meetings in Punjab, [Apr.–July 1931], H.Poll.33/30/31.

opportunity of the post-Pact situation to strengthen his Khudai Khidmatgars against the still very authoritarian imperial regime there.[33] In Bengal, in the midst of a debilitating faction fight between Subhas Bose and Sen Gupta, considerable cooperation was developed between certain Congressmen and certain terrorists.[34] In Bihar Rajendra Prasad put together a long list of complaints against the 'war mentality' of the government.[35] In UP Nehru soon plunged into the leadership of a major agrarian agitation.[36] In Madras Rajagopalachari, with feline skill, issued a circular on 22 April, which, whilst carefully cataloguing the steps Congressmen could *not* now take, emphasised the boycott of liquor and foreign cloth, the collection of new funds, the enrolment of new members and other measures which they *could* now take – a consummate exercise in backhanded 'ambiguity' if ever there was one.[37] Whilst in Gujarat Vallabhbhai Patel traipsed around many a village, fulminating against the government's ejectments and confiscations of the previous year and their now pressing demands for land revenue arrears.[38] It was during the course of this further campaign that the position of Gandhi's principal lieutenants in the provinces became entrenched: Abdul Ghaffar Khan in the Frontier, Rajendra Prasad in Bihar, Nehru in UP, Rajagopalachari in Madras, Vallabhbhai Patel in Gujarat.

As a consequence the Congress movement in India soon showed itself to be a great deal more formidable than ever before, and a whole series of highly charged local conflicts soon multiplied across the land.[39] That placed a great many officials of the British Raj in some often new and exceedingly difficult circumstances. Many of them had been considerably troubled by the Viceroy's negotiations with Gandhi.[40] They were deeply dismayed by the euphoria which accompanied the release of their

---

[33] Memorandum [nd, 1931] H.Poll.33/24/31; Rittenberg, *Ethnicity, Nationalism and the Pakhtuns*, pp. 100–9.   [34] Sarkar, *Bengal 1928–1934*, ch. 3.

[35] H.Poll.33/5/31 passim; Henningham, *Peasant Movements in Colonial India*, pp. 143–5.

[36] *SWJN* 5, section 2; H.Poll.33/24/31 passim; Nehru's mss. note, [June 1931], AICC 63/1931; Gopal, *Nehru*, I, ch. 11; Pandey, *Ascendancy of the Congress in Uttar Pradesh*, ch. 6.

[37] Rajagopalachari's Circular Instructions to Congress Workers, 22 Apr. 1931, H.Poll.33/30/31. Emerson even seems to have been well pleased with it, Gandhi to Rajagopalachari, 17 May 1931, *CWMG* 46, p. 163. See more generally H.Poll.33/9/31, 33/30/31 passim; Arnold, *The Congress in Tamilnad*, pp. 133–7; Arnold, *Police Power and Colonial Rule. Madras 1859–1947*, Delhi 1986, pp. 196–7.

[38] E.g. Surat Police reports, 30 Apr., 2, 5 May 1931, H.Poll.33/3/31. See more generally Hardiman, *Peasant Nationalists of Gujarat*, pp. 234–9.

[39] Even a broad survey cannot be attempted here, but see *inter alia* AICC 2 & KWs, 3 & KW, 32, 53, 75, and G140 & KW/ 1931; H.Poll.14/8/31, 33/5/31, 33/23/31, 33/24/31, 33/30/31, 33/5/31.

[40] E.g. Montmorency to Irwin, 11 Mar. 1931, H.Poll.33/2/31. See also Irwin to Hailey, 20 Mar. 1931, HP 34.

satyagraha prisoners and the loud proclamations of a Congress victory,[41] and before very long they became profoundly disturbed by the agitations erupting all around them, and particularly by the impotence the Pact had newly imposed upon them in holding these at bay.[42] They were soon appalled, moreover, by the mounting evidence that the prestige upon which so much of their imperial hegemony had rested in India was now being quite devastatingly sapped.[43] As a consequence many of them hardened their hearts, flexed their muscles, and gave the Congress many a cause to complain of their obstructive tactics, all of which often aggravated the situation even more.[44]

In consequence of all this a highly fraught situation soon developed in India. Whilst both sides were committed to 'peace' and to following the ordinary law of the land, and were, moreover, committed to upholding the Pact, and to the holding of talks on constitutional reforms by the end of the year, the major conflict between the accumulating legions of Indian nationalism and the hard rock of British imperialism had hardly ever been more intense. Peace there could be; but there were endlessly multiplying conflicts too. Ambiguity bred further ambiguity, and was soon performing some further twists as well. Everyone was caught in its enveloping coils. Whilst the Government of India did a great deal to try to handle the situation with openness and discretion, because of its absolute determination to hold its ground, that simply served to fan the fires of public agitation. On the Congress side open civil disobedience was for the time being altogether ruled out, but the resourcefulness and novelty which characterised its renewed agitation not only perfectly reflected the ambiguous stance of the British, but soon led to a myriad of disputes and confrontations with agents of the Raj.[45]

In this situation Gandhi found himself in an extremely difficult position. The total commitment of the Congress to the fulfilment of the precise conditions of the Pact was absolutely vital both to his own reputation for good faith and to that of the Congress too.[46] Should the Pact collapse there could be no assurance that a renewal of civil disobedience

[41] E.g. Dep. Comm., Rae Baraeli to Comm. Lucknow, 12 Mar. 1931, H.Poll.33/11/31; Hailey to Stewart, 25 Apr. 1930, HP 20.

[42] E.g. Reid, CS Bengal to Emerson, 11 May 1931, H.Poll.33/7/31.

[43] E.g. Montmorency to Emerson, 13 May 1931, ibid.; UP CID report 28 Mar. 1931, Mudie to Harper, 30 Mar. 1931, Kemp 'Report on Political Situation', 31 Mar. 1931, Fazli Husain's Note, 22 June 1931, H.Poll.33/11/31; Reid to Emerson, 13 July 1931, ibid. 13/8/31.

[44] E.g. H.Poll.33/5/31; various UP reports for July 1931, H.Poll.33/23/31.

[45] E.g. Hallett to Emerson, 19 May 1931, H.Poll.33/5/31.

[46] For characteristic statements see his Interview to the press, 18 Apr. 1931, CWMG 46, pp. 10–11.

would be supported by India's crucially important merchant communities, and there was every probability that the government would suppress it swiftly and decisively. To Gandhi's intense dismay, moreover, a violent spirit was evidently spreading amongst his younger followers;[47] whilst communal divisions across the land had never looked more serious.[48] It was far from certain too that the Round Table Conference (to which he had promised to go)[49] would produce any useful outturn. Whilst he continued to enjoy the full support of his provincial lieutenants, he was soon under mounting pressure from them to involve himself directly in a whole series of local issues where they asserted the government was behaving contumaciously. Clearly it was quite impossible for him to exercise effective charge over all the eruptive possibilities now pervading India. Yet to maintain his own credibility with his followers and with the British too he clearly had to do something, since sooner or later one or more of the local encounters could easily escalate into something a great deal more portentous. In these lowering circumstances he grasped at a quite particular personal opening. Selecting from amongst the large number of complaints he was receiving about the malice and malevolence of the government, he took hold of the opportunity to renew his earlier contacts with the highest reaches of government so as to secure their resolution.

In the ominous circumstances now prevailing the Government of India was caught in its own duality. It was necessarily all but irrevocably committed to the Pact. It had no wish to revert to open repression once again. As it was now central to British policy to get Congress to participate in the constitutional discussions in London and attend the second Round Table Conference, that could only be assured so long as the Pact remained in being. The Government of India was in no position, therefore, to abrogate it. If the Pact was to collapse it would in any event be vital to its own standing both in India and in Britain that the responsibility for this should lie firmly with the Congress.[50] Short of surrendering – which it had absolutely no intention of doing – it was imperative therefore that it should maintain the Pact in every way it could. At the same time so perturbed did it become that the highly charged situation now erupting all around it might suddenly explode into a major confrontation, that it very soon set about ensuring that should Civil Disobedience be in any

---

[47] Sukhdev to Gandhi [23 May 1931], ibid., pp. 397–9; Gandhi to Nehru, 20 June 1931, H.Poll.21/8/31.

[48] This large subject cannot be elaborated upon again here, see the major studies, Page, *Prelude to Partition*, pp. 229–45; M. Hasan, *Nationalism and Communal Politics in India, 1885–1930*, Delhi 1991.

[49] 'To proud Gujarat', *Navajivan*, 15 Mar. 1931, *CWMG* 45, pp. 295–7.

[50] E.g. Crerar to Hailey, 11 July 1931, H.Poll.33/16/31; Emerson to Bell, 23 July 1931, H.Poll.33/19/31.

form renewed it would be assured of all the powers it needed to suppress it.[51]

Short, however, of any renewal of Civil Disobedience, the options before the Government of India, given the skill and magnitude of the Congress campaign, and its own absolute determination to hold its own corner, were otherwise very limited. Ambivalence was writ large all over its face. It could urge its subordinates to display patience, and instruct them to employ no more than the ordinary law.[52] Everyone knew, however, that that could in the end be quite ineffectual against the agitations now springing up all about them, and that in a very short while much more substantial measures could all too easily be required. In these circumstances almost the only opening available to it, so it soon concluded, would be to resume the earlier talks that had been held with Gandhi, and to seek to place upon him the responsibility for curbing the more threatening activities of his followers.[53] Since in their different ways both Gandhi and the Government of India had an overriding interest in holding down the lid upon the seething cauldron that was now India, a quite exceptional sequence of events soon ensued.

During the course of the negotiations which had preceded the Gandhi–Irwin Pact the personal relations between Gandhi and some key figures in the Government of India had, as we have seen, become in the end very cordial.[54] When, therefore, each of them found themselves caught in the maelstrom spreading across India their relatively good personal relations now made it seem advantageous to both sides to revive their earlier conversations. As it happened the further discussions on which as a consequence they soon embarked took on a very unusual character. That principally arose from the quite fortuitous fact that in mid April 1931 Irwin left India and was replaced by a new Viceroy, Willingdon. Accordingly neither of them was in a good position to conduct the resumed discussions with Gandhi which entailed any point of detail.[55] As a consequence it suited both Viceroys to entrust the critical talks that now took place between the Government of India on the one hand and Gandhi on the other to the one Indian Civil Service officer who

---

[51] E.g. Emerson to LGs, 11 June 1931, ibid. 13/8/31, 209/31 passim; Emerson to Reid, 17 June 1931, H.Poll.33/7/31.   [52] E.g. Emerson to LGs, 11 Apr. 1931, H.Poll.33/7/31.

[53] For two explicit statements see Emerson to Lambert, 7 Apr. 1931: I 'have some hope that Gandhi himself will successfully check activities of which he appears to have been largely ignorant and some of which he certainly disapproves', to which Lambert (Acting G UP) replied, Lambert to Emerson, 12 Apr. 1931, that he hoped 'Mr Gandhi can carry out his side of the bargain and call off his wolves', H.Poll.33/11/31.

[54] E.g. Gandhi to Emerson, 6 Mar. 1931, H.Poll.5/45/31; Gandhi to Chintamani, 31 May 1931, CWMG 46, pp. 266–7.

[55] See Irwin's Note on his interview with Gandhi, 19 Mar 1931, CWMG 45, p. 314; Emerson to Gandhi, 15 July 1931, H.Poll.33/23/31.

during the negotiation of the Pact had won his approbation: the Home Secretary of the Government of India, Herbert Emerson.

In a way that has not been sufficiently recognised, the protracted discussions which took place between these two men over the summer months of 1931, which is the principal focus of this chapter, constituted the high peaks of Indo–British relations in the immediate aftermath of the Gandhi–Irwin Pact, and comprised a quite remarkable personal embodiment of their singular quality. Such talks would have been inconceivable during the 1930s in Indonesia or Vietnam;[56] superfluous in the Philippines. They epitomised the paradox in Indo-British relations during these years in that at their cutting edge and at their apex the principal encounter between the British and the main forces of Indian nationalism now came to be conducted not in the clash of mass agitations followed by mass repression, nor in the minueted form of a conference in the imperial capital, but in a series of one-on-one talks on a great miscellany of local details between two principal actors in the story sitting down quietly on their own.

The two men made an incongruous pair; the one short, the other six feet tall; 'the contrast', Irwin noted, 'between the broad-shouldered, robust Briton and the small, fragile, Mr. Gandhi was sharp'.[57] There were more substantial matters too. By now Gandhi was the hugely experienced, immensely respected leader of the world's most powerful nationalist movement; Emerson an archetypical member of the British Indian Civil Service, soon to be the Governor of his old province the Punjab. To judge from the minutes which Emerson compiled of their meetings, he was a man of considerable ability. Certainly two successive Viceroys, together with several of his senior colleagues, were prepared to entrust him with the key discussions which now took place with much the most astute political operator the British Raj ever faced; whilst to judge from their later correspondence the two of them developed a remarkably warm regard for each other.[58]

Their ensuing meetings proved to be extraordinary occasions. Whilst India pullulated all around them, Gandhi and Emerson sat down with each other on their own on six successive occasions usually for several hours if not days on end to discuss a great many pressing details from right across the country, as well as large issues of principle relating to the

---

[56] It has been suggested to me that Ho Chi-minh's negotiations with Saiteny in 1946 were on a par with these Gandhi–Emerson talks, but in the aftermath of the declaration of the Democratic Republic of Vietnam in September 1945 the circumstances were altogether different, see Marr, *Vietnam 1945*, passim.   [57] Halifax, *Fulness of Days*, p. 148.

[58] E.g. Gandhi to Emerson, 27 Jan., 13 Mar. 1932, and Emerson to Gandhi, 2 Mar. 1932, IOL R/3/1/289.

whole governance of India to which these variously gave rise. Each brought to their talks a great store of knowledge based upon their apical position in one of the two hierarchies of political information which now extended throughout India. Gandhi was extensively briefed by his provincial lieutenants who channelled up their concerns to him (as if to the barrister he was by profession), whilst Emerson sat at the centre of the elaborate (usually telegraphic) network of communications which the Government of India maintained, both with its provincial governments and with a host of others – the police, the military, the customs department etc. Despite their strong mutual desire to reduce the points of conflict, each pressed his case with very considerable energy. To Emerson his principal objectives were to harness the authority Gandhi could exercise over his followers so as to bring the agitations spilling across the Indian countryside to an end and to ensure that there was no breakdown in the Pact until at least the second Round Table Conference had convened; while on Gandhi's side his persistent interest was to press the government to respond to the detailed demands that his followers were constantly urging upon his attention.

It is vital, however, to understand that Gandhi had a further major interest too. This he variously specified in the following terms:

If Congressmen . . . fully implement the conditions applicable to them [he declared] . . . Congress will obtain an irresistible prestige[59] . . . observance of the conditions . . . will make the Congress an irresistible power for vindicating the national position[60] . . . there is a big principle which the Government has to face . . . that principle is an integral part of the Pact, namely, that between the people and the Government the Congress is the intermediary.[61]

Back in 1929 (we may recall) he had been greatly troubled by the weakness of the Congress and the national movement much more generally. Thereafter he had been in two minds about how to respond to the Irwin declaration, and about how to proceed with Civil Disobedience. Once, however, his salt satyagraha had been launched, the Congress movement proved to his immense satisfaction to be far more formidable than he had earlier expected. Yet while it had severely damaged British prestige in the country, it had totally failed to break the hold of the British over India – let alone secure the Congress's now avowed objective of *purna swaraj*.

It happened, however, that these developments became entwined with one other to which he now attached great importance. That stemmed from the succession of attempts by the British to retrieve the fiasco of the

[59] Statement to the press, 5 Mar. 1931, *CWMG* 45, p. 255.
[60] 'How to do it', *Young India*, 12 Mar. 1931, *CWMG* 45, p. 282.
[61] Interview to the Associated Press, 18 Aug. 1931, *CWMG* 47, p. 312.

'all-white' Simon Commission of 1927 by mounting an escalating series of conciliatory initiatives to bring the Congress leaders to the negotiating table. First in 1929 Irwin had sought to secure Congress's cooperation by issuing a declaration of his own *ex cathedra*. When that failed, he proceeded, nine months later, to entrust the so-called Yeravda negotiations with the Congress leaders to two *Indian* intermediaries. When that also failed Irwin went to the lengths early in 1931 of opening direct personal negotiations with Gandhi himself. That was a quite extraordinary step for any Viceroy to take at this time. For here was the principal agent of the British Raj negotiating on all but equal terms with India's principal nationalist leader in a supreme effort to recover the position needlessly squandered in 1927. When that eventually culminated not only in the Gandhi–Irwin Pact but in a remarkably warm exchange of personal letters between the two of them,[62] Gandhi fastened upon the possibility that there could well be here an altogether new opportunity to propel Indo–British relations onto an entirely new basis. He was always acutely aware that whilst his innumerable followers in Congress were becoming extensively involved in a major new campaign against the British, which in line with the ambiguities in the Pact was soon bringing immense pressure upon them, there was nevertheless no realistic chance that ultimately (as Irwin had been at pains to remind him) they would permit this to overwhelm them. It accordingly became vital for him to seek to effect some breakthrough upon another front. Sensing what he saw as an opening here, he soon began to invoke the readiness of the British during the negotiation of the Pact to accept him as India's principal political plenipotentiary as an indelible precedent which necessitated that henceforth they should recognise the Congress which he led as the accredited intermediary of the Indian people which in the determination of any issue of importance should stand upon an equal footing with the government. In the aftermath of the Pact this ploy became his principal concern during all his post-Pact talks with Emerson.

In the end, however, it proved to be fatefully unattainable, since despite the considerable personal goodwill which both Irwin and Emerson expressed towards him personally, there was simply no getting away from the pervasive ambivalence of the British. Whilst they wanted round table discussions upon India's developing constitution and an end to open conflict, and whilst they showed a remarkable disposition to discuss with Gandhi disputed issues arising out of the Pact and other matters too, before long they made it absolutely plain that they were in no mind, as to his increasing chagrin he came to realise, to share their

---

[62] Irwin to Gandhi, 6 Mar. 1931, Gandhi to Irwin, 7 Mar. 1931, *CWMG* 45, p. 268.

executive dominion over India with the Congress or its principal leader in any way that mattered.[63] Although they did everything they could to get him to use his authority on their own behalf to restrain his often considerably less accommodating followers, in the end they invariably rebuffed his reiterated claim that in these and other connections they should acknowledge the interlocutory role he and his associates played on behalf of the Indian masses. To a far greater degree than many of his lieutenants Gandhi wanted peace, and so did the British. But the fundamental ambiguity at the core of the British position inexorably ensured that peace without conflict lay well beyond their reach.

It was that which eventually tore at the vitals of the extraordinary series of discussions which Gandhi and Emerson held together over the summer months of 1931 and finally emasculated the newly hard-won position he had earlier secured with the British. It is to the successive acts of that very distinctive drama that we now need to turn.[64]

Upon the conclusion of the Gandhi–Irwin Pact in March 1931, Gandhi set about justifying it to his followers. In a series of statements and speeches he variously argued that, although *purna swaraj* had not been secured, it would be folly

to go on suffering when the opponent makes it easy for you to enter into a discussion with him upon your longings . . . As a satyagrahi it was my duty to seek for such an opening . . . This settlement is not the end of the struggle. That will come only after securing swaraj . . . We did not know in 1929 or while I was at Yeravda what stand the British parties and our people would take at the Round Table Conference . . . Today we know that the leaders of India have asked for a fully responsible government. The British have accepted that demand. It is true that all those who attended the Round Table Conference have agreed to retain the Empire link. We of course are asking for the right to snap that link at our discretion. We have complete freedom to demand this right at the Round Table Conference . . . Moreover, on those two occasions, we did not have a complete measure of our strength. Today we have some idea of it. If a weak man undertakes negotiations, he is a beggar. A strong man is always ready for parleys . . . Therefore, by effecting a settlement, the Congress has shown its wisdom and enhanced its prestige.[65]

---

[63] There were many forceful expressions of this attitude, e.g. by Sir Frederick Sykes, *From Many Angles. An Autobiography*, London 1941, p. 412; Punjab to HD, 16 May 1931, H.Poll.33/7/31; Hailey to Peel, 25 May 1931, HP 20; Willingdon to Hoare, 28 Aug. 1931, TwP 5. Willingdon was to tell Hoare: 'You may confidently rely . . . that we should never do anything . . . in the nature of surrendering on the lines of the Irish Treaty', Willingdon to Hoare, 15 Sept. 1931, ibid.

[64] For an informative but differently focused account see Brown, *Gandhi and Civil Disobedience*, pp. 192–241.

[65] Statement to the press, 5 Mar. 1931, Interview to journalists, 6 Mar. 1931, Speech at

From the outset, however, he had to contend with the profound emotions stirred by the impending execution of Bhagat Singh.[66] He found himself, moreover, at odds with Jawaharlal Nehru,[67] Subhas Bose,[68] and more particularly with Vallabhbhai Patel.[69] And a number of violent episodes now occurred.[70] At the same time there were widespread uncertainties concerning the degree of picketing that was permissible, and there were soon mounting complaints about the Government's illiberal interpretations of the Pact.[71] The Government of India indicated that it was ready to enquire into a number of matters which Gandhi and others brought to their attention,[72] but for their part they were deeply shocked by the highly conditional attitude many Congressmen were taking towards the Pact,[73] and within a fortnight of the making of the Pact the two sides had a tart exchange of telegrams about the picketing of a number of cloth merchants.[74]

Gandhi, however, was already committed to attending a meeting of the prospective delegates to the second Round Table Conference on 21 March. and Irwin sent him a message saying he would be happy to see him beforehand. And he then added: 'as to particular matters mentioned in your telegram . . . it would probably be most convenient if you could have a talk to Emerson'.[75] Gandhi accordingly saw Irwin on 19 March and proceeded to discuss a number of issues, particularly concerning his complaint about the inflexibility of a recent Government statement in London about 'financial safeguards' in any new constitution for India,[76] and it was upon that evening that there occurred the first of the six sets of discussions which he was to have with Emerson over the months that

Borsad, 12 Mar. 1931, 'To proud Gujarat', *CWMG* 45, pp. 250–6, 263–7, 284–7, 295–7. See also 'An Englishman's dilemma', Gandhi to Gregg, 29 Apr. 1931, *CWMG* 46, pp. 3–8, 52–3.

[66] E.g. Interview to the press, 26 Mar. 1931, *CWMG* 45, pp. 344–5.
[67] Jawaharlal Nehru's note on Provisional Settlement, nd, ibid. pp. 431–2.
[68] Interview to Bose, 16–17 Mar. 1931, ibid. pp. 301–2.
[69] E.g. Gandhi to Irwin, 4 Mar. 1931, *CWMG* 46, pp. 245–6; H.Poll.33/3/31 passim.
[70] 'The Cult of Violence', *Young India*, 16 Apr. 1931, *CWMG* 46, pp. 1–3.
[71] AICC 2/1931 contains a considerable number of telegrams reporting clashes between Congressmen and government agents, 4–11 Mar. 1931; Amrital Seth to Gandhi, tel., 20 Mar. 1931, ibid.; see also Gandhi's, 'Their part of the obligation', *Young India*, 19 Mar. 1931, *CWMG* 45, pp. 312–13.
[72] E.g. Gandhi to Emerson, 8, 11 (tel.) Mar. 1931, Emerson to Gandhi, 8, 13 Mar. 1931, ibid., pp. 275, 277. See also further Emerson letters to Gandhi, e.g., 11, 13 Mar. 1931, AICC 2/1931.
[73] E.g. Emerson Note, 12 Mar., Irwin's Note 14 Mar. 1931, H.Poll.33/2/31; Collins (Bombay) to Emerson, and encs., 17 Mar. 1931, H.Poll.33/3/31.
[74] HD to Bombay (incorporating message for Gandhi), tel., 15 Mar. 1931, Gandhi to Emerson, tel., 18 Mar. 1931, *CWMG* 45, pp. 438, 307.
[75] PSV to Gandhi, 17 Mar. 1931, ibid. p. 298.
[76] Interview with the Viceroy, 19 Mar. 1931, ibid. pp. 313–16.

followed. They met together in Emerson's house in New Delhi, and were ensconced together for around three hours.

Gandhi led off with some complaints about the attachment of some property of the Raja of Kalakankar for arrears, and about the case of a Mamlatdar in Colaba – hardly the stuff of nationalist confrontation. But he soon proceeded to protest at some length against the government's illiberality over the release of certain political prisoners – to which Emerson responded at still greater length that while inflammatory speeches were still being made, it was impossible to release those who had been in any way involved in violence. When it was Emerson's turn to make the running he took the opportunity to complain first about the impact of Congress's swadeshi campaign on a number of mills and the importers of British cloth, and then protested vigorously against the circular Nehru had sent out to Congress officials (which we have already noted). There were clear indications, he said, of a Congress-inspired anti-rent, anti-revenue, anti-landlord campaign in UP which the government could in no way tolerate. He then proceeded to complain too about the activities of Vallabhbhai Patel, and the likelihood that in the event a good deal of land revenue might deliberately not be paid in Gujarat. That in turn led Gandhi to raise questions about the restoration of land and offices in Gujarat, about which he was now under considerable pressure from Patel and others.

The pattern of their future talks was thereby set. Gandhi would raise a number of complaints about the manner in which the government was implementing, or not implementing, the Pact, whilst Emerson would respond by expressing the deepening impatience of the government with the failure of the Congress to fulfil the Pact in the spirit in which it had been framed. Whereas Gandhi argued for redress, by clear implication Emerson called upon him to use his considerable influence to ensure that the Pact was held to unequivocally by the Congress and its following.

Despite some animated exchanges this first meeting was nonetheless thought to have been useful. Emerson concluded (as indeed did Irwin) that 'Mr Gandhi is anxious to implement the settlement and to obtain a genuine solution'; while Gandhi himself seemed pleased that his recently attained direct access to the highest reaches of government was still intact.[77]

And the very next day there was a telling exchange. A meeting had been called that evening in Delhi at which Subhas Bose was to stoke the campaign for Bhagat Singh's reprieve. Seizing upon the new relationship the government had established with Gandhi, Emerson sent him a brief note

[77] Emerson's Note on interview with Gandhi, 19 Mar. 1931, dated 20 Mar. 1931, H.Poll.33/1/31, *CWMG* 45, pp. 438–46.

asking him to restrain his followers. 'Government', he wrote, 'will much appreciate any assistance you feel able to give . . . to check the creation of conditions which, if uncontrolled, may have serious consequences'.[78] Seeing here a prime opportunity to nail the point he was seeking to make that the government should henceforth leave any matter within his purview to him alone to handle, Gandhi promptly replied:

I have already taken every precaution possible [he wrote to Emerson] . . . I suggest that there should be . . . no interference . . . Irritation is undoubtedly there. It would be better to allow it to find vent through meetings, etc.[79]

Emerson accepted the Mahatma's advice (in a way he was never to do again), and on his side Gandhi then attended the meeting of Indian delegates to the Round Table which Irwin had called for the next day. During the following weekend he and Emerson, moreover, had an amicable exchange of letters upon a number of other matters.[80]

Gandhi then travelled to Karachi, where Congress was due to meet in full session to consider the Gandhi–Irwin Pact. On his arrival he had a near-violent reception from some of Congress's younger, more radical supporters, distraught at the hanging of Bhagat Singh on the Monday evening.[81] Gandhi had pleaded with Irwin both verbally and in writing for Bhagat Singh's life.[82] But the Viceroy had told him he would not only not commute the sentence, but that it would not be right to postpone it until after the Congress had held its meeting.[83] The execution cast a large shadow over the Karachi Congress, and forced Gandhi to renew his praise for the self-denial of Bhagat Singh.[84] There was another very large cloud as well: horrendous Hindu–Muslim riots in Kanpur, which made him despair of the possibility of any agreed constitutional progress.[85] His confidence, however, that the Karachi Congress would ratify the Gandhi–Irwin Pact nonetheless proved correct.[86] Nehru even moved its

[78] Emerson to Gandhi, 20 Mar. 1931, ibid. p. 446, AICC 2/1931.
[79] Gandhi to Emerson, 20 Mar. 1931, *CWMG* 45, p. 316, AICC 2/1931.
[80] Discussion at meeting of Round Table Conference delegates, Delhi, 21 Mar. 1931, Gandhi to Emerson, 20(3) Mar. 1931, Emerson to Gandhi, 20, 21 Mar. 1931, *CWMG* 45, pp. 320–6.
[81] Gandhi's own account, Speech at Karachi Congress, 26 Mar. 1931, Discussion with Naujawan Bharat Sabha, 27 Mar. 1931, *CWMG* 45, pp. 320–6, 316–17, 446–7.
[82] E.g. Gandhi to Irwin, 23 Mar. 1931, ibid., pp. 333–4.
[83] Irwin to Gandhi, 23 Mar. 1931, ibid. p. 34; Irwin to his father, 24 Mar. 1931, IP 27.
[84] Statement on execution of Bhagat Singh and comrades, 23 Mar. 1931, 'Bhagat Singh', *Navajivan*, 29 Mar. 1931, Resolution on Bhagat Singh and Comrades, 29 Mar. 1931, *CWMG* 45, pp. 335–6, 359–60, 363.
[85] Statement on the Kanpur riots, 26 Mar. 1931, Speech on Kanpur riots, ibid. pp. 345, 353–4. There were both UP Govt and Congress enquiries, Pandey, *Ascendancy of the Congress*, pp. 135–41.
[86] Gandhi's remarks to Irwin, Interview with Viceroy, 19 Mar. 1931, *CWMG* 45, p. 315.

adoption. Despite Bhagat Singh's execution the Pact accordingly held, and Congress thereupon appointed Gandhi as its sole delegate to the second Round Table Conference (seemingly at his own suggestion).[87]

Thereafter Gandhi travelled to Gujarat – and promptly found himself in the midst of a hornets' nest. From the outset many of his most devoted supporters there had been incensed that in his Pact with Irwin he had not secured full relief for all the sacrifices they had made in his cause.[88] Many of them were facing substantial demands for land revenue arrears. Many were fearful that they might not recover their confiscated lands; whilst several village headmen who had given up their posts were outraged by their replacements. Gandhi found himself in very considerable difficulty.[89] He had necessarily to uphold the Pact, but Vallabhbhai Patel was soon deeply troubled that the whole Congress position in Gujarat was at serious risk unless substantial amends were made upon all these points.[90]

At the same time the Government of India found itself under no less pressure from its own subordinates too.[91] Quite typically the Government of the Central Provinces wrote to it on 29 March to say that:

While Congress has outwardly at least carried out the settlement in [some] respects, in other ways the situation has deteriorated to a marked extent. The leaders have done lip service to what they call 'the truce', but their followers have made a number of inflammatory speeches containing abuse of Government and incitements to violence which the leaders have made no effort to restrain. In all important centres the settlement has been represented as a victory for the Congress and as merely affording a breathing space before the struggle will ensue upon the inevitable failure of the Round Table Conference. In Congress circles at any rate there is no acceptance of the settlement as a peace honourable to both sides and as a preliminary to the calm discussion of the future constitution. There is also a distinct tendency to camouflage the above activities by accusing the Government of not carrying out the spirit of the agreement, because it has not yet released certain prisoners convicted of incitement to mutiny and violence.[92]

To which the Government of Bombay then added that in Gujarat

---

[87] Resolution on Provisional Settlement, 29 Mar. 1931, ibid. p. 363; V to SoS, tels., 2, 11 Apr. 1931, H.Poll.136/31.

[88] This was already being reflected in Gandhi's speeches in Gujarat immediately after the announcement of the Pact, e.g. speeches at Borsad, Ras, Sunav, Karadi, 12, 14 Mar. 1931, *CWMG* 45, pp. 284–9.

[89] See Collector, Broach, to Gandhi, 18 Mar. 1931, AICC 2/1931.

[90] E.g. Surat Police reports, 30 Apr., 2, 5 May 1931, H.Poll.33/3/31.

[91] E.g. Emerson to Gandhi, 1 Apr. 1931, H.Poll.33/5/31, re complaints from B & O; Collins (Bombay) to Home Dept, 1 Apr. 1931, and encs., Bell to Emerson, 2 Apr. 1931, H.Poll.33/3/31; Hallett to Emerson, 4, 14 Apr. 1931, H.Poll.33/5/31.

[92] CS CP to HD, 29 Mar. 1931, H.Poll.33/1/31. See also B & O to HD, 22 Apr. 1931, H.Poll.33/7/31.

though Mr. Gandhi has advised the payment of land revenue, the advice has been hedged in by so many qualifications and interpretations that its effect has been almost worse than useless . . . Vallabhbhai Patel has harped on the clause that those who cannot pay need not pay . . . The effect of this preaching has been that everywhere in the affected talukas people plead poverty and inability to pay anything, although . . . the crops were *first-rate*.[93]

Emerson became especially worried by the agrarian position in UP (in which Nehru was soon playing a leading role).[94] Accordingly on 3–4 April Emerson visited the acting Governor, Lambert, and came away with the clear impression that the UP Congress was actively mounting an agitation 'to stir up the tenants against their landlords and against Government and to consolidate their position in rural areas'.[95]

Irwin thereupon called a meeting of his Executive Council on 6 April which decided that Gandhi should be very specifically informed that while the Government of India desired to avoid drastic action, the operation of the ordinary law would no longer be suspended; that in view of the non-payment of land revenue in Gujarat the Bombay government could soon be resuming 'coercive processes' there; that in UP the government 'trusted that the Congress would at once stop the agitation' 'which was of a political character', and that if matters deteriorated there any further 'special measures' might need to be taken.[96] The extent to which the Government of India was already writhing in its own ambiguity was neatly summarised by Irwin when on the same day he told the Secretary of State that:

The truth really is . . . that no remedy can be found except by . . . suppressing [Congress] with all the forces at our disposal . . . [but] that, in spite of everything that can be said on the other side, I believe at this juncture to be unprofitable and unwise.[97]

As it happened Gandhi was now due to travel to the Punjab. In view of all that was happening all about them it suited both sides to arrange a further meeting between him and Emerson as he passed on his way through Delhi. The two of them accordingly met for their second series of talks on the evening of 6 April, and this time were closeted together for five hours.

[93] Bell to Emerson, 2, 4 Apr. 1931, H.Poll.33/3/31. See also Emerson's Note, 4 Apr. 1931, H.Poll.33/11/31.
[94] Nehru to Jagdish Prasad, 11 Mar. 1931, Nehru's 'Note on Economic Distress in the United Provinces [23 Mar. 1931], etc., *SWJN* 5, pp. 55–66; Nehru to Pant, Nehru to Jagdish Prasad [March 1931] AICC 63/1931; Bomford, Collector, Allahabad to Maharaj Singh, Comm. Allahabad, 17 Mar. 1931, Emerson to Jagdish Prasad, 28 Mar. 1931, H.Poll.33/11/31; Emerson to Gandhi, 21 Mar. 1931, Gandhi to Emerson, 23 Mar. 1931, AICC 2/1931; Emerson to Gandhi, 23, 31 Mar. 1931, *CWMG* 45, p. 334.
[95] Emerson's notes, 3, 4 Apr. 1931, H.Poll.33/11/31.
[96] Orders in Council, 6 Apr. 1931, ibid.   [97] Irwin to Benn, 6 Apr. 1931, IP 6(2).

They talked to begin with of communal matters, about which they were both now very despondent. They also discussed a number of detailed problems in Gujarat: the replacement of village headmen, the recovery of confiscated lands, and the government's growing anxiety about the non-payment of land revenue. From all this Emerson inferred that 'Vallabhbhai Patel and his friends are making it as difficult as possible for Gandhi to honour the settlement'. All the same he was 'inclined to think that when he returns to Gujarat he [Gandhi] will play the game'. In particular he welcomed his suggestion that when he did so he should speak to the Commissioner of the Northern Division (which covered the Gujarat area) about the problems there.

They then talked for two hours about UP. Emerson protested that in UP 'under cover of economic distress, the Congress were in fact carrying on the campaign for political purposes'. To which Gandhi responded that it must be remembered that there was 'brutal treatment of tenants by landlords'. And thereupon he seized the opening this gave him to express his principal concern throughout these months that:

the real problem was how the Congress could cooperate with Government in regard to the situation . . . [there] was no reason why the matter should not be put on the right lines . . . in each tahsil there should be a Congress Committee which should cooperate with the local officers in land revenue matters . . . in times of distress the Congress would collect facts and figures themselves, would ascertain the views of the zamindars and the tenants and would make representations to the Collector which the Collector would examine.

Emerson saw his purpose promptly, and a vigorous discussion soon ensued. When Emerson rejected the whole idea, Gandhi avowed 'that this showed distrust of Congress'. Since 'Government were now at peace with the Congress [and] had entered into a settlement with it . . . there could be no reason why this principle should not be extended'. Emerson would not hear of it: 'the settlement', he averred, '. . . related to the abandonment of . . . civil disobedience . . . it was a different matter for Government to use Congress as an intermediary in matters in which other parties were concerned'. Whereupon Gandhi remarked 'that Congress had always supported the cause of tenants and . . . it would be impossible to stand by and see tenants ill-treated by landlords without trying to help them'. During the coming months it was upon these matters that the crucial discussions turned. This time, however, only the preliminary markers were set out.

The two of them then concluded this second, and considerably longer, meeting by discussing the boycott of mills and foreign cloth and the non-release of certain prisoners, and in the end Emerson recorded that he 'found Mr. Gandhi very friendly and reasonable'. 'He was pleased', he said, 'with his success at Karachi, but depressed about the communal sit-

uation'. Whilst anxious to go to the Round Table Conference and 'obtain
a settlement which . . . he can honourably accept', he was not, however,
over confident. He was, moreover, 'quite candid in saying that, in the
meantime, Congress will attempt to consolidate their position in case
there is another fight', which prompted Emerson to make 'it quite clear to
him that the so-called consolidation of the Congress position might easily
produce a situation which Government could not tolerate'. Emerson was
nonetheless well satisfied that Gandhi did 'not want a breach of the settlement'; that he 'would do what he could to stop the present activities in the
United Provinces'; and that he would be prepared to see the UP's
Governor. On Gandhi's departure he left behind with Emerson a memorandum of complaints which Emerson agreed to read. Despite the vehemence of their discussion both men were still evidently anxious to see the
Pact fully implemented. Each was seeking to use the other to ensure that
this should be done.[98]

But there was then an ominous follow-up. Three days later whilst travelling by train on his way back from Punjab to Gujarat Gandhi wrote to
Emerson to say that:

We have been thinking at cross-purposes . . . The Congress could not possibly
implement the terms of the settlement if the local authorities refused to recognize
and treat with sympathy the advances of the Congress when speaking for the peasantry. The difficulties . . . [in] U.P. . . . could all have been solved if the local
authorities had sent for the Congress officials in their respective districts. Many of
the Congress officials are well known to them. I suggest that any other attitude
would be contrary to the spirit of the settlement and must defeat the very purpose
we have in view.[99]

Emerson once again saw Gandhi's intention very clearly and once again
would in no way entertain it. 'Mr Gandhi is evidently uneasy', he noted
on the file, 'lest he gave away too much in his discussion with me on the
6th', and thereupon he deliberately refrained from sending any reply.[100]
The clouds on this issue were starting to build up in the sky.

In the days that followed Emerson nevertheless busied himself with for-
mulating the Government of India's official response to the very many
complaints provincial governments were now making about the
Congress's failure to uphold the Pact faithfully. Nothing should be done,
he emphasised, that would in any way destroy the Pact. He retained some
hope, moreover, that Gandhi would restrain his more activist followers.

[98] 'Note by Mr. Emerson of an interview between himself and Mr. Gandhi on 7th April
1931', H.Poll.33/1/31, CWMG 45, pp. 450–8. See also Emerson to Gandhi, 7 Apr.
1931, H.Poll.33/3/31, AICC 2/1931.
[99] Gandhi to Emerson, 9 Apr. 1931, CWMG 45, pp. 404–5, H.Poll.33/3/31.
[100] Emerson's Note (circulated to the Viceroy and Executive Council), 12 Apr. 1931, ibid.

He was careful, however, to assure the governments of both Bombay and the UP that he had warned Gandhi quite specifically that if the current level of agitation continued, they would not hesitate to repress it.[101] But then (in a manner that was characteristic of the Government of India on such occasions) he circulated a general letter to provincial governments in which whilst acknowledging the provocation under which they were all labouring, and the inevitability of action being taken against imminent disorder and incitements to violence, he nevertheless laid it down firmly that any necessary action should only be launched under the ordinary law, and that the Government of India should be consulted before any fateful step was taken.[102] Since he was clearly determined to keep Gandhi impaled on the hook of close association with the government where the Pact had placed him, and well understood the difficulties he was facing in Gujarat, he then took special steps to ensure that upon his return there he should see Garrett, the Commissioner for the Northern Division.[103] On his arrival in Gujarat Gandhi pressed for this as well, since he believed this was precisely how government–Congress relations ought to proceed in the aftermath of the Pact. Consequently on 12 April 1931 the Gandhi–Emerson talks were supplemented by two hours of Gandhi–Garrett talks.[104] These marked the beginning of a further series of discussions in Gujarat on which so much was in the end to turn.

Gandhi and Garrett first discussed the reinstatement of village headmen. In Gujarat, it now transpired, their appointments were ordinarily made for fixed periods of between two and ten years. Their replacements, Gandhi accordingly claimed, were not 'permanent' as the Pact required that they should be if they were to be upheld, and accordingly they should be replaced by their predecessors who had previously resigned. Garrett sensed that some concession would have to be made here.[105] But when Gandhi went on ('in studiously moderate language', as Garrett allowed) to complain that those who wanted to recover their confiscated land were in very great difficulty as they had not been told whether it had been sold or not, Garrett was quite unsympathetic. All the necessary information, he said, was readily available, and it was not for the government to publish it formally. When Gandhi then sought to raise a number of other matters, Garrett turned his fire upon Congress's moves to stir up trouble over land revenue arrears, on which Gandhi unequivo-

---

[101] Emerson to Bell, 7 Apr. 1931, ibid.; Emerson to Lambert, 7 Apr. 1931, H.Poll.33/11/31.
[102] HD to LGs, 11 Apr, 2 May 1931, H.Poll.33/7/31. They did not demur, see their replies, ibid.   [103] Emerson to Bell, 7 Apr. 1931, H.Poll.33/3/31.
[104] On the arranging of the meeting see Emerson's Note, 7 Apr. 1931, Gandhi to Garrett 10 Apr. 1931, CWMG 45, pp. 452, 413, H.Poll.33/4/31; Bell to Emerson, 11 Apr. 1931, H.Poll.33/3/31, Sykes to Irwin tel., 11 Apr. 1931, Bell to Emerson, 20 Apr. 1931, H.Poll.33/4/31.   [105] For later developments see Bombay to HD, 10 July 1931, ibid.

cably assured him 'that he would on no account permit any contumacious refusal to pay land revenue'.[106]

These discussions accordingly mirrored those between Gandhi and Emerson. Garrett concluded that 'MKG is . . . being pressed by his followers to get these points cleared up and I think the chief object of his meeting me was to get the help of Government officers to secure this end'. Since for his own part he was looking to Gandhi to curb his followers, Vallabhbhai Patel not least, there was clearly a good deal of mutual exploitation operating on both sides.[107]

Less than a week later Gandhi went to Bombay to bid farewell to Irwin who was leaving India on 18 April. There he not only saw Irwin but had a three-hour talk with Sykes, the Governor of Bombay, in the course of which he repeated his complaints about the confiscation of lands, the replacement of village headmen and suchlike, and reiterated his claim that Congress should be recognised as the people's intermediary with the government.[108] Sykes, however, was very resistant and particularly rejected his larger claim. So the 'meeting ended inconclusively'.[109]

In Bombay Gandhi also, however, held his third post-Pact talk with Emerson. It was the shortest of them all. It was almost entirely devoted to the single issue of confiscated land in Gujarat. Gandhi protested that the precise prices paid by its purchasers must be made known to its former owners so that they could begin negotiations to buy it back as provided for in the Pact. Since he had not been fully briefed on the point by the Bombay Government, Emerson was in some difficulty, and his stalling response – that the Government ought to remain neutral in such matters – was clearly quite unconvincing. Since he was worried 'that this matter will be exploited as a grievance', he suggested to the Government of Bombay that the necessary information should be provided.[110] But they chose to continue to drag their feet.[111]

Before very long rather more important issues supervened. For in the aftermath of this third meeting there was a sudden crisis that very nearly

---

[106] Garrett's 'Note of discussion with Mr. M.K. Gandhi on 12th April 1931', ibid.
[107] For the immediate follow-up see Gandhi to Garrett, 13 Apr. 1931, *CWMG* 45, pp. 415–19, AICC 3/1931; Gandhi to Maxwell, 13 Apr. 1931, Garrett to Gandhi, 13, 15 Apr. 1931, ibid.
[108] Sykes had agreed to this meeting on 1 Apr., Sykes to Irwin, tel., 11 Apr. 1931, H.Poll.33/4/31. Four weeks after the meeting Gandhi was sent a long reply to the representations he made, Maxwell to Gandhi, 13 May 1931, *CWMG* 46, pp. 422–4; Collins to Gandhi, 9 May 1931, AICC 3/1931.   [109] Sykes, *From Many Angles*, pp. 412–13.
[110] Emerson's Note, 22 Apr. 1931, H.Poll.33/3/31.
[111] Hudson to Crerar, 28 Apr., 4 May 1931, Garrett to Hudson, 30 Apr. 1931, ibid.

ended the relations between the Mahatma and the government. Already Gandhi had corresponded with Emerson about some notices of dismissal issued by the Mamlatdar of Borsad in Kheda district in Gujarat against village headmen who were partipicating in a no-tax campaign.[112] When in spite of his talk with Garrett he then came across a further notice from the Mamlatdar which he not only found to be most objectionable but which had been issued without any reference to the conversation he himself had had with Garrett, Gandhi protested to Garrett vehemently.[113] Garrett conceded that the notice required some amendment, but then brusquely rejected Gandhi's more general claim that in sending it out the Mamlatdar had totally ignored the position of 'the Congress as the intermediary between the Government and the people'. That, Garrett riposted, was 'not one of the matters agreed upon in the Settlement'.[114]

This cut to the core of the position Gandhi believed he had established with the government and he was profoundly incensed. Brushing aside the particulars of the case, he informed Garrett that his response raised 'a question of the first magnitude',[115] and immediately appealed over his head to the Government of Bombay.

If His Excellency too takes the same view as Mr Garrett does about the Congress mediation, [Gandhi wrote to Maxwell, the Chief Secretary of Bombay, on 22 April] I feel that it nullifies the whole settlement. It was only when the Government of India and the British Government recognized that the Congress virtually represented the people that there was a Settlement between it and the Government. To repudiate the Congress as the intermediary between the people and the Government means repudiation of the Settlement.[116]

And to Emerson he then wrote with some passion that

the Settlement, so far as Gujarat is concerned, is in imminent danger of a breakdown . . . I am straining every nerve to prevent a breakdown. I am trying all the powers of persuasion I can command. But the strain is proving unbearable.[117]

Garrett's view of what was occurring was scarcely less vehement, and went to the heart of the central question between Gandhi and the government at this time:

---

[112] Notices by Mamlatdar of Borsad, 9, 11 Mar. 1931, H.Poll.33/4/31, AICC 2/1931; Gandhi to Emerson, 20 Mar. 1931, *CWMG* 45, p. 316, H.Poll.33/4/31.

[113] Gandhi to Garrett, 20, 26 Apr. 1931, *CWMG* 46, pp. 19, 42, H.Poll.33/4/31, 33/11/31, AICC 3/1931.

[114] Garrett to Gandhi, 21 Apr. 1931, H.Poll.33/11/31, *CWMG* 46, pp. 394–5, AICC 3/1931.

[115] Gandhi to Garrett, 21 Apr. 1931, *CWMG* 46, p. 21, AICC 3/1931, H.Poll.33/4/31, 33/11/31. See also Gandhi to Andrews, 29 Aug. 1931, *CWMG* 46, pp. 50–1.

[116] Gandhi to Maxwell, 22 Apr. 1931, ibid., pp. 23–4, H.Poll.33/4/31.

[117] Gandhi to Emerson, 22 Apr. 1931, *CWMG* 46, p. 25; H.Poll.33/11/31.

It is perfectly plain [Garrett wrote to Maxwell] that Mr Gandhi aims at maintaining the influence of the Congress by making it appear to the villagers that without their help nothing can be done. I noticed during my tour in the Surat District that the same tactics are being tried there. I accordingly advised Kothawala [the Deputy Collector] to be very cautious in his dealings with Congress workers and agents. He has fully appreciated the position and demands that the persons concerned should make an application in any matter requiring action by the Government. Mr Gandhi realises that if the villagers are allowed to approach Government officials direct the hold of the Congress will rapidly disappear. There is nothing in the terms of the Settlement which requires the intervention of the Congress in implementing the settlement. Nor can I accept the position that there is any reason why the Congress should be invited to assist the Government officers in carrying out the terms of the Settlement. The obligations on each side are entirely independent and distinct from one another. It was never contemplated that they should work together. It would be fatal to the position of Government officers to have to work under such conditions and would merely be playing into the hands of those (including Mr Gandhi) who have been so zealously arguing that this is a mere suspension of hostilities. If Mr Gandhi means that unless the Congress Workers are to be treated as the Agents and spokesmen of the villagers he will not carry out the terms of the Settlement, I can only regard it as a breach of faith. Assuming this to be so, I consider that it would be necessary to face the consequences and ignore the Congress entirely.[118]

Nevertheless at Emerson's instance the Government of India took very great care with their considered response.[119] Over the course of recent days they had become very concerned about some pamphlets Nehru and Purushottamdas Tandon had been issuing to tenants in the UP advising them about their rent payments,[120] and by the news that the Allahabad Congress Committee was taking 'active steps to promote reasonable settlements between zamindars and tenants and between zamindars and Government regarding the payment of rent and revenue'.[121] Crerar, the Home Member of the Viceroy's Council, noted: 'This is a palpable manoeuvre . . . It is certainly very ominous for the settlement.'[122] The question for the Government of India had therefore now become, 'Who rules India? Congress or the government?'. In these circumstances it became absolutely essential for the government that it should firmly rebut

---

[118] Garrett to Maxwell, 22 Apr. 1931, H.Poll.33/4/31, 33/11/31. Garrett's attitude was endorsed by G Bombay, Sykes to Willingdon, 24 Apr. 1931, H.Poll.33/4/31.

[119] E.g. HD to PSV, tel., 24 Apr. 1931, HD to Bombay, tel., 24 Apr. 1931, Bombay to HD, 25 Apr. 1931, Emerson's Note, 28 Apr. 1931, ibid.

[120] Tandon, 'An Appeal to the Zamindars of Allahabad', 5 Apr. 1931, Nehru, 'An Appeal to the Tenants of Allahabad District', 13 Apr. 1931, H.Poll.13/4/31; Emerson's Note, 23 Apr. 1931, Office Note, 30 Apr. 1931, H.Poll.33/11/31.

[121] Malaviya to Emerson, 15 Apr. 1931; see earlier notice by Sitla Sahai, 8 Mar. 1931, ibid.

[122] Crerar's Note, 23 Apr. 1931; see also Emerson to Hailey, 24 Apr. 1931, ibid.

the claim that Congress could in any way stand between it and its imperial subjects. But in doing so it had to be very careful indeed not to forfeit the hold it had established over Gandhi. Caught in the vice of its own ambidexterousness it had to respond with very considerable circumspection.

After very careful consideration[123] Garrett was accordingly authorised to repeat to Gandhi his earlier robust response, but then (at his own suggestion) to add[124] – and Gandhi immediately noted the distinction[125] – that:

There is nothing to prevent the Congress advising people as to what they should do, nor can any restriction be placed on the duty of Government officers to perform their functions directly with those concerned. This is a quite different thing from the meeting and discussion of matters of importance between Congress representatives and Government Officers which is being carried on where necessary.

The prevailing ambiguity in the whole situation was thus epitomised in the very fine line which this drew. Thereafter following consultations with Emerson, Maxwell, the Chief Secretary of Bombay, wrote to Gandhi on 24 April in the same spirit that the government was quite sure he did not claim that

the people can have no dealings with one another except through the Congress . . . [They understood he was ready] to acknowledge the extent to which the Government have been prepared to recognize your own representative position . . . [For their part they readily accepted] the great influence for good which you are in a position to exercise in securing faithful observance of the spirit of the Settlement among your supporters [Should, however, he wish] to claim for the Congress any status which is not implied in the treatment which you as its representative have already received . . . your correct course would be to approach the Government of India yourself.[126]

Gandhi was all the same exceedingly vexed about Garrett's reply: 'the way you are going', he replied, 'is the way of war'.[127] Since, however, he remained determined that over any major matter in dispute the government should enter into direct consultations with himself, he now wrote to Emerson to say that:

If the matters brought to your notice are not clear to you and if you think it necessary you may drag me to Simla . . . I want your help in preventing a breakdown of the Settlement. I have pledged my honour to Lord Irwin that I shall do nothing

[123] Bombay to Emerson, 24 Apr. 1931, ibid.; Sykes to Willingdon, 24 Apr. 1931, H.Poll.33/4/31.   [124] Garrett's draft [24 Apr. 1931], ibid.
[125] Gandhi to Maxwell, 26 Apr. 1931, *CWMG* 46, pp. 43–4, H.Poll.33/4/31.
[126] Maxwell to Gandhi, 24 Apr. 1931, ibid., *CWMG* 46, pp. 395–6.
[127] Gandhi to Garrett, 26 Apr. 1931, ibid., p. 42, H.Poll.33/4/31.

that I could honourably refrain from doing to prevent a breakdown. But it takes two to play a game.[128]

Emerson did not think a breakdown was in any way imminent, but since it was obviously of critical importance to keep the Mahatma in play he soothingly replied that since

there are several matters in regard to which Government think a personal discussion with you will be of value . . . reluctant as I am to drag you up to Simla at this time of year, I am sure that, if we have a heart to heart talk, we shall find the difficulties much less than they seem to be at a distance.[129]

As, however, Gandhi seemed bent upon insisting that the Settlement gave him and the Congress coordinate functions with the government on issues relating to administrative matters, whereas the government had no intention whatsoever of sharing any executive authority with him or the Congress, Emerson took the precaution before he reached Simla of ensuring that there was no Achilles' heel in the government's case. Accordingly the Law Member of the Viceroy's Council, Sir B.L. Mitter, was asked for a formal Opinion on this aspect of the Gandhi–Irwin Pact.

Mitter fully endorsed the government's position.

In so far as the performance of its part of the settlement is concerned [Mitter opined], the Congress is a principal party vis a vis the Government. The Government may look to it to perform its part and the Congress may look to the Government to perform their part . . . In the performance of the obligations of the Settlement, the Government are entitled to look to Gandhi as the author of the Civil Disobedience movement and not to 'the people'; and similarly, Gandhi and not 'the whole' can look to the Government for the performance of their part . . . If in the performance of any Congress obligation for the discontinuance of the Civil Disobedience Movement, 'the people' have to do or abstain from doing certain things, it is for the Congress or Gandhi to see to it. [Gandhi was entitled] to correspond with Garrett, and interview representatives of the Government. [But:] Any claim beyond this is untenable . . . Gandhi can not claim to stand between the Government and tenants . . . Gandhi's claim to be recognised as an intermediary is invalid . . . if by 'intermediary' Gandhi means that, in fulfilling their part of the settlement, the Government must act through him or the Congress that would constitute Gandhi or the Congress the agent of the Government. That is neither the intention nor the effect of the settlement.[130]

The ambidexterousness of the British position couched in lawyer's language could hardly have been better stated, and Emerson felt the ground under his feet firming up.

[128] Gandhi to Emerson, 27 April 1931, *CWMG* 46, pp. 47–8. (The hill station of Simla was the summer capital of the Government of India.)
[129] Emerson to Gandhi, 2 May 1931, H.Poll.33/30/31, *CWMG* 46, pp. 396–7, AICC 2/1931.   [130] Mitter's Opinion, 30 Apr. 1931, H.Poll.33/4/31.

Momentarily, moreover, Gandhi seems to have realised that he might have overstepped the mark, since in an article in *Young India* on 30 April he appeared to moderate his previous demands:

I may say [he wrote] that great difficulties are being experienced in establishing friendly touch with local officials. The result is that many things that should have long ago been done on behalf of the Government are still not being done . . . They do not seem to realize that there is peace now . . . between the people and the Government and that efforts are being made to make enduring what is today only temporary and provisional. The difficulties in the way are enormous. But I have pledged my word to Lord Irwin that so far as is humanly possible, I shall prevent the Truce from breaking . . . I know that Lord Irwin was sincerely anxious to see that it is fully carried out by the Government's agents, as he testified more than once that I was to see it being fully carried out by the Congressmen.

On reading this Emerson swiftly remarked that the 'general question of Congress acting as an intermediary between Government and the people has rather faded from the picture', and so it seemed for the moment.[131]

In the intervening fortnight before Gandhi eventually went to Simla[132] both sides did all they could to hold the prevailing situation in check. Emerson sent a further letter to provincial governments in which, whilst again acknowledging the very considerable difficulties that they faced, he not only reiterated the wish of the Government of India that the Pact should be upheld, but went so far towards meeting Gandhi's position as to suggest that government officials should bring 'specific instances of objectionable methods to the notice of responsible Provincial Congress leaders . . . who might be able and disposed to exert a good influence'.[133] Already several of Gandhi's principal provincial lieutenants, Nehru, Prasad, Rajagopalachari, Patel, were variously in touch with their provincial governments;[134] while Gandhi himself tried once again to resolve the details of the old disputes in Gujarat.[135] There Vallabhbhai Patel remained very disgruntled.[136] Gandhi nevertheless remained emphatic

---

[131] Gandhi later confirmed that for a while he allowed this to happen, *CWMG* 47, pp. 319–20.

[132] His impending visit to Simla had been fixed by 2 May, HD to Bombay, 2 May 1931. It was also arranged that Garrett should visit Simla to brief Emerson on the matters likely to arise, idem, 4 May 1931, H.Poll.33/4/31.

[133] Emerson to LGs, 2 May 1931, H.Poll.33/7/31.

[134] E.g. Nehru to Jagdish Prasad, 11 Mar., 17, 27 (2) June, to Maharaj Singh 9 Apr. 1931, *SWJN* 5, pp. 56–9, 79–80, 96–8, 66–8, and more generally AICC 63/1931; Kothawala to Bell, 7 May 1931, H.Poll.33/3/31; Gandhi to Nehru, 20 June 1931, ibid. 21/8/31; Hallett's Notes, 16, 19 July 1931, H.Poll.33/5/31.

[135] He was much involved with the attempt to buy land back from Sardar Framroze Garda, *CWMG* 46, AICC 3/1931 passim. See also 'Notes', 3 May 1931, ibid., pp. 102–4; Kothawala report, 28 Apr. 1931, H.Poll.33/3/31.

[136] Police reports Surat, 30 Apr., 2, 5 May 1931, Kothawala's reports, 3, 8 May 1931, Collins to HD and enc., 26 May 1931, ibid.

that the Pact must be upheld.[137] On 28 April, moreover, he had a conciliatory two and a half hours with Perry, the Collector of Kheda district[138] – of whom he was soon to say 'I with my co-workers have been . . . getting on like a happy family'[139] – while Patel saw Kothawala, the District Magistrate of Surat, on 7 May.[140] Gandhi then issued a number of pamphlets emphasising that whilst those who had suffered from their participation in civil disobedience were not obliged to borrow to pay for their land revenue, others were not so protected.[141] More generally, however, he became at the same time increasingly worried by all the much more general uncertainties attending the Pact,[142] and he was especially concerned about the worsening state of Muslim–Hindu relations particularly at the highest level.[143] As a consequence he started to hold back from his earlier assurances that when the time came he would go to London.[144]

On his eventual arrival in Simla on 13 May, a personal note was awaiting him from Emerson suggesting that they should meet at a private house, 'Richmond', near to where he was to stay.[145] Their ensuing discussions spread over four days. Emerson's note upon them ran to over 7,000 words.[146] They were therefore far more protracted than any of their earlier talks. That reflected the fact that down in the plains the post-Pact conflict, bred in the ambiguity of the British position and the ordinary Congressman's corresponding response, was throwing up an increasing number of contentious issues which called for skilful handling.

The two of them this time began by discussing all the old issues of revenue arrears, the reinstatement of village officials, and the repurchase of lands in Gujarat, though in rather better humour than before. They discussed as well the non-release of certain prisoners, the return of confiscated arms, the restoration of forfeited pensions, and the assurances being sought by educational establishments from politically active students.

[137] 'To the Satyagrahi Farmer', 19 Apr. 1931, 'Advice to Peasants, Bardoli', 24 Apr. 1931, 'The Gujarat Farmer', 30 Apr. 1931, 'Statement to the press', 2 May 1931, Gandhi to Andrews, 5 May 1931, *CWMG* 46, pp. 13–15, 36, 57–9, 68, 88–9.
[138] Perry to Collins, 33/4/31, H.Poll.33/4/31; Gandhi to Perry, 3 May 1931, *CWMG* 46, p. 77, AICC 3/1931, H.Poll.33/3/31.
[139] Gandhi to Garrett, 8 May 1931, H.Poll.33/4/31.
[140] Kothawala to Bell, 7 May 1931, H.Poll.33/3/31.
[141] Indian News Agency telegram, 29 Apr. 1931, H.Poll.33/4/31; encs. in Bell to Emerson, 7 May 1931, H.Poll.33/3/31.
[142] E.g. Gandhi to Emerson, 4 May 1931, Gandhi to Nanda, 6 May 1931, *CWMG* 46, pp. 84–5, 96–7.
[143] Again the details cannot be properly elaborated here, see Page (note 48 above), and e.g. Gandhi to Tucker, Gandhi to Andrews, 5 May 1931, *CWMG* 46, pp. 87–9.
[144] For an early expression of this see Gandhi to Sapru, 22 Apr. 1931, SP 6, G14.
[145] Emerson to Gandhi, [13 May 1931], H.Poll.33/9/31.
[146] 'Note by Mr. Emerson on an interview between himself and Mr. Gandhi on the 13th, 14th, 15th, and 16th May 1931', H.Poll.33/9/31, *CWMG* 46, pp. 400–16.

When they then discussed the question of salt manufacture they very soon agreed that the Pact's provisions about this required considerably greater clarification.[147]

As in recent weeks both Gandhi and the Government of India had become increasingly worried by the growing confrontation between Abdul Ghaffar Khan and the Government of the Frontier Province,[148] Emerson called in its Chief Secretary to discuss the situation there, and reached agreement with Gandhi that he would send for Abdul Ghaffar Khan and do what he could to calm it.

When they then talked about the deleterious effect on influential British opinion of the boycott of British cloth, Gandhi took the opportunity to express his deepening concern that in the absence of a communal settlement it would be fruitless for him to go to London and present a claim for the self-government of a much divided India. About this Emerson made the revealing comment that any postponement of constitutional advance

was not possible for Government to accept . . . Government had often been accused of Machiavellian methods, and if it adopted the line taken by Mr. Gandhi himself, there would be an immediate outcry accompanied by political agitation on an intense scale.

Constitutional reform still constituted, that is, a vital ingredient in the dualist policy of the British towards India, and they were quite determined to proceed with it.

When they then moved on to talk of agrarian matters Emerson gained the distinct impression that 'Mr. Gandhi was more happy about Gujarat than he was when I last saw him'. He was especially pleased with the cooperation Congressmen had now established with government officials in Kheda district.[149] More strikingly Gandhi appeared (or so Emerson thought) to have 'dropped the claim, if he ever seriously entertained it, that Congress should be recognised as an intermediary between Government and the people'. Whilst Gandhi still insisted that Congress 'was not able to accept the idea of Congress standing aside from helping persons in distress', he accepted Emerson's statement 'that there was no Government in the world that would allow a political organization to come between them and the tax-payer'. Nor did he contravene Emerson's assertion that because of the febrile situation in the provinces 'the outstanding danger was the war mentality of the Congress and the

[147] See the subsequent communique, *CWMG* 46, p. 241.
[148] HD to Chief Comm. NWFP, nd, H.Poll.33/8/31 KW; Gandhi to Emerson, tel., 1 May 1931, Emerson to Gandhi, 2 May 1931, *CWMG* 46, pp. 66, 396–7.
[149] On how this worked see Bell to Emerson, 15 July 1931, H.Poll.3/17/31.

constant advocacy in the country of preparations for a further struggle', except to complain that this 'suggested a wide-spread suspicion of the objects and activities of the Congress, that these were in fact good and that they did want a peaceful solution'. Emerson was well satisfied, moreover, that he fully accepted that 'any renewal of the civil disobedience movement would compel Government to hit hard'. And whilst Gandhi now seemed increasingly reluctant to go to London, because he remained fearful of so much that was happening in India, he nonetheless told the press when the talks eventually concluded that so far as he was concerned they had been 'healthy and good' and that 'he was on the whole satisfied with his visit'.[150] Emerson emerged content as well. Gandhi, he reflected,

is always very impressed by practical difficulties than by theoretical principles and he is often ready to see the dangerous results of a particular course of action, when he will not admit the action itself is wrong. He has a keen sense of humour, and I found it useful, when we got to a sticky patch to have a comparatively frivolous diversion. He is fair in seeing the other side of the case and is ready quietly to argue any point at issue. He is very sensitive to the personal touch, but does not mind and, in fact, rather welcomes plain speaking.[151]

More generally Emerson felt the ambidexterous course the Government of India had been pursuing with him was now working pretty effectively.

Personal contact with various officers of Government [he noted] has increased his desire to co-operate and while I realize only too well the difficulties and dangers in the way of closer cooperation with Congress leaders so long as Congress are out to increase their prestige and influence at the expense of Government and other parties, I feel that, where it is possible to avoid these difficulties and dangers, personal contact will definitely help to relieve the situation. This will be particularly the case if, as I hope, Mr. Gandhi tries with success to tone down the war mentality. If there is no response by Government, we will get back into the same vicious circle

of coercion and repression; and that must if at all possible be avoided.[152]

At the end of this fourth set of discussions the links between Gandhi and the Government of India therefore remained intact. That by any account was a notable achievement for both sides. Yet as the monsoon months supervened, political storm clouds finally broke as well, and all – or almost all – was swept away.

---

[150] Interviews to the press, 15, 17 May 1931, *CWMG* 46, pp. 153, 164. Sapru met him at this time in Simla and found him 'in a reasonable state of mind', Sapru to Sankey, 24 May 1931, SP 23 S6/4.
[151] Emerson to Hailey, 16 May 1931, and Note, IOL R/3/1/289.
[152] Emerson's Note [13–16 May 1931], see footnote 146 above.

Long prior to this fourth set of talks, agreement had been reached in principle that Gandhi should see the Governor of UP about the problems there.[153] Sir Malcolm Hailey had been on leave (having a hernia operation). The acting Governor of UP had recognised that the severe drop in agricultural prices as a result of the world slump called for a reduction in rent and revenue levels, but Hailey needed time to explore the issues for himself.[154] Like other British officials he was not prepared to acknowledge that the Congress or Gandhi could act as an intermediary between government and the peasants.[155] He did nonetheless hope that he might be 'able to utilise his [i.e. Gandhi's] influence to assist in solving the difficulty which has arisen in our rural areas'. By the beginning of May he decided that, because of the leading part a good many Congressmen were playing in the agrarian agitation in the province, some selected prosecutions had become unavoidable. He hoped, however, that they could be effected 'without giving support to the notion that we are attempting anything like a general movement against Congress speakers'. At the same time he concluded that in a number of districts there must be even more remissions in UP than had already been agreed, 'for if we allow matters to go on as at present', he wrote, 'we shall completely lose hold over them'. Having reached these conclusions he was ready to see Gandhi.[156]

Accordingly at the conclusion of the Gandhi–Emerson talks in Simla, Gandhi journeyed to Naini Tal to speak with Hailey. They met there on 20 May. They began by traversing the familiar ground of the non-release of prisoners, the confiscations of arms licences, the plight of rusticated students, and picketing. But they soon concentrated on agrarian matters. Hailey complained that the Congress campaign for substantial reductions in rent could all too easily lead both to no rent being paid, and to increasingly violent clashes with landlords. About this Gandhi commented (as was his wont) that such problems 'could only be solved by enlisting the effective cooperation of Congress in persuading tenants to pay for their rents'. He made, moreover, three proposals: either, he suggested, the Government could 'accept the figures [about appropriate rent reductions] arrived at by Congress workers'; or 'officers might hold a kind of summary enquiry with selected Congressmen in each district'; or

---

[153] Emerson to Hailey, 20 Apr. 1931; Emerson to Malaviya, 24 Apr. 1931, H.Poll.33/11/31; for the detailed arrangements see ibid. and H.Poll.33/4/31.
[154] Emerson to Gandhi, 30 Apr. 1931, CWMG 46, pp. 399–400; Hailey to Willingdon, 27 Apr. 1931, HP 20.   [155] Cf. Sykes to Willingdon, 24 Apr. 1931, H.Poll.33/4/31.
[156] Emerson to Gandhi, 30 Apr. 1931, Emerson to Hailey, 28 Apr., 2 (tel.), 8 May 1931; Hailey to Emerson, 27, 29 Apr., 2, 4 May 1931, Jagdish Prasad to all Comms. 7 May 1931, Hailey to Crerar, 8 May 1931, H.Poll.33/11/31; Hailey to Montmorency, 29 Apr. 1930, HP 20.

'Government itself should hold a public enquiry at which Congressmen could give evidence as to the capacity of tenants to pay rentals'. Hailey responded that generalised figures did not work effectively; an enquiry would take too long; and the capacity of peasants to pay was greater than was being suggested. He did allow that Gandhi felt 'deeply that Congress cannot entirely retire from its position of championship of tenants and smallholders', but he was in the end disappointed not to secure any more definite undertakings from him other than 'to discountenance . . . a no-rent campaign or . . . Congress tribunals'. 'It is not a very satisfactory conclusion', he told Emerson, but 'we left the matter there'.[157]

Before Gandhi left Naini Tal three days later it did not, however, remain there. In the course of their conversation Hailey had carefully 'avoided any point of principle', but he had made it quite clear that while he and his officers were quite ready to hold talks with the UP's Congress leaders, they would not share any executive authority with them. Gandhi by now had set aside his claim for Congress to be recognised as the 'intermediary' between government and the people, but he remained totally committed to ensuring that Congress should play a major role in the resolution of any major public matter in dispute, and in protracted talks with his UP associates and a selected group of landlords in Naini Tal he soon reached the conclusion that the agrarian situation in the province had now become so serious that only a major intervention upon his own part would in any way meet the case. So in a bold and audacious move he wrote to Hailey on 23 May[158] to say that since the government's proposals for rent remissions were altogether too limited, 'in the absence of response by the Government to any of the proposals made by me', he would be issuing a manifesto 'to the Kisans of the UP' to advise those who lived in certain districts to pay only half their due rentals and others no more than three-quarters.

That was a head-on challenge to the government,[159] and he gave Hailey no more than a few hours to respond to it before he left Naini Tal by train. Hailey, however, kept his head. While fully acknowledging Gandhi's accompanying condemnation of violence, he made it very clear in reply that 'I could not associate myself in any way with the manifesto as a whole', and then proceeded to give his reasons in some detail;[160] 'it was

---

[157] Sir Malcolm Hailey's Note on discussions with Gandhi, 20 May 1931, H.Poll.33/11/31, *CWMG* 46, pp. 417–19. See also Hailey to Emerson, 21 May 1931, H.Poll.33/11/31, *CWMG* 46, p. 419. Gandhi evidently thought likewise, Gandhi to Mahmud, 21 May 1931, ibid., p. 191.

[158] Gandhi to Hailey, 23 May 1931, *CWMG* 46, pp. 199–200, H.Poll.33/11/31.

[159] For the consequences see Jagdish Prasad to Emerson, 16 July 1931, H.Poll.33/24/31.

[160] Hailey to Gandhi, 23 May 1931, H.Poll.33/11/31, *CWMG* 46, pp. 420–1.

clearly impossible for me', he told Emerson, 'to agree to anything that would look like a joint manifesto from myself and him'.[161]

This was a crucial episode.[162] For it indicated that the situation on the ground in a province like UP was far more intractable than the armchair talks in Simla could control.[163] And it marked the moment when Gandhi made his first open move to usurp the authority of the British upon an important issue of public policy in India – and broke the bonds which his Pact with Irwin had cast around him.[164] More ominously it opened up a breach in the personal links he had formed with Emerson. On reading Hailey's report Emerson responded:

Personally I feel that Gandhi has let me down badly . . . I can only hope that he gave Congress workers personal advice which may mitigate the effects of his manifesto.[165]

The consequences were soon apparent. On 27 May the Viceroy's Council decided that the situation was now so threatening that, for the first time in the history of British India, they should authorise the preparation of a full-scale Emergency Powers Ordinance which upon its promulgation would provide for an immediate declaration of a country-wide state of emergency, and the prompt arrest without trial of a great many Congressmen:[166] 'civil martial law' as we have seen one official pointedly dub it.[167] By 11 June Emerson was inviting provincial governments to send their comments to him upon the draft.[168]

At the same time during the last few days of May Gandhi decided that owing to the increasing number of clashes which were occurring between Congress supporters and the government, and the now parlous communal divide, he could not now go to London.[169] On 9 June the Working Committee decided he should, however, still go – Rajagopalachari in par-

---

[161] Hailey to Emerson, 23 May 1931, H.Poll.33/11/31, *CWMG* 46, p. 421; Hailey to Dawson (editor, *The Times*, London), 7 June 1931, HP 21.

[162] For a further account see J.W. Cell, *Hailey. A Study in British Imperialism, 1872–1969*, Cambridge 1992, ch. 13.

[163] Pandey, *Ascendancy of the Congress*, ch. 6 and e.g. Nehru to Jagdish Prasad [June 1931], AICC 63/1931.

[164] 'To the Kisans of the U.P.', *CWMG* 46, pp. 200–3. See also Speech at Zamindars' meeting, Nainital, 23 May 1931, 'To the U.P. Zamindars', 28 May 1931, ibid., pp. 204, 233–5.   [165] Emerson to Hailey, 2 June 1931, H.Poll.33/11/31.

[166] Order in Council, 17 May 1931, Emerson to LGs, Emerson to India Office, 11 June 1931, H.Poll.13/8/31. See also Collins to Emerson, 5 June 1931, Stewart to Emerson, tel., 30 June 1931, Emerson to Stewart, 4 July 1931, ibid., and H.Poll.209/31.

[167] On all this see D.A. Low, '"Civil Martial Law": the Government of India and the Civil Disobedience movements 1930–34', in Low (ed.), *Congress and the Raj*, pp. 199–224.

[168] Emerson to LGs, 20 June 1931, H.Poll.21/8/31.

[169] E.g. Gandhi to Willingdon, tel., [before 22 May 1931], Gandhi to Sastri, tel., 23 May 1931, Gandhi to Nag, 26 May 1931, Gandhi to Shirer, tel., [after 30 May 1931], *CWMG* 46, pp. 197, 199, 226, 253–4.

ticular argued strongly for this[170] – and Gandhi reluctantly acquiesced.[171] But by now right across India, and not just in UP and Gujarat, there was a rising tide of local clashes between groups led by Congress activists and police and subordinate officials of the British government which in varying ways became deeply worrying to both sides.[172] Gandhi remained strong in his private condemnations wherever the fault evidently lay upon the Congress side. 'I am very clear', he wrote to Nehru on 20 June about two episodes in UP, 'that we must not be in any shape or form, directly or indirectly, party to the breach',[173] while Hailey later admitted privately that

> you know what the young district officer is like when you let him off the leash; one or two of them undoubtedly splashed about a little too widely and did things that were definitely incautious and impolitic.[174]

In view, however, of the wide range of matters in dispute, and the now surging belief that open conflict was just around the corner, any effort to exercise restraint now stood at a large premium upon both sides. Gandhi continued to take the line that

> at the present moment the Government and the Congress are supposed to be cooperating with each other and therefore they should trust us and work with us, making use of us wherever they feel there is any breach on the part of any of our workers.[175]

But that required a measure of trust which in view of the disputes and clashes that were now occurring in so many parts of India was beginning to crumble fast.

> There is constant talk [Emerson noted on 11 June] of a future struggle . . . many Congress workers . . . are preparing the people for a renewal of civil disobedience . . . great activity is manifest in rural areas . . . behind the screen of agrarian distress

---

[170] Rajagopalachari to Gandhi, 2 July 1931, H.Poll.33/30/31.   [171] *CWMG* 47, pp. 1–3.

[172] For details about some early clashes in e.g. UP and Madras as reported from the two sides see Bomford to Maharaj Singh, 23 Mar. 1931, H.Poll.33/11/31, and Gurumurti to Patel, 11 Apr. 1931, AICC 17/1931. Then: Gandhi to Emerson, 19, 24, 25 May 1931, Emerson to Gandhi, 20 (2), 28 (2) May 1931, Gandhi to Maxwell, 29 May 1931, *CWMG* 46, pp. 245–7, H.Poll.33/9/31; Emerson to Gandhi, 25 May, 5 June 1931, Gandhi to Emerson, 25 May 1931, H.Poll.33/5/31; Maxwell to Gandhi, 25 May 1931, H.Poll.33/4/31; Chhatari to Hailey, 8 June 1931, Hailey to Emerson, 12 June 1931, H.Poll.33/11/31; Gandhi to Emerson, 5, 14, 18, 20 June 1931, H.Poll.33/30/31; Sulakhe to Gandhi, 5 June 1931, Sulakhe to Patel, 8 June 1931, Patel to Sulakhe, 16 June 1931, AICC 17/1931; B & O to HD 28 June, 13 July 1931, H.Poll.33/23/21; Nehru to Pant, 18 June 1931, Sahai to Nehru, 28 June 1931, AICC 63/1931; Duni Chand to Ogilvie, 14 June 1931, AICC 2/1931; Indian National Congress, *Agrarian Distress in the U.P.*, Allahabad 1931; H.Poll.33/50/31 passim.

[173] Gandhi to Nehru, 20 June 1931, H.Poll.21/8/31.

[174] Hailey to Crerar, 24 July 1931, HP 21. See also idem to idem, 3 July and enc., 11 July 1931, H.Poll.33/16/31.   [175] Gandhi to Nehru, 20 June 1931, H.Poll.21/8/31.

... attempts are being made by Congress ... to assume an authority coordinate with Government ... outside the legitimate scope of a political party ... their continuance constitutes a grave menace to ... present policy.[176]

Gujarat remained a major flashpoint.[177] Gandhi was soon once again there wrestling with the continuing plethora of disputes over confiscated lands, village headmanships, rusticated students, salt, picketing and unreleased prisoners.[178] Since it remained central to British policy that he should still go to London, Emerson, in an effort to see that he was not given any excuse to withdraw from doing so, urged the Government of Bombay to advise its officers to see 'that Gujarat situation should be kept easy and notices of forfeiture of land avoided as far as possible at present'.[179] But his own attitude was clearly hardening,[180] and that of officials in Gujarat too. On 29 May Gandhi and Patel had had a stiff meeting with Kothawala, the District Magistrate of Surat[181] (and were to have another one too on 13 July), and they were soon at odds with him over the collection of land revenue arrears and a number of other issues.[182] Gandhi and Patel fell into a succession of disputes with Bhadrapur too, Perry's successor as Collector of Kheda, particularly over a village headmanship.[183]

There were now all sorts of other issues elsewhere.[184] On a number of

[176] Emerson to LGs, 11 June 1931, H.Poll.33/8/31.
[177] E.g. Gandhi to Patel, tel., 18 May 1931, Interview to the press, 28 May 1931, *CWMG* 46, pp. 168, 245; Bombay to SoS, tel., 8 June 1931, H.Poll.33/3/31; Bhadrapur to Gandhi [15 July 1931], H.Poll.33/17/31; Kothawala's report, 18 July 1931, H.Poll.33/9/31.
[178] Interview to the press, 1 June 1931, *CWMG* 46, pp. 273–4; 'Advice to Farmers, Borsad', 22 June 1931; Gandhi to Bhadrapur 24, 25 June, 2 July 1931, Gandhi to Shirras, 24, 30 June, 3, 11 July 1931, *CWMG* 47, pp. 36–7, 46, 62, 96, 49–50, 79–80, 99, 124–5; Bombay Educational Department Circular, 26 June 1931, Emerson to Gandhi, 2, 4 July 1931, AICC 2/1931; Maxwell to Gandhi, 1, 12 July 1931, AICC 3/1931.
[179] HD to Bombay, tel., 21 May 1931, Emerson to Bell, 25 June 1931, H.Poll.33/3/31.
[180] Emerson's Note, 23 June 1931, ibid.; Emerson to Gandhi (2), 24 June 1931, H.Poll.24/11/31, AICC 2/1931.
[181] Kothawala's report, 30 May 1931, H.Poll.33/4/31.
[182] Gandhi to Kothawala, 30 May 1931, *CWMG* 46, pp. 249–50; Kothawala to Gandhi, 1 June, 5 July 1931, AICC 3/1931; Surat report, 6 July 1931, H.Poll.3/17/31; Kothawala's report on interview with Gandhi on 13 July 1931, 14 July 1931, H.Poll.33/19/31.
[183] Gandhi to Bhadrapur, 7 June 1931, Interview to the press, 14 June 1931, *CWMG* 46, pp. 346, 382; Bhadrapur to Gandhi, 23 June 1931, AICC 3/1931; Gandhi to Maxwell, 5 July 1931, Gandhi to Bhadrapur, 2 July 1931, *CWMG* 47, pp. 110, 96; Gandhi to Bhadrapur, 28 June 1931, Bhadrapur to Gandhi, 29 June 1931, H.Poll.33/3/31; Maxwell to Gandhi, 7 July 1931, Gandhi to Maxwell, 10 July 1931, AICC 3/1931; Bhadrapur to Gandhi [15 July 1931], H.Poll.33/17/31.
[184] E.g. Gandhi to Emerson, 19, 24 (3) May 1931, 'Notes', 21 May 1931, Gandhi to Hailey, 23 May 1931, Gandhi to Maxwell, 29 May 1931, 'An Honest Doubt', 4 May 1931, Gandhi to Saxena, 15 June 1931, Gandhi to Nehru, 17 June 1931, *CWMG* 46, pp. 181, 207–9, 184–8, 203, 245–7, 310–14, 384, 390; Gandhi to Andrews, 24 June, Gandhi to Nehru 28 June, 1 July, Gandhi to Hotson, 3 July 1931, 'Terrible if True', 'Serious Allegations', 'Notes', 'Kisan Troubles in the U.P.', *CWMG* 47, pp. 48, 69–70, 98, 85–90, 54–6, 59–62, 92–4; Maxwell to Gandhi, 18 July 1931, H.Poll.33/4/31.

these Gandhi now exchanged letters with Emerson,[185] and in an effort to resolve some of the issues in dispute he proposed in mid June (in full accord with his conception of the form that government–Congress relations should now take) that 'boards of arbitration' should be established consisting of one government and one Congress nominee to deal with them.[186] But Emerson would not hear of this. 'If . . . questions of policy affecting Law and Order or the effective working of the administration' were referred to such a Board, he told Gandhi on 4 July, that would not 'be consonant with the discharge by Government of fundamental responsibilities'.[187]

By early July a general crisis thus stood well within the offing.[188] Amongst other things, the Government of India was yet again exceedingly troubled about the activities of Abdul Ghaffar Khan in the Frontier Province.[189] In UP Hailey was privately admitting that rental demands were still a great deal too high, but since he was not prepared to make all the reductions this implied without a comprehensive enquiry, the conjunction there of a slump, inordinate rents, and much political excitement, was now a sure recipe for all the Congress-led tenant–landlord confrontations that were now occurring there.[190] Late in June Gandhi had told the press that 'he had been receiving reports from all over India . . . that a deliberate policy of repression of strictly peaceful picketing, in the shape of faked prosecutions, physical interference and lathi charges was hindering the work of the Settlement',[191] and during the first week of July Congress's Working Committee meeting in Bombay put together a compendium of the information they had about the clashes right across the country.[192] Thereupon Gandhi on 9 July wrote an article in *Young India* beneath the title 'Is it crumbling?' in which he stated 'that it almost looks as if the Government was at war with the Congress'.[193] So assailed did he feel by all the allegations of breaches of the Pact on both sides that,

[185] Gandhi to Emerson, 3, 14 June 1931, *CWMG* 46, pp. 286–7, 379–81; idem 19 (2), 20, 24 (3), 30 (4) June, 5 July 1931, *CWMG* 47, pp. 8, 12–13, 20, 43–4, 75–8, 109–10; Gandhi to Emerson, 24 June 1931, Emerson to Gandhi, 10 July 1931, H.Poll.33/21/31; Gandhi to Emerson, and enc., 2 July 1931, H.Poll.33/30/31.

[186] Gandhi to Emerson, 14 June 1931, Gandhi to Rajagopalachari, 16 June 1931, *CWMG* 46, pp. 379–81, 387; Gandhi to Emerson, 20 June 1931, *CWMG* 47, pp. 19–20.

[187] Emerson to Gandhi, 4 July 1931, ibid., pp. 428–9; Surat report, 6 July 1931, HD to Bombay, 9 July 1931, Bell to Emerson, 15 July 1931, H.Poll.33/17/31.

[188] E.g. Emerson to Jagdish Prasad, 13 July 1931, H.Poll.33/24/31. See also Office Note on communications from CP and UP, 24 June 1931, H.Poll.33/11/31; Fazli Husain Note on some speeches, 26 June 1931, H.Poll.247/31; Kamlapati to Sahai, 26 June 1931, H.Poll.33/9/31; Patel to Nehru, 21, 29 July 1931, AICC G60/1931.

[189] Gandhi to Emerson, 13 June 1931, *CWMG* 46, pp. 373–4; H.Poll.33/4/31.

[190] Hailey to Crerar, 24 July 1931, HP 21; AICC 63/1931 passim; Dep. Comm. Sultanpur to Jagdish Prasad, 20 July 1931, H.Poll.33/23/31.   [191] *CWMG* 47, p. 63.

[192] Nehru to PCCs, 16 July 1931, *SWJN* 5, pp. 8–9.   [193] *CWMG* 47, pp. 115–18.

supported by the Working Committee, he now decided that the only thing to do was to approach the Government of India once again,[194] and upon receiving Willingdon's invitation of 12 July to a further 'discussion between you and Emerson', promptly took the train to Simla once again,[195] this time taking Nehru with him.[196]

The fifth set of discussions which then ensued between Emerson and Gandhi following the Gandhi–Irwin Pact extended from 15 to 21 July and thus became the longest of them all. They started with the two of them holding talks over two days once again at 'Richmond', mostly on their own.[197] Early in June Gandhi had remarked to Charlie Andrews: 'Thank God, I do receive help from Central Government. I believe Mr Emerson knows me and will play the game.'[198] But the atmosphere had by now greatly changed. Whilst in May Gandhi had presented Emerson with a memorandum of complaints, this time he brought with him a 'charge-sheet' based upon the compendium the Working Committee had composed in Bombay.[199] Emerson believed most of the accusations to be totally unwarranted, but in order to ensure that the government should not be held responsible for any breakdown of the Pact, he arranged for each of them to be investigated.[200]

Once more the two of them discussed Gujarat. Gandhi protested that coercion was being used there in revenue collections, though he and other Congressmen were quite ready to ensure that appropriate payments should be made. Emerson expressed his scepticism about this – as indeed about Rajagopalachari's anti-liquor campaign in Madras, and Congress's picketing of cloth shops in UP. They then spoke about the Frontier Province, and Bengal.[201] They spent most of their time, however, on UP.[202] Emerson now castigated the anti-rent campaign there,[203] which he said was being 'organised by Congress on a very large scale'. Gandhi riposted that in UP there was now an 'active war going on against the Congress as such'. That, Emerson insisted, 'was because Congress were

---

[194] Gandhi to Willingdon, tel., 10 July 1931, ibid., p. 122.
[195] Willingdon to Gandhi, tel., 11 July 1931, Gandhi to Willingdon, tel., 12 July 1931, ibid., p. 126. For Gandhi's various press interviews during his Simla visit see ibid. pp. 127, 133–4, 146–7, 149, 150, 164–5, 177, 181–4.
[196] Who had been trying to see Hailey, who had been unresponsive, Nehru to Gandhi, 30 June 1931, H.Poll.33/9/31; Jagdish Prasad to Nehru, 30 June 1931, H.Poll.33/16/31; Hailey to Willingdon, 15 July 1931, H.Poll.33/23/31; Nehru to Jagdish Prasad, [23] July 1931, AICC 63/1931.   [197] Emerson to Gandhi, 15 July 1931, H.Poll.33/23/31.
[198] Gandhi to Andrews, 2 June 1931, CWMG 46, pp. 275–6.
[199] CWMG 47, pp. 166–77; H.Poll.33/23/31.
[200] Emerson to LGs, 21 July 1931, H.Poll.33/23/31.   [201] On Bengal see H.Poll.14/8/31.
[202] For the kind of information Emerson was receiving see Jagdish Prasad to Emerson, 30 June, 9 July 1931, H.Poll.33/24/31.
[203] See also Emerson to Gandhi, 24 June 1931, and Emerson's note, 1 July 1931, H.Poll.33/11/31; Jagdish Prasad to Emerson, 16 July 1931, H.Poll.33/24/31.

responsible for a campaign which was definitely assisting towards the creation of dangerous conditions'. To which Gandhi replied (as he had so often before) that 'Congress could not dissociate themselves from the interest of the peasants without renouncing their creed'. To which Emerson retorted that 'the close identity of interest [between the Congress and the peasantry] had been developed since the Settlement and was part of the policy of consolidation in rural areas as preparation for a new fight, that it was mainly the last feature that inevitably made all local Governments look with suspicion on Congress activities'. While to Gandhi's reiterated plea that in such matters 'Government should definitely associate Congress with them and accept the advice of the Congress as to what rents should be collected', Emerson roundly objected 'that this would mean that Government would abrogate its functions in favour of a political party that had taken up the side of the tenants against the landlords'.

When they went on to speak about the upcoming Round Table Conference, Gandhi avowed that he could hardly now go to London whilst all these conflicts raged in India. To which Emerson responded 'that the only way of securing reasonable peaceful conditions was for the Congress to close down agitation and to suspend war preparations, at any rate for the next 3 or 4 months'. Gandhi countered that he 'felt Provincial Governments were out to kill the Congress'. And then once more avowed that 'the settlement between Government and Congress placed the latter in a special position . . . and that Government and Congress should work together in close unity'. Emerson now dismissed this out of hand.

The really telling exchanges came on the two or three occasions when in the course of these first two days of talks Gandhi enquired why, if the Government believed that Congress was breaching the Settlement, they did not denounce it altogether. For in framing his replies Emerson found himself trapped in the thicket of British ambiguity. All he could remark was that the government was still hoping the situation would settle down, when the truth was that they were exceedingly anxious that Congress should not slip the noose of constitutional negotiations which at such political cost they had cast about it.

All in all it was thus a very different conversation from most of their previous ones.[204] Crerar, the Home Member and Emerson's chief, soon called it all 'deadlock'.[205] Hitherto the two of them had managed to keep

---

[204] 'Note by Mr. H.W. Emerson of his discussion with Mr. Gandhi on July 15th and 16th 1931', H.Poll.33/23/31, *CWMG* 47, pp. 430–41.
[205] Crerar to Hailey, 17 July 1931, H.Poll.33/11/31.

their heads above the pent-up turbulence that was sweeping across the provinces. But its tide now washed right over them, and they were sucked into its swirling rip.

On 17 July Gandhi had had an hour and a half with the Home Member, Crerar,[206] and on the next day three hours with Willingdon. Over the following two days Emerson had two lengthy meetings with Nehru, which were principally devoted to UP. On this Emerson commented: 'The Pandit seemed to me to appreciate more clearly than Mr. Gandhi the complexity of the problem.' They spoke as well about the Round Table Conference, as to which, so Emerson affirmed, Nehru 'admitted that there was an "outside" chance . . . that it might produce a constitution acceptable to Indian opinion'.[207] Thereafter Gandhi saw Willingdon for a second time on 21 July.

By then however the general atmosphere had turned exceedingly bleak. On the previous day Hailey had made a major pronouncement[208] on the agrarian situation in UP in which he outlined his plans for its amelioration in terms Gandhi generally found acceptable.[209] But in the course of the past few days Gandhi had been receiving a string of despairing telegrams from Vallabhbhai Patel about police parties raiding villages in Bardoli enforcing land revenue arrears there.

Police broke open backdoor of a Mohammedan of Bardoli. [just one of these reported] two children hurt. property taken out for twenty four rupees arrears for past year. he had paid last year two years full dues . . .[210]

Gandhi put these straight into Emerson's hands: 'I hold the position to be entirely unbearable', he inveighed, 'and a distinct breach of the Settlement'.[211]

As a consequence his second meeting with Willingdon concentrated not upon UP but upon Gujarat. Willingdon and his advisers told him they wanted to avoid a break 'if this is reasonably possible'.[212] They therefore agreed to consider his request that certain details of the Pact should be referred to an impartial tribunal for adjudication,[213] and they assured him

---

[206] 'Note by the Hon'ble Sir J Crerar of his discussion with Mr. Gandhi on July 17th 1931', H.Poll.33/23/31, *CWMG* 47, pp. 441–2.

[207] 'Confidential Note by Mr. H.W. Emerson of his discussion with Pandit Jawahar Lal Nehru on the 19th and 20th of July 1931', H.Poll.33/23/31, *SWJN* 5, pp. 9–11.

[208] Text in H.Poll.33/16/31.

[209] Interview to *The Pioneer*, *CWMG* 47, p. 181. For accounts of what was involved see Hailey to Benn, 1 Aug 1930, HP, 21 and Hailey to Willingdon, 12 Aug. 1930, HP 20.

[210] Patel to Gandhi, tels., 19, 20, 21 (2) July 1931, H.Poll.33/39/31; Patel to Nehru, 21 July 1931, AICC G60/1931.

[211] Gandhi to Emerson, 19, 20, 22, 24 July 1931, H.Poll.33/16/31.

[212] Emerson to Bell, 23 July 1931, H.Poll.33/19/31.

[213] Gandhi to Emerson, 21 July 1931, *CWMG* 47, pp. 179–80. For some of the background

the government would abide by the Pact's specific provisions, and examine the charge sheet that he had given them. Having, however, now concluded that, with an eye to 'world opinion', he was looking for some symbolic concession to 'save the face of Congress', and justify a break with the government should this be refused him, they showed themselves completely adamant on other issues.[214] Once again they rejected his claims for a special status for the Congress. They told him starkly that should the Congress's agitations persist, not only would they take decisive action against it. If it came to the point they would not hesitate to publish their own version of events.[215] All of which left Gandhi in very great despair. He had come to Simla, so he told Willingdon on his departure,

in the hope that the difficulties would be removed. But our protracted conversations have not advanced matters . . . Reports pour in upon me . . . showing that Congressmen are being harassed . . . I have suggested several ways out. But I am sorry they have not commended themselves to you.[216]

While in a press interview he affirmed that:

I don't want to humiliate the Government of India and I don't want to set up a parallel Government but I do want the district authorities to allow responsible Congressmen to assist in assessing the ability of the peasants to pay.[217]

Privately he emitted a *cri de coeur*: 'They no longer trust the Congress', he declared.[218] That was now the essential truth.

Emerson was sufficiently worried, however, by the likely repercussions of the Bardoli situation on the general position that he now sent a sheaf of communications to the Government of Bombay over the next few days impressing upon them the need to

give quiet hint to Collector to go slow . . . Gujarat at present is comparatively unimportant factor in situation . . . If accounts of coercive action in Bardoli are even substantially true such action at present time is likely seriously to prejudice general situation and to make Gujarat instead of United Provinces cause of complaint . . . if a break comes it seems to us of vital importance that the responsibility should be clearly laid on Congress . . . Gandhi's general position has been that he and his lieutenants in Kaira District have co-operated wholeheartedly with the local officials and largely through their assistance the greater part of the revenue

to this see Gandhi to Haksar, 19 July 1931, and Ramaswamy Aiyar to Sapru, 21 July 1931, SP I, 2, A 143.

[214] 'Then (to make matters worse) there is Gandhi trying to back out of the Round Table Conference and trying to pick a quarrel in one way or another', General Smuts (South Africa) to Mrs Gillett, 28 July 1931, SmP 49, 193.

[215] HD to LGs, tel., 22 July 1931, H.Poll.33/23/31; Emerson to Bell, 23 July 1931, HD to Bombay, tel., 24 July 1931, H.Poll.33/19/31.

[216] Gandhi to Willingdon, 21 July 1931, *CWMG* 47, p.178.

[217] Interview to *The Pioneer*, 21 July 1931, *CWMG* 47, p.182.

[218] In a letter to Birla, 20 July 1931, ibid. p. 164.

has been collected . . . The present danger [is] . . . that the Collector [of Bardoli could] . . . involve himself in a tug of war with the Congress . . . with consequences that may be very grave.[219]

In addition he was particularly careful to keep in close contact with Gandhi.[220] That was just as well for on reaching Bardoli Gandhi's patience finally snapped.[221]

By this time there were very grave conflicts in both the Frontier Province and UP,[222] in both of which he once again became involved. However, there was very little he could do to influence either. Whilst Abdul Ghaffar Khan was deeply devoted to Gandhi personally, and strongly committed to non-violence, Gandhi was not fully informed about the details of the conflict there and was not in a good position to ameliorate it from a distance.[223] Whilst in UP the persisting agrarian conflicts were at least as much between tenants and landlords as between peasants and government – and Hailey as he had already recognised was belatedly trying to do something about them.[224] Gujarat by contrast was his own ground, and he knew its details intimately. Later Hailey came to remark: 'I was delighted when he got wrapped up in his funny little problem about his eleven villages in Gujarat . . . when they might have been playing havoc with six or seven million tenants in the U.P.'[225] Gandhi, however, had chosen his ground very deliberately.

In line with his persistent purpose throughout these months he believed that he, Vallabhbhai Patel and their associates had undertaken to ensure that those Congress supporters in Gujarat who were liable for land revenue arrears should pay all that they could, short of having to borrow to do so, on the clear understanding that the government would not thereupon coerce them. By early July, however, the figures available to Kothawala, the District Magistrate of Surat, showed that the largest arrears in his district were in areas particularly subjected to Congress influence, and that crop returns, in Bardoli and Valod Mahal more particularly, clearly called for larger payments. When his reiterated demands for

---

[219] HD to Bombay, tels., 21, 22, 25, 28, 29 July 1931, Emerson to Bell, 23 July 1931, Bombay to HD, tels., 25, 29 July 1931, H.Poll.33/19/31.

[220] Emerson to Gandhi, 23, 25 (tel.) July 1931, ibid.

[221] Gandhi to Emerson, tel., 24 July 1931, CWMG 47, p. 200.

[222] Gandhi to Emerson and enc., 19 July 1931, H.Poll.33/16/31.

[223] Gandhi to Maxwell, 1 Aug. 1931, Gandhi to Emerson, 28 Aug. 1931, CWMG 47, pp. 240, 375.

[224] Gandhi to Hailey, tel., 5 Aug. 1931, CWMG 47, p. 250; Interview to The Pioneer, ibid. p. 181.

[225] Hailey to Haig, 10 Oct. 1931, HP 22. For their expectations that UP would be the flashpoint see Crerar to Hailey, 17 July 1931, UP to HD, tel., 20 July 1931, H.Poll.33/11/31.

arrears were unyieldingly ignored, he accordingly picked on 13 villages to make an example of out of the total of 137, and sent his revenue officers with police parties to afforce revenue collections there.[226] Gandhi was quite outraged. His personal honour, he told Emerson, was at stake: 'it is matter deepest grief', he cabled to him on 24 July, 'to see incessant labours four months on behalf government thus reduced to nought'. He sent a copy of his detailed protest against Kothawala to the Government of Bombay, and made it plain that unless there was either immediate redress in Bardoli or the appointment of 'an impartial open tribunal', he would regard the settlement as having been totally disrupted, and himself free to take any future action which he chose.[227] He had a fruitless two-hour meeting with Kothawala on 27 July.[228] He had better meetings with Bhadrapur in Borsad,[229] and with the Governor of Bombay on 4 August,[230] but despite the urgent problems in both the Frontier Province and UP, the litmus test now turned for him on the Government of Bombay's formal response to the charges he had levied against Kothawala. 'I have written a letter in the nature of an ultimatum to the Government', he wrote to G.D. Birla on 26 July, 'and am awaiting a reply'.[231] In view of the gravity of the situation Willingdon alerted the Secretary of State in London to the possible need for an early promulgation of the Emergency Powers Ordinance,[232] while at the same time seeking to calm Gandhi with a string of conciliatory messages.[233] The

---

[226] 'Note on the Land Revenue Situation in Gujarat' [July 1931], H.Poll.33/23/31; Bombay to HD, tel., 25 July 1931, Kothawala's report on 'Interview with Mr. Gandhi', 28 July 1931, Kothawala to Bell, 29 July 1931, H.Poll.33/19/31; V to SoS, 17 Aug. 1931, H.Poll.33/24/31.

[227] Gandhi to Kothawala, Gandhi to Emerson, Gandhi to Maxwell, 24 July 1931, Gandhi to Sapru, 25 July 1931, CWMG 47, pp. 198–201, 203–4; Gandhi to Garrett, 24 July 1931, H.Poll.33/19/31.

[228] Kothawala's report on 'Interview with Mr. Gandhi', 28 July 1931, Bombay to HD, tel., 27 July 1931, ibid.

[229] Interview with the press, 31 July 1931, Gandhi to Bhadrapur, 1, 7 Aug. 1931, CWMG 47, pp. 238, 241, 266.

[230] Bombay to HD, tel., 29 July 1931, HD to Bombay, 29 July 1931, H.Poll.33/19/31; Interview to the press, 4 Aug. 1931, CWMG 47, p. 249.

[231] Gandhi to Birla, 26 July 1931, ibid., p. 219; Gandhi to Mirabehn, 25 July 1931, Gandhi to Tyabji, 28 July 1931, Gandhi to Bolton, 7 Aug. 1931, Gandhi to Maxwell, 8 Aug. 1931, Speech at AICC meeting, 8 Aug. 1931, ibid., pp. 204, 221, 267, 269, 271–3; Hailey to Irwin, 15 Aug. 1931, HP 21.

[232] V to SoS, HD to LGs, tels., 25 July 1931, SoS to V, tel., 27 July 1931, H.Poll.33/19/31, 33/24/31; V to SoS, tel., 4 Aug. 1931, H.Poll.13/8/31; idem, tel., 6 Aug. 1931, H.Poll.14/12/31; SoS to V, tels., 6, 14 Aug. 1931, ibid.

[233] Emerson to Gandhi [25 July 1931], Gandhi to Emerson, 25 July 1931, Willingdon to Gandhi, 23, 31 July 1931, Gandhi to Willingdon, 29 July 1931, CWMG 47, pp. 202, 222, 444–5; Emerson to Gandhi in HD to Bombay, 25 July 1931, Gandhi to Emerson, tel., 25 July 1931, H.Poll.33/19/31.

crunch, however, had now come. Everyone was sitting anxiously perched on the edge of their chairs.[234]

On 30 July the Government of India formally rejected Gandhi's proposal to refer the disputed provisions of the Pact to an impartial tribunal for consideration (a typical example of their tortuous ambivalence since during their recent meeting in Simla they had agreed to consider doing this). It was impossible, Emerson wrote,

for Government to agree to any arrangement ... which included the appointment of an external authority to whom Government would delegate the responsibility for reaching decisions in matters closely affecting the administration, or ... would ... provide special procedure ... of which members of the Congress would lay claim and from which other members of the public would be excluded.[235]

Then on 5 August Hailey sent Gandhi a telegram rebutting earlier claims he had made about tenant evictions in UP.[236] These replies were bad enough. But when on 10 August the Government of Bombay sent him their eventual response to his complaints about Bardoli, it was quite unyielding too. Amongst other things it affirmed that 'neither the Government nor the Collector have ever accepted the position that the collection of land revenue should be dependent on the advice of the Congress'.[237] To Gandhi that was totally unacceptable. In his view it quite directly contravened the entire spirit that had marked his Pact with Irwin. And that sliced a breach. Following a fruitless exchange of telegrams with Willingdon, he announced that he would not now be going to London to attend the forthcoming Round Table Conference.[238] On 14 August Congress's Working Committee emphasised that this did not mean that the Gandhi–Irwin Pact had been totally abrogated.[239] But on the following day Gandhi failed to board his ship for England. And with that the government's sustained attempt to suck the Congress into direct involvement in discussions about constitutional reforms as a principal

---

[234] E.g. Patel to Nehru, 21, 29 July 1931, AICC G60/1931; Emerson–Collins correspondence and attached notes, 20 July–22 Aug. 1931, H.Poll.33/28/31; HD to Bombay, tel., 25 July 1931, V to SoS, tel., 27 July 1931, H.Poll.33/19/31; HD to LGs, tel., 31 July 1931, H.Poll.33/23/31; HD to Bombay, tel., 4 Aug. 1931, H.Poll.33/24/31.

[235] Emerson to Gandhi, 30 July 1931, H.Poll.33/17/31, *CWMG* 47, pp. 442–4; HD to LGs, tel., 31 July 1931, H.Poll.33/23/31.

[236] Hailey to Gandhi, tel., 6 Aug. 1931, Gandhi to Hailey, 28 Aug. 1931, *CWMG* 47, pp. 488–9, 370–1, AICC 63/1931; Hailey to Lambert, 6 Aug. 1931, HP 21.

[237] Maxwell to Gandhi, 10 Aug. 1931, *CWMG* 47, pp. 445–8.

[238] Gandhi to Willingdon, tels., 11, 12 Aug. 1931, Gandhi to Maxwell, tel., 11 Aug. 1931, Willingdon to Gandhi, 13, 14 Aug. 1931, Interview to the press, 13 Aug. 1931, Gandhi to Bernays, 14 Aug. 1931, ibid., pp. 281–2, 286–90.

[239] Nehru to PCCs, 14 Aug. 1931, *SWJN* 5, pp. 12–13; Gandhi to Willingdon, 14 Aug. 1931, H.Poll.14/30/31; V to SoS, tel., 18 Aug. 1931, H.Poll.33/24/31.

means of sustaining the British Raj in India appeared to be collapsing in ruins all around them, with renewed repression soon an almost certain prospect.[240]

Gandhi for his part was by now utterly despondent. On 20 August he summarised the situation as he saw it in an article in *Young India* under the headline 'The Real Issue'. That went to the heart of the case he had been earnestly pressing over the preceding six months.

In the very first days of the Settlement [he wrote] Mr. Emerson . . . contended that the Congress could not act as intermediary between the Government and the people. I had no desire to . . . humiliate the Government. I was therefore content so long as in practice the Congress mediation was accepted . . . The refusal [however] of the Government to concede the very natural implication of the Settlement shows how far the authorities in India are from recognizing the fact that the power is passing to the people, nor are they willing to acknowledge that the Congress represents the people and that its voluntary co-operation should be thankfully accepted. In their opinion, cooperation should mean acceptance of their orders and authority and not mutual trust and accommodation between parties to a contract . . . The Settlement never contemplated that the Congress should alter its goal and its goal is to destroy the existing system of government . . . If the Congress was unworthy of confidence, or its demand was distasteful or unacceptable to the British Government, the Settlement should not have been entered into . . . to have commenced with distrust when the ink was hardly dried on the paper on which the Settlement was written was, and still is, difficult for me to understand . . . It has been said that in concentrating upon matters of detail I have missed the opportunity of helping decisions on matters of higher interest. I do not look at the two things separately. The Government of India is but part of the whole imperial scheme . . . and the closest association with the Government of India during the past four months has left on me the impression that the Civil Service is not ready to recognize the right of India to full freedom . . . Bardoli . . . for me was the acid test.[241]

In the same issue of *Young India* the 'charge-sheet' he had presented to Emerson in July was also published.[242]

That brought matters to a head. For the Viceroy's Council was quite adamant that whatever might be the cost to their general position this had to have a very sharp reply.[243] In deference to the remonstrances of the

---

[240] Jayakar Diary, 20, 21 Aug. 1931, JP; Sapru and Jayakar to Gandhi, tel., nd, Gandhi to Sapru, tel., 21 Aug. 1931, Gandhi to Willingdon, tels., 21, 23 Aug. 1931, Gandhi to Nehru, 21 Aug. 1931, Gandhi to Aney, 22 Aug. 1931, Statement to Associated Press, 22 Aug. 1931, 'Alone yet not alone', *CWMG* 47, pp. 330–1, 352–3, 339, 342–3, 349–50, 369–70; Emerson to Crerar, tel., 19 Aug. 1931, H.Poll.14/30/32.

[241] *CWMG* 47, pp. 319–22.

[242] For the material on which it was based, and associated matters, see H.Poll.33/23/31 and 33/24/31 passim.

[243] HD to PSV, tel., 19, 20 Aug. 1931, PSV to HD, 19 Aug. 1931 (2), ibid.

Secretary of State,[244] they refrained from issuing a blunt statement,[245] but in a special number of the official *Gazette* on 24 August 1931 they nonetheless set out their responses in very extensive detail.[246] A total impasse was thus reached.

As the position had quite palpably started to deteriorate badly so a number of people attempted to relieve the situation as best they could. Back on 12 August the recently appointed Law Member of the Viceroy's Council, Ramaswamy Aiyar, had met Gandhi and discussed with him whether he might see some Gujarat officials once again.[247] That same day the Secretary of State had suggested that Gandhi should once more be invited to hold a further round of talks with Emerson.[248] Sensing that the hegemony of their dominion in India was now under very serious and direct challenge, and feeling the eyes of both political India and their own supporters beadily fixed upon them to see if they would be the first to blink in this growing stand-off with Gandhi, the Viceroy's Council impatiently dismissed this suggestion out of hand.[249] They were now absolutely determined to stand their ground lest completely fatal damage should be done to their political primacy in India. Over the following two days Sapru and Jayakar thought they secured Gandhi's agreement to their suggestion that should the government institute an enquiry into the Bardoli affair his larger concerns would be assuaged.[250] Whilst the Government of Bombay was prepared to consider this,[251] on three successive occasions with Emerson in the van the Viceroy's Council flatly refused to contemplate this, and believed themselves justified in doing so[252] when Gandhi now declared that if this was granted it would not stop him from pressing his concerns on other matters too.[253]

[244]   SoS to V, tels., 18, 19, 20 (4), 21, 23 Aug. 1931, V to SoS, tels., 19 (3), 22 Aug. 1931, HD to PSV, tel., 20 Aug. 1931 (2), PSV to HD, tels., 19, 20 Aug. 1931, H.Poll.33/23/31, 33/24/31, 14/30/32.   [245]   Draft 'Summary for the Press', ibid.

[246]   *The Gazette of India Extraordinary*, 24 Aug. 1931. For Nehru's reaction see Nehru to all members AICC and CWC, 27 Aug. 1931, H.Poll.33/24/31.

[247]   Note by Law Member, 12 Aug. 1931, ibid.

[248]   SoS to V, tel., 12 Aug. 1931, H.Poll.14/30/32.

[249]   V to SoS, tels., 11, 13 Aug. 1931, ibid.

[250]   Desai to Jayakar, 1 Aug. 1931, JP 474; Jayakar Diary, 13–14 Aug. 1931; Jayakar and Sapru to Willingdon, tels., 14 Aug. 1931 (2), Willingdon to Jayakar and Sapru, tel., 14 Aug. 1931, PSV to Home Sec., 16 Aug. 1931, H.Poll.4/30/32.

[251]   Willingdon to Hotson, tel., 15 Aug. 1931, Hotson to Willingdon, tel., 16 Aug. 1931, H.Poll.14/30/32.

[252]   PSV to Rainy, tel., 17 Aug. 1931, HD to PSV, tel., 17 Aug. 1931, V to SoS, tels., 18 (3), 21 Aug. 1931, Rainy to PSV, tels., 18, 20 Aug. 1931, Emerson to Crerar (enclosing Memorandum), 18, 19 (tel.), Aug. 1931, Note by Fazli Husain, 19 Aug. 1931, H.Poll.14/30/32.

[253]   Nariman to Desai, nd, Gandhi to Nariman 16, 17 Aug. 1931, Nariman to Gandhi, 16 Aug. 1931, Interview to *The Hindu*, 19 Aug. 1931, *CWMG* 47, pp. 299, 305; SoS to V, tel., 16 Aug. 1931, Hotson to Willingdon, tel., 16 Aug. 1931, H.Poll.14/30/32.

Faced with this rigid stance Gandhi was, however, in a far from strong position. Having failed to embark for London he was himself effectively in breach of his solemn Pact with Irwin. Despite his own despair and the energetic activities of so many of his followers, there was, moreover, next to no support in the Congress at this time for a total break with the government and an early renewal of civil disobedience[254] – which everyone knew would be very swiftly suppressed. Following a communication from Willingdon which emphasised that the government would continue to abide by the Pact but would not allow its discretion to be fettered in any other way,[255] Gandhi felt trapped. Accordingly he wired to Willingdon on 21 August suggesting he should come to Simla for one further round of talks. Willingdon jumped at this.[256] 'He has begged for an interview', Emerson went out of his way to tell a passerby in Simla, 'Government did not go on its knees asking him to come here'.[257]

As a consequence there thereupon ensued the last of the six sets of discussions which Emerson and Gandhi held with each other during the summer months of 1931. This time Gandhi very deliberately took with him to Simla Patel, Abdul Ghaffar Khan, and Nehru, his principal lieutenants in the three provinces which were now primarily affected, with the clear intention of securing their participation in the conclusions that were reached.[258] Gandhi and Emerson met each other once again at 'Richmond' at 3 pm on 25 August.[259] Over recent days Gandhi had been concentrating once again upon seeking an enquiry into the affairs in Bardoli.[260] Since it had been Gandhi who had asked for these further talks, and since there could be here a lever to get him to go to London after all, Emerson judged that such an enquiry might just perhaps now be conceded so long as it was extremely strictly circumscribed and that

---

[254] E.g. Gandhi to Willingdon, 14 Aug. 1931 (also H.Poll.14/30/32), Interview to the press, 14 Aug. 1931, Statement to Associated Press, 18, 22 Aug. 1931, *CWMG* 47, pp. 290–3, 312–13, 349–50; Hailey to Irwin, 15 Aug. 1931, HP 21; Hotson to Willingdon, tel., 16 Aug. 1931, Surat report, 18 Aug. 1931, H.Poll.14/30/32.

[255] Willingdon to Gandhi, 19 Aug. 1931, ibid.; HD to PSV, 20 Aug. 1931; V to SoS, tel., 21 Aug. 1931, H.Poll.33/24/31.

[256] Gandhi to Willingdon, tels., 21, 23 Aug. 1931, Willingdon to Gandhi, 22 Aug. 1931, *CWMG* 47, pp. 330–1, 352–3, H.Poll.14/30/32; V to SoS, tel., 22 Aug. 1931, HD to Bombay, tel., 22 Aug. 1931, HD to LGs, 22 Aug. 1931, H.Poll.33/24/31, 14/30/32.

[257] Sarda to Thakurdas, 23 Aug. 1931, ThP 104.

[258] Gandhi to Nehru, tel., 23 Aug. 1931, Gandhi to A.G. Khan, tel., 23 Aug. 1931, 'Alone, Yet Not Alone' 28 Aug. 1931, *CWMG* 47, pp. 353, 367–8.

[259] Emerson to Gandhi, 25 Aug. 1931, H.Poll.14/30/32.

[260] Note by Law Member, 12 Aug. 1931, ibid.; Gandhi to Nariman, tel., 17 Aug. 1931, Interview to the Associated Press, 18 Aug. 1931, Interview to *Bombay Chronicle*, 20 Aug. 1931, 'Burnt Rope Retains Twist', *Navajivan*, 23 Aug. 1931, *CWMG* 47, pp. 305, 313, 328, 351–2.

Gandhi undertook to go to London after all.[261] Once that point was taken the two of them began to draft an agreed statement. On the following day they both saw Willingdon; and the Viceroy's Council met. That afternoon Gandhi telephoned to ask for an amendment which would reserve Congress's right to pursue other matters. That evening the Viceroy's Council flatly rejected this. On 27 August the Council met again, and made itself available should further decisions be required later in the day. In the course of that day Gandhi and Emerson exchanged letters three times; Sir Cowasji Jehangir, a Bombay businessman, acted as a go-between; whilst Emerson spoke to Gandhi on the telephone.[262] By evening he had ground him down to setting all other matters except the Bardoli case aside, and on that basis Gandhi and Willingdon eventually agreed a so-called 'Second Settlement' on 28 August.[263] Under this Gandhi undertook to attend the Second Round Table Conference after all, while the Government of India established a formal enquiry into whether more had been collected in July in the thirteen villages in Bardoli and Valod Mahal by coercion than in villages where no police had been employed.[264] At the same time Willingdon and his advisers insisted that this 'Second Settlement' should also state that:

In regard to any further matters of complaint . . . [these] will be dealt with in accordance with the ordinary administrative procedures . . . and the decision as to whether any enquiry will be held . . . will be made by the local government concerned.

It was, therefore, for Gandhi a humiliating and contemptuous outcome.[265] As he quite correctly avowed the Second Settlement was

---

[261] Hailey to Emerson, tel., 19 Aug. 1931, Emerson's Note, 24 Aug. 1931, V to SoS, tels., 24, 25 Aug. 1931, HD to Bombay, tels., 24, 25 Aug. 1931, Bombay to HD, tel., 25, 26 Aug. 1931, H.Poll.14/30/32.

[262] Gandhi to Emerson, 27 Aug. 1931 (3), Emerson to Gandhi, 27 Aug. 1931(3), Emerson's Note, 28 Aug. 1931, H.Poll.14/30/32.

[263] Willingdon in retirement later recalled that 'after Mr.Gandhi left, Emerson and I were sitting and congratulating each other on the result of our talks when suddenly the telephone bell rang . . . It was Mr. Gandhi – who having got back to his friends and showed them the document, informed Emerson that he had found after all that it was quite unsatisfactory and that he would be unable to agree to go over to London . . . I am afraid my language was not of a very Parliamentary character, but . . . I said to Emerson that he might make any observations he chose as to my feelings . . . but that I was going to have no more negotiations on the matter . . . What Emerson [said] down the telephone I do not know . . . but I think . . . his words must have been forceful, they were certainly effective'. Though undated it looks as if this occurred on the evening of 28 August, Willingdon's undated note, WP 20 (I am grateful to Dr Gyanesh Kudaisya for bringing it to my attention).

[264] 'The Second Settlement', 28 Aug. 1931, *CWMG* 47, pp. 449–50. For the eventual *Report of the Special Officer* . . ., and the Congress's withdrawal from the enquiry see Kothawala's comment 13 Nov. 1931, Bell to Emerson, 19 Nov. 1931, Press note nd, and Patel to Emerson, H.Poll.33/39/31.

[265] 'Gandhi has accepted all the conditions imposed by Govt at Simla and is going to sail for England on Saturday next', NMML Khaparde Diary, 27 Aug. 1931.

'bereft of all grace'.[266] It contained nothing of the reciprocity between the government and the Congress he believed he had secured at the time of the Gandhi–Irwin Pact. It represented a far cry from Emerson's request to him at the time of the Bhagat Singh meeting in Delhi in April to use his good offices to see that nothing untoward occurred. It was leagues away from the joint Congress–Government consultations he had striven for so consistently – let alone his *de facto* claim in Naini Tal that Congress should determine the settlement of a public issue which the government should then accept. There was no mention here of the reiterated claim he had made that the government should acknowledge Congress as its intermediary with the people. There was no reference to the joint Government–Congress boards of arbitration he had called for in June, nor to the independent enquiry into the interpretation of the Pact he had asked for in July, nor to his insistence in Simla that Congress should remain free to pursue other existing grievances. In the event there was nothing here but the Bardoli enquiry, and even that was to be at once exclusive, very narrowly drawn, and placed in the hands of an ICS officer of the Bombay cadre acting entirely upon his own.[267] For all the personal goodwill he and Emerson had displayed towards each other, their readiness to canvass issues at considerable length, their strong mutual interest in ensuring there was no breakdown in their talks, and even their joking relationship, it eventually became quite clear that in view of the manifold disputes erupting right across India no longer term accommodation of the kind he had had in mind was at all possible. The one was seeking what the other was quite determined to deny. The position of the Government of India at this stage was epitomised by Willingdon when he told the new Secretary of State that whilst the Gandhi–Irwin Pact,[268]

may have had its good points, [it established] in the minds of the people . . . that Gandhi had acted as a plenipotentiary . . . with the Viceroy himself, and that there therefore seemed to be two kings of Brentford[269] in India. My job has been to reassert the authority of the administration.[270] [Under the Second Settlement] claims for arbitration and for special treatment by Congress have, we hope, been finally dismissed. These gains are of great importance and will we hope more than counteract the grant of an enquiry in Gujarat.[271]

---

[266] 'Alone Yet Not Alone', Interview to *Bombay Chronicle*, 28 Aug. 1931, 'Statement on Bardoli Inquiry', post 29 Aug. 1931, *CWMG* 47, pp. 369, 378–80, 385.

[267] For this appointment see HD to Bombay, tel., 25 Aug. 1931, Bombay to HD, tel., 26 Aug. 1931, H.Poll.14/30/32.

[268] With the creation of the National government in Britain, Sir Samuel Hoare had just been appointed.

[269] The reference is to William Cowper's line in *The Task*, Book i: 'So sit two kings of Brentford on one throne'.

[270] Willingdon to Hoare, 28 Aug. 1931, TwP 5. See also idem, 12 Oct. 1931.

[271] V to SoS, tel., 28 Aug. 1931, H.Poll.14/30/32. See also: 'It was my main purpose in the early years of my Viceroyalty to make Gandhi understand quite clearly that he was not a

The resistant face of Britain's ambiguity was thereby redisplayed in all its fearsome bleakness.

Yet quite characteristically the Second Settlement did nonetheless display just a glimmer or two of its other face. For not only did it give Gandhi an approximation to the enquiry which he had demanded. By clear implication it showed that the government remained anxious to maintain their connections with him and prevent him from terminating his relations with them, while still being strongly committed to holding constitutional talks with the Congress in London. In another letter earlier that same month Willingdon had, moreover, sought (albeit in somewhat tendentious terms) to put the overall British position rather more comprehensively.

I cannot understand [he told M.R. Jayakar] what we are all fighting about, for we are surely all working for the same thing i.e. self government for India . . . my [earlier] negotiation with Mr. Gandhi failed . . . for the reason that he conducted them with me as if he were the head of a parallel administration.[272]

A basic dualism still characterised, therefore, British policy towards India. Sometimes it sought to show its conciliatory face, as in the Gandhi–Irwin Pact: on other occasions its repressive one, as in the Second Settlement. Which of the two constituted its true face remained a riddle worthy of the sphinx itself.

The paradox at its core, and the spell that this cast, were rarely more intimately revealed than in an extraordinary exchange of letters which as Gandhi started on his way to London, he now had with Emerson:

This is to tell you how grieved I felt in Simla [he wrote to Emerson as he travelled to Bombay to catch another ship to England] over what appeared to me to be your obstructive tactics. I hope I am wrong in my fears and that you were not responsible for the exasperating situation that led to the waste of precious three days. The securing of a constitution is nothing to me compared to the joy of discovering human contacts by which one could swear. I shall soon forget the sad memories of the past three days and I know you will forgive me if I have unwittingly misjudged you. But the future fills me with fear and misgivings. If you will distrust Sardar Patel, Pandit Jawaharlal and Abdul Ghaffar Khan an explosion is almost unavoidable . . . I have written thus freely in the exercise of a privilege of friendship and therefore hope not to be misunderstood.[273]

Bitterness here battled with personal regard; despair mixed with anguished appeal. Emerson fastened on the two latter sentiments, and his reply was almost bantering:

parallel authority with the Viceroy in dealing with the affairs of India, though it is true that he might have got this idea into his head after his discussions as a plenipotentiary on one side in his discussions with my predecessor over the Delhi Pact', Willingdon's undated note (above, note 263).   [272] Willingdon to Jayakar, 2 Aug. 1931, JP 455.
[273] Gandhi to Emerson, 28 Aug. 1931, *CWMG* 47, p. 374.

I confess [he wrote to Gandhi on 1 September] that I was very annoyed with you when I got your letter – but have now forgiven you . . . considering I did more rapid thinking and achieved more important results on Thursday the 27th than on any day I remember – and mostly on your behalf – I thought it hard to be accused of obstructive tactics.[274]

And he went on:

You have claimed the privilege of friendship for telling me off. I am going to claim the same privilege for making to you a suggestion . . . Start with the assumption that the British statesmen and the British public want to do the best they can for India . . . until convinced to the contrary.

And, incredibly, he then ended this letter – this principal spokesman of the British Raj (whose Viceroy had just called Gandhi 'one of the most astute politically-minded and bargaining little men I ever came across')[275] – by quipping: 'And, as I told you when I said good bye at the Viceregal Lodge, don't get into mischief now that I am not there to look after you.'[276]

Sucked into the stygian abyss of British ambiguity, two inherently honourable men, who had developed a remarkable personal rapport with each other, remained nevertheless held upright by the human lifelines within it.

---

[274] Among other things Emerson arranged for cars, rail seats, motor driver, money for fares, passport, and a shipping berth, Emerson to Gandhi, 1 Sept. 1931, IOL: R/3/1/289; Emerson to Police Comm. Bombay, 27 Aug. 1931, Emerson to Mackinnon Mackenzie, 27 Aug. 1931, H.Poll.14/30/32.

[275] Willingdon to Hoare, 28 Aug. 1931, TwP 5.

[276] Emerson to Gandhi, 1 Sept. 1931, IOL: R/3/1/289.

5   Thrust and parry: the Mahatma at bay, 1932–1933

> We are once more engaged in fighting an agitation for civil disobedience. I suppose that the world at large must look on this fact with something of amazement. We have just welcomed Congress to our Round Table Conference and we have just made lavish promises to India of the introduction of a responsible government. Within a month we are putting every member of Congress in prison by means of regulations, ordinances and all manner of things that to the outside world must reek of the middle ages . . . We cannot avoid a combat, yet I suppose there are few of us who really like it.
>
> > Hailey, Governor, UP, to Katherine Mayo, 10 January 1932

> I frankly cannot grasp the British policy. It seems to me a sheer muddle to put the Congress in gaol, to alienate the Moderates, and yet to think of going forward with the grant of a new Constitution . . . I can appreciate frank reaction or the Strong Hand. I can also appreciate a more or less liberal policy of Trust . . . But what is this monstrosity, which now keeps in gaol the people who must necessarily work the new Constitution?
>
> > General Smuts (South Africa) to Mrs Gillett, 15 August 1932

1933 was a checkerboard year in Monsoon Asia. In China it saw a 'decisive fight between the two ways'. As the year opened Chiang Kai-shek and the Kuomintang were advancing with 500,000 troops in their Fourth Encirclement of the Chinese Communists under Mao Zedong in their key Soviet in Kiangsi. But in February and March the Communists inflicted more than one severe defeat upon the KMT, and by April were within striking distance of Kiangsi's provincial capital, Nanch'ang. Only Chiang's swift despatch of reinforcements saved the KMT troops who were congregated there. During the summer months the Communists proposed not only a truce but the formation of a common front against the Japanese. But this came to nothing; and the two sides now made preparations for a final round of fighting. Chiang built a ring of blockhouses around the Communists and a network of roads, while the Communists created two new Army Corps and made preparations against the probability of a further assault. In August – a fateful month as

174

we shall see elsewhere too – the KMT's Fifth and final Encirclement of Mao's Chinese Soviet began, with Chiang at the head of seventy-five divisions marching in four columns. The Kiangsi Soviet now comprised seventy counties, and was defended by a Red Army of 100,000 men, bent on 'halting the enemy beyond the gate'. In October the KMT's 19th Route Army in neighbouring Fukien defected to the Communists, but as the year ended Chiang's forces surged forward in a major strike. In the new year the Communists managed to inflict a few defeats on their opponents, but nine months later, in October 1934, the main remaining force of China's southern Communists was forced out of its shrinking Kiangsi bailiwick, and Mao eventually led out his followers upon their Long March to Yenan in the far distant northeast of China.[1]

Whilst the destinies of China thus revolved in 1933 around a bitter civil war, the future of the Philippines was meanwhile being determined in the course of year-long negotiations between the new American Administration of the lately elected Democratic President, Franklin Delano Roosevelt, and the principal Filipino elite politician, Manuel Quezon.

Under pressure from the American sugar, labour, isolationist, and anti-imperialist lobbies, the United States Congress late in 1932 had accepted the advocacy of the Philippines' Ninth Independence Mission, headed by Quezon's two main rivals for primacy in the Philippines, Sergio Osmena and Manuel Roxas, and agreed to the Hare–Hawes–Cutting Bill, under which a new constitution was to be framed for the Philippines which would be followed by full independence ten years later. On 13 January 1933, however, the outgoing Republican President, Herbert Hoover, vetoed the Bill, lest it should upset the existing balance of power in the Far East. But the Congress promptly overrode him, and shortly afterwards Roosevelt appointed the former Mayor of Detroit (and later Supreme Court Judge), the anti-imperialist Irishman, Frank Murphy, as his new Governor-General of the Philippine Islands. As Murphy left Michigan in May 1933 on his way to the Philippines he dramatically told his brother (as we have noted): 'I have one ambition, I'm going to set these people free.'[2]

It was not, however, to be quite such smooth sailing. In March 1933 Quezon, seemingly outsmarted by his two main rivals, had gone to Washington, and had there dubbed the Hare–Hawes–Cutting Act 'a disgraceful piece of legislation', while in Murphy's presence he had proceeded to denounce the Stars and Stripes as 'an alien flag'. Upon his

[1] J. Chen, *Mao and the Chinese Revolution*, Oxford 1965, chs. VIII and IX.
[2] Fine, *Murphy*, p. 38.

return to the Philippines, he then forced the resignations of Roxas as Speaker of the Philippines' House of Representatives and of Osmena as President of the Senate; and – as Chiang mounted the Fifth Encirclement of the Kiangsi Communists – vigorously campaigned against the Hare–Hawes–Cutting Act until in October 1933 he prevailed upon both houses of the Philippines' legislature to reject it. Early the next month he left for Washington once again, this time as leader of his own mission, to secure a new independence act which would not only bear his own stamp, but would give better access for Philippines' products to the American market, and more Filipino say over the provisions for American military and naval bases in the Philippines than the Hare–Hawes–Cutting Act had done. Early in the new year he secured agreement on a number of changes in these respects, and on 4 March 1934 Roosevelt eventually signed a new Philippines Independence Act, the Tydings–McDuffie Act. Eighteen months later that was followed by Quezon's election as the first President of the Commonwealth of the Philippines, a development which was principally punctuated by the suppression in May 1935 of the strongly anti-elitist Sakdalistas revolt. With that the shape of the Philippines' polity for many decades to come – the Japanese occupation from 1942 to 1944 notwithstanding – was largely settled.[3]

Whilst Filipino nationalist leaders thus managed to move decisively in 1933 towards attaining formal political independence for their country, in the Netherlands East Indies 1933 saw the Dutch turning upon Indonesia's nationalists in a totally repressive manner. At the beginning of the year a great deal of Indonesian elite opinion had become deeply angered by the so-called Wild Schools Ordinance. Because of the world slump severe cuts had been made in Dutch support for Indonesian education. That forced the Indonesian elite to turn more than before to their own European-type schools. The Dutch, however, feared that these might foster anti-government attitudes, and thus promulgated the Wild Schools Ordinance to control them. But so vehement was the Indonesian outcry that even the new exceedingly conservative Governor-General, de Jonge, was forced to suspend the ordinance in February 1933.

Such was the unity and success of this campaign that the Indonesian nationalist movement was thereby given a very considerable boost. Late in 1931 the principal Indonesian nationalist leader, Sukarno (who had been imprisoned by the Dutch in 1930) had been suddenly released. In August 1932 the other leading nationalist figure, Mohammed Hatta, had returned from the Netherlands. For reasons to which we will come in the

[3] B.R. Churchill, *The Philippine Independence Missions to the United States*, Manila 1983, chs. XI and XII.

next chapter, they failed to join hands, and proceeded to put themselves at the head of two separate parties. By the early part of 1933 both, however, were drawing substantial followings, at all events in the towns, and as a consequence Governor-General de Jonge, much perturbed by the Wild Schools agitation and by a recent naval mutiny, started to send his police to seize party newspapers, break up public meetings, and on 1 August 1933 – a date to which we must return – finally arrested Sukarno and his prime supporters. Hatta remained at large till February 1934, but he and his associates were then arrested too, and while Sukarno was exiled to Endan in Flores, Hatta was despatched to the Indies' penal settlement at Bogun Digul, both of them ostensibly for life. It was only with the Japanese conquest in 1942 that Sukarno, Hatta, and their associates were finally released.[4]

Events in India in 1933 followed a very different course; and yet the resemblances and the distinctions serve to mark their distinctive characteristics. In 1933 a new constitution was being fashioned in London, as it was for the Philippines in Washington. Not only, however, was there never a chance that it would lay down a fixed date for India's independence as both the American Acts did for the Philippines. For all the concessions that were made to India's nationalist aspirations, the new constitution was being chiefly fashioned with an eye to ensuring that British supremacy was maintained in India into the long foreseeable future.[5] There was, moreover, next to no involvement in its making by India's principal nationalist leaders of the kind that Osmena, Roxas, and above all Quezon enjoyed in the making of the new Philippines' constitution. Unlike the Americans who were now prepared to give the Philippines' nationalists their head, the British were quite determined to maintain their ultimate control over India.

Yet unlike the Dutch the British were not bent on suppressing Indian nationalism altogether. Early in 1932, following an extensive resumption of civil disobedience, they once more swept most of India's nationalist leadership into jail. But they never thought of removing them from public life altogether (let alone of eliminating them entirely as the French had gone far towards doing in Vietnam).[6] But because unlike the Americans the British had no intention of 'setting these people free' the old conflict between the British Raj and Indian nationalism still persisted, and during much of 1932–3 a new and quite distinctive battle royal soon ensued. As compared with the contemporaneous clash between Sukarno and Hatta

[4] J. Ingleson, *Road to Exile. The Indonesian Nationalist Movement 1927–1934*, Singapore 1979.   [5] C. Bridge, *Holding India to the Empire*, Delhi 1986.

[6] J. Buttinger, *The Smaller Dragon: A Political History of Vietnam*, New York 1958, pp. 436–7.

and the Dutch, it was a great deal less dire; but as compared with the confrontation in 1933 between Quezon and the Americans (which was an all but entirely specious affair, having far more to do with intra-elite conflict in the Philippines than with any great issue with the Americans) it was in every way more substantial.

There were of course major contrasts with events in China. Mao's eventual move out upon the Long March involved immense physical effort over vast and daunting terrain, constant armed conflict, and the close management of initially large but eventually shrinking cohorts of people. Meanwhile in India the major conflict in 1932–3 took the form of a quite extraordinarily personal confrontation between the British and Gandhi acting almost entirely upon his own in what was essentially a propaganda war conducted for much of the time from behind his prison walls. Yet there are some intriguing parallels even so. The Gandhi–British encounter never, of course, involved actual armed conflict. But it did entail a sustained attempt by each side to 'encircle' the other. Moreover, as in August 1933 Chiang advanced upon his Fifth and final Encirclement of Mao's southern Communists, so the British launched their *coup de main* against Gandhi. Furthermore it was at this point that both Mao and Gandhi revealed their quite exceptional skills as leaders of great insurgent movements. For, with equally dazzling success, if in very different ways, they succeeded in extricating the remnants of their following from very evident disasters in ways that kept their key forces intact – with the consequence that in a far shorter time than anyone could have expected, via the Sian Incident in China in 1936, and the provincial elections in India in 1937, the position of their two movements came to be restored, which paved the way for their final triumphs in the late 1940s.

We left Gandhi in the previous chapter on his way to London for the Second Round Table Conference. The discussions there proved to be just as fruitless as he had anticipated, and by the time he returned to India in December 1931, the situation there had deteriorated sharply. There had been a spate of terrorist outbreaks in Bengal. Civil disobedience had begun to be renewed in the Frontier Province. And a no-rent campaign was escalating in UP. Following upon the Gandhi–Irwin Pact British officials had been expected to ride out the consequences, but as the situation worsened so it had become necessary to assure them that if civil disobedience were to be in any way renewed swift and decisive action would be taken against both it and the Congress. As a consequence early in December 1931 Emergency Powers Ordinances were promulgated in Bengal, NWFP, and UP, and on 17 December the Viceroy's Council formally decided that if Gandhi on his return to India should seek an interview with the Viceroy this should be refused 'so long as the No-Rent campaign is in progress'. Should, moreover, Congress take any step towards supporting the provincial campaigns, that would be immediately treated as a *casus belli*.

Upon his return to India on 28 December 1931 Gandhi did indeed seek an interview with the Viceroy.[7] Willingdon only agreed to this so long as he repudiated his associates.[8] That was impossible for Gandhi to contemplate, and under his leadership the Working Committee of the Congress thereupon resolved to reinstitute countrywide civil disobedience forthwith should the government continue obdurate.[9] Gandhi's further request[10] for an interview was in these circumstances instantly rebuffed;[11] and with that the crisis climaxed. On 4 January 1932 the Government of India in a highly dramatic step issued the first countrywide Emergency Powers Ordinance it had ever promulgated in India; arrested all the Congress leaders and a great many of their followers; and forthwith suppressed every other Congress activity wherever this could be found. Minor episodes spluttered on through 1932 and into 1933, but as a result of sustained police action the Civil Disobedience campaign was very effectively halted.[12]

All of which placed Gandhi in an exceedingly difficult position. Not only was he once again behind bars. Before long tens of thousands of Congressmen were in jail too.[13] He still wholly abjured the use of violence (to which in their frustration numbers of the Bengali Hindu elite had now – abortively – reverted).[14] For him non-violent satyagraha remained both his personal creed and his ruling passion. Throughout 1930–1 it had, moreover, from his point of view been working very effectively. His Dandi march and the extensive civil disobedience episodes which followed it had constituted a countrywide satyagraha of a most successful kind. In due course it had been matched by what he always saw as the essential outcome: talks between combatants to the dispute. During 1931 there had followed both his Pact with Irwin and his talks with Emerson. That

---

[7] Gandhi to Willingdon, tel., 29 Dec. 1931, *CWMG* 48, p. 459.

[8] PSV to Gandhi, tel., 31 Dec. 1931, ibid., pp. 500–2.

[9] Resolution of the Working Committee [1 Jan. 1932], ibid., pp. 469–72.

[10] Gandhi to PSV, tel., 1 Jan. 1932, ibid., pp. 472–6.

[11] PSV to Gandhi, tel., 2 Jan. 1932, ibid., pp. 502–3.

[12] D.A. Low, 'Civil Martial Law', in Low, ed., *Congress and the Raj. Facets of the Indian Struggle 1917–1947*, London 1977, ch. 5.

[13] 60,000 according to Sarojini Naidu as Acting President of Congress to all provincial workers, 18 Mar. 1932, H.Poll.14/22/32. The government had reported 14,660 in V to SoS, tel., 28 Jan. 1932, H.Poll.5/29/32, and later 32,500 at the end of April, and 24,000 at the end of July 1932, V's speech to the central legislature, 5 Sept. 1932, H.Poll.24/10/32.

[14] Tanika Sarkar, *Bengal Politics 1928–1934. The Politics of Protest*, Delhi 1987, passim.

was how he believed the procedure which he had now brought the great Indian nationalist movement to adopt should most properly operate. For a while the British seemed to go along with him. But there then occurred first his contretemps with Emerson and Willingdon in July–August 1931, and then Willingdon's refusal to see him upon his return from London except on quite unacceptable conditions which was swiftly followed by the clamp down on his movement. Over the next two years not only were these rebuffs endlessly repeated. It became clear that for the Government of India they constituted the ultimate symbol of their utter determination to maintain their imperial rule over India. When on top of this they insisted that civil disobedience – the primary instrument in a satyagrahi's armoury – should be unilaterally called off before they would even consider the suggestion of further talks, his predicament became even worse. No self-respecting Indian nationalist would in these circumstances have bent his knees to the British Raj. Yet that was precisely what the Government of India appeared determined to make him do.

For a brief moment from behind his prison walls he wondered whether he should embark on a fast unto death as a protest against all the fierce repression to which so many of his supporters had been subjected.[15] But he soon realised that that was not the best course to take. For upon this issue if upon no other the British would certainly resist him to the end (as Linlithgow was to do in 1943). Rather than courting a head-on collision with them, he had therefore to find another way forward.

This was all the more important because the national movement had now reached one of its most critical stages. The essential point here can perhaps best be illustrated by recalling a thesis which has already been propounded elsewhere.[16] This stems from the indications that there was something of a repetitive rhythm to the three great countrywide campaigns which Gandhi mounted – between 1919 and 1922, 1929 and 1934, and 1939 and 1944. Each was prompted by some great insult to Indians' *amour propre* – the Rowlatt Bills of 1919; the Simon Commission in 1927; the Viceroy's unilateral declaration that India was at war in 1939. Upon each occasion there followed the first of the two waves of agitation which each campaign then engendered – the Rowlatt satyagraha of 1919; the first Civil Disobedience movement in 1930; the individual satyagraha movement in 1940. Thereafter on all three occasions there ensued a mid-term break, when the Congress's leaders went a considerable distance towards effecting an accommodation with the British – at the Amritsar Congress in 1919; in the Gandhi–Irwin Pact of 1930; during the Cripps

[15] Gandhi to Hoare, 11 Mar. 1932, *CWMG* 49, pp. 191–2.
[16] Low, *Congress and the Raj*, 'Introduction', pp. 7–10.

negotiations in 1942. All of which were then swept aside by the movement's unfulfilled agitational propensity, and a second agitational wave invariably ensued – the Khilafat/Non-Cooperation movement of 1920–2; the second Civil Disobedience movement of 1932; the 'Quit India' campaign of 1942. It was in their efforts to deflect these upsurges that the British made their principal political concessions, first as the first waves began to mount, and then at those very significant mid-term breaks.[17] They never, however, made any further concession in response to the second waves. They merely went ahead with the changes they had already announced. At the same time whilst second nationwide agitations always did rise up, for reasons that are still not altogether clear, once these had passed their peak, countrywide agitational propensity soon lost its potency.

It was at these last points that the Indian national movement faced by far its most critical moments. For if nothing were now done to sustain the morale of its supporters, it could all too easily have fallen into disastrous disarray. That placed a quite special pressure upon its principal leader. It was, however, precisely at these moments that Gandhi made some of his most conspicuous contributions to its success.

Upon the first occasion, following his own calling off of the joint Khilafat/Non-Cooperation movement in early 1922, he seized the opportunity of his subsequent trial speech to proclaim the ardour of his nationalist faith and openly to accept the full impact of the law as he taught that a true satyagrahi ought to do.[18] Two decades later, once his third great agitational campaign had been crushed in late 1942, at exactly the same stage in the by then common rhythm of these movements, he proceeded to embark early in 1943 on his 'Epic' Fast, so as to anathematise the Government of India's attempt to fasten responsibility for the unwonted violence of the Quit India movement upon the Congress.[19] On both occasions he brilliantly seized the moral advantage, and upheld the integrity of his nationalist cause at exactly the moment when it threatened to break apart.

Following his incarceration in January 1932 he found himself in precisely the same situation on this second occasion too. It was soon clear that British repression had broken the back of the second wave of Civil Disobedience, and there were a great many signs that it would not easily be renewed. For the moment at least, the Indian nationalist movement appeared completely mired. It was patently suffering a major reverse at

---

[17] E.g., on the second occasion, the Irwin Declaration in October 1929, and Macdonald's 'responsibility-at-the-centre' statement in January 1931.
[18] F. Watson, *The Trial of Mr Gandhi*, London 1969.   [19] *TOP* III, ch. 2.

the hands of the British. Nor was it at all easy to see what exactly might be done. On this occasion neither Gandhi nor any of his senior colleagues was placed on trial (at all events to begin with), so there could be no repetition of his trial speech of a decade earlier; while the Government of India's fierce rebuttal of the 'charge-sheet' Congress had levied against it in August 1931 (as we saw in the previous chapter) made it very difficult to sustain the kind of outraged protest he was to make against its actions a decade later. As upon those other occasions what he needed to do was to find some issue amidst the parlous state of the national movement that would allow him to exploit his personal moral potency so as to uphold the integrity of the national cause, and if possible belabour the British for their infamy too. In due course opportunities came his way because of the inherent ambiguity of the British – absolutely determined to retain their imperial hold over India, yet never quite able to disown their own liberal political values.

During the course of the middle and later months of 1931, British officials in India had become increasingly concerned at the impression that was now spreading that the days of the British Raj were numbered, and those of the Congress stood just around the corner. With the effective imposition of full emergency powers in January 1932 and the country-wide arrests of Congress activists, they began before very long to feel confident once again that they had reestablished their imperial hold over India.[20] But having lived through all the political trauma from their point of view of 1931 they, and the Government of India more especially, were now adamant that Britain's imperial supremacy should never be thrown in doubt again. Not only, they insisted, should civil disobedience be completely banned. No settlement should be contemplated till it had been renounced altogether. Nothing, moreover, should be done ever again to give any impression – to their Indian employees and supporters in particular – that they had lost the will to maintain British dominion in India. As a consequence they were inflexibly opposed to 'peace talks' of the kind which Gandhi and others were soon demanding of them and, above all, to anything that remotely resembled the Gandhi–Irwin Pact, since from their point of view nothing was more likely to destroy, perhaps this time for ever, the dominance they had now reestablished in India than even the suspicion that they would be prepared to renew the bargaining so extensively conducted with him in 1931. In these and other ways they now displayed a far more hostile stance towards the Indian national movement

---

[20] E.g. Willingdon to Hoare, tel., 10 Jan. 1932, TwP 5; Chief Comm. Delhi to Emerson, 16 Jan. 1932, V to SoS, tels., 17 Jan., 27 Mar. 1932, H.Poll.5/46/32; Madras to HD, 16 Mar. 1932, H.Poll.14/21/32.

than at any time between the Punjab clash of 1919 and the 'Quit India' crisis of 1942.[21]

Yet for all the decisive firmness with which they suppressed the second Civil Disobedience movement and their steely determination to maintain their hold thereafterwards, the more general stance of the Government of India and its officers always remained carefully nuanced. They displayed no inclination to destroy the national movement altogether, as the French had sought to do in Vietnam, and as the Dutch were soon to do in Indonesia. They refrained from proclaiming martial law (except in quite particular circumstances), putting anyone on trial, putting anyone to death, or banishing India's nationalist leaders to some distant island for life. Those fates were reserved for open terrorists which Gandhi and his lieutenants assuredly were not. The Government of India deliberately decided moreover not to proscribe the Congress,[22] and they were soon specifically warning their officers not to resort to any arbitrary, vindictive or humiliating measures. What was more, on the very day that Willingdon promulgated his Emergency Powers Ordinance he wrote to Hoare, the Secretary of State for India in London, to say: 'And now for the future . . . our policy must be to push on as rapidly as possible with regard to these reforms.'[23] Paradoxical as it may seem throughout their simultaneous repression of the civil disobedience movement that remained their persistent policy. In April 1932, for example, Sir Harry Haig, the Home Member of the Viceroy's Council, told Gandhi's English friend, Charlie Andrews, that:

If preventive action were the sole feature of Government policy, I might share your pessimism as regards the future. But it is only one part and that, I hope, an ephemeral one. Constitutional advance is the other and more important side. Government . . . will press forward with this as rapidly as possible.[24]

They always made it clear too that should Congress formally renounce civil disobedience, they would be quick to rescind 'Ordinance' rule, set Gandhi and his associates free, and allow the Congress to operate without any let or hindrance.[25] Furthermore in the second half of 1932 the London government convened a third Round Table Conference to

---

[21] E.g. Willingdon to Hoare, tels., 21 June, 1, 4 (2), 5 (2) Oct. 1932, TwP 11; Emerson's note, 30 Jan. 1932, H.Poll.14/8/32; Haig to Mieville, 13 Apr. 1932, HgP 1.

[22] HD to LGs, tel., H.Poll.14/2/32.

[23] Willingdon to Hoare, 4 (also 10) Jan. 1932, TwP 5. See also V to SoS, tel., 24 Jan. 1932, Emerson to Haig, 30 Jan. 1932, H.Poll.14/8/32.

[24] Haig to Andrews, 23 Apr. 1932, H.Poll.40/2/32. See also Haig to Hailey, 2 May 1932, HP 23.

[25] Hoare was emphatic that Gandhi understood this, Hoare to Willingdon, 21 June 1932, TwP 11.

advance the programme of constitutional reform, and as soon as there then seemed some prospect of a new constitution being instituted for India they started to consider how they could ensure its acceptance there. Since there was no chance that it would provide for the kind of early independence the Americans were now promising to the Philippines, they knew[26] that with most of the Congress leaders still in jail this would be all but impossible to effect. Whilst, therefore, the Government of India was quite determined that there would be no repetition of the general jail deliveries of early 1931, by the beginning of 1933 they were becoming increasingly embarrassed by the large number of Congress *détenus* they were still holding in jail without trial, and soon started to arrange that increasing numbers of them should be set free in unannounced driblets.[27]

Gandhi well understood that there was nothing here that in any way implied that they were ready to compromise with him over civil disobedience. Yet in view of the anxiety they always displayed to proclaim the high moral standing of their imperial dominion in India, it was plain that the opprobrium which their repression of the national movement was soon generating in quarters both in India and in Britain which they could not easily ignore would sooner or later prey upon their political sensitivities. He correctly perceived, moreover, that their ever-present ambiguity made them peculiarly vulnerable to the ethical imperatives of an issue of high principle if only he could find one to exploit. For several months all his probings here failed to strike. But then in what at the outset had seemed no more than a half-expected opportunity he quite suddenly found exactly the kind of opening he was looking for and with consummate skill exploited this to the full. When that then yielded substantial dividends, with uncanny skill he built upon it to proclaim himself the champion of a great humanitarian cause, and, despite the fact that he remained a political prisoner, to demand that he be allowed to promote this in full public view. That was an extraordinary ploy. Since, however, the British were fully alert to the exceptional personal prestige he had now built up not only in India but (particularly following his recent visit there) in Britain, they found themselves completely unable to withstand the challenge which this posed to their public standing, and were soon forced to give way.

The consequences were astounding. At a time when the Indian nationalist movement stood at a disconcertingly low ebb, Gandhi not only restored his former position as the cynosure of every eye concerned with India, but revived the battered morale of his Congress followers,

---

[26] Despite the momentary bluster of Haig's Note, 28 Dec. 1932, H.Poll.31/97/32.
[27] Ibid.

entrenched the moral preeminence of the cause that they served, and this time, as compared with 1922 and 1942, went a major step further. In a quite remarkable way he now forced the British to enter upon a sustained open personal encounter with him even whilst he remained their political prisoner. Although by their comprehensive repression of his Civil Disobedience movement they had successfully excluded him from the open political arena where they had always confronted him before, by seizing upon a stretch of high moral ground he now impelled them to confront him where, with his deadly weapon of a threat to fast unto death, he was uniquely well armed to meet them.

In an extraordinary way the struggle between the two titans at the apex of the Indo–British conflict now took the form therefore, not of a clash between competing armies, as was contemporaneously occurring in China, nor of a myriad of local encounters mediated through a series of high-level negotiations, as had been the case in India in the previous year, nor of a confrontation in a parliamentary election, as was to be the case in India in 1937, but in the highly rarefied form of an intensely personalised propagandist duel between Gandhi and the Government of India. In this each side sought to put the other morally in the wrong so as to propel them into an ignominious public relations retreat that would ravage their public posture.

Gandhi generally made the first thrust. The British would then parry and counterthrust, forcing him to parry in turn. Given the novelty of this way of proceeding it is not to be wondered at that each side periodically hesitated and sometimes fumbled. They were frequently left guessing as to what the other would do next. Upon more than one occasion Gandhi forced the British back upon their heels. But twice they caught him out unawares and very nearly nonplussed him altogether. It is difficult to conceive of a more astonishing way in which to conduct a major nationalist–imperialist encounter. Yet for a full twelve months from August–September 1932 to August–September 1933 this was the form that it took in India. It derived its character principally from the self-doubts which existed at the core of the British position (which battled there with their absolute determination to hold Gandhi at bay) in interaction with the inimitable skill of the Mahatma in exploiting those to the full.

For present purposes it is, however, of central importance to see at the same time just how vividly this exceptional encounter exposed the tensions that the ever-present ambiguities in the British position could from time to time engender within the British camp itself. Although Willingdon and the Government of India stood constantly on the *qui vive* lest any false move on their part should allow Gandhi to undermine the position to which they had now restored the Raj, they not only found themselves periodically at odds with each other, but twice at least with the Government of Bombay, and much more seriously and for a while all but continuously with the Cabinet in London. Increasingly, moreover, they found themselves having to resort to sophistry, deviousness, and in the end to sheer animal cunning, whilst more than once they very nearly took what could have been a quite disastrous step. Although most of this occurred behind closed doors, enough was publicly apparent to give Gandhi the opportunities he needed to maintain his attack, and a variety of others a sufficiency of grounds to excoriate the Government of India for its intransigence and to force it to bend.

In the absence of any other engrossing affair, and to a degree which does not seem to have been sufficiently appreciated, the high politics of India during late 1932 and into much of 1933 was focussed upon this drama.[28] In its own terms it went to the heart of the situation created by the suppression of the great satyagraha campaigns of 1929–32; Gandhi's utter determination to maintain the thrust of the Indian national movement in their aftermath; and the Government of India's equal determination not to compromise in any way with him over civil disobedience. It reached its climax in those self-same days in August 1933 when, elsewhere in Asia, Chiang started to close in on Mao, Quezon pressed forward his personal campaign to win a still more advantageous Independence Act for the Philippines, and the Dutch finally turned on Sukarno and the Indonesian nationalist parties with the intent of expelling them from its political life altogether. It is to the details of the successive stages of this saga that we now need to turn.

Within days of his arrest in January 1932 Gandhi started to probe for any cleft he could find in the British armour. He wrote to the Viceroy to suggest that negotiations should take place after all,[29] and to Hoare to protest against the government's interpretation of recent events – for which he laid the blame squarely on the Viceroy.[30] He remonstrated with the Governor of Bombay about the excesses of 'Ordinance' rule,[31] and

---

[28] See, for example, the V's weekly reports to SoS during the first half of 1933, which while reporting periodic minor civil disobedience activities, ordinarily reported very little open conflict upon any great scale, H.Poll.3/1/33; or Madras to HD, 24 Jan. 1933, H.Poll.14/21/32.   [29] See V to SoS, 16 Nov. 1932, H.Poll.31/11/32, 31/95/32.

[30] Gandhi to Hoare, 15 Jan. 1932, CWMG 49, pp. 10–11; idem, 11 Mar. 1932, Hoare to Gandhi, 13 Apr. 1932, H.Poll.31/113/32.

[31] Gandhi to Sykes, 23 Jan. 1932, CWMG 49, pp. 19–20.

upbraided Emerson for the Government's decision to sell the land of certain villagers who had refused to pay land revenue.[32] Then in June 1932 he became involved in an altercation with the government over its refusal to allow his English follower, Miss Slade, to visit him upon her release,[33] and shortly afterwards protested about the delays in his correspondence because of their censorship regulations.[34] None of these, however, gave him the leverage he needed to raise his stakes against the British. It was not until Macdonald, the British Prime Minister, issued in August 1932 his so-called Communal Award that quite suddenly he was able to grasp hold of the kind of opportunity he was looking for.

The story here had its origin in the debate at the second Round Table Conference over the demand of the accredited leaders of India's Untouchables for separate electorates along the lines already granted to Muslims. Gandhi had then announced that he would fast unto death against any such provision as a nefarious attempt to divide India's Untouchables from the rest of its Hindu population just when Indians were already being disastrously divided into 'Hindus' and 'Muslims'.[35] No agreement could be reached, and the tangled issue of voting provisions for India's minority communities was then left to the British Prime Minister to determine. In March 1932 Gandhi had told Hoare that if he were to provide for separate electorates for Untouchables he himself would carry out his threat.[36] Hoare had assured him that the government understood his position,[37] but when the Communal Award was announced in August 1932, it was the principal Untouchable leaders' demand which prevailed, and not Gandhi's.[38]

Gandhi immediately sprang into action. On 18 August he wrote to Macdonald to say that unless 'the British government, of its own motion or under pressure of public opinion' changed its mind, he would 'resist

---

[32] Gandhi to Emerson, 28 Mar. 1932, ibid. p. 244, and Notes by Emerson and Haig, 18, 19 Mar. 1932, H.Poll.14/17/32. But see also the remarkably civil exchange, given the circumstances, on the general position, Gandhi to Emerson, 27 Jan., 13 Mar., and Emerson to Gandhi, 2 Mar. 1933, India Office Library R/3/1/289 (I am grateful to Gyanesh Kudaisya for this reference).

[33] Gandhi to Doyle, Gandhi to Mirabehn, 18–19 May 1932, *CWMG* 49, pp. 452–3; Gandhi to Doyle, 9, 18 June 1932, *CWMG* 50, pp. 21, 58. See also NMML, ThP 107 passim. Ansari was also refused permission to see him, H.Poll.31/9/32 passim.

[34] Gandhi to Doyle, 9, 13, 22, 24 July 1933, *CWMG* 50, pp. 174, 237–8, 272–3, 279–80.

[35] *CWMG* 48, passim, especially his speech at the Minorities Committee, 13 Nov. 1932, p. 298.   [36] Gandhi to Hoare, 11 Mar. 1932, *CWMG* 49, pp. 190–1.

[37] Hoare to Gandhi, 13 Apr. 1932, ibid. pp. 534–5.

[38] The GoI clearly anticipated the possibility that he would fast, and canvassed what they would do, Hallett's note, 29 July 1932, H.Poll.31/113/32, Willingdon to Hoare, 30 July 1932, TwP 5.

your decision with my life' and begin to fast on 20 September.[39] He fully realised how fateful such a challenge might be, but he regularly reaffirmed his determination to carry it through.[40] Nevertheless he was careful to emphasise that the fast was directed 'only against separate electorates and not against statutory reservation of seats',[41] and he confided to Vallabhbhai Patel that 'it will be the limit of wickedness if they [the British] let me fast . . . and they certainly are not the people to go further than is necessary'.[42]

At his own instance his threat remained secret whilst the government considered it. Politically he could not have chosen a better moment. The Communal Award had generated intense public interest, and a good deal of controversy too.[43] Willingdon immediately placed his own gloss on Gandhi's intention. As 'civil disobedience is at a very low ebb', he told Hoare, '. . . this is . . . his last desperate effort to regain his prestige and authority'.[44] The British could, of course, have overridden him (as they had just done over the Communal Award), or (theoretically at least) have given in. But characteristically they did neither. They finessed.[45] Knowing full well the immense damage which his death in prison would do to their public image, they first offered to release him for its duration.[46] When he immediately grasped their purpose and refused,[47] they calculated that it would be safe to hold him in jail at least till his life stood in danger.[48] And thereupon they took evasive action. Seizing upon the explicit provision in the Communal Award that it could be amended if those principally affected by it were agreed, they instructed their subordinates to publicise widely that: 'It is a question not between Gandhi and His Majesty's Government, but between Gandhi and the Depressed Classes.'[49] Macdonald responded to Gandhi's letter in similar vein,[50] and

---

[39] Gandhi to Macdonald, 18 Aug. 1932, *CWMG* 50, pp. 383–4, H.Poll.31/113/32; idem, 9 Sept. 1932, *CWMG* 51, pp. 31–2. For his accompanying discussion with Mahadev Desai and Vallabhbhai Patel, 17–22 Aug. 1933, see *CWMG* 50, pp. 466–9.

[40] See his extensive correspondence once the news of his decision became public, 13–25 Sept. 1932, *CWMG* 51, pp. 50–139.

[41] Interview to the Press, 20 Sept. 1932, also Statement to the Press, 16 Sept. 1932 and Interview with Mate, Rajbhoj and Limaye, 21 Sept. 1932, *CWMG* 51, pp. 117, 64, 126; G Bombay to V, tel., 10 Sept. 1932, H.Poll.31/11/32.

[42] Discussion with Patel, 6 Sept. 1932, *CWMG* 51, p. 457.

[43] GoI to SoS, tels., 22, 26 Aug. 1932, H.Poll.41/4/32.

[44] Willingdon to Hoare, 4 Sept. (also 22 Aug.) 1932.

[45] Hallett's Note, 21 Aug. 1932, H.Poll.31/113/32.

[46] Several items 11–15 Sept. 1932, ibid.

[47] Gandhi to PSV, tel., 16 Sept. 1932, *CWMG* 51, p. 60.

[48] Numerous items, 16–25 Sept. 1932, H.Poll.31/113/32.

[49] HD to LGs, 27 Aug. 1932 and enclosure; idem, tel., 11 Sept. 1932, ibid.

[50] Macdonald to Gandhi, 8 Sept. 1932, Gandhi to Macdonald, 9 Sept. 1933, ibid.

Haig, the Home Member of the Viceroy's Council, hammered the point in the central legislature.[51]

Their guile worked. They successfully avoided being dragged into any detailed negotiations on the Award. Instead, by the time Gandhi started on his fast on 20 September 1932, those two seasoned negotiators, Sapru and Jayakar, along with a number of others were already busily engaged in seeking a *pis aller*. Cannily the Government of India now declared that although Gandhi remained their political prisoner they were

> most anxious . . . that opportunities for discussion of the Depressed Classes problem . . . should be available to him . . . they have therefore decided that . . . he should receive in the jail all reasonable facilities for private interviews with such persons . . . as he may wish to see, and that there should be no restrictions on his correspondence.[52]

Intense pressure was then placed on the Untouchable leaders, Ambedkar in particular, to grant the concessions which Gandhi sought, and by 24 September these were embodied in the so-called Poona Pact.[53] Thereupon Gandhi made a further attempt to wrongfoot the government by demanding that they should accept the agreed changes unconditionally.[54] But following upon speedy consultations with their provincial governments, and with London this was soon done.[55] Whereupon he called off his fast – though not without declaring that should the position of the Untouchables not be more generally improved he would before long renew it.[56]

Although the Government of India had skilfully deflected his more pointed thrusts, it was for Gandhi a stunning coup. Not merely had his moral stature both in India and abroad[57] been enormously enhanced. By very successfully challenging a very deliberate British decision, he had

---

[51] Haig's speeches, 15, 20 Sept. 1932, ibid.

[52] HD to Bombay, Bombay to HD, tels., 17–19 Sept. 1932, Haig's speech in Legislative Assembly, 20 Sept. 1932, ibid.

[53] R. Kumar, 'Gandhi, Ambedkar and the Poona Pact', in J. Masselos, *Struggling and Ruling. The Indian National Congress 1885–1985*, Delhi 1987, pp. 87–101. For the text of the Pact see *CWMG* 51, App. II.

[54] Bombay to HD, tel., 24 Sept. 1932, G Bombay to V, tel., 25 Sept. 1932, H.Poll.31/113/32; Message to Great Britain, Statement to the Press, 25 Sept. 1932, *CWMG* 51, pp. 141–2.

[55] HD to LGs, 24, 25 Sept. 1932, LGs to HD, 25, 26 Sept. 1932, SoS to GoI, tel., 25 Sept. 1932, H.Poll.41/5/32; Andrews to Tagore, 6 Oct. 1932, AP. Haig announced in the Legislative Assembly the British Government's acceptance of the Pact at 11 am on 26 Sept. 1932.

[56] Statements to the Press, 25, 26 Sept. 1932, Gandhi to Polak, 17 Oct. 1932, *CWMG* 51, pp. 141–5, 252–3.

[57] E.g. 'Gandhi has made a great achievement. He is really one of the wariest calculators I have ever seen, and his threat of starvation has brought the Hindus to heel and sent his stock soaring up', General Smuts (South Africa) to Mrs Gillett, 27 Sept. 1932, SmP 49, 271.

once again shown just how formidable an opponent of the Raj he could be.[58] As a consequence he managed to revive much of the sunken morale of his Congress followers. 'Congressmen have . . . been busy making the most of the opportunity of coming before the public eye', the Government of Madras typically reported.[59] What was more there now sprang up a widespread campaign for his unconditional release.[60]

Yet by far the most troublesome consequence for the Government of India emanated not from India – where their clamps on the civil disobedience movement were very successfully maintained – but from London. There back in 1931 there had been a good deal of concern about the imposition of emergency powers, and it appears possible that the former Labour Secretary of State, Wedgwood Benn, might well have vetoed them. Hoare and the National Government (which came into office in August 1931) soon however approved them, and at the outset they were insistent that

while Gandhi should be treated with consideration . . . he should have no facilities for communication with persons outside . . . and in particular no press interviews should be allowed[61] . . . we intend [Hoare declared] to win a crushing victory and . . . until this victory is won we cannot think of peace terms.[62]

But it was not very long before their attitude changed quite markedly. As early as March 1932, Macdonald, the Prime Minister, was writing to Willingdon, for example, to ask:

what is to come after the Ordinances because the weakness of government by Ordinance is that the longer it lasts the more ineffective and faulty it becomes . . . If, at the end of six months, the Government of India simply says that it must have a renewal of the Ordinances, there will be a very strong reaction here and the effect on some foreign countries will be serious. The Ordinances method has never been welcomed by us and I would not be at all surprised if a simple renewal led to resignations . . . Will a point come when Mr Gandhi will be allowed to enter into political conversations for the purpose of reaching an agreement; or must we go on keeping him in prison, whilst a policy of smashing Congress is being pursued by Ordinance methods?[63]

---

[58] For the levels at which he pitched and won his challenge see, for example, Gandhi to Shirer, tel.,[23 Sept. 1932], Statement to the Press, 23 Sept. 1932, Gandhi to Housman, tel., Message to Great Britain, Statement to the Press, 25 Sept. 1932, Statements to the Press, 26 Sept. [27 Sept.] 1932, and numerous letters, 30 Sept.–12 Oct. 1932, ibid. pp. 128–9, 132–3, 138–45, 146, 154–233; LGs to HD, tels., 25, 26 Sept. 1932, H.Poll.41/5/32.   [59] Madras to HD, 23 Sept. 1932, ibid.

[60] E.g. Sir Sivaswamy Aiyar to Willingdon, Sir Montagu Webb to Willingdon, President, Deccan Merchants Association, Bombay, Shaukat Ali to PSV, 6 Oct. 1932, H.Poll.31/106/32; Willingdon to Hoare, tel., 9 Oct. 1932, TwP 6.

[61] SoS to V, tel., 12 Jan. 1932, (and PSV to Edward Thompson, 26 Jan. 1932) H.Poll.31/11/32.   [62] Hoare to Hailey, 9 Feb. 1932, TwP 15.

[63] Macdonald to Willingdon, 31 Mar. 1932, copy in HgP 1.

To this Haig, the Home Member, drafted an emphatic reply:

first and foremost [he averred] every effort should be made to reach practical conclusions about the constitution . . . It is the constructive side of the 'dual policy' and it is vital that it be pushed on . . . [but] side by side with this we must maintain the other wing of this dual policy, we must defeat the menace of civil disobedience.[64]

For the moment Macdonald left the matter there, but in June 1932 Hoare resumed the argument following representations from the Archbishop of York that a settlement with Gandhi ought now to be attempted.[65] Hoare assured Willingdon that he was of course 'as strongly opposed as ever' to negotiations, but that he would nevertheless like to see some prominent Indian – or some 'official of standing' – visiting Gandhi in order that he might

be in a position to say that there is no obstacle whatever in the way of advances from him . . . I am prepared to accept your view [Hoare told Willingdon] that Gandhi has no intention of making his peace with Government . . . But the people I am concerned with do not accept your view and . . . the question reduces itself to this – are the conditions of Gandhi's confinement such as to make it possible for a man of his antecedents to make advances without humiliating himself? I want to be able to say they are.[66]

Willingdon, however, would not hear of this.[67] 'Anything that looks like negotiation', he riposted, 'will seriously upset those who support us and we simply cannot afford to shake the confidence of the army and the police'.[68] And for a second time the matter was allowed once again to rest there.

These, however, were only the ranging shots in what soon became an intense and wordy battle. For when in the aftermath of Gandhi's fast and the Poona Pact the Government of India decided to foreclose upon the special facilities which they had granted to him whilst the negotiations were in train,[69] on the grounds that

it is not consistent with position of Gandhi as State prisoner to allow him to conduct campaign in country even if it is not connected with civil disobedience, and to allow him this latitude will indirectly strengthen his position as civil disobedience leader.[70]

---

[64] Haig to Mieville, 13 Apr. 1932, ibid.
[65] The Archbishop and others had written to *The Times* on 26 May.
[66] Hoare to Willingdon, tels., 18, 23 June 1932, TwP 11.
[67] Willingdon to Hoare, tel., 18 June 1932, ibid.
[68] Willingdon to Hoare, tel., 11 June 1932, ibid.
[69] HD to Bombay, tel., 27 Sept. 1932, Bombay to HD, 28 Sept. 1932, H.Poll.31/11/32, 31/113/32.   [70] HD to Bombay, 29 Sept. 1932, ibid.

Hoare and Macdonald and their colleagues returned to the attack, and thereupon to the intense dismay of the Government of India subjected it to a seven-week-long telegraphic bombardment in which they not only gave vent to their concern that in the aftermath of the Poona Pact, which had so enormously enhanced Gandhi's reputation, his continuing imprisonment was becoming exceedingly difficult to justify in London, but their increasing worry that the absence of any move to bring about a political settlement in India was putting seriously at risk all the sustained efforts they were making – not least against considerable Conservative opposition – to restore political calm in India through constitutional reform.[71] In taking this line they unveiled that deep substratum of perplexed aversion in British public life to unbending opposition to nationalism overseas,[72] which was one side of Britain's ambidexterousness towards India. Whilst the Government of India vehemently argued from the other side that anything that smacked of weakness on their part – Gandhi's release; further negotiations with him; even the appointment of an intermediary to sound him out – would quite fatally undermine their dominion in India.

Hoare fired the first shot on 29 September. 'Do you contemplate keeping him in prison indefinitely?' he enquired of Willingdon. Presumably Gandhi would continue to be allowed to conduct his depressed classes' campaign; but should not the opportunity also be taken, he asked, to set him free 'on the plea of convalescence' and thus

improve relations generally by liquidating civil disobedience movement and endeavouring to restore cooperation in the hope of getting new constitution launched by agreement?[73]

The Prime Minister (he added the following day)

is strongly of opinion that we must exploit to the full what appears to be the better atmosphere . . . [in particular] we must on no account prevent . . . Gandhi having communications with his friends . . . [or] we shall be accused of . . . inflicting grave injury on the Depressed classes . . . [The Prime Minister] certainly thinks . . . [that] it is well worth considering . . . releasing Gandhi on the ground that he must be given a chance of implementing the pact and that it is impossible for a state prisoner . . . to have constant communications with the outside world . . . this [we believe] . . . would involve no embarrassing negotiations . . . rightly or wrongly we feel that if there is to be a change . . . [it] must take place whilst the atmosphere is in this improved condition.[74]

---

[71] E.g. Hoare to Willingdon, 29 Sept. 1932, TwP 11.
[72] In relation to Latin America, Greece, Italy, Canada, Australia, New Zealand, white South Africa, eastern and central Europe, and even (remember Gladstone) Ireland, that record, whatever else cut across it, speaks for itself.
[73] Hoare to Willingdon, tel., 29 Sept. 1932, TwP 11.
[74] Hoare to Willingdon, tel., 30 Sept. 1932, ibid. For the kind of pressure to which Macdonald was being subjected see General Smuts (South Africa) to Mrs Gillett, 5 Oct.

Willingdon immediately saw that this amounted to a frontal attack upon the Government of India's whole current policy, and accordingly mobilised both his own Council[75] and his provincial governors,[76] and vehemently rebutted any such suggestion as constituting a quite fatal threat to their whole recently resecured position. If, he told Hoare, Gandhi were to be provided with special facilities for his campaign, that would 'indirectly strengthen his position as civil disobedience leader', while to release him to enable him to conduct it openly simply raised the 'possibility of rearresting him if he engaged in any other political activities':

it would be quite impossible [he inveighed] to distinguish between Gandhi the social reformer and Gandhi the leader of civil disobedience. It would be an ideal position [which] he would exploit . . . to the utmost . . . we would be releasing him at a moment when his stock stands highest . . . his release would be hailed . . . as triumph over Government . . . this would have most damaging effect on our supporters, including Muslims and . . . Army, Police and government servants generally . . . we should . . . lose all the advantages we have secured by our consistent policy of last nine months . . . his release would be interpreted as showing that Government wanted to negotiate with him . . . We feel most strongly that . . . there must be no relaxation of effort . . . the first move . . . must come from the opposite side. Gandhi fully appreciates that he can secure his release if he definitely repudiates civil disobedience . . .[77]

Hoare reeled under this onslaught and was careful not to press for Gandhi's release again. He insisted, however, that an announcement shortly to be made by the Government of Bombay that Gandhi's recent special privileges would now be discontinued should be modified,[78] and emphasised his strong endorsement of its specific provision that 'special applications for interviews will be considered by the Government of Bombay in consultation with the Government of India on their merits'.[79] Shortly afterwards he reiterated, moreover, his earlier suggestion that 'it would do more good than harm if people like Rabindranath Tagore had opportunities of making Gandhi realise futility of civil disobedience'.[80] That for the Government of India called for a further emphatic reply,

---

1932, SmP 49, 273: 'Take Gandhi . . . you know how fatal in my opinion has been the blunder of the British Government and of Willingdon . . . I told the P.M. my opinion . . . Gandhi has scored greatly over this untouchable business . . . His stock has gone up enormously, and I can't understand his being secluded in gaol. The British seem to lose their political instinct at certain points.'
[75] Meetings, 29 Sept., 1 Oct. 1932, H.Poll.31/95/32.
[76] Willingdon to Hoare, tels., 4 (2), 5 (2) Oct. 1932, TwP 11.
[77] Willingdon to Hoare, tel., 1 Oct. 1932, ibid.
[78] Hoare to Willingdon, tel., 2 Oct. 1932, ibid.
[79] HD to Bombay, tel., 3 Oct. 1932, Hallett's Note, 30 Sept. 1932, H.Poll.31/11/32, 31/95/32.   [80] Hoare to Willingdon, tel., 5 Oct. 1932, TwP 11.

and Haig sat down for the second time to spell out its firmly considered position in another lengthy note.

We are definitely not prepared to enter into negotiations with Mr. Gandhi [he avowed] . . . Mr. Gandhi is not prepared to call off civil disobedience unconditionally . . . It would be an admission of defeat, and his influence is very largely based on the prestige of his success against government . . . If that is a fair appreciation . . . interviews . . . with a view to his abandoning civil disobedience would be infructuous . . . I recognise the difficulties of going back to the precise position we were in before the fast . . . many people honestly believe that the change in the situation may enable Mr. Gandhi to . . . call off civil disobedience. I do not myself believe that that is a contingency that can be contemplated . . . if conversations are allowed and make any progress, we shall undoubtedly be placed in a very difficult position . . . our whole position will be seriously weakened, and distrust in our resolution would spread once more through India . . . All this talk will keep Mr. Gandhi in the limelight, which is exactly what he wishes to secure; whereas we want to put him back in the comparative oblivion in which he was before the Pact began.[81]

Willingdon told Hoare at the same time that whilst they might be prepared to allow someone to see Gandhi 'to encourage him to give up civil disobedience, in which case he would of course be let out', they were adamant that they should never again enter into any negotiations with him, and for their part could not see how these could possibly be avoided once such a visit had taken place.

Government policy as it has existed during the past year [he declared] has proved fairly successful. We have always acted on the principle of trying to crush civil disobedience . . . and at the same time to push forward our reforms . . . Therefore, if Gandhi comes out, he must come out unconditionally; if he tries to do the *bania* and make terms he must remain where he is.[82]

Macdonald and other members of the Cabinet were, however, in no way assuaged, and during the next fortnight they continuously pressed the point that if any restrictions were to be placed upon Gandhi's visitors, not only would they be accused of putting difficulties in the way of implementing the Poona Pact. They would also be making it much 'more difficult for him to call off civil disobedience' – which was now becoming their chief concern.[83]

Following consultations with both Haig and the Governor of Bombay, Willingdon assured Hoare that Gandhi was being 'allowed to see the intimate members of his family and also those people who we are satisfied

[81] Haig's Note, 9 Oct. 1932, H.Poll.31/11/32.
[82] Willingdon to Hoare, 9 Oct. 1932, TwP 6.
[83] Hoare to Willingdon, tel., 14 Oct. 1932, TwP 11.

wish solely to discuss with him the question of untouchability'.[84] But, he went on:

We feel strongly that interviews other than those . . . solely connected with . . . untouchability . . . would give . . . the impression that negotiations were in progress between the Government and Congress . . . consequently there would be a corresponding fillip to the civil disobedience movement and a most damaging effect on prestige of the Government and the morale of the Services, involving, as it would undoubtedly do, the loss of ground which we have gained in the last nine months . . . I would ask you once again to impress our views upon the Prime Minister and your colleagues.[85]

The Cabinet nonetheless remained unsatisfied. 'We agree with you entirely', Hoare telegraphed to Willingdon on 20 October, 'as to negotiations'. But clutching at Willingdon's statement of 9 October – pulled completely out of context – that some latitude might be given 'to certain people to see Gandhi in order to encourage him to give up civil disobedience', he then added:

I shall undoubtedly be pressed on the subject in Parliament. I am not unduly influenced by outside propaganda[86] nor by pressure from Opposition, but Prime Minister and other colleagues have a strong feeling, which I to a large extent share, in favour of latitude for interviews such as you describe . . . I should accordingly be glad, with your concurrence, to be able, if pressed, to follow your language. If interviews . . . give rise to intimation that Gandhi is ready to desist from civil disobedience and devote himself to better cause, we should like to consider the upshot. . .[87]

This irritated Willingdon greatly. On 23 October he told Hoare that while like the Cabinet he too was 'being smothered with applications', and could well understand that 'the appeals to your Christian spirit must be numerous and strong', nonetheless he was now

getting rather bothered by . . . the very constant way you suggest that some of your colleagues, and to some extent you yourself, are of the opinion that we are not giving Gandhi sufficient opportunities of crying off civil disobedience . . . the unanimous view of myself and my colleagues [is that] . . . Gandhi has been the *fons et origo* of the whole of our troubles during the last two or three years . . . He may be in some aspects a saint, but he is certainly a very astute politician. He was put in prison . . . because he deliberately declared war against us . . . the result has been that we have restored confidence throughout the country . . . If we now give any suggestion that we are opening negotiations . . . then that confidence . . . will rapidly disappear . . . Gandhi is in prison because he is the chief promoter of the

---

[84] See also Bombay to HD, 6 Nov. 1932, H.Poll.31/11/32.
[85] Willingdon to Hoare, tel., 17 Oct. 1932, TwP 11.
[86] E.g. Andrews to Tagore, 9, 10 Oct. 1932, AP.
[87] Hoare to Willingdon, 20 Oct. 1932, TwP 11.

civil disobedience movement. There he must stay until he unconditionally with-draws this movement or until a moment arrives when we can feel strong enough to let him and his friends out without any restrictions.[88]

The Cabinet, however, remained unpersuaded.

My colleagues and I [Hoare replied on 25 October] are still afraid that the rigid line defined in your telegram of 22 October will prove difficult to maintain . . . many will say that is no reason for preventing people attempting to dissuade him from his present attitude.

And he reiterated that whilst they had no wish 'to override your strong and repeated view', they would still like someone like Rabindranath Tagore to see Gandhi in order to try and persuade him to call off civil dis-obedience.

Once more Willingdon mobilised his Council, and once again they stood foursquare behind him:

both I and my colleagues [he replied to Hoare on 27 October] are strongly of opinion that the adoption of any halfway line is going to prove . . . impossible to maintain . . . if interviews are allowed regarding civil disobedience we shall inevitably be led on from one point to another, and if and when we do take a stand we shall be much more heavily attacked than if we took a stand at the beginning . . . interviews such as you have in mind will certainly be misrepresented as nego-tiation . . . The present agitation . . . for the release of Gandhi . . . is, in our opinion, being largely maintained owing to the belief . . . that His Majesty's Government are weakening in their attitude . . . We consider it of the greatest importance to do nothing to lend colour to that view.[89]

– hardly the language in which a subordinate government ordinarily addresses its superiors. But that was not to be the end of it. For once again Hoare pushed his point, though he now did trim a little.

I still feel [he replied to Willingdon on 28 October] you have misunderstood my reasons for pressing you to allow at least one interview not confined to Depressed Class question. I agree with you that it is unlikely that anyone like Tagore could persuade Gandhi to abandon civil disobedience. But there are many people who do not think this out of the question and I want to meet their complaint that we are making it impossible for anyone to try to move Gandhi . . . I see from the Press that you have just issued a letter making it quite clear the Government is not weakening . . . it should be possible to allow an interview of the kind I have in mind without risk of misunderstanding . . . it would be in our power to stop discussions at any time . . . it would be a great help to me here if you could meet me to this extent.[90]

[88] Willingdon to Hoare, 23 Oct. 1932, TwP 6.
[89] Willingdon to Hoare, 27 Oct. 1932, TwP 11.
[90] Hoare to Willingdon, tel., 28 Oct. 1932, ibid.

For another fortnight this hammer and tongs went on. Despite periodic suggestions that there were no real differences between them,[91] the cross-fire between the two sides not only vividly highlighted the polarities at the heart of British policy towards India. It also showed the extent to which the deep ambivalences at its core could wind themselves in remorselessly convoluted ways around both of its two principals at once. For while on the one hand the Cabinet pressed hard for active steps to be taken to bring the confrontation in India to an end, and urged in particular what it saw as the most minimal approach to the problem, it was never in the last resort prepared to override the vehement objections of the Government of India that in current circumstances even that would fatally undermine the British position in India. Yet at the same time while the Government of India quickly fended off the suggestion that they should take the present opportunity to release Gandhi forthwith, and firmly stood their ground against the attempt to pressurise them into doing no more than permit someone to interview him over civil disobedience, not only had they now clearly been put on notice that in relation to any further matter concerning untouchability they should treat Gandhi with the utmost sensitivity. The pressures were henceforth firmly upon them to effect a settlement in India at the earliest possible date, and meanwhile to ensure that the situation there never deteriorated any further. The cat's cradle of British ambiguities was rarely more explicitly exposed.

This exchange could well have persisted had it not quite suddenly been cut short by a second dramatic move by Gandhi.[92] During the greater part of October he had been slowly recovering from his fast.[93] Over this period it had become increasingly clear (as indeed the government's secret correspondence with London amply confirmed) that the public demand for his release was making no headway, and that the Government of India was absolutely determined to retain 'Ordinance' rule till civil dis-obedience had been completely renounced.[94] Given the effectiveness of their repression many a lesser man could well have sought a compromise, and some did. In due course a number of lesser Congressmen suggested that they would be ready to return to more constitutionalist paths if these were reopened to them.[95] Gandhi, however, was never cast in that mould.

---

[91] Willingdon to Hoare, tel., 8 Nov. 1932, ibid.
[92] For subsequent correspondence see Willingdon to Hoare, tel., 8 Nov. 1932, Hoare to Willingdon, tel., 9, 14 Nov. 1932, ibid.
[93] E.g. Gandhi to N. Gandhi, 2 Oct. 1932, *CWMG* 51, pp. 174–5.
[94] E.g. PSV to Sir Sivaswamy Aiyar, 9 Oct. 1932, H.Poll.31/106/32.
[95] By March 1933 Gandhi's British friend, H.S.L. Polak, estimated that the number was 'at least 50%', Haig's Note, 18 Mar. 1933, H.Poll.79/33.

He had no intention of risking the disintegration of all that he had striven for by renouncing civil disobedience unilaterally. Nor could he ever forget the countless sacrifices so many Congress followers had made in his cause. He nevertheless faced enormous difficulties. Despite his lustrous success over the Communal Award he remained the Government of India's closely confined political prisoner.

Yet with quite astonishing insight he now seized upon one central fact. Whereas the Government of India was obviously totally unbending over the issue of civil disobedience, their actions at the time of the Poona Pact confirmed their vulnerability to an issue of moral significance. Were he – he judged with quite masterly skill – to accept their susceptibilities on the question of civil disobedience, whilst in no way altering his own commitments to it, perhaps building on the precedent of the Poona Pact, he might so exploit their sensibilities on the question of India's Untouchables as to force them to permit him to mount a major public campaign for the 'uplift' of Untouchables, Harijans, 'children of God', as he now invariably called them,[96] even whilst he remained in jail. Not only would he thereby be able to propel himself back into the public eye once again, and in the process help to shore up the ravaged zeal of his civil disobedience supporters. By vigorously promoting the Harijan cause, and exploiting any further lapses in the reactions of the British to it, he might even find a way of unhorsing them altogether. By proceeding in this way there must just be here a classic opportunity to turn the ambivalences of the British right around upon themselves.

This story began as early as 27 September 1932 when he blandly told his jailors that he expected the special facilities recently granted to him for seeing visitors and conducting correspondence in the Harijan cause to be continued.[97] So soon as he was informed two days later that 'all restrictions previously in force' would on the contrary 'be reimposed at once',[98] he vigorously protested. When a week later he had heard no more, he pressed for a formal response.[99] This was not readily forthcoming.

His main point [officials in Delhi variously noted] is that we have stopped his work in connection with untouchability. This was the deliberate intention of the Government of India ... the purpose for which facilities were granted [have] now been served ... it is not possible to contemplate Mr Gandhi being allowed to conduct an elaborate campaign from prison.[100]

---

[96] He had only recently been calling them 'Antyajas', Discussion with Vallabhbhai Patel, 6 Sept. 1932, *CWMG* 51, p. 457.   [97] Gandhi to Doyle, 27 Sept. 1932, ibid. p. 148.

[98] HD to Bombay, tel., 28 Sept. 1932, H.Poll.31/11/32.

[99] HD to Bombay, tel., 28 Sept. 1932, ibid.; Gandhi to Bhandari, 29 Sept. 1932, Gandhi to Doyle, 6 Oct. 1932, *CWMG* 51, pp. 151–2, 197–8, H.Poll.31/95/32.

[100] Hallett's Note, HD to Bombay, tel., 3 Oct. 1932, Haig's Note, 9 Oct. 1932, ibid.

But under strong pressure from Hoare (as we have seen) Willingdon and the Governor of Bombay eventually agreed on 16 October that he could have 'a reasonable number of interviews with persons approved by government', though on the strict understanding that no reports of these, or of any of his correspondence, should reach the press.[101] When in connection with an interview with Ambedkar[102] (who seems to have been the only person to have especially asked to see him) he was told about this condition, he reacted strongly.[103] He not only now demanded an authoritative reply to his protest of 29 September and a clear statement of government policy, but forcefully declared that he held it

to be essential that I should be permitted to see people and carry on correspondence, strictly regarding untouchability, without let or hindrance. You may know that my fast has only been suspended. It has to be resumed if the Hindu public do not play the game by the Harijans. My contact with the public is thus inevitable if the reform is to be carried out.[104]

Because the Government of Bombay was fully aware of the decision of the Viceroy and the Governor of Bombay on 16 October about these matters, they coolly told him that no general facilities would be granted to him.[105]

That brought Gandhi to his feet. If by 1 November, he told them, the restrictions upon his visitors and correspondence were not lifted, he would forthwith restrict his diet.[106] And when a week later there had still been no response from the government he embellished his challenge further:

it is incumbent [he told his jailors] upon the government either to publish my correspondence . . . or . . . inform the public . . . of my request and their refusal to accede to it.

And then added:

if the Government would that I died rather than I lived to work for the removal of untouchability I cannot help it.[107]

---

[101] Hoare to Willingdon, tels., 29, 30 Sept., 2, 5, 14 Oct. 1932, Willingdon to Hoare, tel., 17 Oct. 1932, TwP 11; HD to Bombay, 7 Oct. 1932, Haig's Note, 17 Oct. 1932, Bombay to HD tel., 28 Oct. 1932, H.Poll.31/95/32, Haig's Note, 9 Oct. 1932, Bombay to HD, 11, 28 Oct., 6 Nov. 1932, H.Poll.31/11/32.
[102] Discussion with Ambedkar, 17 Oct. 1932, *CWMG* 51, pp. 462–3. Gandhi carefully evaded Ambedkar's request *inter alia* 'to give up civil disobedience and to join the Round Table Conference'.
[103] He interpreted this decision incorrectly as 'punishment' for having tried to wire Shaukat Ali, Gandhi to Shaukat Ali, tel., 7 Oct. 1932, Gandhi to Doyle, 24 Oct. 1932, *CWMG* 51, pp. 201, 289–90, but see Bombay to HD, tel., 14 Oct. 1932, HD to Bombay, tel., 15 Oct. 1932, Haig's Note, 17 Oct. 1932, H.Poll.31/11/32.
[104] Gandhi to Hudson, 18 Oct. 1932, *CWMG* 51, pp. 255–6.
[105] See Bombay to HD, tel., 28 Oct. 1932, H.Poll.31/11/32.
[106] Gandhi to Doyle, 24 Oct. 1932, *CWMG* 51, pp. 288–9, H.Poll.31/95/32.
[107] Gandhi to Bhandari, two letters, 31 Oct. 1932, *CWMG* 51, pp. 320–2, H.Poll.31/95/32.

As the Government of Bombay believed he should be firmly faced down, they did not inform the Government of India of this challenge till four days after it was first received.[108]

So soon as the Government of India heard of it, however, they immediately realised that they had a major crisis on their hands.[109] Not only had they just saved themselves from falling into one trap he had laid for them, and were thus particularly anxious not to fall into the next. In recent weeks they had been insistently told by the Government in London that he must be given every facility he needed for his campaign. They knew, therefore, they were not going to be supported from there if they refused to provide these.[110] At the same time their principal concern had been that any special privileges granted to him might be used to sustain his civil disobedience campaign. Here, with a wondrous twist, it was Gandhi who came to their rescue: 'Naturally these interviews and correspondence should have no reference to civil disobedience and must be strictly limited', he told them, 'to the removal of untouchability'.[111]

The Government of India seized upon this as its lifeline. On the one thing that really mattered to them they thought they now had him cornered. They accordingly told him that they were proposing to the Cabinet that he

should be allowed complete freedom in regard to visitors and correspondence on matters strictly confined to removal of untouchability and that there should be no restriction on publicity.[112]

To which Hoare quickly gave his assent.[113]

When the Government of Bombay learned of this they were outraged, and once again the tensions that could accumulate on the British side were laid bare. Having initially been more relaxed about continuing Gandhi's special privileges than the Government of India,[114] they had nonetheless faithfully implemented the restrictive orders they had received – against indeed Gandhi's triple protests.[115] Now, however, they found themselves in the humiliating position of having to rescind those orders against their own better judgment.[116] Not only were they

---

[108] Bombay to HD tel., 28 Oct. 1932, H.Poll.31/11/32, 31/95/32. They were subsequently reprimanded for their delay, HD to Bombay, 7 Nov. 1932, ibid.

[109] Hallett to Mieville, 31 Oct. 1932, H.Poll.31/11/32 (arranging an urgent meeting of the V's Council at 10 am the next morning), V to SoS, 'Most Immediate' tel. in two parts, 1 Nov. 1932, HD to Bombay, 1, 2 Nov. 1932, ibid., H.Poll.31/95/32.

[110] HD to Bombay, 16 Nov. 1932, ibid.

[111] Gandhi to Doyle, 24 Oct. 1932, CWMG 51, p. 289, H.Poll.31/95/32.

[112] HD to Bombay, tel., 1 Nov. 1932, CWMG 51, pp. 290–300, H.Poll.31/11/32, 31/95/32.

[113] SoS to V, tel., 1 Nov. 1932, ibid., HD to Bombay, 2 Nov. 1932, ibid., H.Poll.31/95/32.

[114] Bombay to HD, tel., 28 Sept. 1932, H.Poll.31/11/32.

[115] Bombay to HD, 28 Oct. 1932, ibid.

[116] HD to Bombay, Bombay to HD, tels., 1 Nov. 1932, H.Poll.31/95/32.

extremely angry. They were deeply perturbed at the spectre of the Government of India crumbling for the second time before his threats to fast.[117] Their angry complaints, however, were briskly thrust aside in Delhi.[118] There in the late autumn of 1932 the paths of effective government seemed to be crossed by a triplicate of flailings – by Gandhi, by the Cabinet, and now by the Government of Bombay. Had, however, the Government of India rejected Gandhi's demands for special privileges, not only would they have been faced by a Gandhian fast, from which given his public standing they could only have extricated themselves by an ignominious retreat. As it was, in parrying his further blow they not only ensured that they suffered no fatal wound themselves.

We think there may be definite advantages [they unblushingly told Hoare] in getting Gandhi involved in untouchability. It will rouse strong feeling on both sides and will divert attention from strictly political issues and civil disobedience.[119]

Initially Gandhi agreed to suspend his fast with some reluctance,[120] but when he heard of the Cabinet's approval he graciously welcomed the concessions he had secured.[121]

They constituted for him his second major triumph over the British within a mere five weeks.[122] Not only had he forced them to overturn a quite formal and very public decision once again.[123] During the months that followed there was the incredible spectacle of Britain's principal Indian antagonist holding open court in his prison yard to a continuous throng of visitors,[124] while freely communicating upon an almost daily basis a constant stream of major public statements to the press.[125] Not only did he thereby thrust himself back into the public eye once again. He had given himself a standpoint from which, whenever the opportunity

---

[117] Bombay to HD, 6 Nov. 1932, H.Poll.31/11/32, 31/95/32.

[118] HD to Bombay, 16 Nov. 1932, ibid.

[119] V to SoS, tel., 1 Nov. 1932, ibid.; see also Willingdon to Hoare, tel., 8 Nov. 1932, TwP 11.

[120] Gandhi to Home Sec. GoI, tel., 2 Nov. 1932, CWMG 51, pp. 327–8, H.Poll.31/95/32.

[121] HD to Bombay, 2 Nov. 1932, Gandhi to Home Sec. GoI, 3 Nov. 1932, CWMG 51, pp. 337–8, H.Poll.31/11/32.

[122] The fact became public with an Associated Press of India report on 6 November; see also Bombay to HD, 6 Nov. 1932, and Haig's statement in the Legislative Assembly, 7 Nov. 1932, H.Poll.31/95/32.

[123] HD to Bombay, tel., 3 Oct. 1932, Haig's Note 9 Oct. 1932, ibid.

[124] See the lists of his visitors, 4–15 Nov., 16 Nov.–31 Dec. 1932, Gandhi to Bhandari, 24 Dec. 1932, CWMG 51, pp. 451–3, CWMG 52, pp. 315–26, 280–1, which the GoI carefully noted (by December it was common for there to be two to three dozen a day), H.Poll.31/95/32 passim.

[125] CWMG 51, 52 passim, e.g. his thirteen successive 'Statements on Untouchability', 4 Nov.–30 Dec. 1932.

came his way, to widen the breach in the British defences even further. It was an astonishing achievement for any political detenu to have attained.

Yet ambiguity clearly left its mark as well. For the price he had had to pay was by no means negligible.

Neither these interviews nor this correspondence shall have any reference to civil disobedience matters [he assured the government] outside removal of untouchability. This trust shall never be abused.[126]

As a consequence they were able to confine their concessions very strictly to his Harijan cause. When, for example, he tried to send a wire to the Muslim leaders, Shaukat Ali, Maulana Azad, and Dr Ansari, to support them in their now forlorn efforts for Hindu–Muslim unity (which he said had nothing to do with civil disobedience),[127] they told him emphatically, and with Hoare's support, that whilst for exceptional reasons they had permitted him

facilities for carrying on his programme in regard to the social and moral problem of the removal of untouchability . . . as the leader of civil disobedience . . . and as a prisoner he cannot expect to take part in the ordinary life of the country or the discussion of political questions, even though they have no connection with civil disobedience.[128]

When, moreover, soon afterwards he drafted an uncompromising reply to a public appeal to him by the Labour Chancellor, Lord Sankey, to make some gesture towards calling off civil disobedience[129] (in which he boldly reaffirmed not only that civil disobedience was for him 'an article of faith' designed to destroy 'the unnatural relation of conquerors and conquered', but that 'the only gesture I can make . . . is to drink cup of suffering to dregs'),[130] they had no compunction in suppressing it.[131]

On his side Gandhi understood their position very well.

---

[126] Gandhi to Home Sec. GoI, tel., 3 Nov. 1932, *CWMG* 51, pp. 336–7.

[127] Gandhi to Home Sec. GoI, 7 Nov. 1932, ibid. pp. 368–9, H.Poll.31/95/32.

[128] HD to Bombay, 16 Nov. 1932, *CWMG* 51, p. 369, H.Poll.31/95/32, SoS to V, 13 Nov. 1932, ibid., V to SoS, tel., 12 Nov. 1932, ibid., H.Poll.31/11/32, 210/32, 24/10/33. Earlier they had stopped Gandhi to Ansari, tel., [1 Oct. 1932], Gandhi to Shaukat Ali, tel., 7 Oct. 1932, and Gandhi to Azad, tel., [20 Oct. 1932], *CWMG* 51, pp. 161, 201, 265, but had allowed him to send Gandhi to Iyengar, Gandhi to Zamorin (re Kelappan, see below), tels., 3 Oct. 1932, Gandhi to Doyle, 6 Oct. 1932, Gandhi to Kelappan, 15 Oct. 1932, ibid., pp. 177, 197–8, 242, see generally Hallett's Note, 8 Oct. 1932, Haig's Note, 9 Oct. 1932, HD to Bombay, tels., 9, 11 Oct. 1932, H.Poll.31/95/32.   [129] Newspapers for 12 Nov. 1932, *CWMG* 51, fn. p. 413.

[130] Gandhi to Sankey, tel., Gandhi to Private Sec. G Bombay, 13 Nov. 1932, ibid. pp. 413–16.

[131] V to SoS, tel., 16 Nov. 1932, SoS to V, 18 Nov. 1932, H.Poll.31/11/32, 31/95/32. See also Gandhi to Bhandari, 19 Nov. 1932, *CWMG* 52, pp. 20–1, H.Poll.31/95/32.

I can fully appreciate the Government standpoint [he told Charlie Andrews in December 1932]. So long as they feel that civil disobedience must be put down at any cost and that their plan might be frustrated or checked if I was left free to carry on civil disobedience propaganda, they are bound to keep me under detention unless I would give them an assurance, be it even verbal, that I would not carry on civil disobedience propaganda.[132]

And that of course he would never do.

It was all the same not at all easy for him to hold to this position. When, for example, he dealt with a tart question which was put to him by a newspaper correspondent at this time as to whether in pursuing his Harijan campaign he was not retarding the political emancipation of India, he could only say:

that those who know me at all should understand that I draw no hard and fast line of demarcation between political, social, religious and other questions . . . the solution of one brings nearer the solution of the other.[133]

Whilst in reply to a similar question shortly afterwards the most he could bring himself to say was that: 'I don't regard my life as divisible into so many watertight compartments.'[134]

These responses[135] soon led a leading Bombay Congressman, Jamnadas Dwarkadas, who was out on bail and saw him on 26 December, to ask whether that meant that people should now give up political work altogether and concentrate upon untouchability.[136] To which he once again could only reply in very delphic terms. A good many Congressmen were as a consequence now finding it increasingly difficult to gauge what he really had in mind, and were beginning to turn their backs on civil disobedience altogether.

For his part he plainly calculated, however, that in adjuring any attempt to attack the British where they were overpoweringly well armed against him, he was by no means allowing himself to become politically sidelined. Twice already he had forced them to retreat before him over a lapse upon their side over a Harijan issue. If he kept his eyes skinned there might yet be an opportunity to force a further such reverse upon them and this time

---

[132] Gandhi to Andrews, 9 Dec. 1932, *CWMG* 52, p. 158. The Government took careful note of this letter, Maxwell to Hallett, 15 Dec. 1932, H.Poll.31/11/32, 31/95/32.

[133] Statement on Untouchability, 17 Nov. 1932, *CWMG* 52, p. 4; see also Interview with *Times of India*, 10 Nov. 1932, *CWMG* 51, p. 466.

[134] Interview to the Press, 21 Nov. 1932, *CWMG* 52, p. 37.

[135] Interview to *Free Press* [3 Dec. 1932], ibid. p. 112.

[136] For his refusal to be drawn see Discussion with Natarajan and Devdhar, 18 Dec. 1932, ibid. pp. 438–40; Interview with Associated Press, 2 Mar. 1933, *CWMG* 53, pp. 447–8; Maxwell to Hallett, 12 Jan. 1933, H.Poll.24/10/33, 44/35/33.

perhaps unhinge them altogether. During the next six months he assiduously explored a number of opportunities when he might have done just that.[137]

The beginnings of this further stage in the story came as early as October 1932 when he was just recovering from his fast at the time of the Poona Pact. It was then that he learnt that Kelappan, one of his associates from the time of the Vykom satyagraha of 1924–5, had begun to fast against the continued closure to Harijans of the Guruvayur Temple in the territory of the Zamorin of Calicut. This greatly troubled him.[138] So that there should be no confusion with his own fast he had insisted that no one should emulate it.[139] There were no signs, moreover, that Kelappan's fast would successfully arouse countrywide support, let alone provide any opening against the British. Kelappan's cause, however, was very much his own and he could not easily disown him. He decided therefore to tell Kelappan to suspend his fast for three months on the grounds that as a satyagraha follower he should have secured his leader's sanction for it, and given longer notice to those who controlled the temple. In view of the authority which Gandhi wielded in such matters Kelappan obeyed, though not without protest.[140] Thereupon Gandhi pressed the Zamorin of Calicut to exercise his influence to have the temple opened,[141] and so as to press his point decided somewhat hesitantly to say that if this were not done by 2 January 1933 he would join Kelappan in a renewed fast to

---

[137] The British view was variously stated as: 'amid his devotion to the problem of untouchability, Mr Gandhi's adherence to the creed of civil disobedience as an article of faith appears to remain unshaken'; 'there is little doubt that he would welcome any development which would enable him to divert the issue against Government', Maxwell to Hallett, 7 Dec. 1932, H.Poll.31/11/32, 31/95/32; idem, 12 Jan. 1933, H.Poll.24/10/33, 44/35/33. See also the much respected V.S. Srinivasa Sastri to Gandhi: 'It might be said by an observer who wasn't prejudiced against Government that, while Harijan uplift was dear to you, putting blame on Government was dearer. It has been said in my hearing by well-disposed persons that you would love nothing so much as to die in gaol and leave Government burdened with the responsibility', 27 Aug. 1933, *CWMG* 55, p. 455. Gandhi denied that his proposed fast on the Guruvayur issue (see below) was political, but allowed that 'the last fast [against the Communal Award] had a political tinge about it and superficial critics were able to say that it was aimed at the British Government', Gandhi to Tagore, 10 Nov. 1932, *CWMG* 51, p. 395; see also Gandhi to Bhandari, 31 Oct. 1932, Gandhi to Home Sec. GoI, 2 Nov. 1932, Gandhi to Sankey, tel., 13 Nov. 1932 (as withheld by the Government), ibid. pp. 320–2, 327–8, 413–15.

[138] Gandhi to M.K. Nair, tel., [27 Sept. 1932], *CWMG* 51, p. 145.

[139] E.g. Statement to the Press, 16 Sept. 1933, and telegrams to Mehta, Mor, and Nair [23 Sept. 1933], *CWMG* 51, pp. 64, 130–1.

[140] Gandhi to Kelappan, tels., 29 (2) Sept., [1 Oct.] 1932, and Kelappan's replies, and 15 Oct. 1932, Gandhi to Nair, 29 Sept. 1932, ibid. pp. 150–1, 162, 242; Gandhi to Michael, 16 Nov. 1932, *CWMG* 52, pp. 5–6.

[141] Gandhi to Zamorin, tels., 27 Sept., 3 Oct., [9 Nov.] 1932, and letter, 15 Oct. 1932, *CWMG* 51, pp. 147, 177, 387–8, 243.

bring this about.[142] Since any fast by Gandhi whilst still their political prisoner posed ominous difficulties for the British that became a smoking fuse.

Nothing emerged, however, initially from this affair to allow him to turn it against the British. Soon afterwards, however, there seemed a much more promising possibility. That arose from the high-principled decision of one of his other associates, Appasaheb Patwardhan, to confine himself to reduced rations as a protest against the reiterated refusal of his jailors to permit him to do conservancy work which was ordinarily reserved for Harijans. So soon as Gandhi heard of this he upbraided the government for its obduracy.[143] In reply it told him they had plenty of labourers to do the work already, and had no intention of acceding to Patwardhan's demand.

Gandhi immediately seized upon the opening here. He promptly told Doyle (the Inspector-General of Prisons of the Government of Bombay) that he too wished to do conservancy work, and that if Patwardhan was not to be permitted do so as well, he himself would start a complete fast upon the issue on 3 December.[144]

For a brief moment there seemed here to be all the makings of a fateful confrontation between the British and the Mahatma.[145] For to begin with they played straight into his hands. His jailors had recently become irked by the series of demands he had been making of them.[146] 'I am afraid', Doyle remarked, 'Mr. Gandhi is like Oliver Twist – he always wants more'.[147] While they immediately accepted that he could do conservancy work himself, they once more told him firmly that they could not have him interfering on Patwardhan's behalf.[148] Whereupon Gandhi immediately announced that he would start to fast.[149] Ready once again to face him down if necessary, the Government of Bombay set about making

---

[142] Gandhi to Zamorin, tel., 3 Oct. 1932, Gandhi to Doyle, 6, 24 Oct. 1932, Statement on Untouchability, I, 4 Nov. 1932, Interview to the Press, 7 Nov. 1932, ibid. pp. 177, 197, 288, 343, 376–8; Statement on Untouchability VII, 16 Nov. 1932, Discussion with *Times of India* representative, 21 Nov. 1932, Discussion with Macrae, 8 Dec. 1932, *CWMG* 52, pp. 1, 422–3, 429–30.

[143] Gandhi to Doyle, 28 Nov. 1933, ibid. pp. 88–9.

[144] Gandhi to Doyle, 30 Nov. 1933, ibid. pp. 94–5, Gandhi to Subbiah, 17 Jan. 1933, *CWMG* 53, p. 71.

[145] Its political aspect was clear to Gandhi, Gandhi to Andrews, 20 Dec. 1932, *CWMG* 52, p. 244.

[146] Gandhi to Home Sec. Bombay, 24, 29 Nov. 1932, Gandhi to Bhandari, 24 Nov. 1932, ibid. pp. 50–1, 90–1, 51; Bombay to HD, tel., 29 Nov. 1932, HD to Bombay, tel., 30 Nov. 1932, H.Poll.31/95/32, Maxwell to Hallett, 7 Dec. 1932, H.Poll.31/11/32, 31/95/32.   [147] Doyle to Maxwell, 29 Nov. 1932, H.Poll.31/108/32.

[148] HD to PSV, 5 Dec. 1932, ibid.

[149] Gandhi to Doyle, 3 Dec. 1932, *CWMG* 52, pp. 108–10.

arrangements in accord with the government's policy at the time of his Communal Award fast for his immediate release once his life stood in danger, and drafted a justificatory press statement which could then be issued.[150]

Cautioned, characteristically, by a telegram from Hoare,[151] the Government of India immediately realised, however, that they would have to confront this challenge a good deal more perspicaciously than the Bombay Government had done. As a consequence there then followed an all but unbelievable piece of political decision-making at the highest levels of British government in India which turned on the altogether momentous question of whether one obscure Congress detenu should be allowed to clean out his own prison latrines or not. For if Patwardhan were permitted to do so Gandhi would once more have put one over them. If not, a Gandhian fast, with all the dire consequences which could flow from that, would thereupon proceed.

With the Viceroy travelling away from Delhi, Haig, the Home Member of the Viceroy's Council, telegraphed Hoare 'most immediate' to tell him that they had it in mind to inform Gandhi that if he and Patwardhan both called their fasts off, the latter's request would be reconsidered. But they then calculated that this could be a bad mistake.

It would be said [he wired] that merely upon a point of prestige we were refusing to examine reasonable claim and thereby endangering Gandhi's life.[152]

Once again Gandhi came to their rescue. He seems to have concluded that it was unlikely that there would be much popular support for Patwardhan's demand, and wondered whether he should proceed with his fast after all.[153] That enabled Doyle to work out a compromise with him by which Patwardhan would be allowed to do conservancy work; both fasts would be called off; while the Government of India would accept, and Gandhi would acknowledge, that he had raised a larger issue of policy which it would take the Government of India several weeks to determine.[154]

Clearly concerned not to upset the Government of Bombay once again, the Government of India, in a steep descent into sophistry, fell for this formula with alacrity.[155]

---

[150] Bombay to HD, tel., 3, 4 Dec. 1932 (the latter containing a long draft press statement that was never in the event issued), H.Poll.31/108/32.

[151] SoS to V, tel., 2 Dec. 1932, ibid.

[152] GoI to SoS, tel., 'Most Immediate', 4 Dec. 1932, ibid.

[153] Statement on Fast to Anti-Untouchability Committee, 4 Dec. 1932, half a dozen brief messages, 4/5 Dec. 1932, Interview to the Press 5 Dec. 1932, CWMG 52, pp. 112–19, 125–7; Maxwell to Hallett, 7, 15 Dec. 1932, H.Poll.31/11/32, 31/95/32.

[154] Gandhi to Doyle (2), Doyle to Gandhi, 4 Dec. 1932, CWMG 52, pp. 115–16, 424–5, H.Poll.31/108/32.   [155] GoI to SoS, tel., 6 Dec. 1932, ibid.

Advantage of this line of action [Haig wired to Hoare] is that we do not refuse examination of . . . not unreasonable request . . . [By] making it an all-India question we do not embarrass Bombay . . . [At] the same time Gandhi is not able to secure what he no doubt desires, namely immediate change of policy in response to his hunger strike. If he still continues to strike his conduct will appear unreasonable.[156]

On 4 December Gandhi first agreed with Doyle to suspend his fast,[157] and when he learnt of the Government's decision to accept their compromise persuaded Patwardhan to do so too.[158]

Over the following weeks Gandhi nevertheless regularly pressed for their decision.[159] On 7 February when none seemed forthcoming, Patwardhan resumed his fast.[160] Gandhi, however, held back, and pressed the government yet again.[161] When eventually their decision was announced later that month it was yet another subterfuge. High-caste Hindus, they declared, would be permitted to do conservancy work – not as a matter of general policy, but at the discretion of each individual jail superintendent.[162]

In the meanwhile this tilt at arms had been overtaken by another. That stemmed from the still pending question of Harijan entry into the Guruvayur Temple.[163] On this Gandhi had been facing increasing opposition from orthodox Hindus, and many a plea from his closest associates against fasting over it.[164] His British captors soon received the distinct impression indeed that 'he is funking his so-called "contemplated fast" on 2nd January and is casting around for any excuse to be rid of it'. As a *pis aller* Gandhi called for a scrupulously conducted local referendum

---

[156] GoI to SoS, tel., 4 Dec. 1932, ibid.

[157] Statement on Fast, Gandhi to Doyle, 4 Dec. 1932, *CWMG* 52, pp. 112–15; Bombay to HD, tel., 4 Dec. 1932, Maxwell to Hallett, 5 Dec. 1932, H.Poll.31/108/32.

[158] Gandhi to Patwardhan, 6 [and Patwardhan's reply], 13 Dec. 1932, Interview with Associated Press [7 Dec. 1932], *CWMG* 52, pp. 128–9, 183, 142–3; Bombay to SoS, V to SoS, tels., 6 Dec. 1932, SoS to V, tel., 7 Dec. 1932 (expressing pleasure at the outcome), Maxwell to Hallett, 8 Dec. 1932, H.Poll.31/108/32.

[159] Gandhi to Doyle, 8 Dec. 1932, 10 Jan. 1933, *CWMG* 52, pp. 145, 412; Gandhi to Home Sec., GoI, tel., 16 Jan. 1933, *CWMG* 53, p. 60. For developments on the British side see HD to SoS, tel., 6 Dec. 1932, H.Poll.31/108/32, Maxwell to Hallett, and encs., 9 Dec. 1932, Hallett to LGs, 10, 15 Dec. 1932, Hallett to Maxwell, 15 Dec. 1932, H.Poll.31/108/32.   [160] Maxwell to Hallett, 14 Feb. 1933, H.Poll.44/35/33.

[161] Interview to Associated Press, 9 Feb. 1933, Gandhi to Doyle, 10 Feb. 1933, Gandhi to Home Sec. Bombay, 11 Feb. 1933, *CWMG* 53, pp. 251–2, 269–70.

[162] Patwardhan was given this permission and on 12 Feb. abandoned his fast, Maxwell to Hallett, 14 Feb. 1933, H.Poll.44/35/33; Gandhi's Interview to Associated Press, 13 Feb. 1933, *CWMG* 53, pp. 297–8.   [163] H.Poll.31/108/32.

[164] Interview with *Times of India*, 10 Nov. 1932, *CWMG* 51, pp. 465–8; Maxwell to Hallett, 7, 15, 22 Dec. 1932, H.Poll.31/11/32, 31/95/32. He recognised his undertaking was 'misunderstood by many', Gandhi to Andrews, 20 Dec. 1932, *CWMG* 52, p. 244.

on the issue,[165] and 300 volunteers immediately went to work upon this.[166] When at the end of December the results became available it showed a substantial majority in favour of Harijan entry to the temple.[167]

By then, however, the whole matter had taken a further twist.[168] This followed upon the seemingly sudden discovery that the application to India of the British law on trusts in India meant that temple trustees could not be forced to open their temples against their will. A prominent Madrasi, Dr Subbarayan, thereupon took steps to introduce a Bill in the Madras Legislative Council[169] to amend the law upon this point. That, however, presented the Government of India with the very difficult question of whether they should give their approval for its introduction (as on a matter of this kind the law required), since it very directly challenged their longstanding determination never to take sides in any contentious religious question. At the end of December[170] they accordingly announced that they could make no decision upon a matter of this moment before mid January 1933. Whereupon Gandhi announced that he would not be fasting on the Guruvayur issue on 2 January as he had earlier promised, and persuaded Kelappan not to do so either.[171]

But by then a second bill was being planned, this time for introduction into the central legislature by Ranga Iyer. Gandhi, moreover, clearly implied that if the Government in the end refused permission for any temple entry bill to be introduced he would have no option but to fast in protest.[172]

---

[165] Gandhi to Kelappan, Interview with Women, 23 Nov. 1932, Gandhi to Menon, tels. and letter, [1], 9, 21 Dec. 1932, Gandhi to Gujarati student, 6 Dec. 1932, Gandhi to R. Malaviya, 24 Dec. 1933, *CWMG* 52, pp. 42–5, 48, 99, 155–6, 135, 275; Maxwell to Hallett, 7 Dec. 1932, H.Poll.31/11/32, 31/95/32.

[166] Interview with Khimji and Mehta, 25 Nov. 1932, Statement on Untouchability IX [26 Nov. 1932], Interview with *Times of India*, 26 Nov. 1932, Discussion with Macrae, 12 Dec. 1932, Interview to Press, 5 Dec. 1932, and fn. to *Times of India*, 7 Dec. 1932, *CWMG* 52, pp. 67–72, 77–8, 430, 125; Gandhi to Patwari, 11 Jan. 1933, *CWMG* 53, p. 15.   [167] Statement on Untouchability XIII, 30 Dec. 1932, *CWMG* 52, pp. 304–8.

[168] Interview to *The Hindu*, 12 Nov. 1932, *CWMG* 51, pp. 408–11; Interview to the Press, 5 Dec. 1932, Gandhi to Andrews, 20 Dec. 1932, Gandhi to Rajagopalachari, 21 Dec. 1932, Gandhi to Subbarayan, 1 Jan. 1933, *CWMG* 52, pp. 125, 245, 248–9, 330; Maxwell to Hallett, 22 Dec. 1932, H.Poll.31/95/32. For further copies of items on this episode see H.Poll.31/108/32.   [169] Its jurisdiction covered the Camorin area.

[170] See also Haig's Note of talk with Birla, 22 Dec. 1932, H.Poll.50/1/33.

[171] Gandhi to Rajbhoj, 8 Dec. 1932, Gandhi to Mashruwala, 11 Dec. 1932, Statements on Untouchability XI, XII, 14, 15 Dec. 1932, Discussion with Kelappan, 29 Dec. 1933, Gandhi to PSV, tel., 30 Dec. 1932, and for subsequent developments see Gandhi to Zamorin, 1 Jan. 1933, Gandhi to Nathan, 11 Jan. 1933, *CWMG* 52, pp. 147–8, 169, 185–6, 198–99, 304–10, 328–9, 443, and *CWMG* 53, p. 6; Maxwell to Hallett, 2 Jan. 1933, H.Poll.44/35/33.

[172] Gandhi to PSV, tel., 30 Dec. 1932, Gandhi to Menon 31 Dec. 1932, Interview on Subbarayan's Bill, 2 Jan. 1933, *CWMG* 52, pp. 309–10, 313, 346; Maxwell to Hallett, 12 Jan. 1933, H.Poll.24/10/33, 44/35/33.

Once more this could very easily have precipitated an actual head-on collision with the Government of India. For following upon their consultations with provincial governments,[173] they firmly decided to decline permission for a bill's introduction.[174] They accepted the force of Gandhi's reiterated argument that the bill would only be permissive and simply provide for a temple to be opened if a local majority were agreed. They recognised too that 'this is a Bill to which Gandhi attaches importance'. And they were well aware that for all the hesitations he was displaying as to whether this was the most propitious issue on which to take a stand,[175] if it came to the point he would almost certainly do so. They not only decided, however, 'without reference to consequence of his fasting', that permission for a Bill's introduction should be refused, but that it must 'be quite clearly understood that there can be no question of any subsequent modification of attitude on our part' should he should then proceed to fast.[176]

They soon found themselves, however, pushed from this perch by the leading Muslim member of the Viceroy's Council, Sir Fazli Husain, who had been sick when the original decision had been made. On his recovery he slyly argued that Subbarayan's bill

does not affect religious beliefs ... It only determines whether, in the case of a particular temple, administration should vest in the orthodox or in the reformed section of worshippers ... Politically it would be a wrong move [to disallow its introduction, he said]. The [Harijan] movement at present is a social and religious question. As soon as Government has declared itself against the reformer, the movement will assume a political aspect and will gain in strength and momentum. [Were on the other hand a major debate to take place on the Bill] the current of thought in the country will be distinctly in religious and social grooves; and the Civil Disobedience movement will finally disappear.[177]

Hoare also thought the decision mistaken, and provided his own artful compromise. The Madras Bill, he suggested, should be refused since it related to an all-India issue. However:

---

[173] All of whom, other than the Government of the Punjab, were strongly opposed to a bill's introduction, both on the traditional grounds that legislation on a religious matter was quite inappropriate, and on the more pragmatic grounds that it could seriously alienate many orthodox Hindus, GoI to SoS, tel., 9 Jan. 1933, H.Poll.50/2/33; see also Secretary, Sanatan Dharma Mahamandal, Calcutta, to Willingdon, 8 Jan. 1933, H.Poll.50/14/33.

[174] See, for example, the Notes of the Law Member, Sir B.L. Mitter, 19, 20 Dec. 1932, H.Poll.50/2/32, and generally ibid., and 50/1/32, 50/3/32.

[175] His criticism of a report in *The Hindu* on 16 Jan. 1933 suggests that he had had second thoughts about fasting on this issue, *CWMG* 53, pp. 488–9, 80, 87–8, 104–5, 181–2; Maxwell to Hallett, 23 Jan. 1933, H.Poll.44/35/33.

[176] GoI to SoS, tel., 9 Jan. 1933, H.Poll.50/2/33.

[177] GoI to SoS, reporting Husain's minute, tel., 11 Jan. 1933, H.Poll.30/2/33.

As regards Central legislation . . . refusing permission to introduce bill . . . will at once have effect of putting Government in wrong in eyes of substantial bodies opinion both in India and elsewhere . . . refusal of permission to introduce will afford Gandhi opportunity for renewing his fast with show of justification for which he appears to be looking and though I entirely agree with view that Government cannot allow itself to be coerced by threats of this kind it seems unnecessary to present him with excuse for fasting if it can be avoided.[178]

Willingdon was not persuaded, nor one of his Indian Councillors either. But over the next few days the rest of the Viceroy's Council began to take the Secretary of State's point, and so in the end – 'in deference to the very strong wishes expressed by you' – did Willingdon. It was accordingly agreed that Ranga Iyer's Bill might be introduced in the central legislature, but that Subbarayan's Bill should be vetoed in Madras.[179] The bad humour which accompanied this decision was explicitly expressed in the public announcement which the Government of India then made. Whilst they would allow the central legislature to discuss the Untouchability Bill, they made it plain

that the consideration of any such measure should not proceed unless the proposals are subjected to the fullest examination . . . not merely in the legislature, but also outside it.

They insisted too that they were in no way committed to the Bill's passage, and retained the right to take any action over it which they thought necessary.[180]

When Gandhi heard of their decision he was far from pleased, but he recognised that: 'It clears the issue',[181] and thereafter followed the course of the discussion upon the bill very closely, especially when he learnt that as a private measure it was unlikely to secure an easy passage.[182] As to

---

[178] SoS to GoI, tel., 12 Jan. 1933, ibid.   [179] GoI to SoS, tel., 19 Jan. 1933, ibid.

[180] Statement, 19 Jan. 1933, ibid.; GoI to Gandhi [17 Feb. 1933], CWMG 53, p. 497.

[181] Statement on V's Decision, 24 Jan. 1933, Interview with Associated Press, 21 Jan. 1933, Gandhi to Andrews, 27 Jan. 1933, ibid. pp. 128–32, 112–13, 162–3; Maxwell to Hallett, 30 Jan. 1933, H.Poll.44/35/33.

[182] Maxwell to Hallett, second letter, 30 Jan. 1933, ibid.; Gandhi to PSV, Gandhi to Andrews, 1, 2 Feb. 1933, Interviews to Associated Press, 2, 7 Feb. 1933, GoI to Gandhi, nd, Gandhi to Home Sec. GoI, 19 Feb. 1933, Messages to Members of the Legislative Assembly, 11, 18 Feb. 1933, Gandhi to Malaviya, tel., 14 Feb. 1933, 'Agreeing to differ', 18 Feb. 1933, CWMG 53, pp. 202–5, 209, 213–14, 245–6, 497, 350–1, 277, 328, 298 (see also H.Poll.50/2/33 which includes Hallett's Note, 28 Feb., and Hallett to Maxwell, 12 Feb. 1933); Jayakar to Sapru, 6 Feb. 1933, JP 360; Maxwell to Hallett, 6 Feb. 1933, H.Poll.44/35/33. See also Haig's Note, 6 Feb. 1933, and Hallett's Notes, 8, 10 Feb. 1933, H.Poll.50/2/33. He secured strong support for it from, among others, Sapru and Jayakar, Gandhi to Jayakar, 20 Jan., 1, 14, 19 Feb., 2 Mar. 1933, Gandhi to Sapru, 16, 19 Feb. 1933, 'Dr Sapru on Untouchability Bill', 25 Feb. 1933, CWMG 53, pp. 101, 205, 353, 302, 444–5, 315, 351, 394–5; Sapru to Gandhi, nd, 2, 11, 18 Feb. 1933, SP 6, G16, G19, G20, G22; Sapru to Iyengar, 2 Feb. 1933, SP II A53; Jayakar to Willingdon, 12 Feb. 1933, H.Poll.50/2/33.

whether he would then fast upon it should it be rejected in the legislature, that was left as an open question.[183] It soon transpired, however, that he was not in fact prepared to do so.[184] Thereafter the Bill foundered before the foot-dragging of the orthodox,[185] which deprived him of any effective leverage it might perhaps have given him against the government.[186]

During March and April 1933 he once again however succeeded in niggling the Government of India upon yet another issue. This centred upon the decision of one of his lesser followers, Poonamchand Ranka, to fast against what he alleged to be the harsh jail regime for Civil Disobedience prisoners in his Central Provinces prison.[187] Gandhi refused to endorse this protest as being quite unworthy of a satyagrahi,[188] and attempted to send Ranka a message telling him to desist.[189] The government, however, would not hear of this. It could not, it told him, permit him to interfere in the jail discipline of other prisoners.[190] He immediately protested that he had been allowed to do this in 1922 and again in 1930.[191] Whereupon it curtly told him their policy had now changed. Anxious, however, not to be led once more into a crisis it then quite disingenuously arranged that Ranka should be sent a message along the lines Gandhi wanted by a person outside his jail even though it still refused to allow Gandhi to do this himself.[192] On this issue there was once more a good deal of anxious discussion at the highest reaches of the

---

[183] Interview to Associated Press, 25 Jan. 1933, *CWMG* 53, p. 151.

[184] Talk with Bhandari, 24 Jan. 1933, Gandhi to Rajagopalachari, letter and tel., 12/13 Feb. 1933, Gandhi to Birla, 14 Feb. 1933, 'When is it possible ?', 18 Feb. 1933, *CWMG* 53, pp. 491–2, 286–7, 303–4, 323–3.

[185] Rajagopalachari's report to Gandhi, 28 Feb. 1933, *CWMG* 53, p. 436. See also Gandhi to Rajagopalachari, 22 Apr. 1933, *CWMG* 54, p. 495.

[186] Gandhi to Andrews, 17 Feb. 1933, Gandhi to Home Sec. GoI, 19 Feb. 1933, *CWMG* 53, pp. 320–1, 350–1.

[187] Gandhi to Raghavendra Rao, tel., 24 Feb. 1933, Gandhi to Supt Seoni Jail, 25 Feb. 1933, ibid. pp. 383, 407. For a major collection of papers on this episode see H.Poll.31/108/33.

[188] Gandhi to Bachraj, tel., 1 Mar. 1933, Gandhi to Bajaj, 8 Apr. 1933, Gandhi to Ranka, [10 Apr. 1933], *CWMG* 54, pp. 54, 345, 362.

[189] The text is set out in Maxwell to Hallett, 22 Apr. 1933, H.Poll.44/35/33.

[190] Gandhi to Home Sec. Bombay, 18 Mar. 1933, *CWMG* 54, p. 118; Maxwell to Hallett, 23 Mar. 1933; Hallett's Note, 23 Mar. 1933, H.Poll.44/35/33.

[191] Gandhi to Home Sec. Bombay, 23 Mar, 1 Apr. 1933, *CWMG* 54, pp. 165–6, 271; Bombay to HD, tel., 28 Mar. 1933, and Hallett's Note, 29 Mar. 1933, H.Poll.44/35/33. Gandhi variously pressed his case, Gandhi to Home Sec. Bombay, two letters, 28 Mar. 1933, Gandhi to Bachhraj, tel., 30 Mar. 1933,Gandhi to Bhandari, 8, 10 Apr. 1933, *CWMG* 54, pp. 228–9, 245, 341–2, 362–3. See also Gandhi to Doyle, 3 Dec. 1932, *CWMG* 52, pp. 109–10.

[192] HD to Bombay, tels., 29 Mar. (see also H.Poll.31/108/33), 12 Apr. 1933, Maxwell to Hallett, 31 Mar., 7, 11, 15, 22 Apr. 1933, H.Poll.44/35/33; CP to Hallett, 18 Apr., 1 June 1933, Haig's Note, 9 May 1933, Hallett to CP, 13 May 1933, H.Poll.31/108/33; Gandhi to Home Sec. Bombay, 12 Apr. 1933, *CWMG* 54, pp. 377–8.

Government of India,[193] where it was pointedly admitted that 'Gandhi put us in a difficult position over this case, and the sooner it is ended, the better'. 'It is a difficult case', Haig averred, 'but I think the position at present reached is not unsatisfactory'.[194]

On several occasions, therefore, between November 1932 and March 1933 Gandhi managed to provoke the Government of India to exasperation whilst he remained their political prisoner. On each occasion the ambiguity in their position forced them to extricate themselves from a quite untenable position in ways that were essentially spurious. They were lucky that the Guruvayur case could not in the end be turned against them. In Patwardhan's case their replies to Gandhi's protests were entirely meretricious. Over the Untouchability Bills, they were only rescued from the distant corner into which they had backed themselves by the cynical advice of Sir Fazli Husain and the cool calculation of Sir Samuel Hoare. While in Ranka's case they simply resorted to open casuistry. In each instance they just about managed to hold their own, and despite Gandhi's feline skill he never finally succeeded in opening up another issue with which he might have inflicted another major reverse upon them. All the same for the Government of India it was all too often a close call.

Their position in the middle of all this was peculiarly difficult since at the same time they found themselves having to fight a further round with the Cabinet in London.

During the late autumn of 1932 the Third Round Table Conference had been held in London with a view to completing the refashioning of India's constitution. Whilst this was taking place the Government of India was largely left in peace. But once it was over two of the conference's principal figures, Sapru and Jayakar, made a public appeal in London for Gandhi's release, and clearly received some support for this from Hoare.[195] Just before Christmas 1932 to the Government of India's intense dismay Willingdon received a telegram from Hoare, who was increasingly anxious that his handiwork, a new constitution for India, should be accepted there,[196] which proposed that he should announce in

---

[193] See also Hallett's Notes, 4 Apr. 1933, H.Poll.44/35/33.
[194] Hallett's Note, 19 Mar. 1933, Haig's Note, 20 Mar. 1933, H.Poll.44/35/33. For yet one more contretemps see Gandhi to Home Sec. Bombay, 19 Apr. 1933, *CWMG* 54, p. 448.
[195] Sapru to Pole, 22 Jan. 1933, SP 6, G128/2; Sapru to Iyengar, SP II, A53.
[196] For this sentiment see Hoare to Willingdon, tel., 29 Sept. 1932, TwP 11; for Haig's anxiety about 'the general atmosphere which appears to prevail in England of trying to seek agreement with Congress' see Haig to PSV, tel., 27 Dec. 1932, H.Poll.31/97/33; and for Willingdon's appreciation that 'there is a general feeling at home that no reforms are possible without Mr. Gandhi as one of the chief participators', see Willingdon to Hoare, 1 Jan. 1933, TwP 6.

London that upon their return to India Sapru and Jayakar would be allowed to see Gandhi in order to give him a first-hand account of the reforms that were now proposed.[197] Willingdon was aghast.

Interview [he wired back on Christmas Day] will undoubtedly be regarded in India as initiating negotiation . . . especially if formal announcement is made by you.[198]

At the very least Sapru and Jayakar should first see him before any announcement was made. In reply Hoare declared that he was, of course,

alive to the dangers of public misunderstanding . . . but trust they could be overcome as I attach real importance to Sapru and Jayakar . . . conveying to Gandhi their impression of position resulting from last Round Table Conference.[199]

Once more the Government of India was being subjected to the kind of Cabinet pressure under which they had lived previously, and this time they replied with all their guns firing. 'I wd. rather let Gandhi out now than have an announcement by S/S', Hallett, the Secretary of the Home Department, proclaimed,[200] and thereupon proceeded to write a long note explaining just how disastrous both the Sapru/Jayakar–Yeravda negotiations of 1930 and the Gandhi–Irwin Pact had been.[201] Haig too [202] was no less emphatic, and once again spelt out the uncompromising position of the Government of India at considerable length.

My general conclusion [he summarised] is that we should not be afraid of our own policy just as it appears to be succeeding. We can, in my opinion, do without the goodwill of Congress, and in fact I do not believe we shall ever have it, but we cannot afford to do without the confidence of those who have supported us during the long struggle against the Congress.[203]

Sykes, the Governor of Bombay, bent to the extent of suggesting that a strictly private interview between Gandhi and Sapru and Jayakar could perhaps be allowed,[204] but all the other Governors remained just as opposed to any discussion with him as they had been back in October.[205] 'There isn't a doubt', Willingdon protested to Hoare early in January 1933, that if Sapru and Jayakar were upon their return allowed to see Gandhi

---

[197] Hoare to Willingdon, tel., 24 Dec. 1932, TwP 11.
[198] Hoare to Willingdon, tel., 25 Dec. 1932, ibid. based on Hallett to PSV, 25 Dec. 1932, H.Poll.31/97/32.   [199] Hoare to Willingdon, tel., 29 Dec. 1932, TwP 11.
[200] Hallett to Haig, 25 Dec. 1932, H.Poll.31/97/32.
[201] Hallett's 'A brief history of the negotiations undertaken by Messrs Sapru and Jayakar in July 1930 . . .', 2 Jan. 1933, ibid.
[202] For his initial reactions see Haig to PSV, 27, and tels., 27, 28 Dec. 1932, H.Poll.31/97/32.
[203] Haig's Note, 28 Dec. 1932, ibid., H.Poll.24/10/33, and Willingdon's concurrence, PSV to Haig, tel., 28 Dec. 1932, H.Poll.31/97/32.
[204] Sykes to Willingdon, 1 Jan. 1933, ibid.   [205] Gs to V, 28 Dec.–2 Jan. 1933, ibid.

there will be a general cry that history is repeating itself . . . the inevitable result will be that they will come back to me . . . to agree to Gandhi's conditions of release . . . We have always had a perfectly definite policy; the pushing on with Constitutional Reforms and insisting on law and order . . . I can quite understand your wish . . . after the Round Table Conference . . . [to] ease the situation . . . but . . . if we give way . . . at this particular moment we shall ruin the whole . . . effect . . . we have achieved with the many loyal subjects of His Majesty out here.[206]

Once again his Council backed him, and, after reviewing the Governor's letters, Willingdon then forcefully told Hoare that:

Gandhi . . . has shown no sign of modifying his political views . . . He would be likely to adopt the same line as . . . in July 1930, when Sapru and Jayakar intervened . . . Congress would again become predominant and . . . adopt the more insidious methods used after the pact in 1931 and . . . destroy the results of the admirable work you have been able to achieve in London. We can justify our position . . . by reiterating . . . that it is open to Gandhi and other Congress leaders to take a part in constitutional discussions by . . . giving up civil disobedience.[207]

Publicly Macdonald and Hoare supported this position,[208] but privately they were quite unpersuaded.

We are neither of us happy over Gandhi's position [the latter telegraphed to Willingdon on 12 January] . . . Gandhi is not in the least likely to make a retraction . . . do you desire to keep him in prison for an indefinite time? . . . it will be extremely difficult to maintain the position here during many months and perhaps years.[209]

To which, on Haig and Hallett's prompting, Willingdon replied:

I quite agree that Gandhi is not at all likely to make a formal retraction of civil disobedience, and that at some point we will have to let him out without any kind of gauarantee. That, however, would not in my opinion be safe as long as there is any possibility of reviving civil disobedience.[210]

So the old debate raged on.

Once again it was quite fortuitously cut short by another move by Gandhi. By the turn of the year he had become increasingly perturbed about the uncertainties which various Congressmen now released from jail were expressing over his attitude towards civil disobedience, and early

---

[206] Willingdon to Hoare, 1 Jan. 1933, TwP 6.
[207] Willingdon to Hoare, tel., 7 Jan. 1933, H.Poll.31/97/33, TwP 11; Haig to PSV, 10 Jan. 1933, ibid.
[208] Macdonald to Jayakar, 4 Jan. 1933, enc., Macdonald to Sapru 4 Jan. 1933, JP 360; Macdonald to Thakurdas, 6 Jan. 1933, ThP 132; Hoare to Willingdon, tel., 9 Jan. 1933, H.Poll.31/97/33. A press report from London about the differences between the governments there and in Delhi was vigorously denied, Willingdon to Hoare, tels., 30, 31 Dec. 1932, Hoare to Willingdon, tel., 30 Dec. 1932, H.Poll.31/97/32.
[209] Hoare to Willingdon, 12 Jan. 1933, ibid.
[210] Enclosure in Haig to PSV, 28 Jan. 1933, Hallett's Note, 25 Jan. 1933, ibid.

in January he drafted a statement, which he hoped the government would allow to be published, in which he stated that:

I have used all the talents I have for civil disobedience. I found that I had also talents for the service of Harijans . . . In so doing I have abated nothing from my existing dharma . . . I have added service to the untouchable to it.

Because of his commitments to the British he was, he wrote, in no position to advise those outside prison as to how they should proceed. They must make up their own minds.[211] The purpose of his statement, so he told the Government of India, was to make sure that those out of jail 'know clearly that they must not look to me for guidance in the choice between civil disobedience and untouchability work'.[212]

In view of the recently renewed bombardment to which they had been subjected from London,[213] several of those in the Viceroy's entourage seized upon this to mean 'that if the leaders outside choose to concentrate on untouchability, he would have no objection . . . indeed he gives a pretty clear hint that that might be the wise policy', and they thereupon decided that there might just be the possibility here of an opportunity to set him free without impairing their own position.

It is the kind of opening, [Haig noted] for which His Majesty's Government have probably been looking . . . there will be a feeling that we could not reasonably expect more from Gandhi in way of dissociation from civil disobedience.[214]

They agreed therefore to allow his statement to be published.[215]

It fell, however, completely flat,[216] and only made confusion worse confounded. A number of Congressmen took it to contain another call to arms.[217] Dwarkadas, however, who had seen Gandhi in December,[218] now renounced civil disobedience altogether,[219] whilst a number of other Congressmen concluded he must have lost all interest in it.[220] He soon

---

[211] Statement to the Press, *CWMG* 52, pp. 379–81; Maxwell to Hallett, 12 Jan. 1933, H.Poll.24/10/33, 44/35/33.

[212] Gandhi to Home Sec. Bombay, 7 Jan. 1933, *CWMG* 52, p. 381.

[213] For the GoI's final, half conciliatory response see Haig's draft for Willingdon to Hoare, 28 Jan. 1933, and correspondence about the V's meeting with returned Round Table Conference delegates, Jan. 1933, passim, H.Poll.31/97/33.

[214] Haig to PSV, tel., 11 Jan. 1933, H.Poll.50/15/33. The Bombay Government took a similar view, Maxwell to Hallett, 12 Jan. 1933, H.Poll.44/35/33.

[215] Bombay to HD, tel., 11 Jan. 1933, ibid.

[216] Hallett's Note, 25 Jan. 1933; Haig's draft for Willingdon to Hoare, 28 Jan. 1933, H.Poll.31/97/33.

[217] E.g. Jayakar to Polak, 19 Jan. 1933, JP 360; Maxwell to Hallett, 23 Jan. 1933, H.Poll.44/35/33.

[218] Maxwell to Hallett, 12 Jan. 1933, reported Dwarkadas' disillusion, ibid.

[219] Maxwell to Hallett, 23 Feb., 8 Mar. 1933, ibid.

[220] Maxwell to Hallett, 23, 30 Jan. 1933, ibid.

explained, however, to one of these that: 'My statement has not the meaning you have assigned to it';[221] and thereafter whilst regularly reiterating in statements that reached the press that he was 'civilly dead',[222] he responded to a rather more precise question in March 1933 about whether he had lost all interest in contemporary politics by saying that 'if the ban is lifted . . . I can, without any difficulty, speak on questions of policy and fundamental principles'.[223]

In view of all this Hoare held his fire, whilst upon their return to India, Sapru and Jayakar, while vigorously expressing their vexation with the Government of India, decided not to invite the inevitable rebuff from them by asking to see Gandhi.[224]

By the early spring of 1933 a grating deadlock had thus been reached in which both sides in India felt remorselessly trapped. For its part the Government of India was still quite determined to have no dealings with Gandhi, or with any of his associates, over anything to do with civil disobedience.[225] This they forcefully demonstrated in a twice adjourned debate in the central legislature,[226] and in their decision to send in their police at the end of March to suppress a bold attempt to hold a Congress session in Calcutta.[227] Yet at the same time they lived under the constant threat of renewed Cabinet pressure to mitigate the conflict in India, while Gandhi was soon on their tail once again, this time over the obstruction he was facing in sending a telegram to V.J. Patel who, he heard, was ill in Europe.[228] With all this pressing hard upon them they felt themselves caught in an increasingly unhappy double gridlock.

[221] Gandhi to Thenge, 24 Jan. 1933, *CWMG* 53, p. 132.
[222] E.g. Gandhi to Aney, 13 Feb. 1933, ibid., p. 296.
[223] Quoted in Maxwell to Hallett, 8 Mar. 1933, H.Poll.44/35/33.
[224] They saw Willingdon on 25 January 1933, Jayakar Diary; Sapru to Iyengar, 2 Feb. 1933, SP 11, A53; Sapru to Hoare, 5 Feb. 1933, SP 8, H227; Sapru to Irwin, Sapru to Simon, 18 Feb. 1933, SP S9/8.
[225] In mid March Haig gave Gandhi's British friend, H.S.L. Polak, a long and very stiff interview, Haig's Note, 18 Mar. 1933, H.Poll.79/33.
[226] 15 Feb., 1 Mar., 1 Apr. 1933, see H.Poll.24/10/33; for Haig's responses on 1 Mar. see H.Poll.4/3/33; Willingdon to Hoare, 2 Apr. 1933, H.Poll.3/1/33.
[227] Hallett's Notes, 30 Jan., 13 Mar. 1933, Haig's Note, 3 Feb. 1933, Husain's Note, 18 Feb. 1933, GoI to SoS, tel., 18 Feb. 1933, SoS to GoI, 23 Feb. 1933, AICC to PCCs, 6 Mar. 1933, Bengal to HD, tel., 7 Apr. 1933, H.Poll.4/3/33; Willingdon to Hoare, tels. 12 Mar., 2 Apr. (2), 9 Apr. 1933, H.Poll.3/1/33; 25 Members of the House of Assembly to Haig, 11 Apr. 1933, Bengal to Hallett, 15 May 1933, GoI communique, 29 May 1933, H.Poll.3/13/33. About the same time correspondents of the London *Daily Herald* and the *Philippines Free Press* were refused permission to interview Gandhi, Maxwell to Hallett, 31 Mar., 7 Apr. 1933, H.Poll.44/35/33.
[228] Gandhi to Home Sec. Bombay, 19 Apr. 1933, *CWMG* 54, p. 448; Maxwell to Hallett, 28 Apr. 1933, H.Poll.44/35/33. There were earlier problems too, Hallett's and Haig's Notes, 4 Apr. 1933, ibid.

But Gandhi was in an even more difficult position. During the early months of 1933 the special privileges granted to him for his Harijan campaign continued to bring him considerable public attention. In February the first English edition of his newspaper, *Harijan*, appeared, and was soon followed by several Indian-language editions;[229] while in March a number of his associates who were out of jail formed the Harijan Sevak Sangh.[230] None of this, however, compensated in any way for all the troubles that were now impacting on him. The Government of India remained as flint hearted as before. His efforts to impale them upon some further Harijan issue had all failed. A great many of his followers still languished ineffectually in jail; while outside there was mounting criticism of his still uncompromising commitment to civil disobedience which was now on its last legs.[231] Worse still, he was now being subjected to severe criticisms by Untouchable leaders, Ambedkar especially, for quite improperly appropriating their cause,[232] while the Orthodox in increasingly large numbers were now fulminating against the whole thrust of his Harijan cause.[233] He was much upset too by two quite personal matters. His Sabarmati Ashram at Ahmedabad (where he had established his

[229] Statements on *Harijan*, [5], 25 Feb. 1933, *CWMG* 53, pp. 226–7, 406–7; Gandhi to Birla, 8 Jan. 1933, 25 Jan. 1933, *CWMG* 52, pp. 392, 140–1. Gandhi's prolific contributions are reprinted *in extenso* in ibid, p. 262 et seq. The Government followed *Harijan* closely, e.g. Maxwell to Hallett, 14, 23 Feb., 8, 15 Mar., 15, 22 Apr. 1933, H.Poll.44/35/33.   [230] For its constitution see *CWMG* 54, pp. 17–22.

[231] Upon this and the government's self-imposed difficulties over forwarding letters to him about this see Maxwell to Hallett (re Rohit Mehta to Gandhi), 15 Mar. 1933, Wilson to Williamson, 17 Mar. 1933, Hallett's two Notes, 4 Apr. 1933, H.Poll.44/35/33.

[232] Discussion with Untouchables Deputation, 15 Dec. 1932, *CWMG* 52, pp. 435–6; Statement to Associated Press, 11 Jan. 1933, Gandhi to Nathan, 11 Jan. 1933, Discussion with Ambedkar, 4 Feb. 1933, 'Dr Ambedkar and Caste', 11 Feb. 1933, Ambedkar's Statement, 13 Feb. 1933, Interview to Associated Press, 14 Feb. 1933, ibid. pp. 1–3, 6–9, 498–500, 259–61, 503–4, 305–8; Maxwell to Hallett, 14, 23 Feb. 1933, H.Poll.44/35/33; 'A True Servant', *Harijan*, 11 Mar. 1933, *CWMG* 54, pp. 47–9. He took some comfort from the Memorial of the deputation of Representatives of Depressed Classes to Willingdon and Willingdon's reply, 29 Mar. 1933, H.Poll.50/4/33. See 'Harijans and Temple Entry', *Harijan*, 8 Apr. 1933, *CWMG* 54, pp. 335–7.

[233] Statements on Untouchability, 4, 9 Nov. 1932, *CWMG* 51, pp. 344, 384–7; Discussion with Poona Sanatanists, 7 Dec. 1932, Gandhi to Iyer, 24 Dec. 1932, Gandhi to T.S.K.R. Iyer, 25 Dec. 1932, Interview to Associated Press, 2 Jan. 1933, Statement on Untouchability, 3 Jan. 1933, Gandhi to Bhambania, 3 Jan. 1933, Appeal to Sanatanists, 4 Jan. 1933, Gandhi to Rao, 7 Jan. 1933, Gandhi to Patwardhan, 10 Jan. 1933, *CWMG* 52, pp. 425–6, 276–7, 284–5, 343–5, 347–50, 351, 358–61, 383, 413; Gandhi to Patwari, 11 Jan. 1933, Gandhi to R.S. Aiyar, 12 Jan. 1933, Interview with Associated Press, 16 Jan. 1933, Gandhi to Shah, 18 Jan. 1933, Gandhi to Andrews, 27 Jan. 1933, Interview to Associated Press, 27 Jan. 1933, Gandhi to Gujarat Caste Hindus, [30 Jan. 1933], Gandhi to Hindu Central Committee, 13 Feb. 1933, Gandhi to Nehru, 15 Feb. 1933, *CWMG* 53, pp. 13–24, 30–1, 68–9, 85–6, 163, 169–71, 192–3, 291–5; 'A True Servant', 'Truth the only way', *Harijan*, 11, 18 Mar. 1933, *CWMG* 54, pp. 47–9, 66–8; Deputation of Orthodox Hindus to Willingdon and Willingdon's reply, 17 Mar. 1933, H.Poll.50/4/33.

base nearly two decades before) was in his absence falling into great disarray,[234] while towards the end of April he was greatly unnerved by the sexual confessions of one of the young European women in his entourage.[235] On top of all this his greatest concern stemmed from the undertaking he had made at the time of the Poona Pact to resume his then abandoned fast should there be no sustained progress in Harijan 'improvement'. In the course of the intervening months he had harped constantly on his readiness to fast again in this cause, but so far had baulked at every opportunity to do so.[236] All of which led him to fret about his own public standing and to ponder deeply how best he might relieve his growing psychic tension. 'Mr Gandhi seems to be becoming impatient at his continued eclipse in the political world', his jailors reported late in March, 'and is likely to assert himself'. Upon which Hallett wryly commented: 'This indeed is not unlikely.'[237] By late April 1933 he badly needed to find some way to cut through the thickets threatening to engulf him. Some dramatic new move was now urgently called for.

Gandhi, it must always be remembered, was a deeply religious man. With all these pressures now bearing down upon him, it is in no way surprising that he should have sought to confound them in religious terms. The saint in him always remained his surest armour.[238] The eventual resolution of his problem came quite suddenly. The catalyst seems to have been the onset of 'Harijan Day', which he had himself fixed for 30 April.[239] Given the wide range of controversies he had been provoking it could very easily have fallen appallingly flat; his own moral ascendency and his Harijan cause with it. That he could never allow.

---

[234] Gandhi to Narandas Gandhi, *CWMG* 54, 55 passim.

[235] Gandhi to 'N', *CWMG* 53, 54 passim; Gandhi to N. Gandhi, 19 Apr. 1933, *CWMG* 54, p. 454.

[236] On his fixation see Discussion with *Free Press* representative, 3 Dec. 1932, Gandhi to Chintamini, 1 Jan. 1933, Gandhi to Madeleine Rolland, 6 Jan. 1933, Gandhi to Kapadia, 8 Jan. 1933, *CWMG* 52, pp. 423–4, 329–30, 376–7, 399–400; Statement on V's decision, 24 Jan. 1933, Interview with Associated Press, 25 Jan. 1933, Discussion with Rajagopalachari, 31 Jan. 1933, Gandhi to Andrews, 27 Jan., 2 Feb. 1933, 'When is it possible?', 18 Feb. 1933, *CWMG* 53, pp. 128–32, 151, 163, 209, 494–6, 332–3; 'The Law and the Heart', 7 Apr. 1933, 'Thinking Aloud', 15 Apr. 1933, *CWMG* 54, pp. 426, 413–14; Maxwell to Hallett, 30 Jan. 1933, H.Poll.44/35/33.

[237] Bombay's Inspector General of Prisons, and Maxwell to Hallett, 31 Mar. 1933, and Hallett's Note, 4 Apr. 1933, H.Poll.44/35/33.

[238] J.M. Brown, *Gandhi. Prisoner of Hope*, New Haven 1989, passim. In February he had urged people to dismiss from their minds the 'remote possibility' of another fast against untouchability and 'accept my assurance that, if such a fast does come, it will have come in obedience to the call of Truth which is God', 'When is it possible?', and see also Gandhi to Andrews, 7 Apr. 1933, *CWMG* 54, pp. 332–3, 328–9.

[239] 'Remember 30th April', ibid. pp. 481–3.

A tempest has been raging within me for some days [he thereupon told the press]. I have been struggling against it . . . But the resistance was vain.[240]

Following three days without sleep, the climax, so he told Vallabhbhai Patel, came at around 11 pm on 29 April, within an hour of the start of his 'Harijan Day', when:

I woke up, I watched the stars, repeated Ramanana . . . [and then at] half past twelve came the clear, unmistakable voice: 'you must undertake the fast'. . . If I don't do this much the rot in the Harijan work will reach the heart and destroy it altogether.[241]

'Whenever a great reformation . . . is going on', he explained, 'people in order to ensure purity and acceleration of their object, undertake a fast'.[242] He determined now to fast. His intention, he said, was

to remove bitterness, to purify hearts and make it clear that the movement is wholly moral, to be prosecuted by wholly moral means.[243]

The fast would begin, he said, on 8 May and end on 29 May. It was not, he insisted, directed against anyone, not even the orthodox.

When Nehru heard of it he was quite bewildered. Rajagopalachari, Dr Ansari, and the South African Prime Minister, General Smuts, were amongst the many who urged him to desist. Momentarily he wondered whether he would arrange for his Ashram followers to embark upon a subsequent 'unbroken chain of fasts till untouchability is completely abolished', but soon thought better of it. He tried to reassure his wife, a number of his English friends, and some of his older associates in the nationalist movement about the wisdom of his throw since he certainly did not expect to die,[244] and then at precisely 12 noon on Monday 8 May 1933 he began to fast, whereupon he issued a further statement to the press elaborating its whole purpose.[245] It was a spectacular stroke, brilliantly composed to confound each of his various adversaries.

Nothing, however, went to plan. Instead of embarking forthwith on a sustained atonement in the Harijan cause, he suddenly found himself immediately plunged into a major clash with his jailors. For at 7 pm that evening the British released him from jail quite unconditionally, and in the course of the next twenty-four hours the thwack of verbal onslaughts stung the ears.

---

[240] Statement on Fast [30 Apr. 1933], *CWMG* 55, pp. 74–5.
[241] Discussion with Vallabhbhai Patel, 30 Apr. 1933, ibid. p. 76.
[242] Interview to the Press, 1 May 1933, ibid. pp. 82–5.
[243] Statement explaining object of fast, 8 May 1933, *CWMG* 55, pp. 156–7.
[244] Upon all this see ibid. pp. 77–157 passim.
[245] Statement explaining object of Fast, 8 May 1933, 'All about Fast', 8 July 1933, ibid. pp. 156–7, 254–8.

A week earlier he had told the Government of India that his 'fast might have been commenced at once but for my . . . anxiety to enable local authority receive instructions for arrangements'.[246] The Medical Officer at Yeravda Jail advised that although he would probably survive the first week, he was unlikely to last the full three.[247] That meant that the Government of India had to decide what they would do.[248]

They faced a number of acute problems. On the occasion of his previous fast prior to the Poona Pact they had offered to release him for its duration, but he had deftly refused. They had no wish to invite another rebuff. At the same time they could not allow him to die in jail; the ensuing uproar would be impossible to contain. But neither could they forcibly feed him.[249] Very probably therefore they would have to set him free sometime, and would almost certainly then have to do so without conditions.[250]

As they sized up the situation they quickly sensed that he had suddenly presented them with a quite unexpected opportunity, both to resolve their own dilemmas, and to place him at a severe political disadvantage. During the past seven or eight months they had lived under the immense strain of having to reconcile the deep dualities in Britain's imperial stance in two distinct respects. On the one hand they had been constantly plagued by Gandhi, who with great ingenuity had found a way of putting inordinate pressure upon them even whilst he remained their political prisoner. On the other hand they had found themselves persistently pressurised by the Cabinet in London to secure a settlement with him when they were absolutely determined not to drop their guard. As recently as mid April 1933 Hoare had once more urged upon them that although

in the absence of entirely new factors . . . no question arises of inviting or consulting any prisoner . . . if any person of substance who is more or less of Congress persuasion, but is not under restraint . . . is willing to be called into consultation, I see . . . real advantage in securing his presence.[251]

They had then bent to the extent of permitting an informal meeting of released Congress leaders which Aney, the acting President of Congress, had called 'to take stock of our losses and gains during the past 16 months'[252] on the grounds that this 'might have interesting

---

[246] Gandhi to Home Sec. GoI, tel., 30 Apr. 1933, ibid. p. 77; Bombay to HD, tel., 1 May 1933, forwarded to SoS, ibid., H.Poll.44/56/33.
[247] Bombay to HD, tel., 2 May 1933, ibid.   [248] HD to Bombay, tel., 1 May 1933, ibid.
[249] Hallett's note, 2 May 1933, ibid.   [250] GoI to SoS, tel., 3 May 1933, ibid.
[251] Hoare to Willingdon, 16 Apr. 1933, TwP 12.
[252] Aney to Ansari, 19 Apr. 1933, H.Poll.4/4/33. Aney had been in Poona in mid March to discuss future policy (but had not seen Gandhi), Hallett to Maxwell, 15 Mar. 1933,

result'.[253] They could not, however, countenance anything more.[254] Yet (they now deviously calculated) if so soon as Gandhi began his fast they set him free without conditions, not only would they no longer have to stand on the defensive against him. The Cabinet could be assuaged as well. No one, moreover, could say they had been forced into releasing him. Nor could anyone readily foist negotiations with him upon them.[255]

There are distinct advantages in releasing Gandhi [they accordingly preened themselves to tell Hoare on 3 May] on ground of humanity connected with a definitely non-political development. His release whenever it comes will be an embarrassment, and present conditions seem to afford a comparatively unembarrassing opportunity. We think it likely to render easier rather than more difficult pursuance of our general policy of avoiding anything like an amnesty to political prisoners . . . for some considerable time after fast he could not [moreover] with show of decency . . . take part in subversive activities against government.[256]

Such, however, were the strains that anything to do with Gandhi now generated within their own ranks that the details of how this should all be managed put them at odds once again with the Government of Bombay, who were not only worried about the possibility of major demonstrations upon his release, but wanted him retained in jail till his life stood in danger.[257] The Government of India would not hear of this.

Nature of his present fast [they declared] which is not directed to achievement of particular end, would seem to preclude spectator demonstrations which we apprehended in September . . . If we are releasing him unconditionally we get some credit for doing this at the beginning.[258]

Their own preference was to do so two days before his fast began, and tell him a day earlier of their intention.[259] Hoare, however, told them that 'in view of public opinion here' they should wait till his fast had actually begun.[260] Clearly angered with the Government of India the Bombay Government then pressed to be allowed to send him to Ahmedabad and only there set him free once he became immobile.[261] The Government of

---

H.Poll.44/35/33; and Malaviya, Aney, Asaf Ali, Khaliquzzaman, Azad had met with Sapru in Benares on 26 Mar., Sapru to Pole, 27 Mar. 1933, SP 6, G128/6.

[253] HD to UP, tel., 24 Apr. 1933, H.Poll.44/35/33; Aney to Ansari, Sapru to Pole (above, note 252).

[254] Haig to Chhatari, 5 May 1933, H.Poll.4/4/33. As it happened there were problems in convening an appropriate group, Malaviya to Aney, tel., 26 Apr. 1933, ibid.

[255] HD to Bombay, tel., 4 May 1933, H.Poll.44/56/33.

[256] GoI to SoS, tel., 3 May 1933, ibid.

[257] Bombay to HD, tel., 2 May 1933, Maxwell to Hallett, tel., 16 May 1933, ibid.

[258] GoI to SoS, tel., 3 May 1933, HD to LGs, 3 May 1933, ibid.   [259] Ibid.

[260] SoS to GoI, tel., 3 May 1933, HD to Bombay, tel., 4 May 1933, ibid.

[261] Bombay to HD, tels., 4, 5 May 1933, Maxwell to Hallett, tel., 16 May 1933, and Hallett to Maxwell, tel., 17 May 1933, ibid.

India agreed that he might be moved – though in the end he was retained in Poona – but otherwise declared that:

We adhere to the view that there are definite advantages in releasing Gandhi as soon as he commences his fast . . . In particular we feel that if Gandhi is released some time after fast has begun, it will appear that we have been driven out of our position and have been forced by public opinion to change our policy.[262]

There was a last-minute hitch on Sunday 7 May which was one of Gandhi's days of silence. It was impossible therefore to hold the explanatory discussions with him which had been planned.[263] Accordingly he was only told of the government's intentions at 6.45 pm on the following day, and immediately thereafter, after a passing thought that he might ask to proceed to Sabarmati, he accepted Lady Thackersey's offer to stay at her house nearby the prison in Poona,[264] and was thereupon released at 7 pm that evening.[265] Greatly relieved – for the Mahatma had to be handled with the utmost care if there was not to be a loud outcry[266] – the Government of India congratulated the Government of Bombay on the smoothness of the operation,[267] and then at the moment of his release delivered its *coup de main*. In a blistering communique it first quoted in full his telegram to them of the week before that 'for reasons wholly unconnected with Government and solely connected with Harijan movement' he proposed to fast, and then unctuously declared that:

In view of the nature and objects of the fast and the attitude of mind it discloses, the Government of India have decided that Mr. Gandhi should be set at liberty. He was released this evening.[268]

It was a swingeing blow. Just when he had steeled himself for an extraordinary personal sacrifice in the Harijan cause, the last thing the Mahatma wanted to do was to have to give his mind to anything else. To all appearances the government seemed to be treating him with the utmost personal consideration, but at the same time they had quite mercilessly leapt at the opportunity to strike hard at the root of his commitment to civil disobedience. The extent of their guile was clearly manifested in the steps they simultaneously took to placate their numerous subordinates by emphasising that the Mahatma's release,

[262] HD to Bombay, tel., 4 May 1933, ibid.   [263] Bombay to HD, tel., 5 May 1933, ibid.
[264] Interview to Associated Press and footnote, 8 May 1932, *CWMG* 55, p. 157.
[265] Maxwell to Hallett, 12 May 1933, H.Poll.44/35/33.
[266] The GoI had in the last stages pressed the Bombay Government about his proposed place of residence 'as it is very desirable not to give grounds for criticism' after he had given a week's notice, HD to Bombay, tel., 6 May 1933, ibid.
[267] Hallett to Maxwell, tel., 16 May 1933, H.Poll.33/56/33.
[268] GoI's communique, 8 May 1933, H.Poll.44/56/33.

indicates no change whatsoever in Government's general policy towards release of civil disobedience prisoners . . . Release is based on nature and circumstances of fast and inferences that may reasonably be drawn from it . . . present fast has no bearing on politics . . . It has been represented for some time that he has lost interest in Civil Disobedience and intends to devote himself solely to work in connection with the social and religious problem of untouchability. The present occasion constitutes a good opportunity of testing the truth of these contentions . . . If Government are wrong in the conclusions . . . they have drawn, they will not hesitate to deal with him in such manner as situation may demand.[269]

But they had entirely failed to size up Gandhi himself to the full. For whatever else he was he remained a consummate politician to his fingertips. Not only did he immediately see their game. Within two and a half hours of his release[270] he plunged back at them with a no less devastating statement of his own. His acute distress at all this diversion from his Harijan cause was clearly seen in the even more rambling structure of his prose in this than usual, but he not only now made it crystal clear that he could in no way be bounced into renouncing civil disobedience. He speedily turned the attack against the government by calling for the suspension of civil disobedience whilst his fast lasted and by demanding that 'peace' and negotiations should follow once it was completed.

I cannot regard this release with any degree of pleasure [he publicly proclaimed] . . . The whole purpose of the fast will be frustrated if I allowed my brain to be occupied by any extraneous matter . . . for the moment I can only say that my views about civil disobedience have undergone no change whatsoever . . . during these three weeks it would be better if the President of Congress . . . were to officially declare suspension for one full month or even six weeks . . . I would make an appeal to the Government. If they want real peace in the land . . . they should . . . unconditionally discharge all the civil resisters. If I survive the ordeal . . . I would like to take up the thread at the point where I was interrupted on my return from England . . . If there is a will on the part of the Government, I have no doubt that a *modus operandi* can be found.[271]

The highly effective nature of this riposte was vividly exemplified when the press messages that were sent to London that night for the next morning's newspapers emphasised heavily that he had held out the hand of friendship.[272]

---

[269] HD to LGs, tel., 5 May 1933, ibid.   [270] See *CWMG* 55, footnotes pp. 157 and 160.

[271] Statement suspending Civil Disobedience, 8 May 1933, ibid. pp. 157–60, H.Poll.44/57/33. For an extensive collection of relevant items (particularly newspaper abstracts) between this date and Sept. 1933 see H.Poll.4/11/33.

[272] V to SoS, tel., 10 May 1933, ibid. Reuters also reported that the Cabinet would shortly consider the mass release of prisoners and the suspension of emergency powers – which had speedily to be denied, GoI to SoS, tel., 10 May 1933, Willingdon to Hoare, Hoare to Willingdon, tels., 9 May 1933, ibid.

His call for 'peace' at this critical juncture when his own prestige stood at a peak now suddenly threatened to destroy the Government of India's whole carefully crafted stance. They very soon calculated that there must have been collusion with Aney, who had been permitted to see him on 6 May, and who as acting President of the Congress now issued instructions on 9 May that, whilst civil disobedience would be in no way abandoned, it would now 'be suspended for six weeks'.[273] Gandhi needed, however, no help from Aney to stiffen his response. Nor is it likely that he would have reneged upon his commitments to the Government about conversations with his visitors. The profound annoyance of the Government of India at this point bore all the marks of their intense frustration at finding themselves devastatingly outsmarted at exactly the moment when they thought they had delivered their own crushing blow.[274]

For a brief moment they were minded to treat Gandhi's own statement calmly, but within hours of Aney's announcement – which they went on to interpret as 'part of a preconceived plan to embarrass Government by creating the impression that the release of political prisoners was under consideration' – they quickly concluded that there was an 'urgent necessity of reasserting the Government's policy unambiguously' in order 'to prevent the confidence of our supporters being seriously shaken'.[275] And with their backs to the wall they reached for a broadsword.

The release of Mr Gandhi [so the communique they issued hurriedly on 9 May stated] indicates no change whatever in the Government's policy towards the release of civil disobedience prisoners . . . A mere temporary suspension of the civil disobedience movement intended to lead up to negotiations with the Congress leaders in no way fulfils the conditions which would satisfy the Government of India that in fact the civil disobedience movement has been definitely abandoned. There is no intention of negotiating with the Congress for withdrawal of the civil disobedience movement or of releasing the leaders of that movement with a view of arriving at any settlement with them in regard to these unlawful activities.[276]

That appeared to do the trick. 'It was difficult', they were soon cabling to London, 'to foresee immediate developments, but it seems fairly certain that our Communique will have served its purpose'.[277]

---

[273] Aney's Statement, 9 May 1933, *CWMG* 55, pp. 443–4; GoI to SoS, tel., 10 May 1933, Maxwell to Hallett, 12 May 1933, H.Poll.44/35/33. Aney had originally been refused permission to see Gandhi, but this was eventually granted, Maxwell to Hallett, 31 Mar. 1933, Aney to HD, HD to Aney, HD to Bombay, tels., 4 May 1933, Bombay to HD, May 1933, ibid.

[274] E.g. GoI to SoS, tel., 10 May 1933, H.Poll.44/57/33, Hallett to Maxwell, tel., 16 May 1933, H.Poll.44/56/33.

[275] GoI to SoS, tel., 10 May 1933, H.Poll.44/57/33; Willingdon to Hoare, 15 May 1933, TwP 6.   [276] GoI communique, 9 May 1933, H.Poll.44/56/33, 22/43/33, 44/57/33.

[277] GoI to SoS, tel., 10 May 1933, ibid.

It had, however, been a hugely clumsy stroke, and had evidently affronted even some of the government's own most assured supporters. As a direct reflection of this there was over the coming weeks an angry exchange behind the scenes between the Government of India and the traditionally pro-government newspaper, *The Pioneer* of Lucknow. A new editor, Desmond Young, had started to write a series of articles which were highly critical of the government's proceedings.[278] Haig concluded that the government's position needed to be defended once again even if this had to be in private, and set about doing so with much zeal.

I see that the Pioneer has joined the ranks of the Congress papers [he inveighed to its proprietor Sir J.P. Srivastava and to Young as well] . . . I cannot suppose that anyone who . . . has followed . . . the history of the last few years and the tactics of Mr. Gandhi would suppose [that a settlement with him] could have any other result than that of re-establishing the authority of Congress . . . No one who forms part of the administrative machinery of the country could contemplate without grave disquiet any prospect of the conditions which prevailed two years ago being renewed . . . The great merit about the policy which has been maintained since January 1932 has been that it has been consistent, and that the public generally, and particularly the loyalist section of it, have known precisely where they stood. Gandhi's action was clearly designed to cause Government to vacillate, and had it not been made perfectly clear immediately by the official communique (which I can quite understand having struck you as being rather 'aggressive' in tone), that that policy remained unchanged, the general effect throughout the country would have been most unfortunate. It cannot, I think, be denied that conditions are now vastly better than they were when the present policy was inaugurated, and it seems commonsense that Government should not allow themselves to be jockeyed out of it.[279]

Young had little difficulty in replying. Prisoners, he agreed, need not have been released immediately, but some delay in order to see how the Congress leaders would respond, and some acknowledgement that the temporary calling off of civil disobedience was 'evidence of a desire for reconciliation', would not have been amiss; while to respond in the way that the Government had done 'when the man will probably be dead within three weeks' was, he said, 'unnecessarily brutal'.[280]

It is not a sign of weakness [he went on] to be ordinarily polite to an individual who is, after all, regarded with respect by most hindus . . . whether or not Mr

---

[278] E.g. 'A Last Chance for Generosity', 30 Apr., 'A Lost Opportunity', 11 May, 'On a Question of Tactics', 18 May, see also *The Pioneer*, 6, 8, 12, 13, 28 May, 7 June, 17, 19 July 1933. Between 10 May and 7 June no fewer than eighteen letters flew back and forth, H.Poll.85/33.
[279] Extracts from Haig to Srivastava, 13 May 1933, and Stephens to Young, 10 May 1933, H.Poll.85/33.   [280] Young to Stephens, 10 May 1933, ibid.

Gandhi's gesture was sincere . . . it would have been better tactics to acknowledge it politely, with whatever reservations, than to reject it in a manner which has, to my knowledge, offended Indians of all shades of opinion. The tone of the communique seemed to me to put Government morally in the wrong, however much they may have been technically and practically in the right.[281]

A similar view, he noted, had been taken by the *Manchester Guardian*, *The Spectator*, the *New Statesman*, and *The Times of India*.[282] Once more the duality in British imperial thinking was quite vividly exposed.

Gandhi meantime pursued his three weeks' fast to the end. Whilst at the outset there were a number of meetings across the country in its support, a hush soon settled across the land.[283] As early as 14 May there was a strong rumour that he had died. The Government of India ordered that no official notice should be taken of this if it occurred.[284] When he then started to recuperate it was soon evident that he was greatly exhausted.[285] Aney's original suspension of civil disobedience had therefore to be extended till the end of July.[286] It was soon clear too that, while he had succeeded in entrenching his position at the centre of public attention, the chief purpose of his fast had been entirely aborted. Neither the Orthodox nor the Harijan leaders were assuaged,[287] and the supreme irony was that the prime consequence of the exchanges that occurred at the time of his release, that were designed on both sides to fasten attention on the Harijan issue, was to bring the issue of civil disobedience back to a centre-stage position once again.

Nevertheless for the Government of India his fast and the further suspension of civil disobedience gave them a breathing space which they had not really had since 1931. Despite the drumming they had received, there was, moreover, now one major difference in their position. They had successfully cast off the coils which had been wound around them by Gandhi and the Cabinet.[288] That meant they had an opportunity to undertake careful contingency planning of a kind they had not been able to do since their duel with Gandhi began; and they now made good use of

---

[281] Young to Stephens, 10, 24 May 1933, ibid.
[282] *The Times* (London) was privately critical too, Brown to Stephens, 8 June 1933, H.Poll.44/57/33.
[283] See V's weekly reports to SoS for May, June, July 1933, H.Poll.3/1/33.
[284] HD to Punjab, 15 May 1933, H.Poll.44/57/33.
[285] E.g. Gandhi to Asaf Ali, 26 June 1933, Gandhi to Mirabehn, 6 July 1933, *CWMG* 55, pp. 221, 251.
[286] Willingdon to Hoare, tel., 18 June 1933, H.Poll.3/1/33.
[287] For Harijan–Sanatanist conflict, see Willingdon to Hoare, tel., 21 May 1933, ibid.
[288] Willingdon to Hoare, tel., 1 July 1933, TwP 12.

their time.[289] As always they needed to tread the narrow space between what was essential to the maintenance of the British Raj in India and what was acceptable to their mentors in London.[290]

They began by reaffirming their basic stand.[291] On 25 May they sent a letter to provincial governments – which was promptly leaked to the press[292] – in which they reiterated their continuing refusal to negotiate with the Mahatma. Since civil disobedience had only been 'temporarily' suspended, and since Gandhi had 'expressly declared his views ... to have undergone no change whatever', the 'value to Government of offer made' by him, they avowed, '. . . is *nil*'. Since civil disobedience 'had manifestly failed', by demanding 'peace' he had simply been trying to revivify his movement – which 'was precisely what happened in 1931'. His principal concern seemed to be to revert to the Gandhi–Irwin Pact, 'the assumption being that Government has already forgotten the lessons that experiment taught them'. The only 'peace' that would be in any way acceptable to them would, they said, have to be preceded by an unequivocal Congress declaration indicating a 'definite determination to substitute constitutional for unconstitutional methods', and of that there was as yet no sign.[293]

Characteristically they nevertheless sought at the same time to mitigate the conflict as best they could.[294] Earlier in the year they had accepted a call from the Cabinet to speed up their release of Congress prisoners.[295] By May 1933 the numbers had fallen to around 11,000 and there was now some debate in the Viceroy's Council about how they should proceed further.[296] Several members believed that only an unconditional undertaking to desist from illegal activity would justify further releases,[297]

---

[289] Over the ensuing months they carefully collected, for example, successive statements by Gandhi and Nehru, H.Poll.4/11/33.

[290] Hoare to Willingdon, tel., 27 June 1933, Willingdon to Hoare, 1 July 1933, TwP 12; but see also Stephens (Director, Public Information) to Brown (*The Times*), 26 May 1933, Brown to Stephens, 8 June 1933, Stephens to Haig, and Haig's Note, 24 June 1933, H.Poll.44/57/33.

[291] For various expressions of their determination see e.g. Willingdon to Hoare, 26 May 1933, TwP 6; Willingdon to Hoare, tel., 1 July 1933, TwP 12; Hallett's Note, 6 June 1933, H.Poll.44/57/33; Hallett to LGs, 26 June 1933, H.Poll.4/2/33.

[292] Bracken to Hallett, 2 June 1933, and Notes, H.Poll.44/57/33.

[293] Hallett to LGs, 25 May 1933, ibid.; see also Trivedi's note, 24 May 1933, H.Poll.4/7/33, and Willingdon to Hoare, 28 May 1933, TwP 6.

[294] For a retrospective comment see Willingdon to Hoare, 15 July 1933, TwP 12.

[295] SoS to GoI, tel., 20 Feb. 1933; HD to LGs, 9 Feb. 1933; Hallett to LGs, 25 Feb. 1933 (also H.Poll.10/2/33); Statement concerning the anticipated numbers in jail between January and August 1933, nd, H.Poll.4/2/33.

[296] On this whole issue for Apr.–June 1933 see H.Poll.3/10/33. Hallett first reviewed the position in his note, 14 May 1933, H.Poll.4/2/33.

[297] About 20 per cent of prisoners had already done so, Husain to Haig, 7 June 1933, H.Poll.3/11/33.

but Sir Fazli Husain argued that the great majority ought to be set free as 'a fair and good response to the gesture by Congress'.[298] Here the Home Department decided to cleave to the middle. Provincial governments, they declared, should retain their freedom of action, but wherever possible they should speed up their releases.[299] 'The principle to be borne in mind throughout', Hallett specified, 'is that there is no amnesty, and that the action to be taken depends on local conditions'.[300] That policy seems to have worked quite successfully, and it was not long before most Civil Disobedience prisoners were released without either a general jail delivery or a victory claim by the Congress. As a consequence the issue was effectively removed from public attention.[301]

But all this was only a beginning. Once they narrowed their focus they first considered what they would do if the Congress leaders out of jail tried to hold a meeting. They quickly rejected Gandhi's reiterated suggestion that until all of the Working Committee had been released, Congress could not possibly bring an end to civil disobedience.[302] That, Hallett stated, 'would involve a recreation of the situation at the beginning of 1931' – of which he would not hear. Back in April 1933 (as we have seen) they had decided that if an informal meeting of Congress leaders was called, they would not prevent this. That decision was now reaffirmed and provincial governments were told to 'take no notice of the participators in the meeting'.[303]

Next they discussed what they should do if they had to confront Gandhi once again. They were much concerned that he might now adopt some new procedure for which they would be quite unprepared.[304] They therefore remained upon a constant *qui vive*.[305] At the same time they discussed with the Government of Bombay the proposal that if he attempted to revive civil disobedience, they should, instead of detaining him under emergency powers, arraign him under the ordinary law. It might be difficult, they said, to argue that an emergency still existed. However, by prohibiting him from visiting certain areas, and then, when he inevitably

---

[298] He had first raised the question in April, Husain to Haig, 5 Apr. 1933; see also Hallett's Note, 21 Apr., Hallett to Husain, 22 Apr., Husain to Haig, 7 June 1933, H.Poll.3/11/33; Hallett's Notes, 6, 14 June 1933, H.Poll.44/57/33; Husain to Hallett, and Hallett's Note, 20 June 1933, H.Poll.4/2/33.   [299] Hallett to LGs, 26 June 1933, ibid.

[300] Hallett's Notes, 2 July 1933, H.Poll.10/2/33, 1 July 1933, H.Poll.4/7/33, and 4 July 1933, H.Poll.44/57/33, 4/2/33.

[301] e.g. Clay (U.P.) to Hallett, 1, 22 July 1933, ibid.; Willingdon to Hoare, tel., 15 July 1933, TwP 12.

[302] Set out in his Statement suspending Civil Disobedience movement, 8 May 1933, *CWMG* 55, p. 159.   [303] Hallett's note, 14 June 1933, H.Poll.44/57/33.

[304] E.g. Maxwell to Hallett, 5 June 1933, ibid.

[305] E.g. Hallett's notes 14, 15, 16 June, 4 July 1933, ibid.; Haig's Note, 16 July 1933, H.Poll.117/1933; HD to Bombay, 18 July 1933, H.Poll.3/17/33.

refused, formally sentencing him to a definite period of imprisonment, they would not only be able 'to emphasise that what we are doing . . . is merely the enforcement of the law', but since he would now be a convicted prisoner they would be under 'no necessity to continue the facilities . . . which he enjoys at present in connection with the untouchability movement'.[306]

The Bombay Government was not persuaded: 'proof of an offence', they advised, '. . . is by no means a simple matter'; 'Mr Gandhi would have the whole strength of the Bombay Bar at his disposal.' There would be distinct 'possibilities of a prolonged trial and a subsequent appeal accompanied by public excitement, a press campaign and concomitant tactics'. It would be better to detain him again under the emergency powers since 'the public are . . . by now so familiar with this procedure that it is not likely to give rise to special comment in Mr. Gandhi's case'.[307] Whilst taking the point,[308] the Government of India evidently concluded – to judge from their subsequent actions – that these difficulties could be avoided.

They discussed too what they would do if Gandhi again sought an interview with the Viceroy. Upon this they soon found themselves at odds with Hoare, who was very concerned about the possible reactions amongst Indians and in Britain to any further maladroit move against him. If Gandhi made 'an unconditional and unprovocative request', he insisted, it must not be abruptly rejected.[309] With this the Government was far from happy. Till civil disobedience had been completely renounced, they believed, all such requests should be refused.[310] They did allow, however, that should this occur the Viceroy 'could not refuse an interview to Gandhi to discuss constitutional but not administrative questions'.[311]

Such finely tuned contingency planning was then supplemented by face-to-face talks between Haig and several Governors,[312] more especially, in view of Gandhi's presence there, with the Governor of Bombay and his colleagues. Sir Patrick Kelly, Bombay's Police Commissioner, believed that although Gandhi still had 'a tremendous hold over the

---

[306] Hallett to Maxwell, 27 May 1933, H.Poll.44/57/33.

[307] Maxwell to Hallett, 5 June 1933, ibid.

[308] Hallett to Maxwell, Hallett to Peel, 9 June 1933, Haig's (second) Note (also H.Poll.3/17/33, 10/2/33, 117/33), 10 July 1933, H.Poll.44/57/33.

[309] Hoare to Willingdon, 6 July 1933, TwP 12.

[310] Hoare to Maxwell, 27 May 1933, Hallett's Note, 14 June 1933, H.Poll.44/57/33.

[311] Willingdon to Hoare, tel., 8 July 1933, TwP 12; Hallett's Note, 4 July 1933, H.Poll.44/57/33.

[312] For the discussions with Gs of Punjab and NWFP see Hallett's Note, 4 July 1933, H.Poll.4/2/33, 44/57/33, and G. UP, Haig's Note, 16 July 1933, ibid., H.Poll.117/33.

people in Bombay, and . . . would retain this', not only were they 'generally tired of civil disobedience, and thoroughly discouraged', Congress
would not 'be able to work up any new enthusiasm on a new programme'.
For its part the Government of Bombay did not think Congress would
call off civil disobedience unconditionally, but they did not think he
wanted to return to jail either, and in general they found the situation
'extremely satisfactory'. All the same they had no doubt that there was

a definite danger of Mr Gandhi and the Congress restoring their position if we
give them any chance, and His Excellency the Governor is strongly opposed to
taking any risks in this matter.[313]

It was with a mind considerably resharpened in these ways that the
Government of India finally stalked Gandhi in the dramatic final round of
their year-long duel with him in July and August 1933.

By mid summer 1933 there was much disillusion in Congress circles
about civil disobedience, and an increasingly weary concern to call it
off.[314] Yet there was also a determination to see that this was done with
dignity. On 3 July Jamnadas Dwarkadas saw Haig and asked him if all the
remaining political prisoners would be set free if Civil Disobedience were
to be called off. But Haig would not be drawn.[315] During the weeks which
Gandhi required to recover his strength he himself never flinched. Keenly
aware that 'the peace of the cemetery' stretched across the land, his
commitment to civil disobedience stood as firm as ever.[316]

There is no intention whatsoever on the part of the Indian Civil Service to give up
power [he said] . . . nor . . . on the part of Mr Baldwin and Sir Samuel Hoare.
[There was, he went on] no cause for despair, for there is the certainty of the final
triumph.[317]

Yet in major contrast with the previous autumn, his political ingenuity
now failed him quite disastrously. Whilst the Government of India had
taken the opportunity of the interlude to refurbish its likely tactics, he all
but entirely failed to do so. Although he came up with two new ploys (and
may well have considered a third), neither of which cut very much ice, for
the rest he clearly intended to rely upon three of his old, much used
weapons, none of which was now likely to lay the British low. Against all of
them they were much better armed than before.

---

[313] Haig's Notes on his visit to Bombay, 9 July 1933, H.Poll.4/2/33, 117/33; two Notes, 10
July 1933, ibid., 10/2/33, 44/57/33 (the second also in H.Poll.3/17/33).
[314] E.g. Sri Prakash to Sita Ram, 20 May 1933, NMML, Sita Ram Papers 29 (106);
Willingdon to Hoare, tels., 1, 15 July 1933, TwP 12.
[315] Haig's Note, 9 July 1933, H.Poll.4/2/33, 117/33; Willingdon to Hoare, tel., 1 July 1933,
TwP 12.   [316] Talks with Rajagopalachari, 1–2 June 1933, *CWMG* 55, pp. 445–8.
[317] Gandhi to Andrews, 15 June 1933, ibid. pp. 196–9.

On 12–14 July a considerable group of Congress leaders who were out of jail held a private three-day meeting with him in Poona.[318] In accordance with the government's decision not to interfere, this was allowed to proceed. During the first two days there was much support for the abandonment of civil disobedience. But Gandhi would not hear of this. 'I would rather', he said, 'be reduced to dust than surrender'. What he wanted was an 'honourable settlement'. Should that not be forthcoming mass civil disobedience, he recognised, might no longer be feasible, but that did not mean that it should be abandoned altogether. On the third day he accordingly put forward his alternative proposal for 'individual' civil disobedience,[319] which, he said, anyone who was ready to do so could embark upon.[320] That was his first new ploy. The meeting meekly fell in behind him.[321]

Thereupon he unsheathed his first well-worn weapon:

will His Excellency grant interview with a view to exploring possibilities of peace?

he wired to Willingdon on 15 July.[322] Couched in these terms it could only provoke a swift rebuff. During the immediately preceding days the differences between the Cabinet and the Government of India over the response to be given to any such approach had led Hoare (deeply concerned about the possible reactions both in Britain and amongst Indians to any further clumsy move) to draw a fine line between a call by Gandhi for negotiations, 'and the more likely alternative of his simply asking for an interview'.[323] Since Gandhi's request was framed in the former sense the potentially disruptive effects of this distinction were never tested, and with no more than a minor amendment Hoare readily agreed to Willingdon's reply[324] that since civil disobedience had not been called off no such interview could be granted.[325]

Gandhi expatiated on the distress he felt at his appeal for peace being

---

[318] For a list of major figures released see Note, 12 June 1933, H.Poll.4/4/33; Hallett's Note, 14 June 1933, H.Poll.44/57/33; Bombay FR mid July 1933, H.Poll.18/8/33; V to SoS, tel., 15 July 1933, H.Poll.3/1/33. For Gandhi's invitation see Circular Letter 2 July 1933, *CWMG* 55, p. 235.

[319] Talks with Rajagopalachari, 1–2 June 1933, ibid. pp. 445–8.

[320] Speeches at Leaders' Conference, Poona, 12, 14 July 1933, ibid. pp. 262, 265–6

[321] Bombay to HD, tel., 14 July 1933, H.Poll.44/57/33; V to SoS, two tels., 15 July 1933, H.Poll.3/17/33; Bombay FR, mid July 1933, H.Poll.18/8/33.

[322] Gandhi to PSV, 15 July 1933, *CWMG* 55, p. 264, H.Poll.3/17/33.

[323] Hoare to Willingdon, tels., 11, 12 July 1933, Willingdon to Hoare, tel., 13 July 1933, TwP 12.

[324] Willingdon to Hoare, tel., 15 (2), 16 July 1933, Hoare to Willingdon, tel., 16 July 1933, ibid.

[325] PSV to Gandhi, tel., 16 July 1933, *CWMG* 55, p. 264; on its receipt see Intelligence Secret Report, 15 July 1933, H.Poll.3/17/33.

rebuffed,[326] and repeated his request.[327] This time Willingdon was blunt.

His Excellency had hoped the position of the Government was plain [the Private Secretary to the Viceroy cabled back on 17 July] . . . there can be no question of the Government holding conversations with a representative of an association which has not abandoned [its civil disobedience] movement.[328]

That put paid to any possibility of a meeting between the two men, and on 22 July Aney proceeded to make a formal declaration suspending mass civil disobedience, but authorising individual civil disobedience in its place.[329]

Gandhi then went to Ahmedabad[330] where the personal relations in his Ashram had by now fallen into great disarray.[331] During the next few days the Government of India became unnerved by a rumour that he planned to despatch forty to sixty of its members across India to fast unto death in protest against the government's actions.[332] But that proved to be quite unfounded. Instead Gandhi – clearly concerned to retain his moral ascendancy – then produced his second novel ploy by announcing that as so many others had made sacrifices in the national cause he would do so too – by closing his Ashram, and handing all of its land to the government.[333] Then in very evident replication of his Dandi march in 1930 he unsheathed his second old weapon, and on 30 July announced that on

---

[326] He had never been very hopeful, but he was vexed that the Government should have taken notice of confidential discussions in Poona, Gandhi to Andrews, 15 June 1933, Interviews to the Press, 18, 30 July 1933, Interview to Associated Press, 19 July 1933, *CWMG* 55, pp. 197, 274, 332, 280–1.

[327] Gandhi to PSV, tel., 16 July 1933, ibid. pp. 270–1, H.Poll.3/17/33.

[328] PSV to Gandhi, tel., 17 July 1933, *CWMG* 55, p. 271; on the leaders' quite mistaken expectations that it would be 'reasonable' see Intelligence Secret Report, 18 July 1933, H.Poll.3/17/33.

[329] Aney's Statement, 22 July 1933, Gandhi's Statement on Aney's Statement, [26 July 1933] *CWMG* 55, pp. 450–1, 295–301; HD to Bombay, tel., 18 July 1933, Bombay to HD, tel., 20 July 1933, HD to LGs, tel., 23 July 1933, H.Poll.3/17/33.

[330] Bombay to HD, tel., 20 July 1933, ibid.

[331] District Magistrate, Ahmedabad to Bombay, 27 July 1933, ibid., *CWMG* 54, 55 passim.

[332] CID Poona, 2 tels., 18 July 1933, Williamson's Note (Director, Intelligence Bureau), 19 July 1933, Bombay to HD, tel., 20 July 1933, Hallett's Note, 20 July 1933, HD to Bombay, tel., 21, 23 July 1933, Bombay to HD, tel., 22 July 1933, V to SoS, tel., 27 July 1933, H.Poll.3/17/33; Hallett to UP and NWFP, 18 July 1933, H.Poll.4/2/33. There was also a suggestion that he would embark on a 'penitential fast to death', UP to HD, 27 July 1933, and Hallett's and Haig's Notes, 31 July 1933, H.Poll.4/10/33.

[333] Gandhi to Bajaj, 22 July 1933, Interview to Associated Press, 25 July 1933, Gandhi to Home Sec. Bombay, 26 July 1933, Interview with *The Hindu*, 26 July 1933, Interview with *Daily Herald*, 27 July 1933, *CWMG* 55, pp. 289, 294–5, 301–4, 310–11, 315; Bombay to HD, tel., 25 July 1933, H.Poll.3/17/33; Hallett Note, 2 Aug., on Bombay letter, 30 July 1933, H.Poll.3/17/33.

1 August he would leave his Ashram with his associates[334] and march to the neighbouring village of Ras and there call for volunteers to begin his individual civil disobedience campaign.[335]

The Government of India stood ready for him.[336] The Director of the Intelligence Bureau and the Government of Bombay had argued some days earlier that he should immediately be arrested. Haig and Hallett generally concurred,[337] but, absolutely determined not to be wrong-footed once again, they decided to wait for exactly the right psychological moment.[338] So soon, however, as he issued his 30 July statement they promptly decided that he must be stopped before he left Ahmedabad on 1 August, and immediately put their contingency plans into operation.[339]

Away in Indonesia 1 August was the day on which for the second time the Dutch arrested Sukarno and this time exiled him for life. A few hours earlier, on the evening of 31 July, Gandhi was arrested too, along with thirty-six of his followers.[340] Speedily arraigned before the District Magistrate of Ahmedabad,[341] he was despatched to Poona, and at 9 am on 4 August was set free under an order confining his movements to Poona City.[342] That he inevitably refused, whereupon he was rearrested for disobeying a court order and was then formally sentenced – as he had never yet been during these civil disobedience years – to a carefully crafted twelve months' imprisonment.[343] Although given the usual

---

[334] Although as late as 27 July he said he had not decided 'what definite steps will be taken', and still seemed uncertain two days later (Interview with *Times of India*, 27 July 1933, Interview with Associated Press, 29 July 1933, *CWMG* 55, pp. 316, 325) the GoI were forewarned, Bombay to HD, tel., 25 July 1933, V to SoS, tel., 26 July 1933, HD to PSV, tel., 28 July 1933, H.Poll.3/17/33.

[335] Statement to Associated Press, Gandhi to Home Sec. Bombay, and 'Appeal to the People of Gujarat', 30 July 1933, *CWMG* 55, pp. 326–9.

[336] Haig's notes, 10 July 1933, H.Poll.3/17/33, 10/2/33, 117/33, 44/57/33; HD to UP and NWFP, 18 July 1933, H.Poll.4/2/33; HD to Bombay, tel., 23 July 1933, Bombay to HD, 29 July 1933, H.Poll.3/17/33; Haig's Notes, 24 July 1933, H.Poll.34/7/33; Hallett's Notes, 27, 31 July 1933, Haig's Note, 31 July 1933, H.Poll.4/10/33.

[337] Williamson's Notes, 19, 21 July 1933, Haig's Note, 19 July 1933, Haig to Hallett, 20 July 1933, Hallett's Note 20 July 1933, PSV to HD, tel., 29 July 1933, H.Poll.3/17/33.

[338] Haig's Note, 19 July 1933, HD to PSV, tel., 28 July 1933, ibid.

[339] They saw the 'full statement' by 28 July, HD to PSV, tel., 28 July 1933, PSV to HD, Bombay to HD, HD to Bombay, tels., 29 July 1933; V to SoS, tel., 30 July 1933; SoS to V, tel., 30 July 1933, ibid.   [340] V to SoS, tel., 1 Aug. 1933, ibid.

[341] Statement before District Magistrate, Ahmedabad, 1 Aug. 1933, *CWMG* 55, p. 336.

[342] Order restraining Gandhi's movements, 4 Aug. 1933, H.Poll.3/17/33, *CWMG* 55, pp. 452–3; Bombay to HD, tel., 5 Aug. 1933, H.Poll.3/17/33.

[343] Haig pressed for this procedure, and had originally suggested three months; however, the Bombay Government 'had always pressed for deterrent sentences and did not wish to see any exception in the case of Mr Gandhi', so twelve months it was: Haig's Notes, 10 July 1933, ibid., H.Poll.4/2/33, 10/2/33, 117/33, 44/57/33. See also Hallett's Note, 27 July 1933, on UP to HD, 25 July 1933, H.Poll.4/10/33.

opportunity to address the court he made no attempt to replicate his trial speech of 1922.[344]

So soon, however, as he was back again in jail he immediately demanded that he should be granted all the facilities he had previously enjoyed for his Harijan campaign.[345] There was some delay whilst the government considered his request, whereupon he unleashed his third old weapon, and told his jailors he would start to fast if by 14 August his demands had not been met.[346]

Both the Governments of Bombay and of India insisted that as a convicted prisoner he should not this time be granted any special privileges.[347] They were confident, moreover, that in view of the widespread opposition in India to both his Harijan and individual civil disobedience campaigns they could now hold the line against him.[348] Not for the first time, however, their masters believed differently, and as they all went down to the wire the duality in the British position was exposed yet again. 'My main concern', Hoare wired to Willingdon – Gandhi's success in exploiting the ambivalence of the British corrosively at work once again – 'is that it should not be open to anyone to say we have repressed Gandhi's work for social reform'.[349] Hoare approved, however, a reduction in the extent of the facilities previously granted to him, and, to the relief of the Government of India, declared that he would stand firm upon that.[350]

Tired and at the end of his tether – subject, moreover, to mounting public criticism for the course he had taken[351] – Gandhi now fell headlong into the traps the British had set.[352] On 16 August – so finely honed

[344] Statements 3, 4 Aug., 'Trial at Poona', 4 Aug. 1933, *CWMG* 55, pp. 340–3; Bombay to HD, 5 Aug. 1933, H.Poll.3/17/33; V to SoS, tel., 6 Aug. 1933, H.Poll.3/1/33.

[345] He had taken it for granted these would be allowed him, Associated Press interview, 28 July 1933; Gandhi to Advani, 1 Aug. 1933, Gandhi to Martin, 5, 7 Aug., Gandhi to Home Sec., Bombay, 4, 6, 8, 10 Aug. 1933, *CWMG* 55, pp. 319, 338, 344, 346–50.

[346] Gandhi to Home Sec., Bombay, 14 Aug., Gandhi to Martin, 14, 15, 16 Aug. 1933, ibid. pp. 353–6. For the details to this point see Bombay to HD, 16 Aug. 1933, H.Poll.18/17/33.   [347] See Haig's Note, 2 Dec. 1933, H.Poll.4/19/33.

[348] HD to Bombay, tel., 5 Aug. 1933, and subsequent items, 11 Aug. 1933, esp. Bombay to SoS, tel., 16 Aug. 1933, H.Poll.3/17/33.   [349] SoS to V, tel., 11 Aug. 1933, ibid.

[350] SoS to V, tel., 15 Aug. 1933; V to SoS, tels. 16, 18 Aug. 1933, ibid. The V's Council accepted this way of proceeding, Haig's Note on SoS to V, tel., 11 Aug., V to SoS, tel., 13 Aug., Bombay to SoS, 16 Aug. 1933, ibid.

[351] Interview to the Press, and Interview to *The Hindu*, 18 July 1933, Interviews to Associated Press, 19, 29 July 1933, Statement on Aney's Statement, [26 July 1933], Gandhi to Nehru, 14 Sept. 1933, Sastri to Gandhi, 27 Aug. 1933, Gandhi to Sastri, 30 Aug. 1933, *CWMG* 55, pp. 273–7, 280–1, 324–5, 295–301, 426–30, 455–6, 381–2; FRs end July 1933, H.Poll.18/8/33; V to SoS, tel., 30 July 1933, H.Poll.3/1/33; B & O, Assam, Madras, CP, and Bombay (esp. App. A and B) to HD, variously 1–11 Aug. 1933, H.Poll.4/10/33.

[352] E.g. V to SoS, tel., 6 Aug. 1933, H.Poll.3/1/33; Punjab to HD, 8 Aug. 1933, Bombay to HD (and Hallett's Note 14 Aug.) 11 Aug. 1933, H.Poll.4/10/33; though see V to SoS, tel., 13 Aug. 1933, H.Poll.3/1/33, and FR for mid Aug. 1933, H.Poll.18/9/33 for the episodes which did occur.

were now the terms of the conflict between the Mahatma and the Raj, and so sphinx-like the deal the British decreed – that he at first accepted Hoare's terms, and then, realising they did not meet his demands, changed his mind, and began his fast after all.[353]

Thereupon the Government of India sprang the first of their traps.[354] They issued[355] a long and deeply scornful statement in which they declared that: 'It was noticeable that when Mr. Gandhi was at liberty he did not appear to devote the major part of his time or attention to [his Harijan] movement', and then drew political blood:

If Mr. Gandhi now feels [they stated] . . . that life ceases to interest him if he may not do Harijan service without let or hindrance, the Government is prepared, provided Mr Gandhi is willing to abandon all civil disobedience activities and incitements to set him at liberty at once so that he can devote himself wholly . . . to the cause of social reform.[356]

It was a lacerating thrust. On 18 and 19 August Charlie Andrews met Gandhi and pleaded with him to accept the government's terms, but he adamantly refused.[357] Then on 20 August, as his health deteriorated, they removed him to the nearby hospital[358] where the climax came on 23 August. On his prison doctor then advising that 'he is entering the danger zone',[359] the government unleashed their two final, pulverising thrusts. Once more they set him free unconditionally,[360] and then in an utterly disdainful manner stated they had done so because

Mr Gandhi was apparently determined to commit suicide. Government was not prepared to allow him to die in jail nor to order forcible feeding to save his life.[361]

It was an altogether himalayan put-down and he was quite devastated.[362] His fast had aroused little or no public stir.[363] By releasing him in

---

[353] Gandhi to Martin, 16, 17 Aug. 1933, *CWMG*, 55, pp. 356–8; see also Bombay to HD, tel., 16 Aug. 1933, H.Poll.3/17/33.

[354] Bombay to HD, 5 Aug. 1933, Hallett's Note, 8 Aug. 1933, HD to Bombay, tel., 23 July 1933, Bombay to HD, tel., 26 July 1933, ibid.; Hallett's and Haig's Notes, 31 July 1933, on UP to HD, 27 July 1933, H.Poll.4/10/33.

[355] GoI communique, 17 Aug. 1933, H.Poll.3/17/33 was a brief preliminary one.

[356] GoI communique, 18 Aug. 1933, ibid., H.Poll.22 84/33, *CWMG* 55, pp. 453–4. This was commended by the SoS, SoS to V, tel., 19 Aug. 1933, but strongly criticised by Andrews, Andrews to Haig, 23 Aug. 1933, H.Poll.3/17/33.

[357] Gandhi to Home Sec., Bombay, 19 Aug. 1933, *CWMG* 55, pp. 361–2; Bombay to HD, tel., 19 Aug. 1933, H.Poll.3/17/33.

[358] Bombay to HD, tels., 20, 21, 22 Aug. 1933, ibid.

[359] Bombay to HD, tel., 23 Aug. 1933, ibid.; Advice to Friends [before 3 Sept. 1933], *CWMG* 55, p. 393; Andrews to Tagore, 31 Aug. 1933, AP.

[360] Bombay to HD, tel., 23 Aug. 1933; for the decision to proceed in this way see Bombay to HD, 5 Aug., HD to Bombay, 8 Aug. 1933, H.Poll.3/17/33.

[361] *Times of India*, 26 Aug. 1933.

[362] Tel. to Tagore, 23 Aug. 1933, 'The Breath of My Life', *Harijan* 26 Aug., Gandhi to Tyabji, 24 Aug., Gandhi to Patel, 24 Aug. 1933, *CWMG* 55, pp. 367, 366, 368, 370; Bombay to HD, tel., 27 Aug. 1933, H.Poll.3/17/33.

[363] V to SoS, 9, 20 Aug. 1933, H.Poll.3/1/33; FR for late Aug. 1933, H.Poll.18/9/33.

this humiliating manner the Government of India had finally trounced him as they had never managed to do before.

When Gandhi was released last August [Hallett, the Home Secretary later crowed] his prestige was not increased, nor is there anything to show that Government was regarded as having acted in a weak or timid manner ... The preventive effect of punishment has thus been secured, without any loss of prestige by Government.[364]

Gandhi for his own part declared: 'This discharge is a matter of no joy to me.' 'The most unexpected event of my life has happened.' 'Who knows what God means by this play?' 'My release has placed me in a most embarrassing position.'[365] Andrews attempted to persuade the Government of India of his basic good intentions, but was brusquely swept aside.[366] With three swift resounding blows they had finally dislodged him from the high moral ground he had so skilfully commandeered just a year before. There was never a greater nadir in his fortunes.

Yet, it was not the end of the story. During the next three weeks Gandhi was at a loss what to do next.[367]

As a rule [he confessed], during my long course of public service the next moment's step has been clear to me, but since my unexpected release from prison ... darkness has surrounded me.[368]

Yet, in an altogether mesmerising way, after a quite fatal lapse of three months, his extraordinary political ingenuity finally sprang to his rescue once again. After three or four days of talks with Jawaharlal Nehru (who was briefly out of prison) and two or three others,[369] he suddenly saw his way through, and on 14 September 1933 announced that since he would not 'be a willing party to an undignified cat-and-mouse game if the

---

[364] Hallett's Note, 16 July 1934, H.Poll.3/9/34. For a poignant reflection on this attitude see Andrews to Haig, 10 Nov. 1933, H.Poll.169/33.

[365] Press interview, 25 Aug., 'The Breath of my Life', 23 Aug., 'I shall dance to his tune', 27 Aug., Press statement, 14 Sept. 1933, also Gandhi to Tyabji, Gandhi to Patel, 24 Aug., Interview to Associated Press, 2 Sept. 1933, Gandhi to Alam, 2 Sept. 1933, *CWMG* 55, pp. 373–6, 366, 378, 425, 392, 389.

[366] Bombay to HD, tels., 30 Aug., 4 Sept. 1933, H.Poll.33/17/33; see especially Haig's Note, 26 Oct. 1933, H.Poll.169/33. The GoI was quite prepared to rearrest Gandhi if necessary, but decided that by confining him to a designated bungalow rather than putting him back in prison, and leaving him free to pursue his Harijan campaign, they could then withstand any further threat by him to fast, V to SoS, tel., 1 Sept., SoS to V, 2 Sept. 1933, H.Poll.3/17/33; Haig's Note, 2 Dec. 1933, H.Poll.4/19/33.

[367] Andrews to Tagore, 31 Aug. 1933, AP; Interview to Associated Press, 2 Sept. 1933, *CWMG* 55, p. 392; Bombay to HD, tel., 4 Sept. 1933, H.Poll.3/17/33.

[368] Statement to the Press, 14 Sept. 1933, *CWMG* 55, p. 425.

[369] Nehru to Gandhi, 13 Sept. 1933, Gandhi to Nehru, 14 Sept. 1933, ibid. pp. 457–60, 425–30; Indian News Agency tel., 12 Sept. 1933; Bombay's FR for mid Sept. 1933, H.Poll.18/10/33.

Government have any such thing in contemplation', he would for the remaining period of his one year's sentence embrace a self-denying ordinance and 'not court imprisonment by offering aggressive civil disobedience'.[370] With this one inspired leap he scrambled back therefore to the moral high ground once again. It was an astonishing reprieve from the very jaws of defeat.

By any standards this intensely personal, elongated duel was a most unusual conflict. Throughout the British played it ambidexterously. They remained quite determined not to forego their political supremacy in India, and had no compunction in using the resources of their police and their prison services to make sure of that. But whilst holding firm to their ultimate power, they nevertheless continuously sought to assuage their opponents by proffering some limited constitutional reforms, and following the collapse of their mid-term settlement with Gandhi allowed themselves to be dragged into a protracted political duel with him in which they endlessly fended off a series of his threats to fast for fear of the catastrophic furore that would follow upon his death in prison. In the end their dexterity paid off. It not only laid Gandhi himself prostrate. It destroyed his civil disobedience movement altogether.[371] That was not, however, without those who had to make the fine decisions having to undergo some grinding debates amongst themselves.

On his side Gandhi ensured that the overwhelming majority of his tens of thousands of supporters conducted his Civil Disobedience campaign without violence, and with consummate skill maximised the opportunities the British gave him to fight his duel with them. At no time did he consider surrender (as we now know Sukarno offered to do at just this time in Indonesia),[372] while like Mao on a much larger scale in these same years in China, he succeeded in defeat in snatching some crucial brands from the burning, so that in the end the honours stood at even. Whilst the Civil Disobedience movement was no more, the integrity of its leader and thus of the Congress under his command emerged intact. Further battles could thus be fought, with the contestants no less evenly matched than before.

---

[370] Statement to the Press, 14 Sept. 1933, *CWMG* 55, pp. 425–6, H.Poll.3/17/33.

[371] For the GoI's monitoring of its final stages and their refusal to take any chances see Haig's Note on interview with Andrews, 26 Oct. 1933, H.Poll.169/33; Bombay to HD, tel., 26 Sept. 1933, V to SoS, tels., and Hallett's (and Trivedi's) Notes, 27 Aug., 1, 3, 10, 17, 24 Sept., 1, 8, 16, 22 Oct., 5 Nov. 1933, H.Poll.3/1/33, FR for Aug. and Sept. 1933, H.Poll.18/9/33; Husain to Haig, 5 Oct., Hallett's Note 6 Oct., Haig to Husain, 7 Oct. 1933 H.Poll.3/11/33; and H.Poll.4/8/33, 4/19/33 passim. They remained on the *qui vive*, e.g. Hallett to Brett, 23 Sept. 1933, ibid. Even in October 1933 they refused to allow the full AICC to meet, H.Poll.4/8/33 passim, though they agreed that the Working Committee could do so in December, HD to CP, tel., 2 Dec. 1933, H.Poll.4/19/33.

[372] Ingleson, *Road to Exile*, pp. 216–22.

Nothing like this occurred in the Philippines; there was no occasion for any such encounter there. Nor was there anything like it in Indonesia and Vietnam. At this stage nationalist leaders in Indonesia were being banished to distant islands for life, whilst lately many of those in Vietnam had been shot down or executed. Whilst the Indian encounter constantly exemplified Gandhi's own exceptional qualities, it endlessly betrayed at the same time the duality-ambiguity-duplicity – according to one's point of view – which lay at the heart of the British position. Without that any such duel would have been quite inconceivable. The persistent two-sidedness of the British once more stamped its distinctive imprint on events.[373]

[373] In his retirement Willingdon looked back on these events: 'we clearly stated', he wrote, 'that our policy was of a dual nature. In the first place to insist on the due observance of the laws of the country and to support our officers whole heartedly in securing this end; and in the second place we stated we would do everything in our power to push forward the new Reform Scheme, but we stated further that the progress of the latter must obviously depend on the peaceful and orderly condition of the country', undated memo, TwP 20.

The road is wide open whereby India can attain to the independence
represented by the Statute of Westminster as quickly as she develops
political parties and constitutional habits strong and wise enough to
carry the strain of all-India government and defence.
Ruling powers and ruling classes have not been known in history to
abdicate willingly.

Lord Lothian to Jawaharlal Nehru, Nehru to Lothian,
December 1935–January 1936

As has been variously noted in earlier chapters, eighteen months before
the Indonesian nationalist leader, Sukarno, was finally exiled ostensibly
for life he was prematurely released from jail on 31 December 1931 after
having been sentenced a year previously to four years' imprisonment for
his nationalist activities. The decision to set him free was taken by the
rather more liberally minded Governor-General de Graeff a few days
before his term ended. By the time it occurred de Graeff had been
replaced by a new Governor-General, de Jonge, 'an unashamed conservative determined to tolerate no nonsense from upstart Indonesian political
agitators', who eventually decided, as we have seen, to arrest him again on
1 August 1933.

It is of considerable interest in the present context that in the course of
the intervening nineteen months not only did a classic debate develop
within the Indonesian national movement as to how it should now
proceed, but that the parameters within which this was set were substantially determined by the new posture in Dutch policy which
Sukarno's release seemed to signify. For while the Dutch remained
absolutely determined to make no move towards meeting the vociferous
demands of Indonesia's nationalist leaders for Indonesia's independence,
they refrained for a while at least from any repression of its nationalist
movement. For a brief period, that is, they played, very much as the
British so often did, an ambidexterous hand. As a consequence
Indonesia's nationalist leaders now had an unexpected opportunity to
embark upon a far greater mobilisation of Indonesia's nationalist forces

than had recently seemed at all feasible. As to how precisely they should proceed became, however, a matter of considerable debate – and as we shall see the debate which took place correlated remarkably closely with that which was to occur three years later in an intriguingly comparable situation in India. In both cases the differences turned in part on some basic ideological differences that were widely prevalent in a number of countries at this time, but it seems as if they turned as well upon the degree of opportunity which each situation gave for the pursuit of two comparably divergent alternative procedures.

In Indonesia the form that the debate took became centred upon a division between Pendidikan Nasional Indonesia Baru (the 'new' PNI party) on the one hand, and its rival party, Partindo, on the other. The differences between the two sides were then aggravated by keen personal rivalry between Indonesia's two major nationalist figures at this time: Mohammed Hatta, who became the principal leader of PNI Baru, and Sukarno, who following his release from prison eventually moved into the leadership ranks of Partindo. Following a long sojourn in the Netherlands prior to his return to Indonesia in August 1932 Hatta had become much attracted to the socialist doctrines which were then circulating in Europe, and at his instance PNI Baru became committed during 1932–3 to conjoining class struggle with the nationalist struggle, and to this end 'concentrated on recruiting and educating a well disciplined cadre and building an organisational structure, rather than on holding spectacular large-scale public meetings'. Partindo on the other hand, with Sukarno eventually in its van, not only rejected any such conjunction between class struggle and the nationalist struggle, but, drawing upon his own exceptional skills as a public orator, set out to create a broadly based Indonesian national movement composed of all levels of Indonesian society, high and low, rich and poor, which through mass action in 'a spontaneous eruption from the masses' would proceed to break the hold of the Dutch.

The debate between these two positions persisted throughout the latter part of 1932 and beyond the middle of 1933 till it was summarily checked by Sukarno's second arrest, and finally killed early in 1934 when Hatta and his associates were arrested too. Thereafter, because of the absolute determination of the Dutch to suppress any nationalist agitation, nationalist mobilisation in Indonesia upon any significant scale became totally out of the question, and it was not until the Japanese conquest of the Netherlands Indies in 1942 that a new era eventually opened up.[1]

---

[1] Ingleson, *Road to Exile*, chs. 6 and 7 (the quotations are from pp. 158, 177, 188); Legge, *Sukarno*, chs. 5 and 6; Rose, *Hatta*, chs. 4 and 5.

During the mid 1930s three debates concerning the strategy which the Indian National Congress should pursue in its long-run conflict with the British became intertwined with each other. One of these closely resembled this Indonesian debate and became of special importance during 1936–7. A second saw a continuation through two further stages of the earlier debate we have already considered in chapter 2 – over whether anything was to be gained by the Indian national movement in accepting the partial constitutional reforms the British had on offer, or not. While a third – which will be considered in the next chapter – concerned the more specific point of whether Congress should accept provincial office under the Government of India Act of 1937, or not. All three debates reached their denouement in India in 1937. Each was deeply coloured by the distinctive ambiguity of the British.

By 1932 the forces arraigned in the second of these three debates differed very greatly in size. On the one side stood tens of thousands of Congressmen under the leadership of Gandhi and his closest lieutenants, Jawaharlal Nehru, Vallabhbhai Patel, Rajendra Prasad, Rajagopalachari, and Abdul Ghaffar Khan, who, confronted by Britain's adamantine opposition to granting India the independence Congress demanded, flung themselves into two successive Civil Disobedience campaigns in two sustained attempts to compel the British to change course. In so doing they displayed an astonishing commitment to Gandhi's doctrines of non-violence and won a great deal of popular support. Since, however, the British possessed all the coercive forces they needed to suppress these movements, large numbers of Congressmen soon languished in jail for many months on end. Their commitment to the course they had chosen remained, however, quite unabated, while the resoluteness they displayed in accepting the incarceration to which they were subjected spoke even more loudly than the pronouncements of their most eloquent leaders of their determination to resist any kind of accommodation with their imperial suppressors as constituting a gross betrayal of India's national interests.

Throughout this period, as indeed both before and after, there was, however, always a small minority of people on the other side who, believing themselves to be no less committed to India's freedom than any Congressman, were deeply convinced that to proceed in the way Congress had chosen to do when the British seemed quite prepared to discuss, and even grant, some constitutional reforms (in a way the Dutch were never prepared to do) constituted a major disservice to India's national cause. Whilst they fully accepted that the British were not going to grant India the independence which it sought within an easily foreseeable future, negotiations with them, they earnestly believed, were much more likely to bring that within sight than the course Congress had espoused.

A particularly cogent expression of this other point of view was put by one of its principal proponents, Sir Tej Bahadur Sapru, at that particularly bleak moment in the history of the Indian national movement, a full year after the Government of India had instituted countrywide emergency rule in January 1932. In a letter to a relatively unknown correspondent from Bihar dated 22 January 1933, Sapru set out the two main points which he and his kind were always concerned to make.

I thank you very much for your letter of 17th instant which has come to me as an agreeable surprise [he began]. I note . . . with satisfaction that you have now become convinced, in the present state of the country, that the methods which have been hitherto pursued will bear no fruit . . . I have never believed that Civil Disobedience movement can bring you nearer Swaraj. It may embarrass the Government and make the task of administration difficult. Indeed it has done all that. But situated as we are with all our differences and with all the weakness inherent in our social system and political organisations I do not think that it can effectively paralyse the Government or bring the Government on to its knees . . . I put it to you frankly that 60000 to 70000 men went to jail this time and a similar number of men went in 1930 and yet what has been the result. Their sufferings and sacrifices which I clearly recognise have neither melted the heart of the British nor wrecked the Government. I do not deny that the activities of the Congress have exercised pressure on the Government but only up to a certain point. Situated, therefore, as we are our only course lies at the present moment in negotiations. When you enter into negotiations you do not always get all that you want. But if you do get a position of vantage you must not lose it . . . I am fully aware that views such as mine are in the circumstances of India extremely unpopular and they give rise to all sorts of suspicions, distrust and ridicule. Nevertheless I hold these views very strongly. I have not concealed them from some of the distinguished leaders of the Congress and I should not hesitate to press my views before others when they come out of jail.

He then turned to a more specific point:

We have no reason to feel alarmed or disappointed [he went on] that the proposed constitution [the British were fashioning by 1933] will give us neither independence, whatever that may mean, nor immediate Dominion Status. We are of course entitled to examine critically the nature of the safeguards and the reservations [in it] . . . Nevertheless it is my conviction that with all these safeguards that if we can send the right sort of men in the Legislative Assembly and the Provincial Councils, that is to say, men who will not hesitate to resign their offices if the interests of the country should require such a course . . . the safeguards will not and cannot interfere with the responsibility of the Ministers. In the constitution of Canada some safeguards exist even today, but they have never prevented the Canadians from working responsible Government. I shall beg of you to note that it is one thing for the Governors and the Governor-General to overrule Indian Ministers at the present moment when they are only a fraction of their

Governments and when there is always an official block and a nominated block ready at hand to support the official point of view. It will be quite another thing when the whole of the Government in the Provinces will be Indian and 7 out of 9 Ministers of the Central Government will be responsible to the Legislature. No Governor and no Viceroy can, in my opinion, easily interfere with the discharge of their responsibility by the Ministers provided of course they are men of the right sort . . . if the right sort of men can be persuaded to go in they will hold such a powerful weapon in their hands that within a few years they can traverse the rest of the ground . . . when they are in possession of the machinery they will be able to achieve much greater success in expanding the constitution than we can at present hope to do. It is for this reason that I am clearly of the opinion that the advanced section of politicians such as the Congressmen should clearly face the situation and take charge of the machinery of Government.[2]

These were potent arguments with which to conjure.

A further and more notable round in this debate came three years later just as the new Government of India Act of 1935 came into operation. In bringing the Act to fruition the British government had held to its earlier promise to institute Responsible Government in the provinces and to establish an All-India Federation at the centre, and had successfully fended off the Conservative 'diehard' attacks against any further reform in India. They had completely failed, however, to assuage the Congress, and had even managed to annoy greatly Sapru and his like as well.[3]

There had been a curtain raiser to this further stage in the debate during 1934 when following the collapse of the second Civil Disobedience movement a number of Congressmen had sought to persuade the Congress to reenter India's legislative politics once again. Amongst those making this case was Rajagopalachari, Gandhi's chief lieutenant in southern India. On 21 April 1934 he wrote to Gandhi

strongly pleading that the parliamentary programme should be done in the name of the Congress . . . It is only if the magic of the Congress name and memory of its past sacrifices are utilized that the tremendous difficulties . . . can be at least hoped to be overcome.[4]

That advice seemed to be vindicated later in 1934 when in the elections to the central Legislative Assembly Congress and its allies secured a 'national triumph'[5] by winning fifty-three of the seventy-five seats open to Indian members.[6] That did not, however, resolve the ongoing debate

---

[2] Sapru to Janakdhari Prasad, 22 Jan. 1933, SP I, 19, P384.

[3] See Prasad's Presidential speech, Bombay Congress, 26 Oct. 1934, *RPCSD*, 1, pp. 237–42.   [4] Rajagopalachari to Gandhi, 21 Apr. 1934, H.Poll.4/4/34.

[5] Pant to Ansari, 25 Nov. 1934, NMML Ansari Papers (which contain details about the election campaign). 'Singularly unfortunate', the Viceroy called it: 'a great triumph for little Gandhi', Willingdon to Hoare, 19, 26 Nov. 1934, TwP8.

[6] *Return showing the results of the General Election for the Legislative Assembly of India, 1934*, 1934, Cmd. 4939, 1935; AICC G9/1934.

between those who saw an unbridgeable gulf here between British imperialism and Indian nationalism,[7] and those who believed that this was nowhere near as wide as was being suggested. Rather, over a year later it fell to two particularly articulate men to give this ongoing debate much the most precise and explicit form that it ever took.

When in 1958 Jawaharlal Nehru compiled his collection of *A Bunch of Old Letters*, he included in it four letters he received during the mid 1930s from the British Liberal peer, Lord Lothian, together with two of his own replies. A few years later when in 1962 he revised an earlier and smaller collection of letters, which had originally been published in 1936, and dropped half a dozen items from it and added four in their place, he seems to have gone out of his way to include extracts from one of these Lothian letters – it was the only item in this smaller collection he did not write himself – along with his own reply. There seems little doubt therefore that he saw his exchange of letters with Lothian during the mid 1930s as being of quite particular importance, privately conducted though it was at the time.[8]

By the latter part of 1935 Nehru was due to be the next President of the Congress. Upon a number of points he and Gandhi differed greatly, but he was now firmly established as the Mahatma's principal younger colleague, the most outstanding of Congress's younger leaders, by far its most articulate spokesman, and both a seasoned nationalist campaigner and a preeminent ex-political prisoner. His correspondent, Philip Kerr, 11th Marquess of Lothian, had originally made his mark as one of the small group of young assistants whom Lord Milner had taken out to South Africa when he had been British High Commissioner there at the turn of the century who came to be known as 'Milner's kindergarten'. Thereafter he was a leading member of the 'Round Table' group which then and later became closely associated with British imperial and later Commonwealth issues.[9] During the First World War and into its immediate aftermath he held the very influential position of Principal Private Secretary to Lloyd George, the British Prime Minister. Subsequently he became a leading member of the British Liberal Party delegation to the

---

[7] E.g. Rajendra Prasad's Congress Presidential Address, 26 Oct. 1934, *RPCSD* 1, pp. 232–49. Essential parts of the text are most accessible in M. Gwyer and A. Appadori, *Speeches and Documents on the Indian Constitution*, Bombay 1957, vol. I, pp. 323–76.

[8] For the text of the letters see Nehru, *Bunch of Old Letters*, pp. 137–51; Nehru, *India's Freedom*, London 1962, pp. 73–93; *SWJN* 7, pp. 49–51, 62–75. Parts of Nehru to Lothian, 17 Jan. 1936, were published in J. Nehru, *India and the World*, London 1936, pp. 177–99.

[9] J.R.M. Butler, *Lord Lothian (Philip Kerr) 1822–1940*, London 1960; J. Turner, ed., *The Larger Idea: Lord Lothian and the Problem of National Sovereignty*, Exeter 1988. For some more on the background here see J.E. Kendle, *The Round Table Movement and Imperial Union*, Toronto 1975.

first two Indian Round Table Conferences; briefly during 1931–2 Under-Secretary of State for India under Sir Samuel Hoare; and in 1932 chairman of the Indian Franchise Committee. Eight years later he was to die whilst serving as British Ambassador to the United States. Having long been involved in the protracted gestation of the Government of India Act of 1935 he was deeply concerned, like so many other interested British politicians at the time, that the Act's provisions for full Responsible Government in the provinces and for an All-India Federation at the centre should be put into operation as soon as possible so as to advance India an important step further along what they saw as the open road towards its eventual self-government. During the latter part of 1935 Lothian attempted to see Nehru whilst he was on a visit to Europe in order to discuss these issues with him. Nehru had by now read a number of Lothian's writings with a certain amount of interest and agreed to meet him. They were unable, however, to arrange a mutually convenient time, so on 31 December 1935 Lothian sent to Nehru his more than once reprinted and remarkably lengthy letter.

In this he began by canvassing a number of issues concerning the state of the world, marxism and socialism, the attempts being made through the League of Nations to bring all war to an end, the likelihood of 'religion race and language' becoming of ever 'increasing political importance', and a number of other topics in which Nehru had a considerable interest. His principal concern, however, was to persuade him of the critical importance of working the new Act to the full as providing India with an altogether new opportunity to advance its national cause.

Britain and India have different roles to play at the moment [Lothian wrote as he warmed to his theme]. Britain is shedding the old imperialism and is actively concerned with trying to find the way to prevent the anarchy involved in universal self-determination from ending in fresh wars or in a new deluge of imperialism . . . India has the tremendous task of assuming responsibility for her own government and enacting the social and economic reforms which are urgently needed without losing her unity . . . You will ask me how it is possible for India to accomplish her ends through the Constitution which has been passed . . . Unfortunately, in politics, we none of us start with a clean slate. We have always to start from facts emerging from history . . . The . . . risk [of] acquiescence in domination by Britain . . . has disappeared . . . because of the strength of the Indian national movement and of the decision taken by Great Britain to overrule the diehards and transfer the ultimate keys of power through the Constitution Act . . . I don't think . . . there has ever been, as a matter of practical politics, any alternative to the present constitution . . . within the constitution there is room for indefinite growth . . . the road is wide open whereby India can attain to the independence represented by the Statute of Westminster . . . while the safeguards may be of vital value in preventing a breakdown of government . . . they cannot possibly . . . resist the onset of public opinion . . . in demanding the transfer of responsibility to ministries responsible to popularly elected legislatures . . . The whole history of responsible government proves this everywhere . . . the constitution itself contains possibilities of unlimited growth by constitutional means. Under the system of responsible government the most fundamental changes, at any rate in the transference of power and responsibility to new hands, take place through alterations in the conventions and practice rather [than] in the letter of the constitution . . . Congress has now to choose between the catastrophic and the constitutional road and I feel I ought to give you what seem to me some reasons, derived from European experience, in favour of the latter and against the former.

All of which was essentially Sapru's earlier argument reexpressed for a new occasion and with very particular urgency.

Nehru clearly gave Lothian's letter very close attention since in mid January 1936 he wrote a letter in reply at around twice its length. Like Lothian he traversed a series of wider issues, but in due course came to Lothian's central point and promptly dismissed it out of hand.

I do not see any shedding of the old imperialism [he declaimed], but repeated and strenuous attempts to hold on to it . . . though a new facade is presented to public view . . . You refer . . . to the 'constitutional road' in India . . . The mere fact that it is impossible for the great majority of the people of India to make their will effective shows that they have no constitutional way open to them . . . To talk of democracy and constitutionalism in India, in the face of what has happened and is happening there, seems to me to distort utterly the significance of these terms. Ruling powers and ruling classes have not been known in history to abdicate willingly. And if the teaching of history was not enough, we in India have had enough experience of hard facts . . . If this new constitution is a liberal one it is difficult for me to imagine what an illiberal constitution can be like . . . Very recently one of the most eminent leaders of the Indian Liberals described the new constitution as 'the quintessence of the most venomous opposition to all our national aspirations'. Is it not remarkable that even our moderate politicians should think so and yet you, with all your broad sympathy for Indian aspirations should approve of it and say that it 'involves the transfer of the citadel of power in India to Indian hands'? Is the gulf between our ways of thinking so vast? . . . If catastrophe is to be avoided it will have to be for the British Government to retrace its steps.

Three months later Nehru seized the opportunity of his presidential address to the Lucknow Congress in April 1936 to deliver what he evidently intended as the *coup de grâce* to what he saw as this wholly pernicious argument.[10] After reviewing the world situation, capitalism, imperialism, nationalism, socialism, and fascism, much as he and Lothian had both done, he came to the central point. 'Between Indian nationalism, Indian freedom and British imperialism', he inveighed, 'there can be no common ground'. The new Government of India Act was simply 'the

[10] The text, which is extensively quoted in the sections that follow, will be found in *SWJN*, 7, pp. 170–95.

new charter of slavery' deliberately designed 'to strengthen the bonds of imperialist domination'. Against

the federal part of this unholy structure . . . we shall fight [he declared] . . . to our utmost strength, and the primary object of our creating deadlocks in the provinces and making the new Act difficult of functioning, is to kill the federation. With the federation dead, the provincial end of the Act will also go and leave the slate clean for the people of India to write upon.

Long ago, he recalled, Congress had

discarded the old sterile creed of reformism. Are we to go back again to that blind and suffocating lane, after all these years of brave endeavour and to wipe out the memory of what we have done and achieved and suffered?

His answer was pellucidly clear. In a series of pungent sentences he brushed aside the essence of Sapru's case and Lothian's plea as both being obtusely fallacious. Later that year Lothian and he had a further exchange of letters.[11] In December 1936 they met in Allahabad;[12] while eighteen months later Nehru seems to have stayed with him on a further visit he made to England.[13] Despite these gentlemanly courtesies it would be difficult, however, to find a starker example of the totally different interpretations which two men who clearly had a good deal of respect for each other could each put upon precisely the same British policy. As so often in this story its pervasive ambiguity presented at exactly the same time two totally different faces.

If, however, Congress was not to take the 'constitutional way' – 'tactical action' as Kwame Nkrumah of Ghana was later to call it – while being in no position for the moment to mount a further agitation – 'positive action' as Nkrumah dubbed this[14] – it was absolutely vital that some other way of proceeding should now be urgently found. Upon the point at issue here there had already been a good deal of discussion in the Congress ever since the Civil Disobedience campaign had finally petered out in 1934. Some leaders – Nehru especially amongst them – were deeply perturbed

---

[11] For the texts see *Bunch of Old Letters*, pp. 223–5, 231–3, and *SWJN* 8, pp. 74–5. Cf. 'If Indians can agree to work the new system, India will be a free Dominion at any time she likes. Andrews' letters and speeches about the Indian attitude seem to indicate a great chance is going to be missed by India', General Smuts (South Africa) to Mrs Gillett, 23 Feb. 1935, SmP 53, 194.

[12] Nehru to Krishna Menon, 20 Dec., Nehru to Agatha Harrison, 23 Dec. 1937, *SWJN* 8, pp. 633–4.

[13] Shortly after his meeting with the principal British Labour Party leaders at Filkins, *Bunch of Old Letters*, p. 287.

[14] *The Autobiography of Kwame Nkrumah*, Edinburgh 1957, chs, 10, 13.

at the many signs that support for the Congress had dropped away amongst the generality of the Indian population precisely at the moment when a greatly strengthened nationalist movement was badly needed to reinvigorate its conflict with the British. In the circumstances of the time the issue here became focused upon a sharp difference of opinion between the so-called 'Gandhians' in the Congress largely composed of those with commercial, industrial, rich peasant, and professional interests, and those now clustering about the Congress Socialist Party newly formed in 1934. The latter considered it to be of crucial importance that the freedom struggle should now become a great deal more socially radical, and to that end wanted to establish a 'united front' between the Congress and very specifically constructed peasants' and workers' organisations.[15] For the 'Gandhians' this was all anathema. To them it was vital that Congress should continue as a broadly based rally of the Indian people – under their own collective leadership. Insofar as they sought new ways of proceeding they took their cue from Gandhi's efforts following the collapse of Civil Disobedience to recruit dedicated 'Gandhian' workers so as to develop such things as his Village Industries Associations.[16] By the time of the Lucknow Congress of April 1936 it was clear that this division was starting to generate a serious rift within the Congress, and conscious that this was so Nehru devoted more of his presidential address to this one topic than to any other.

His starting point was to declare that in recent years Congress had lost its way.

Sixteen years ago [he recalled], under the inspiration of our leader, we took a new and long step converting this Congress from an ineffective body, feebly functioning amongst the upper classes, into a powerful democratic organization with its roots in the Indian soil and the vast masses who live upon it . . . The exhilaration of being in tune with the masses and with world forces came upon us, and the feeling that we were the agents of historic destiny . . . [Since then however:] We have largely lost touch with the masses and, deprived of the life-giving energy that flows from them, we dry up and weaken and our organization shrinks and loses the power it had.

'How', he asked, 'is this problem to be solved then?' 'Inevitably', he declared, 'we must have middle class leadership'. But if Congress was ever to secure the greatly increased support which it needed in its campaign against the British it was vitally necessary that it should 'look more and more towards the masses and draw strength and inspiration from them'. It was therefore essential to

---

[15] H.K. Singh, *History of the Praja Socialist Party in 1934–59*, Lucknow 1959.

[16] Tomlinson, *The Indian National Congress*, pp. 45–6. For the anxious British reaction see Craik's Note, 6 Nov., Williamson's Note, 16 Nov., GoI to LGs, 23 Nov. 1934, H.Poll.3/16/34.

find a new link and a new connection . . . which allows for the growth of mass consciousness within the Congress . . . [since] the real problem for us is . . . how we can make a broad front of our mass elements with the great majority of the middle classes which stands for independence . . . sweep away the defeatist mentality of some people, and . . . build up our organization with its mass affiliations.

As to how this should not be done, he was in no doubt.

There has been some talk [he said] of a joint front but, so far as I can gather, this refers to some alliance among the upper classes, probably at the expense of the masses. That surely can never be the idea of the Congress . . . The essence of a joint popular front must be uncompromising opposition to imperialism, and the strength of it must inevitably come from active participation of the peasantry and workers.

And thereupon he made three specific suggestions. The Soviet Union, he declared,[17] had succeeded in establishing 'a vast democratic organization' in which 'scores of millions of men and women are constantly taking part in the discussion of public affairs'. Congress should follow in its footsteps and 'try in our own limited way to develop democracy in the lowest rungs of the Congress ladder and make the primary committee a living organisation'. At the same time:

An additional method for us to increase our contacts with the masses [would be] to organize them as producers and then affiliate such organizations to the Congress or have full cooperation between the two. Such organizations of producers as exist today, such as trade unions and peasant unions, as well as other anti-imperialist organisations, could also be brought within this sphere of mutual cooperation for the good of the masses and for the struggle for national freedom. Thus the Congress could have an individual as well as a corporate membership, and retaining its individual character, could influence, and be influenced by, other mass elements.[18]

'The subject', he declared, 'is fascinating but complicated'. It should be 'tackled by an expert committee which I trust will be appointed on behalf of the Congress'.

His chief purpose in proposing such a committee was to try to propel the Congress into making itself 'not only *for* the masses . . . but *of* the masses', both in the interests of the masses themselves (whom he clearly saw as being appallingly disadvantaged), and because he believed their far greater mobilisation was crucial to the success of Congress in its struggle with the British. Yet in couching his concern in the socialist terms that he did, far from closing the breach that was threatening to divide the Congress, he opened it a great deal wider than he ever intended.

---

[17] Following upon S. and B. Webb, *Soviet Communism: A New Civilisation*, 2 vols., London 1935.
[18] During a recent visit to Europe he had discussed this idea with two men who had long been involved in the Indian Communist movement, Palme Dutt and Ben Bradley, Gopal, *Jawaharlal Nehru*, I, ch. 14.

Prior to his presidential address three Congress Socialists, Achyut Patwardhan, Kamaladevi Chattopadhya, and A.P. Sinha, had already submitted identical draft resolutions for adoption by the Lucknow Congress which declared that:

The Congress recognises the need for a closer association of the toiling masses in the struggle for independence ... [and to] this end, the Congress asks the Working Committee to work out, in consultation with Trade Union and Peasant Organisations, amendments to the Congress constitution providing for the representation of organized workers and peasants.[19]

When this proposal came before the 'Subjects' Committee which was held prior to the main Congress to consider the issues that should be listed for open debate this formula was swiftly transformed by the Gandhians who held the majority there to say no more than that moves should be taken 'to bring about closer cooperation with other organisations of peasants, workers and others' so as 'to make the Congress a joint front of all the anti-imperialist elements in the country'.[20] The Socialists, however, were not to be brushed aside quite so easily, and when the issue came up for plenary debate on 14 April 1936, the evening of the third day of the Congress, a major clash ensued. At the outset two 'Gandhians', Purushottamdas Tandon and Acharya Kripalani, moved a bland Subjects Committee resolution that did no more than take up Nehru's central suggestion that a three-man Committee should be established 'to examine the question of bringing about closer contact between the Congress and the masses'. The Socialists' spokesman, Sampurnanand, thereupon immediately moved a Socialist amendment that called for the direct representation of worker and peasant organisations in the Congress. In the course of the animated debate which followed Jairamdas Doulatram eventually stood forth as the 'Gandhians'' principal proponent to protest that if the Congress were to 'consist of class organisations, then it would bring about a clash of interests and result in loss of strength'. And in the end when Sampurnanand's amendment was put by Nehru from the chair, it 'was lost by a large majority', 255 to 487.[21] Whereupon the original Subjects Committee's resolution was agreed to.

As a consequence there then came into existence the Congress Mass Contacts Committee of 1936 (later the Congress Constitution Committee) which over the following months was to provide the principal arena for a classic debate over how the Congress should go about

[19] Patwardhan, Kamaladevi and Sinha to General Secretary AICC, 30 Mar. 1936, AICC 16/1937. For a general survey see Tomlinson, *Indian National Congress and the Raj*, esp. chs. 2–4.   [20] AICC G31/1936.
[21] Ibid.; A.M. & S.G. Zaidi, *Encyclopaedia of Indian National Congress*, Delhi 1980, II, p. 265.

securing greatly increased public support for its cause. It was chaired by
Doulatram, a Sindhi and a journalist, who had been General Secretary of
the Congress in 1931 and following a period in jail had worked for
Gandhi's Village Industries Association and for the Congress Labour
Organisation.[22] He was joined on the one side by a man of a similar cast of
mind, the foremost Congressman from Bihar, Rajendra Prasad,[23] and on
the other by the young Bihari Socialist, Jayaprakash Narayan.[24] The split
within the Congress which the debate of 14 April had exposed accordingly came to be directly replicated within the Committee itself.

In view of the importance of the issues the Committee needed to consider it was under great pressure to conclude its business at an early date.
Accordingly on 6 May 1936 it issued to every District Congress
Committee a small four-page printed questionnaire, and asked for
responses to it to be sent to their Provincial Congress Committees so that
they could send their consolidated replies to Doulatram by the end of
June.

The returns which were received presented a striking picture of
Congress organisation at the time. Very few Congress Committees
managed to send in their replies even by the end of the year let alone by
the end of June, and in the event Doulatram received no more than a miscellany of responses. Apart from ten which came from Provincial
Congress Committees, no more than a dozen or so originated from
District Congress Committees direct, whilst six to eight came from other
organisations. Some were quite extensive. The Gujarat PCC, for
example, provided nineteen pages of typed foolscap; the Bengal PCC
forty (though these were based upon responses from only twenty of its
thirty-one DCCs). Many, however, were extremely brief.[25]

At the outset the questionnaire posed a number of questions about the
'primary, i.e. the lowest Congress Committees in your province' – their
number, their memberships, their modes of working, and their influence
upon decision-making. From the answers received it was clear that there
was a goodly number of DCCs. What, however, they actually amounted
to was a very different matter. In Mahakoshal, for example, the Hindi-
speaking parts of CP, it was reported that only four DCCs had offices,
whilst the other eleven were said to 'remain in the pockets, drawers and
almiras of some one gentleman of the District'! Membership lists were

[22] S.P. Sen, ed., *Dictionary of National Biography*, vol. II, Calcutta 1973, pp. 227–8.
[23] R. Prasad, *Autobiography*, Bombay 1957.
[24] A. Bhattacharjee, *Jayaprakash Narayan. A Political Biography*, Delhi 1978.
[25] For the questionnaire, replies, and draft reports and the extracts cited below from these,
    see AICC G13/1936 and G30(a)/1937, and NMML, J.P. Narayan Papers, Ser. II, file no.
    116, and RPP IX/36/1,2,4.

much like those for branch memberships of many another political party elsewhere – the numbers varying from between a few hundred, to, here and there, several thousands. What was particularly striking, however, was how common was one central set of complaints. The primary committees at the bottom of the organisational structure, so it was often said, were only rarely consulted. They sometimes did not meet for a year at a time and had little or no influence upon the decisions of higher committees. 'The policy, programme and resolutions rarely reach the rural masses', as the Bengal PCC put it. As a consequence there were numerous suggestions about the need to improve communications within the Congress organisation. It was frequently suggested, for example, that before new policies were adopted by superior bodies it should be mandatory for consultations to be held with primary committees. There were numerous calls too for an enlargement in the party's full-time cadres; and especially for a reduction in the Congress's annual subscription from four annas to two, and even one.

To the question 'to what extent do primary committees associate themselves with the daily life of the people in their areas?', the answers were no less disconcerting. 'Not in any way', said the Karaikudi DCC in Tamilnad. 'Never', said the Nasik DCC. 'Not generally' said the Bihar PCC. 'Hardly at all', said the Rajshahi DCC. There was, the Murshidabad DCC declared, an 'unabridgeable gulf' here. Although some committees were more encouraging – Kaira DCC affirmed, for example, that 'a majority of members are from the masses who are familiar with the real conditions of the people' – the most characteristic expression of the essential point here was articulated by the Walluvanad Taluka Congress Committee in Malabar:

Congress membership [it reported] is mainly confined to the upper layer of society. Educated middle class forms the largest percentage in its roles. Higher peasantry, petty shopkeepers, junior members of aristocratic families etc. are the main props of the organisation. Actual tillers of the soil are practically absent, not to speak of the agricultural labourers on conditions of semi serfdom. Industrial labour is practically non-existent in the Taluk.

The gloomy picture Nehru had drawn of the general state of the Congress at this time was upon all this evidence all too close to the mark.

When the Mass Contacts Committee then asked in a couple of further questions what were the most promising ways in which close contact with the masses could be established, the answers were again very revealing. The unprecedented floods of 1927 and 1933, so the Broach DCC explained, had afforded 'an opportunity to serve the afflicted and thus brought the masses and the workers in very close contact'. There had been a bad frost in 1935, and a drought in 1936, and local Congress

leaders had been able to make very good use of the openings these provided for securing popular support. 'Epidemics', the Broach DCC
further stated, 'afford good opportunities to all that love to serve the suffering humanity'.

It may be said in confidence [so the UP PCC declared] that our real contact of
rural influence among the peasantry is due to our championing their cause against
the Govt., the Big Zaminders and Teluqdar, the money-lender and many others
who harass them. We have had with some success widespread no tax movements
among the peasants. It is to this that we owe our real influence with the masses of
this province.

'The participation of the Congress in movements for removal of the
grievances of the masses did lead to the development of closer relations
between the Congress and the masses', wrote the Basti DCC; while the
Surat DCC declared that:

Villagers are many a time harassed by money lenders, zamindars and petty officials. The best way to come into direct touch with the masses is to help them in
removing these harassments.

It is significant that these last replies largely paralleled the Government
of India's view of precisely where the critical battleground in the struggle
for India now lay. 'The greatest risk in this country of violent upheaval',
the Viceroy, Willingdon, had declared in 1935, 'lies in the grievances of
the tenantry. The longer they remain unredressed, the greater the scope
of subversive propaganda.'[26] On learning of Nehru's address to the
Lucknow Congress the Government of India had thus become especially
worried about 'the present agrarian movement developing on the lines
which the Congress President clearly has in view', and in a circular letter
of 12 June 1936 to their provincial governments urgently reminded them
that because of Congress's ability to 'make capital out of grievances'
which had 'thereby largely increased its prestige in the local area', it was
essential that prompt steps should be taken to 'redress legitimate grievances, so as to leave no room for Congress to exploit them': 'there are', it
stated, 'many minor matters in regard to which tenants and cultivators
have grievances'; 'first hand information on matters such as complaints of
corruption' should therefore be procured, and 'when suitable opportunities present themselves, prompt action should be taken within the scope
of the funds available' to improve village amenities.[27]

[26] Letter of 5 Sept. 1935, D. Rothermund, *Government, Landlord and Peasant in India. Agrarian Relations under British Rule, 1865–1935*, Wiesbaden 1978, p. 124.
[27] Hallett's Note, 5 May 1936, and 'Appreciation' of Lucknow Congress in Craik to Gs, 12 June 1936, H.Poll.4/8/36. See also the notorious Court of Wards letter of 9 July 1936, AICC E1(a)/1936, and H.Reforms 29/37G(B).

It was, however, in answer to a range of other questions that the Mass Contacts Committee received the responses it needed on the central issue it had to consider. Question 11, for example, stated:

It is suggested that Congress will be strengthened by giving special representation on Congress committees to certain sections of the nation (peasants and workers) on their class basis. It is contended, on the other hand, that this will weaken the Congress, as it will emphasise class antagonisms in a national organization. What is your opinion on this question?

The most vehement support for this whole idea came from Professor N.G. Ranga of the South Indian Federation of Agricultural Workers and Peasants writing from the Andhra Peasants Institute in Nidubrole, who roundly declared that

the policy so far followed by the Congress . . . has not succeeded . . . in the Peasants coming to actively associate themselves as a class with the Congress and its organisations . . . The sooner we realise that the formation and promotion of the organising strength of Peasants is the most revolutionary and creative thing we can do, the better it is for the Congress.[28]

He was joined in this view by Swami Sahajanand Saraswati of the Bihar Provincial Kisan Sabha, and by a number of DCCs, from Bengal and UP in particular.[29] Meeting on 8 June 1936, with Jawaharlal Nehru present, the UP Political Conference declared, for example, that Congress should give direct representation to organised groups of peasants and workers, subject only to their readiness to accept the broad outlines of Congress policy.[30] General support for this idea of special representation for worker and peasant organisations in the Congress came too from the Secretary of the Walluvanad Taluk Congress Committee, E.M. Sankaran Namboodimpad – the EMS of post-independence Kerala.[31]

But at the same time there were very much louder voices on the other side. Two thirds of the Bengal DCCs declared, for example, that they were opposed to special representation for peasants and workers in the Congress. So did most of the Maharastrian DCCs; whilst the Delhi DCC declared that:

We are emphatically of the opinion that special representation on class basis will weaken the Congress . . . Already the labour classes have begun to entertain strange notions of socialism.

When, moreover, on 13 July Jayaprakash Narayan proposed in the Bihar PCC that Kisan Sabhas and Labour Unions should be given direct repre-

---

[28] See also Ranga to Nehru, 24 Nov. 1936, AICC G5A(1)/1936.
[29] Sahajanand to Prasad, 10 Aug. 1936, RPP 36/IV/2.   [30] *IAR*, 1936, pp. 361–5.
[31] V. M. Fic, *Kerala, Yenan of India*, Bombay 1970; T.J. Nossiter, *Communism in Kerala*, Delhi 1982.

sentation in the Congress, his motion was badly defeated by forty-two votes to seven. While in the midst of all this the Gujarat PCC was particularly vehement.

Giving special representation to peasants and workers on their class basis [they declared] would necessarily accentuate class struggle and raise a class war as is presumably intended by the section making this suggestion. This is entirely against the existing policy and creed of the Congress and would result only in weakening the Congress and giving a set-back to the national movement. This Committee is therefore definitely against such representation on class basis.

Their statement was drafted and signed by their Secretary – the forty-year-old Morarji Desai.

Such divisions in the evidence before it reinforced the divisions that already existed within the Committee itself. These would have made it very difficult in any event for it to have produced an agreed report, but those difficulties were multiplied when according to one source two of its members (according to another all three) fell ill.[32] In these circumstances Doulatram does not seem to have taken any particular lead himself, and it was that that gave an opportunity to both of his colleagues, Prasad the 'Gandhian' and Narayan the socialist, to try to preempt the Committee's report by producing a draft text of his own. As a result they now proceeded to produce as notable an expression of the division of opinion upon this issue as the exchange between Lothian and Nehru had been upon that of 'the constitutional way'.

When one puts their drafts side by side it is clear that upon several points Prasad and Narayan stood in broad agreement. They took a similar line, for instance, on the course the Indian national movement had taken since the First World War. They were agreed too in thinking that support for the Congress and sympathy with its aims extended well beyond its present formal membership, and they used exactly the same terms in discussing the importance of Congress's involvement in ameliorating the distresses of the peasantry.[33] Like the PCCs, the DCCs, and the Government of India, they were, moreover, at one in believing that there was here an issue of major importance for the whole future of the Indian national movement.

Work by Congress to relieve distress [each of them averred] caused by flood or famine, disease or pestilence, oppression by landlords, Government petty officials and others – has naturally received its due meed of praise and a certain consideration at the hands of the masses in the form of attachment. It is also well known

---

[32] AICC Foreign Dept Newsletter, no. 7, 10 Sept. 1936, AICC Misc.6/1936; Patel to Nehru, 23 Sept. 1936, AICC E1/1936; Kripalani to PCCs, 28 Oct. 1936, AICC P1/1936.   [33] So there seems to have been some contact between them.

that even where the Congress has done no such appreciable service it has commanded respect and confidence on account of the suffering its members have undergone for the larger cause of Swaraj. The Congress must therefore extend its sphere of activity in all directions, making itself serviceable in every way to the masses, taking up every cause which touches them and trying to remedy it.

Accordingly they both made great play of the need for Congress to identify itself with the lives of the masses, and as a consequence they each enlarged on the need for primary committees and primary members to be fully consulted on any significant issues for decision. They were agreed too that primary committees should meet much more frequently and debate much more fully. They both emphasised the need for existing worker and peasant organisations to be closely linked with the Congress, and they specifically concurred in recommending that the annual subscription for membership of the Congress should be reduced from four annas a year to two.

This extensive measure of agreement only served, however, to highlight the depth of the differences between them on the issue of the precise manner in which the peasantry and the working classes should be linked to the national movement. Here the split between them could scarcely have been wider.

The Committee [so Narayan's draft sought to have it] feels that the peasantry is the backbone of the national movement. The more the struggle for independence identifies itself with the desires and needs of the peasantry, the greater will be its strength . . . A harassed, oppressed, demoralized peasantry cannot take its place in the national revolution. The peasantry must be put on its feet, it must be made conscious of its strength and power, it must be organized and welded together. With the strength of the peasantry will grow the strength of the nation and the fight for freedom . . . The strength of an organized working class will be of inestimable value to the National movement. In fact, if that movement is to reach its destiny and end in the liberation of the Indian people from political and economic slavery, the workers must be in the forefront because they stand most consistently opposed to exploitation.

Prasad, however, would have none of this.

The Congress [he wrote as if in reply] is not a class organisation. It has been always and is today a national organisation having as its members persons belonging to all classes and strata of society. It has undoubtedly extended its sphere more and more and from being at one time an organisation of a small number of persons educated in schools and colleges has now become the largest organisation of the common people drawn very largely from the village population and counting amongst its members lakhs of peasants and cultivators and a sprinkling of industrial and field workers . . . The ideal of national independence is spacious enough for all and any other ideal can be achieved only after this has been achieved. Emphasis therefore may not be laid at this stage on the conflict of interests as between class and class in the Congress and its organisation. By its very nature and composition the Congress is bound to work for the removal of grievances and amelioration of the condition of the vast bulk of the people who constitute the masses of peasants and workers and further it is bound in all conflicts to take the side of the weaker i.e. the less organised and less resourceful of the parties viz. the masses. It has done so in the past and will do so in an ever increasing measure in the future.

So profound were the differences between the two men on this basic issue that they struck out at each other too. By clear implication Narayan accused Prasad of being fearful of the masses, whilst Prasad seized upon a clumsy phrase in Narayan's draft to lambast him for preferring the interests of the rich peasantry to those of the poorer. They were seriously at odds too over other matters. Narayan's draft piled up the arguments for basing Congress on Trade Unions and Kisan organisations, whilst Prasad marshalled every objection he could to any such idea, and fastened instead upon the urgent need for Congress to have a considerably increased number of 'Gandhian' workers working full time for it.

In view of these two deeply conflicting drafts, and seemingly no attempt by the chairman to bring them together, it was hardly to be wondered at that the Committee failed to report to the Congress Working Committee when it met in Bombay on 9–11 December 1936 as had evidently been intended. In an effort to take matters forward it was there decided to create a new sub-committee composed of the three previous members together with Jawaharlal Nehru (who for the second year in succession was about to be the Congress President) and Acharya Kripalani, one of the Congress's General Secretaries.[34] At the same time in a very evident move to ensure that the results should be to its liking the 'Gandhian' majority on the Committee redrafted the terms of reference for this new sub-committee so as to instruct it to do no more than 'consider changes in the Congress Constitution with a view to increase the initiative of primary members and to make Congress a more effective organisation'.[35]

Nehru was clearly very unhappy with this move and in his presidential address to the Faizpur Congress on 27 December 1936 went out of his way to express his personal interest in the Socialists' proposals by saying that:

Action to be effective must be mass action . . . it is argued that functional representation will give far greater reality to the peasants and workers in the Congress.

[34] AICC G29, G31, G85(VI)/1936; Report of the Constitution Committee, AICC G28/1937. I cannot confirm the report that M.N. Roy was added to the committee, cf. J.P. Haithcox, *Communism and Nationalism in India: M.N. Roy and Comintern Policy 1920–1939*, Princeton 1971, p. 269.
[35] AICC G29, G31, Misc.41/1936; Zaidi, *Encyclopaedia*, pp. 159–60.

This proposal has been resisted because of a fear that the Congress will be swamped by new elements . . . now or later some kind of functional representation in the Congress is inevitable and desirable.[36]

And in a further effort to shift Congress's policy in this direction a number of Congress Socialists tabled resolutions at Faizpur to 'provide inter alia for the direct representation of organised peasants and workers' in it. 'The Congress', so Achyut Patwardhan's wording ran, 'therefore considers that participation in the work of organization of workers and peasants should be the main item in the constructive programme of the Congress in the coming year'.[37] Like other such moves, however, these were soon stopped in their tracks by the 'Gandhian' majority in the Congress, though there were no signs that the argument was in any way thereby foreclosed.[38]

There was a remarkable congruence here, we may suggest, not only with the substance of the earlier debate we have considered in Indonesia in 1932–3, but with its significance in the present context. There was for a start a remarkable symmetry in the policies of the two imperial powers at these particular points in time. Upon his release from prison in December 1931 Sukarno and his fellow Indonesian nationalists had been left free by the Dutch to pursue their nationalist activities as they wished, just as most Congressmen had been by the British as soon as the Civil Disobedience movement had collapsed. Likewise in the same way that there was no possibility of the Dutch instituting any constitutional reforms at this time, so there was no likelihood following the enactment of the Government of India Act of 1935 that the British would grant any further constitutional reforms beyond those they had already agreed. At the same time just as following their suppression of the Communist revolts in Java and Sumatra in 1926–7 the Dutch were most unlikely to tolerate for very long any nationalist activity which was really threatening, so after 1934 the British were seemingly always quite prepared to suppress any resurgence of Civil Disobedience. Both powers, that is, pursued at these particular points in time very comparable dualist policies of 'no repression but no concession'. These both had ambiguities at their core. In each case 'no repression' stood at odds with 'no concession', and vice versa.

The nationalists' response was not only remarkably similar. It was significantly conditioned by the duality in the imperial position. On the one hand that precluded any thought of constitutional negotiations. At the

[36] The address is in *SWJN* 7, pp. 598–614.
[37] Notes by Patwardhan, AICC Misc.25/1936; see also AICC Misc. 28, 85(v)/1936.
[38] Zaidi, *Encyclopaedia*, pp. 207–8. For Gandhi's continued opposition to 'class war' because 'it created atmosphere of violence' see notes of Working Committee meeting, Allahabad, 28 Apr. 1937, AICC Misc.42 1936.

same time, whilst effectively debarring civil disturbance and civil disobedience, it did little to prompt any resort to violence or to revolutionary
insurrection. Within the limits it fixed and the opportunities it allowed
there was, that is, just enough space for each movement to go about determining how it could best mobilise much more popular support than it
had enjoyed before. There was even room, particularly in view of the
uncertainties attending the eventual reactions of the imperial powers, to
allow two competing agendas to open up. In each instance the divide
between them took its colouring from the widely prevalent debate at the
time between those who were espousing the new socialist principles that
were around and those who abhorred these altogether.

What is particularly striking, however, is just how comparable the two
sets of proposals that were advanced in each movement turned out to
be. Whilst both PNI Baru and the Congress Socialists looked to the
deliberate mobilisation of a class-based nationalist movement, Partindo
and the 'Gandhians' each sought to generate a cross-class nationalist
movement that would constitute a single whole. Both alternatives, moreover, stood quite close to the midpoint of conceivable nationalist activities (in Nkrumah's terms neither involved 'tactical action' nor 'positive
action', but only, if one may coin the phrase, 'organisational action').
More particularly both operated, for the time being at least, strictly
within the dualities which the two imperial powers had established.
Given these correspondences it is difficult to avoid the conclusion that it
was the particular matrix of imperial power that once again conditioned
the corresponding nationalist alignments to a degree that still warrants
emphasis.

In the event in each instance the debate was very soon quite suddenly
cut short – in Indonesia by the arrests of Sukarno and then Hatta and
their associates in August 1933 and early in 1934, and in India, not as in
Indonesia by renewed resort to imperialist repression, but quite to the
contrary by the astonishing outturn of the provincial election's campaign
and the ensuing results in the provincial elections of 1936–7.

In the course of his presidential address at the Lucknow Congress in
April 1936 Nehru had, albeit reluctantly, acknowledged that as a consequence of the very considerable success Congressmen had had in the
central and municipal elections since 1934, a great many of them were
determined to contest the forthcoming provincial elections in spite of the
substantial objections which were levied against the new Government of
India Act under which they would be held. He seems to have reconciled
himself to this by accepting that an election campaign could well give the

Congress an invaluable opportunity to develop closer associations with the Indian masses which remained his principal concern.

One of the principal reasons for our seeking election [he had accordingly declared] will be to carry the message of the Congress to the millions of voters and to the scores of millions of the disenfranchised, to acquaint them with our future programme and policy, to make the masses realise that we not only stand for them but that we are of them and seek to cooperate with them in removing their social and economic burdens.

So soon as the election was called he therefore set off on a protracted speech-making tour right across the length and breadth of India so as to proclaim the Congress creed.

The results he found quite astonishing. To his complete amazement and huge delight wherever he went, in the large cities, in the smaller townships, along the highways and byways of India, he found himself received during a frenetic 130 days on tour with quite extraordinary enthusiasm. As he moved about, 'often in remote parts of the country, addressing enormous audiences everywhere . . . and probably covered over fifty thousand miles by railway train, motor car and aeroplane', he recorded, he found himself speaking to as many as a dozen meetings and upwards of 100,000 people a day, and at the end reckoned he had addressed something like ten million people all told.[39] 'Apart from these huge audiences', he recalled, 'I have met vast numbers of others on the road sides as I motored through rural areas. The enthusiasm everywhere was astounding.'

Nothing like this had been anticipated; and it radically changed the whole situation. The pervasive impression of institutional patchiness and ideological divisions within the Congress which had been thrown into such high relief in the answers to the Mass Contacts Committee's questionnaire in 1936, whilst no doubt quite correct in themselves, turned out to be of no consequence whatsoever. Some degree of local organization was no doubt necessary to the Congress if it was to be provided with a network of local contacts for its leaders, formal institutions for decision-making at the local level, and a mechanism for selecting delegates to the annual Congress meeting. Yet as Nehru travelled about India, far from being hamstrung by either Congress's institutional inertia or its ideological divisions, he found himself overwhelmed by the seething crowds peering up at him wherever he went.

All of which was triumphantly confirmed by the dramatic electoral victories Congress won in the provincial elections which ensued where they

---

[39] *SWJN* 7, sections 4, 5, 8, 9; 8, sec. 1. See also AICC General Secretary's (Kripalani's) report for 1937, AICC G47/1937.

astonished both themselves and virtually everyone else by winning overall majorities in five of the eleven provinces of India (Madras, Bihar, Orissa, CP, and UP) and emerging as the largest party in three more (Bombay, the Frontier, and Assam).[40] Upon the announcement of the results Nehru was ecstatic. Whilst in the contests for the provincial upper houses, with their much narrower franchises, Congress had not been very successful:

In the Assembly elections [he told the British Labour MP, Sir Stafford Cripps] we carried all before us and our majorities were prodigious, varying as a rule between twenty thousand and fifty thousand . . . With the present electorate of about ten percent of the population (for the Lower House) we have gained ninety percent of the seats in the general constituencies. We could have won 100% of those seats but for the tremendous pressure of vested interests, and sometimes the questionable tactics played against us. If this is any indication of the Congress strengths, as it undoubtedly is, then the position is even stronger so far as the 90% of non-voters is concerned.

It was of crucial importance, he emphasised, to note

what we were contending against. We had the Government apparatus and all the other vested interests against us and all means, fair and otherwise, were employed to defeat us. But the enthusiasm for the Congress was so tremendous that it swept everything before it. Our majorities have been enormous. Remarkable as the election victory has been the really significant feature of the election campaign has been the shaking up of the masses. We carried our message not only to the thirty million and odd voters but to the hundreds [sic] of non-voters also. The whole campaign and the election itself have been a revelation of the wide-spread anti-imperialist spirit prevailing throughout the country.[41]

A number of reports written by British officials following the election soon confirmed this conclusion.

It was to be expected [so the Government of Bengal was soon reporting] that a year which marked the introduction of such vast political changes should see a great increase in the number of political and quasi-political meetings assembled in mufassal centres . . . but it is the number of local meetings held on all kinds of occasion in different places all over the province that is of interest. The size of these gatherings and the deep and sustained interest in their proceedings seem to indicate that the attention of the 'masses' has really been awakened and that new ideas are finding a ready hearing.[42]

---

[40] D. Taylor, 'The Reconstruction and Use of the Statistics of the Provincial Elections of 1937', *Bulletin of Quantitative and Computer Methods in South Asian Studies*, 2 Mar. 1974. Only in three of the Muslim-majority provinces (Bengal, Sind, and Punjab) were they significantly less successful.   [41] Nehru to Cripps, 22 Feb. 1937, *SWJN* 8, pp. 31–4.

[42] Govt of Bengal, 'A Brief Summary of Political Events in the Presidency of Bengal during the year 1937', H.Poll.132/38.

'In this Province', an intelligence officer from the CP put it,

the success of the Congress in the Assembly elections has upset all forecasts both official and non-official. Many of the Congress candidates with no individual status defeated their strong opponents by thumping majorities . . . The electioneering campaign of the Congress which was carried on on an organised wide scale has resulted in mass awakening and a spirit of contempt is created against the Government and its supporters.[43]

Nehru's personal elation soon became unbounded.

As a whole [he told Cripps] India is wide awake and expectant . . . Politically the masses are wholly anti-imperialist, so also the middle-classes, except the top fringe. My extensive touring has been a revelation to me of the suppressed energy of the people and of their passionate desire to be rid of their burdens. The Congress is supreme today so far as the masses and the lower middle classes are concerned . . . It has hardly ever been in such a strong position.

A watershed had been crossed.

The significance of all of this may now be spelt out. Two sets of considerations would seem important: one relating to the 'mass contacts' debate we have considered, with its Indonesian analogue; the other to the much more protracted debate between the major Congress leaders (and Nehru in particular) with the likes of Sapru on the Indian side and Lothian on the British. Both, we have suggested, bore the marks of British ambiguity.

As to the former,[44] whilst Nehru would in due course slide down from his high peak of February 1937, one central point had now been made. Less than a year previously he had been deeply perturbed at the apparent divorce between the Congress and the Indian masses. So convinced had he then been that there was an issue here of crucial importance to the very

---

[43] Report by Deputy Central Intelligence Officer, Nagpur, 24 Feb. 1937, H.Poll.4/9/37.

[44] The enlarged Mass Contacts Committee eventually proposed in August 1937 a new category of 'Associate Members' of the Congress who would pay no subscription but by accepting the Congress creed would become members of 'Ward and Village Panchayats', though without the right to elect members of other committees. Even this was vigorously resisted, and when a new Constitution Committee appointed by the Haripura Congress 1938 eventually submitted its support, no such idea received a mention. The only Congress Mass Contacts campaign that was launched in 1937–8 was for Muslim 'mass contacts', and that proved an egregious failure, Working Committee, Wardha, 27 Feb.–1 Mar. 1937 and Allahabad, 26–28 Apr. 1937, AICC Misc.42/1936; Presidential Circular 24, 2 May 1937, Presidential Circular 37, Kripalani to all PCCs, 27 Aug. 1937, AICC P1/1937–8; Report of the Constitution Committee, 17–18 Aug. 1937, AICC G28/1937; see also AICC G80/1937–8, G42, G43, G80/1938, G31/1939 (4 parts), G43/1939–40, and Misc.36/1936 and 40/1937; Haithcox, *Communism and Nationalism*, pp. 268–9; M. Hasan, 'The Muslim Mass Contacts Campaign: Analysis of a Strategy of Political Mobilisation', in R. Sisson and S. Wolpert, *Congress and Indian Nationalism*, Berkeley 1988, ch. 10.

future of the national movement that he had seized upon his position as Congress President to press for a major investigation of the ways in which the disjunction could be overcome and had put forward two proposals as to how this might be done.

At that stage the British had shared his doubts about whether the greater part of the rural populations of India was as yet all that closely attached to Congress. Over recent decades British officials had shown a great deal of ingenuity in cultivating the acquiescence of large numbers of India's peasantry in their rule.[45] An investigation they made in the aftermath of the establishment of emergency rule in January 1932 had indicated that whilst in a great many urban areas support for the Congress was now running very strongly, beyond such areas as Gujarat and a number of Telegu and Tamil districts, in most of the rural areas it still seemed at best patchy and uncertain.[46] The 1936–7 election campaign put paid to all of that. As the British now fully realised there could be no doubt that the Congress enjoyed very considerable mass support in the country.

The corollary on the Congress side was even more substantial. The urgent need to build up its 'mass contacts', on which Nehru had pressed it so hard considerably less than a year before, proved to be entirely supererogatory. Congress had no need, moreover, to trouble itself any further with the issue of organisational reconstruction of either a 'Gandhian' or Socialist kind.[47] Hostility towards the British for the repressive measures they had taken against the Congress had substantially eroded their position. The sufferings endured by so many Congress members had evidently not been in vain. Whilst the magnetic figure of the Mahatma led countless numbers to cast their votes for his party.[48] Far from bemoaning its lack of mass contacts, Congress was soon overwhelmed by the huge number of applications it was receiving for membership from almost every quarter.[49] As a result the debate that Nehru had brought to a head in his Lucknow address, and that had so riven the Mass Contacts Committee, quite suddenly ended.

[45] Rothermund, *Government, Landlord and Peasant*, passim.

[46] D.A. Low, 'The Forgotten Bania: Merchant Communities and the Indian National Congress', in Low, *Eclipse of Empire*, Cambridge 1991, ch. 4.

[47] Presidential Circulars 11, 19 Feb. 1937, AICC P1/1936; *SWJN* 8, pp. 26–7.

[48] Presidential Circular 30, 10 July 1937, AICC Misc.41/1936–7. On the erosion of British authority see Kudaisya, 'State Power and the Erosion of Colonial Authority', passim. On voting for Gandhi, see Dep. Central Intelligence Officer, Nagpur, 25 Feb. 1937, and Bihar, UP, CP FR1, H.Poll.4/9/37.

[49] In his Annual Report on the Congress for the year 1937 the General Secretary, Acharya Kripalani, pronounced that Congress now had 'the biggest individual membership that any organisation has, the world over. It is perhaps bigger than that of the Communist party in Russia'. See generally AICC G78/1937, G43/1938; *IAR* 1938, II, pp. 299–300.

The 1937 election results produced a denouement in the other, more protracted debate we have considered too. Despite the anathemas that had been rained upon it the 'constitutional way' had proved its capacity to serve a critically important national purpose. The immense support the Congress now enjoyed in so many parts of the country had in the event been principally registered in a parliamentary election which the imperial rulers themselves had mounted, and to which in their own way of thinking they always attached a quite special significance. No longer therefore would the contest for popular loyalties between the British and the Congress principally revolve around competitions over the relief of peasants' afflictions, as both of them had hitherto believed would primarily be the case. It had now been determined in the course of an election campaign and the ensuing election results. Whilst (as we shall see in the next chapter) Nehru continued to resist every suggestion that Congress should go on to accept provincial office, from this moment onwards even he was at least a partial convert to the case Lothian, and previously Sapru, had been making. Along with the great majority of Congress's supporters he showed himself to be all but invariably ready after Congress's great success in 1936–7 to take the parliamentary road whenever there seemed a chance that this would advance the Congress cause. There were certainly traumas to come, especially during the Second World War, particularly when the next great wave of Congress agitation culminated in the great Quit India campaign of 1942. Yet despite the vehemence with which that was suppressed, so substantial was now the switch by the principal Congress leaders to the parliamentary way of proceeding whenever there seemed a plausible case that this could be used to good effect, that as soon as they came out of jail, just as the war was ending, they promptly set about organising, not another nation-wide agitation (let alone an armed revolt), but the Congress's campaign for the central and provincial elections of 1946.[50] All this was done, we may note, at the time when their counterparts in Indonesia, not to mention those in Vietnam, were limbering up for armed conflict with their imperial rulers.

In tracing this further impact of British ambiguity on the Indian story it is instructive to consider the issue of Congress's mobilisation of support for its cause within the wider context of the other Asian imperialist–nationalist struggles we have noted. For so soon as that is done some further revealing contrasts open up, yet again as between the Philippines on the one hand, and Indonesia and Vietnam on the other.

In the Philippines the generally accommodating policy of the Americans made it very largely unnecessary for its nationalist elite to

[50] See e.g. Nandurkar, ed., *Sardar's Letters*, ch. 1.

generate the widespread mass support for its cause which the Congress believed to be absolutely essential against British dominion in India. During the 1930s (and in the 1940s too, following the American expulsion of the Japanese) little more than elite mobilisation seemed to be necessary to secure their nationalist objectives. In Indonesia by contrast even during that brief period during 1932–3 when Dutch policy appeared to approximate more to the dualism of the British, both sides into which the nationalist movement split committed themselves to adopt rather more sharply pointed programmes than their later counterparts in India. PNI Baru aimed to build up a tightly organised, cadre-based party, well beyond anything the Socialists at this time contemplated in India, whilst Partindo sought to generate a mass uprising of the kind about which the 'Gandhians' always remained very wary. When following the Dutch suppression of all nationalist activity after 1934 the Japanese in 1942 liberated Indonesia's nationalist leaders, not only did Sukarno and Hatta join together. Upon the defeat of the Japanese in 1945 their followers propelled them into a revolutionary movement in which thousands of *pemuda* (young men) first threw themselves into armed struggle against the Dutch and in which in the end a critical component proved to be the hastily constructed Indonesian Republican army.[51] Meanwhile in Vietnam, with its still more draconian imperial rulers, there was never any doubt after the French White Terror of 1930–1, even during the brief Popular Front years of the later 1930s, that it would be absolutely essential for its nationalist leaders to mobilise popular mass support in a far more rigorous and systematic way than generally appeared to be necessary elsewhere. During the 1940s the Vietminh (under Communist leadership) therefore developed not only a revolutionary army but a cadre-led movement too, both of which proved to be vital to the final destruction of French rule.[52] While, therefore, the depth of popular mobilisation which the Philippines' nationalist leaders needed to effect against the Americans was never very deep, as against the Dutch in Indonesia and *a fortiori* the French in Vietnam not only did nationalist mobilisation need to strike very much deeper but in both cases to be in the end militarily supported too.

In India, precisely because of the fundamental dualism in the British position, it was essential that the Indian national movement should secure a great deal more mass support than proved to be necessary against the Americans in the Philippines. Yet by the same token it never seems to have been necessary to embark on the extensively generated mass

---

[51] Reid, *The Indonesian National Revolution.*
[52] E.J. Hammer, *The Struggle for Indochina 1940–1955*, Stanford 1954; A.B. Woodside, *Community and Revolution in Modern Vietnam*, Boston 1976.

mobilisation, or the creation of armed forces, that in the end were clearly necessary both in Indonesia and in Vietnam. What the INC needed to do was to make sure that it could draw upon a very widespread, generalised support for the nationalist cause that, after 1937, could be effectively registered in parliamentary elections. Anything else was either superfluous or ineffectual (as the events of the 1940s were to show).[53] In all this one can see Britain's inherent ambiguity characteristically inducing in the Indian national movement the distinctive, singular, intermediate *modus operandi* that in the contemporary southern Asian situation proved to be its hallmark.

Beyond this there are two further comments to be made. During 1936 the prevailing view both in Indian 'moderate/liberal' and in Congress circles was that the new Government of India Act of 1935 was an essentially negative construct. That in many respects it certainly was. Yet, quite typically of the British, it was also ambiguous. Whilst it was principally designed to ensure that British control at the centre was firmly entrenched, since it provided for a significantly larger franchise than before, especially in the Provinces, it served at the same time to open the door to a decisive advance in Indian nationalist fortunes. Earlier studies in this book have all but invariably reported on episodes and encounters which, whatever may have occurred whilst they were in train, saw a generally negative result in the end for the Indian side. The form that these took was to a very large degree determined, so it has been endlessly argued, by the persistent ambiguity of the British. The essential point, however, about ambiguity is that it is indeed double-edged. The eventual outcome could not therefore be predetermined. On many occasions that was in fact very negative. But, if the thesis has any validity, on occasion some positive outcomes should have occurred as well, and in 1937, and in an important respect in the last case to be considered in this book, a clearly positive outcome for the Indian National Congress did in fact occur. That serves to underscore the further point that whenever Congress was in agitational mode, the British could, with a clear conscience within their own self-imposed frame of reference, very easily bring themselves to suppress it. But so soon as Congress moved into constitutional mode, that same frame of reference made it all but impossible for them – as Sapru and Lothian had been much concerned to emphasise – to do other than live with the consequences, however threatening these might be to their imperial hold. One should, of course, not lean here too far the other way as both Sapru and Lothian were too prone to do and assert that a decid-

---

[53] The cadre organisation of 1940–1 and the Quit India movement were both a great deal less effectual than the electoral victories of 1946.

edly positive outcome could well nigh be assured if one was only to take the accommodatory road. For that would be to deprive Britain's persistent ambiguity of precisely its ambiguousness. There was nothing to suggest in anything that happened at this time that the British would never again resort to coercion, particularly if agitation came to be revived. Yet neither could it be said – as Nehru discovered in 1937 – that there was never any chance of the Congress cause being in any way well served by taking the constitutional road to its goal. Ambiguity could cut both ways, and after their experience of 1937 Congress leaders were a great deal more alert to this than before.[54]

[54] They interacted far more closely with the British in 1937–9, at the time of the Cripps mission, and between 1945 and 1947 than they had ever done since before the First World War.

7 The spider's web: Congress and provincial office 1937–1939

> The British Government know that the Congress is out for complete independence. It seems to me that the British Cabinet resent this attitude . . . If so, they should plainly tell the world that they will not tolerate complete independence and should cease to play with the word 'autonomy'. If on the other hand they do not mind national evolution of India to its destiny . . . they must treat the Congress with consideration . . .
>
> Gandhi, 6 May 1937

> For many years I have regarded our position and policy in India as that of fighting a rearguard action. We are deliberately surrendering our power and we ought to do it with good-will; but we must not let the rearguard turn into a rout. There are times when we have to stand and fight, even though at the end of it we continue to retire; and I think we may perhaps before long reach such a stage.
>
> Haig, Governor, UP, to Linlithgow, 4 December 1939

If the election campaign and the provincial election results early in 1937 largely resolved the debates within the Congress both over whether it should take the 'constitutional way' and over what it should do about establishing its 'mass contacts', they served at the same time to bring to a head the third argument running through the years 1935–7 over whether Congress should take provincial office if they won the provincial elections or not. This debate continued into the middle of 1937 and only then did the Congress leaders who won a clear majority, or who emerged at the head of the largest party in their province, eventually agree to take office. Nearly two and a half years later, they resigned *en bloc*. This whole story has been recounted in various forms before. It is not the purpose of the present chapter to provide a further extended account.[1] Its concern is

---

[1] E.g. Lord Glenderon, *The Viceroy at Bay: Lord Linlithgow in India 1936–43*, London 1971; Tomlinson, *The Indian National Congress*, chs. 2–5; Arnold, *The Congress in Tamilnad*, ch. 6; G. Rizvi, *Linlithgow and India*, London 1978, chs. 1, 2, 5; A.R.H. Copley, *The Political Career of C. Rajagopalachari: 1937–1954*, Delhi 1978, Pt I; D.E.U. Baker, *Changing Political Leadership in an Indian Province. The Central Provinces and Berar 1919–1939*, Delhi 1979, ch. VIII; M.C. Rau, *Govind Ballabh Pant. His Life and Times*, Delhi 1981, chs. 14–18; R.D. Shankerdass, *The First Congress Raj: Provincial Autonomy in Bombay*, Delhi

simply to point up the striking examples this further story provides of the way in which British ambiguity once again suffused Indian political developments during these years.

The 1937 elections were held under the terms of the new Government of India Act of 1935. That Act was ambiguity institutionalised. At the all-India level it provided for ministers in an All-India Federation government to be drawn from members of the federal legislature and to that extent established 'responsibility at the centre'. Because, however, of its provision for the special allocation of seats in the Federal Assembly to Muslims and to the Indian Princes, there was no likelihood that the Congress would ever secure a majority there. The Government of India's own calculations showed indeed that even were Congress to have as great a success in federal elections as it had had in the 1937 provincial elections, it would win no more than 100 out of a total of 332 seats.[2] There were, moreover, innumerable imperial 'safeguards' operating at the centre which gave the Viceroy considerable 'reserve' powers over external affairs, defence, the public services, currency, credit, etc., along with that overall matter, 'any grave menace to the peace or tranquillity of India'. The provincial arrangements were rather less tightly drawn. There was to be 'provincial autonomy' and 'responsible government in the provinces'. Popular majorities were thus to be free to determine the composition of provincial governments and their provincial policies, and to have full jurisdiction over a long list of subjects which included public order, the police, local government, education, health, etc., together with a number of concurrent powers with the centre. Provincial governors were under firm instructions, moreover, to employ their 'best endeavours to select . . . Ministers . . . in consultation with the person who . . . is most likely to command a stable majority in the Legislature'. Yet at the same time the 1935 Act gave governors considerable 'reserve' powers over the public services, the rights of minorities, 'the peace and tranquillity of the province', and not least – under section 93 of the Act – over any 'situation

1982; Shankerdass, *Vallabhbhai Patel*, London 1988, chs. 4–6; Henningham, *Peasant Movements in Colonial India*, ch. 6; M.R. Dove, *Forfeited Future. The Conflict over Congress Ministries in British India 1933–1937*, Delhi 1987; Rittenberg, *Ethnicity, Nationalism and the Pakhtuns*, ch. 6; R.S. Vasudevan, 'Why the Congress Accepted Office in 1937', *Studies in History*, 4, 1 & 2 n.s., 1988, pp. 37–84; Reeves, *Landlords and Governments in Uttar Pradesh*, ch. 5; Damodaran, *Broken Promises*, chs. 1–2; Kudaisya, 'State Power and the Erosion of Colonial Authority', ch. 4. The important parallel stories in these years of mounting Hindu–Muslim, Congress–Muslim League conflict is reviewed in A.I. Singh, *The Origins of the Partition of India, 1936–1947*, Delhi 1937, chs. 1 and 2, and Rizvi, *Linlithgow* ch. 4; of Congress intra-party conflict in Tomlinson, *Indian National Congress*; and of the negotiations with the Princes to bring about Federation in Rizvi, *Linlithgow*, ch. 3, and Copland, *Unwanted Allies*, ch. V.

[2] Menon's Note, 5 May 1937, H.Reforms 29/37 G(B).

. . . in which the government of the province cannot be carried on in accordance with the provisions of this Act'.[3] 'Responsible government in the provinces' was not in any way therefore untrammelled.

These dualisms at the heart of the regime constituted by the Act were well understood by leading figures on the British side. Characteristically there were marked differences amongst them. The Viceroy, Lord Linlithgow, was quite clear that: 'To Dominion Status [the British] are committed, though they are not committed as to its date . . . [and] they are not committed in any way to surrendering their freedom of judgment.'[4] To the Liberal peer, Lord Lothian, however, the Act held out all sorts of possibilities for the Indian electorate; 'as the diehards have ceaselessly pointed out', he told Gandhi, it 'is based on a dualism which cannot last indefinitely'.[5] Gandhi comprehended its duality too,[6] though in significantly different terms. The Act, he said in mid 1937,

is an honest effort to make the Provinces autonomous . . . The honest effort is, however, vitiated by the fact that simultaneous effort is being made to maintain the British connection practically by force.[7]

When following the final collapse of the Civil Disobedience movement Congressmen came to confront the regime which was due to be established by the Act they very soon faced a considerable challenge. Since the Act provided nothing of the *purna swaraj* they had been demanding since 1929, it left them very far short of their nationalist objectives. As so many of its provisions – its allocation of seats in the federal legislature and the reserve powers it granted the Viceroy and governors – would significantly limit any elected government's capacity to govern in accord with a popular mandate, and in any event vividly illustrated the extreme distrust in which the Congress was still held by the British, a great many Congressmen denounced the Act as totally unacceptable to the Indian people. They saw in its provision for 'responsible government in the provinces' a trap that was to be avoided at all costs, since to take provincial office under it could so easily drag them into the suffocating arms of an imperial embrace which could soon completely hamstring their larger ambitions.[8]

Yet in directly challenging the Act Congress was faced with formidable

[3] For convenient extracts see Gwyer and Appadori, *Speeches and Documents*, I, pp. 323–82.
[4] V to Haig, 1 Dec. 1939, HgP 2B.   [5] Lothian to Gandhi, 10 June 1937, SP13.
[6] See also Prasad's Presidential speech, Bombay Congress, 26 Oct. 1934, *RPCSD*, 1, pp. 236–7.
[7] Gandhi's discussion with an American [3 July 1937], *CWMG* 65, p. 359. See also 'My Meaning of Office Acceptance', 4 Sept. 1937, *CWMG* 66, pp. 104–5.
[8] E.g. Speeches by Nehru at Bombay, 18 May, Madras 6 Oct. 1936, Lucknow 6 Mar., Bombay, 10 Aug. 1937, *SWJN* 7, pp. 237, 495, and 8, pp. 55, 297–8.

problems. Although with Nehru in the van it had deeply committed itself both to 'destroying' the Act and to establishing a popularly elected Constituent Assembly to draft an independence constitution in its place, no one had any convincing ideas as to how either might be effected.[9] All the while, moreover, there were a good many other Congressmen who found it exceedingly difficult to close their eyes to the possible opportunities 'responsible government' in the provinces would bring to them if their leaders would now swallow their scruples and take provincial office. Even under the more limited 'dyarchy' provisions of the Government of India Act of 1919 Unionist ministers in the Punjab had managed to carry through a series of reforms which had significantly benefited their followers,[10] whilst in Madras those in the Justice Party in Madras had done a good deal to reward their adherents and disadvantage their opponents.[11] Congress ministers could well do likewise. In Bombay, for example, they could set about restoring the lands that had been confiscated during the course of the Civil Disobedience movement,[12] while in Bihar and UP they might carry through some badly needed agrarian reforms. There was nothing to suggest that provincial governors would attempt to suborn the Act and frustrate Congress ministries from proceeding with such reforms. In these circumstances to forswear provincial office might well be an egregious mistake.

There was as a consequence from at least mid 1935 onwards a continuing debate in the Congress on this issue that paralleled the two other debates we considered in the last chapter.[13] In putting this into context we may rehearse again the ongoing argument. There was no such debate in these years in the Philippines, since it was quite obvious by 1935 that Philippines' leaders should stand for the Philippines' Presidency and for other significant political offices, since this clearly now promised to be the penultimate step prior to securing full political independence from the United States. At the same time there was no corresponding debate in either Indonesia or Vietnam, since in neither place had any moves been made to throw significant executive positions open to nationalist leaders. There was, however, a debate in India both because that opportunity lay open there and because the British were still not offering anything like Indian independence.

In this third debate there stood on one side those like the UP politician Rafi Ahmed Kidwai who was greatly troubled about

---

[9] SWJN 7–9, passim.   [10] E.g. A. Husain, *Fazl-i-Husain*, Bombay 1946, ch. VIII.
[11] Baker, *The Politics of South India*, passim.
[12] Hardiman, *Peasant Nationalists of Gujarat*, ch. 9.
[13] Reddy to Rajagopalachari, 1 Aug. 1935, Rajagopalachari to Prasad, 3 Aug. 1935, Ansari to Prasad, 8 Aug. 1935, Prasad to Ansari, 12 Aug. 1935, RPP V/35/1.

Congress leaders occupying ministerial chairs and [being] merged with the Government Executive . . . The reaction . . . will be simply disastrous. We shall have to cease to talk of revolution and independence.[14]

Others, however, thought differently. Office acceptance, M.A. Ansari typically argued,

would not do much to bring independence or even the substance of independence much nearer, [but it] would have at least achieved respite to the war weary people and would have done a good deal of spade work for the future advance.[15]

When the Working Committee first considered this question at Wardha in August 1935, and again when the AICC met in Madras in the following month, they both found the issue already too hot to handle, and decided to defer a decision until the full Congress convened. At this stage Rajendra Prasad, the Congress President, did not think an early decision was required,[16] and for his own part was quite undecided as to which course it would be best to take.[17] By the end of 1935, however, the whole issue was arousing such 'a great deal of controversy'[18] that he asked the lately reconstituted Congress Parliamentary Board for its views.[19] The result was a considerable surprise.

Nobody could have imagined [Kripalani, the Congress Secretary, reported back to him] that there was such a strong opinion for accepting office. Excepting Punjab and Bengal, all the other Provinces were for acceptance of office . . . The main reasons . . . were 1. that other parties . . . would consolidate their power by means of office and make our work more difficult. 2. that there was no hope of any alliance with the minority parties . . . unless office was accepted . . . all . . . leaders responsible for Congress work in their respective provinces felt they had no choice if they had to consolidate the Congress position.

'If Jawaharlal does not fall in line', he added, 'the position will be a little difficult'.[20]

From the very outset Nehru had been quite determined that Congress should in no circumstances have anything to do with office under the 1935 Act.[21] He had made his position crystal clear in a number of statements he made on a recent visit to London,[22] and in his address to the Lucknow Congress in April 1936 dismissed the whole idea out of hand.

[14] Kidwai to Prasad, 4, 5 Aug. 1935 and enc., RPP III/35/2.
[15] Ansari to Nehru, 11 Feb. 1936, JNP Ansari file.
[16] Prasad to Dalvi, 24 Sept. 1935, RPP III/35/3.
[17] Prasad to Caveesher, 7 Sept. 1935, AICC G30/33 [sic]; Prasad to Nehru, 19 Dec. 1935, RPP VI/36.   [18] Pant to Prasad, 27 Dec. 1935, RPP III/35/5.
[19] Prasad to B. Desai, 19 Dec. 1935, ibid.
[20] Kripalani to Prasad, 15 Feb. 1936, RPP III/36/1.
[21] 'S.S.' review of Nehru's correspondence, 4 Dec. 1935, H.Poll.4/13/35.
[22] Ibid.

To accept office and ministry, under the conditions of the Act, [he inveighed] is to negative our rejection of it . . . as ministers under the Act, we could do very little to give relief and we would have to share responsibility for the administration with the apparatus of imperialism . . . Imperialism sometimes talks of cooperation but . . . the ministers who accept office will have to do so at the price of surrender of much they might have stood for in public. That is a humiliating position . . . disillusion with us will spread across the land . . . It will be a pit from which it would be difficult to come out.[23]

But he soon found that a majority of Congressmen were against him. So he played for time, and not only arranged that a decision should once again be postponed,[24] but over the ensuing months was very careful over what he said on this issue.[25]

When the AICC next met in Bombay in August 1936 it once more stalled on a decision, and this time deferred it till after the provincial elections had been held.[26] During these months Nehru began to feel that opinion was swinging to his side.[27] But support for office acceptance nevertheless remained strong, particularly in Madras, from where back in February 1936 Rajagopalachari had told Prasad that

no futile wrecking should be attempted, but as much benefit should be wrung out of the Councils as possible for strengthening the prestige and position of the Congress.[28]

That position was strongly endorsed by the Tamil Nadu PCC when in July 1936 it voted unequivocably in favour of office acceptance.[29] Nehru neverthelesss persisted and in a forthright speech in Madras in October 1936 once more declared that

it will be fatal for . . . Congressmen to accept office . . . it will lead to cooperation with British imperialism [and] tone down our struggle against imperialism.[30]

That simply provoked, however, a vigorous rebuttal from the Tamil Nadu PCC President, Satyamurti,[31] whereupon Nehru took the opportunity of his further Presidential address to the Faizpur Congress in December

[23] Speech 12 Apr. 1936, and see also Speech 11 Apr., *SWJN* 7, pp. 185–8, 167–9.
[24] See AICC G16/36, G25/36, G31/36, passim; Nehru to K. Menon, 28 Sept. 1936, ibid. pp. 470–1. [25] See speech and interview, Bombay 15 May, ibid. pp. 222–3, 226–7.
[26] Election manifesto, 22 Aug. 1936, ibid. p. 463.
[27] Nehru to K. Menon, 28 Sept. 1936, ibid. p. 471.
[28] Rajagopalachari to Prasad, 24 Feb. 1936, RPP VIII/36.
[29] Satyamurti to Kripalani, 11 July 1936, enclosing resolution of Tamil Nadu Congress Working Committee of 9 July, AICC P19/36.
[30] Speech, Madras, 6 Oct. 1936, *SWJN* 7, pp. 495–6.
[31] Satyamurti's speech, Vellore, 17 Nov. 1936, AICC P19/36. Around the same time Rajagopalachari told Erskine, G. Madras, that he had no doubt that 'if they got a majority' Congress would form a government there, see V to SoS (repeating Erskine's tel.), tel., 3 Feb. 1937, *TF* 1, item 91.

1936 to exhort the Congress yet again to have 'nothing to do with office and ministry . . . It would inevitably', he said, 'mean a kind of partnership with British imperialism'.[32]

Over the course of the intervening months Rajendra Prasad had been discussing the issue privately with a number of his closest colleagues. Like many others he was much troubled about whether those who took provincial office 'could be kept strictly to the Congress programme'. They might, he told Vallabhbhai Patel, simply 'settle down to routine administration which . . . will destroy the spirit of resistance'. At the same time he was also concerned that if Congress took office on

a programme of immediate deadlock . . . our opponents will be able to say . . . we were out to create deadlock . . . and my fear is [then] that if a re-election becomes necessary on account of our attitude . . . we may lose at it. If such is likely . . . I would frankly . . . prefer non-acceptance . . . [On the other hand] if we lay out a definite programme of action . . . such as to strengthen the people in their resistance and change their outlook . . . a deadlock would take some time in coming and in the meantime . . . we shall be doing [much] which will . . . please the people.[33]

By the middle of February 1937 he therefore seems to have come down in favour of office acceptance so as to secure a modicum of reforms, but at the same time remained fearful that if Congress stayed in office too long 'there is every likelihood of converting the Congressmen to moderate views'. Accordingly he proposed (so it was reported) that

a crisis should be created on an important issue as soon as possible after creating public opinion against the Act [in order to] compel the Governor to make use of special powers.[34]

In the aftermath of Congress's major successes in the provincial elections early in 1937 a decision about office acceptance could no longer be avoided.[35] Arrangements were accordingly made in February 1937 to consult PCCs for their views.[36] That proved to be quite unhelpful. Upon Nehru's prompting the UP PCC came out against office acceptance. So by two votes did the Maharashtrian PCC. But in Bombay three other PCCs voted in favour of office acceptance, as did the PCCs in Madras, the Central Provinces, and Bihar.[37] Successive postponements of a deci-

[32] Presidential address, Faizpur, 27 Dec. 1936, *SWJN* 7, pp. 608–9.
[33] Prasad to Patel, 14 July 1936, (and see also 14 Aug. 1936) RPP III/1936/1.
[34] Report by Deputy Central Intelligence Officer, Nagpur, 24 Feb. 1937, H.Poll.4/9/37.
[35] As it might have been if it had been generally necessary to form coalitions with others. See V to SoS, 15 Feb. 1937, Gowan to V, 26 Feb. 1937, Erskine to V (reporting conversation with Subbarayan), 1 Mar. 1937, Laithwaite to Stewart, 5 Mar. 1937, *TF* 1, items 66, 82, 87, 95. See also *SWJN* 8, pp. 48–75.   [36] Nehru to PCCs, 9 Feb. 1937, ibid. p. 47.
[37] FR, mid Mar. 1937, H.Poll.18/3/37. The Madras PCC's resolution is conveniently printed in *CWMG* 65, pp. 456–7.

sion over the preceding eighteen months had done nothing therefore to resolve the differences over this issue and had simply entrenched them even further. The dualism that lay at the heart of the 1935 Act was now threatening to tear the Congress apart.[38]

Hitherto Gandhi had kept his own counsel, but in his inimitable way he now came to the rescue. His chief concern was to wheel the disputants away from confronting each other and turn them into withstanding the British instead.[39] In precisely the same way that the British so often did, he proceeded to do this by tying together two completely contradictory positions into one composite formula. In mid February 1937, after talking to both Prasad and Rajagopalachari, and making himself fully apprised of Nehru's position,[40] it began to be reported that whilst he was 'in favour of working the reforms for three years at least without any attempt at wrecking' (clearly an elaboration of Prasad's formula)

he was at heart against acceptance of office, but in order to prevent a split will agree to it subject to conditions – these conditions, however, will be such that they cannot be accepted by Governors.[41]

The crunch came at the end of February 1937 when the Working Committee met at Wardha. Officially it concentrated on drafting an instruction to Congress's newly elected legislators 'to combat the Act', to maintain strict discipline, to secure the release of political prisoners and to effect agrarian reforms.[42] Such, however, was now the importance of the office acceptance issue that in spite of Nehru's insistence that no decision should be taken till the full AICC met a fortnight later: 'Most of the 28th [February] was occupied by informal discussion of . . . office acceptance.' 'The Socialist group maintained its hostile attitude.' The majority, however, argued strongly in its favour. With impeccable timing Gandhi now showed his hand. Whilst emphasising that the new constitution 'only deserved to be wrecked', 'Mr Gandhi', it was reported, 'was definitely in favour of acceptance'. But

with a view to placate the Socialists recommended office acceptance on the condition that Government gave an assurance that Ministers would be allowed full scope to use the constitution for the good of the people and that the safeguards and special powers would not be abused by the Governor.[43]

---

[38] E.g. Nehru's successive statements against the talk of office acceptance, 19 Feb.–23 Mar. 1937, *SWJN* 8, pp. 48–70.

[39] Emerson, now Governor of the Punjab, who had negotiated with Gandhi in 1930 (see chapter 4 above), anticipated much of this, Emerson to V, 19 Feb. 1937, *TF* 1, 73.

[40] See Erskine to V, 3 Feb. 1937, ibid. 45.   [41] CP FR, mid Mar. 1937, H.Poll.18/3/37.

[42] CWC Resolutions, 1 Mar. 1937, *TF* 1, 84.

[43] CP & Berar, FR late Feb. 1937, ibid. 85.

Nehru and the Socialists maintained their objections,[44] but when the AICC met in Delhi in mid March the decision was taken along these lines – to take provincial office but only on condition that each provincial leader was

satisfied and is able to state publicly that the Governor will not use his special powers of interference or set aside the advice of ministers in regard to constitutional activities.[45]

This Janus-faced resolution was a wonderfully crafted riposte to the double-think at the heart of the 1935 Act. It rescued the Congress from a threatening breach in its ranks. At the same time, as Gandhi clearly intended, it turned the heat against the British.

Late in 1936 Rajagopalachari had assured Lord Erskine, the Governor of Madras, that Gandhi was in favour of 'office acceptance', and that Congress would soon agree to this.[46] By January 1937 provincial governors were generally agreed that this was now likely.[47] But shortly after the Working Committee met at Wardha, and Gandhi made his intervention, while Rajagopalachari told Erskine that he was still 'fairly certain' Congress would take office, he now added that it would

make it much easier for Congress as a whole to agree to office acceptance, which was really complete reversal of their former policy, if they could get a written assurance . . . that Governors would not use the safeguards in ordinary course of Government business.

But Erskine told him promptly that a written assurance was inconceivable,[48] and Linlithgow, and Zetland, the Secretary of State, backed him to the full.[49] An attempt was then made to get Linlithgow to intervene, but he made it very plain that he would not take the issue out of the hands of the governors, and that he had no intention of allowing Gandhi to become its arbiter.[50] At the same time he told his provincial governors that the resolution passed in Delhi, it seemed to him, 'unquestionably

[44] Note, 15–22 Mar. 1937, AICC Misc. 42/1936 [sic]; Nehru's speech at Convention of Congress Legislators, 19 Mar. 1937, and interview, 23 Mar. 1937, *SWJN* 8, pp. 70, 72–4.
[45] AICC Resolution, 16 Mar. 1937, *TF* 1, 115, see also *CWMG* 65 App. I and AICC 42/36.
[46] Erskine to V, 3 Feb. 1937, *TF* 1, 45.
[47] Brabourne (Bombay), 15 Jan., Sifton (Bihar) 9 Feb., Haig (UP) 13, 17 Feb., Emerson (Punjab) 19 Feb., Griffith (NWFP) 22 Feb., Gowan (CP), 26 Feb., Erskine (Madras) 1 Mar., all to V, Laithwaite to Stewart, 5 Mar. 1937, V to SoS, 5 Mar. 1937, HD to Lgs, 16 Mar. 1937, Cabinet Paper 24/269, 19 Mar. 1937, ibid. 19, 55, 61, 69, 73, 79, 82, 87, 95, 96, 113, 117.   [48] V to SoS (repeating Erskine's tel.), tel., 3 Mar. 1937, ibid. 91.
[49] V to SoS, 4 (tels.), 12 Mar. 1937, V to Erskine, tel., 7 Mar. 1937, SoS to V, 8 Mar. 1937, Zetland's Cabinet Memo. 12 Mar. 1937, and see also Emerson to SoS, 19 Feb., Lothian to Nehru, 4 Mar. 1937, Nehru to Lothian, 25 Mar. 1937, ibid. 92, 106, 99, 102, 107, 73, 93, 130.
[50] V to SoS, 13 Mar., 9 Apr. 1937, ibid. 109, 182; V to SoS, 12 Mar. 1937, ibid. App. III.

represents a victory for the right wing of Congress',[51] and that since it did not specifically call for a governor's 'assurance' (and thus intriguingly replicated the ambiguity of the British), if they were to proceed with the utmost care they might shoehorn the Congress into government.[52] There was certainly a widespread belief at the time that the opponents of office acceptance had been badly worsted at Delhi and that Congress would very soon be taking provincial office.[53]

That, however, proved to be a grievous mistake.[54] For whilst there had been 127 votes in favour of Gandhi's recommendation at the Delhi meeting, the Socialists had nevertheless marshalled a significant minority of 70 votes against it,[55] and that meant that with a third of their colleagues remaining opposed to it the supporters of office acceptance had to step very warily indeed. The result was that when the Congress's provincial leaders now called on their provincial governors they each sought an assurance that he would not use any of his special powers nor ever reject his minister's advice.[56] Such an undertaking was inevitably rejected,[57] whereupon the Congress leaders abruptly refused to take office.[58]

By the end of March 1937 that brought about a total impasse.[59] Hitherto Gandhi had not spoken out openly on the subject but now proceeded to do so. The condition he had formulated for office accep-

---

[51] This was not entirely unwarranted, since the AICC 'went further than many of us wanted', Nehru to Lothian, 25 Mar. 1937, and Nehru's interview, 23 Mar. 1937, *SWJN* 8, pp. 130, 72–3. See also Birla to PSV, 17 Mar. 1937, G.D. Birla, *Bapu. A Unique Association*, Bombay 1977, Vol. II, p. 334, Gandhi to Nehru, 5 Apr. 1937, *CWMG* 65, p. 55, Zetland's Cabinet Memo, 12 Mar. 1937, SoS to V, 5 Apr. 1937, *TF* 1, 107, 169.

[52] V to SoS, tel.(quoting his tel. to Gs), 18, 19 Mar. 1937, ibid. 116, 119.

[53] See further, 'Confidential Appreciation of the Post-Election Situation in India', Cabinet Paper 24/269, 19 Mar. 1937; and Rajagopalachari's interview to *Justice*, 23 Mar. 1937, ibid. 117, 126.

[54] Erskine had been warned about this by Rajagopalachari at a further interview on 9 Mar., Erskine to Linlithgow, 9 Mar. 1937, IOL Erskine Papers 11.

[55] AICC 42/37; 'a very narrow majority', Linlithgow called it, V to SoS, 18 Mar. 1937, *TF* 1, 116.

[56] On the background to this see Nariman to Kripalani, 16 Apr. 1937, Kripalani to Nariman 21 Apr. 1937, AICC G39(i)/37; Gandhi's Interview, 19 Mar. 1937, *CWMG* 65, p. 8.

[57] On Linlithgow's instructions, tel., 22 Mar. 1937, V to SoS, 30 Mar. 1937, Zetland's Cabinet memo. 31 Mar. 1937, *TF* 1, 124, 147, 152.

[58] FRs early Apr. 1937, H.Poll.18/3/37; Haig to V, tel., 24 Mar. 1937, V to SoS, 28 Mar. 1937; Rajagopalachari tried but failed to find an acceptable compromise formula, see his statement, 27 Mar. 1937, and V to SoS, tel., 26 Mar. 1937, ibid. 129, 141, 139, 136; Gandhi to A. Harrison, tel., 27 Mar. 1937, *CWMG* 65, p. 26; tels. to and from Prasad, 25 Mar. 1937, Das's letter (Orissa), 29 Mar. 1937, *RPCSD* 1, pp. 32, 278–9; Arnold, *Congress in Tamilnad*, p. 182.

[59] E.g. Nehru's statement, 29 Mar. 1937, *SWJN* 8, p. 76, *TF* 1, 141; Pant to Prasad, 2 Apr. 1937, ibid. 162, *RPCSD* 1, pp. 34–5; 8 Apr. 1937, RPP 2/37/2.

tance, he declared, was one that 'could be easily accepted by the Governors'. Congress had not asked for any amendment of the constitution. It accepted that 'Governors have discretionary powers'. What it asked for was a 'gentlemanly understanding' that Congress ministers would not be put 'in dread of interference at the will of the Governors'.[60]

The response from the British side came on 8 April in a speech by Zetland, the Secretary of State for India, in the House of Lords, in which he declared[61] that to grant the demand Congress was making would amount to

a grave breach of faith with the minorities and others in India who have been promised the protection against the arbitrary rule of a majority ... reserve powers are an integral part of the Constitution ... they cannot be abrogated except by Parliament itself and ... the Governors therefore cannot treat the Congress as a privileged body which is exempt from the provisions ... by which all other Parties are bound.[62]

That refusal[63] generated a very great deal of bitterness in the Congress,[64] and led to a flood of words both in India and in Britain.[65] At Zetland's prompting Lothian wrote to *The Times* criticising Gandhi's stance,[66] while he wrote to Gandhi too.[67] Gandhi responded both publicly and privately,[68] and others joined in as well.[69] On receiving legal advice that 'Governors could give the required assurance without infringement of the Act',[70] Gandhi now suggested that if this was not agreed a joint tribunal should be established by the Congress and the

---

[60] Gandhi's statement, 30 Mar. 1937, *CWMG* 65, pp. 36–8, *TF* 1, 146.

[61] Linlithgow briefed him, V to SoS, tels., 28 Mar., 7 Apr. 1937; see also Reforms Comm's Note, 2 Apr. 1937, SoS to Hoare, 5 Apr. 1937, SoS to V, 5 Apr. 1937, Hoare to SoS, 6 Apr. 1937, Cabinet Paper 2388, 7 Apr. 1937, ibid. 141, 176, 158, 168, 169, 170, 177.

[62] Parliamentary Debates, House of Lords, 8 Apr. 1937, ibid. 178.

[63] Deliberately so, SoS to V, 12 Apr. 1937, ibid. 190.

[64] Gandhi to A. Harrison, 9, 10 (tel.) Apr. 1937, *CWMG* 65, pp. 64, 72; Nehru's interview, 9, 14 Apr. 1937, message to *News Chronicle*, 16 Apr. 1937, Nehru to A. Harrison, 18 Apr. 1937, *SWJN* 8, pp. 81–2, 83–5. At the same time it was received with considerable relief elsewhere, Ambedkar's statement, 9 Apr. 1937, *TF* 1, 180.

[65] E.g. ibid., M.N. Roy's article, 4 Apr. 1937, ibid. 180, 165, and Indian and British newspapers mid April 1937 passim. For running commentaries on events over the next two months see *SWJN* 8, pp. 86–103 passim, and *Bapu*, II, pp. 340–81.

[66] Lothian to *The Times*, 6, 9 Apr. 1937. See the prompting he received from the India Office, Stewart to Lothian, 2 Apr. 1937, Lothian to Stewart, 4 Apr. 1937, *TF* 1, 160–1, 164.

[67] Lothian to Gandhi, 9 Apr. 1937, ibid. 184; idem, 10 June 1937, copy in SP 13.

[68] Gandhi's statement, 10 Apr. 1937, Gandhi to Lothian, 24 June 1937, *CWMG* 65, pp. 70–2, 332–3, *TF* 1, 187, 324; Gandhi to Lothian, 8 May 1937, copies in SP 13.

[69] Sapru, for example, made a number of statements, SP 13 passim; Sapru to Datt, 11 Apr. 1937, Sikander Hayat Khan in the Punjab Legislature, 8 May 1937, *TF* 1, 188, 246.

[70] Gandhi's statement, 10 Apr. 1937, *CWMG* 65, pp. 70–2, *TF* 1, 187; Gandhi to Munshi, 4 Apr., Munshi to Gandhi, 9 Apr. 1937, *CWMG* 65, pp. 52, 65.

British to make a decision on the matter. When his suggestion was abruptly rejected, his ire rose.[71]

My advice to the Congress [he now declared on 14 April] has always been that office acceptance would be a fatal blunder without a previous understanding regarding safeguards which are in the Governors' discretion . . . A refusal to submit [this] interpretation to examination by a legal tribunal will raise the strong presumption that the British Government had no intention of dealing fairly by the majority party whose advanced programme they dislike. I prefer an honourable deadlock to dishonourable daily scenes between Congressmen.[72]

But by now things were not all going Congress's way. Non-Congress governments were already taking office in five provinces.[73] In each of the six where Congress had secured a majority, minority governments were being installed.[74] There were suggestions, of course, that this was unconstitutional,[75] but under the terms of the 1935 Act they could remain in office for six months before needing to face their legislatures, and were soon exploiting the opportunities available to them.[76] As the weeks passed, moreover, there were a good many signs that whilst Congressmen everywhere remained completely loyal to the AICC's formal position, a great many of them were becoming increasingly frustrated at Congress's continued refusal to take office.[77]

Amidst this disturbing situation[78] the AICC met again in Allahabad on 26–29 April. They lambasted Zetland for his 8 April speech and supported the position Gandhi had taken up.[79] But they now narrowed down the point at issue to say no more than that, whilst they did not seek to

---

[71] Gandhi's statements 10, 14, 15 Apr. 1937 (he had been none too pleased earlier, Gandhi to A. Harrison, 5 Apr. 1937), ibid. pp. 70–2, 84–5 (and 54–5), *TF* 1, 187, 196; V to SoS, 14 Apr. 1937, Gandhi to Rajagopalachari, 17 May 1937, ibid. 192, 257.

[72] Gandhi's statement, 14 Apr. 1937, *CWMG* 65, pp. 83–4, *TF* 1, 196.

[73] Emerson (Punjab), 22 Feb. 1937, Anderson (Bengal), 9 Mar. 1937, Reid (Assam), 12 Mar. 1937, Graham (Sind), 22 Mar. 1937, all to V, V to SoS, 30 Mar. 1937, Zetland's Cabinet memo. 31 Mar. 1937, FR NWFP, 17 Apr. 1937, *TF* 1, 78, 103, 122, 147, 152, 201.

[74] V to SoS, 25 Mar. 1937, Zetland's Cabinet Memo., 31 Mar. 1937, ibid. 132, 152; Arnold, *Congress in Tamilnad*, p. 183. The greatest difficulty for the British was in UP, but the Nawab of Chhatari (a longstanding UP minister under 'dyarchy') eventually did so, Haig to V, 31 Mar., 1, 7 Apr. 1937, V to Haig, 1 Apr. 1937, ibid. 154, 156, 175, 157; see also Reeves, *Landlords and Governments*, pp. 229–30.   [75] V to SoS, 7 Apr. 1937, ibid. 173.

[76] On their position see SoS to V, 17 (tel.), 22 Mar. 1937, Haig to V, 23 Apr., 7 May 1937, Cunningham's report, 4 May 1937, Chhatari to Sapru, 30 May 1937, Chhatari to Haig, 23 June 1937, ibid. 114, 123, 212, 238, 231, 283, 320.

[77] E.g. FRs mid and late Apr. 1937, H.Poll.18/4/37; Pant to Prasad, 8 Apr. 1937, Birla to Lothian, 15 Apr. 1937, Erskine to V, 18 May 1937, *TF* 1, 179, 194, 260.

[78] E.g. Gandhi's speeches at Gandhi Seva Sangh meeting, 17, 20 Apr. 1937, Gandhi's interview with *The Hindu*, 22 Apr. 1937, his interviews, 25, 26 Apr. 1937, *CWMG* 65, pp. 104–5, 120–7, 140–1, 154–6.

[79] Gandhi's interview with *The Hindu*, 22 Apr. 1937, *TF* 1, 209.

deprive a Governor of the right to dismiss a government or dissolve a legislature if a serious dispute should arise, they had

grave objection to ministers having to submit to interference by Governors with the alternative of themselves having to resign office instead of the Governors taking responsibility of dismissing them.[80]

Cast in those terms the argument was becoming much too abstruse for many people to follow,[81] and only made confusion worse confounded.

Around this time Congress leaders in both UP and in CP tried to undermine the 1935 Act by summoning private meetings of legislators in their provinces which they invited ministers in their minority governments to attend; but to no avail.[82] On 6 May Zetland made a more conciliatory speech in which he stressed that the governors' reserved powers 'will not normally be in operation', and that

there can be no possible question of the Governors interfering constantly and embarrassingly in the responsibilities and work of the Ministries.[83]

Coupled, however, with some ill-judged remarks by the Governor of Bombay, that failed to break the impasse.[84] During the course of these weeks both Gandhi and Rajagopalachari attempted to get the government to concede that should there be a 'serious disagreement' between a Governor and his Congress ministers the Governor should either dismiss them or insist that they should themselves resign.[85] But Linlithgow, Zetland, and their Governors remained unmoved.[86] So on 2 June Gandhi tried again by telling *The Times of India* that he was

very anxious that Congressmen should take office – but only if Government show their willingness to conciliate the Congress.[87]

---

[80] CWC Resolutions, 26–29 Apr. 1937, ibid. 216.
[81] Gandhi's interviews, 30 Apr., 6 May 1937, *CWMG* 65, pp. 158–9, 174–5.
[82] Khare to Gowan, 13 Apr. 1937, Gowan to Khare, 17 Apr. 1937, Khare's statement 3 May 1937, Chhatari to Pant, 4 May 1937, Tandon to Haig, 10 May 1937, Donaldson to Tandon, 16 May 1937, CP G's FR mid May 1937, Cabinet Paper 24/270, 23 June 1937, *TF* 1, 191, 199, 228, 232, 249, 252, 253, 319; Pant to Prasad, 8 Apr. 1937, *RPCSD* 1, pp. 38–9.
[83] Zetland speech, House of Lords, 6 May 1937, following a discussion in Cabinet the day before, Cabinet Paper 23/88, *TF* 1, 237, 233; *CWMG* 65, pp. 462–4.
[84] Gandhi's interviews, 6, 12, 14 May 1937, Desai to Birla, 14 May 1937, Gandhi to A. Harrison, and to Rajagopalachari, 17 May 1937, Gandhi to Latthe, ibid. pp. 175–6, 190, 209, 197–8, 214–16, 244–5; Patel to Prasad, 24 May 1937, *RPCSD* 1, p. 42, 9 June 1937, RPP II/37/3.
[85] Ibid., and Erskine to V, tel., 27 May 1937, V to SoS, 28 May 1937, *TF* 1, 278-80.
[86] Zetland's Cabinet Memo., 29 Apr. 1937, SoS to V, 13 June 1937, Erskine to V, 16 June 1937, V to SoS, 16 June 1937, ibid. 219, 305, 308, 309.
[87] Gandhi's statement to *The Times of India*, 2 June 1937; 'I want a sign from them before I take office, and I regard that sign as indispensable', Gandhi to Rajagopalachari, 11 June 1937, *CWMG* 65, pp. 261–3, 291–2, *TF* 1, 285, 304; Patel to Prasad, 7, 9 June 1937, RPP II/37/3.

That was now the central issue. For older Congressmen a decision was now becoming increasingly urgent since there were mounting signs that the Socialists had become very impatient at Gandhi's seeming readiness to brush aside 'our decisions of combating the Act or of fighting for Independence' and might well soon create a crisis.[88] On 11 June Rajagopalachari accordingly anxiously told Erskine that:

If Congress took office without an understanding, they would not be able to control their extreme wing, but if there was some understanding with Governors then they would find it easier to do so.[89]

Till this point Linlithgow had very deliberately refrained from making any move himself. There had been a good deal of pressure on him from some Cabinet members in London to reach a settlement, and he had been strongly criticised for his dilatoriness in the Anglo-Indian press. But he was determined not to be rushed.[90] During the course of May he carefully considered how to proceed, and quite typically came up with a double-headed policy. Should Congress continue to decline office (he told his provincial governors) legislatures in the Congress majority provinces should be summoned, and if that led to their minority governments losing a vote of confidence, they should necessarily be required to resign. If provincial Congress leaders persisted in refusing office, governors should then take emergency powers under Section 93 of the 1935 Act. Thereafter, however, legislatures should not be summoned, but they should not be dissolved either, since that would allow Congress to increase its majority at an ensuing election, which could only deepen the crisis. Linlithgow was quite confident when outlining this course of action that the control the British exercised in India remained sufficient to secure their position there.

It was, however, of the very essence of the British stance that it very rarely faced in one direction only. And so it was that in quite classic manner Linlithgow coupled his contemplation of a constitutional breakdown with the quite contrary consideration of an

immediate constructive policy towards Congress, [to see] whether any step can be taken . . . within the terms of the Act and of the policy we have hitherto adopted . . . to facilitate office acceptance.

What he had in mind was to make a public statement that would

---

[88] Kidwai to Kripalani, 7 June 1937, S. Rao to J.P. Narayan, 2 June 1937, Patel to Prasad, 7 June 1937, *TF* 1, 297, 286, 296. Gandhi acknowledged that he had toned down his conditions, though not altogether, Gandhi to Prasad, 6 June 1937, *CWMG* 65, pp. 284–5.   [89] Erskine to V, tel., 11 June 1937, *TF* 1, 303.

[90] V to SoS, tels., 14, 16 Apr. 1937, ibid. 192, 197. On the background to all this see Glendevon, *Viceroy at Bay*, pp. 50–67, Rizvi, *Linlithgow*, pp. 34–48, and Marquess of Zetland, *'Essayez'*, London 1956, pp. 217–23.

gather up the threads of this business, [emphasise the] anxiety of Governors not merely not to provoke a conflict in the area of their special responsibilities, but to leave nothing undone to avoid such conflict arising . . . and [end by] expressing hope that misunderstandings and misconceptions have now been removed.

In framing this possible course of action he had two considerations particularly in mind. It would avoid 'giving ground to any suggestion at home that we are adopting a stiff and legalistic policy'.[91] And since 'after mature consideration of the arguments on both sides' the reforms embodied in the 1935 Act had very deliberately provided for responsible government in the Provinces:

So long as the present Act is in operation, and so long as Congress represent the largest party in the legislatures, it must inevitably be our object to secure the help of Congress in carrying on the administration.[92]

The provincial governors and the Secretary of State soon endorsed this approach,[93] and in mid June Linlithgow sat down to draft his proposed 'message'.

I have worded my statement [he told his governors] in the most conciliatory manner possible, but it involves no modification of position on which we have throughout stood . . . [Moreover:] We are clear as to the line to be taken in the event of a complete breakdown.[94]

His plan was to stretch to the full the ambiguity in the British position and ensnare the Congress in its enveloping coils.[95]

In a broadcast message on 21 June 1937 he played his ace, and in a published statement the next day he resolutely refrained from backing down, gave nothing away, and made no concessions to the Congress's demands. He reminded his hearers too that if

a deplorable outcome should emerge from the present situation . . . it might be beyond the power of any of us rapidly to reverse the circumstances that would then supervene.

But at the very same time he played every conciliatory note in his repertoire. He referred to 'a great political party'. He endorsed Gandhi's suggestion that any breakdown in a governor–minister relationship should be strictly limited to a 'serious disagreement'. He acknowledged

[91] He had been warned about this, SoS to V, 22 Apr., 3 May 1937, ibid. 210, 227; see also V to SoS, tel., 28 Mar. 1937, ibid. 141, Butler to Brabourne, 21 May 1937, Brabourne Papers, IOL, 21.   [92] See also SoS to V, 28 June 1937, TF 1, 332.

[93] Haig, 21 May, Erskine, Gowan 24 May, Hallett 25 May, Cunningham, Brabourne 26 May, Hubback 27 May 1937, Zetland 6 June, all to V, ibid. 263, 270, 273, 274, 275, 276, 277, 294.

[94] V to Gs, tel., 16 June, also 9 June 1937, ibid. 310, 298; V to Haig, 11 June 1937, HgP 3A.

[95] On all this see V to Gs, 18 May 1937, V to SoS, 21 May 1937, ibid. 259 (Brabourne's copy), 264.

the sincerity of those who had opposed the 1935 Act, and he committed himself 'to strive unstirringly towards the . . . final establishment in India . . . of parliamentary government'. He was careful, moreover, to spell out in very precise terms the exact position concerning a Governor's role.

Three months' experience . . . of the Constitution [he affirmed] . . . has conclusively shown . . . that the apprehensions . . . that Governors would seek . . . [to] challenge the Ministers in the day to day administration of the Province, have no shadow of justification . . . it [is] clear beyond any possibility of question that . . . in all matters falling within the ministerial field . . . the Governor will ordinarily be guided . . . by the advice of his Ministers.[96]

Nehru captured the point precisely when three days later he remarked that:

The Viceroy has spoken softly but the meaning of his utterance is hard as British imperialism is hard.[97]

The two-facedness of the British had scarcely ever been quite so expressly displayed before.[98]

Gandhi deliberately refrained from commenting upon the Viceroy's statement[99] till the Working Committee had met at Wardha on 6–7 July. By then, however, he 'was receiving [letters] from various parts of the country', that 'were making him incline more and more to office acceptance'.[100] Linlithgow was reasonably content with the reception his pronouncement had received, but remained very wary about what precisely the outcome would be.[101] At Wardha Gandhi strongly rebutted the charge that he had steadily emasculated the Congress's demands, though he accepted that the assurances he had sought had not as yet been given.[102] By now, however, it was quite clear that very many Congressmen had become very impatient indeed at Congress's continuing refusal to take office.[103] Three days before the meeting began Nehru arrived in Wardha threatening 'open revolt if a resolution in favour of acceptance

[96] V's speech, 21 June 1937, *CWMG* 65, pp. 467–71. For an all too brief extract see *TF* 1, 316.   [97] Nehru's statement, 24 June 1937, *TF* 1, 322.

[98] E.g. V to Haig, 30 June 1937, HgP 3A.

[99] Gandhi's interview 22 June 1937; privately he admitted it was 'an improvement', Gandhi to Lothian, 24 June 1937, *CWMG* 65, pp. 329–30, 332–3, *TF* 1, 324.

[100] M. Desai to Birla, 16 July, 1 Aug. 1937, *TF* 1, 366, 390. For the plethora of local Congress resolutions urging Congress to accept office see FR Mar.–July 1937, H.Poll.18/3/37–18/7/37.

[101] See Linlithgow's correspondence 24 June–1 July 1937 (there was in particular a last-minute contretemps with Rajagopalachari), ibid. 323, 324–34, 337–9, 342.

[102] Gandhi's speech at CWC, 6 July 1937, *CWMG* 65, p. 372, *TF* 1, 349.

[103] E.g. Erskine to V, 18 May, 11 June (tel.), 1937, Haig to V, 21 May, 23 June 1937, Dep. Comm. Nagpur to Comm. Nagpur, 24 May 1937, Brabourne to V, 5 June 1937, Roy to Gandhi, 4 July 1937, ibid. 260, 303, 263, 321, 272, 288, 345; FR mid and late June 1937, H.Poll.18//6/37; Nehru's statement 16 June 1937, *TF* 8, pp. 100–1; Kishore to Pant, 21 June 1937, NMML Pant Papers 4/8; FRs June 1937, H.Poll.18/6/37.

was passed'. He was, however (so it was reported), 'brought into line by Gandhi in the course of lengthy private discussions', and at the ensuing meeting: 'With Nehru controlled, the voice of the Left was hardly raised.'[104] As a result whilst continuing to emit defiance, the Working Committee finally announced on 7 July that as recent statements from the British side appeared to ensure 'that it will not be easy for the Governors to use their special powers', Congress provincial leaders were now being authorised to take office.[105] Nehru put a brave face on the decision. Those who opposed office acceptance, he declared, had

> feared that acceptance involved grave risk of our getting involved in petty reform-ist activities and forgetting for a while the main issue . . . Thus it is not to work the constitution . . . that we . . . accept offices. It is . . . to stultify the constitution . . . prepare the ground for . . . independence . . . strengthen the masses and . . . give some relief to them . . . If we accept office we do so for a longer purpose in view, and we have to leave it when that purpose can be better served otherwise.[106]

They would enter 'the cage',[107] that is, but be exceedingly careful to hold the key to its exit in their own hands.[108]

Linlithgow had pulled off a major coup; 'we have won the first round', Zetland crowed, 'and that may well turn out to be the most important'.[109] In its characteristically insidious way the imperial spider had succeeded, for the time being at least, in luring the Congress into its finely wrought and glutinous web.

In the course of the next few days the minority governments all resigned, and in five and eventually seven provinces Congress ministers took office.

---

[104] CID note, PSV to Croft, 12 July 1937, Gowan to V, 21 July 1937, *TF* 1 359, 378. 'Jawaharlal was more than good throughout', Gandhi to Amrit Kaur, 10 July 1937, *CWMG* 65, p. 380; Nehru to A. Harrison, 24 June 1937 and his interviews, 7, 10, 13 July 1937, *SWJN* 8, pp. 103, 105–10.

[105] CWC resolution, 7 July 1937, *CWMG* 65, pp. 373–4, *TF* 1, 347, AICC 42/37; Gowan to V, 6 July, Gandhi's speech at Wardha, 7 July (see also *CWMG* 65, p. 372), Laithwaite to Croft (forwarding CID note), 12 July 1937, *TF* 1, 348, 349, 359. Behind the scenes these events coincided with a crisis on the British side consequent upon an apparent move by Zetland to compromise with Gandhi, which brought Linlithgow to the verge of resignation; the Wardha decision, however, dissipated this, and Linlithgow was warmly congratulated on his success in securing the outcome, Glendevon, *Viceroy at Bay*, pp. 64–7.

[106] Nehru's statement, *Times of India*, 12 July 1937, *TF* 1, 353. See also Nehru in Bombay, 11 Aug. 1937, *CWMG* 8, p. 434.

[107] Rajagopalachari's term, Copley, *Rajagopalachari*, p. 65.

[108] See especially Katju's remarks as recorded in Haig to V, 23 June 1937, *TF* 1, 321. For extensive AICC correspondence on the whole issue see AICC G18, G39, G62 1937.

[109] Zetland to Linlithgow [12 July 1937], IOL Zetland Papers 8(2), quoted Copley, *Rajagopalachari*, p. 64.

Both sides approached the new circumstances with a good deal of apprehension. Haig (who had become Governor of UP in 1934) believed 'that a Congress Government could not function in this province without leading to a very rapid breakdown',[110] while Gandhi opined that:

If this thing lasts beyond a year, I shall either infer that the Britishers have become angels or that our ministers are completely kow-towing to them![111]

The first six months were accordingly crucial. Of the principal Congress leaders only Rajagopalachari became Premier of his province, Madras; B.G. Kher became Premier of Bombay, N.R. Khare of CP, G.B. Pant of UP, S.K. Sinha of Bihar and Biswanath Das of Orissa.[112] After a visit by Rajendra Prasad in September 1937, Dr Khan Sahib formed a Congress-led government in the Frontier Province,[113] while a year later a similar Congress-led government was formed in Assam under Bardoloi.[114] So as to ensure that these ministries operated effectively and did not become too ensnared in the imperial embrace, a 'Parliamentary Sub-Committee' consisting of three members of the Congress 'High Command' was formed, in which Vallabhbhai Patel took charge of Bombay, Madras, CP, and Sind, Rajendra Prasad of Bihar, Orissa, and Assam, and Maulana Azad of UP, NWFP, Punjab, and Bengal.[115]

A series of moves was then made to signify that despite its acceptance of office Congress had in no way abandoned its ultimate objectives. Its ministers were instructed to have no social contacts with governors or any officials.[116] They were enjoined to move resolutions in their legislatures denouncing the 1935 Act and demanding the establishment of a Constituent Assembly.[117] They were directed to remove all restrictions on 'unlawful' publications and organisations; and to effect the early release of any remaining political prisoners.[118] Most of these things the governors

---

[110] Haig to V, 10 Jan. 1938, HgP 17.   [111] Desai to Birla, 1 Aug. 1937, *TF* 1, 390.

[112] They were variously called Chief Minister, Premier, Prime Minister, e.g. V to Brabourne, 13 Sept. 1937, *TF* 1, 459.

[113] Cunningham to V, 6 Sept. 1937, Prasad to Patel, 17 Sept. 1937, *TF* 1, 447, 463.

[114] On this story and its background see K. Ogborn, 'The Development of Nationalist Politics in the Assam Valley 1920–1939', University of Western Australia PhD thesis 1982.

[115] See also CWC resolution, 30 Sept. 1938 (copy), HgP 2A. For their activities see *RPCSD* 1–4 passim. Nehru as President continued to exercise authority too, e.g. Nehru to Khare, 4 Nov. 1937, *TF* 1, 532.

[116] Desai to Birla, 1 Aug. 1937, V's note on meeting with Gandhi, 4 Aug. 1937, ibid. 390, 396; Haig to V, 9 Feb. 1937, HgP 17B.

[117] Nehru to Premiers, 30 July 1937, *SWJN* 8, pp. 287–8; Erskine to V, 7 Aug. 1937, Rajagopalachari's speech, 31 Aug. 1937, Brett to HD, 16 Sept. 1937, *TF* 1 404, 438, 462.

[118] Nehru to Premiers, 16 July 1937, *SWJN* 8, pp. 280–1; Gandhi, *Harijan*, 21 July 1937, *TF* 1, 374.

took in their stride.[119] On two matters, however, they dug in. They refused to allow Congress flags to be hoisted over government buildings, or when they themselves were present.[120] Over the ensuing year this caused a number of passing problems, but the point was eventually conceded. On Linlithgow's instructions they insisted too that they must preside at Cabinet meetings.[121] Congress at first vehemently resisted this;[122] but a compromise was eventually reached whereby whilst ministers would hold their own meetings beforehand, a formal protest would be recorded every time a governor took the chair.[123]

Over the first six months there were some considerable problems over political prisoners. The largest number of them came from Bengal, many of whom had been exiled to the penal settlement in the Andaman islands.[124] Because Congress did not hold office in Bengal there was little it could do but campaign for their release.[125] Where, however, it did hold office Congress ministers immediately set about demanding the immediate release of all remaining political prisoners.[126] Since it could not easily be argued that releasing a few prisoners in each province could entail 'a grave menace', and as generally the country remained 'quiet', Linlithgow's early dictum to his governors that upon such issues they 'would be unwise to press disgreement with Ministry about any of these to point of break' was mostly followed.[127] Governors did nonetheless do their best to make sure that any releases to which they agreed should not embarrass their fellow Governors. They pressed, moreover, for each case to be considered individually; for assurances to be provided of good behaviour by anyone who had been convicted of violence; and for

[119] V to Brabourne, 10 Aug. 1937, ibid. 410. The social boycott was soon being honoured in the breach, Lumley to V, 25 Sept. 1937, Cunningham to V, 23 Oct., 10 Nov. 1937, ibid. 470, 508, 541; Mrs Pandit, Nehru's sister and a minister in UP, had lunch with the Governor around the end of November, Haig to V, 9 Dec. 1937, HgP 17B; by mid 1938 the CWC were relaxing the injunction, Glendevon, *Viceroy at Bay*, p. 97; while by December 1938 Rajagopalachari was attending the St Andrew's Day dinner in Madras, Copley, *Rajagopalachari*, p. 53.

[120] V to Brabourne, 17 Aug. 1937, V to Gowan, 25 Aug. 1937, Haig to V, 15 Oct. 1937, V to Haig 25 Oct. 1937, *TF* 1, 421, 427, 495, 511; Haig to V, 8 Nov. 1937, HgP 17B; Gandhi, 'The National Flag', *Harijan*, 24 Oct. 1938, *CWMG* 68, pp. 47–9. No exception was taken, however, to Congress ministers flying Congress flags at their own residences, V to Erskine, 23, 24 July 1937, *TF* 1, 380–1.

[121] V to Gs, 13 July 1937, V to SoS, 15 July 1937, V to Brabourne, 25 July 1937, *TF* 1, 360, 362, 382.

[122] Pant to Nehru, 7 Aug. 1937, ibid. 406; Nehru to Khare, 14 Nov. 1937, *SWJN* 8, p. 356.

[123] CWC Minutes, 26–31 Oct. 1937, *TF* 1, 520.

[124] Anderson to V, 27 July 1937, Stewart to PSV, nd, ibid. 385, App. IV.

[125] E.g. V to Haig, tel., 4 Aug. 1937, Anderson's note of conversation with Gandhi (copy), 11 Nov. 1937, HgP 22A; Nehru, *Amrita Bazar Patrika*, 7 Aug. 1937, *TF* 1, 405.

[126] CWC Minutes, 14–17 Aug. 1937, ibid., 416; Nehru's speech, Bombay, 11 Sept. 1937, *SWJN* 8, p. 325.   [127] Haig to V, 16 July 1937, *TF* 1, 364.

consideration to be given to the concerns of those responsible for law and order (the police in particular) when any release was made.[128] Along these lines they managed to drag out the process for several months, even though considerable numbers of political prisoners were indeed released.[129]

There were all the same a number of early encounters upon some rather incidental matters. In October 1937 there was, for example, a complex run-in between Das, the Premier of Orissa, and Hubback, the Governor, over several matters where Das believed Hubback should have consulted him before making a decision. Hubback defended himself. But Das insisted that he 'should be regarded as the constitutional adviser of the Governor in all cases, including such cases', and in the end got his way.[130] There was a brief contretemps too over a confidential circular by the Bihar Chief Secretary saying that unless an order had been signed by a government official it should not be acted upon – which seemed to preclude any orders by a minister – until this was rectified.[131] More extensively there were disputes over officials' pay. Congress had decided that ministers' salaries should be limited to Rs.500,[132] and they wanted a significant cut in officials' pay as well. Governors unanimously resisted this, and as this clearly fell within their own 'special responsibilities', despite a particularly vigorous tussle in Madras, they eventually won out.[133]

The most likely flashpoint had always been Gujarat.[134] Back in 1930 Irwin had promised to uphold the land confiscations there at the time of the first Civil Disobedience movement. Patel had been outraged that the Gandhi–Irwin Pact of 1931 had made no amends about this.[135] Since this threatened Congress's entire hold upon Gujarat, Congress had thereupon committed itself to a restoration of these lands so soon as it was in any position to do so. In August 1937 Kher and his colleagues in the Bombay Cabinet accordingly immediately broached the issue with the

---

[128] E.g. V to Haig, tels., 15, 17, 18 July 1937, Haig to V, 15, 16 July 1937, V to SoS, tel., 6 Aug. 1937 (copy), SoS to V, tel., 13 Aug. 1937 (copy), Anderson to Haig, tel., 9 Aug. 1937, Hallett to Haig, 2 Nov. 1937, HgP 22A.

[129] E.g. V to Haig, tels., 23, 24 July 1937, ibid.; Bombay Government's Note, 6 Aug. 1937, *TF* 1 402.

[130] Das to Patel, 15 Oct. 1937, Patel to Prasad, 10 Oct. 1937, *RPCSD* 1, pp. 199–202, 109, *TF* 1, 491. See for some further contretemps, which nevertheless led to no breach, Copley, *Rajagopalachari*, pp. 66–7.

[131] Nehru to Sinha, 11 Dec. 1937, *SWJN* 8, p. 369; Hallett to V, 12 Dec. 1937, *TF* 1, 590.

[132] CWC Minutes 14–17 Aug. 1937, ibid. 416.

[133] Nehru's statement, 24 July 1937, *SWJN* 8, pp. 284–6; Nixon to PSV, 3 Aug. 1937, PSV to Stewart, 5 Aug. 1937, Note of Discussion at Simla, 6 Sept. 1937, *TF* 1, 394, 398, 445; Haig to V, 23 Aug. 1937, HgP 17A; Copley, *Rajagopalachari*, pp. 49–52.

[134] Prasad to Patel, 14 July 1936, RPP III/36/1; V's Note on meeting with Gandhi, 4 Aug. 1937, *TF* 1, 396.   [135] Hardiman, *Peasant Nationalists of Gujarat*, ch. 9.

governor, Brabourne. He was already alert to their determination in this matter and seems to have been very careful not to resist them head on. Instead he sought to ensure that no government pressure should be placed on those who had bought the land to return it,[136] and that attempts should be made to negotiate 'a free and equitable price' with them. There were sharp differences on this matter with Garrett the Commissioner involved (who had carried through the original confiscations in 1930), but when, as chance had it, he was promoted to be Governor of Sind, after considerable debate legislation was eventually passed through the Bombay legislature by the late summer of 1938 which met the Congress's demand almost totally.[137] It then happened that under the 1935 Act the Bill needed the Viceroy's assent and that at the critical moment Linlithgow was away on leave and Brabourne was acting-Viceroy in his place. In a last-minute attempt he tried to persuade the Bombay ministers to reach an agreed settlement with the owners, but when they would not resile he eventually gave way. No break in the relationship thus occurred and at least to begin with nowhere else as well.[138]

In the event the flashpoints came in UP and Bihar. Immediately upon his installation as Premier of UP Pant summarily lifted restrictions on a number of publications and organisations and ordered the release of a variety of non-political prisoners.[139] That led to an early encounter with the governor, Sir Harry Haig, who believed that he had some jurisdiction here.[140] But the two men then began to work together, and when Pant agreed to make a statement stressing his government's complete opposition to violence,[141] Haig in a particularly difficult case agreed to release the prisoners convicted in the Kakori conspiracy case of ten years before.[142] To the intense annoyance of both of them, and of Gandhi too, those released were publicly feted in Kanpur, Lucknow, and elsewhere.[143] When pressed the men agreed to make a statement abjuring any further terrorism, but Haig made it plain to Pant that he would not be so accom-

---

[136] Brabourne to V, 5 Aug. 1937, Note of Discussion at Simla, 6 Sept. 1937, ibid. 399, 445.

[137] Gandhi, 'The Confiscated Lands', *Harijan*, 22 Oct. 1938, *CWMG* 68, pp. 36–7.

[138] M. Desai, *The Story of My Life*, vol. I, Delhi 1974, chs. 18 and 19.

[139] Pant to Nehru, 19 July 1937, Pant's statement, 2 Aug. 1937, *TF* 1, 370, 391; see also Haig to V, tel., 10 Oct. 1937, HgP 21.

[140] Haig to Pant, Pant to Haig, 20 July 1937, ibid.; Haig to V, 21 July 1937, *TF* 1, 377.

[141] Pant to Haig, 14, 18 Aug. 1937, Haig to Pant, 16 Aug. 1937, HgP 22A.

[142] Haig to V, tels., 5, 7, 9, 12, 13 Aug. 1937, V to Haig, tel., 8 Aug. 1937, Haig to Pant, 11 Aug. 1937, ibid. For Nehru's interest see Interview 12 Aug. 1937, *SWJN* 8, p. 305.

[143] Panna Lal to Owen, 27 Aug. 1937, V to Haig, 1, 14 (tel.) Sept. 1937, HgP 22A; Haig's Note to Pant, 29 Aug. 1937, Haig to V, 30 Aug., 6 Sept. 1937, Prasad to Patel, 28 Sept. 1937, *TF* 1, 433, 434, 448, 472; Gandhi's Notes, *Harijan*, 4 Sept. 1937, *CWMG* 66, pp. 101–2. For Nehru's more equivocal position see 'The Right Perspective', 30 Aug. 1937, *SWJN* 8, pp. 312–14; also Desai to Birla, 6, 22 Sept. 1937, *Bapu*, III, pp. 82, 95.

modating again.[144] Amidst a disquieting situation, with industrial conflict in Kanpur,[145] Muslim demonstrations against British policies in Palestine, reports of 'parallel governments' and agrarian conflicts in many districts in the province, and attacks upon the police,[146] Haig nonetheless continued to try to work closely with his Congress ministers.[147] So much so indeed that Linlithgow in November 1937 went to the length of rebuking this most senior of Indian Civil Servant Governors for allowing the administration of this key province to slip out of control,[148] and reinforced his criticism in December[149] when he read a circular issued by the UP's Chief Secretary to District Magistrates instructing them to institute 'relations of mutual confidence and harmony' with 'leaders of the Congress organisation in the districts'[150] as going altogether too far. Haig defended himself.[151] Not only had a corresponding circular from the Congress been issued to its subordinates,[152] but, he insisted, to work so far as possible with Congress was precisely the way to check the growth of parallel governments in the province, and to calm the position generally.[153] He was not backward, moreover, upon other fronts. Early in November he formally warned Pant about the denunciations that were being made against the police and about 'revolutionary speeches',[154] and at the end of the month, incensed by a speech advocating violent revolution and the desertion of troops by a lately released prisoner named Parmanand, he insisted that Parmanand must be prosecuted.[155]

That created a crisis. Pant was deeply troubled. Shortly beforehand Rajagopalachari had been strongly rebuked by Nehru and other Congress leaders over a comparable prosecution in Madras.[156] Since unlike Rajagopalachari Pant was not in the front rank of Congress leaders

[144] *The Pioneer*, 31 Aug. 1937, *TF* 1, 437; Haig to V, 4, 10 (tel.), Sept., 5, 15, 20 (tel.), 24 Oct. 1937, Haig's Note, 3 Oct. 1937, V to Haig, 25 Oct. 1937, HgP 22A.

[145] For Congress's involvement see e.g. Nehru to Mill Workers of Kanpur [27 Sept. 1937], *SWJN* 8, pp. 328–34.

[146] UP Police reports, 11, 18 Sept., 16, 23, 30 Oct. 1937, HgP 12; Haig to V, 22 Sept., 8, 28 Nov. 1937, ibid. 17B; Haig to V, 6 Sept. 1937, *TF* 1, 448.

[147] E.g. Haig to V, 4 Aug. 1937, V to Haig, 28 Aug. 1937, ibid. 401, 431; Haig to V, tel., 16 Sept. 1937, HgP 22A; 22 Sept., 9 Dec. 1937, ibid. 17B.

[148] V to Haig, 15 Nov. 1937; see also Ewart's Note, 28 Nov. 1937, *TF* 1, 549, 571. Linlithgow had evidently been earlier critical too of Hallett, Bihar's Governor, as had Zetland more generally; they were clearly still very apprehensive about the general situation, SoS to V, 18 Sept. 1937, Hallett to V, 25 Sept. 1937, ibid., 464, 469.

[149] V to Haig, 24 Dec. 1937, 1 Feb., 10 Mar. 1938, HgP 12.

[150] Gwynne's circular, 10 Nov. 1937, V to Haig, 24 Dec. 1937, *TF* 1, 543, 612.

[151] Haig to V, 17 Nov. 1937, ibid. 550.   [152] *The Pioneer*, 9 Dec. 1937.

[153] Haig to V, 12 Feb. 1938, HgP 12.   [154] Haig to Pant, 3 Nov. 1937, *TF* 1, 529.

[155] Haig to V, tel., 27 Nov. 1937, HgP 15.

[156] Nehru to Subbarayan, 21 Nov. 1937, Nehru to CWC members, 24 Nov. 1937, *SWJN* 8, pp. 359–60, 363.

he was in an even weaker position to withstand the strictures of his colleagues than Rajagopalachari, and in any case his own policy was in such situations to issue a preliminary warning first. Since, however, all his efforts to reach Parmanand failed, he found himself in a trebly difficult position: fearful of his colleagues' reactions on the one side, frustrated in executing his own policy on the other, and despite lengthy talks with Haig confronted by an unbending Haig on the third.[157] It then happened that Parmanand was arrested on a lesser charge in Delhi.[158] Pant clutched at this to suggest to Haig that they should now drop the earlier proposed prosecution in UP. Haig insisted, however, that Parmanand must be arraigned in UP too. Both sides soon recognised that there was a resigning issue here for Pant.[159] Haig did not relish that idea, since it would entail 'Governor's rule' in the province, and could very soon lead to an early breakdown in the constitution as a whole.[160] Linlithgow did not want that to happen either.[161] Nor did Gandhi.[162] So in the end a compromise was reached whereby Parmanand's prosecution in UP was dropped and Pant issued a further strong public declaration saying his government would not be prepared any longer to tolerate 'irresponsible language or subversive activities' by Parmanand or anyone else.[163]

No sooner had this crisis been overcome, however, than an even more serious one erupted, which this time extended to Bihar as well.[164] It turned on the classic ambiguity in the 1935 Act under which while provincial governments were given full responsibility for law and order, both the Governor and the Viceroy retained overriding reserve powers. In Bihar in the latter part of 1937 the Governor, Sir Maurice Hallett had been resisting the release of a number of political prisoners because of their connections with some Bengali terrorists. Following his earlier experience over the Kakori prisoners, Haig was now resisting too the further

---

[157] Haig to V, tels., 27, 29 Nov. 1937, Pant to Haig, 28 Nov. 1937, *TF* 1, 568, 570, 572; see also V to Haig, SoS to Haig, tels., 30 Nov. 1937, HgP 15.

[158] V to Haig, 6 Dec. 1937, ibid.

[159] Haig to V, 7 (tel.), 15 (tels.) Dec. 1937, V to Haig, tels., 10 Dec. 1937, SoS to Haig, tel., 11 Dec. 1937, Haig to Pant, 11 Dec. 1937, V to SoS, tel., 15 Dec. 1937, ibid.; Pant to Haig, Haig to Pant, 11 Dec. 1937, Haig to V, 12 (tel.), 13 Dec. 1937, V to Haig, 15 Dec. 1937, *TF* 1, 588, 589, 592, 594.

[160] For which Haig started to make preparations, Haig to V, 14 Dec. 1937, ibid. 596.

[161] V to Haig, 15 Dec. 1937, ibid. 597; idem. (tel.),16 Dec. 1937, HgP 15.

[162] Police report in V to Haig, tel., 20 Dec. 1937, ibid.

[163] SoS's Cabinet Memo. 24/273, 21 Dec. 1937, V to Emerson, 22 Dec. 1937, SoS to V, 28 Dec. 1937, *The National Call*, 30 Dec. 1937, *TF* 1, 602 & 607, 608, 615, 618; also drafts by Haig, Haig to Pant, 23 Dec. 1937; Haig to V, tels., 15, 17, 18, 21, 23 (2) Dec. 1937, V to Haig, 17, 19 (tel.), 20 (2 tels.) Dec. 1937, HgP 15; Haig to V, 10 Jan. 1938, ibid. 17B. See also Desai to Birla, 18, 21, 22 Dec. 1937, Birla to Desai, 21, 31 Dec. 1937, *Bapu*, III, pp. 119, 123–7, 132–3.

[164] For the earlier story see e.g. Hallett to V, 5 Oct. 1937, *TF* 1, 480.

release of political prisoners who might foster 'ideas of revolutionary vio-lence', particularly since in UP these now included the last six Chauri Chaura prisoners.[165] Early in November 1937 Bihar's Premier, Sinha, had told Hallett that he was 'no longer prepared to examine individual cases' and that all remaining political prisoners should be released forth-with.[166] Hallett doubted whether the gradual release of Bihar's remaining prisoners would 'under present circumstances have very bad results', but he was adamant that 'it will be necessary to take into account both condi-tions in the province and reactions outside'.[167] Linlithgow, moreover, made it plain that he was quite determined that there should be no 'indis-criminate clemency', since that would 'undoubtedly constitute a grave menace' he said to law and order in the country.[168]

Following upon a brief but threatening hunger strike in January 1938 by a number of political prisoners in Bengal, Punjab and Bihar,[169] both the Bihar and the UP Ministers then pressed their demands even more strongly for the immediate release of all remaining political prisoners in their provinces. This, they declared, was a critical element in the Congress programme which could no longer be postponed. In any event there was no evidence that the freeing of a dozen or so prisoners in each province could possibly upset the peace of either.[170] Early in February Sinha told Hallett that it was 'impossible to consider individual releases' any further,[171] whilst Pant now informed Haig that his ministers 'could wait no longer' either.[172] When Linlithgow heard about these demands he told Haig that while he was ready to see the 'release in driblets of individ-ual prisoners whose release cannot be regarded as constituting grave menace', he explicitly forbade any 'indiscriminate or general release' even if that should lead to a major crisis. Any general release of political prison-ers would, he declared, compromise the position of non-Congress governments (in Bengal, where there were 387 such convicts, and Punjab where there were 44). Moreover: 'If . . . we give way' on this issue

---

[165] Hallett to V, 24 Oct. 1937, V to Hallett, 25 Oct. 1937, HgP 22A; idem, 23 Nov. 1937, Hallett to V, 30 Jan. 1937, ibid. 15; Haig's Note, 11 Jan. 1938, ibid. 22B. On Chauri Chaura see S. Amin, *Event, Metaphor, Memory: Chauri Chaura 1922–1992*, Delhi 1995.

[166] Hallett to Haig, tels., 10 Nov., 6 Dec. 1937, ibid.

[167] Hallett to V, 9, 10 Dec. 1937, ibid. Hallett analysed the situation from his point of view in considerable detail for the Bihar ministers, Mainwaring to PSV, 22 Nov., 7 Dec. 1937, V to Hallett, 22 Nov. 1937, *TF* 1, 561, 584, 562.

[168] V to Haig, 26 Nov. 1937, HgP 22B; V to Gs, tel., 11 Dec. 1937, *TF* 1, 587.

[169] PSV to Donaldson, 2 tels., 27 Jan. 1938, Mainwaring to PSV, 28 Jan. 1938, HgP 22B.

[170] Haig's Notes 11, 28 Jan. 1938, Hallett to Haig, tels., 30 Jan., 1, 2 (2) Feb. 1938, Haig to Hallett, tel., 31 Jan. 1938, Pant's Note, 9 Feb. 1938, ibid.; Haig to V, 22 Jan., 9 Feb. 1938, ibid. 17B; Haig to V, 30 Jan. 1938, ibid. 8.

[171] Hallett to Haig, tels., 11, 12 Feb. 1938, ibid. 22B.

[172] Haig to V, and tel., 10, 14 (tel.) Feb. 1937, ibid. 8; idem. 24 Jan. 1938, ibid. 22B.

'Congress ministries will think they can force our hands on other issues' which he was in no mind to contemplate.[173]

The climax came on 14 February 1938 when Sinha ordered the Chief Secretary of Bihar to release all the twenty-three remaining political prisoners in the province straight away.[174] Linlithgow promptly instructed both Hallett and Haig to reject any demand for a 'general release',[175] whereupon both of their Congress ministries resigned.[176] Pant, whose patience had been sorely tried for several months,[177] now protested that it was inconceivable that the release of fifteen more prisoners, such as was demanded in UP, could possibly constitute 'a grave menace to the peace and tranquillity of any province in India', and in some anger then added that:

The responsibility for maintaining law and order in the province is that of the Ministers. No Council of Ministers can discharge its functions satisfactorily if its considered opinion is disregarded arbitrarily in respect of momentous questions strictly falling within their purview by outside authority.[178]

That position was endorsed by Congress's Working Committee at its Haripura meeting on 18 February.[179] The Viceroy's intervention, the Working Committee declared,

not only exposes the utter inadequacy of the Act . . . but also shows the intention of the British Government to use it . . . not for the expansion of liberty but for its restriction.

To which Linlithgow tartly riposted that:

To acquiesce in the immediate and indiscriminate release of prisoners with records of violent crime would have been to strike a blow at law and order in India.

Both sides, however, soon started to draw back.[180] The Working Committee was careful not to order other Congress ministries to resign (they were clearly very reluctant to do so),[181] whilst Linlithgow empha-

---

[173] V to Haig, tel., 11 Feb. 1938, ibid. 8; see idem, tels., 31 Jan., 3, 12 Feb. 1938, ibid. 22B.
[174] Hallett to Haig, tel., 14 Feb. 1938, ibid.
[175] V to Haig (also to Hallett), tel., 15 Feb. 1938, ibid. 8.
[176] UP Official Communique, 15 Feb. 1938, ibid.
[177] See Haig's frank summary, 30 Jan. 1938, ibid.
[178] Pant to Haig, 15 Feb. 1938, ibid. 22B.
[179] Gandhi drafted the resolution, see his speech and statement, 16 Feb. 1938, *CWMG* 66, pp. 373, 375.
[180] Though Gandhi still challenged the right of Governors to consider individual cases, Gandhi's statement, 23 Feb. 1938, ibid. pp. 383–5.
[181] Glendevon, *Viceroy at Bay*, p. 90. For Nehru's hesitations, see his Jhansi address, 7 Feb. 1938, *SWJN* 8, p. 377. See also Subbarayan to Nehru, 21 Feb. 1938, AICC PL3(i) 1937 (sic).

sised that 'there is no going back on a policy of readiness to examine individual cases'.[182] In the event the Congress-supporting industrialist, G.D. Birla, smoothed the path to an agreed settlement.[183] Following upon a long talk between Haig and Pant on 24 February,[184] they eventually issued a joint statement the next day which announced that Congress ministers would be resuming office; that following a renewed examination of individual cases a number of further prisoners were now being released while others would follow soon; and then stated:

There is no reason to fear any usurpation of or interference with the legitimate functions of the responsible Ministers. We are both desirous of maintaining healthy conventions and with goodwill on both sides we hope that we will succeed.[185]

That position was held to over the next eighteen months. Nehru declared that 'the British Government [had] climbed down completely'[186] – which was pretty near the mark. The British had, however, kept Congress within the spider's web that the 1935 Act had wrapped around them, and from their point of view that was their principal concern.

From time to time thereafterwards governors became apprehensive as to whether the settlement would indeed continue to hold,[187] and there were a number of minor scuffles.[188] There was, for example, a further episode in Orissa when the Governor, Hubback, appointed a British rather than an Indian official to be acting Governor whilst he went on leave. In the ensuing furore the Congress ministry threatened to resign. Hubback eventually resolved the crisis by abandoning his intention to go on leave.[189] There was then a sizeable issue for Congress over a leadership

---

[182] CWC Resolution, and Gandhi's interviews with *Daily Herald* and *The Times*, 18 Feb. 1938, *CWMG* 66, pp. 376–81; Nehru to K. Menon, 5 Mar. 1938, *SWJN* 8, p. 379; V's statement [22 Feb. 1938], HgP 22B; V to Haig, tel., 22 Feb. 1938, ibid. 8; Zetland, '*Essayez*', pp. 225–6; Gwyer and Appadorai, *Speeches and Documents*, I, pp. 397–404.

[183] Birla to Gandhi, 20, 25 Feb. 1938, *Bapu* 3, pp. 149–57.

[184] Haig to V, tel., 24 Feb. 1938, HgP 8.

[185] Haig–Pant statement [25 Feb. 1938], ibid. 22B; see also Pant to Haig, 24 Feb. 1938, ibid. 8. In the rush there was some confusion in telephone messages about Linlithgow's views on this wording, and he was none too pleased with the outcome, but it did no damage, V to Haig, 27 Feb. 1938, Haig to V, 5 Mar. 1938, ibid.; Donaldson to Haig, 28 Feb. 1938, ibid. 22B.

[186] Nehru to K. Menon, 5 Mar., and to A. Sen, 11 Mar. 1938, *SWJN* 8, pp. 379–80; Nehru's London speech, 13 July 1938, and article, *Labour Monthly*, Aug. 1938, ibid. 9, pp. 41, 124–5.   [187] E.g. Haig's lengthy memorandum, 19 Dec. 1938, HgP 2A.

[188] E.g. Haig to Linlithgow, 3 Apr. 1939, ibid.; also between Erskine and Rajagopalachari over the appointment of a High Court judge in Madras, Copley, *Rajagopalachari*, p. 58.

[189] Gandhi's statements [31 Mar. 1938], 29 Apr. 1938, *CWMG* 66, p. 455, and 67, pp. 51–2; Pant to Prasad, 6 May 1938, *RPCSD* 2, p. 48; Nehru, *Daily Worker*, 7 Sept. 1938, *SWJN* 9, p. 141; Glendevon, *Viceroy at Bay*, pp. 97–8.

crisis in CP. There had been two earlier Congress provincial leadership crises when in 1936/7 Rajagopalachari had supplanted Satyamurti in the leadership of the Madras Congress (and had gone on to become Chief Minister there),[190] and when Patel and his associates had arranged for Kher rather than K.F. Nariman to lead the Bombay Congress (and become its Premier too).[191] The rivalry, however, in CP between Shukla from the Hindi areas and Khare, the Premier, from the Marathi-speaking areas, became a great deal more protracted. At a critical moment in July 1938 Khare arranged with the Governor, Sir Francis Wylie, that his principal opponents in the Cabinet should be dismissed. For his pains Khare not only lost the Chief Ministership but was proscribed by the High Command, while the Governor was vigorously denounced by the Congress as well.[192] Neither of these episodes threatened, however, to destroy the pragmatic concordat Haig and Pant had worked out, and as it happened, despite several stresses and strains,[193] there were not to be others at the provincial level either.

Rather throughout 1938 and most of 1939 Congress governments in the six (and with Assam eventually seven) provinces in which they held office set about exercising to the full the powers that the 1935 Act had granted them. Many of the details have been recounted elsewhere and should not detain us here. Apart from a number of educational reforms, along with the handling of several sizeable industrial and communal conflicts, some attempts were made to introduce prohibition; while a great deal of energy was expended, especially in Bihar and UP, on carrying through some agrarian reforms.[194] Governors kept a close watch upon all these events. But even when they sought to use their good offices to ease a complicated situation forward, they always showed themselves careful not to place any obstacles in the way of Congress governments doing what they had set their minds to do.[195] As a consequence to a varying, yet sometimes a notable, degree there developed some remarkably close working relations between many a British Governor and his Congress Chief Minister, of the kind that Emerson and Gandhi had gone far to establish

---

[190] Copley, *Rajagopalachari*, pp. 40–4.   [191] E.g. Desai, *Story of My Life*, pp. 141–2.
[192] CWC Resolution, 30 July 1938, Gandhi's 'Functions of the Working Committee', 6 Aug. 1938, *CWMG* 67, pp. 450–1, 222–6; Nehru's interview, *Daily Worker*, 6 Sept. 1938, *SWJN* 9, p. 141. For a full account see Baker, *Changing Political Leadership*, pp. 177–85. For Nehru's reflections see article in *National Herald*, 5 Mar. 1939, *SWJN* 9, pp. 503–5.
[193] E.g. over Congress's attitude towards the administrative services, e.g. Haig to V, 23 Oct., 22 Nov. 1938, HgP 102; 4 Dec. 1938, ibid. 101.
[194] Reeves, *Landlords and Governments*, pp. 230–47; Damodaran, *Broken Promises*, pp. 89–157.
[195] E.g. HgP 1938–9 passim. See especially Shankerdass, *First Congress Raj*; Baker, *Changing Political Leadership*, VIII; Copley, *Rajagopalachari*, Part I; Damodaran, *Broken Promises*, chs. 1 and 2; Rau, *Pant*, chs. 15 and 16.

between themselves in 1931, and which Nehru and Mountbatten were famously to establish ten years later on.[196] As a result there soon developed on both sides a widespread impression that 'broadly speaking things have gone better than one would have been justified in expecting'.[197] Even as early as October 1937 Nehru conceded that 'office acceptance has benefited us'.[198] Though he periodically became troubled at Congress ministries 'tending to become counter-revolutionary',[199] and remained much dissatisfied with a good deal of what they were doing,[200] nevertheless by early in 1938 he was allowing that they had 'functioned bravely . . . and have a substantial record to their credit',[201] while by March 1939 he was even saying that 'the resignation of ministers with a view to creating deadlocks is entirely wrong tactics'.[202] The British received the distinct impression indeed that he was now welcoming the strength provincial office had brought the Congress.[203] Linlithgow was well content too:

the longer the Congress Government remains in office [he remarked early in 1938] the more do the ordinary reactions of political forces come into play . . . the essential thing is to play for time, and to let Congress settle into the business of administration . . . Every month that a breakdown . . . can be postponed is . . . a real and substantial contribution.[204]

And by mid 1939 he was expressing his warm satisfaction that:

Provincial Autonomy could be regarded as working smoothly . . . as a result of the last 2¼ years we have not merely convinced ministers that provincial autonomy is no sham, but that it confers real and substantial powers on them.[205]

The spider's web, that is, within which the 1935 Act had enmeshed the Congress, was now serving the purposes of the British very well.[206] As

---

[196] E.g. Haig to Brabourne, 15 Sept. 1937, Haig to V, 23 Oct. 1938, HgP 2A; V to Haig, 4 Feb., 26 May 1939, ibid. 3B.

[197] V to Haig, 13 Aug. 1937, ibid. 3A; Haig to V, tel., 23 Dec. 1937, ibid. 5; Gandhi, *Harijan*, 24 June 1939, *CWMG* 69, p. 361.

[198] Nehru's Calcutta AICC speech, 30 Oct. 1937, *TF* 1, 522; Allahabad speech, 4 Oct. 1937, Garhdiwala speech, 11 Oct. 1939, *SWJN* 8, pp. 261–2, 265–6; Haig to V, 22 Jan. 1938, HgP 17B.   [199] Nehru to Pant, 25 Nov. 1937, *TF* 1, 566.

[200] Nehru to Premiers, 4 Nov. 1937, his Harduaganj speech, 31 Dec. 1937, his Bombay speech, 13 May 1938, *SWJN* 8, pp. 348–90, 372–5, 389–90, article, 28 Mar. 1937, articles, *National Herald*, 28 Feb.–6 Mar. 1937, ibid. 9, pp. 325–6, 499, 502, 505.

[201] Nehru's Haripura AICC speech, 16 Feb. 1938, Ayodhya speech, 2 Jan. 1939, Madras speech, 25 July 1939, ibid. p. 757, and *SWJN* 9, pp. 313, 591.

[202] Speech at Subjects Committee, 11 Mar. 1939, ibid. p. 523.

[203] V to Haig, 6 Jan. 1938, HgP 3A, Haig to V, 10 Jan. 1939, ibid. 2A. See also Nehru's Presidential speech to the UP Provincial Conference, Ayodhya, 30 Dec. 1938, *SWJN* 9, p. 313.

[204] V to Haig, 6 Jan. 1938, HgP 3A; V to Gowan, 12 Aug. 1937, *TF* 1, 413. See also V to Haig, 9 July, 30 Sept. 1937, HgP 3A, and 23 Jan. 1939, ibid. 3B.

[205] V to Haig, 26 May, 3 July 1939, ibid.

[206] E.g. M.N. Roy to Prasad, 19 Oct. 1939, *RPSCD* 4, pp. 119–24.

Nehru himself put it: 'The British are a clever people. The Act they have introduced is to divide Indians and make them look at things from a provincial point of view.'[207]

While following the Haig–Pant agreement of February 1938 there was, therefore, really no further ambiguity about the way provincial autonomy would operate – Congress governments had full control of provincial executive powers – that, however, did not mean that the underlying ambiguity in British relations towards political India as a whole had somehow magically been whisked away. It might very largely have been removed from the provinces. But it was still to be found in the sharp contrast which existed between the provincial regimes and that which was to be found – and that which was provided for – at the centre. During the years 1937–9 Nehru accordingly spent a great deal of his time and energy keeping alive the flame of Congress's ultimate commitments to the final elimination of British imperial power in India.[208] Nothing, however, for most of these years served to bring this issue to the fore at the provincial level, as we have seen, nor at the all-India level either.

It is possible to visualise two possible eventualities at the all-India level which might well have created a confrontation. Had the much hated Federation embodied in the 1935 Act been brought into operation, a countrywide eruption could very well have occurred.[209] Throughout these years Congress continued to denounce the whole idea, and its opposition was soon echoed by the newly reviving Muslim League. Under the terms of the Act the Federation's inauguration was critically dependent, however, upon a plurality of the Indian Princes agreeing to enter into it. That gave them endless opportunities to haggle over the terms of entry which they would accept, and despite Linlithgow's persistent attempts over three long years to bring negotiations on these to a conclusion, talks finally collapsed in mid 1939.[210] As a result the opportunity that might well have occurred to allow the Congress to mount a further countrywide assault upon the British on this issue disappeared on the wing.[211]

---

[207] Nehru's Bombay speech, 9 Aug. 1937, *SWJN* 8, p. 298.
[208] E.g. his 'National Demand' resolution, Tripuri, 11 Mar. 1939, *SWJN* 9, pp. 521–2.
[209] E.g. Nehru's Note, 6 Sept. 1939, ibid. p. 136; Prasad to Sinha, 4 Mar. 1939, *RPCSD* 2, p. 8.   [210] Copland, *Unwanted Allies*, Ch. V.
[211] In 1938–9 Gandhi became embroiled in the abortive Rajkot satyagraha which if successful could have undermined the Princes' 'blocking third' in the Federal legislature if that had ever been established, see J.R. Wood, 'Indian Nationalism in the Princely Context: the Rajkot Satyagraha of 1938–9', in R. Jeffrey, ed., *People, Princes and Paramount Power*, Delhi 1978, ch. 7.

A countrywide conflagration might, alternatively, have occurred, however, if S.C. Bose had had his way in the conflict that broke out between him and the right-wing leadership of the Congress particularly during 1939. Following his eventual release from prison in 1937 Bose had become President of Congress in 1938. Against the wishes of Gandhi and the right wing Congress 'High Command' he campaigned in the following year to become President of the Congress for a second year in succession. In doing so he castigated his opponents on the right of the party for their readiness to work the Federation as soon as it came into being. Any such intention was vehemently denied, but there were just enough straws in the wind to lend it credibility. His principal demand, however, was that Congress should forthwith renounce its compromise with the British, which office acceptance in the provinces had entailed, send them a stiff ultimatum, and upon its rejection mount a further mass civil disobedience movement so as finally to win full independence for India.[212] So hostile, however, had the entrenched Congress's leadership become towards Bose through what became a protracted and bitter intra-party struggle, that they, and Gandhi in particular, refused to have anything to do with this. Gandhi was now deeply apprehensive, moreover, that in any further major mass agitation it would no longer be possible to avoid violence, and since he was as totally opposed to that as he had ever been, he shrank from taking any fateful step which might conceivably bring that about.[213] So riven did the two sides become upon this and various related issues that Gandhi and his cohorts not only forced Bose to resign from the Presidency soon after his second election in 1939. When he then defied them by establishing his 'Forward Bloc' and organised a day of protest against what he saw as the anodyne position they had adopted in some resolutions they passed at the end of June, they went on to eject him from the Presidency of the Bengal PCC as well.[214] In all this turmoil any idea of launching a further major campaign against the British simply disappeared in the sand.[215] For two years and more, therefore, after Congress accepted office in the provinces in 1937 there was not only no insuperable crisis with the British at the provincial level, there was no major anti-imperial confrontation at the all-India level either. The spider's web remained intact.

When a crisis did eventuate it came about all but inadvertently, not as a consequence of any special event within India itself, but as a result of a

---

[212] E.g. Bose to Gandhi, 31 Mar. 1939, *CWMG* 69, App. VI.
[213] E.g. Gandhi's interview with Steel [17 May 1939], *CWMG* 69, p. 279.
[214] CWC resolution, 11 Aug. 1939, *CWMG* 70, pp. 84–5.
[215] On the whole story see Gordon, *Brothers against the Raj*, chs. 8 and 9. For Nehru's role see *SWJN* 9, pp. 477–602.

series of occurrences following upon the outbreak of war in western Europe.

There had been three warning signals. Congress had regularly reiterated its sustained opposition to any involvement of India in any war that did not have the agreement of the Indian people.[216] More specifically in the aftermath of the Munich crisis in Europe late in 1938, when the British decided that they would need to amend the 1935 Act to ensure that they could exercise full control over the provincial governments in time of war, Congress leaders expressed their profound anger at any such move to strengthen the Act's already abhorrent 'reserve powers'.[217] When, moreover, in August 1939 the Government of India decided to despatch Indian troops to Aden, Egypt, and Singapore, Congress ordered its members in the central legislature to boycott the next session in denunciation of a quite unwarranted step that was 'against the declared will of the Indian people'.[218]

Upon the outbreak of war in Europe on 3 September 1939 Linlithgow, in a much discussed episode, immediately declared India to be at war without ever consulting any Indian public body. That proved, as has so often been remarked, a fateful step. So far as he was concerned, however, questions of war and peace for India were still matters that constitutionally lay solely in the hands of its British rulers, so that once Britain had gone to war with Germany, it was his duty on his own authority to declare that India was at war with Germany too.

On the day before war broke out he saw Gandhi,[219] who promptly declared that India should support Britain unconditionally in the crisis that now confronted it.[220] But within days Gandhi was effectively sidelined by Nehru, the best informed of the Congress leaders upon international affairs, who had become increasingly angered by the unending failures of the British to withstand the Japanese over the invasion of China, the Italians in Abyssinia, the Fascists in Spain, the Germans in Czecho-Slovakia, and who was now deeply distrustful of their whole

---

[216] E.g. Resolution moved by Nehru (and his supporting speech) at the Madras Congress in 1927, *SWJN* 3, pp. 25–30; his editorial in the *National Herald*, 28 Apr. 1939, ibid. 9, pp. 294–5; AICC resolution, 1 May 1939, P. Sitaramayya, *The History of the Indian National Congress*, Delhi 1969, vol. II, p. 126.

[217] Nehru to Pant, 21 Feb. 1939, Nehru to Menon, 24 Feb., 26 Apr., 4 May 1939, Nehru's speech at Allahabad, 13 Apr. 1939, and at Calcutta, his editorials in *National Herald*, late Apr. 1939, *SWJN* 9, pp. 320–1, 570, 299, 284, 301, 293, 296–7; Haig to V, 8 Mar. 1939, HgP 2A; Bose to Gandhi, 20 Apr. 1939, AICC Resolutions 29 Apr.–1 May 1939, *RPCSD* 3, pp. 54–5, 393.

[218] CWC resolution [11 Aug. 1939], *CWMG* 70, App. VIII.

[219] Gandhi to Prasad, tel., 2 Sept. 1939, ibid. p.152.

[220] Gandhi's statement, 5 Sept. 1939, and *Harijan*, 16 Sept. 1939, *CWMG* 70, pp. 161–2, 171.

international position.[221] When, moreover, the Working Committee met on 14 September to consider the situation, he had ready for them a lengthy draft resolution which whilst vehemently denouncing Germany's aggression in Europe first declared that 'the issue of war and peace for India must be decided by the Indian people', and then avowed that 'India cannot associate herself in a war said to be for democratic freedom when that very freedom is denied to her'.

In view . . . of the gravity of the occasion [his draft went on] . . . the Committee desire to make no final decision at this stage, so as to allow for a full elucidation of the issues at stake, the real objectives aimed at, and the position of India in the present and in the future . . . The Working Committee therefore invite the British Government to declare in unequivocal terms what their war aims are in regard to democracy and imperialism and the new order that is envisaged, in particular how these aims are going to apply to India and to be given effect to in the present.[222]

That was endorsed with little argument by the Working Committee, and by the AICC when it met on 9–10 October which simply added: 'In particular, India must be declared an independent nation and present application should be given to this status to the largest possible extent.'[223]

In a private conversation on 21 September with Desmond Young, the editor of *The Pioneer* of Lucknow, Nehru spelt out what was meant by all of this. Young had the 'very strong impression that he [Nehru] is personally anxious to assist to the full in the prosecution of the war', but that

Congress wanted a clear declaration that [India] should be free to determine her own destinies after the war . . . [That in the meanwhile] the two countries [should] fight the war together as equal partners [which in turn meant] that India should be . . . free to determine the extent of her war effort . . . [and] have the right to decide, like Canada and Australia, whether she should raise an expeditionary force in addition to the present regular army . . . it is no use [Young reported Nehru as saying] either Mahatma Gandhi or I pledging the full support of India . . . unless we can convince Indians that the war is in their interests and not merely in the interests of Great Britain . . . He . . . quite realised that the difficulty lay in giving Indians responsibility at the centre at once . . . At the same time . . . he thought it would be easier to bring [this] about in war time when there was no need to give constitutional form to such changes . . . some sort of National War Council . . . was the sort of organisation that was necessary.[224]

---

[221] E.g. articles in *National Herald*, 30 Mar., 21 Apr. 1939, Speeches at Allahabad, 10 Jan., 13 Apr. 1939, and at Calcutta, 2 May 1939, Interview with *Hindustan Times*, 3 Sept. 1939, *SWJN* 9, pp. 327–9, 289, 226, 283–4, 566, 129–30.

[222] See the successive drafts, 11, 12, 14 Sept. 1939, *SWJN* 9, pp. 122–38, and final versions of CWC Manifesto and AICC Resolution, 14 Sept. 1939, *CWMG* 70, Appendices X & XI. See also Prasad to PSV, 16 Sept. 1939, *RPCSD* 4, pp. 86–90, 239–43; Gandhi's statement, 15 Sept. 1939, *CWMG* 9, pp. 175–7.

[223] AICC resolution, *CWMG* 70, App. XI; Prasad to PSV, 11 Oct. 1939, *RPCSD* 4, pp. 99–102.   [224] Young's note [21 Sept. 1939], HgP 7.

These propositions immediately ran headlong, however, into the unrelenting side of British ambiguity towards India which still remained completely intact. Earlier in the year Linlithgow had remarked in a letter to Zetland on some rumours circulating in Calcutta that while:

No one can, of course, say what in some remote period of time, or in the event of international convulsions of a particular character, may be the ultimate relations of India and Great Britain . . . that there should be any general impression (if it in fact exists) that public opinion at home, or His Majesty's Government, seriously contemplate evacuation in any measureable period of time, seems to me astonishing.[225]

And when he saw the Working Committee's resolution in September he immediately told Haig that:

It is clearly out of the question for us to consider undertakings of the nature suggested, or equally to commit ourselves to vague promises of Dominion Status at the end of the war or the like. There would be no hope of securing Parliament's approval for that, and apart from that we have to consider legitimate claims of, and reactions on, the Princes, the Muslims and parties other than Congress.[226]

Quite suddenly therefore irresistible political force was once more ramming its head against immovable imperialist object.

Linlithgow nevertheless did embark on a lengthy series of discussions with a wide array of Indian political figures to see whether anything could be agreed, but after correspondence with the Cabinet the most that he and they were prepared to offer in a major statement he made on 18 October was that at the war's end there would be

consultation with representatives of the several communities, parties, and interests in India, and with the Indian Princes, with a view to securing their aid and cooperation in the framing of such modifications [to the 1935 Act] as may seem desirable . . . [and in the meanwhile] a consultative group, representative of all major political parties in British India and of the Indian princes . . . [would] be summoned at his invitation.[227]

This provoked deep and widespread disappointment in India:[228]

if the substance of the statement could have been put in a different way [Rafi Ahmed Kidwai, a minister in the UP government, put it] with emphasis on the future, it might not have been unacceptable; if it had been said, for instance, that H.M.G. hoped that it would be possible for India to get Dominion Status at an early date after the war [that could have made a considerable difference].[229]

---

[225] Zetland, 'Essayez', p. 265.

[226] V to Haig, tel., 22 Sept. 1939, ibid. See also Hoare's speech, 26 Oct. 1939, *CWMG* 70, pp. XIV.

[227] V's declaration, 18 Oct. 1939, ibid. App. XII; V to Prasad, 16 Oct. 1939, *RPCSD* 4, pp. 105–11.

[228] Gandhi's statement, 18 Oct. 1939, *CWMG* 70, pp. 267–8; Prasad to V, 18 Oct. 1939, Prasad's statement, nd, *RPCSD* 4, pp. 119, 257–8.

[229] Haig reporting Kidwai to V, tel., 19 Oct. 1939, HgP 7.

But that was precisely what Linlithgow would not say. There were still many in Congress, including Gandhi, who hoped against hope that an agreed settlement could be reached,[230] but when the Working Committee met at Wardha on 22 October to consider Linlithgow's statement they declared it to be 'wholly unsatisfactory', and an impasse ensued.[231]

From the very beginning Linlithgow had been well aware that this gathering crisis could very soon lead to a major break with the Congress that would involve the resignation of its provincial ministries and the establishment, under section 93 of the 1935 Act, of 'Governor's rule' in the provinces. He and his Governors were quite confident, however, that they could once again hold the line in India, and soon set about making the necessary dispositions.[232] Linlithgow made a thirteenth-hour attempt to entice both the Congress and the Muslim League into accepting places in his Executive Council, but as in every other respect his 18 October statement stood that proved to be entirely fruitless.[233]

Thus to no one's surprise[234] following a Working Committee meeting at Wardha on 22 October Congress's Parliamentary Sub-Committee now called upon all Congress's provincial ministers to resign in protest against the British stance.[235] Very many of them were reluctant to do so. But so soon as the Viceroy had brushed aside Congress' central demands and had thereby brought to the fore once again the sharp contradiction between British autocracy at the centre and Congress cooperation in the provinces, the Congress leadership had really no option but to revert to their former fundamentally hostile attitude.[236] 'The least the Ministers could do', Gandhi declared, 'was to resign to show the hollowness of autonomy'.[237] It was the only shot they had at this time in their locker: 'the principles and past commitments of Congress', as one of the ministers put it, 'made it inevitable'.[238] The spider's web that had entwined the

[230] E.g. Haig to V, tels., 17, 21, 25, 29 Sept. 1937, ibid.; Kingor to Prasad, tel., 26 Oct. 1939, *RPCSD* 4, p.129.

[231] CWC resolution, 22 Oct. 1939, *CWMG* 70, App. XIII; Prasad to V, 23 Oct. 1939, *RPCSD* 4, pp. 126–7. For Nehru's stance throughout these weeks see *SWJN* 10, pp. 117–261. For Linlithgow's side see Glendevon, *Viceroy at Bay*, pp. 134–59.

[232] E.g. V to Haig, 22 Sept., 10, 15 Oct. 1939, Haig to V, 23 Sept., 18 Oct. 1939, Haig's Memo. 19 Oct. 1939, HgP 7.

[233] E.g. Shiva Rao to Prasad, 21 Oct. 1939, Prasad to Shiva Rao, 28 Oct. 1939, V to Prasad, 2 Nov. 1939, Prasad to V, 3 Nov. 1939, *RPCSD* 4, pp. 124–6, 131, 135–8. Prasad to V, 3 Nov. 1939, V's broadcast, 5 Nov. 1939, V to Gandhi, Prasad and Jinnah, 5 Nov. 1939, Zetland's speech, 7 Nov. 1939, *CWMG* 70, Appendices XVI-XIX.

[234] The CWC had warned that this could well be so, Resolution on the War, 11 Aug. 1939, ibid. Appendix VII.   [235] For some details see Rau, *Pant*, p. 234.

[236] E.g. Patel to Prasad, 31 Aug. 1939, ibid. p. 66; Haig to V, tel., 19 Sept. 1939, HgP 7; Copley, *Rajagopalachari*, pp. 67–71.   [237] *Harijan*, 18 Nov. 1939, *CWMG* 70, p. 344.

[238] Haig reporting Sampurnanand to V, tel., 22 Oct. 1939, HgP 7. Since the Government of India's wartime emergency powers curtailed their autonomy, they might well have resigned anyway, e.g. Prasad's speech to AICC meeting, 9–10 Oct. 1939, *RPCSD* 4, pp. 262–5.

Congress in the provinces was thus summarily ripped apart. The destructive blade of British ambiguity tore asunder the Indo–British relationship once again.

As it did so there was, however, a parting glimpse of the other face it bore. Congress ministers took several days to vacate their positions whilst their provincial assemblies passed resolutions denouncing the British position.[239] When Pant then formally submitted his resignation to Haig, he wrote him a remarkable letter to say that he and his colleagues wanted

to take this opportunity to express our thanks to you for the courtesy and guidance which we have received from you in the discharge of your office.

On 3 November Haig formally accepted the Congress ministers' resignations, and in so doing arranged that those present should pose with him for a final photograph,[240] and then since Pant was ill and could not attend, wrote to him in similar vein

to tell you how greatly I have appreciated working with you in conditions which were bound to be difficult. I should like to say that I have the highest regard for you personally.[241]

To which Pant responded in equally generous terms to say that he hoped he might see Haig before he left UP shortly upon retirement, since:

You will be retiring after a strenuous life of more than thirty years, having devoted the best of your time, talents and energy to the conscientious discharge of multifarious duties and responsibilities attached to the high offices filled by you. I wish you the joyful peace of a well earned and active rest for many a happy year.[242]

Thereafter when early in 1940 Erskine retired as Governor of Madras, Rajagopalachari, his former Premier, wrote to him in very comparable terms.[243] Such cordiality at precisely the moment when a complete political rupture between Congress and the British had opened up is striking testimony yet again to the quite extraordinary ambidexterousness that lurked within this whole immense encounter.[244]

---

[239] Draft resolution for provincial legislatures, *CWMG* 70, p. 189.
[240] Haig to V, 23 Oct. 1939, Pant to Haig, 30 Oct. 1939, HgP 7, Haig to V, 8 Nov. 1939, ibid. 2B.
[241] Haig to Pant, 4 Nov. 1939, ibid. 7.
[242] Pant to Haig, 14 Nov. 1939, ibid.
[243] Rajagopalachari to Erskine, 8 Mar. 1940, Copley, *Rajagopalachari*, p. 72.
[244] For Haig's recollections see Sir H. Haig, 'The United Provinces and the New Constitution', *Asiatic Review*, 36, 1940, pp. 423–34, and for Erskine's see Lord Erskine, 'Madras and the New Constitution', *Asiatic Review*, 37, 1941, pp. 12–22.

8   Working with the grain: Sir Tej Bahadur Sapru and the antecedents to the Cripps Declaration 1942

> If you are in a place where you are not wanted, and where you have not the force, or perhaps the will, to squash those who don't want you, the only thing to do is to come out.
>
> Hugh Dalton, British Labour Cabinet Minister

On 2 January 1942 the distinguished Indian 'moderate', Sir Tej Bahadur Sapru, sent a letter to the Private Secretary to the Viceroy enclosing a copy of a telegram he had sent on behalf of himself and a dozen others of his kind – the veteran 'moderate' Sir Srinivasa Sastri, and the subsequent President of India, Radhakrishnan, amongst them – to Winston Churchill, the British Prime Minister, in Washington to impress upon him the vital importance of making some major changes forthwith in the way Britain governed India. Following upon the Japanese attack on the American fleet in Pearl Harbor, and the consequential entry by the United States into the Second World War, Churchill had gone to Washington to consult with President Roosevelt. Sapru's telegram was thus despatched at a critical moment in world affairs. It made a careful, urgent appeal to Churchill for some 'bold stroke far-sighted statesmanship . . . without delay' so as to transform 'entire spirit and outlook administration India' (sic: telegraphese). It called for the immediate establishment of a wholly non-official National Government for India 'subject only responsibility to Crown'. It asked for the re-establishment of 'popular governments broadbased on confidence different classes and communities' in those Provinces of British India which were currently 'ruled autocratically' by their British Governors, and it sought agreement with the propositions that India should be represented on all important war and peacekeeping bodies at the instance of its own National Government, which should generally be treated on an equality with the other governments of the British Dominions. While the telegram was careful to state that detailed questions on the ultimate constitution of a self-governing India should 'wait more propitious times, until after victory achieved in this titanic struggle against forces threatening civilisation', it nonetheless pressed on Churchill the immediate question: 'Is it not possible for you declare this juncture that India no longer be treated as dependency to be ruled from Whitehall, and henceforth her constitutional position and powers identical with those other units British Commonwealth?'[1]

For Sapru this appeal represented the climax to a year's energetic labour,[2] and derived its character from a lifelong involvement in such matters. He and his associates were by no means the only ones who at this tense moment in the course of the war believed that 'something should be done about India'.[3] He had, however, shaped and directed his approach with quite impeccable skill. Whilst Churchill's immediate reaction was to fulminate against Sapru's appeal root and branch,[4] he quite failed to dispose of it as he wished. For Sapru's long experience of how such things should be handled had led him to send copies of his telegram to the press in India, and to make sure that it received extensive press coverage in Britain too. As soon as it was published in London it was promptly treated there with very considerable seriousness, and in a short while became the central peg upon which the momentous discussions which now ensued in Britain over 'what should be done about India' were hung.

Following his return to London from Washington later in January 1942, Churchill, for all his other immense wartime preoccupations, and for all his intense hostility to the Sapru telegram, found not only he could not ignore it, but that it had become the principal focus of attention of his hard-pressed Cabinet as they came to consider the extremely important question of their future policy towards India – with the Japanese pressing at its gates. The essential case which the Sapru telegram made was taken up by the Labour leader and Deputy Prime Minister, Clement Attlee, and early in February 1942 actually precipitated an extraordinary single-handed attempt by none other than Churchill himself to draft a major, and much more conciliatory statement on Indian affairs than could otherwise have possibly been expected of him. Owing to the press of other business – this was, after all, a peculiarly critical moment in the course of the Second World War – it proved impossible to bring the issue to a prompt conclusion. So on 20 February Churchill sent Sapru a conciliatory interim reply to his 2 January telegram, which when published served to emphasise the centrality to British decision-making on India which

[1] *TOP* I, item 2.
[2] For Sapru's earlier formulation of much of this language see Sapru to Prasad, 17, 27 Sept. 1941, SP 18; Sapru to Shiva Rao, 13 Sept. 1941, SP 20; Sapru to Ahmad, 23 Sept. 1941, SP 1.
[3] R.J. Moore, *Churchill, Cripps and India 1939–45*, Oxford 1979, pp. 45–70; *The Times*, 23 Dec. 1941; *Manchester Guardian*, 17, 22, 24 Dec. 1941.
[4] Winston S. Churchill, *The Second World War*, vol. III, *The Grand Alliance*, London 1950, pp. 614–15.

Sapru's initiative had so skilfully achieved; and when on 11 March 1942 Churchill eventually announced in the House of Commons that the British Government had decided to send the Lord Privy Seal, Sir Stafford Cripps, to India to discuss a new draft declaration on British policy towards India with India's major political leaders, Churchill simultaneously sent a message of a quite personal kind to Sapru saying that he hoped he would take his announcement as obviating the need for a more direct reply to his 2 January telegram since it was 'in effect the answer to that telegram'.[5] It was in the glare of the publicity which the Sapru telegram secured in London that the British Cabinet held its momentous discussions on India which eventually led to the Cripps mission and the Cripps Declaration of 1942.

The broader background to these events will be clear from what has been said earlier in this book, and in many another account as well. There are several matters, however, that warrant emphasis.

During the 1930s, as we have seen, Conservative reformers in Britain had worked out a way of institutionalising the ambiguity at the core of mainstream British attitudes towards India. Their solution was to institute some constitutional reforms, but to ensure that in doing so (in Irwin's words) the British kept their hands 'pretty firmly on the things that matter'. As a consequence they showed themselves ready to transfer power over those circumscribed matters that were managed at provincial level in India to those who could command an elected majority in its provincial legislatures. At the same time they held to their commitment to uphold Macdonald's announcement in 1931 to grant India 'responsibility at the centre'. This, however, was only to be to an All-India Federation which would be so constructed as to ensure that any popularly elected majority in its legislature would invariably be frustrated by a combination of specially elected Muslim members and the undemocratically appointed nominees of India's still autocratic Princes. In addition the British would retain control over those matters such as foreign affairs, defence, currency and banking, etc., which they believed to be of crucial importance to maintaining their ultimate dominion over India, and gave themselves power as well to restore their full administrative control over the provincial governments of India should in their view any occasion for that become necessary.

As Viceroy between 1936 and 1943, Lord Linlithgow was all but wholly consistent in giving effect to this stance in its various guises.

---

[5] Pinnell to Sapru, 14 Mar. 1942, SP 13.

When, following the provincial elections in 1937, the Congress majorities in the Hindu-majority Provinces and the Frontier Province held back from taking control of the 'responsible governments' which were there open to them, Linlithgow, as we have seen, had first refused to respond to their peremptory demands, but in the end had shown himself quite prepared to make an emollient public statement to get them to change their minds – and had succeeded in so doing. Thereafter he had been far more assiduous than was once appreciated in trying to get the All-India Federation concocted by the Government of India Act of 1935 brought into being. More than once he pressed the Political Department of the Government of India to bring the negotiations with the Indian Princes over their instruments of accession to the Federation to a successful conclusion. If his efforts here eventually failed, he was not himself to blame. Congress and the Muslim League, each for its own reasons, displayed great hostility to the whole idea. There was only equivocal support for his efforts in London; while the Princes, with the backing of Britain's diehard Conservatives, strung out the negotiations for so long until with the outbreak of war in 1939 they had to be abandoned.[6]

Thereafter whilst Indians were understandably affronted by Linlithgow's decision in September 1939 to declare that India was at war with Germany before any Indian public body had even been consulted, by his own lights Linlithgow was being quite consistent once again. No affront was intended. Constitutionally he was entirely correct. India was not as yet an independent nation-state. Its external affairs were still in Britain's own unencumbered hands; and thus as Britain's Viceroy it was for him to make decisions about India's war and peace on his own.

When Congress then demanded not only that 'the British Government [should] declare in unequivocal terms what their war aims are in regard to democracy and imperialism' but that: 'In particular, India must be declared an independent nation and present application should be given to this status to the largest possible extent',[7] Linlithgow found himself forced into making a reply. Had the British already made up their minds that they would grant India full independence within a foreseeable future, as the Americans had declared they would do in the Philippines, or had they, like the Dutch in Indonesia or the French in Indochina, been quite clear that any such thought was out of the question, he could in so doing have been able to be a good deal less equivocal than he was. As it was,

---

[6] Rizvi, *Linlithgow and India*, chs. 2 and 3; Glendevon, *Viceroy at Bay*, chs. 2–12. On the Federation story more generally see B. Ramusack, *The Princes of India in the Twilight of Empire*, Columbus, Ohio, 1978; S.R. Ashton, *British Policy towards the Indian States 1905–1939*, London 1982, chs. V and VI; Copland, *Unwanted Allies*, ch. V.

[7] Gwyer and Appadorai, *Speeches and Documents*, p. 485.

although Britain was irrevocably committed to granting India full self-government at some stage in the future, there was still a firm determination in ruling British Conservative Party circles to put that off to the kalends. There was no question therefore of Linlithgow undertaking to establish a 'National Government' in India, nor indeed of his taking any steps that would involve transferring control over India's war effort to Indian political hands, since any such moves could very directly have threatened the maintenance of Britain's ultimate dominion over India. As an intensely loyal Conservative reformer Linlithgow – with the government in London firmly behind him – remained quite unmoveable on such issues.

After all [he wrote to Zetland, the Secretary of State, in December 1939] we framed the Constitution as it stands in the Act of 1935, because we thought that way the best way – given the political position in both countries – of maintaining British influence in India. It is no part of our policy, I take it, to expedite in India constitutional changes for their own sake, or gratuitously to hurry the handing over of controls to Indian hands at any pace faster than we regard as best calculated on a long view, to hold India to the Empire.[8]

And yet, in accord with the carefully honed stance which the British had now adopted towards India, it was no longer possible for him to be completely negative either. In particular the failure to effect constitutional change at the centre clearly left him worried. Accordingly, in reply to the Congress demands, the statement that he made on 18 October 1939 was couched in full conformity with the Conservative reformers' well-entrenched position, and presented a vintage version of Britain's ambidexterousness. Whilst, so he announced, Britain would 'at the end of the war be prepared to regard the [existing Government of India] Act as open to modification in the light of Indian views', and while he was ready to establish an all-India 'consultative group', on which leading Indian politicians and public figures would be invited to serve so as to assist him in forwarding the Indian war effort, that was all.[9]

For the Congress this was totally unacceptable. There was nothing here about war aims; and every indication that the British were as determined as ever to hold on to all real power at the centre. A deep cleavage opened up. Congress provincial governments, as we have seen, soon resigned their posts. In extensive talks with Gandhi, the Muslim leader, Jinnah, and others, Linlithgow sought to avoid a total rupture, since its import was far more serious than might meet the eye. For with the onset of the Second World War the Conservative reformers' carefully crafted

---

[8] Marquess of Zetland, '*Essayez*', London 1956, p. 277.
[9] V's statement, 18 Oct. 1939, Gwyer and Appadorai, *Speeches and Documents*, pp. 490–3.

Indian strategy was suddenly losing its crucial dual character. Upon the one side Linlithgow's declaration that India was at war with Germany without consulting any Indians was an emphatic reminder of the continued dominance of the British. That was given further emphasis by their refusal to make provision for anything more than advisory roles for Indian leaders in its conduct. It was still further emphasised, following the resignation of the Congress ministries, by the establishment of Governor's Rule in the Provinces where Congress ministries had been holding office since 1937. And that was only the half of it. For, at the same time, the establishment of Governor's Rule in all of these Provinces (popularly elected 'responsible governments' remained in three Muslim-majority Provinces only) effectively put paid to one of the two most important concessions – the grant of 'responsible government in the provinces' – which Conservative reformers in the 1930s had been prepared to make so as to assuage Indian nationalist feelings; whilst the continuing failure to establish the All-India Federation, followed as it was by a decision soon after the war began to abandon the attempt *sine die*, entailed the collapse of the other concession on which (whatever its flaws) the Conservative reformers had placed great store as well. As a consequence even in appearances there was now very little to mitigate the autocratic character of British imperial rule in India, despite all the efforts of the previous quarter century. Suddenly the mailed fist had slipped its velvet glove.

That placed the British in more of a quandary than has generally been appreciated. *Au fond* they remained deeply wedded to the maintenance of British imperial control over India. In holding to this whilst the war was being fought they did not find it too difficult to argue that, in the midst of what became a 'titanic struggle', it was quite impossible for them to make major decisions about India's future. They could even insist that it was not possible to plan for an altogether problematic peacetime outcome either, let alone forgo their firm control in the meanwhile. Yet at the same time they could never quite put out of their minds the fact that for all their protracted efforts in the early 1930s, something was badly awry once again in India. Nor could they easily rebut the argument that India's contribution to the war effort would almost certainly be a good deal less wholehearted if its own political leadership was to have no hand in it. While inevitably there were both lingering concerns as to whether a totally autocratic Raj consorted at all well with Britain's more finely tuned imperial instincts, and nagging doubts too as to whether this was in any way consistent with the fervent rhetoric of a war being fought to preserve freedom.

These conflicting thoughts surfaced and sank in the minds of various

leading British figures in very uneven sequence throughout the first two
and a half years of the war, and the central fact was that the British now
stood in great confusion as to what precisely they should do next. For on
the one side any move they made seemed to threaten the collapse of their
power, either very abruptly, or at all events in a not-so-distant future.
Many of them were at the same time very discomfited that they seemed to
have lost their previous skill in assuaging India, and found themselves
confronted again by its mounting animosity. Linlithgow persisted with his
efforts to bring Indian political leaders into consultation with him over
wartime matters. But late in 1939 he allowed his efforts to become sub-
merged in Congress–Muslim League divisions, and when faced by a
number of more radical proposals from the Labour politician, Sir
Stafford Cripps, he immediately took fright, and strongly argued for
'lying back'. By then the Conservative Cabinet had unanimously decided
not to concede India's right to independence after the war. In the new
year Zetland, the Secretary of State, did nevertheless persuade
Linlithgow to take a new initiative, and in a speech to the Orient Club in
Bombay he emphasised that he was quite prepared to enlarge his
Executive Council to include representatives of the main political parties,
and even went so far as to declare that 'full Dominion Status of the
Statute of Westminster variety' might be granted to India before the war
was over. Conservative circles in London, however, were greatly dismayed
by this pronouncement, and soon more Congress–Muslim League dis-
putation killed any progress upon it in India. Zetland now tried his hand
at spelling out a programme for early post-war independence in India, but
with much Cabinet support Linlithgow held his coat tails firmly. Some
thought it was a chance sorely missed. Not only did all of this entail a
good deal of debilitating indecision on the British side. More seriously it
left British policy in India in the unaccustomed, and ultimately very
uncomfortable, position of standing upon a single leg only.[10]

In May 1940 there was a change of government in London. The arch
diehard on Indian affairs, Winston Churchill, became Prime Minister,
and Leopold Amery, a Conservative reformer, became Secretary of State
for India, while for the first time the Labour and Liberal parties joined the
wartime government. When shortly afterwards France fell to the
Germans, the war took a grave turn for the worse. Congress thereupon
returned to the fray with an urgent demand for the immediate establishment of a National Government in India. Amery now characteristically

[10] Upon all this see Moore, *Churchill, Cripps and India*, chs. 1 and 2; Rizvi, *Linlithgow and
India*, ch. 5; Glendevon, *Viceroy at Bay*, chs. 13 and 14; Zetland, *'Essayez'*, chs. 27 and 28;
J.H. Voight, *India in the Second World War*, Delhi 1987, ch. II; A.I. Singh, *The Origins of the
Partition of India 1936–1947*, Delhi 1987, ch. 2.

expressed the uneasiness which Conservative reformers almost invariably felt when their India policy became suddenly stuck in authoritarian grooves.

There is a risk [he remarked to Linlithgow] of our missing the moment for action . . . We may very well have to continue to govern India autocratically, but it will make it much easier . . . if you can announce . . . the future stages towards Indian self-government.[11]

He even suggested to Linlithgow that he should 'appoint an Indian Minister of Defence'.[12] For the Viceroy that was going too far. But having rebuffed Amery, he was nonetheless ready to agree with him that the Government might now accept the principles Zetland had sought to propound earlier in the year under which the British would agree to

abide by conclusions of any representative body of Indians on which various political parties could agree . . . [and] spare no effort to bring about Dominion Status within a year of the conclusion of the war.[13]

They were both, however, pulled back sharply by Churchill, who told Amery that he would

rather go out in the wilderness and fight, than to admit a revolution which meant the end of the Imperial Crown in India.[14]

And thereupon he proceeded to emasculate the draft public statement which Linlithgow and Amery had been preparing.

The 'Offer', which Linlithgow was then authorised to issue publicly in India on 8 August 1940, was consequently even more equivocating than had hitherto been customary. Whilst it stated that the Viceroy would appoint a majority of Indians to his Executive Council (it was well understood that these would be mainly drawn from the political parties), not only was there no suggestion that they would constitute a National Government of the kind the Congress had been demanding. It was made clear that the British would still retain the key portfolios of Finance, Defence, and Home in official hands. Moreover, while the Offer contained an undertaking that at the end of the war and 'with the least possible delay' the British would establish 'a body representative of the principal elements in India's national life' and would 'lend every aid in their power to hasten decisions on all relevant matters to the utmost degree', not only was there nothing here to meet the Congress demand for independence. Everything was constrained by the statement that all

---

[11] Amery to Linlithgow, 13 June 1940, in J. Barnes and D. Nicolson, eds., *The Empire at Bay. The Leo Amery Diaries 1929–1945*, London 1988, p. 607.

[12] Amery to Linlithgow, 13 June 1940, ibid.

[13] Linlithgow to Amery, tel., 17 June 1940, ibid.   [14] Ibid., 26 July 1940, p. 637.

change would be 'subject to the due fulfilment of the obligations which Great Britain's long connexion with India has imposed upon her', and that could clearly have been crippling – as was evidently Churchill's full intention. 'I have got pretty well three quarters of what I wanted', Amery declared. But it was that missing quarter which set the scene.

Hedged in by so many conditions [Sapru called the August Offer. It] is so incomplete in the enunciation of the aim and so non-committal in regard to its being implemented within any reasonable distance of time that it can afford no satisfaction whatever to the people of this country.[15]

It was swiftly rejected out of hand by the Congress President, Maulana Azad.[16]

The straits to which even Britain's Conservative reformers were by now reduced by the loss of the palliative side to their policy were simultaneously illustrated by two expedients to which Linlithgow now resorted. From the beginning of the war he had been busy elevating Jinnah, the President of the All-India Muslim League, not just to be the sole spokesman of India's Muslims to the all but total exclusion of the elected Muslim Premiers of the Muslim majority Provinces of Bengal and the Punjab, who, unlike Jinnah, each had an established electoral base behind them, but to placing him on a par with Gandhi, the leader of the much more substantial Indian National Congress. Thereafter he not only gave Jinnah a long rope. He allowed him to impose many a veto upon any Congress move. His purpose here was plain:

however tiresome Jinnah may be . . . [he told Amery in a characteristic letter in May 1941] I remain unshaken in my view . . . that it is desirable if possible to keep the Muslim League together because of the post-war discussions, because it represents the only organised opposition to Congress . . . Nor do I want to risk a combination against us of the Congress and the Muslim League.[17]

That soon became Amery's position too. Though in August 1940 he had conceded to a friend that: 'It is no good our . . . saying "When you have agreed we will think about doing something"',[18] by the end of the year he was congratulating himself that:

I have at any rate got it into the head of the public here and even in India that the major deadlock is that between Indians . . . [and] that we are ready . . . to move as soon as India will let us.[19]

[15] Statement of 1–2 November 1941, *Indian Annual Register,* 1941, vol. II, pp. 270–1.
[16] On the genesis of the August Offer, see also Moore, *Churchill, Cripps and India,* pp. 31–8; Rizvi, *Linlithgow and India,* pp. 152–60; Glendevon, *Viceroy at Bay,* ch. 15; Voight, *India in Second World War,* pp. 45–51; and *Empire at Bay,* ch. 9.
[17] Amery to Linlithgow, 5 Apr. 1941, LP 10. For a survey of this story see Rizvi, *Linlithgow and India,* pp. 105–21.   [18] *Empire at Bay,* p. 661.   [19] Ibid., p. 670.

At the same time Linlithgow, in company with his Home Member, Sir Reginald Maxwell, worried by the possibility of another Congress agitation (which Congress had been threatening ever since the previous March) had set about preparing nothing less than a 'Revolutionary Movements Ordinance' that was deliberately designed to be a great deal more draconian than the Emergency Powers Ordinance that had successfully halted the Civil Disobedience movement in 1932. This was approved in principle by the Cabinet on 1 June 1940, and on the very day Linlithgow issued the August Offer, he simultaneously went to the lengths of telling his provincial Governors

that the only possible answer to a 'declaration of war' by any section of Congress in present circumstances must be a declared determination to crush that organisation as a whole.

On this matter the latent hesitations on the British side nevertheless rose up against him. Sir Maurice Hallett, the Governor of UP (who had been Secretary of the Home Department in Delhi in 1932 and thus was no neophyte in these matters), roundly told Maxwell that it made no sense to say that subject to certain safeguards Indians could frame their own constitution and then to 'go out and smash the Congress' altogether. While shortly afterwards when Linlithgow asked if he could put his Revolutionary Powers Ordinance into effect against a new agitation by the Congress, Amery with the Cabinet fully behind him told him to use much less portentous measures first. They and their predecessors had long since recognised that it was neither in them nor in their electorate to suppress Indian nationalism wantonly, and were not, at this time, prepared to do so.[20]

The consequence of all this was that by the end of 1940 British imperial strategy in India stood in almost complete disarray. All the efforts during the preceding decade or so to create a more resilient framework for British rule in India had now collapsed. Recourse was now being made (as in Churchill's August Offer) to some very deliberate obfuscations, and (in Linlithgow's hands) to some very subterranean machinations of an altogether bankrupt kind. At the same time there were clearly limits to the extremes to which the Government of India was being permitted to go, and even Linlithgow had allowed himself to envisage the grant of Dominion Status at the end of the war in India. Away in London Amery, moreover, remained instinctively aware that British policy towards India could never remain entirely still, and early in 1941 in an attempt to keep some momentum going he arranged for two academic enquiries to be

[20] On all this see H.Poll.3/13/40, 3/14/40, 6/13/40, 3/16/40, 3/19/40, 3/22/40, 3/14/40 passim; *Empire at Bay*, pp. 641–2, 667–8.

made into India's constitutional problems, one by the Oxford Professor Coupland, the other by the new Reforms Commissioner, H.V. Hodson.[21] Neither, however, brought any relief, and for the most part Britain's imperial policy towards India now reached its nadir. Having lost anything like its reformist garb, it stood unfrocked in its underlying armour. 'I cannot imagine all this happening in the time of Reading, Halifax and Willingdon', Sapru remarked to a British Indian Civil Servant friend. Amery himself called it 'deadlock'.

By late 1940 the position, however, was little better on the Congress side. From the beginning of the war many of its leaders had been considerably frustrated by not being allowed to share in the fashioning of India's war effort.[22] They had agreed to Congress ministers resigning their provincial offices in protest against the churlish treatment the British were doling out. But they had then found themselves in an altogether novel situation. Hitherto they had always been able to oscillate fairly easily between office acceptance and nationalist agitation. So soon as they abandoned the one they had embarked on the other. But this time, having abruptly abandoned office, civil disobedience seemed well beyond their grasp.[23] There was no great agitational potential to propel it along. It had been there in the late 1930s, in places like Bihar and the United Provinces, but rather than using it to drive a further agitation forward, Congress governments in both provinces had set about suppressing or assuaging it themselves with some very modest land reforms.[24] In the vacuum which resulted a number of bolder spirits sought to take the initiative on their own. Subhas Bose built up the Forward Bloc (and in January 1941 fled to join the Axis powers). Jayaprakash Narayan and various other Congress Socialists set about organising a larger following – from which the Congress right was deliberately excluded. Right-wing extremists flexed their muscles too. The Hindu Mahasabha marshalled its growing following, and the semi-militarised Rashtriya Swayamsevak Sangh spread its net as well.[25]

In these circumstances the inability of the Congress High Command to carve out a clear road along which to lead the increasingly disparate forces

---

[21] Ibid. pp. 674–6. See R. Coupland, *The Indian Problem*, 3 vols., Oxford 1944; H.V. Hodson, *The Great Divide. Britain–India–Pakistan*, London 1969; Note on Reforms Comm.'s tour, 27 July–21 August 1941, LP 136.

[22] E.g. Gopal, *Jawaharlal Nehru*, vol. I, ch. 16.

[23] Gandhi, 'The Only Way', 19 Nov. 1939, *CWMG* 70, item 428; Damodaran, *Broken Promises*, ch. 3.

[24] Henningham, *Peasant Movements in Colonial India*, ch. 6; Reeves, *Landlords and Governments*, ch. 5c; Damodaran, *Broken Promises*, ch. 2.

[25] E.g. Gordon, *Brothers against the Raj*, pp. 404–20; Kudaisya, 'State Power and the Erosion of Colonial Authority', pp. 240–5.

of the Indian national movement was then compounded by a fruitless debate within its ranks over precisely what its attitude should be towards the war. Whilst Gandhi upheld his longstanding commitment to non-violence, and even suggested to the warring western powers that it contained the means by which to resolve their conflicts, Nehru and others were strongly of the view that the war was being waged against the Fascist evil, and that the Indian nation should participate fully in it.[26]

Congress frustration was then gravely aggravated by what was happening on the Muslim side. The outrage of the Muslim leadership in the Muslim minority provinces in the late 1930s at their exclusion from provincial office at the hands of an overweening Congress had now become a major force. After 1939 Muslim-led governments continued to hold office in Bengal, Sind, and Punjab, and under Jinnah's extraordinarily skilful leadership the All-India Muslim League had swept back to prominence on a wave of sustained hostility towards the Congress and its alleged Hindu dominance. The one thing Congress chose to unite upon during these months was its call for complete independence for India and a constituent assembly based upon a full adult franchise. Not only, however, were these things ruled out by the British. They were anathema to a great many Muslims who saw here a plot to deliver them into the hands of an always rapacious Congress. When in March 1940 the All-India Muslim League then passed its so-called 'Pakistan' resolution at its Lahore session, which called for the creation of separate Muslim states in northeastern and northwestern India, Congressmen were outraged. To them this represented a quite monstrous distraction from India's longstanding conflict with the British, and Muslim bitterness was soon reciprocated.

When (in addition to the points we have already noted) the British then spelled out in the August Offer their first major response to the League's 'Pakistan' resolution, Congress's dismay was even further deepened. For the British now declared that they would never transfer power to any government in India 'whose authority is directly denied by large and powerful elements in India's national life. Nor could they be parties to the coercion of such elements into submission to such a Government.' Thereafter these sentences became Jinnah's sheet anchor, and despite Gandhi's attempts to maintain some discourse with him, relations between the Muslim League and the Congress leaders soon reached a total impasse.[27]

Following Congress's total rejection of the August Offer Gandhi never-

---

[26] Gopal, *Jawaharlal Nehru*, vol. I, ch. 16; *CWMG* 71–2 passim.
[27] A. Jalal, *The Sole Spokesman. Jinnah, the Muslim League and the Demand for Pakistan*, Cambridge 1985, ch. 2; *CWMG* 70–72 passim.

theless made a determined effort to impel the Indian national movement forward once again. He seems to have judged that a mass agitation still remained out of reach. In any event it might still further alienate the Muslims, and it could very well create divisions within the Congress too. His experience of the suppression of the second Civil Disobedience movement in 1932 – and perhaps some knowledge of Linlithgow's draft Revolutionary Powers Ordinance – made it plain, moreover, that the British now knew how to suppress a mass movement and would be quite ready to do so again. He had, however, lost none of his old political skill, and now announced the inauguration, not of a mass, but of an 'individual satyagraha' campaign in which one by one Congress figures would utter their defiance of British rule, force the British to arrest them, and thereby revivify the nationalist cause.[28] In two respects the individual satyagraha campaign proved a great success. By 1941 no fewer than 26,000 Congressmen had displayed their devotion to the Congress cause, by going to jail. At the same time since the individual satyagraha campaign involved no great political upheaval Linlithgow was unable to justify the enactment of his Revolutionary Powers Ordinance to his London masters. Once again Gandhi had found the cleft between Britain's two Janus faces, and had turned his knife within it. Even more than before, however, he failed to shift the British.[29] While more seriously his otherwise remarkably ingenious campaign never really succeeded in arousing the public enthusiasm his previous campaigns had secured.

All in all therefore by late 1940 Congress's strategies stood in as parlous a state as those of the British. Despite the latent support on which it could usually draw it seemed to be making no headway against the British. Unable to mount a threatening agitation, its insistent demands for complete independence were wafting away upon the wind. And meanwhile the Hindu–Muslim chasm widened. Even Gandhi and Jinnah had ceased to talk. There was stalemate all along the line.

It was at this moment that a retired Indian Civil Servant and former member of the Viceroy's Executive Council, Sir Jagdish Prasad, who had lately become active in non-Congress politics in northern India, called on Sir Tej Bahadur Sapru, at his home in Allahabad, and urged him to come out of his political hibernation, take an active role in Indian politics once again, and try to resolve the current impasse.[30]

[28] Gandhi, 'Civil Disobedience', 15 Oct. 1940, ibid. 73, item 83.
[29] H.Poll.3/31/40 passim.
[30] Sapru to Dalvi, 9 Dec. 1940, SP 15; Shiva Rao to Sapru, 13 Nov. 1940, Sapru to Shiva Rao, 16 Nov. 1940, SP 20.

Sapru was by now sixty-five. As we saw in an earlier chapter he belonged to the same community and the same city as the Nehrus. Over the previous two decades he had been leader of the Allahabad Bar, and besides appearing occasionally in Calcutta and Madras had long been the leading lawyer in all of northern India too. In his younger days a Congressman, he had great respect for Gandhi; but in view of his strong belief in the necessity for the rule of law, he could never go along with the Mahatma and support civil disobedience. During the early 1920s he had been Law Member of the Viceroy's Council, and had then turned himself into India's foremost constitutional lawyer. Thereafter he had been a leading figure in all the constitutional discussions which had taken place in the 1920s, and in all three Round Table Conferences in London in the early 1930s. Along with his principal associate, M.R. Jayakar, he had been intimately involved too, as we have also seen, in a number of intricate negotiations between two successive Viceroys and the Congress leaders, Gandhi in particular.[31] In his own terms he was a staunch Indian nationalist. But ever since he had refused to endorse civil disobedience and had participated in the Round Table Conferences he had been spurned by the Congress leadership, not least in his own United Provinces. Late in 1940 Prasad nonetheless sought him out, not only because he was widely renowned in India for his integrity, contacts, and political skill, but also because he enjoyed a higher repute in London than any other Indian. To begin with Sapru was in no way impressed with Prasad's entreaty that he should once again employ his talents in the public cause. He issued a statement of his views to the press. But he firmly declined to accept the suggestion that he should head a deputation to the Viceroy, since as things stood he saw no point in doing so.[32]

In view of the parlousness of the times his press statement seems, however, to have caught the eye of a number of leading political figures in the country. When, for example, the United Provinces Provincial Muslim League met in Allahabad in Christmas week 1940, two of its principal leaders, Nawab Mohammed Ismail and Liaqat Ali Khan, spoke with him, and Sapru was left with the impression that on the major Congress–Muslim League issue, whilst 'the task of settlement would present great difficulties it was by no means hopeless'.[33] And thereafter he

[31] Low, 'Sapru and the First Round Table Conference'.

[32] Press statement, 14 Dec. 1940, SP 56; Sapru to Shiva Rao, 16 Nov., 12, 17 Dec. 1940, 3, 7 Jan. 1941, SP 20; Sapru to Natesan, 28 Nov. 1940, SP 40; Sapru to Sinha, 9 Dec. 1940, SP 56 and enc.; Sapru to Roy, 10 Dec. 1940, SP 50; Sapru to Prasad, 1, 26 Jan. 1941, SP 26.

[33] Sapru to Prasad, 27 Dec. 1940, ibid.; Sapru to Bajpai, 27 Dec. 1940, SP 5; Sapru to Gandhi, 28 Jan. 1941, SP 6.

seems to have changed his mind. At any rate shortly afterwards he for the first time in six years wrote an article for a political journal which appeared under the title 'The Needs of the Hour' in the January 1941 number of the monthly review *Twentieth Century*. In it he set out a distinctive strategy. He urged that Gandhi and Jinnah should get together once again. He called for the complete Indianisation of the Viceroy's Executive Council, and emphasised that on psychological grounds it was especially important that its Defence portfolio should now be put in Indian hands. Employing his old connections he was careful to send copies of this article to the editors and correspondents of the quality newspapers both in India and in Britain – significantly to the latter because on the basis of his long experience of the British he knew that it was sometimes of vital importance to appeal over the head of the Government of India to Caesar.[34]

Shortly afterwards his old Junior at the Allahabad bar, Dr S.N. Katju – long since a staunch Congressman – came to see him to explore what practical steps might be taken. He was soon followed by other Congressmen, Purushottamdas Tandon among them.[35] From several quarters there was now beginning to be mounting pressure on Sapru to play a major political role once again.[36] In particular he was being quite specifically pressed to act as mediator between Gandhi and Jinnah. He himself had a strong aversion to exposing himself upon such matters unless he was assured of the definite support of some of those who were more involved.[37] Katju took his point, and wrote to Gandhi to give him a full account of their conversation.[38]

For several weeks the Mahatma had been encouraging a number of people – Rajkumari Amrit Kaur, G.D. Birla, and Sir Purshottamdas Thakurdas – to make contact on his behalf with Jinnah, but had not had much success.[39] He now clutched at a straw, and, greatly to Sapru's surprise – they had not communicated with each other for nearly nine years – on 25 January 1941 he wrote to Sapru personally to say that: 'I have just finished reading your article in the XXth Century.' He much agreed that Jinnah and he should get together again: yet 'my impression is', he went on, 'that Jinnah does not want a settlement till he has consolidated the

[34] Sapru to Low, 3 Jan. 1941, SP, II, L90; Sapru to Prasad, 1 Jan. 1941, SP 26; Natesan to Sapru, 20 Jan. 1941, SP 40.   [35] Sapru to Prasad, 10 Jan. 1941, SP 26.

[36] Shiva Rao to Sapru, 2 Jan. 1941, SP 20; Natesan to Sapru, 20 Jan. 1941, SP 40; Prasad to Sapru, 25 Jan. 1941, SP 26.   [37] Sapru to Natesan, 24 Jan. 1941, SP 40.

[38] Sapru to Prasad, 10 Jan. 1941, SP 26; Sapru to Shiva Rao, 10–13 Jan. 1941, SP 20; Sapru to Katju, 20 Jan. 1941, Katju to Sapru 20 Jan. 1941, SP 32; Sapru to Natesan, 24 Jan. 1941, SP 40.

[39] Prasad to Jayakar, 14 Jan. 1941, JP 576; Birla to Thakurdas, 22 Dec. 1940, ThP 177.

League position'. Even so, he declared, 'if you have faith why don't you see him without being asked by anybody'.[40]

Gandhi's letter put Sapru upon his mettle. There was, he noted, very little of substance in it; but it did contain the Mahatma's blessing for any personal explorations he might make; and in the deadlocked circumstances which prevailed that was of great importance. Accordingly, after some further correspondence – and in the end somewhat to Gandhi's alarm – Sapru wrote to Jinnah (with whom he had had an amicable conversation back in Bombay in the previous August) suggesting that he should once again meet Gandhi to see if they could not arrange to hold a conference and settle their differences before the rift between them grew even wider. At the same time he wrote to the two Muslims, Nawab Mohammed Ismail and Liaqat Ali Khan, who had spoken to him in Allahabad back in December, in the hope that they would use such influence as they had with Jinnah to evoke a favourable response from him.[41]

Within a few days Sapru received a formally courteous reply from Jinnah in which he declared that he was always prepared to meet 'Mr Gandhi or any other Hindu leader on behalf of the Hindu community'. To describe Gandhi, however, in this way was to deny him the whole basis of his position in India as he saw it, and accordingly the whole exchange terminated abruptly before it had ever begun.[42]

Its outcome, however, was quite decisive for Sapru. In the preceding weeks he had been pressed to preside over a 'non-party conference' in Bombay. It had been urged on him, not only that his personal friends, but that the Viceroy himself, and a number of both Congressmen and Muslims too were anxious that he should bend his efforts to resolve the prevailing impasse.[43] To begin with Sapru strongly resisted this idea,[44] both because he had no confidence in the associated idea of sending a deputation to the Viceroy, and because he believed that it was much more important to get Gandhi and Jinnah together first. But when his own attempt to do so failed, he set his doubts aside and eventually agreed to attend the conference.[45] His resolution was strengthened by a conversation he had with Gandhi in Allahabad on 28 February 1941 at which the

[40] Gandhi to Sapru, 25 Jan. 1941, Sapru to Gandhi, 28 Jan. 1941, SP 6. For Linlithgow's very different response see Linlithgow to Amery, 10 Jan. 1941, LP 10.
[41] Gandhi–Sapru correspondence for this period, SP 6 and *CWMG* 73, items 372, 393, 413, 441, 455, 484 and Appendices IX, X.
[42] Sapru to Prasad, 13–14, 18 Feb. 1941, SP 26.
[43] Prasad to Sapru, 8, 16, 20 Feb. 1941, SP 26.
[44] Sapru to Prasad, 12–13 Jan. 1941, SP 26.
[45] Sapru to Prasad, 29 Jan., 12–13 Feb. 1941; Prasad to Sapru, 8 Feb. 1941 and enc., SP 26; Sapru to Shiva Rao, 6 Feb. 1941, SP 20; Jayakar to Sapru, 8 Feb. 1941, Sapru to Jayakar, 11 Feb. 1941, SP 10.

Mahatma told him he would not oppose any settlement which Sapru might effect with the government (and would advise Congress not to do so either).[46] Whereupon Sapru threw himself into the Bombay conference very much more fully than he had originally intended, and soon agreed to become its President.[47]

When the conference met on 13–14 March 1941 in Bombay, only thirty-four people attended. They included, however, a number of 'the knights of the round table', those 'prominent' non-Congress figures who had attended the Round Table Conferences in London ten years previously. They also included representatives of a wide array of political groups that did not belong either to the Congress or to the Muslim League. Sapru gave the presidential address, and played a major part in drafting the conference's resolutions. These set out his proposals for meeting the prevailing deadlock; and their thrust was double-pronged. They proposed that in the first place the British should make a declaration promising India Dominion Status within a fixed period after the war, and in the second that in the interval all central government portfolios should be transferred to the hands of non-official Indians (the Sapru programme of the previous November–December). Sapru deliberately said nothing about the distribution of portfolios between Hindus and Muslims: in his view this did not present insuperable problems (and, surprising as it may seem, experience in the interim government of 1946–7 suggests that he was right). At the same time he made it clear that the details of any such arrangements should be without prejudice to the future. He explained too that the Bombay proposals (like his own earlier ones) differed from Congress's current proposals in two important respects. They did not call for immediate independence, and they proposed that the central executive in India should (for the duration of the war at least) remain responsible *to the Crown*. Ostensibly this was because, as almost everyone believed, the existing central legislature, to which Congress wished it to be responsible,[48] was for the moment, at least, a most inappropriately composed body.[49] But there was a further consideration too. For 'responsibility to the Crown' played with great ingenuity upon the entrenched dualism which Sapru knew to be the preferred posture of the British. For whilst proposing that they should

---

[46] Sapru to Gandhi, 2, 10 Mar. 1941, Gandhi to Sapru, 7 Mar. 1941, SP 6 and *CWMG* 73, pp. 362–3; Sapru to Jayakar, 4 Apr. 1941, SP 10; Sapru to Reed, 30 Apr. 1941, SP 50; Gandhi's Statement to the Press, 6 Mar. 1971, *CWMG* 73, 478.

[47] Sapru to Prasad, 2 Mar. 1941, SP 26.

[48] CWC resolution, Delhi, 7 July 1940, Gwyer and Appadorai, *Speeches and Documents,* pp. 500–1.

[49] Sapru to Laithwaite, 24 Mar. 1941, SP 30; 'Report of the Non-Party Conference...', and 'Memorandum on the Bombay Conference Resolutions', SP 29, Misc. 31.

concede executive positions in the central government to some of India's political leaders, it left them with the power to deprive them of these if circumstances seemed to them in any way to warrant this. At the same time Congress and/or others who took office could along these lines secure executive positions at the pinnacles of power in India, and thereby be immeasurably well placed to confront and shape its future. There could, of course, be a breakdown; but short of the British announcing that they would quit, of which there was as yet very little sign, one foot in the door seemed to be much the most promising way forward. Later Kwame Nkrumah called this 'tactical action', in contrast to the 'positive action' of agitation. It involved a decision very akin to Congress's assumption of provincial office in 1937–9, and to the Congress High Command's entry into the Interim Government in September 1946.

The Bombay conference's resolutions received very considerable publicity. It was clear that Gandhi and his immediate entourage were watching Sapru's moves very closely. Both Rajagopalachari and Mahadev Desai, Gandhi's secretary, were quick to collect details about the conference, and when Gandhi was asked whether he would be contributing to the discussion which it had set on foot, he promptly replied that he was doing so – by keeping quiet.[50] There was, moreover, a notable moment in the central legislature shortly afterwards when Jinnah appeared to trim his sails on the Pakistan issue. Such indeed were the expectations that the Bombay conference had aroused that Sapru was soon being asked by the Governor of his own United Provinces if he was going to see the Viceroy. Not to be caught out, he replied stiffly that he had no intention of making the first move himself. It was up to the Viceroy.[51]

In view of the unusually high regard in which Sapru was held in many quarters both in India and in Britain, Amery and Linlithgow were both well aware that they had to treat his overtures very circumspectly. They accordingly embarked on an extensive correspondence over exactly how they should respond. From the start Linlithgow was, however, entirely dismissive. His influential Private Secretary, Laithwaite, put it about that nothing could be done till Congress and the Muslim League had composed their differences; while Linlithgow himself was reported as having privately been very disparaging about 'those amiable leaders' in Bombay.[52] On substantive matters, moreover, he would not budge.

---

[50] Shiva Rao to Sapru, 18 Mar. 1941, SP 20; Desai to Sapru, 23 Mar. 1941, SP 6; Jayakar to Sapru, 1 Apr., Sapru to Jayakar 4 Apr. 1941, SP 10; Jayakar to Prasad, 2 Apr. 1941, JP 576; Sapru to Shiva Rao, 5 Apr. 1941, SP 20. See also *CWMG* 73, 536.

[51] Sapru to Kodanda Rao, 19 Mar. 1941, SP 22; Sapru to Shiva Rao, 22, 25 Mar. 1941, Shiva Rao to Sapru, 22, 23 Mar. 1941, SP 20; Prasad to Jayakar, 1 Apr. 1941, JP 576.

[52] Sapru to Jogendra Singh, 21 Mar. 1941, SP 24; Sapru to Prasad, 24 Mar. 1941, SP 26; Sapru to Shiva Rao, 21, 22 Mar. 1941, Shiva Rao to Sapru, 19–21, 25 Mar. 1941, SP 20.

Other objections apart [he brusquely told Amery] we could not transfer Defence or Finance to non-officials or concede the Dominion position in Imperial or International relations without hopelessly prejudicing post-war discussions . . . Further reflection confirms and emphasises my view of the importance of the safeguards and indeed of all the protective safeguards in [the Government of India Act of 1935]. Were we to give way now and to accept the proposal, we would have lost all hope of maintaining those protective arrangements in such degree as may be necessary in any post-war constitutional scheme.[53]

As for Sapru's call for an entirely Indianised Viceroy's Council, that was out of the question too.

I should be most reluctant [he told Amery] . . . to consider an all-Indian Non-official Executive Council. I am perfectly certain that this would with little delay lead us into serious difficulties over defence and probably finance . . . We would then be far worse off than we are now if we were to have resignations either collective or communal on such an issue and I would be strongly opposed to any change of policy in this regard.[54]

Amery for his part, however, was having to think of not one but two political flanks. On many matters he was in full agreement with Linlithgow. But his initial instinct − because of the inherent ambiguity in the British position − was to explore some of the issues Sapru had raised. Congress 'having ruled itself out', he mused to Linlithgow. 'If Jinnah really were prepared to come in himself you might go a fairly long way over details.'[55] Moreover:

Demand for all-Indian non-official executive might be said at a stretch to come within framework of our declared policy provided that it is clearly understood that responsibility to the Crown implies that the last word on all policy rests with the Viceroy.[56]

As this was precisely what Sapru had been propounding at the Bombay conference, he had clearly made his point. Amery was nevertheless acutely aware that he had still to face Churchill, and Churchill's response proved once again decisive.

I got another Minute from Winston [Amery soon recorded in his diary], this time a petulant protest, having read my telegraphic correspondence with Linlithgow about what to say to Sapru, against stirring up the constitutional question and suggesting that the best service I could do towards the war would be to leave it alone. I wrote him a long letter explaining that the situation stirred itself up, that some sort of answer had to be given to Sapru and that unless the policy agreed between us was interpreted in a positive sense I could not hold it either in the

---

[53] Linlithgow to Amery, 30 Mar., 2 Apr. 1941, LP 20.
[54] Linlithgow to Amery, 6 Apr. 1941, LP 20.
[55] Amery to Linlithgow, 5 Apr. 1941, LP 10.
[56] Amery to Linlithgow, 5 Apr. 1941, LP 20.

House or in India. The trouble is that Winston just dislikes the idea of anything being done in India at all and though he reluctantly drafted the Statement of August 8th he does not really believe in it and just hopes that we can sit back and do nothing indefinitely.[57]

Even before Linlithgow eventually saw Sapru, therefore, not only was the Viceroy's own mind firmly closed,[58] but the Prime Minister's veto was in the offing too.

All the same on 2 April 1941 Linlithgow sent an invitation to Sapru to come and stay with him at Viceroy's House in New Delhi, and thereafter on 7 April 1941 the two men were closeted together in two successive meetings over nearly five hours. Sapru pressed the Bombay proposals one by one. Linlithgow was careful to indicate that he was listening closely. On the issue of Dominion Status he told Sapru that while he personally was in favour of fixing a post-war time limit for this, London had rejected the idea (he refrained from mentioning his own determination to hold to all the old safeguards). On the Pakistan issue, on which Sapru pressed him strongly, he refused, however, to be drawn. When they then turned to discuss 'responsibility to the Crown', Sapru explained that in ordinary circumstances this meant that

the executive would be irremovable . . . [because] in the first place it was not desirable that during these critical times there should be any instability and in the next place responsibility to the [present] legislature would be open to much criticism.[59]

Sensing a weakness here Linlithgow pressed Sapru to explain what would happen if the legislature opposed the executive persistently. Sapru had his answer. That, he said, would be

an extreme case [when it would be] obvious that they must make room for others who would be appointed by the Crown. [However, given its existing varied membership he] had had no reasons to believe that the legislature could not be managed or that it would be so unreasonable as to completely paralyse the new government.[60]

Linlithgow even so persisted.

I suggested to him [he told Amery] that he had repeatedly commended the workability of his scheme on the ground that members of the new Council would be reasonable men. Could one feel so sure that his successors would be all of them so reasonable? . . . Tested on his intentions in regard to the Governor-General's dis-

[57] *Empire at Bay*, 8 Apr. 1941, p. 679.
[58] For further correspondence see Linlithgow to Amery, 6, 21–23, 29 Mar., 6 Apr. 1941, LP 10, 29 Mar. 1941, LP 20; Amery to Linlithgow, 19–22 Mar. 1941, LP 10.
[59] Sapru's 'Summary of the Conversations I had with . . . the Viceroy on Apr. 7, 1941. . .', SP 29, Misc. 32.   [60] Ibid.

cretions ... [Sapru] made it clear at once that ... on the assumption that we were dealing with reasonable men, we could avoid a difference of view between Council and the Governor-General in 8 cases out of 10. In any event, if the Viceroy did in any such matter disagree, the Viceroy's view must prevail.[61]

– which would seem clear enough. Yet in reporting immediately afterwards to Amery, Linlithgow dismissed Sapru's whole approach out of hand.

Main general impression left on me [he cabled] was that he had not applied his mind with anything like his customary thoroughness to the constitutional and practical difficulties involved in the Bombay plan. When tackled he more than once showed a disposition to dodge the substance of a difficulty by turning argument into less awkward channels. His approach throughout was sketchy and superficial.[62]

That was clearly unfair. No such conclusion is borne out either by his own two subsequent accounts,[63] or by Sapru's note on the two meetings which stretched to forty-five detailed paragraphs.[64]

The fact was that Sapru had pushed Linlithgow to the edge.[65] Within the parameters of maintaining Britain's ultimate control over India whilst the war was still on, he had presented him with two quite feasible proposals. Linlithgow evidently had some personal sympathy with the call for a more accommodating statement about Britain's constitutional intentions at the conclusion of the war. But with Churchill in the way there was nothing that could as yet be done over that. Sapru's other proposal, moreover, for a non-official central executive was less than Linlithgow's provincial governors had had to operate in 1937–9. It was essentially what the Governor of Ceylon was operating concurrently – and which many a British African governor had to manage later. On this, however, Linlithgow refused to budge. Even Amery found his reports

very negative all around and with a good many arguments which did not seem to me wholly conclusive. The fact is that when it comes to it he is alarmed – perhaps rightly – at any effective surrender of power and in this he will have Winston, Simon, and, to a lesser extent, Anderson, behind him. So I can only mark time and prepare the public mind for the future. . .[66]

---

[61] Linlithgow to Amery (longer tel.), 10 Apr. 1941, LP 20. In all this Sapru was simply repeating what he had said in his two speeches at the Bombay Conference, 'Report', SP 29, Misc 31. See also Statement by Standing Committee of Bombay Conference, nd, SP 29, Misc. 29 # 12.   [62] Linlithgow to Amery (shorter tel.), 10 Apr. 1941, LP 20.

[63] Linlithgow to Amery (longer tel.), 10 Apr. 1941, LP 20; 'Note of discussion . . . [in the] Executive Council', 7 May 1941, LP 136.

[64] Sapru's 'Summary. . .' SP 29, Misc. 32; Shiva Rao to Srinivasan, 9 Apr. 1941, JP 576; Sapru to Jayakar, 12 Apr. 1941, SP 10.

[65] This is exemplified by the great length of his disquisitions in Linlithgow to Amery, 25 Apr. 1941, LP 10, and see footnote 63.   [66] *Empire at Bay*, 11 Apr. 1941, p. 680.

At the end of their meeting Linlithgow nonetheless undertook to let Sapru know how his ideas fared in London. To begin with Sapru was mildly optimistic.[67] Certainly Linlithgow had been very polite. Soon, moreover, advanced opinion both in Congress and in the League was becoming greatly concerned lest Sapru and his Bombay men should succeed in effecting a political breakthrough. Some Congressmen (both Satyamurti and Vallabhbhai Patel were explicitly named) let it be known, for example, that they would be considerably disconcerted if the Government were to settle with Sapru and his associates,[68] while the *National Herald*, Jawaharlal Nehru's organ in Lucknow, now proceeded to attack the Bombay proposals with very considerable vigour.[69] More significantly, Jinnah took some quite deliberate steps both in speeches and in circulars to his lieutenants at this time to denounce the Sapru programme as a Congress plot, and during May there was an acrimonious exchange between the two men.[70]

Within a fortnight of their meeting, however, Sapru received a letter from Linlithgow saying that the Secretary of State saw 'difficulties in the degree of advance represented by the changes advocated by you',[71] and in a speech in the House of Commons on 22 April Amery thereafter attempted to justify the Government's complete rejection of the Bombay resolutions. Their suggestion, he said, that India could be treated for external purposes as if she were already a Dominion must be quite unacceptable to Parliament – though, as Sapru was quick to point out, the principle had been conceded as long ago as 1919 when India had sent special representatives to the Versailles Peace Conference. On the demand for Dominion Status after the war, by saying very little Amery by implication rejected the plea for some more definite assurance on this. On the proposal to transfer all central portfolios to Indian hands, he remarked in lordly tones that this was 'certainly something going beyond what we think practicable in the midst of the ever-increasing strain and injury of the war situation'. And (whilst being careful like Linlithgow to be very courteous to Sapru personally) he ended by playing what was now his 1941 theme song. The Bombay proposals, he avowed, had been sent 'to the wrong address'. They had been denounced by Jinnah as a trap by

[67] Prasad to Jayakar, 10 Apr. 1941, JP 576; Sapru to Jayakar, 12 Apr. 1941, SP 10.
[68] Sapru to Prasad, 12 Apr. 1941, SP 26; Sapru to Kodanda Rao, 2 Apr. 1941, SP 22; Sapru to Shiva Rao, 15 Apr. 1941, SP 21.
[69] Sapru to Jayakar, 4 Apr. 1941, SP 10; Sapru to Prasad, 16 Apr. 1941, SP 26; Shiva Rao, 18 Apr. 1941, SP 21.
[70] Sapru's statement, 4 May 1941, SP 29; Sapru to Shiva Rao, 8 May 1941, SP 21; Sapru to Sinha, 13 June 1941, SP 25; Sapru to Kodanda Rao, 2 Apr. 1941, SP 22; Prasad to Jayakar, 5 Apr. 1941, JP 576; see SP 29, Misc. 33.
[71] Linlithgow to Sapru, 20 Apr. 1941, SP 13.

'Congress wirepullers'. 'My appeal to Sir Tej and his friends would therefore be', he declared, 'not to cease from their efforts, but to concentrate,
first and foremost, upon bringing the contending elements in India
together'.[72]

The interesting point about this speech is that in it Amery rejected as
out of the question a number of items which he had previously been ready
to advance himself; a number too that the Government of which he was
still a member conceded within a year; and that he laid down as a *sine qua
non* for any advance a condition – of communal agreement – which he was
to ignore within weeks.

His speech, moreover, failed to settle the matter. Even within the
Viceroy's Council Linlithgow found himself having 'to clear the atmosphere in regard to the talks between Sir Tej Sapru and himself' by
rehearsing, often with considerable pedantry, the issues they had discussed, before concluding lamely that: 'The expansion of Council
involved would, if the terms suggested were accepted, inevitably and very
definitely prejudice the future.'[73] Whilst his Home Member, Sir Reginald
Maxwell, gave vent to the desperation which some of his kind felt when he
affirmed that:

Sapru's move was a move . . . to reopen the bidding for Congress [which] is not
and never will be a real national party: it is a sectarian movement completely anti-
national in character . . . by the time we have finished with the war . . . our business
will be to see that the Congress is forgotten. . .[74]

Others however spoke very differently. Sir Zafrullah Khan bluntly called
the situation 'an unsatisfactory one and a cause of uneasiness . . . a barren
position', while, in contradistinction to Maxwell, Linlithgow, and Amery
alike, one of the other British members of the Council, Sir Andrew Clow,
stated

that Sir Tej Sapru was right in thinking that His Majesty's Government ought to
take a hand in settling the bigger issue. There was no hope, if the attitude that
Indians must reach agreement among themselves was to be the permanent attitude of His Majesty's Government.[75]

Amery, moreover, knew that a good deal of informed opinion about
India both in the House of Commons (where there were a number of crit-
ical speeches, by, for example, Sir George Schuster, a former Finance
Member of the Viceroy's Council) and in the British quality press was

---

[72] 'The Provinces and the Constitution', House of Commons, 22 Apr. 1941, L.S. Amery,
India and Freedom, Oxford 1942, pp. 77–89.
[73] 'Note of Discussion . . . [in the] Executive Council', 7 May 1941, LP 136.
[74] Maxwell's Note, 22 May 1941, LP 136.
[75] 'Note of Discussion . . . [in the] Executive Council', 7 May 1941, LP 136.

very unhappy about the Government's altogether one-sided posture towards India.[76]

> There was an undoubted feeling of disappointment [he told Linlithgow] both in the House and in the press, and a desire, likely to become more vocal before long, that we should not merely leave the onus on the other side, but shall make clear our own positive intention, within the limits of our policy, to do what we can to promote unity and a measure of advance.[77]

For the moment, however, there was little which could now be done – and there was no effectual pressure from the Congress side either to bring about any change.

For his part Sapru was, of course, much disappointed. He had presented the government with an ingenious *pis aller*, which they had promptly turned into a dead end. He was especially perturbed at what he called Amery's grant of a veto to Jinnah. Whilst the full force of that only lasted a month or two, there can be little doubt that in one vital respect Amery's April 1941 speech enabled Jinnah to consolidate his position in India as never before. Sikander Hyat Khan and Fazl Huq, the Premiers of the Muslim majority provinces of Bengal and the Punjab, were most unhappy with his proceedings. They were both, however, ignored in London and by the Viceroy, even though it was in their provinces that Pakistan would have to be based. Jinnah alone was given attention; and when the British kowtowing to him reached its climax with Amery's April 1941 speech, he was quick to use the added prestige it brought him to bring both Sikander and Huq to heel. When later in the year they were minded to accept invitations to serve on the Viceroy's Defence Advisory Council against his direct instructions, he forced both of them to retreat.[78] Thereafter they grumbled continuously at Jinnah's imperiousness in private, but as Sapru for one clearly understood, they were now irredeemably hesitant to stand up to him in public.[79]

For the rest Amery's speech did nothing but widen the breach between Congress and the League, and in all the circumstances of the time his homily to Sapru about communal agreement was at once unctuous and unwarranted.

However, as both the newspaper correspondents in Delhi and existing members of the Viceroy's Council were soon to avow, his efforts were not entirely ineffectual.[80] Quite characteristically both Amery and Linlithgow

---

[76] *Empire at Bay*, p. 663; Amery to Linlithgow, 5, 9, May 1941, LP 20. See also Sapru to Reed, 30 Apr. 1941, SP 22; Sapru to Shiva Rao, 11 May 1941, SP 21.
[77] Amery to Linlithgow, 25 Apr. 1941, LP 10.   [78] H.Poll.17/4/41 I.
[79] Sapru to Shiva Rao, 5 Nov. 1941, SP 21.
[80] Shiva Rao to Sapru, 9 June, 25 Oct. 1941, SP 21.

knew that the Government could not stand altogether pat for very long.[81] There were too many Members of Parliament with Indian experience, and others, who had been stirred into action by Sapru's Bombay conference and would need to be assuaged. That impression was confirmed when on 15 May the Archbishop of Canterbury, that bell-wether of British elite opinion, called upon Amery and 'earnestly urged' that without opening up 'political fissures' the Viceroy should 'definitely declare' his wish 'to associate Indians as Indians' on his Executive Council.[82]

With this lesser matter the Government soon decided to proceed. It proved necessary to wear down Churchill's inevitable opposition, but eventually in July 1941 Linlithgow announced that because of the increased administrative burdens of the war, his Executive Council would now be enlarged by the appointment of three new Indian members, which for the first time would give it an Indian majority;[83] and, in a further Commons speech, Amery took credit for the quality of the men appointed.[84] Jinnah was clearly affronted when he realised the change had been made without his agreement.[85] Whilst there was, as Sapru noted, still no transfer of the crucial Finance, Defence, and Home portfolios, he nevertheless recognised that this was a small step in the right direction, and he hoped that it would not be too long before the Indian majority in the Council would begin to flex its muscles.[86] Encouraged, moreover, by the support he was receiving in London,[87] he undertook to preside over a second session of the Bombay Conference at the end of July,[88] this time in Poona, at which he vehemently denounced the government's continuing intransigence on the other issues which really mattered.[89]

The second half of 1941 was even so a fallow period. In September there was some considerable stir when Churchill appeared to deny that

[81] Amery to Linlithgow, 25 Apr. 1941, Linlithgow to Amery, 26 Apr. 1941, LP 10; Linlithgow to Amery, 19 May 1941, *Empire at Bay*, p. 663.

[82] Amery to Linlithgow, 15 May 1941, Mss. Eur. 125/20.

[83] E.g. *Empire at Bay*, 20 May–29 July 1941, pp. 690–9 passim; Amery to Linlithgow, 5, 24 May 1941, Linlithgow to Amery, 19 May 1941, LP 20; Shiva Rao to Sapru, 12 May 1941, SP 21; Linlithgow to Sapru, 8 July 1941, SP 13.

[84] 'Expansion of the Executive Council', House of Commons, 1 Aug. 1941, Amery, *India and Freedom*, pp. 90–100.

[85] Shiva Rao to Sapru, 4 July 1941, SP 21; Jinnah to Suhrawady, 1 Aug. 1941, H.Poll.17/1/41; Prasad to Sapru, 22 Aug. 1941, SP 18.

[86] Sapru to Sarkar, 11 Aug. 1941, SP 52; Sapru to Shiva Rao, 16, 18 Aug. 1941, SP 21; Sapru to Srinivasan, 16 Aug. 1941, SP 57.

[87] E.g. Sapru to Reed, 30 Apr. 1941, SP 50.

[88] E.g. Sapru to Shiva Rao, 16 May 1941, SP 21; Sapru to Natesan, 15 May 1941, NMML Natesan Papers.

[89] Sapru to Mehta, 3 May 1941, SP 7; Sapru to Prasad 10 May 1941, SP 26; Shiva Rao to Sapru, 6 June 1941, SP 21; Sapru to Amery, 16 Aug. 1941, SP 1.

the recently signed Atlantic Charter would have any reference to India.[90] There was now a good deal of evidence that the Viceroy was once again 'lying back'.[91] Hodson, the newly appointed Reforms Commissioner, saw Sapru in Allahabad in August, and vehemently defended Amery.[92] The trouble, he declared, was Churchill, who was as diehard over India as ever.[93] During these months there was some stirring over India in Labour Party ranks in Britain. Following upon a discussion at the party conference in June, the National Executive Committee had a meeting with Amery on 18 July, which was, however, quite inconclusive.[94] From time to time the party leader, Attlee, and Bevin, the Minister of Labour, gave vent to their growing concerns over India to Amery privately; but they were not as yet ready to confront Churchill.[95] In October an all-party group in London suggested that a parliamentary commission should be sent to India; but that came to nothing too.[96] There was some anxiety at this time in the United States about the Indian position, but Sumner Welles, Roosevelt's Under-Secretary of State, twice squelched any attempt to raise the issue with the British Government.[97]

At the beginning of December 1941 there was even so one tell-tale development. Several months previously Linlithgow had started to contemplate a general release of all the remaining satyagraha prisoners (Maulana Azad and Jawaharlal Nehru principally amongst them). In due course the new Indian members of the Viceroy's Council (with whom Sapru was by now in close touch)[98] joined him in pressing this upon the Cabinet in London. This inevitably ran into strong opposition from Churchill, and Amery was soon fearful that the Viceroy's new Council might find itself being overruled.[99] On this matter it soon became clear, however, that Churchill did not in the end have the Cabinet with him, and eventually, as Amery noted in his diary of a meeting on 1 December: 'Winston looked around the room and said: "I give in." And then added *sotto voce*: "When you lose India don't blame me."'[100]

---

[90] Churchill, *The Second World War*, vol. III, ch. XXIV, and vol. IV, *The Hinge of Fate*, London 1951, p. 786.

[91] e.g. Linlithgow to Amery, 30 Aug. 1941, *Empire at Bay*, p. 664.

[92] Sapru to Prasad, 19 Aug. 1941, SP 18; Sapru to Holland, 20 August, SP II H234.

[93] Shiva Rao to Sapru, 21 Aug. 1941, SP 21.

[94] P.S. Gupta, *Imperialism and the British Labour Movement, 1914–1964*, London 1975, p. 268.

[95] E.g. *Empire at Bay*, 28 May, 27 June, 4, 25 Sept., 30 Oct. 1941, pp. 691, 695, 713, 716–17, 741.   [96] Ibid. p. 45.

[97] For a useful summary see Moore, *Churchill, Cripps and India*, pp. 47–9.

[98] Chiefly through Shiva Rao, Delhi correspondent of *The Hindu* and the *Manchester Guardian*, SP 21 passim.

[99] *Empire at Bay*, 8 Nov.–1 Dec. 1941, pp. 743–51; Churchill, *Grand Alliance*, pp. 748–9; Amery to Linlithgow, 22, 25 Nov. 1940, LP 10; Shiva Rao to Sapru, 21 June 1941, SP 21; Sapru to Prasad, 19 Aug. 1941, SP 18.   [100] *Empire at Bay*, 1 Dec. 1941, p. 751.

It was a telling moment. Several members of the Cabinet, like some in the press, the House of Commons, and even the Viceroy himself, were now starting to show signs of wanting to see Britain's policy towards India presenting a more defensible posture than it had shown over the past year or so. Ultimately repression never satisfied them. As ever they needed a palliative aspect to what they were doing as well. Earlier in the year Sapru had presented them with an opportunity to put this matter right. Privately Amery had long had half a mind to do this, but Churchill remained adamant. So for the most part did Linlithgow. Within India itself there was some talk in the latter part of the year of Congress taking office once again.[101] But for the moment no further move was made. Everyone seemed to be waiting upon events.

They came in a great rush, and from a quite novel quarter. On 7 December 1941 the Japanese attacked the American fleet in Pearl Harbor and launched their sweep southwards into Southeast Asia. That immediately put India right at the forefront of the war. It served, moreover, to bring to a head the growing anxiety in Britain over the Government's stance towards India. On 17 December the Labour Party established an India committee. On 19 December, to Churchill's dismay, Bevin raised the question of Britain's policy towards India in the Cabinet, and on the following day Attlee sought an urgent discussion with Amery about it.[102] Already some Conservative backbenchers were openly discussing the matter,[103] while a number of the British popular newspapers – the *Evening Standard* and the *Sunday Pictorial* amongst them – were starting to comment on it as well. On 23 December *The Times* called for a positive move to be made by the Muslim League and the Congress, while on 24 December the *Manchester Guardian* called upon the Viceroy to consult their respective leaders.[104] Sensing a change in the air Nehru's London friend, Krishna Menon, pressed him to take a 'positive initiative for National . . . Government'. 'May I use discretion', he telegraphed to Nehru, 'to see Amery and others?' Along with many others in the Congress Nehru, however, was at this time in no mood to parley. 'Undesirable your interviewing British official', he replied tartly.[105] In any

---

[101] Inglis to Laithwaite, 20 Aug. 1941, LP 136; Nanna to Kamladevi, 12 Oct. 1941, H.Poll.4/8/41; Birla to Thakurdas, 8 Nov. 1941, ThP 239; Low to Laithwaite, 26 Nov. 1941, Laithwaite's Note, 4 Dec. 1941, LP 136; Cunningham to Linlithgow, 9 Jan. 1942, *TOP* I, 8.   [102] *Empire at Bay*, 20 Dec. 1941, p. 755.

[103] E.g. *The Times*, 18 Dec. 1941.

[104] *Sunday Pictorial*, 13 Dec., *Evening Standard* 17 Dec., *The Times*, 23 Dec, *Manchester Guardian*, 17, 22, 24 Dec., also *Daily Herald* and *News Chronicle*, 14 Dec. 1942.

[105] H.Poll.4/5/41.

case Congress was soon enmeshed in its own tortuous problems, first over whether to hold to Gandhi's non-violence creed with the Japanese at the gates, and then over Gandhi's resignation on this issue from all of his formal positions within it. As a consequence they had at this moment in time nothing new to say to the British, and no new cudgel to brandish against them either.[106] The Muslim League noted the new mood, but the most it did was to warn the British not to appease the Congress.[107]

It was in this situation, when his long-tutored antennae told him that an exceptional opportunity to make a decisive move had quite suddenly arrived, that Sapru alone took the key initiative. Sensing the suddenly renewed interest which was being taken in Indian affairs in London, he consulted two new members of the Viceroy's Council[108] with whom he had been in close touch, drummed up his principal Bombay following, and launched his masterstroke. Quite deliberately bypassing the Viceroy (with whom Congress, the Muslim League, and he himself had always previously negotiated) he despatched directly to Churchill the long telegram of 2 January 1942 which we noted at the outset. As Churchill had just gone over to Washington for urgent discussions with Roosevelt about the conduct of the war, Sapru seized the dramatic opportunity to send it to him there, and with one stroke tore a very large hole in the patched and tattered fabric of Britain's policy wraps over India.[109]

Since an associate of Sapru's sent, moreover, copies of his telegram to two American press agencies,[110] Roosevelt seems to have very soon received a copy. At all events, having himself, following the Japanese attack upon Southeast Asia, promptly reiterated the now longstanding American undertaking to grant early independence to the Philippines, he proceeded to raise the question of India's future in one of his meetings with Churchill. Churchill rounded on him with all the vehemence of a totally unrepentant diehard. As a close association with Churchill was absolutely vital to Roosevelt for the future prosecution of the war, and as Churchill was clearly being entirely obdurate over India, Roosevelt thereafter trod very carefully, and made no further move till after some crucial

---

[106] E.g. Birla to Thakurdas, 8 Nov. 1940, ThP 239; Linlithgow to Amery, 17, 18 Jan. 1942, CWC Resolutions, Bardoli, 30 Dec. 1941, *TOP* I, 16, 17, and Appendix III.

[107] Muslim League Working Committee Resolution, Nagpur, 27 Dec. 1941, *TOP* I, Appendix IV.

[108] Sapru to Jayakar, 29 Dec. 1941, SP 10; Sapru to V. Sastri, 29 Dec. 1941, SP 23. Sapru had had a meeting in his house on 18 December of 125 people to discuss the war situation, Sapru to Jayakar, 20 Dec. 1941, JP 576.

[109] *TOP* 1, 2; Sapru to various, 27 Dec. 1941, SP 29, Misc. 35; Sapru to Jayakar, 29 Dec. 1941 SP 10; Sapru to Prasad, 29 Dec. 1941, Prasad to Sapru, 12 Jan. 1941, SP 18.

[110] Shiva Rao to Sapru, 3 Jan. 1942, SP 21.

decisions had been taken in London.[111] Yet for the next nine months he kept up the pressure on him even so.[112]

Churchill was clearly greatly angered by the Sapru telegram (as he had been by Bevin's intervention in Cabinet on 19 December), for on 7 January, within four days of its receipt, he went out of his way to thunder at his Cabinet colleagues against any suggestion of any change in their Indian policy.

> The Indian troops are fighting splendidly [he boomed in a message to them], but it must be remembered that their allegiance is to the King-Emperor, and that the rule of the Congress and the Hindu priesthood machine would never be tolerated by a fighting race ... I trust we shall not depart from the position we have deliberately taken up.[113]

But on his return to London on 16 January he soon discovered that any such stance was no longer tenable. For Sapru's acumen in sending his telegram direct to Churchill in Washington, and then, as was his practice, sending copies of it not only to the newspapers in India,[114] but to all of the main newspapers in Britain, had had precisely the effect he had desired. As the principal exponent of Indian moderate opinion for the past twenty years his forceful intervention had quickly caught the London eye. It was immediately reported in *The Times*, the *Manchester Guardian*, *The Scotsman*, *The Yorkshire Post*, the *News Chronicle*, the *Daily Express*, the *Daily Herald*, *The Star*, and elsewhere. Thereafter leader writers, not least in *The Times* and the *Manchester Guardian*, but in weeklies like *The Spectator* and *Time and Tide* too, and in more popular Conservative papers such as the *Sunday Pictorial*, the *Standard*, and the *Sketch* as well, were soon lending their strong support to Sapru's plea for the Government to take a new initiative in India.[115] Whilst, moreover, in the course of the general debate on the war which took place in the House of Commons after Churchill's return from Washington, Churchill himself said nothing about Indian politics, a number of other members did,[116] and it was soon clear that there was growing concern not only in the Labour Party but amongst some Conservatives and Liberals also about the essentially negative posture which the Government had adopted

---

[111] Rizvi, *Linlithgow and India*, canvasses the details, pp. 175–6; Roosevelt to Churchill, 11 Mar. 1942, *TOP* I, 311.   [112] Churchill, *Hinge of Fate*, pp. 185–90.

[113] Churchill, *Grand Alliance*, pp. 614–15.

[114] *Pioneer, Hindustan Times, National Herald, Hindu, Tribune, Statesman*, etc., 5 Jan. 1942.

[115] Shiva Rao to Sapru, 3 Jan. 1942, SP 21; Sapru to V. Sastri, 6 Jan. 1942, SP 23; *Manchester Guardian*, 5, 6 Jan., 7 Feb., *The Times*, 5, 8, 17, 23 Jan., 2 Feb., *Daily Herald*, 17 Jan., *Spectator*, 16 Jan., *Time and Tide* 15 Jan. 1942; Turnbull to Rowan, 20 Jan. 1942, *TOP* I, 21.

[116] Gupta, *Imperialism and the British Labour Movement*, p. 269; for a comment to Sapru see Shiva Rao to Sapru 30 Jan. 1942, SP 21.

towards India. As a consequence Churchill found himself having to think again.

Early in February 1942 three provincial meetings – in Calcutta, Madras, and Nagpur – of Sapru's Non-Party Conference (as it was now called) were held; and on 22 February a third meeting of the full conference (which was fully reported in London) took place in New Delhi. That was also extensively reported – in London by *The Times*, the *Manchester Guardian*, *The Daily Telegraph*, the *News Chronicle*, amongst others, and in the United States by such influential newspapers as the *New York Times* and the *Christian Science Monitor*.[117] Though sick and unable to read his own presidential speech, Sapru once again reiterated his earlier demands – which had the continuing merit of still working within the bounds of Britain's persistent ambiguity towards India. The British should still for a while, he argued, retain their ultimate control, but Indian leaders should be placed in positions of 'central' power.

It is significant that even now there was no further move either by the Congress or by the Muslim League.[118] In January indeed Nehru had sharply rebuked Rajagopalachari for toying with the Sapru line: 'it is much too late for real compromise', he wrote;[119] whilst Jinnah now simply repeated his earlier creed.[120] There was, however, one important move by Britain's new Asian ally, China. Its leader, Chiang Kai-shek, made an official visit to India in mid February and there issued a statement saying that the 'vast majority of the world's opinion is in full sympathy with India's aspirations for freedom'.[121] On 22 February, moreover, seven weeks after he had sent his telegram to Churchill and on the very day his conference was to meet in Delhi, Sapru eventually received a personal message from Churchill, in which the Prime Minister said that:

In the normal course, I should have replied earlier to the telegram which you and your distinguished colleagues sent to me in Washington. The press of public business connected with the grave events of recent weeks has however prevented my doing so . . . You will be aware that on two of the points . . . effect has been given to your views in that an invitation has been issued to the Government of India to be represented . . . in the formulation of policy in the War Cabinet in London and on the Pacific War Council. We shall welcome unreservedly . . . whoever may be chosen to fulfil these responsible duties.

---

[117] For summaries see *The Times*, 23 Feb. 1942, and Linlithgow to Amery, 23 Feb. 1942, *TOP* I, 168.   [118] Shiva Rao to Sapru, 26 Jan. 1942, SP 21.

[119] Nehru to Rajagopalachari, 26 Jan. 1942, JNP, Rajaji file; Prasad to Sapru, 18–20 Jan. 1942, SP 18.   [120] Lumley to Linlithgow, 15, 24 Jan. 1942, *TOP* I, 13, 24.

[121] See Linlithgow to Amery, 23 Feb. 1942, ibid. 173. Its importance can be measured from the attention Amery and Churchill gave to it, *Empire at Bay*, 22 Feb., 3 Mar. 1942, pp. 778, 782.

What was more there was an unexpected boon in the tail. 'The other pro-posals which you put to me', Churchill went on, 'are far-reaching issues in regard to which I hope to give you my considered answer before long'.[122] Considering that just a month before he had told the Commons that he did not think the raising of Indian constitutional issues when the enemy was at its gates would be at all advantageous, this was a major about-turn. All the evidence indicates that it was principally prompted by the stir over Britain's policy towards India that had been so skilfully catalysed in London by Sapru's trenchant telegram.

Prior to the Prime Minister's return to London in January Amery had begun to consider with Linlithgow 'a suitable answer to Sapru and Co. and generally of Press agitation here and in India' – to which he was evi-dently very alert. 'The memorial is of course treated here', he told Linlithgow, 'as having far more importance' than by those who knew their India. 'But', he added, 'I am sure the Prime Minister will be well advised to reply in as conciliatory a spirit as he can'.[123] For his part Linlithgow was in no two minds about the right response: 'we should stand firm', he told Amery, 'and make no further move'.[124] Amery essentially agreed; 'there is nothing', he told Churchill, 'to be done at this moment with the Sapru proposals or with any suggestions of a fresh constitutional advance',[125] and along these lines he drafted a reply to the Sapru tele-gram. This held to the established line. (On 'responsibility to the Crown', for example, it asked: 'Is the Governor-General to become a personal autocrat . . . or is the final . . . authority . . . to rest in a majority vote of the new Executive', thus failing to take Sapru's point, as Linlithgow had earlier before him, that whilst ordinarily the latter would be the case, in the minority of cases where the Viceroy's view differed from his Council's the Viceroy's view should prevail.[126])

Linlithgow soon endorsed Amery's draft,[127] which was consonant with the view that he himself took.

It may be necessary . . . [he opined] to alter the general line of our policy . . . after . . . the war . . . [but] policy as it stands . . . can only be successfully implemented from a strong position. [Sapru's scheme] would make it impossible for us after the war to regain any ground given now . . . What we have to decide . . . is whether . . . we intend to stay in this country for our own reasons . . . If we accept that India is too important for us to take any chances then I would face such troubles we may

---

[122] Pinnell to Sapru, 20 Feb. 1942, SP 13; see also *Daily Telegraph*, 21 Jan. 1942.
[123] Amery to Linlithgow, 10, 11, 20 Jan. 1942, *TOP* I, 9, 10, 11, 22.
[124] Linlithgow to Amery, 21 Jan. 1942, ibid. 23.
[125] Amery to Churchill, 22 Jan. 1942, *TOP* I, 27.
[126] Enc. in Amery to Attlee, 16 Jan. 1942, ibid. 15.
[127] Linlithgow to Amery, 23–7, 26 Jan. 1942, ibid. 30, 37.

have . . . His Majesty's Government will naturally wish to appear as constructive as possible in debate. I suggest . . . that the general line could be . . . to harp again on the depth and reality of Indian differences. . .[128]

Fully confident that he would have little difficulty over it, Amery then sent his draft reply to three of his ministerial colleagues for their comments, Attlee amongst them.[129]

But in one critical respect his confidence proved to be very seriously mistaken, and in a very short while everything was overturned. For whilst Attlee accepted Amery's draft for Churchill's reply to Sapru, he at the same time added ominously:

but I feel that it will have to be followed by some action . . . There is a lot of opinion here which we cannot ignore which is not satisfied that there is nothing to be done, but to sit tight on the declaration of August 1940. This opinion exists in your party as well as mine.[130]

Amery responded by saying that he thought he could nevertheless 'hold the House'.[131] But Attlee demurred. 'I still think the position most unsatisfactory', he told Amery, 'and I very much doubt if it can be held'.[132] Amery then prepared two lengthy memoranda for the Cabinet,[133] but these only served to propel Attlee into making a major intervention.

Attlee had been greatly incensed by Linlithgow's remark (when canvassing the Government's proposed reply to Sapru) that 'India and Burma have no natural association with the Empire, from which they are alien by race, history and religion . . . and are both in the Empire because they are conquered countries'.[134] Hitherto he had done little but suggest that a Royal Commission composed of the Chief Justice of India, Sir Maurice Gwyer, should be established.[135] But now, drawing deep upon his fifteen years' experience of Indian affairs since his earlier days on the Simon Commission, he proceeded to write his seminal Cabinet memorandum of 2 February 1942 in which he first accused both Linlithgow and Amery of 'a dangerous ignoring of the present situation', and then went on to affirm that:

the East is now asserting itself against the long dominance of the West. . . . hand to mouth policy is not statesmanship . . . I find it quite impossible to accept . . . the

---

[128] Linlithgow to Amery, 21 Jan. 1942, Linlithgow to Churchill, 21 Jan. 1942, ibid. 23, 25, 26.

[129] Amery to Simon, 16 Jan. 1942, Amery to Attlee, 16, 22 Jan. 1942, Amery to Churchill, 22, 29, 31 Jan. 1942, Anderson to Amery, 23 Jan. 1942, Amery to Linlithgow, 24, 30 Jan., 2 Feb. 1942, Simon to Amery 5 Feb. 1942, ibid. 14, 15, 28, 27, 544, 52, 32, 33, 48, 58, 65.   [130] Attlee to Amery, 24 Jan. 1942, ibid. 35.

[131] Amery to Attlee, 26 Jan. 1942, ibid. 38.   [132] Attlee to Amery, 27 Jan. 1942, ibid. 42.

[133] Amery's Cabinet Memoranda, 28 Jan., 1 Feb. 1942, ibid. 43, 57.

[134] Linlithgow to Amery, 21 Jan. 1942, # 14, ibid. 23.

[135] Amery to Linlithgow, 13 Jan. 1942, ibid. 11.

crude imperialism of the Viceroy . . . it is fatally short-sighted and suicidal . . . A renewed effort must be made to get the leaders of the Indian political parties to unite . . . Durham saved Canada to the British Empire. We need a man to do in India what Durham did in Canada . . . a Cabinet Committee should be appointed to draw up terms of reference and powers.[136]

It would be difficult to think of a more striking tribute to the very considerable stir which Sapru's initiative had so forcefully served to crystallise in London.

When the Cabinet discussed the Attlee memorandum on 5 February, Churchill quickly grasped that the end was nigh even for the Conservative reformers' stand, let alone for his own unrepentant diehardism. Two months previously his Cabinet had overruled him on the issue of the satyagraha prisoners. Now it proceeded to overrule both the Secretary of State and the Viceroy by deciding that 'the proposed answer to Sir Tej Bahadur Sapru should be deferred'.[137] Worried by American and Chinese pressure, Churchill now flew into orbit,[138] and in a dramatic gesture proposed to his colleagues that the Indian Defence Council should be greatly enlarged by the inclusion of a considerable number of elected members, that it should be given a greatly enhanced role in the conduct of India's war effort, and that it should be authorised to frame a new constitution for India at the end of the war. He even suggested that he himself should fly out to India to make the announcement, and when that seemed out of the question proposed that he should make a broadcast to India instead. Amery was bewitched ('a stroke of genius', he called it).[139] Linlithgow was scandalised ('I am, for the first time in my life, really cross with you all . . .', he expostulated to Amery. 'I do . . . beg of you to see that . . . I should be cushioned . . . from the full impact of these explosions in the Prime Minister's mind').[140]

The bubble, however, soon burst. Linlithgow rained so many strictures upon Churchill's scheme that it was quickly killed.[141] With the fall of Singapore to the Japanese on 15 February Churchill necessarily had to turn, moreover, to other things. Since decisions about India now had to be delayed, Amery arranged – particularly since Sapru's conference would soon be reconvening – that he should be sent the message of

---

[136] Attlee's Memo, 2 Feb. 1942, ibid. 60. Unspoken, financial, commercial, and military considerations were tending in the same vein; for a brief summary see Low, *Congress and the Raj*, pp. 12–14, reprinted in Low, *Eclipse of Empire*, pp. 72–4.

[137] War Cabinet 16th Conclusions, 5 Feb. 1942, *TOP* I, 66.

[138] Churchill to Linlithgow, 13 Feb. 1942, ibid. 113.

[139] *TOP* I, 66–145 passim; *Empire at Bay*, 5–17 Feb. 1942, pp. 767–76 passim.

[140] Linlithgow to Amery, 16 Feb. 1942, *TOP* I, 135.

[141] Linlithgow to Amery, 13, 16, 21 Feb. 1942, Linlithgow to Churchill, 14 Jan. 1942, ibid. 121, 129, 160, 124.

20 February from Churchill already quoted above.[142] Thereafter a Cabinet Committee on India was set up[143] – as the press noted, and as Attlee had earlier proposed – which in Churchill's absence Attlee chaired.

I shall now have to face a determined attempt [Amery moaned to his diary] by Cripps [who had lately joined the government] and Attlee to find some immediate Indian solution with a Congress bias to it and possibly with an attempt to get rid of Linlithgow.[144]

In retrospect, however, one can see that the key decisions had already by now been taken.

Hitherto every British declaration about India since 1939 had quite deliberately refused to grant India *carte blanche* in the fashioning of her own post-war constitution. When, however, following the Cabinet meeting on 5 February which discussed the Attlee memorandum,[145] Amery had come to draft a possible broadcast for Churchill to India, he had adumbrated three momentous changes, which Churchill and the Cabinet evidently endorsed.[146] Steps would be taken, the draft read,

after the war . . . without delay to hammer out India's future constitution . . . [while that must express] the desire of the people of India as a whole [a euphemism to meet Muslim demands] the procedure by which effect is to be given to this principle will be discussed . . . as soon as practicable . . . [And] I, on behalf of the British Government, now declare that we undertake to accept in advance a constitution so arrived at.[147]

Moreover, even while 'emphatically insist[ing] that the discontinuance of official membership should not be . . . part of any declaration', and that 'in my view the necessity does not arise primarily from difficulties here' (i.e. but rather from the ferment aroused in London), Linlithgow proposed that in the statement Churchill would make:

At the outset . . . Her Majesty's Government [should] declare that they had no intention of impeding the attainment of India's independence . . . for the preservation of purely British interests . . . [should further] undertake to do all in their power within the shortest practicable time after the end of the war, to promote the peaceful setting-up of autonomous government in India [and would] accept in advance . . . any constitution . . . representing the will and desire of India as a whole.[148]

---

[142] Amery to Churchill, 19 Feb. 1942, Amery to Linlithgow, 19 Feb. 1942, ibid. 151, 152.
[143] Minutes, 1st meeting, War Cabinet Committee on India (chaired by Churchill), 26 Feb. 1942, ibid. 185.   [144] *Empire at Bay*, 19 Feb. 1942, p. 777.
[145] War Cabinet meeting, minute 3, 5 Feb. 1942, Amery to Linlithgow, 9 Feb. 1942, *TOP* I, 66, 89; *Empire at Bay*, 5 Feb. 1942, p. 768.
[146] *Empire at Bay*, 11–12 Feb. 1942, pp. 772–3.
[147] Amery to Linlithgow, 13 (see also 21) Feb. 1942, *TOP* I, 111, 163.
[148] Linlithgow nonetheless continued to be opposed to any declaration being made, Linlithgow to Amery, 25, 26 Feb., 6 Mar. 1942, *TOP* I, 183, 184, 250.

Both statements were sharply at odds with the line that the two of them had been assuming the government would hold to only a short while before. Ineluctably they had now accepted that following Attlee's memorandum the Cabinet had thrown the rudder over. It was for the Cabinet Committee to settle the details. Over the next fortnight they wrestled with the attempt to do so.[149] They did not focus on the formula Sapru had offered them. Rather they resurrected the proposal the Labour leaders had discussed with Nehru at Sir Stafford Cripps' house at Filkins back in 1938 for 'the summoning of a Constituent Assembly to decide on India's future' which would be called so soon as the war was over.[150]

Throughout the last days of February and the first days of March 1942 political circles both in Britain and in India were increasingly agog with what was going on. On 28 February *The Times* (with whom Linlithgow had by now become very angry)[151] affirmed that: 'Above all a change of spirit is required – not least on the British side.' Early in March 1942 *The Sunday Times*, the *Daily Herald*, the *News Chronicle*, the *Daily Mail*, even the *News of the World* ran hot upon the trail as well; and on 6 March the *Manchester Guardian* forecast that Churchill's statement 'in reply to the Sapru overtures' would be made very shortly.[152]

Five days later on 11 March 1942 Churchill eventually rose in the House of Commons to reiterate the August 1940 promise of Dominion Status after the war, but then went on to say that 'in order to clothe these general declarations with precision and to convince all classes, races and creeds in India of our resolve, the War Cabinet have agreed unitedly upon . . . a constructive British contribution to aid India in the realization of full self-government', and that Sir Stafford Cripps would now fly to Delhi to discuss a draft declaration along these lines with India's political leaders.[153]

Two days later Sapru received a personal letter from the Private Secretary to the Viceroy.

His Excellency has been asked by the Prime Minister [this read] to convey to you a message relative to your telegram of January 2nd. The Prime Minister

---

[149] Moore, *Churchill, Cripps and India*, ch. 3; *Empire at Bay*, 26 Feb.–11 Mar. 1942, pp. 779–95; *TOP* I, 185–310 passim.

[150] 'This was in fact the proposal which Cripps carried to India on behalf of the wartime Cabinet on the so called Cripps Mission', C.R. Attlee, 'Nehru in Retrospect', reprinted in K. Natwar-Singh, *The Legacy of Nehru*, Delhi 1996, p. 17. For the 1938 meeting see Moore, *Churchill, Cripps and India*, p. 4.

[151] Linlithgow to Amery, 21, 23–7 Jan. 1942, Linlithgow to Churchill, 21 Jan. 1942, *TOP* I, 23, 30, 26.

[152] *Manchester Guardian*, 6 Mar. 1942, and the London press passim during the first few days of March 1942.   [153] Gwyer and Appadorai, *Speeches and Documents*, pp. 519–20.

observes that as you will no doubt appreciate his statement in Parliament and the mission of Sir Stafford Cripps are in effect the answer to that telegram, and he hopes that you will therefore excuse him from sending a detailed reply at this juncture.[154]

Sapru's superbly timed intervention had spawned a quite momentous response.

The ensuing collapse of the Cripps negotiations need hardly detain us here. Details are readily available elsewhere.[155] So far as Dominion Status after the war was concerned Cripps' 'draft declaration' had none of the deliberately debilitating qualifications which had earlier hamstrung all previous declarations. There was even the possibility of the transfer of the Home and Finance Departments to Indian hands. Unsurprisingly the stumbling block was Defence. Prior to the Japanese attack the former Commander-in-Chief, Auchinleck, had shown himself responsive in conversations in March 1941 with Sapru and others to its transference to Indian hands.[156] But with Japanese aircraft already flying over India there was arguably a case for not making the change now. Yet very understandably this became the touchstone of British good faith for India's leaders, and it was over this that the talks collapsed.

Sapru visited Delhi to be one of a number of people who saw Cripps. He was in close touch with Rajagopalachari (who had written to him in warm appreciation of all of his earlier efforts),[157] and while he did not see many Congressmen (he had recently had no more than limited social contact with Nehru and Azad)[158] he did see Gandhi, and when the conflict over Defence reached its climax, after consulting Rajagopalachari, and in association with his old companion-in-arms, M.R. Jayakar, he and Jayakar issued a statement insisting that a satisfactory division of responsibility between the British C-in-C and an Indian Defence Member really could be made.[159] The Cabinet in response authorised Cripps to attempt a solution along the lines they proposed. But to no avail. The details could not be agreed, and when the Congress leaders met resistance here they correctly drew the conclusion that the British were even now not prepared to install a 'National Government' in India. That may have been hard on Cripps, but it was certainly Churchill's view and Linlithgow's too. Not only did they make no attempt to rescue the negotiations. Some believe they seized an opening which Cripps gave

[154] Pinnell to Sapru, 14 Mar. 1942, SP 13.
[155] *TOP* I, ch. 4; Moore, chs. 4 and 5; Rizvi, *Linlithgow and India*, ch. 6; Voigt, *India and Second World War*, pp. 122–32.   [156] See Shiva Rao to Sapru, 25 Mar. 1941, SP 22.
[157] Rajagopalachari to Sapru, 26, 28 Feb., 13, 23 Mar. 1942, SP II, R32.
[158] Sapru to Shiva Rao, 3, 5 Apr. 1942, SP 21.   [159] JP 753.

them to kill the talks.[160] Certainly they were both very relieved when they failed.

Two features of the outcome to which quite inadequate attention is generally given need to be emphasised here. Following the collapse of the Cripps negotiations the Cabinet, including its Labour members, and, judging from the reactions of the British press, the greater part of British elite opinion too, not only accepted the outcome with equanimity. They did nothing to press for a 'national government' in India during the course of the war. They never questioned the continuance of Governors' authoritarian rule in the provinces, and six months later they gave Linlithgow and the Government of India full support in their vigorous repression of Gandhi's 'Quit India' movement in August 1942. The apparent anomaly here stemmed once again from the ambiguity in British proceedings which has so pervaded this book. Many in the British elite had been exasperated by the response of the Congress leaders to the Cripps proposals. They were then incensed that Congress should seek to destroy the British position in India at the very height of its major crisis in the war with Japan. There was never any intention that the Cripps declaration would lead to the ending of British rule in India during the course of the war. But it had laid down quite unequivocally that this would be done at the conclusion of the war. In these respects the Cripps 'offer' was, yet again, a typically Janus-faced British declaration. But now that the British Government had made its firm commitment about complete independence for India after the war, the British saw themselves as no longer standing upon a single leg only in India, but once again upon two, and that made them feel once more entirely comfortable in resisting Congress's onslaught particularly whilst the war had yet to be won.

But they had nevertheless paid a price for having recovered their preferred position, a price which British Cabinets had hitherto invariably refused to pay. For whilst the Cripps negotiations might have failed, and the Cripps 'Offer' was then withdrawn, given the way that British policies always evolved, once things had been said they could not readily be unsaid, and on the ultimate issues the Cripps Offer had been quite unambiguous. It had laid down 'in precise and clear terms the steps [that would] be taken for the earliest possible realization of self-government in India'. In the first place this was to be as 'a Dominion', but one 'in no way

---

[160] Cripps and Attlee both believed on the other hand that it was Gandhi who killed the Cripps mission, see *TOP* 2, 227, and Attlee's statement that it 'unfortunately failed owing to the opposition of Mahatma Gandhi', Attlee, 'Nehru in Retrospect' in Natwar-Singh, *Legacy*, p. 17. For another view see Moore, *Churchill, Cripps and India*, pp. 127–8; R.J. Moore, *Escape from Empire, The Attlee Government and the Indian Problem*, Oxford 1983, p. 73.

subordinate in any aspect of its domestic or external affairs' to any other body. Moreover: 'immediately upon cessation of hostilities steps shall be taken in India', it said, – note not in London – to establish 'a constitution-making body' so as to bring that consummation about. What was more: 'His Majesty's Government undertake to accept and implement forth-with the constitution so framed' – except in so far as any Province or State chose to stand out. Whilst a treaty would be required to

cover all necessary matters arising out of the complete transfer of responsibility from British to Indian hands [and] for the protection of racial and religious minorities [this] will not impose any restriction on the power of the Indian Union to decide in the future its relationship to the other member States of the British Commonwealth.

Complex as some of this language clearly was, its clarity of commitment was not to be gainsaid. Henceforth it held the field. In the event because of the major head-on collision between Congress and the Muslim League, and the latter's absolute determination to secure Pakistan, things worked out on some significantly different lines.[161] But in all this there was no reneging on the essential elements in the Cripps offer. Its unequiv-ocal language deserves to be closely read. India would be free.

The broad circumstances here warrant a final word. The ambiguity in the British position in respect of India emerges from this story as clearly as in any other we have followed. For the most part it does so in negative terms. With the failure of the federal negotiations by 1939, the resignation of the Congress ministries, and the consequential declaration of Governor's rule in so many provinces, Britain's imperial policy in India suddenly forfeited its carefully constructed equilibrium. For two and a half years thereafter the British failed to counterbalance the authoritarian rule on which they were once more solely relying with anything that represented what Rab Butler called 'progress'. They hobbled along on a single leg only, and many of them found that increasingly uncomfortable. Undiluted autocratic rule was not, they felt, Britain's style. As it hap-pened, at this time, despite their extensive latent support, neither the Congress nor the Muslim League possessed any potent weapon to wield against the British.

In the ensuing impasse the way stood open for a seasoned mediator like Sapru to try his hand. Knowing from his long experience where the broader instincts of India's British rulers lay, he knew too that there was no point in trying to push them out forcefully or immediately. They were past masters at knowing how to resist that. What one had to do was to find some way of getting them to display their more accommodating side once

[161] Ibid.

again. Early in 1941 he had set about doing this, not to salve their *amour propre*, but because *this was the one means by which to get them to move*. In March–April 1941 his first efforts failed. They succeeded, however, in emphasising just how intransigent they had become, and that made many interested British figures increasingly ill at ease. His second, more ambitious, and (apart from his Bombay supporters) single-handed throw in January 1942 then brilliantly succeeded in forcing them to be true to that part of themselves which they had lately set aside. Characteristically – for underneath all of this British ambivalence stood just as firm as ever – that provided India with nothing straight away. But it did secure the critical assurances for the attainment of India's independence once the war was over.

The inwardness of all of this may be briefly stated once again. During the 1930s Britain's inherent imperialist ambiguity had been institutionalised in the Government of India Act of 1935 so as 'to hold India to the Empire'. When for a variety of reasons that strategy broke down following the outbreak of war, it could only be again put together at the cost of undertaking to 'lose India to the Empire' once the war was over. But given the depth of the British need to see the positive and not just the negative side of their contending instincts towards India in evidence, they much preferred to settle for that rather than persist in presenting their absolutist imperial face on its own.

By this stage it will be tedious to remark that as between the Filipinos and the Americans on the one hand, and the Vietnamese and the French, and the Indonesians and the Dutch, on the other, the critical issues took very different forms. In India great skill was required to seize upon those moments when an effective thrust to exploit Britain's ambiguous attitudes might bring about a change. On the ultimate issue of securing from the British a precise undertaking that, despite their earlier, quite deliberate equivocations, they would no longer resist India's demand for complete independence so soon as the war was over, Sapru's thrust in January 1942 was a masterly achievement. Backed by the inherent force of the Indian national movement which its various leaders had put together, India was thereby placed irrevocably on the road to the independence it had sought for so long. That was a crucial moment in Indian history, and in that of the western empires too.

With the ending of the Second World War in August 1945, following the dropping of the two atomic bombs on Japan, the climatic end to the western empires in Asia soon ensued. The three other main colonial powers in Asia now ran true to form. The Americans, having by the end of the war reconquered the Philippines, granted full political independence to it in 1946 (just a year later, owing to the war, than they had earlier promised). Amid a continuing Japanese presence in their countries as the war ended, nationalist leaders in Indonesia and Vietnam[162] quickly seized the opportunity to proclaim their country's independence. Both the Dutch and the French showed themselves quite determined, however, to restore their imperial control. Since both the Indonesian nationalists and the Vietnamese had a modicum of armed backing, violent conflict soon ensued in both countries. Each proved quite disastrous for the imperial power. Following their two euphemistically named 'police actions', the Dutch were eventually forced by international pressure to grant independence to Indonesia in 1949, while following upon their defeat at Dien Bien Phu in 1954 the French were likewise compelled to concede independence to a bifurcated Vietnam.[163]

Meantime the British had finally set aside their earlier equivocations and upon the conclusion of the war had proceeded to grant India the independence they had promised in the Cripps Offer of 1942. As independence dawned there was great trauma. Not because of any remaining doubt about whether the British would go. Rather (as in so many other instances at this stage elsewhere) over the distribution of power upon their departure. That eventuated in the partition between India and Pakistan upon the attainment of independence in August 1947.[164]

It was not, however, from these two Asian countries only that the British now departed; they granted independence to Ceylon in 1948.[165] The really revealing case was Burma. Upon its reconquest from the Japanese in 1945 the British found themselves confronted, as the Dutch were in Indonesia and the French in Vietnam, by a determined nationalist opposition backed by a significant armed force. Yet in striking contrast to both the Dutch and the French they very quickly bent before it. Burma thereupon became independent in 1948.[166] The exception here was Malaya, the one major Asian colony following the ending of the war where colonial rule was relatively peacefully reinstated; partly, in a country dominated by 'native states', because nationalism had not advanced here very far; above all, it would seem, because – in another characteristic end-of-empire situation – its Malay majority was deeply fearful of losing out upon independence to its relatively

[162] See especially Marr, *Vietnam 1945*.
[163] Reid, *Indonesian National Revolution* and Hammer, *Struggle for Indochina*.
[164] Moore, *Escape from Empire*.
[165] K.M. de Silva, ed., *Sri Lanka, BDEEP*, Series B, vol. 2, London 1997.
[166] H. Tinker, ed., *Constitutional Relations between Britain and Burma: the Struggle for Independence 1944–1948*, 2 vols., London 1983–4.

large Chinese minority. Malaya nonetheless attained its independence in 1957.[167]

That was in full accord with Britain's new, and much more general, post-war colonial policy upon independence. That was not without its qualifications. For nearly twenty years these were especially salient where there were white settler communities. More generally they took the form of the condition the Americans installed in the Jones Act of 1916 for the Philippines – that independence would come 'as soon as a stable government can be established therein'. It was formally stated, for example, in Britain in 1950 that: 'There is no intention to abandon responsibilities prematurely.' Yet from at least 1946 onwards the persistent mantra had now become:

The central purpose of British Colonial policy is simple. It is to guide the Colonial Territories to responsible self-government within the Commonwealth.

Around the same time it was formally declared too that: 'British "Imperialism" is dead . . . One illustration of this is our policy in India.' British officials, moreover, now commonly avowed that 'in the process of granting self-government it was safer to move a little too fast than to move a little too slowly';[168] while it was realistically added in 1954 that: 'This process cannot now be halted or reversed, and it is only to a limited extent that its pace can be controlled by the United Kingdom Government.'[169] It all involved, as Sir Harry Haig had put it back in India in 1939, 'a rearguard action':

We are deliberately surrendering our power [he mused], and we ought to do it with goodwill; but we must not let the rearguard action turn into a rout. There are times when we have to stand and fight, even though in the end we continue to retire.[170]

---

[167] A.J. Stockwell, ed., *Malaya, BDEEP,* Series B, vol. 3, London 1995. See also W.R. Roff, *The Origins of Malay Nationalism*, New Haven 1967, T. Harper, *The End of Empire and the Making of Malaya*, Cambridge 1997.

[168] 'The colonial empire today; summary of our main problems and policies' [May 1950], 'Notes on British colonial policy', Mar. 1949; 'Projection of Britain Overseas', 17 August 1946, Sir Angus Gillan at 'International study conference on overseas territories of Western Europe', Amsterdam 9–12 June 1948 (see, moreover, for striking testimony to the different policies of the European governments there represented), reported in Gage to Bevin 26 June 1948, R. Hyam, ed., *The Labour Government and the End of Empire 1945–1951, BDEEP* Series A, vol. 2, London 1992, 72, 71 (or see 'The Colonial Empire 1947–48', Cmd 7433, p. 1), 179, and e.g. Arden Clarke to Cohen, 5 Mar. 1951, R.Rathbone, ed., *Ghana, BDEEP* Series B, vol. 1, pp. 293–7, Sir H. Foot, *A Start in Freedom*, London 1964, p. 106. See also Colonial Secretary Oliver Stanley's statement, 13 July 1943, S.R. Ashton and S.E. Stockwell, *Imperial Policy and Colonial Practice 1925–1945, BDEEP* Series A, vol. 1, 36, fn 4.

[169] Report of the Official Committee on Commonwealth Membership, D. Goldsworthy, ed., *The Conservative Government and the End of Empire 1951–1957, BDEEP* Series A, vol. 3, London 1994, 192.   [170] Haig to Linlithgow, 4 Dec. 1939, HgP 2B.

As in India all this involved very extensive debate within the imperial edifice, that was never the monolith it has sometimes been portrayed to be.[171] Once, however, British ambiguity had been finally resolved in India, the terms of the conflicts in the remaining British empire outside the white settler colonies changed significantly.[172] By 1945 the ambiguity that pervades this book had in all essentials run its course.[173] Twenty years on there was very little of the British empire left.

[171] *BDEEP* passim.

[172] For one summary account see 'The End of the British Empire in Africa', D.A. Low, *Eclipse of Empire*, Cambridge 1991, ch. 9.

[173] The notion in 1954 that Cyprus would not be granted independence was always an aberration (as was 'Suez'). Interestingly – to take the cases with which this book began – when the Irish finally decided to leave the British Commonwealth in 1949 there was no British resistance; when that year India decided to remain within the Commonwealth it was permitted to do so without committing itself to 'the common allegiance to the Crown'; while in 1951 when the Egyptians abrogated the Anglo–Egyptian Treaty of 1936 there was very little British fuss. The contrasts with the pre-war years were extensive.

Biographical notes

Baldwin, Stanley, 1867–1947. Educated Harrow and Trinity College Cambridge. Conservative MP for Bewdley, Worcestershire, 1908–37. Financial Secretary to the Treasury 1917–21. President of the Board of Trade 1921–2. Conservative Prime Minister 1923–4, 1924–9, 1935–7. Lord President of the Council 1931–5. Chancellor Cambridge University 1930–47. Created Earl Baldwin of Bewdley 1937.

Bose, Subhas Chandra, 1897–1945. Educated Calcutta and Cambridge. Passed 4th place Indian Civil Service exam 1921 but resigned. Participated Non-cooperation movement 1921–2, Civil Disobedience movements 1930–1, 1932–4, and imprisoned. Chief Executive Calcutta Corporation 1924, Mayor 1930. Imprisoned 1924–7. President Bengal Congress Committee 1927–31, 1937–9. President Indian National Congress 1938 and 1939 but forced by 'Gandhians' to resign. Founded Forward Bloc 1939. Arrested 1940 but escaped 1941 to Berlin. Moved to Japan 1943 and led Indian National Army. Killed in aircraft accident 1945.

Emerson, Sir Herbert William, 1881–1962. Educated Calday Grange Grammar School and Magdalene College Cambridge. Entered Indian Civil Service, Punjab cadre, 1905. Chief Secretary Punjab 1927–8. Home Secretary Government of India 1930–2. Governor of Punjab 1933–8. High Commissioner for Refugees, League of Nations 1935–47.

Erskine, John Francis Ashley, Lord, 1895–1953. Educated at Eton and Christ Church Oxford. Unionist MP Weston-super-Mare 1922–3, 1924–34. Assistant Government Whip 1932. Governor of Madras 1934–40. Unionist MP for Brighton 1940–1.

Gandhi, Mohandas Karamchand, Mahatma ('Great Soul'), 1869–1948. Inner Temple London 1888–91. Indian political leader in South Africa 1893–1914. Led Champaran, Kaira, and Ahmedabad satyagrahas 1917–18. Became dominant leader of Congress from 1919–20. Led Rowlatt satyagraha 1919, Khilafat and Non-cooperation movements 1920–2, Civil Disobedience campaigns 1930–1, 1932–4, Individual satyagraha 1940–1, Quit India revolt 1942–4, and regularly imprisoned. 'Father of the Nation'. Murdered 1948.

Haig, Sir Harry Graham, 1881–1956. Educated Winchester and New College Oxford. Entered Indian Civil Service, UP cadre, 1904. Secretary Indian Fiscal Commission 1921–2. Private Secretary to the Viceroy 1925. Home Secretary Government of India 1926–30. Home Member Government of

India 1932–4. Governor of UP 1934–9. Regional Commissioner for Civil Defence in Northwestern and then Southern Region UK 1940–5.

Hailey, Sir William Malcolm, 1872–1969. Educated Merchant Taylors' School and Corpus Christi College Oxford. Entered Indian Civil Service, Punjab cadre, 1895. Chief Commissioner Delhi 1912–18. Finance Member Government of India 1919–22. Home Member Government of India 1922–4. Governor of Punjab 1924–8. Governor of UP 1928–34. Created Lord Hailey of Shahpur and Newport Pagnell 1936. Director, African Research Survey 1935–8. *Native Administration in the British African Territories*, 5 vols. 1950–3.

Hallett, Sir Maurice Garnier, 1883–1969. Educated Winchester and New College Oxford. Entered Indian Civil Service, Bihar and Orissa cadre, 1907. Chief Secretary Bihar and Orissa 1930–2. Home Secretary Government of India 1932–6. Governor of Bihar 1937–9. Governor of UP 1939–45.

Hoare, Sir Samuel John Gurney, 1880–1959. Educated Harrow and New College Oxford. Conservative MP for Chelsea 1910–44. Secretary of State for Air 1922–4, 1924–9, 1940. Secretary of State for India 1931–5. Foreign Secretary 1935. First Lord of the Admiralty 1936–7. Ambassador to Spain 1940–4. Created Lord Templewood 1944.

Irwin, Edward Frederick Lindley Wood, Lord, 1881–1959. Educated at Eton and Christ Church Oxford. Fellow of All Souls College Oxford 1903. Conservative MP for Ripon 1910–25. Parliamentary Under-Secretary for the Colonies 1921–2. Minister of Agriculture 1924–5. Viceroy of India 1926–31. President of the Board of Education 1932–5. Succeeded his father as Viscount Halifax 1934. Secretary of State for War 1935. Lord Privy Seal 1937–8. Foreign Secretary 1938–40. Ambassador to the United States of America 1941–6. Chancellor of Oxford University 1933–59.

Linlithgow, Victor Alexander John Hope, 2nd Marquess of, 1887–1952. Educated at Eton. Chairman Royal Commission on Agriculture in India 1928. Chairman Joint Select Committee of British Parliament on Indian Constitutional Reforms 1933–4. Viceroy of India 1936–43.

Lothian, Philip Henry Kerr, 11th Marquess of, 1882–1940. Educated Oratory School, Birmingham, and New College Oxford. South African administration 1905–9. Editor *The Round Table* 1910–16. Secretary to the Prime Minister (Lloyd George) 1916–21. Secretary, The Rhodes Trust 1925–39. Parliamentary Under-Secretary for India 1931–2. Chairman Indian Franchise Commission 1932. Ambassador to the United States of America 1939–40.

Macdonald, Ramsay, 1866–1937. Labour MP for Leicester 1900–18. Published *The Awakening of India* 1910. Chairman Independent Labour Party 1906–9. Member Royal Commission on the Public Services in India 1912. Chairman Parliamentary Labour Party 1911–14, 1922–31. Labour MP for Aberavon 1922–29. Labour (and then National Labour) MP for Seaham 1929–35, for Scottish Universities 1935–7. Labour Prime Minister 1924, 1924–9. Prime Minister of National Government 1931–5. Lord President of the Council 1935–7.

Malaviya, Pandit Madan Mohan, 1861–1946. Educated Muir College Allahabad and Calcutta University. Practised law 1893–1909. Journalist: founded

Leader 1909; Chairman *Hindustan Times* 1942–6. Attended Congresses 1886–1936. President Indian National Congress 1909, 1918, 1932, 1933. Founder member Hindu Mahasabha 1910. Member UP Legislative Council 1902–9. Member Imperial Legislative Council 1909–19, 1923–30. Founder Benares Hindu University 1915, Vice-Chancellor 1919–38, Rector 1939–46.

Maxwell, Sir Reginald Maitland, 1882–1967. Educated at Marlborough and Corpus Christi College Oxford. Entered Indian Civil Service, Bombay cadre, 1906. Home Secretary Bombay 1931–5. Home Secretary Government of India 1936–7. Home Member Government of India 1939–44. Adviser to the Secretary of State for India 1944–7.

Narayan, Jayaprakash, 1902–79. Educated Patna Collegiate School and Benares Hindu University. Iowa, Chicago, Wisconsin, California, and Ohio Universities 1922–9. Professor of Sociology Benares Hindu University 1929. Acting General Secretary Indian National Congress 1932–3. General Secretary Congress Socialist Party 1934–9. Imprisoned 1939–46 (once escaped). President Praja Socialist Party 1951–3. Founder Bhoodan movement 1953. Led agitations against Indira Gandhi 1974–5. Founder member Janata Party 1977.

Nehru, Pandit Jawaharlal, 1889–1964. Educated at Harrow, Trinity College Cambridge, and Inner Temple London. Participated in Non-cooperation movement 1920–2, Civil Disobedience movements 1930–1, 1932–4, Individual satyagraha 1940–1, Quit India revolt 1942–4, imprisoned in all for nine years. General Secretary UP Congress Committee 1920–2. Chairman Allahabad Municipality 1923–6. General Secretary 1923–5, 1927–9 and President Indian National Congress 1930, 1936, 1937, 1946, 1951–4. Prime Minister 1946–64.

Nehru, Pandit Motilal, 1861–1931. Educated Muir College Allahabad. Leading UP lawyer 1890–. President UP Congress Provincial Conference 1907. Member UP Legislative Council 1910–19. President Indian National Congress 1919, 1928, 1931. Participated in Non-cooperation movement 1920–2, Civil Disobedience movement 1930–1 and twice imprisoned. General Secretary of Congress 1920–3. Leader Swaraj Party Imperial Legislative Council 1923–6. Chairman Nehru Committee to draft independence constitution 1928.

Pant, Pandit Govind Ballabh, 1887–1961. Educated at Muir College and Allahabad University. Practised law. Member UP Legislative Council 1912–19. Participated in Rowlatt satyagraha 1919, Non-cooperation movement 1920–2, Civil Disobedience movements 1930–1, 1932–3, Individual satyagraha 1940–1, Quit India movement 1942–4 and regularly imprisoned. Leader Swaraj Party UP Legislative Council 1923–30. Deputy Leader Congress Party Central Legislative Assembly 1934–7. Chief Minister UP 1937–9, 1946–54. Home Minister Government of India 1955–61.

Prasad, Dr Rajendra, 1884–1963. Educated at Presidency College Calcutta. Practised law in Calcutta 1911–16, thereafter in Patna, Bihar. Assisted Gandhi in Champaran satyagraha 1917. Participated in Rowlatt satyagraha 1919, Non-cooperation movement 1920–2, Civil Disobedience movements 1930–1, 1932–3, Individual satyagraha 1940–1, and Quit India movement

1942–4, and regularly imprisoned. President Indian National Congress 1934, 1939. Member Congress Parliamentary Board 1937–9. Minister of Food and Agriculture Government of India 1946–8. President of the Constituent Assembly 1948–9. President of India 1950–62.

Rajagopalachari, Chakravarti, 1879–1972. Educated Presidency College Madras. Practised law in Salem 1900–19. Gandhi's leading lieutenant in southern India from 1920, and frequent President Tamil Nadu Congress Committee. Participated in Rowlatt satyagraha 1919, Non-cooperation movement 1920–2, Civil Disobedience movements 1930–1, 1932–4. General Secretary Congress 1921–2. Chief Minister Madras 1937–9, 1952–4. Governor West Bengal 1947. Governor-General of India 1947. Minister without Portfolio Government of India 1950–1, Home Minister 1951. Founder Swatantra Party 1959.

Sapru, Sir Tej Bahadur, 1875–1949. Educated at Agra College and Allahabad University, Ll.D. By the 1920s the most prominent practising lawyer in northern India. Congress supporter, but joined Moderate Congress in 1917. Member UP Legislative Council 1912–16. Member Imperial Legislative Council 1916–22. Law Member Government of India 1920–2. Indian representative Imperial Conference London 1923. A principal architect Commonwealth of India Bill 1924. Member Muddiman Reforms Enquiry Committee 1924, and Nehru Committee 1928. President National Liberal Federation 1927. Attended three Round Table Conferences in London 1930–3. President All-Party Conferences 1941–5. Chairman Sapru Committee on an Indian constitution 1945.

Sinha, Shri Krishna, 1887–1961. Educated at Patna College and Calcutta University. Practised law in Monghyr. Participated in Non-cooperation movement 1920–2, Civil Disobedience movements 1930–1, 1932–3, Individual satyagraha 1940–1, and Quit India movement 1942–4, and latterly regularly imprisoned. Member Imperial Legislative Assembly 1934–7. Chief Minister Bihar 1937–9, 1946–61.

Willingdon, Freeman Freeman-Thomas, 1st Marquess of, 1866–1941. Liberal MP Hastings 1900–6, Bodmin 1906–10. Junior Lord of Treasury 1905–12. Governor of Bombay 1913–19. Governor of Madras 1919–24. Governor-General of Canada 1926–31. Viceroy of India 1931–6.

Zetland, Lawrence John Lumley Dundas, 2nd Marquess of, 1872–1961. Educated Harrow and Trinity College Cambridge. Conservative MP for Hornsey 1907–17. Governor of Bombay (as Lord Ronaldshay) 1917–22. Secretary of State for India 1935–40. Chairman National Trust 1931–45.

Index